DATE DUE

FE 8 '07			

DEMCO 38-290

Robert Schumann

11 Robert Schumann at 29—lithograph by Joseph Kriehuber.
(Photo AKG London.)

ROBERT SCHUMANN

Herald of a
"New Poetic Age"

JOHN DAVERIO

New York   Oxford

OXFORD UNIVERSITY PRESS

1997

Oxford University Press

Oxford   New York
Athens   Auckland   Bangkok   Bogotà
Bombay   Buenos Aires   Calcutta   Cape Town   Dar es Salaam
Delhi   Florence   Hong Kong   Istanbul   Karachi
Kuala Lumpur   Madras   Madrid   Melbourne
Mexico City   Nairobi   Paris   Singapore
Taipei   Tokyo   Toronto

and associated companies in
Berlin   Ibadan

Library of Congress Cataloging-in-Publication Data
Daverio, John.
Robert Schumann : herald of a "new poetic age" / John Daverio.
p. cm.   Includes bibliographical references and index.
ISBN 0 19-509180-9
1. Schumann, Robert, 1810–1856.   2. Composers—Germany—Biography.
I. Title.
ML410.S4B38   1997
780'.92—dc20
[B]   96-23177

1 3 5 7 9 8 6 4 2

Printed in the United States of America
on acid-free paper

For my parents

Preface

Shortly after completing the draft of this book, I reread one of my favorite essays: Roland Barthes's "Loving Schumann." Like the French critic, I, too, must confess to loving Schumann, even at the risk of leaving myself open to the charge implicit in this odd passion: the adoption of a philosophy of nostalgia or untimeliness, as Barthes puts it. Moreover, the Schumann I love is the whole Schumann—not the one known to most everyone, the dreamy composer of quirky piano pieces and gorgeous songs who met a tragic end—and this Schumann, like caviar, is something of an acquired taste. After receiving a gentle nudge from Maribeth Anderson Payne, my editor at Oxford University Press, I decided to write this biography in part to set aside some old myths—that Schumann knew how to write short pieces but not long ones, that we can hear traces of his final illness in his later music—but also, and apart from any polemical intent, to draw a portrait of a composer who was perhaps the first in Western musical history to view the art of composition as a kind of literary activity. And above all, I felt the need to repay a debt, a debt to an artist who has given me untold happy hours as a listener to and performer of his music over the past twenty years. Loving Schumann may be a nostalgic and untimely avocation, but it exacts a price.

Although I'm sure to make some omissions, I would like to thank the many colleagues, friends, and students who have helped me to make good on my debt. Fellow Schumannians Arnfried Edler, Jon Finson, Rufus Hallmark, Claudia Macdonald, Gerd Nauhaus, Nancy Reich, R. Larry Todd, and Markus Waldura all offered much-appreciated advice at various stages during my research. I thank Barbara Barry, Mark Evan Bonds, Reinhold Brinkmann, Berthold Höckner, Klaus-Jürgen Sachs, and Howard Smither for generously sharing with me materials that enriched my understanding of Schumann's life and works. Drs. Mark Allen and Reed Drews provided invaluable insights on the interpretation of Schumann's medical history. I owe my gratitude to other friends and colleagues, including Anna Maria Busse-Berger, Karol Berger, Isabelle Cazeaux, Lewis Lockwood, and Herbert Sprouse, for their sage counsel and unflagging support. To my colleagues at Boston University who have taken a keen interest in this project—Charles Fussell, John Goodman, Phyllis Hoffman, David Hoose, Joy McIntyre, Emilio Ros-Fábregas, Joel Sheveloff, Roye Wates, Gerald Weale, and Jeremy Yudkin—I extend a warm thank you, and reserve a special word for my recital partner and friend, Maria Clodes-Jaguaribe, who, like me, is an incurable Schumann lover. As always, the music-library staff at Mugar Memorial Library— Holly Mockovak, Richard Seymour, and Donald Denniston—responded promptly and cheerfully to my many (too many) requests.

My thanks also go to the students in a seminar on Schumann's music I conducted in the fall of 1993, especially to JoAnn Koh, Marcus Silvi, and Tom Williams, who reminded me that my hero wasn't victorious in every battle. Many current and former graduate students—Paul Bempéchat, James A. Davis, Simon Keefe, Teresa Neff, Eftychia Papanikolaou, and Elizabeth Seitz—lent willing ears to a sometimes obsessed teacher and advisor.

And last, I extend my thanks to the couple whose immeasurable support of my activities extends back forty years: my parents, Margaret and John D. Daverio. I dedicate this book to them, with love.

Boston   J. D.
March 1996

Contents

Robert Schumann

Introduction:

Schumann Today

The Biographical Challenge

To write, near the turn to the twenty-first century, a study of the life and works of Robert Schumann is perhaps both presumptuous and foolhardy; presumptuous, because so many studies of the composer already exist; and foolhardy, because biographies, if some of the latest critical punditry is to be believed, may soon become the museum pieces of writerly genres. Among nineteenth-century composers, probably only Beethoven and Wagner might boast of having served more often as the subject of biographical inquiries than Schumann, whose story has been told and retold, revised and corrected, again and again. Moreover, the biographical method itself is under fire; before long, general studies of an artist's life and works may well be viewed with the same circumspection among scholarly writings as the historical romance is among literary genres. The guiding ideas of the nineteenth century, after all, can hardly be transplanted uncritically into the twentieth. For most of us, art is no longer the unmediated expression or reflection of the artist's inner life. The unity of lived experience and artistic product—so dear to nineteenth-century thinking—was already consigned by Walter Benjamin some three-quarters of a century ago to the realm where it belongs: to myth; fictional heroes, not living subjects, exemplify a perfect synthesis of this sort.[1] Striking a more hyperbolic tone, Roland Barthes has proclaimed the death of the author, whose written work "is the destruction of every voice, of every point of origin." Writing, Barthes maintains, "is that neutral, composite, oblique space where our subject slips away, the negative where all identity is lost, starting with the very identity of the body writing."[2] And if the language spoken by a *literary* text is "neutral, composite, oblique," then the language of a musical text must be all the more hermetic, even if its creator, like Robert Schumann, has been held up by many as the ideal subject for a biography grounded in the nineteenth century's conviction that life and art are mutually reflective. But given recent skepticism of the view of music as a kind of "sonorous confession" on the one hand, and the demise of musical metaphysics on the other,[3] not even Schumann remains a safe subject for biographers. Either an account of the composer's life, pieced together mainly from his diaries and letters, hobbles alongside of an account of the works, or the works, deprived of their metaphysical content, figure as documents in a psychobiography whose hero is cut down to size by being portrayed as a neurotic like the rest of us. In the context of current debates, it is even questionable whether the traditional biography can be salvaged by tracing the transformation of biographical into aesthetic subjects in an artist's works.[4]

Then why should we have yet another biography of Schumann? In the first place, the project poses an interpretive challenge. The antinomy with which Karl Laux begins his compact but still useful study of Schumann's career—"It is easy to write a Schumann biography [because Schumann wrote it himself]. It is difficult to write a Schumann biography [because the modern biographer must chart the composer's relationships to his complicated and contradictory social surroundings]"[5]—is more than a rhetorical ploy. The difficulties entailed in writing a biography of Schumann are rooted not only in the complexities of the composer's world, but also in precisely the wealth of biographical material on which the writer must draw. Thanks to the painstaking editorial efforts of Martin Kreisig, Georg Eismann, Martin Schoppe, and Gerd Nauhaus, scholars have access to the rich fund of materials offered in the diaries and travel notes that Schumann maintained with some regularity from January 1827 to early 1854. Nauhaus's edition of the three volumes of *Haushaltbücher* ("household account books," with entries extending from early October 1837 to 23 February 1854—that is, to just four days before Schumann's suicide attempt) afford us an intimate if sketchily drawn portrait of the Schumanns' daily activities, including a minute accounting of their expenditures. Diaries, marriage diaries (the *Ehetagebücher* jointly kept with Clara from September 1840), travel notes, and household accounts together emerge as richly textured and indispensable sources of information.

Yet Schumann's diaries are easily sensationalized; some of the earlier entries in particular almost seem to invite *mis*interpretation. Consider the following passage from Peter Ostwald's psychobiography:

> Schumann mentioned some of his adventures only in his diaries and not—understandably—in his letters; for example: "Voluptuous scandal during the night with the naked tour guide and the naked waitress"; "The inaccessible barmaid and my decision—unsatisfied—forced gaiety"; "The homosexual who thrust himself on me, and my sudden departure"; "Coffeehouse and the girl constantly looking around, certainly a whore"; "Real fear of ladies."[6]

Schumann did indeed jot down all these phrases, though at widely spaced intervals in the diaries, or, more exactly, in the travel notes documenting his sojourn in Switzerland and Italy from 20 August to 20 October 1829.[7] Restoring one of the quotations to its original context may make an impression quite different from the one suggested above:

> *16 Sept. 1829*
> "Golden sunny sky—Arrival in Brescia and Sambelli[8] angry on account of the passport—Sambelli's sister—cordial leavetaking from the professor—inn—lively trade in prostitution on the streets—coffeehouse—the ladies—the Signora and Signore—the one with a low voice: yes, sir!!—this woman is certainly from the Campagna[9]—I'm quietly 'left on the shelf'[10]—Addio, Signore—bad mood—theatre—a comedy: *The Adopted Son*—of little worth—the pederast who tried to force his company on me and my sudden departure—dinner at the inn—dim moonshine—letter to Therese [Schumann] . . . —reasonably content—the beautiful dreams that I've forgotten—[11]

Ostwald's string of quotes depicts a sexually obsessed teenager. Schumann's full diary entry, on the other hand, is the work of a keenly observant bystander who records isolated impressions stenographically but vividly, as if he were collecting notes for a novel. The montage calls up images of a young libertine; the full entry was made by an aspiring littérateur.

The realistic detail of the diaries, in other words, is easily made into the stuff of myth. Ostwald's strong suspicion that Schumann experienced several homosexual episodes during his late adolescence provides another case in point. A homoerotic Schumann makes for a more sexually complex figure than we might have suspected, but what is the nature of the evidence? Ostwald relates that after a trip to a tavern with Johann Renz on 2 March 1829, Schumann "noted 'pederasty' in his diary,"[12] and further that: "After returning to the tavern the next day, he [Schumann] recorded 'voluptuous night with Greek dreams'."[13] Ostwald's interpretation of the last phrase presupposes an understanding of the rhetoric of our seedier tabloids. Schumann's "Greek dreams," however, were probably populated by figures from ancient tragedy: a year earlier he had translated a portion of the *Antigone* of Sophocles, whom he rhapsodically—we might say "voluptuously"—invoked in a diary entry of May or June 1828: "O magnificent Sophocles, who so many times has stood revealed before my soul in the beautiful and efflorescent form of Apollo."[14] In addition, Schumann would spend "luxurious" (perhaps a better translation of "üppig" than "voluptuous") nights with composers too: "Schwelgen in Chopin" (luxuriating in Chopin) he jotted in his diary on 19 June 1831.[15] In any event, on the evening of the pederasty episode in March 1829, Schumann had no Greek dreams—whatever they may have been—but rather fantasized about Schubert's so-called *Sehnsuchtswalzer*, as he would again on 4 March. If Schumann dreamed at all on 2 March, it was probably of Walter Scott's *Ivanhoe*, portions of which he read just before going to sleep.[16]

To be sure, Ostwald adduces other evidence to make a case for Schumann's homoeroticism—his close relationship with his roommate, the talented and attractive pianist Ludwig Schunke; the lack of references to Christel, Schumann's sometime-mistress, in the diaries of the mid-1830s—but this is flimsy evidence indeed.[17] Schumann's cultivation of close ties with men must be considered in the context of an age when intimate relationships among members of the same sex did not automatically spell sexual relationships. The principal male characters in Jean Paul's *Siebenkäs*, one of Schumann's favorite novels, were close enough that the author could write of his title character that: "he had not yet mustered up enough courage, except in the dithyrambic moments of friendship, . . . to kiss even his [male friend] Leibgeber, much less his Lenette [Siebenkäs's fiancée]."[18] The reader who assumes that Siebenkäs and Leibgeber are lovers is making an error; the biographer who pays insufficient attention to the cultural milieu in which Schumann grew up is making an even graver one.[19] The paucity of diary references to Christel during the mid-1830s likewise means little or nothing so far as the composer's personal dealings with men are concerned. From late March 1833 to July 1836 Schumann did not keep a diary, so that we must rely instead on the sketchy précis of his activities (from March 1833 to the summer of 1837) hastily compiled in Vienna on the evening of 28 November 1838.[20] To sum up, Schumann was undoubtedly more than an ardent bibliophile, but to maintain on the basis of scanty evidence that "he had one and possibly several homosexual encounters," that the death of his sister-in-law Rosalie might have weakened his "already fragile inhibitions against homosexuality," or that "homosexual panic" may

have contributed to his "nearly catastrophic breakdown" in 1833, requires too many leaps of the imagination.[21]

In reviewing the evidence for Schumann's passage through a homosexual phase during his early- and mid-twenties, I have not meant to
engage in a diatribe with the author of one of the most readable and
provocative biographies of the composer. On the contrary, I want only
to suggest that if the meanings of the documentary materials were at
one time transparent, they are no longer. If, as Sigmund Freud once put
it, "biographical truth is not to be had,"[22] then the biographer should
aim less at "setting the record straight" than at entering into a critical
discourse with the surviving documents.

In addition to the hermeneutic challenges posed by Schumann's
diaries, important advances in research contribute to the timeliness of a
new general study. Wolfgang Boetticher's investigations of the compositional process have gone a long way toward debunking the myth of the
unreflecting artist whose works poured forth at the behest of mysterious
voices from the beyond.[23] The sketches, we are learning, are as variously
interpretable as the literary documents. In her work on the manuscripts
for pieces spanning all phases of Schumann's career—the piano sonatas,
opp. 11, 14, and 22; the First and Third symphonies, opp. 38 and 97;
and the string quartets, op. 41, nos. 1–3—Linda Correll Roesner has
called attention to the composer's mosaic-like assembly of fragmentary
ideas, suggesting a kind of composition-as-planned-improvisation that
finds its sources in his earliest experiences at the keyboard.[24] Jon Finson's study of the sketches and drafts for the First Symphony discloses
the links between Schumann's sometimes conventionalized view of form
and his outlook on the symphony as a public genre,[25] while his reconstruction of the sketch materials for a never completed C-minor symphony (drafted in the fall of 1841) sheds new light on Schumann's abilities to compose at breakneck speed.[26] Another reconstructive effort,
Joachim Draheim's completion of a *Konzertsatz* (concerto movement) in
D minor for piano and orchestra, shows the composer grappling in early
1839 with a problem that would occupy him more persistently in 1841:
the mediation of virtuoso display and thematic development.[27] The appearance of the first several volumes in the new edition of the composer's works (*Robert Schumann Neue Ausgabe sämtlicher Werke*, jointly
sponsored by the Robert-Schumann-Gesellschaft in Düsseldorf and the
Robert-Schumann-Haus, Zwickau, and under the general editorship of
Akio Mayeda and Klaus Wolfgang Niemöller) roughly coincides with
renewed attempts at an analytical evaluation of Schumann's output, a
task pursued more systematically by German than by American or Brit-

ish scholars. In arguing for Schumann's continuity with the formal traditions of Viennese classicism, Markus Waldura subsumes the composer's miniature and expanded forms alike under the banner of
monomotivicism.[28] Reinhard Kapp and Michael Struck have both—albeit from different angles and with differing results—devoted themselves
to a much-needed revision of our outlook on the controversial products
of Schumann's later years.[29]

To be sure, much remains to be done on the documentary side.
Perhaps most sorely missed is a comprehensive source-thematic cata-
logue of the composer's works (as of this writing, Margit McCorkle and
Akio Mayeda are compiling one). For Boetticher, the problematic current status of Schumann's correspondence looms as a major concern.
The publication of the Schumann family's special repository of letters,
the so-called *Familienkassette* (which itself suffered severe water damage
as a result of the 1945 bombing of Dresden and survives only because
Boetticher had the foresight to microfilm much of the collection at the
Dresdener Landesbibliothek in 1938) marks but a first step toward the
realization of an important goal: a critical edition of all previously unpublished letters.[30] Even our knowledge of Schumann's activities as a
music critic has its lacunae. Boetticher's comparison of several of the
composer's early diary entries on Beethoven, Spohr, Berlioz, and Liszt
with anonymous notices on the same figures in the *Allgemeine musikalische Zeitung* suggests that many of the unsigned articles may in fact be
attributable to Schumann.[31] Akio Mayeda's projected completion of a
new edition of Schumann's writings on music promises to address these
(and other) aspects of the composer's critical endeavors. And finally, the
new edition of Schumann's works is still in the incipient stages.[32] Its
editors will have a host of issues to confront, among them the problem
posed by works for which several versions or editions exist (e.g., the
Davidsbündlertänze, op. 6; the *Etudes Symphoniques,* op. 13; and *Concert
sans orchestre*/Piano Sonata no. 3, op. 14)[33] or for which the sketchbooks
transmit alternate (and often very different) readings,[34] and the interpretation of the composer's subtle but sometimes idiosyncratic notation
of his keyboard music.[35]

If the purpose of scholarly biography, as Hermann Danuser puts it,
lies in "the precise representation of compositional thought,"[36] then the
present state of Schumann research will at least allow for a general study
that aims at a thorough engagement with the composer's music, even
though we will have to rely in many cases on the less-than-ideal texts of
his works as transmitted in the old collected edition (Breitkopf & Härtel,
1881–93), a project overseen by Clara Schumann and Brahms. To a certain extent, the assertion made over a decade ago by two leading schol-

ars—"For the present, Schumann is . . . only the composer of certain piano pieces, a piano concerto, and the Rhenish Symphony"[37]—still holds today. Works may be "as irreducible as deeds,"[38] but the light in which these deeds are viewed is constantly shifting over time. That significant portions of Schumann's output (in particular, the choral-orchestral music, much of the chamber music, and the works of his last years) play a relatively minor role in contemporary concert life is in part a function of the vagaries of reception history. Brahms's evaluation of the incidental music to *Manfred* and the *Scenen aus Göthe's Faust* as "the most magnificent things" that Schumann had ever written is probably shared by few today.[39] But at the same time, the spotty picture of the composer emanating from our concert halls and recording studios can be traced to the demise of the type of individual that Schumann represented in its purest manifestation: the musican-as-littérateur. Indeed, literature held a place in Schumann's creative life comparable to that of philosophy in Wagner's. Here was a figure who as a youth of fifteen read with his friends practically all of Schiller's dramas,[40] who as a *pater familias* of forty-three reread (in some cases, for the fourth or fifth time) his favorite Jean Paul novels,[41] and whose eclectic taste for literature extended from Aeschylus's *Eumenides* to Harriet Beecher Stowe's *Uncle Tom's Cabin*.[42] Schumann was, to quote Peter Rumenhöller's finely nuanced phrase, "universally cultured" ("universal gebildet"),[43] so that a necessary condition for our understanding of his musical output, especially its less accessible byways, will be an understanding of the literature that the composer knew and loved. We will have to look behind and beyond the works, the "irreducible deeds" forming our point of departure, to the poetic sensibility that informed their creation and to the afterlife they experienced at the hands of Schumann's critics.

Questions and Provisional Answers

In a review of Nigel Hamilton's *JFK: Reckless Youth*, Elizabeth Hardwick notes that "necessity, gap, lack do not always play a part in contemporary biography. Indeed, redundancy is the rule on the celebrated and even for those of a more narrow appeal such as poets, novelists, painters, and composers."[44] As disconcerting as it may be to accept, Hardwick's assessment rings true. We read (and write) biographies in part to confirm what we know about the subjects under discussion and what we think we know about ourselves. But while redundancy may be the justifiable object of the critic's scorn, this is not to say that previously raised questions should not be framed anew.

So far as Schumann is concerned, a complex of biographical, more broadly historical, critical, and analytical issues are certainly worth considering from a fresh perspective. To what extent did Schumann cultivate the musical *Erlebnislyrik* or "lyric of personal experience," represented, most obviously, by his youthful fondness for cryptograms and ciphers? How can we gauge the interplay between subjective utterance and objective treatment in his music? What is Schumann's position relative to the accomplishments of other nineteenth-century artists? Is it possible for us to form a coherent picture of an output in which works of considerable breadth and seriousness rub shoulders with unpretentious miniatures? Is it sensible to link the changes both in Schumann's style and in the direction of his career with the social and economic configurations of the mid-nineteenth century? To what extent do the old caveats—regarding Schumann's undistinguished orchestration, his greater success in smaller than in larger forms, his lack of dramatic talent, and the gradual decline in his creative powers—still hold?

Without promising definitive answers, we might begin by examining the questions critically. Nowhere is this more difficult than in measuring the interpenetration of life and art in Schumann's works, even if the two commingle more thoroughly here than with any other nineteenth-century composer. The notion of music-as-confession finds sustenance in the writings of Schumann himself, who as a young man wrote of his favorite author, "In all his works Jean Paul mirrors himself, but always as two persons: he is Albano and Schoppe [in *Titan*], Siebenkäs and Leibgeber *[Siebenkäs]*, Vult and Walt *[Flegeljahre]*,"[45] and as a more mature journalist said of Liszt, "His own life is situated in his music."[46] What Schumann asserted of one of his most admired predecessors—"Strictly speaking, a sheet of music was for Schubert what for others was a diary"[47]—has been said often enough of Schumann himself. Plentiful evidence suggests that he viewed large segments of his own output in precisely this way. In spite of a tangle of contradictory utterances, it is difficult to rule out some connection between *Papillons*, op. 2, and the literary example provided by Jean Paul's *Flegeljahre*. Copious references from the letters can be marshalled to support the view that many of the piano works from the 1830s—the *Davidsbündlertänze*, op. 6; the F♯-minor Sonata, op. 11; the *Concert sans orchestre*, opus 14; *Kreisleriana*, op. 16; and the *Novelletten*, op. 21—were bound up with conflicts over Schumann's troubled suit for Clara's hand. While arranging Paganini's G-minor Caprice for inclusion in the *6 Studien*, op. 3, Schumann notes in his diary that he was visited by fantastic images of the violin virtuoso "in a magic circle."[48] Similarly, the composer relates that the *Nachtstücke,* op. 23 (originally called *Leichenphantasie* or "Corpse-Fantasy") were conceived under the spell of a visionary premonition of his brother Eduard's death.[49] According to Clara's January 1841 entry in the marriage diary, the impulse for the creation of the First Symphony (its new stylistic profile is often linked by biographers to Schumann's recent marriage) came from a poem by Adolph Böttger.[50] As late as 1850, Schumann writes to Simrock of the Third Symphony, op. 97, that it "perhaps here and there reflects on a slice of [my] life."[51]

No doubt Schumann is an important witness for his own works, but the suspicion arises that his testimony may be colored by an ideology of art and life that runs through nineteenth-century criticism with the obstinacy of a Wagnerian leitmotif. The two spheres can certainly affect one another, but their interaction may result in either reciprocal support or mutual negation. According to Schumann's comments on his creative outpouring during the civil revolutions at mid-century: "It seemed as if the outer storms impelled people to turn inward."[52] At the same time, artistic product and affective state are not always in harmony. Those who treat the Second Symphony, op. 61, as a reflection of Schumann's depressive melancholy are listening only to the somber rhetoric of the Adagio, and not to the dignified joviality of the first movement and Finale, or the irrepressible good humor of the Scherzo.[53]

An accumulation of biographical detail brings with it a paradox: heightened knowledge of a composer's lived experience often belies the connections between life and art that we would like to find.[54] Even an early commentator like Franz Brendel asserted that the descriptive titles of Schumann's collections of miniatures for piano were "the result of reflection," not pre-compositional catalysts.[55] For most biographers, the link between *Carnaval,* op. 9, and Schumann's then-sweetheart Ernestine von Fricken is assured by the encipherment of the name of her hometown, Asch, into the fabric of the music; but the A-S-C-H motive first appears in sketches unrelated to *Carnaval.*[56]

Living in the shadow of Freud, the modern biographer responds to "the imperfection of artificers" at the expense of "the perfection of artifacts."[57] Udo Rauchfleisch, author of yet another psychobiography of Schumann, is not alone in treating the composer's works as documents of his psychological complaints.[58] The focal point of Ostwald's biography is the composer's final illness, which casts a pall over the entire study; witness the author's decision to devote his opening chapter to an account of Schumann's suicide attempt in February 1854 and its immediate aftermath.[59] Biographical narrative and value judgment go hand in hand, for Schumann's works are thus reduced to a therapeutic means of warding off impending madness. To be sure, composing may have been a form of theraphy for Schumann (it probably is for most composers), but my sense is that it was much more besides.

No less difficult than the circumscribed problems of biography are the larger issues of historical position. No doubt, our composer occupies an equivocal place in the nineteenth century. "Schumann," Brahms pointed out in conversation with Richard Heuberger, "went one way, Wagner another, and I a third."[60] But what was "Schumann's way"? The composer came of age as part of the successor generation to Hegel, Goethe, and Schleiermacher. The majority of his works fall within the two decades bounded on the one hand by the rise of the optimistic literary movement known as *Junges Deutschland* and on the other by the failed revolutions of 1848/49. Hence they span a period of transition from faith in philosophical idealism to resigned embrace of political realism. Schumann's music neither accords neatly with his time nor withdraws decisively from it, but rather hovers between the no-longer and the not-yet, between the youthful bloom of Weber and the autumnal reflection of Brahms. This transitional quality can be read in the network of allusions and foreshadowings in a composition such as the First Symphony: the trombone countertheme from the coda of the Finale inverts a characteristic segment from the famous horn tune that opens Schubert's Ninth Symphony; the melody prefacing the return to E♭ in the slow movement looks forward to the main theme of the first movement of Brahms's Third Symphony.

Perhaps Schumann's appearance at a juncture when the musical scene was in flux has made it difficult for biographers to reach a concensus on the number and nature of his style periods. One thing is certain: traditional three- or four-period divisions will not do. Their differences aside, most attempts at a periodization of Schumann's career affirm the presence of two main phases. In doing so, they draw (whether consciously or not) on the paradigm suggested by the nineteenth-century critic and historian Franz Brendel, who argued that the temporal manifestation of Schumann's general tendency to proceed "outward from within" resulted in the passage from a "subjective" phase (represented in the early piano music) to an "objective" phase (in the symphonic, chamber, and contrapuntal works of the early- and mid-1840s), with the songs of 1840 serving as a bridge from one phase to the other.[61] Stripped of its Hegelian overtones, Brendel's scheme is at the heart of the subsequent divisions of Schumann's career into "romantic" and "classic" periods,[62] a bipartition as convenient as it is questionable: the G-minor Piano Sonata, op. 22, begun when Schumann was in his mid-twenties, is in many ways a model of classical form; the late choral-orchestral ballade *Vom Pagen und der Königstochter* is full of romantic whimsy. Examples such as these could be easily multiplied. Schumann himself singled out 1845 (when the Second Symphony was begun) as the year during which he developed "a completely new manner of composition."[63] Still, it is open to debate whether this composition represents a watershed in the sense that, say, Beethoven's *"Eroica"* does. While the Second Symphony demonstrates a notable sophistication in its integration of materials over the entire course of a multi-movement work, Schumann's "new manner" of 1845 is perhaps better understood as a logical outgrowth of his approach to large-scale instrumental composition in the earlier 1840s rather than as a radical break.

Allow me to suggest a way out of the dilemma posed by the search for a cogent periodization of Schumann's output. Perhaps Schumann consistently intermingled "subjective" and "objective" qualities throughout his career, but with varying degrees of emphasis, a hypothesis implying that the passage from a "subjective" to an "objective" phase was hardly abrupt. To insist on a hard-and-fast demarcation of style-periods in time is to miss the point, namely, that Schumann's *oeuvre* unfolds in a series of sometimes parallel and sometimes overlapping phases.[64] The products of his imagination may thus be viewed as points where divergent or complementary trends intersect. Schumann's hopes for a career as virtuoso pianist, dashed in the autumn of 1831 by the realization that his lame finger would not allow for it, run parallel with an intense preoccupation with literature; both factors coalesce in his engaging review of Chopin's virtuoso variations on Mozart's *"Là ci darem la mano."* During the 1830s Schumann not only cultivated the keyboard miniature, but also prepared assiduously for symphonic composition,[65] a dualism evident in many an orchestrally styled passage in the piano sonatas and the *Fantasie*, op. 17. The balance shifts during the course of the Symphonic Year (1841), where we hear, for example, an allusion to the last piece of *Kreisleriana* in a transitional passage from the Finale of the First Symphony.[66] Overlaps and crosscurrents of this sort infiltrate every aspect of Schumann's work: sketchbooks may function as diaries,[67] passages from the diaries often turn up in the critical writings, critical perspectives shape the attitude toward genre, musical genres—the possibilities of which Schumann appears to have explored quite systematically—mutually influence one another.

In order to analyze the dualisms that contribute to the richness of Schumann's work (but that have caused his biographers no end of headaches), let us turn briefly to one of the more problematic corners of his output: the *Hausmusik* (convivial or pedagogical music for piano, voice, or chamber ensemble) of the late 1840s. The bourgeois sensibility of much of Schumann's later keyboard music—one thinks of the *Album für die Jugend,* op. 68 (1848) and the *Waldscenen,* op. 82 (1848–49)—is as unmistakable as it is challenging to fix in technical categories. But the literal meaning of the term aside, *Hausmusik* cannot be defined by its place of performance. Although mainly intended for the delectation of the family circle, *Hausmusik* might just as well find its way into the aristocratic or royal salon; witness Schumann's report on Clara's performance of selections from the *Album für die Jugend* at the Hannoverian court.[68] Nor is a definition on stylistic grounds any easier to formulate. A fine line separates the stylized naïveté of the *Kinderscenen* from the insouciance of the *Album für die Jugend,* a number of whose pieces (especially from the second part of the collection, "for older children") would not sound out of place in the "poetic" collections of the 1830s. What emerges in much of the *Hausmusik* for piano is a delicate tension between simplicity and high art.

In the first piece of the *Waldscenen,* "Eintritt," this tension manifests itself in the discrepancy between the regularity of the larger metric groupings and the irregularity of their inner divisions. The opening phrase falls into two subphrases of three-and-a-half and four measures, respectively, thus causing a slight but telling shift in the metric weight of the closing gesture, marked x in Example I.1. To the eye, both statements of x seem to occupy the same position within two four-bar phrases. But given the beginning of the second subphrase a half-bar "too soon" midway through m. 4, we perceive the stress pattern delineated by *x* in mm. 7–8 as weak-strong-weak, the reverse of the strong-weak-strong pattern of its first appearance (mm. 3–4). What is more, the player who takes the first ending will hear the opening gesture transformed, as if by magic, from a strong to a weak position in the larger metric pattern. The unpretentiousness of the melody is thus belied by syntactic subtleties.

This example should at least give pause to our unquestioning acceptance of one of the oldest clichés of Schumann criticism: the unrelenting four-squareness of much of his music. Another tired claim, that Schumann was an inept orchestrator, also invites reexamination. Half a century ago, Arnold Schoenberg interpreted this claim as a by-product of the conflict between the "New Germans" (Berlioz, Liszt, Wagner) and the "Academic-Classicists" (Schumann, Brahms) that raged so furiously in the second half of the nineteenth century.[69] And indeed, Schumann was capable of producing orchestral effects just as striking as those of the "musicians of the future" if the occasion warranted. The evocative scoring at the opening of the fourth of his *Faust* Scenes ("Ariel. Sonnenaufgang"), featuring richly divided strings and upper wind chords punc-

Example I.1. Waldscenen, op. 82: *Eintritt*, mm. 1–8.

tuated by the harp, provides both a backdrop for Faust's attempts to fall asleep and an apt portrayal of Goethe's designation for Ariel's opening speech: "Gesang, von Äolsharfen begleitet" ("Song, accompanied by Aeolian harps"). The clearly differentiated sound-strata of the subsequent scene ("Mitternacht"), where a nervous figure in the *divisi* violas contrasts sharply with an eerie line in the winds, are worthy of comparison with many a passage in Berlioz. And in order to establish the proper mood for the invocation of the Spirit of the Alps in *Manfred* (no. 6), Schumann fashioned a gossamer texture of muted violin sixteenths, arabesques in the winds, and harp harmonics.

Even more deeply engrained in the popular consciousness is the opinion that Schumann was unable to control larger forms. That he was more than able to do so is easily demonstrated by the final scene-complex of *Das Paradies und die Peri*. The representation of the Peri's third and final descent to earth, her observation of the fearsome criminal turned penitent, and her joyous welcome into heaven, span a series of four numbers (23–26), the first and third of which are likewise parsed into interdependent lyric units. Fundamental for the cohesiveness of the whole is a "progressive" tonal scheme moving from E minor to G major.

The logic of the design also results from a network of melodic cross-references: portions of the lyrical material from the tenor's arioso in No. 23 resurface in the episodes of the rondo-like No. 26; the sinner's prayer at the conclusion of No. 23 provides the tone for the chorus's reflections in No. 24 and its commentary on the tenor solo in No. 25; and finally, a descending figure elaborated in No. 25 recurs, though reconfigured as an emblem of triumph, at the beginning of No. 26. By and large, Schumann makes his referential points unobtrusively; nowhere in the closing scene-complex do the recurrent materials acquire the chiseled character of leitmotifs. Recognition of this fact may help to explain Schumann's peculiar standing as a composer of dramatic music. His preference for the subtle link over the profiled leitmotif colors his epic endeavors with a lyric quality, an inwardness at odds with the confrontational atmosphere we expect in drama. But faulting him for his lyric bent is as unjustified as criticizing a lyric poem because it happens to eschew dialogue.

The uneasy relationship between analysis and value judgment comes into relief more obviously in discussions of Schumann's late works than in any other portion of his output. For some early critics, a dimming of the composer's genius was already apparent at the end of the 1840s in works such as the opera *Genoveva*.[70] By the beginning of the following decade, Theodor Uhlig would find signs in the A-minor Sonata for piano and violin, op. 105, that idiosyncrasy had given way to musical mannerisms such as obsessive repetitions and curious mixtures of the bizarre and the commonplace.[71] Even the more sympathetic Brendel had only muted praise for the *Phantasie* for violin and orchestra, op. 131. The violinist Ferdinand David, he wrote, "lent the work a surprising effectiveness, demonstrating that it really can be successfully performed for a cultured audience receptive to Schumann's compositions."[72] Nor has it helped matters that the events surrounding the creation or reception of some of these works have all the trappings of a ghost story by E. T. A. Hoffmann. By Schumann's own account, the theme of his last set of keyboard variations was dictated to him "by the angels." Jelly d'Arányi and Adili Fachiri, nieces of the violinist Joseph Joachim and themselves violinists of note, were in turn "commanded" by the spirits of their uncle and Schumann to track down the manuscript of the latter's violin concerto and have it published. (This they indeed did, with the help of Wilhelm Strecker, then in the employ of Schott Verlag; the concerto appeared in print, notwithstanding the objections of Schumann's daughter Eugenie, in 1937.)[73] These are intriguing tales, but they have had the unfortunate effect of enveloping the late works in a fog of occultism that has become increasingly difficult to penetrate.

Stemming from the ever-narrowing circle of family and friends around Schumann in his last creative phase—namely Clara, Brahms, and the violinist Joseph Joachim—the myth that portrays the late works as a necessary complement to the final illness has been called into question by more recent appraisals of the documentary and musical evidence.[74] According to this view, Schumann's ultimate descent into madness forfeits its status as the last stage in a disintegrating career. If we want to interpret Schumann's life as a drama, the dementia of his last years will function as the peripeteia or reversal that occasioned an abrupt interruption in the work that had continued apace until January of 1854.[75] Indeed, anyone who scans Schumann's last diary entries (on the trip to Hannover in late January 1854) for signs of mental decay will be disappointed. Likewise, an unbiased look at the late music will disclose qualities too frequently overlooked: a heightened intensity of expression,[76] a rigorous limitation of thematic materials,[77] and a visionary prefiguration of features associated with later composers including Bruckner, Reger, and even Schoenberg.[78]

Consider, for instance, the slow movement of the Violin Concerto, which, in spite of its brevity, unfolds as a fully elaborated sonata form. The movement plays on two ideas (labeled A and B in Example I.2) associated with a solo cello and the solo violin, respectively. The second idea (B) embodies a tension between lyric breadth and motivic economy: a close look reveals that it evolves entirely as a series of melodically filled-in thirds. While this idea serves in both the opening and closing groups, the solo cello's idea (A) turns out to be even more versatile. One could say that the point of the movement resides precisely in the gradual realization of this motive's potential: as principal theme, as countermelody to the violin's theme, as transitional material to the closing group, as main subject in the development, and finally as transition to the finale. Functional multiplicity and motivic limitation go hand in hand. Only a composer in full command of his or her rational powers can realize the consequences of this interdependence of variety and unity. Robert Schumann was such a composer—until February 1854.

Toward a Portrait of Schumann the Composer

Our image of Schumann will vary depending on which segment of his creative output we deem central. The focus on the piano music common

Example I.2. Violin Concerto: slow movement. Violin and piano reduction by Georg Schunemann © B. Schott's Soehne, Mainz, 1937. © renewed. All rights reserved. Used by permission of European American Music Distributors Corporation, sole U.S. and Canadian agent for B. Schott's Soehne, Mainz.

in so many studies represents the continuation of a critical tradition stemming from the later nineteenth century. But whereas the cycles of keyboard pieces from the 1830s and the songs of 1840 have contributed to a view of Schumann as a sentimental lyricist (in *Jenseits von Gut und Böse* [Be*yond Good and Evil*] Nietzsche spoke of "a dangerous propensity . . . for quiet lyricism and sottishness of feeling"), the poetic element in the piano music, embodied in its evocative titles and superscriptions, enabled the composer's supporters in the "New German" camp to make him into a program musician and hence a representative of musical progress.[79] Liszt found further proof of Schumann's modernity in the later works for chorus and orchestra. In arguing for the centrality of works such as the *Faust* scenes, Liszt justified his elevation of Schumann from musical craftsman to *Tondichter*—tone poet. A more recent writer like Peter Rummenhöller also takes Schumann's "literary culture" as a starting point. In Rummenhöller's opinion, the composer's critical activities serve as the focal point for a new, "modern-bourgeois" artistic type: the musician-as-intellectual.[80] For Helmuth Christian Wolff, who emphasizes the contrapuntal works of 1845 (*Studien für den Pedal-Flügel*, op. 56; *Sechs Fugen über den Namen B-A-C-H*, op. 60; *Vier Fugen für Pianoforte*, op. 72), Schumann is a "classicist."[81] If we accept Dahlhaus's pithy description of Schumann's *oeuvre* as "*Hausmusik* for cognoscenti,"[82] then the keyboard and vocal music of the late 1840s will have to be accorded more than marginal significance. And last, Reinhard Kapp, an apologist for the late, "esoteric" instrumental works, views this repertory as the culmination of Schumann's creative life.[83]

The fact that nearly every facet of Schumann's output can be taken as the decisive one is not so disconcerting as it may first appear. Quite simply, it means that the composer was many things: a progressive, a tone poet, a bourgeois intellectual, a classicist, a lover of the bizarre and enigmatic. It also means that no single genre was central to his development. In fact, he was a master of transforming one genre into another, without our being able to pinpoint where one leaves off and the other begins. *Kennst du das Land,* the first of the *Lieder und Gesänge* from Goethe's *Wilhelm Meister,* Opus 98a, compresses all the elements of an operatic *scena*—instrumental introduction, recitative, and aria—into the smallest of spaces. Schumann's fugues (the *Vier Fugen,* op. 72, in particular) often display the techniques of motivic development associated with the character piece. The slow movement of the D-minor Piano Trio, op. 63, is both a character piece for chamber ensemble and a series of contrapuntal variations.

Thus the model for Schumann's creative work is less a perfectly rounded whole, a circle with a midpoint, than a constellation of fragments. But regulating the fragments and imparting them coherence is a single thought: the notion that music should be imbued with the same intellectual substance as literature. Schumann developed this conviction while he was still a teenager; he held to it until the end of his career.

~1~

The Formation of a Musico-Literary Sensibility

A Youth by No Means Lacking in Talent

"The city and its suburbs lie in one of the most beautiful and romantic regions of Saxony, on the left bank of the Mulde, between gardens, meadows, and fertile fields. . . . The entire area around Zwickau has so many natural beauties that one could actually call it a park."[1] It was here in Zwickau, on 8 June 1810 at 10:30 P.M., that Robert Schumann was born the fifth and last child of August Schumann and Johanna Christiana Schumann *née* Schnabel. The young Schumann passed his early years in a milieu conducive to the pursuit of literary studies. His father, by several accounts an active, ingenious, and industrious man,[2] is often described as a book dealer, though the scope of his activities was considerably wider. The author of chivalric romances and an indefatigable lexicographer, August Schumann made a small fortune by publishing pocket editions of Sir Walter Scott's novels and other foreign classics in German translation. Soon before his death in August 1826 he began to issue similar editions of Byron's works; these publications were not lost on his son, who during the summer of 1827 set one of the English poet's lyrics ("I saw thee weep") as a lied entitled *Die Weinende*. Indeed, Schumann spoke of his father's book dealership as "a great formative power for a youth";[3] within its walls he no doubt wiled away many an hour poring over literary classics produced both abroad and at home. A firm believer in the positive force of Enlightenment, *Bildung* (self-cultivation), and the liberal spirit, August Schumann once asserted that "What binds the Germans as a nation is their literature," [4] a conviction he certainly passed on to his youngest and favorite offspring. Even Johanna Christiana dabbled in literature: the thirteen-year-old Robert copied her poem *An Napoleon* into his *Blätter und Blümchen aus der goldenen Aue* (Leaves and Flowerlets from the Golden Meadow), a commonplace-book in which the aspiring *literatus*, under the name "Skülander," recorded his earliest poetic efforts, including lyrics, dramatic fragments, and fictitious letters.[5]

Up to his third year Schumann was, in his own words, "a child like any other." [6] Then, after his mother contracted typhus ("Nervenfieber"), he was placed under the care of a Frau Eleonore Carolina Elisabeth Ruppius, a kindly woman well practiced in the art of child-rearing, who along with her husband had served as witness at Schumann's baptism. The child's stay in the Ruppius household, which was supposed to last no more than six weeks but in fact covered a two-and-a-half-year period, has been viewed as the source of a separation anxiety that fed into the composer's later depressive condition.[7] Yet Schumann seems to have had nothing but fond memories of this phase of his life: he soon grew extremely attached to Frau Ruppius, whom he likened in his earliest autobiographical account to a "second mother." [8] (In any event, such arrangements were not uncommon in the earlier nineteenth century: the gregarious Balzac, for instance, spent several of his childhood years with a foster family). Schumann emerged from the experience "gentle, childlike, and attractive," ready, at the age of six or so, to enroll in the private school of Archdeacon H. Döhner, from whom he soon began to learn Latin, French, and Greek.[9]

When he was about seven, his frequent singing having alerted his parents to their youngest son's musical talent, Schumann began piano lessons with Johann Gottfried Kuntsch, then the organist at Saint Mary's, described in one of the composer's autobiographical sketches from around 1840 as "a good teacher who liked me, but who was himself only a mediocre player." [10] Kuntsch's youthful charge made rapid progress: in short order, Schumann demonstrated a real gift for sight-reading, "though obviously without technical perfection or accuracy," and already by his second year of study, he had made his first attempts at composition in the form of dances, presumably for keyboard.[11] A further spur to the boy's musical imagination dates from about the same time. In 1818, Schumann accompanied his mother to Karlsbad, where she intended to reap the curative benefits of the spot's famed mineral baths (her son would do likewise in the mid- and late-1840s, in the environs of Dresden and on the East Frisian island of Norderney). Schumann remembered their five-week excursion, which flew by so quickly he thought only a week had passed, as the "most beautiful time" in his life; he was up every morning, sometimes as early as 4 or 5 A.M., for a walk along the promenade, read until lunchtime, and then took another stroll in the afternoon, either in the city or alone in the countryside. At an evening concert, Johanna Christiana whispered into her son's ear that the famed pianist-composer Ignaz Moscheles was seated behind them. This fleeting encounter made a lasting impression. Writing to Moscheles many years later, in 1851, Schumann confessed to having preserved a concert program that the virtuoso happened to touch, as if it were a "sacred relic."[12]

Schumann's childhood idyll came to an end by about 1819 or 1820 when, upon entering the fourth class of the Zwickau Gymnasium, he began to feel overladen with schoolwork. "I wasn't always diligent," Schumann admitted in his earliest autobiographical account, "though I was by no means lacking in talent."[13] Along with his brother (probably the next oldest, Carl) and some schoolfriends, Schumann set up a "right pretty theatre" at home and, charging two or three thalers admission, mounted ex tempore theatrical productions that made him into something of a neighborhood celebrity.[14] Beginning in 1821 or 1822, he appeared in *Abendunterhaltungen* (semi-private evening entertainments) organized by Kuntsch, participating in performances of four-hand variations by Pleyel; variation sets for solo piano by J. B. Cramer, Ferdinand Ries, and Moscheles; and Weber's *Aufforderung zum Tanz*.[15] Echoes of this repertoire can easily be heard in some of Schumann's earlier compositional efforts. The *VIII Polonaises* (1828) draw on his youthful exposure to the four-hand literature; the *Abegg Variations*, op. 1 (1830), reflect his close acquaintance with the virtuoso variation tradition; and the diverse influences that fed into *Papillons*, op. 2 (1829–31), certainly include Weber's popular *Aufforderung zum Tanz*.

Thanks largely to the *Lebenserinnerungen* of his schoolmate Emil Flechsig, we can sense the emergence of a well defined personality as Schumann approached adolescence. According to Flechsig, his friend's performance as a gymnasiast was only "middling," his deportment, at least at school, given to dreaminess and inattention. But this is not to say that Schumann was indifferent to his schoolwork, nor that he was lethargic and withdrawn. After all, his diploma from the Zwickau Gymnasium, awarded on 15 March 1828, testifies to a graduation "with honor."[16] Moreover, and again as Flechsig tells it, Schumann was "absolutely convinced" as a teenager "that he would eventually become a famous man." He needed only to settle on the precise area in which to distinguish himself. And although Schumann toyed with the idea of pursuing heraldic or philological studies, Flechsig drew particular attention to his schoolmate's keen intelligence for belles-lettres, his aspirations in this direction encoded in the poems and dramatic fragments of the *Blätter und Blümchen*.

At the same time, Schumann had already developed into an accomplished pianist with a genuine gift for free improvisation. His own autobiographical notes on this phase of his life speak, in even stronger terms, of a "pathological longing for music and piano-playing if I hadn't played for a while," and make further reference to cello and flute lessons with a Herr Meissner, the municipal music director.[17] In addition, a number of ambitious compositional projects stem from these early teenage years. Schumann listed his setting of Psalm 150 for soprano, alto, and an unusual orchestral complement (consisting of two violins, viola, two flutes, two oboes, bassoon, horn, two trumpets, tympani, and piano) as his "oldest completely finished work,"[18] and indeed the manuscript's title page, dated 1822, and unfortunately the only trace of the composition to survive, bears the proud disignation "Oeuv. 1" as well as an imprint indicative of the young composer's wishful thinking: "Leipzig / chez Breitkopf et Härtel." "I'm almost ashamed when I look at it now," Schumann wrote of his fledgling effort many years later, "I had no knowledge [of composition] and even wrote like a child."[19] Nonetheless, the child was already exhibiting a proclivity for systematic production, for another foray into the oratorical genre, an *Ouverture* and *Chor von Landleuten*, "Oeuv 1 . . . No. 3" (again scored for an odd instrumentarium, this time including piano and serpent) followed later in 1822 or early in 1823.[20] An entry in his *Projektenbuch* (project book) for the same years even alludes to the beginnings of an opera.[21]

Thus by the time Schumann reached his thirteenth year, a tug-of-war between poetic and musical pursuits was well under way and would, in one form or another, persist until the end of his career. As he indicated much later in his diary, both urges emanated from the same source: "Already in my earliest years I always felt compelled to produce, if not music, then poetry, and I enjoyed a happiness just as great as any I've since felt."[22] And even at this relatively early stage, there are signs of an attempt to reconcile the dual impulses in his will to production by writing literature *about* music: the *Blätter und Blümchen* contain, together with poetic and dramatic fragments, a series of brief biographical sketches of famous composers and excerpts from F. D. Schubart's *Ideen zu einer Ästhetik der Tonkunst* (1806).

Among the clearest signs of the seriousness with which Schumann intended to cultivate the belletristic side of his talent was his founding, along with ten other students, of a *Litterarischer Verein* (literary club) in the late autumn of 1825. No doubt the young Schumann was the driving force behind the group, which met no less than thirty times between December 1825 and February 1828. Indeed, its statement of purpose begins with a phrase much in keeping with the outlook of Schumann *père:* "It is the duty of every cultivated individual to know the literature of his fatherland. . . ."[23] Dedicated to the study of specifically German literature, every meeting of the *Verein* consisted of a series of readings aloud from the masterworks of German poetry and prose, the biographies of distinguished men of letters, and even the original works of members, followed by a period of discussion. The *Protokollbuch* of the *Verein* likewise laid out the ground-rules for the establishment of a lending library to be owned jointly by the members and toward which every new member was to contribute one volume. Frequently elected *Vorsteher* or chairman, Schumann was responsible for maintaining silence during the readings, distributing parts in plays, correcting errors in delivery, and imposing fines for inappropriate behavior. In the course of its slightly more than two-year existence, the *Verein* provided a forum for the reading and discussion of poetry by acknowledged masters such as Schiller, a particular favorite of the young Schumann, and less well-known figures including Ernst Schulze; biographical articles on Jean Paul, Herder, and Wieland; and essays by Friedrich Schlegel.[24] From the minutes of the group's meetings we can tell that its members planned to explore, systematically, the works of great German authors in turn, and here too it is possible to sense Schumann's guiding hand. Special emphasis was first accorded the dramatic works of Schiller, eight of whose plays were read and studied, either in whole or in part, between 16 January 1826 and March 1827. One of these, *Die Braut von Messina,* provided the inspiration for an overture (op. 100) composed during Schumann's later years.[25] The group's focus on drama thus occurred at the end of a phase designated in Schumann's autobiographical sketches of 1840 as one of "Passion for the theatre," and marked by his first hearing of operas by Weber *(Der Freischütz),* Cherubini *(Les deux Journées* in its German incarnation as *Der Wasserträger),* Rossini *(La Gazza Ladra, Mosé in Egitto),* and Mozart *(Die Entführung aus dem Serail).*[26]

The survey of Schiller's dramas complete, the *Verein* turned to the writer who would loom larger in the young Schumann's literary pantheon than any other: Johann Paul Friedrich Richter, best known by his *nom de plume,* Jean Paul. But the group did not make much progress with its study of this brilliant but idiosyncratic author; only two of his titles figured in their sessions: *Die Neujahrsnacht eines Unglücklichen,* a novella, taken up in June 1827, and his *Conjecturalbiographie*, read in December of that year.[27] During the same period, Schumann had apparently struck out on his own self-designed course of Jean Paul study; in a letter of 25 December 1827, he promised to send his friend Otto Hermann Walther a copy of *Titan*, the novel whose apparent offenses against writerly proprieties he would defend in a school essay, also written in 1827, entitled "Warum erbittert uns Tadel in Sachen des Geschmakes [sic] mehr, als in andern Dingen" (Why Does Censure Provoke Us More in Matters of Taste Than in Other Things?).[28] The *Litterarischer Verein* assembled for the last time on 16 February 1828, its subsequent disbanding surely linked to Schumann's relocation in Leipzig to pursue legal studies.

The formative importance of this coterie of like-minded, aspiring literati for the young Schumann can hardly be overemphasized, not least because it afforded him an outlet for his developing tendency toward systematic study and production. Indeed, the *Verein* was founded on the principle that all of the "great men" of German letters "have sprung from groups such as this."[29] Hence reception and creation were envisioned as flipsides of the same coin, as they undoubtedly were during Schumann's later teenage years as well. His justifiable claim to have been familiar with "the most important poets of a fair number of countries" before his twentieth birthday[30] was complemented by an urge to try his hand at a broad range of literary genres: translation, lyric poetry, drama, critique, and confessional memoir. The same desire to exhaust the possibilities of a genre that arches over Schumann's mature productions is thus present in his youthful literary activities. Some of these projects even foreshadow the chief musico-poetic efforts, the "literary operas" of Schumann's later years. Though none of the seven surviving dramatic fragments of the Zwickau years progressed beyond a first act, two of them dating from early 1827—*Die beiden Montalti*, a *Trauerspiel*, and *Coriolan*, a *Dramatisches Gedicht*—prefigure the dramaturgical forms of *Genoveva* and *Manfred*, respectively.[31]

As a gymnasiast, Schumann had read the classical tragedians and Horace in the original Greek and Latin. No later than 1825, he began to make metric translations (many of them collected in his *Idyllen aus dem Griechischen des Bion, Theocritus und Moschus*) of Anakreon, Homer, and Sophocles, an activity for which he claimed to demonstrate "great talent."[32] As we have already seen, Schumann's earliest original efforts in verse, assembled in the *Blätter und Blümchen aus der goldenen Aue*, date from two years before. Then between 1825 and 1830, he brought together a number of his own lyrics in another album, this one entitled *Allerley aus der Feder Roberts an der Mulde* (All Sorts of Things

from the Pen of Robert on the Mulde), now part of a manuscript containing thirty-two poems and poetic fragments, fugitive notes on Beethoven and Spohr, an exercise in Jean-Paulian prose-poetry, and the beginning of a letter in English.[33] While Schumann's handling of the
standard romantic themes—love, death, honor, artistry—and images—
sunflowers and violets, heaven-bound swans, enchanted gardens—
proves to be somewhat stiff, it is nonetheless noteworthy that he should
have lavished so much attention on his early efforts in the lyric vein.
The manuscript abounds in emendations and marginal notes; in one
extreme case of self-criticism, he even writes: "all this has been said
before—trivial recounting of phrases that convey little."[34]

The young Schumann struck a better balance between reflection
and fantasy in his essays and confessional writings. Their youthful effu-
siveness aside, the extant school essays of 1827, all of them touching on
aesthetic issues, bear the seeds of the keenly developed critical faculty
characteristic of the writings of the next decade. True enough, the young
critic devotes a fair amount of space to assuming what were already
well-worn ideological positions. In "Über die innige Verwandtschaft der
Poesie und Tonkunst" (On the Inner Bond Between Poetry and Music),
written when Schumann was still under the sway of Schiller, he argues
as many had before him for the common source of poetry and music,
though his reluctance to say which is the "higher" art reflects his powerful attraction to both. He shows a greater willingness to subject his own
views to a critique in another essay, "Das Leben des Dichters." Here
Schumann begins by painting an idealized portrait of the literary life,
emphasizing the proximity of the poet's muse to Nature and the Divine:
"The poet lives a charmed life; his eye becomes dark and weak during
the bustling day, but it awakens clear and serene in the solitude of Nature." At the same time, he acknowledges that this stance is at best naïve,
and at worst false, that the discrepancy between ideal vision and quotidian reality is the precise cause of the poet's pain.[35]

Probably the most critically acute of the early essays is "Warum
erbittert uns Tadel in Sachen des Geschmakes mehr, als in andern
Dingen." On the surface a general inquiry into the causes underlying
the stubborn refusal of some individuals to alter their judgments of taste
on matters musical (Schumann mentions Spohr, Rossini, and Weber),
painterly, and literary, the essay evolves into a spirited justification of
the apparent stylistic anomalies in the works of Jean Paul. While an
unnamed but "enlightened man" has criticized Jean Paul's *Titan* for its
abundance of contradictions, its "unnatural" plot, its peculiar imagery,
and its oddly developed characters, Schumann convincingly argues that
these eccentric features are part and parcel of the work's thematic fabric.

As a *Bildungsroman,* or novel of personal formation, *Titan* thematizes the attempts of its central character, Albano, to forge contradictory tendencies and unusual happenings into a meaningful unity. According to this line of reasoning, the contingency of events in the novel, which Schumann calls a "collision of circumstances" and relates to a similarly "romantic" conceit in Goethe's *Wahlverwandtschaften,* merely serves to underscore the capriciousness of Fate.[36] Jean Paul's eccentricity, in other words, is a necessary condition of the genre in which he encapsulates his world view. Schumann's attempt to rationalize the irrational thus belies a more than passing acquaintance, or at least an uncanny affinity, with the esoteric critical strategies of the chief figures of Jena Romanticism: the Schelgel brothers and Novalis.

Lived experience, poetic language, and critique intersect in *Tage des Jüngling-lebens,* the diary Schumann began shortly after New Year's Day, 1827, and maintained for about a month thereafter. Personal confession lies at the heart of such endeavors, and Schumann's earliest diary does not lack in tantalizing glimpses into the creative adolescent's quest for self-definition: "I myself don't clearly know what I actually am; I believe that I possess imagination, and no one denies it, but I'm not a deep thinker: I can't proceed logically with the threads I've perhaps entwined too tightly. Whether I am a poet—for one can't *become* a poet—is for posterity to decide. Further about myself I can't say, for the most difficult thing is to describe oneself, and 'Know thyself' is a powerful phrase."[37] The actual impetus for the diary, however, sprang from Schumann's attempt to cope with a typically adolescent problem: the reconciliation of a current love (for a girl named Liddy Hempel) with a past crush (on Nanni Petsch). "When I think of Liddy," he writes, "the vision of an angry Nanni hovers before my eyes." Like the "lyric I" in a romantic love poem, the young diarist traces an emotional path from doleful longing for an unattainable object—"I am unhappy; the darkest doubts mount in my heart; I thirst for her gaze, and yet I can't contrive to see her"—through nervous joy at having finally stolen a dance—"my hands shook, my voice trembled, I became dizzy"—and nagging doubts over the depth of his beloved's feelings for him—"I tremble, I lose myself in a labyrinth of hellish dreams . . . If only she loved me! I ask myself this the whole day long, and can't form an answer: a cold 'perhaps'—Ugh! How I shudder at the thought. Yet a flatout 'no'—would destroy me"— to repulsion at his inability to restrain his desires for Liddy—"It was a dreadful day; such days shorten one's life; when sensual pleasure prevails, man becomes an animal, as did I. Enough of this. I should be ashamed of myself."[38] Yet Schumann's infatuation with Liddy was further complicated by another factor: thoughts over the "two beloved be-

ings" recently "torn" from him: his father, who had succumbed to a
nervous disorder on 10 August 1826, and his nineteen-year-old sister
Emilie, whose death, perhaps from suicide, probably occurred around
the same time.[39] At once pained by these losses but joyful over the
possibility of union with Liddy, Schumann gives utterance to the feelings
of guilt that naturally arose from the emotional discrepancy: "Can the
outer being mourn, if the inner being perhaps rejoices? Or is inner
mourning a condition for outer mourning?"[40] Yet the potency of his
love for Liddy leads to a resolution of the conflict, or at least to a ratio-
nalization couched as a series of rhetorical questions: "Is it not horrid
enough . . . to be robbed of a father? why shouldn't one try to forget
pain through joy? why not be jolly in jolly company?"[41]

Schumann's first diary, however, is not merely a confessional account, a personal diagnosis of a sensitive and lovesick youth's conflicting
soul states. No less constitutive for its character is an undeniably literary
quality born of reflection. We, as readers, should feel no embarrassment
at peering into the pages of a strictly confidential document, for
throughout there is the sense that Schumann was writing to be read not
just by himself, but by others. Already the affixing of a title, *Tage des
Jüngling-lebens* (uncomfortably close to that of a popular American soap
opera when rendered in English as "Days from the Adolescent Life"),
lifts the diary from a narrowly private into a broader realm. So too do
the self-consciously stylized language, the frequent literary allusions, and
even the newly-minted maxims with which Schumann peppers his account. He relies on nature imagery, the stock-in-trade of the romantic
poet's style, to justify the transfer of his affections from Nanni to
Liddy—"If merry violets, the adornment of golden spring, bloom
around my present love, why should I preserve the wilted, though still
beautiful roses more lovingly in my bosom?"—and to assume the role
of the unrequited lover—"unfortunately those violets grow on a barren
field."[42] His first dance with Liddy becomes the occasion for a long
poem whose opening effectively captures the giddy alternation of dancing couples in short, breathlessly delivered lines:

> In whirling flight on the quaking floorboards
> The fleet-footed soles take wing:
> Little curls fly—
> Little skirts swing—
> All goes swiftly
> And the dance,
> Like a band of elves,
> Like orgiastic springtime,
> Sways from couple to couple.

Subsequent stanzas bring playful allusions to Schumann's friends: Flechsig breaks through the "dense ranks" like a "nobly smiling Adonis"; Ida Stölzel appears with her partner, "radiating modestly, like the violets by the brook"; and of course, "Like a butterfly in the meadow / Flitting through a flowery wreath / *Liddy,* the shepherd's sweet joy, / Floats along in the nimble dance."[43] Personal experience thus nurtures poetic expression, its central image in this case the dance, a long-time favorite of Schumann's.[44]

Yet the aspiring poet was keenly aware that the process whereby emotions were transformed into verse was a "chemical" one contingent upon reflection. As a diarist Schumann intended "to entrust [his] feelings and views to paper, to give a brief account of [his] happier hours," but at the same time he realized that "only when my spirit is more calm, my feelings more moderate . . . my imagination more elevated, and my enthusiasm more subdued, can I think back quietly on those hours when I was so happy."[45] Self-conscious detachment from an emotive source thus becomes a pre-condition for the poetic act: "when my feelings speak most strongly, I must cease being a poet; at best I can only jot down a few disconnected thoughts; but when my actual, feeling self is not involved, when imagination and thought prevail, I poetize with freedom and ease. . . . Thus I couldn't write a poem about Liddy. I feel too strongly about her, [and feelings] are speechless."[46] On the surface a confessional memoir, a window into the developing artist's soul, the adolescent Schumann's diary proves to be a medium of critical reflection.

In spite of the importance of his literary activities, it is still impossible to say which—poetry or music—had the upper hand for Schumann in his mid-teens. His contributions to a "Musikalish-deklamatorischen Abendunterhaltung" (musical-declamatory evening entertainment) held at the Zwickau Gymnasium on 25 January 1828, less than two months before his graduation, are emblematic of a dual will to music and literature: after reciting a monologue from Goethe's *Faust,* he played a movement from Kalkbrenner's Piano Concerto, op. 1.[47]

Though the surviving documents attest more fully to the cultivation of poetry than to music, both artforms were probably pursued with almost equal vigor. While immersing himself in Schiller, Friedrich Schlegel, and Jean Paul in preparation for the meetings of the *Litterarischer Verein,* Schumann demonstrated a comparable attachment to the keyboard music of Haydn, Prince Louis Ferdinand, Ries, and Moscheles; to Mozart's operas; and to Beethoven's string quartets.[48] His skills as the organizer of a literary club were paralleled on the musical side by a complementary entrepeneurial flair; probably in 1827 he planned, di-

rected, and played in a concert held at his home in the Amtgasse, the
ambitious program including choruses from Weber's *Preciosa* and Boieldieu's *Jean de Paris,* an aria from Mozart's *Entführung,* a piano concerto
by Lecour, and a symphony by Ernst Eichner.[49] Although we have no
original compositions for the period from 1824 to 1826, Schumann
probably did continue to compose after having tried his hand at a psalm
setting, an overture and chorus, and an opera in 1822 or 1823. His
father, after all, had approached Weber as a potential teacher for his
talented son, though the plan was disrupted by the death of Weber and
the elder Schumann in 1826.[50] Moreover, one of Schumann's autobiographical sketches of 1840 refers not only to the composition of a psalm
setting and "a few numbers from an opera," but also to "many songs"
and "many piano pieces."[51] While at least some of the early songs are
indeed extant, none of the piano works, among them the beginnings of
an E minor piano concerto dated 1827 in the *Projektenbuch,*[52] appears
to have survived.

   Given the young Schumann's attraction to both music and literature, it is only natural that he should have been drawn to the composition of lieder, for here, as he put it in one of his autobiographical
sketches, "poet and composer [appear] in one person." A diary entry of
13 August 1828 expresses a similar point of view in more highflown
terms: "Song unites the highest things, word and tone, the latter an
inarticulate letter in the alphabet of humanity; it is the purely extracted
quintessence of the spiritual life."[53] Another factor probably contributed
to Schumann's turn to song in the summers of 1827 and 1828: his encounter with Agnes Carus, an attractive woman eight years his senior
and reportedly a gifted singer. Her husband, Dr. Ernst August Carus,
was the nephew of Karl Erdmann Carus, a merchant in whose home
Schumann was a regular guest. It was here during the spring of 1827
that he first met the young Frau Dr. Carus and in all probability
promptly became enamored of her, though whether or not their contact
tipped the balance in favor of Schumann's decision on a musical career
it is difficult to say.[54] Just as the *Tage des Jüngling-lebens* served as a
reflective medium for his feelings for Liddy Hempel, so too did the early
songs emerge, at some level, from the interaction of personal and artistic
concerns. "My songs," Schumann wrote in his diary on 14 August 1828,
"were intended as an actual reproduction of my inner self; but no human being can present something exactly as the genius creates it; even
she [Agnes Carus] sang the most beautiful passages badly and didn't
understand me."[55]

   All told, we know of thirteen songs from this period: four date
from the summer of 1827 *(Sehnsucht, Die Weinende, Verwandlung,* and

Lied für XXX); another eight *(Kurzes Erwachen, Gesanges Erwachen, An Anna, Erinnerung, An Anna II, Hirtenknabe, Der Fischer,* and *Klage)* can be ascribed to June, July, and August of 1828, by which time both Schumann and the Caruses had resettled in Leipzig; a single song, *Im Herbste,* edited by Brahms for the collected edition of Schumann's works, remains undated, but no doubt belongs here as well.[56] Even a cursory glance at these lieder will indicate that in his later teens Schumann had already attained an impressive level of technical mastery as a composer, thus lending further support to the conjecture that his compositional activity continued apace in the immediately preceding years. While the early songs are perhaps not perfect specimens of the art of conjoining word and tone, they are hardly the fledgling attempts of an untutored amateur. Even the lieder of 1827 disclose a notable stylistic range. In *Sehnsucht,* completed in June of that year, Schumann assumes the dual roles of poet and composer. The former, in typical romantic fashion, implores the stars to greet his beloved and the winds to send her a kiss; the latter responds with an unassuming strophic setting in which the eloquently shaped, arching vocal line is supported throughout by a murmuring accompanimental figure. In contrast, Byron's verses elicited an altogether more complicated response in *Die Weinende,* composed during the next month. Here again, the poem turns on a common enough image: the radiant eyes of the poet's beloved, whose glance outshines even the most lustrous sapphire. But Schumann binds the two stanzas of the poem into a continuous thought by means of a nearly through-composed setting, and likewise couples the suggestive imagery of the lyric with a more chromatic musical language. In addition, the varying number of poetic feet per verse motivated a flexible, arioso-like vocal line. A subtle play between *cantabile* and declamation is evident already in the first phrase (Example 1.1), where Schumann regularizes the $3+4$ disposition of feet in the first two verses by welding them into a four-bar unit that begins in a lyric vein but closes with a recitative-like gesture.

Subtleties of this sort aside, the early lieder were nonetheless products of a composer without formal training. After having completed several lieder on Kerner texts by mid-summer of 1828 and anxious for the informed opinion of a recognized professional, Schumann sent his settings to Gottlob Wiedebein, Kapellmeister in Braunschweig, and like the young composer, a devotee of Jean Paul.[57] By early August, Schumann had received an encouraging reply from the older man, who diagnosed the shortcomings of the lieder not as "sins of the spirit," but rather as "the natural sins of youth" that one might easily forgive so long as "here and there a genuinely poetic feeling bursts through."

Example 1.1. Die Weinende, mm. 5–8.

Sounding a theme upon which Schumann's critics would construct all sorts of variations in response to the keyboard music of the 1830s, Wiedebein cautioned that although the young composer had given himself up to inspired fantasy, he should also allow "the calmly testing faculty of understanding" its due. His parting words of advice must have struck a resonant chord with the youthful artist: "Above all, attend to truth. Truth of melody, harmony, and expression—in a word, poetic truth. If you don't find it, or if it is threatened—then cut even your favorite passage."[58]

Wiedebein was perhaps reacting to features evident most obviously in a lied such as *An Anna* ("Lange harrt' ich"), an extended setting in which the composer's inspired fantasy animates practically every phrase. His pursuit of ultra-expressivity manifests itself in the no less than four tempo shifts—spanning a range from the unusually designated opening, *Schwärmerisch* (rapturously), to the concluding *Largo*—and in an abundance of affective indications, *zart* (tenderly), *träumerisch* (dreamily), *steigernd* (intensifying), and *solenne* (solemn) among them. Schumann delivers much of Kerner's text in a flexible *parlando* style, consciously avoiding metric squareness even in the *cantabile* sections. A series of unexpected harmonic turns culminates in an passage initiated from the

♭VI region (G major). Yet Schumann's extravagant approach nonetheless takes its bearings from Kerner's lyric, a thematization of the poet's intense desire for an unattainable beloved, probably deceased, who appears to him in the image of an "angel of peace." The contrasting settings of parallel lines near the end of the Lied ("Sprechen's nach die Stern . . . Sprechen's nach des Tales . . ."), for instance, lend poignancy to the poet's futile exhortation of his unapprehending beloved. The attenuation of the B-major tonic throughout imparts to the music a measure of the anxious longing so prominent in the verses, just as the excursion to an unstable G major beautifully colors the poet's desolate stance "in the distance." In short, Schumann's inspired fantasy turns out to be an agent of poetic truth after all.

The early lieder thus occupy a special place in Schumann's output, and not only because they represent his first extant works in a polished compositional idiom. In the piano music of the next decade, he would turn to these musical lyrics of personal experience more than once as a repository of melodic ideas: *Hirtenknabe*, a stylized *Volkslied*, serves as the basis for the fourth of the *Intermezzi*, op. 4; a significantly reworked form of *An Anna II* surfaces as the second movement, Aria, of the F♯-minor Piano Sonata, op. 11; and *Im Herbste* supplies the principal material for the slow movement, Andantino, of the G-minor Piano Sonata, op. 22. Even in his keyboard music, then, Schumann emerges as poet and composer in one person, deepening and refining tendencies already present in a youth who may not have been a genius, but who certainly was not lacking in talent.

Revelling in Schubert and Jean Paul

According to the generous terms of August Schumann's will of 6 June 1826, his son Robert was allotted 10,323 Reichsthaler in trust, of which he would receive 200 yearly (plus his father's Viennese piano and an additional 100 thalers for the defrayal of examination costs) if he agreed to complete a three-year course of university study in an unspecified field.[59] In deference to the wishes of his mother, who feared that a career in the arts might be rich in spiritual but slim in material rewards, and those of his guardian, a Zwickau merchant named Johann Gottlob Rudel, Schumann agreed to matriculate on 29 March 1828 as a student of law at the venerable University of Leipzig. To be sure, Johanna Christiana did not intend to squelch her son's broadly creative and specifically musical proclivities, talents she hoped he would continue to cultivate for his own enjoyment and that of others as well; but as a parent justifiably concerned for her child's future, she remained steadfastly committed to her Robert's pursuit of a *Brotstudium,* a profession whereby he might earn his daily bread.[60]

From the start, however, Schumann harbored quite different plans. As he put it in one of his autobiographical sketches: "[At] eighteen I went to Leipzig, in accordance with my mother's wishes, to study law, but in accordance with my own still vaguely formed intent, to devote myself entirely to music."[61] Once settled in the city, Schumann responded to his new surroundings in less than enthusiastic terms: "Nature, where will I find her here?" he queried in a letter to his mother of 21 May 1828, "no valley, no mountains, no forest." Nor did he conceal his lack of interest in the "ice-cold definitions" of law, consoling himself with the observation that "philosophy and history will be among my studies."[62] Writing to his mother less than a month later, he described a daily routine including two hours of piano practice, several hours of reading, some "poetizing" in the nearby village of Zweiaundorf, and regular attendance at law lectures.[63] Schumann probably appended the last item to set her mind at ease, for according to Flechsig, with whom he shared lodgings, he "never entered a lecture hall."[64] The same witness supplies us with a compelling and at times colorful report of his friend's student days in Leipzig. The bustling north German trade center may have offered fewer natural beauties than his native Zwickau, but as the center of a flourishing book trade, it afforded him rich opportunities to keep abreast of the latest in literature, his continued study of Jean Paul acting as a further catalyst to original poetic creation.

No later than August, he assiduously pursued his piano studies under the tutelage of Friedrich Wieck, a figure destined to play a major role in Schumann's professional and personal life, who, bemused by his new student's fervor, dubbed him the "hothead at the keyboard," and through whom the youth came into contact with the leading musicians of the city.[65] By late summer, he had developed a passionate attachment to a new musical love: the works of Franz Schubert, which, again according to Flechsig, were just beginning to gain some currency beyond the limited circle of their Viennese devotees. Anxious to get his hands on everything by the composer that he could, Schumann was thrown into such an agitated state by the news of Schubert's death on 19 November 1828 that his roommate "heard him sobbing the whole night long."[66] Composition likewise formed an integral part of the would-be law student's activities, his comical bearing while engaged at his writing desk the subject of an amusing passage from Flechsig's *Lebenserinnerungen:* "[Schumann] always puffed at a cigar [while composing], but since smoke got into his eyes, he pressed it upward with his mouth as far as it would go, at the same time casting his eyes downward in a squint, so that he made the strangest grimaces all the while."[67] The image that emerges from Flechsig's description of this phase of his friend's life is that of a young man situated at once together with and apart from other youths of comparable social background. Like many other university students of his day, Schumann became an avid chess-player, dabbled a bit in fencing, and "enjoyed a drink" in "the spirited company of friends." Yet in spite of his "compatible" nature, he evinced less interest in the "usual trivialities" of student life than many of his colleagues. Soon he became "one of Leipzig's best-known sons of the Muses—because of his talent," and grew "into a singularly handsome fellow [who] bore his attire well, [and] was of a thoroughly noble character, chaste and pure as a vestal virgin."[68]

The idealized tone of Flechsig's description notwithstanding, it supplies us with a convincing portrait of an affable if reflective youth for whom artistic matters counted for more than anything else. The "new life" that Schumann linked with his move to Leipzig had little to do with his formal university studies (from reading his diary alone, it would be difficult to know that he was even studying law) but very much to do with an expanding literary and musical sensibility. For Schumann, university life in Leipzig amounted to a period of "revelling in Jean Paul and Schubert,"[69] each figure in turn providing him with a model for his own creative endeavors.

Although Jean Paul has long been acknowledged as the most significant poetic influence on the composer, it is important to keep in mind the encyclopedic breadth of Schumann's readings, which (to judge from his diaries and other documents) encompassed well over six hundred works ranging from world classics to political journals. As we have seen, Schumann's habit of focusing on one writer at a time, parallelled by his later concentration on individual musical genres in a systematic fashion, was already firmly established in the days of the *Litterarischer Verein*. Having thoroughly explored Schiller's plays in the context of that group, he was poised for a comparably exhaustive encounter with the writings of Jean Paul. Later he would devote phases of similarly intense study to figures including Shakespeare, Byron, Heine, and Rückert. But Jean Paul remained the writer to whom Schumann turned again and again. As late as 1853 we find him rereading—often aloud, and in collaboration with Clara—the novels of his youthful idol.[70]

While still a "mystery" to the sixteen-year-old Schumann,[71] the eccentric world of Jean Paul began to disclose itself to him a year later through a reading of *Titan*. In short order he devoured most of the other major novels: a passage in Schumann's diary entered in May 1828, but reflective of his activities in the previous six months or so, alludes to *Die unsichtbare Loge, Hesperus, Titan, Flegeljahre,* and *Siebenkäs; Der Komet* provided bedtime reading in January 1829.[72] Already by March 1828, he was able to state unequivocally in a letter to Flechsig: "Jean Paul still takes first place with me, and I rank him above all, even Schiller." At the time it was Goethe whose works he failed to comprehend to the fullest.[73] Then in April of the same year, on a trip to Munich with his friend Gisbert Rosen, he passed through Bayreuth, Jean Paul's home for nearly thirty years. Like a pilgrim making his way in a poetic Holy Land, Schumann lost himself in a sombre reverie at the writer's tomb: "Jean Paul, I stood by your grave and wept as you looked on and smiled at my tears." The "deep pain" of this experience gave way to "pleasant memories" when, after a two-hour conversation with the proprietress of the guest-house where Jean Paul plied his writerly trade for twenty-six years, Schumann beheld the author's tiny, sparsely furnished room.[74] On his return journey from Munich in early May, he again stopped in Bayreuth, this time for a visit with Jean Paul's widow, who presented him with a portrait of her late husband—a memento he preserved as if it were a sacred object. Writing to Rosen from Leipzig on 5 June 1828, Schumann felt compelled to observe: "If the whole world read Jean Paul, it would certainly be a better, but unhappier place—he's often brought me close to madness, but the rainbow of peace and of the human spirit always hovers delicately over all the tears, while the heart is wondrously elevated and tenderly transfigured."[75]

Of course, Jean Paul has brought other readers close to madness as well, if for different reasons. A notoriously difficult writer, his language, to quote Thomas Carlyle, "groans with indescribable metaphors . . . flowing onward not like a river, but an inundation, circling in complex eddies, chafing and gurgling now this way, now that, [until] the proper current sinks out of view amid the boundless uproar."[76] A few examples will bear out Carlyle's appraisal. Leibgeber's "Adam Letter" from *Siebenkäs* refers to Adam and Eve, not as our primordial parents, but as our "protoplasts." As Siebenkäs attempts to make headway on his writing projects, the nearly inaudible sounds produced by his wife Lenette's housecleaning attack him "like rabies or podogra, each time putting to death one or two budding ideas, as a loud noise puts to death silkworm or a brood of canaries."[77] Walt and Vult Harnisch, the twin-brother protagonists of *Flegeljahre*, not only exchange costumes during the novel's culminating masked ball scene, they practice an "alternate pupation and depupation." Little wonder, then, that Jean Paul wanted the epitaph on his tombstone to proclaim him the writer who had thought up more metaphors than any other. Given his conviction that it is not the poet's duty to reproduce reality, but rather to unriddle its eternal meaning, decipherment is a necessary condition for even a basic comprehension of the Jean-Paulian text. In *Siebenkäs,* the author describes one of the items in the title character's home as a "copper fish-kettle, which, as long as it remained unmended, could not poison any vinegar," relying on his readers' knowledge that the chemical interaction of copper and acid will produce a poisonous compound to make the point that Siebenkäs and Lenette are too impecunious to pay for the repair of their kitchen utensils.[78]

When Friedrich Schlegel ironically characterized Jean Paul as an author "who hasn't control of the basic principles of art . . . [and] cannot tell a story well, at least not according to what is accepted as good story-telling,"[79] he was undoubtedly thinking of another key feature of the poet's idiosyncratic style: his love for digressions. Whether brief or protracted, humorous or sentimental, these excurses proliferate on the surface of Jean Paul's prose like ivy on a stone wall. Sometimes they take the form of narrative embeddings, or even embeddings within embeddings, as in *Flegeljahre,* where the twins are at work on a novel entitled *Hoppelpoppel* (scrambled egg hash) to which Walt contributes the main plot and Vult the satirical asides. In other cases, the digressions spill over the narrative frame; in *Titan,* for instance, the logbook of Gianozzo, the ill-fated balloonist, and a mock-serious philosophical tract on Fichtean philosophy are consigned to a "Comic Appendix," Schumann's bedtime reading, by the way, on 18 January 1829.[80] Of course, it is not that Jean Paul was *unable* to tell a story well; on the contrary, he stubbornly *refused* to adhere to the accepted principles of unity of plot, if only because he passionately believed that life itself was a motley, variegated affair. Hence the plethora of digressions, excurses, embeddings, interpolations and appendices, however disorienting they may be, serves to affirm what was an essentially epic world view. The patient reader, in any event, will be rewarded with glimpses into Jean Paul's inimitable comic style, his uncanny ability to give a humorous twist to the most solemn subjects. Fichte's idealist philosophy, for instance, comes in for a merciless lampooning in the "Clavis Fichtiana seu Leibgeberiana" from the Comic Appendix to *Titan:* "Kant spent 10,957 ½ nights, or 30 years, on the begettal of his Critique; Fichte probably needed less than 3 months for it (for reading is also making)."[81] Jean Paul even pokes fun at his own narrative convolutions in the *Biographische Belustigungen* (Biographical Entertainments), where he is ordered by the court to desist from telling stories with so many digressions.

What did Schumann find so enthralling about this most bizarre of writers? We should keep in mind, first, that his discovery of Jean Paul amounted in part to a kind of self-discovery. "I've often asked myself," he writes in *Hottentottiana*, the diary he began keeping just after settling in Leipzig, "where I might be had I not gotten to know Jean Paul; yet he seems on the one hand to be interwoven with my inner being, as if I had an earlier premonition of him." [82] Just as Schumann beheld himself in Jean Paul, so Jean Paul "mirrors himself in all his works, but always in two people: he is Albano and Schoppe [from *Titan*], Siebenkäs and Leibgeber *[Siebenkäs]*, Vult and Walt *[Flegeljahre]*, Gustav and Fenk *[Die unsichtbare Loge]*, Flamin and Viktor *[Hesperus]*. Only the single Jean Paul could combine two such different characters into one being; it is superhuman, but still he's done it." [83] The notion of the *Doppelgänger*, a term that Jean Paul himself coined and a prominent theme throughout his *oeuvre*, is a highly unsettling one, yet it was precisely to the disturbing qualities in the writer's works that Schumann was particularly drawn. Based on a dream vision in which Jean Paul saw himself as a corpse, *Siebenkäs* abounds in qualities of just this sort. Its protagonists exchange names as youths, and identities as adults, so that the title character (whom we first meet as "Siebenkäs" though he is in fact "Leibgeber") can go through the pretense of death and burial, thereby liberating himself from a stultifying environment. Schumann found the tale positively "frightful," but like a child fascinated by the stimulating causes of his nightmares, he still wanted "to read it a thousand times." [84]

In a broader and less morbid sense, the disturbances in the Jean-Paulian text result from the writer's fondness for the portrayal of life as a series of unresolved conflicts, a feature neatly encapsulated at the end of *Flegeljahre* in a line from Vult's letter of farewell to his sleeping brother: "I leave you as you were, and go as I come." Striking contrasts abound in Jean Paul's novels, but his intentional refusal to weld them into a harmonious unity often leaves a remainder. Firm in his belief that life is never pure poetry, Jean Paul fancifully juxtaposes prosaic and poetic styles, pigtails and moonlight, the result a kind of dissonance that Schumann found equally compelling: "Jean Paul has seldom appeased but always enchanted me; and although an element of dissatisfaction, like an eternal melancholy, resides in this enchantment, I feel afterward a sense of inner well-being comparable to that of a rainbow arching over the heavens in the wake of a storm." [85] Indulging in a pun on the author's surname, Schumann dubs Jean Paul a "comforting, mild judge *[Richter]*," a "supremely human" writer who "cries over" life but loves it nonetheless. [86] No less a teacher than a judge, he continually nudges his readers into a position of active engagement with his texts, and herein lies, as Schumann well understood, the motivation for the extravagant metaphors, the continual wordplay, and the fantastic digressions. Jean Paul's texts demand critical, not passive, readers, and here too they found a willing student in Schumann, who—drawing on categories that play an important role in the writer's anatomy of the comic modes in the *Vorschule der Ästhethik*—analyzed the Jean-Paulian spirit as an amalgamation of "feeling" *(Gemüth)*, "humor" *(Humor)*, and "wit" *(Witz)*.[87] Analogues of these properties in turn assume special significance in Schumann's music.

Schumann's fascination with Jean Paul was complemented by the veritable outpouring of literary projects undertaken soon after Schumann's arrival in Leipzig. In all of these endeavors, confessional, novelistic, aesthetic, and critical elements intermingle and overlap to such a degree that it is often impossible to unravel them. In many ways, *Hottentottiana,* the diary Schumann began on 2 May 1828 and maintained faithfully until 1 April 1830 (with only one major interruption between August and November 1829 during his travels in Switzerland and Italy), evinces an even more markedly literary quality than the earlier *Tage des Jüngling-lebens.* As a sign of the semi-public character of his musings, Schumann adds fanciful titles to the first and fourth of the diary's volumes: *Das Fuchsjahr, eine komische Autobiographie* ("The Year of the University Freshman, a Comic Autobiography") and *Das Burschenjahr oder die moralische Erziehung* ("The Year of the Upperclassman, or The Moral Education"), respectively. At the end of the second volume, he adds the humorous note: "printed in the thought-offices of the ostensible author, Robert Schumann." Verse mottos and dedications (to his friends Flechsig and Rosen) further contribute to the diary's literary character. The overall title in turn alludes to the "Hottentots"—later a derogatory term for the natives of South Africa, but in Schumann's day a less offensive slang expression for "savage" or "barbarian"—perhaps underscoring the "wild" youth's recently won independence from the watchful eyes of parent and guardian. Not surprisingly then, *Hottentottiana* amounts to considerably more than a mere diary. A congeries of autobiographical analyses, lapidary notices of quotidian activities, drafts for letters, fragments and sketches of various poetic projects, and aesthetic speculations on music and literature, it holds up a mirror to a developing artistic nature.

While *Hottentottiana* colors confessional with self-consciously reflective prose, *Juniusabende und Julytage,* a "Bildchen" or "Idylle" conceived during the summer of 1828, does much the reverse. Viewed by Schumann as his "first work," his "truest and most beautiful,"[88] it focuses on a dilemma already presented in such early romantic novels as

Friedrich Schlegel's *Lucinde:* the threat to individuality posed by a quest for spiritual and physical union with friends and lovers. In tracing the fortunes of his main characters, the couples Julius and Ammali, Gustav and Inna, Schumann certainly drew on personal experience, just as he had in *Tage des Jüngling-lebens* the previous year: Julius projects the author's own persona, his various love entanglements modelled on Schumann's relationships with Nanni Petsch, Liddy Hempel, and perhaps Agnes Carus as well. Yet the reflective quality of the idyll emerges in its connection with the diarist's art in general and Schumann's diary in particular. On the one hand, *Hottentottiana* includes many excerpts from the *Juniusabende;* on the other, the fifth chapter of the idyll opens with entries from the fictional Julius's diary.[89] A precedent for this sort of mutually conditioning exchange between producer and product, confession and reflection, would have been readily at hand in the works of Jean Paul. After the title character in *Siebenkäs,* for instance, decides to become a writer, he sets to work on "Jean Paul's" so-called *Teufels Papieren* (Devil's Papers). Echoes of the Jean-Paulian manner may likewise be detected in Schumann's frequent recourse to wordplay, unusual turns of phrase, neologisms, and even to "Polymeter" or *Streckvers,* Jean Paul's term for freely metred but non-stanzaic prose-poetry.[90]

Though Schumann may have begun an epistolary novel, *Bernard von Nontelliers* at about this time, none of the more ambitious writing projects from his first period in Leipzig owes more to Jean Paul in matters of style and spirit than *Selene,* a fragmentary *Bildungsroman* dating from late in 1828.[91] Indeed, Schumann's reading of Jean Paul's autobiography *(Wahrheit aus Jean Pauls Leben)* in November of that year coincides with his copying of several draft excerpts from *Selene* into his diary.[92] While the novel's heroine takes her name from the title of Jean Paul's last major work, *Selena,* her twin brother Gustav takes his from the hero in *Die unsichtbare Loge.* And just as the theme of the split self or *Doppelgänger* resonates with *Siebenkäs* and *Flegeljahre,* so the migration of characters from one tale to another (we have already encountered a "Gustav" in *Juniusabende und Julytage*) recalls Jean-Paul's practice as well: several of the figures from *Hesperus,* for instance, recur in *Siebenkäs;* Viktor, the hero of the former, reads *Die unsichtbare Loge;* and Gianozzo, whose logbook forms a major part of the "Comic Appendix" to *Titan,* dedicates his journal to Siebenkäs's double, Leibgeber.[93] Drawing as they do on a fixed but variegated cosmos of characters, Jean Paul's novels in a sense constitute a single novelistic system. In his early literary works, we likewise find Schumann attempting to imitate just such a system, even though it will appear in full bloom only in the keyboard works and music criticism of the 1830s, where musical themes wander from piece to piece, and the partly fictional characters of the critical writings put in appearances as the "composers" of character pieces and works in larger forms.

If Julius serves as spokesperson for the author in *Juniusabende*, then Gustav functions similarly in *Selene*. Schumann describes him as a *hoher Mensch*, or "higher human being," hearkening again to a favorite Jean-Paulian conceit. Indeed, the first part of *Die unsichtbare Loge* concludes with a lengthy excursus on the capacity of the *hoher Mensch*, as represented by characters such as Dr. Fenk, the Genius, the hero Gustav, and his friend Ottomar, to rise above the pettiness of everyday life. But fearful that his novel might turn out to be "too much like Jean Paul," Schumann was determined that *his* Gustav "should be neither an Albano, a Gustav, a Woldemar, a Viktor, nor a Flamin; he should be more poetic than Flamin and more powerful than Viktor." [94] Accordingly Schumann departs somewhat from Jean Paul's notion of the *hoher Mensch* as an individual sublimely indifferent to earthly cares, associating the epithet instead with the ability to temper Promethean energy through Olympian restraint: "Gustav must pass through all the schools of life; he must learn both to hate and to love; his youthful demeanor must be tender and mild in order to show that the higher being can submit to the fetters of calm, but that his Promethean sparks remain unextinguished nonetheless." [95] Three years later, Schumann would split the dual personae of the *hoher Mensch* into the respectively dynamic and contemplative "Florestan" and "Eusebius," the fictional producers of much of the criticism and keyboard music of the next decade. The *hoher Mensch*, in other words, emerges in retrospect as a cipher for the author-composer's idealized attempt to neutralize the conflicts in his own being, to rise above his human limitations. Here again Schumann proves himself true to the spirit of Jean Paul through his pre-echo of Nietzsche's conviction that humankind is "a thing to be overcome."

The surviving fragments for Schumann's novel are not only rich in allusions to the favored themes of his beloved Jean Paul, but also to the writer's idiosyncratic style. Consider, for instance, the following description of an eerie, moonlit landscape from the *Mitternachtsstück* in *Selene*, no doubt modelled on the comparably spooky churchyard scenes in *Siebenkäs*:

> The pale stars glimmered magically over the hilltop graveyard, a teary meadow, and the cypresses whispered quietly, and in their own tongue, among themselves—the silent gravediggers towered over the flowers

that staggered in the wind, and the tombstones threw great, long shadows, like the hands of a time-piece wound for eternity, as if to say: "Behold, we mark the spot where you now lie buried"—the moon shone quietly, and long drawn-out swan-songs, monotonous and gloomy, intoned in the ether.[96]

Here, as elsewhere in his youthful prose, Schumann makes generous use of Jean Paul's most characteristic punctuation mark, the dash, the resultant paratactic style a fitting emblem for a worldview that configures reality as a system of mysteriously related fragments. To this feature Schumann adds one of his own, the repeated use of the coordinating conjunction "and" to string together his diminutive thought-fragments into a suggestive mosaic.

Likewise the *Harmonika-Altarblatt* episode, in which Selene, Gustav, Minona, and the Prince enter a dimly lit cathedral by night, recalls one of the most celebrated of Jean Paul's digressions: the "Speech of the Dead Christ of the Universe" in *Siebenkäs,* a proto-Nietzschean vision of man alone in a godless world.[97] As in the *Mitternachtsstück,* parataxis and an additive approach to sentence construction impart a fragmented quality to the language of Schumann's scene, while the many word- and phrase-repetitions lend an unmistakably incantational dimension as well. These features come together in the description of the weird music that Selene and her companions hear emanating from the organ loft: "Silence—then a single, deep tone wandered quietly (as if it were afraid to breathe), hardly audibly, through the nave—new tones joined in— then everything overflowed with tones, then the stones, the statues, and the portraits of the saints seemed to come to life in tones and everything resounded as if bewitched. . . ."[98] Schumann's youthful literary and musical pursuits largely run on parallel tracks; indeed, passages such as this reveal an attempt to fuse them into a musical prose redolent more of Novalis than of Jean Paul. Gustav's pained reaction to the mysterious stranger's organ-playing and the response of the inspirited tones—" 'O ye heavenly sounds from the graves of slumbering bliss, tell me, do tell me, why do I weep when I hear you?' then the tones replied: we are harbingers of the world toward which you weep, but that you will never discover here—we come from the beyond"[99]—touches on a whole panoply of *topoi* associated with the aesthetics of other early Romantics such as Tieck and Wackenroder: music as the voice of Nature's darker forces; tone as an emanation of the divine; the musician as tortured prophet. Schumann's conflation of imaginative prose and aesthetic speculation thus betrays more than a passing acquaintance with a cherished ideal of the Jena Romantics. Just as Friedrich Schlegel, the principal theoretician of the group, envisioned the novel as an amalgam of narrative and criticism, inspired effusion and cool-headed reflection, so Schumann's otherwise Jean-Paulian text aims for a similar blend.

In the months prior to his sustained work on *Selene*, Schumann entrusted his musico-poetic ruminations to the pages of *Hottentottiana*. Indeed, during July and August 1828 the diary begins to read like a preparatory sketch for an aesthetic, or rather synaesthetic, tract. It is certainly no coincidence that Schumann's second burst of song composition fell in the same period. Searching for yet another means of mediating his attraction to both music and poetry and following on the early Romantic tradition that led Tieck, Wackenroder, and E. T. A. Hoffmann to a doctrine of "absolute" music, he decides to recast the former as a more elevated function of the latter. Hence he concludes that "tones are higher words," or, in a variation on the same conceit, "Music is poetry raised to a higher power; spirits speak the language of poetry, but the angels communicate in tones."[100] Taking this conviction a step further, he speculates on a rapprochement between musical and poetic genres. Hence Schubert's *Acht Variationen über ein Thema aus der Oper Marie von Hérold* (*Eight Variations on a Theme from Hérold's Marie*, op. 82 no. 1, D908; published 1827) for piano four hands, a particular favorite at the time, "relate to [Goethe's] *Wilhelm Meister* just as tones generally do to words; in any event, both are the ne plus ultra of Romanticism. After all, tone is but the musically realized word. Schubert's Variations are thus the composed novel that Goethe has *yet to write*"—or, put more succinctly: "Schubert's Variations are the most perfect romantic portrait, a perfect novel in tones *[Tonroman]*."[101] (The same line of thinking culminates, four years later, in the intriguing rhetorical question: "Why shouldn't there be such a thing as an opera without text? Now that would be most certainly dramatic. There's much for you in Shakespeare.")[102]

In the same spirit, Schumann posits analogues for his favorite composers among the great poets, without, however, always settling on a definitive conclusion. Schubert is equated with Goethe, but also with Novalis, and even (in an entry of 15 August 1828) with a chemical compounding of Novalis, Jean Paul, and Hoffmann.[103] At least at this stage, Jean Paul finds a more fixed musical counterpart in the figure of Beethoven, since, according to Schumann, both artists possess the uncanny ability to unite melancholy and enchantment, to make their devotees at once happy and unhappy.[104] Touching on a theme later elaborated in his review of Berlioz's *Symphonie fantastique* and realized in many passages of his own compositions, Schumann imagines a musical syntax liberated from the strictures of metric regularity and modelled on the *Streckverse* of Jean Paul:

Evening Fantasy in X major; the free fantasy unites the highest elements
in music—the law of the measure and alternating, freely lyric, metric
groupings—a union lacking in compositions in the strict style. Poetry
accomplishes this in Jean Paul's Polymeter and in the choruses of classical Greek drama; syntactic liberty *[Ungebundenheit]* is in every instance
more imaginative and more ingenious than metric regularity *[das Geb-
undene]*, hence my displeasure with rhymes.[105]

These citations speak less to a firmly delineated theory than to the quest
for a theory, but taken together, they point toward an evolving notion
of music as a kind of literary activity. Although the particulars of Schumann's youthful musico-poetics will change in time, his outlook on music as a form of literature remains fundamentally the same.

The young Schumann delineates his musical aesthetic in a more
systematic fashion in "Die Tonwelt," an essay dating from late summer
1828, and thus a product of the same impulses articulated in the
musico-poetic aphorisms of *Hottentottiana*. Subtitled "Aus dem Tagebuch der heil. Caecilia" (From the Diary of St. Cecilia), it falls into five
parts, each a self-contained mini-essay; after an introductory section,
"Ueber Ton im Allgemeinen nebst sentimentalen Ausschweifungen" (On
Tone in General along with Sentimental Excesses), come four "Extrava-
ganzen," the first of these and portions of the second probably culled
from a letter written by Schumann's friend Willibald von der Lühe.[106]
Hence the essay is representative of what the Jena Romantics called *Sym-
philosophie*, collaborative theorizing by like-minded thinkers. And to be
sure, both Schumann and Lühe shared a passion for Jean Paul, whose
influence is made palpable through an initiatory motto drawn from
Hesperus—"Ah! All that ye say, ye tones, is denied me!"—pointing to
the inability of words to replicate the affective power of pure tone, and
through the conception of the essay as a colloquy among five *höhere
Menschen* who stroll in a dusky landscape. The process of symphilo-
sophizing is neatly exemplified in the second Extravaganza, where, reacting to the assertion that music, unlike painting, involves unmediated
perception and hence can be understood without reflection, Schumann
supplies the parenthetical observation that the *production* of musical
works does indeed require the exercise of the reflective faculty: "for a
composition conceived without reflection will lack character, and such
a piece is just as reprehensible as a poem without a basic coloration."[107]
Nonetheless, the central tenet of the essay—the notion that music is the
most nearly autonomous of the arts, the freest from material con-
straints—is very much in line with the aesthetic of absolute music implicit in the *Hottentottiana* fragments. Schumann's scoffing at the strictures of the *reine Satz* recalls the "Evening Fantasy in X major," but here

the "strict style" is imaginatively personified as a troupe of "musical sack-carriers and hurdy-gurdy men" reminiscent of those "tedious family scenes" where Grandfather takes the bass, the upright Hausfrau the discant, and the children pipe out the innter parts.[108] Likewise, the view of music as "the true mediator between the beyond and the here-and-now"[109] resonates with the outlook expressed poetically in the *Harmonika-Altarblatt* chapter from *Selene*, once again demonstrating the fluid boundary between imaginative and critical prose for the young Schumann.

In addition, "Die Tonwelt" touches on a problem that will motivate much of Schumann's critical activity during the next decade. The introductory mini-essay is headed with a verse motto that also appears in the entry for 29 July 1828 in *Hottentottiana:* "In man there resides a great, incredible Something which no tongue can proclaim, and which awakens on high mountains or at sunset or in tones."[110] Pellegrini, the first of the *höhere Menschen* to offer a definition of "tone," glosses on this conceit in asserting that music is an "earthly breath from beyond, which, like everything divine and otherworldly, can be neither named nor described, but only felt."[111] Music, in other words, articulates the inarticulable. But as the bearer of mysterious messages from the spirit world, is it therefore inaccessible to rational discourse? Convinced that music, its numinous powers aside, is indeed an object of reflection, Schumann refuses to answer in the affirmative. In "Die Tonwelt," he responds to the problem as a poet would, attempting in the final "Extravaganza," a Jean-Paulian Polymeter entitled "Beethoven," to capture in words an impression of the "dreams" set in motion by the composer's music. During the 1830s, Schumann will record his impressions in the more sober language of the critic. Both responses, however, the poetic and the critical, are grounded in the conviction that although music utters the inutterable, it still embodies an intellectual content.

Among the most intriguing literary products of the summer of 1828 is the playfully entitled essay "Ueber Genial- Knill- Original- und andre itäten." Roughly translatable as "On Genial- Insobr- Original- and other i(e)ties," the title sports with a common German suffix in a manner reminiscent of Jean Paul.[112] Similarly, Schumann's striking play with unusual metaphors in the body of the essay recalls the idiom of his favored author: "Geniality likes to build its temples in wine-cellars and tipsiness [in the Zwickau dialect, *Knillität*] is a quasi-helper or in the end, the left hand itself, while originality is the foot."[113] The fanciful language, however, in no way detracts from the seriousness of Schumann's attempt at a kind of anatomy of creative genius. Nor should his fascination with the effects of alcohol be taken as a paean to insobriety:

the intoxication that often accompanies geniality must be brought on by champagne, not by "schnapps, punch, or Bavarian beer."[114] Hence *Knillität* is neither more nor less than an emblem for the heightened awareness associated with the act of creation.

Of the three terms considered in the essay, *Genialität, Originalität*, and *Knillität*, the first, in Schumann's view, is the highest. It is also devilishly difficult to translate into English. "Geniality," though not inappropriate, is an uncommon locution, and too readily confused with "*con*geniality," a term with very different connotations. As the distinguishing feature of creative geniuses, *Genialität* is perhaps best rendered as "ingeniousness." In any event, Schumann views it as the ability to synthesize opposites: moderation and power, the "lightness of butterflies" and the "ponderousness of elephants," delicacy and destruction. It is, in a word, the hallmark of the *hoher Mensch*, its "highest capacity" being the "aesthetic-beautiful union of the sentimental and the humorous, as we find often in Jean Paul, sometimes in Goethe, seldom in Hoffmann, but frequently in Beethoven, Schubert, and even in Moscheles." What figures in *Selene* as an ethical category is thus granted an aesthetic, and even critical slant, for the "genial" being will know how to synthesize "feeling" and "understanding," *Gefühl* and Kantian *Verstand*.[115] But perhaps most important, the individual rises to the level of genius, thus attaining to the status of *hoher Mensch*, not through the grace of God, but rather through an active program of self-formation or *Bildung*: "Every genius is at once a creative and self-formed *[gebildetes]* individual, . . . [though] not every creative individual is a genius."[116]

Imaginative and critical prose in the Jean-Paulian style thus complement one another. Together they attest to the development of a sensibility that would animate Schumann's artistic endeavors in the years ahead. The motto of the *Freuden- und Schmerzensthränen*, a manuscript collection of aphorisms stylistically and thematically related to "Die Tonwelt" and the essay on *Genialität*, for instance, tells of an angel's request for the creation of something to saturate the human heart with melancholy. In response, God transforms the dewdrops of roses, forget-me-nots, and cypresses into teardrops, saying: "the last is the most beautiful, and a jewel in the heavenly crown."[117] This line strikingly prefigures the completion of the Peri's quest for a suitable gift in Schumann's great oratorio of 1843.

Just as the sphere of Schumann's literary activities broadened during the summer of his first year in Leipzig, so too did his commitment to music. By late August 1828, he was spending much time in the company of the Caruses and his piano teacher, Friedrich Wieck, through whom he gained access to Leipzig's elite musical circles, and at whose home he came into contact with his teacher's daughter Clara, at nine years old a burgeoning concert pianist. Already at this early point, Flechsig detected in the prodigy's engagement of his roommate in "childish teasing" a premonition of their future life together.[118] In the same letter to his mother in which Schumann reports on his studies with Wieck, he also alludes to plans for a four-hand piano recital in the coming winter months with Emilie Reichold, another of Wieck's students;[119] whether the concert took place, we do not know, though there is ample evidence for Schumann's honing of his keyboard skills during that period. According to a series of diary entries for early 1829, he practiced Hummel's *Etudes* assiduously in February, returning in March to the same composer's A-minor Piano Concerto, op. 85, the first movement of which, probably together with Moscheles's *La Marche d'Alexandre*, op. 32, he performed in Zwickau on 28 April 1829.[120]

In the meantime, Schumann had fastened on an idol whose position in his musical pantheon was comparable to that of Jean Paul in the poetic sphere. By mid-summer 1828, he was revelling in Franz Schubert, whose musical creations, no less than Jean Paul's novels, surely provided an important stimulus for the musico-poetic fragments in *Hottentottiana* and the aesthetic of "Die Tonwelt." While Flechsig attests to Schumann's splendid playing of the *Erlkönig*,[121] his attention soon shifted to the four-hand piano repertory. As noted earlier, his synaesthetic speculations led him, in July 1828, to dub the *Acht Variationen über ein Thema aus der Oper Marie von Hérold* a "perfect novel in tones." On 20 August he would describe the same work as "too sublime and otherworldly for contemporary humanity; in spite of the transparency of these variations, one can't grasp them in a single hearing, a trait they share with Beethoven's music."[122] In a diary entry for the day before, he alludes to a session devoted to Schubert's four-hand polonaises (op. 61, D. 824 and op. 75, D. 599) with August Böhner, a student friend described in none too flattering terms as "uncultivated and without character"; in the months ahead, he would continue to play these pieces in convivial gatherings with his sister-in-law Therese (the wife of Eduard Schumann) and a number of other friends and acquaintances.[123]

Schumann's cultivation of this repertory further corresponds to the beginnings of a definitive association between his favored author and his current favorite among composers. As we have seen, several of the aesthetic fragments in *Hottentottiana* for July and early August 1828 link Jean Paul with Beethoven, but in an entry of 15 August 1828 we read: "*Fantasie a la Schubert:* Schubert expresses Jean Paul, Novalis, and Hoffmann in tones."[124] And a little over a year later, Schumann states unequivocally in a letter to Wieck: "Schubert is still my 'one and only'

Schubert, especially since he has everything in common with my 'one and only' Jean Paul; when I play Schubert, it's as if I were reading a novel 'composed' by Jean Paul." [125] It may at first strike us as odd to assert that two such different artists have "everything in common." Schubert possesses even less of Jean Paul's baroque quirkiness than the writer shares in the composer's rarefied elegance. But on reflection, perhaps the two figures are not such polar opposites after all. Neither will have much of an impact on an impatient observer: Schubert's continual invitations for his listeners to pause over leisurely unfolding and subtly varied phrases find a parallel in Jean Paul's demand that his readers linger over a peculiar metaphor or a convoluted sentence whose meaning discloses itself only gradually. Schumann hints at other shared features in his letter to Wieck: "Apart from Schubert's, no music exists that is so psychologically unusual in the course and connection of its ideas, and in the ostensible logic of its discontinuities. . . . What for others was a diary in which to set down momentary feelings was for Schubert a sheet of music paper to which he entrusted his every mood, so that his thoroughly musical soul wrote notes when others wrote words." [126] Similarly, Jean Paul lent his novels an unusual psychological profile by tinging melancholy with humor, and by opting for a discontinuous style in order to emphasize the fragmentary nature of existence. And Jean Paul too, much like Schubert, infused his creations with a powerful confessional element: he "mirrors himself in all his works," to quote again from a diary entry written when Schumann's Jean Paul craze was at its height, "but always in two people." The aspiring poet finds the process "superhuman" *(übermenschlich),* an adjective close to the one he later employed to characterize Schubert's Variations: "otherworldly" *(überirdisch).* [127]

Just as Jean Paul inspired Schumann to literary creation, so Schubert provided a stimulus for musical composition in the late summer and fall of 1828. Composed in August and September while Schumann was at work on "Die Tonwelt" and the essay on *Genialität,* and dedicated to his brothers Eduard, Carl, and Julius, the *VIII Polonaises . . . op. III*[WoO20] for piano four hands were a direct outgrowth of Schumann's passion for Schubert's works for the same medium. The composer's spirits buoyed by the positive response accorded his first significant works for piano in Dr. Carus's circle, he noted in his diary that while Schubert's polonaises may be divine, his own were "highly or at least passably beautiful." [128] Taken as a group, Schumann's polonaises are marked by the exuberant, unbuttoned style typically associated with the genre. Each falls into a straightforward ternary form (ABA), the A section, or polonaise proper, featuring driving dactylic rhythms and glittering textures, the B section comprising a lyric trio in a contrasting key. Several of the latter—their programmatic French titles perhaps a reflection of Schumann's youthful study under Kuntsch of similarly titled pieces by C. P. E. Bach and Türk[129]—are notable either for their improvisatory, rhapsodic flights ("La fantaisie" of no. 7) or for their flirtation with contrapuntal textures ("L'aimable" of no. 6). In some cases (Polonaises II and III) Schumann links the contrasting sections by presaging the theme of the trio in the polonaise proper.

Schubert's influence is felt not only in the generally easy-going style of the *VIII Polonaises*—appropriate for a genre whose *raison d'etre* lies in the delectation of the performers—but also in their harmonic language. The third-related modulations in the A section of Polonaise I, whose E♭-major tonic is colored by both G♭ and B (= C♭), recalls many a similar "flat-side" progression in Schubert's works. So too does the emphasis on the Neapolitan in Polonaise V; obviously, its C-major Trio stands in just such a relationship to the B-minor A section, but the second half of the trio compounds the Neapolitan coloration by climbing a half-step further to D♭. Likewise redolent of Schubert is the general absence of expressive indications; these Schumann leaves to the discretion of the performer, for as he wittily puts it in his diary: "Works in which many 'dolces' appear are usually not very *dolce;* Jean Paul has already said something similar in his *Ästhetik:* comedies with 'laughter to death' in their titles often bring weeping and lamentation to death."[130]

By early October, Schumann had moved on to another composition for the piano four-hand medium, a set of variations on a theme by Prince Louis Ferdinand, a favored composer since Schumann's early and mid-teenage years. Now the recently completed polonaises seemed dull and tedious, but "so it goes with me; the new continually displaces the old, and I prize the latest creative project most highly."[131] While the variations have not survived, another and more ambitious project undertaken shortly thereafter—a quartet in C minor for piano and strings, designated "op. V" on the autograph manuscript—is rich in implications for an account of Schumann's evolving compositional talent. Like the polonaises, his first essay in what he would later call the "higher forms" grew out of an atmosphere that viewed music as a promoter of conviviality. Late in 1828, he formed a piano quartet—comprised of Johann Friedrich Täglichsbeck (violin), Christoph Sörgel (viola), Christian Glock (cello), and Schumann himself as pianist—whose reading sessions were often attended by a circle of select listeners including Wieck, Dr. Carus, and the music-dealer and butt of many of Schumann's jokes, Heinrich Probst. A musical counterpart to the *Litterarischer Verein* of the Zwickau years, the group tackled a broad range of piano quartets and trios by acknowledged masters (Beethoven, Weber, Schubert) and other figures little known today (Prince Louis Ferdinand, Ries, Dussek, Onslow). A diary entry for 13 March 1829 paints a vivid portrait of a typically lively session given over to hearty music-making and good-natured banter:

> Evening: 14th quartet session. Beethoven's ["Archduke"] Trio, op. 97 (bizarre)—Dussek Quartet in E♭ (op. 57)—[Schumann's] Quartet op. V (went well)—much Bavarian beer [the previous night, Flechsig had arrived home drunk, "knill," and broken his bed]—tedious conversation about the students' and peasants' associations—good cheer—late at night the first movement of Schubert's Trio [op. 100, D. 929]—very noble music—gallopade [a lively Hungarian dance]—beautiful sleep." [132]

Again like the *Litterarischer Verein,* the quartet centered around Schumann and his self-designed course of study: its disbanding soon after the seventeenth session on 28 March 1829 immediately preceded his relocation to Heidelberg; and following its first meeting on 14 November 1828, we find him engaged in writing a piano quartet of his own. Therefore the initial work on the composition coincides with the drafting of *Selene,* the fervent melodramatics of its *Mitternachtsstück* and *Harmonika-Altarblatt* episode resonating with the impassioned opening movement of the C-minor quartet. But from the start, Schumann associated his latest compositional effort with the image of his newly found musical hero, word of whose untimely death threw him into a state of emotional anxiety, witness the diary entry for 31 November: "My quartet—Schubert is dead—dismay." [133] The informal quartet sessions at Wieck's or Carus's thus would have provided Schumann with a laboratory for trying out what probably began as an *Hommage à Schubert.* As soon as he had finished a movement and seen to the copying of parts, his friends were on hand for a sympathetic reading. At their tenth meeting on 7 February 1829, the group played through portions of the quartet (probably the first movement) no less than three times to "general laudations." [134] A week later, the *Minuetto* was ready, but the cellist Glock (at the time a student of theology and philosophy, and also an amateur pianist) apparently came to grief over its witty rhythmic turns: "bungled quartet—the breakneck cello" Schumann noted in his diary on 14 February. [135] While the Adagio received a trial performance at the group's next meeting on the evening of 21 February, the last movement was not ready until exactly a month later; and although the work as a whole was accorded a "laudatory aesthetic judgment" at that session,

Glock expressed his dissatisfaction over the fact that "the piano maintains the characteristic rhythm" throughout the vivacious Finale.[136] Schumann spent much of the next week "behind closed doors" checking his quartet "note for note"—and perhaps also tightening some passages as well—his reward being a run-through at the group's final session on 28 March during which the entire composition elicited praise from Carus and Wieck.[137] Then we hear nothing of the work until early January of the following year, when Schumann noted in his diary: "The quartet will be cobbled into a symphony."[138] But while the autograph is peppered with orchestrational designations, the plan for a symphonic realization of the quartet never materialized.

Schumann's C-minor Piano Quartet, a remarkably polished work for someone who was as yet without formal training in composition, is at once a result of convivial musical practice and a document of the young composer's reception of Schubert. If the *VIII Polonaises* drew their inspiration from the latter's dances for piano four hands, then the Piano Quartet reflects a fascination with his E♭-major Piano Trio, D. 929. The mixture of enchantment and disturbance in Schumann's reaction to one of the most impressive products of Schubert's mature style bears a striking resemblance to his reaction to Jean Paul; after hearing Schubert's Trio at a "little gathering" *(Kränzchen)* at Wieck's on 4 December 1828, he arrived "home at 3 in the morning—excited night with Schubert's immortal trio ringing in my ears—frightful dreams."[139] And indeed, elements of Schubert's idiom in general, and of his chamber style in particular, abound in Schumann's quartet. In the first, second, and last movements, the glittering passagework characteristic of the keyboard part—which, a few exceptions aside, Schumann notates on a single staff—seems especially indebted to the older composer's manner. The quartet's harmonic language likewise draws liberally on a variety of Schubertian traits, witness the immediate emphasis on the Neapolitan in the opening movement, the rapid-fire modulations by third in the *Minuetto,* and the interpenetration of major and minor modes in the finale. While the principal rhythm of the last movement ($\srceq$) may have been suggested by the first movement of Beethoven's seventh symphony, its obsessive repetition, the feature that aroused Glock's displeasure, again recalls a favorite strategy in the quick movements of Schubert's maturity. Even the minimization of transitional passages in the first movement hearkens to a quintessentially Schubertian formal device.

But just as Schumann feared that his *Selene* might turn out "too much like Jean Paul," so he took pains to ensure that his piano quartet would amount to more than a mere imitation of Schubert. In the first movement, his will to self-conscious originality as regards tonal and formal relations somewhat misfires: the development's continual reiteration of the minor and major tonic (C), no less than its inclusion of not one, but two retransitional passages, leads to a confusion of elaborative and recapitulatory functions. But the free handling of phrase rhythms in the *Minuetto* (in effect, a Scherzo) is little short of masterful; the division of the main four-bar units into a 1 + 2 + 1 grouping, together with the quirky placement of the overriding rhythmic cell in a strong-weak metric position and the configuration of the central two bars as a hemiola pattern, results in a total effacement of metric squareness (Example 1.2). While Schumann's rhapsodic approach to form has less than satisfactory consequences in the first movement, it comes into its own in the third, an affective Andante whose recapitulation brings the themes of the exposition in reverse order (and likewise shows that these themes are capable of all sorts of contrapuntal combinations), thus effecting an emotional arch that proceeds from melancholy, peaks in a series of dreamily contented dialogues, and sinks back into the opening mood.

Just after drafting the last movement, Schumann noted that it contained a "jovial ferocity that gaily muses on the past as if from another world and transports its bas reliefs into this one."[140] To be sure, the manner in which the finale "gaily muses" on past events constitutes one of the quartet's most striking features. To appreciate the point, though, we should return to the *Minuetto*, or more exactly, its trio. Writing some twenty years later, Schumann accorded this passage a special place in his development as a composer: "I remember very well a spot in one of my works . . . about which I said to myself: this is *romantic*; here a spirit different from that of my earlier music opened up for me: a new poetic

Example 1.2. Piano Quartet in C Minor: second movement, mm. 1–4. (By permission of Heinrichshofens Verlag, Wilhelmshaven, Germany.)

Example 1.3. Piano Quartet in C Minor: second movement, mm. 1–8, 17–24. (By permission of Heinrichshofens Verlag, Wilhelmshaver, Germany.)

life appeared to reveal itself (the spot in question was the trio of a scherzo from a piano quartet)."[141] The new, "romantic" spirit of the Trio section manifests itself in lilting trochaic and dactylic rhythms, piquant appoggiaturas, and, at the beginning of the Trio's second half, a simple but evocative scoring strategy whereby the melody, assigned to the cello, is accompanied by pizzicatos in the violin and viola, and pulsing chords in the piano (Example 1.3). Schumann was obviously taken by his Jean-Paulian blend of "melancholy and enchantment" in this passage, for he recalls the trio theme just before the recapitulation of the third movement and again in the finale, where it occupies a place in a veritable parade of recurrent ideas from earlier movements: the second theme from the first movement (at mm. 121ff. and mm. 496ff., during the exposition and development, respectively) and the opening theme of the Andante (mm. 317ff. of the development). The "romantic" trio theme, however, serves as the peroration of this process of recall when it appears, transformed into an ebullient C major, in the *più presto* coda. Here too we realize in retrospect that the obsessive rhythm of the finale is none other than a quick-tempo variant of the dactylic pattern from the trio. Hence the "new poetic life" that revealed itself to Schumann through his charming but initially unassuming trio theme was closely bound up with a search for coherence on a large temporal scale. Clearly the development of his musico-poetic sensibility was well under way.

～2～

$\mathcal{M}$usic as
Literature

The Budding Virtuoso

Less than half a year after matriculating as a law student at the University of Leipzig, Schumann had already determined to continue his studies elsewhere. Writing to his mother on 3 August 1828, he broached the idea of resettling in Heidelberg, ostensibly to attend the lectures of the great jurists Karl Mittermaier and Anton Friedrich Thibaut, but also for the less clearly defined purpose of counteracting his steadily growing malaise by expanding his range of intellectual contacts. According to his only partially realized plan, he would leave Leipzig just after the winter semester of 1829, spend a year at the University of Heidelberg, and return to Leipzig by Easter 1830 to complete his law degree.[1] At some level, then, Schumann did perhaps intend to see his legal studies through to their conclusion, or, what is more likely, he deluded himself into thinking he might do so. En route to Heidelberg in May 1829, he had an experience that offers a more telling premonition of the direction his future would take. Stricken with an "extraordinary desire" to play the piano while passing through Frankfurt on 14 May, he strolled into a piano dealer's shop, introduced himself as the valet of an English nobleman interested in purchasing an instrument, installed himself at a piano, and played to his heart's content for three hours. Although he promised to return in two days with a definitive answer from his master, he was by that time, as he proudly related the anecdote to his mother, already in Rüdesheim drinking Rüdesheimer beer.[2]

Schumann quickly assimilated himself into the easy-going pace of life in the picturesque university town. In a letter dated 17 July 1829, he assured his mother that he was "jolly, indeed quite happy at times," adding, no doubt for her benefit, "I'm industrious and organized; the law, as taught by Thibaut and Mittermaier, is much to my liking." The former made a particularly deep impression as a lecturer who "overflows with life and spirit, so that he hardly has time or words enough to express his ideas." But as we shall see, Thibaut did far more to deepen Schumann's still evolving musical sensibilities than to kindle his purported liking for juridical matters. In keeping with his penchant for the analysis of people and places alike, Schumann also offered his mother a critique of university life in his new home: the student, he writes, is the most important person in Heidelberg, though he remains unconvinced that the development of a young individual is well served "by entering a town where the student alone rules and flourishes."[3]

Eduard Röller, then a theology student, confirms his friend's indifference to the frivolous existence enjoyed by many of their young colleagues; in Heidelberg, as in Leipzig, Schumann apparently lived "somewhat independently and unruffled by student life." His certificate of study from the University, dated 10 September 1830, likewise attests that he kept his distance from all "forbidden student organizations." In all likelihood he kept his distance from the university's lecture halls as well. Although for the period from summer 1829 through summer 1830 the certificate affirms his enrollment in Thibaut's course on Roman law (with the further notation "especially diligent and attentive"), Karl Zachariä's lectures on natural and church law, and other courses on constitutional and international law, Röller states flatly, echoing Flechsig's report on their friend's commitment to legal study, that so far as he knew, Schumann "didn't attend a single lecture."[4] During his year in Heidelberg, Schumann appears to have devoted his principal academic energies to the study of languages: French, Italian, English, and according to a letter to his brother Carl, even Spanish.[5] In the same letter, he requests a "little check" to help settle his debt (150 gulden) to a local moneylender; for in addition to his tuition expenses (50 gulden), the fees for "special sessions" with a Professor Johannsen (80 gulden), and the cost of private language study, he also had to meet the demands of the "tailor, shoemaker, laundress, piano, the damned cigars, and my own stomach, even though it makes only modest claims."[6] Though largely immune to the frivolities of student life, Schumann thus emerges—at least in the handling of his finances—as a typical student.

Immediately after matriculating at the University of Heidelberg on

30 July 1829, Schumann was smitten with *Wanderlust*, and to justify in his mother's eyes what turned out to be a two-month tour of Switzerland and Italy, he attempted to convince her of its educative benefits. The academic senate of the university, he related in a letter of 3 August, had fixed an eight-week holiday around the feast of Michaelmas precisely so that students could see a bit of the world; how better, then, to improve his French and Italian than by journeying south?[7] According to the most detailed of the autobiographical sketches of 1840, the trip—which extended from 28 August to 25 October—had no musical purpose.[8] Nonetheless, Schumann's Swiss-Italian tour was not devoid of musical stimuli. For the first time in his life, he was exposed to a regular diet of Italian opera, and try though he might, he found it difficult to resist. "By God," he wrote to Wieck soon after returning to Heidelberg, "you can have no notion of Italian music unless you've heard it under the skies that called it forth—that is, the Italian skies. . . . How enchanted I was by Rossini, or rather by [the soprano Giuditta] Pasta." But he quickly tempered his enthusiastic account with the rejoinder that, apart from Pasta, "Italian music is hardly fit to listen to; you can hardly imagine with what fervid sloppiness they hack away at everything."[9] Schumann was not the first Northerner, nor would he be the last, to view the art of the Italians as a kind of forbidden fruit. Like Goethe in the century before and Thomas Mann in the century after, he was at once enthralled by and suspicious of its inimitably sensuous surface. The increasingly shrill denunciations of the shallowness of Italian opera in Schumann's critical writings of the 1830s and 1840s thus served as a defensive mechanism against an artform whose charms he found more than a little alluring.

Schumann's literary production, cultivated so diligently in Leipzig, fell off markedly in quantity during his year or so in Heidelberg. Though he may have planned to elaborate his Swiss-Italian travel notes into the variety of prose narrative that had become increasingly popular in the wake of Goethe's *Italienische Reise* (1816)—a supposition strengthened by the fragmentary *Jünglingswallfahrten* (The Youth's Pilgrimages), a travel reminiscence begun in the winter of 1830—the plan, if intended, was not pursued.[10] And while he continued to add to *Hottentottiana*—its fourth, "Heidelberg," volume subtitled "The Year of the Upperclassman, or the Moral Education"—the entries display a less self-consciously literary and more conventionally diaristic tone.

At least for the moment, then, Schumann channelled his artistic energies into musical pursuits in general and piano-playing in particular. In Anton Töpken, a fellow student and musical enthusiast, he found a willing partner with whom to continue his exploration of the four-hand repertory; not surprisingly, their weekly sessions were frequently given over to favorites such as Schubert's Polonaises, D. 599 and 824, and his Variations, D. 908. Töpken, in turn, was impressed with Schumann's aplomb and artistry, both as interpreter of the first movement of Hummel's A-minor piano concerto, op. 85, and as an improviser from whom "ideas flowed in an inexhaustible stream."[11] But anxious to improve at a more rapid pace, the four-hand partners attempted to shorten the process leading to technical perfection at the keyboard. "Later he recognized his error," Töpken wrote of his friend,[12] in a probable allusion to Schumann's use of the finger-strengthening device (or *Cigarrenmechanik* [cigar mechanism] as he calls it in his diary) that perhaps brought on but certainly exacerbated the "numbness" in the third finger of his right hand, a complaint he first registered in late January 1830.[13]

An amusing series of diary entries for late December 1829 is indicative of the seriousness with which Schumann began to take his pianistic efforts. Here he records the largely adulatory views of his playing voiced by twenty-one individuals ranging from Töpken's landlady ("Come again soon; that sounded so wonderful") to his law professor, Zachariä ("I understand nothing, but your piano playing is extraordinary").[14] By early 1830, Schumann's reputation as a gifted pianist had gained him access into the inner circle of Heidelberg's cultural elite. As he boasted to his brother in a letter of 11 February: "You can hardly believe how generally liked I am . . . and really, without flattering myself too much, how esteemed and respected as well." He goes on to describe the busy round of social calls that keep him occupied at one soirée or another almost every night of the week: Tuesdays at Mittermaier's, Thursdays with a "brilliant circle of Englishwomen," Fridays at Thibaut's, Sundays at "the Grand Duchess's." Owing to a brilliant performance of Moscheles's "Alexander" variations on 24 January—his rendition was greeted with enthusiastic "bravos" and "encores"—he tells his brother that he is now known by the epithet "Darling of the Heidelberg Public."[15] Schumann scored his triumph as a performing artist in a concert sponsored by the Museum, a musical *Verein* composed largely of students. Devoted chiefly to the performance of larger instrumental works, the Museum thus provided an outlet for Schumann's aspirations as a concert artist, much as the Zwickau *Litterarischer Verein* and the Leipzig quartet had nurtured his sense for belles lettres and convivial music-making, respectively.

Schumann's musical horizons broadened immeasurably during his stint in Heidelberg, and in two principal directions: on the one hand, he grew increasingly aware of the historical foundations of music as art and practice; on the other, he became fascinated with the poetic possibilities of musical virtuosity. Schumann may have absorbed few of the particulars of jurisprudence from his professors, but one of them, Thibaut, exercised a lasting influence on his developing mode of music-historical thinking. The author of *Über Reinheit der Tonkunst* (1825), an encomium to the glories of sacred choral music in general and Palestrina and Handel in particular, Thibaut regularly assembled up to seventy singers in his home to read through Handel's oratorios. A frequent participant in these events, Schumann relates that Thibaut, who presided at the keyboard, was often so moved at the conclusion of a run-through that "two great big tears rolled down from his large eyes." Writing to his mother on 24 February 1830, Schumann went on to praise his teacher's "wit, acumen, and feeling for the purest in art; his kindness, incredible eloquence, and tact in all things."[16] The following day, his imagination kindled from a reading of *Samson*, Schumann accorded Handel a literary analogue much as he had Beethoven and Schubert over a year before. While Thibaut had apparently argued for a direct comparison of Handel and Shakespeare, Schumann thought the former too "one-sided" to keep company with "universal geniuses" on the order of Shakespeare, Mozart, and Michelangelo. As an "ideal human being," and thus similar in artistic makeup to Schiller and Raphael, Handel lay somewhere between Klopstock and Shakespeare in Schumann's musico-poetic scheme.[17] During the month before, Schumann formulated a provocative and specifically music-historical paradox. Proceeding from the premise that the "esteemed older masters" from Handel to Haydn "ruled over the passions, squashing and crushing them through the might of their expansive spirits," while in contrast the "recent school" is ruled *by* the passions, Schumann likened the earlier composers "to a lofty, profound youth" and his contemporaries to a "reposing adult." Yet he found his conclusion neither "logical nor natural"; furthermore, it brought him face-to-face with a disturbing question: "What end will history take?"[18] By spring of the same year, however, he had made significant headway toward articulating an answer: "The future," he wrote in May or June, "should be the higher echo of the past."[19] As we shall see, Schumann's solution to the paradox of music-historical development will be raised to the level of an ethical imperative in his work as critic and composer in the years to come. But already by early in 1830, Schumann had most probably adopted as a personal article of faith the opening line of Thibaut's aesthetic tract, "It has never been so generally recognized as now that historical study and understanding of the available classics should be the foundation of all genuine knowledge."[20]

A musical stimulus of a very different kind dates from about the same time. While in Frankfurt on 11 April 1830, Schumann attended one of four concerts given by Paganini, and although Schumann harbored some doubts about the depths of the renowned virtuoso's artistic ideals, suspecting he might "lack that great, noble, priestly serenity characteristic of the genuine artist," still the performance filled the impressionable young man with "incredible enchantment." Gathering afterward at a nearby pub, the *Goldener Schwan,* Schumann and two of his student friends from Heidelberg, Friedrich Weber and Eduard Hille, spoke well into the night of the violinist's captivating playing. Once settled in his hotel room, Schumann gave himself over to "enchantment in bed and gentle dreams," the magical tones of Paganini's concert still ringing in his ears.[21] According to Röller, the artistry of the violinist Heinrich Wilhelm Ernst, a famed performer whose stay in Heidelberg brought him into contact with Schumann, made an equally memorable impression.[22]

Handel and Paganini, Thibaut and Ernst, historicism and virtuosity—the personal, artistic, and intellectual stimuli that greeted the young Schumann during his Heidelberg period make for odd couplings indeed. The virtuoso, after all, practices a kind of high-wire act in which the present moment and its striking effect count for everything; the devotee of history, on the other hand, is concerned with temporal continuities and their role in the establishment of a tradition. Yet the resolution of these divergent tendencies was among the chief tasks Schumann set for himself in his compositions of 1830.

Writing to Hummel in August 1831, Schumann pinpointed the spring of the year before as a period of crisis in another regard: "What do you want of the world?" he asked himself with increasing urgency.[23] Aware that his Heidelbergian idyll could not continue indefinitely, Schumann seems for the first time to have confronted, head on, the difficult issue of settling on a career. A remarkably frank self-analysis, preserved as an appendix to *Hottentottiana,* probably dates from this critical phase:

> S[chumann] is the young man I've loved and observed for a long time. I would like to portray his soul, but I don't know it completely. . . . [He possesses] talent for many things and unusual, individual traits distinguish him from the common horde. . . . His temperament [is] melancholic because therein the power of feeling expresses itself more strongly than the power of observation; hence there is more subjectivity than objectivity in his judgments and creative work. . . . [He has] a lively memory and recollective faculty. Acumen, intellection, and wit

[are] not so strongly developed. . . . [He is] more inclined to artistic activity than to speculation—excellent in music and poetry—but not a musical genius—his talents as musician and poet are at the same level." [24]

This passage indicates that at least on one point Schumann had no doubts: his destiny as an artist. The question hinged less on *whether* he should embrace art than on *what sort* of an artist he should aspire to be. Hence his decisive turn to a musical career in the summer of 1830 was, in all probability, the product of precisely the sort of objective speculation that, according to his self-analysis, was inimical to his fundamental character.

Schumann's conscious decision to devote himself totally to artistic pursuits merely brought to light a desire that was never far removed from the surface. For all intents and purposes, he had already set his sights on a life in art before half-heartedly conceding to legal study in the spring of 1828. Now, however, he would have to broach the issue with a skeptical parent. In a letter to his mother of 1 July 1830, he begins by describing his daily routine: up at 4 A.M., with his law books until 7, two hours of piano practice, lectures, reading, and language study in the afternoons, evenings spent in the company of friends or "with nature." He claims not to have lost his ambition to become a great lawyer, but at the same time begins to prepare his mother for the possibility that his calling might lie elsewhere. In the first place, he lacks two of the qualities that every successful jurist must possess, "practicality" and a "talent for Latin." More important, Thibaut has been discouraging him from pursuing his studies since "Providence didn't make me a born bureaucrat." If Schumann's account of a typical day makes him out to be more diligent than he in fact was, and if his self-deprecating allusion to an impractical character is easily unmasked as a feeble excuse, he strikes a more sincere tone in his closing remarks: "A mechanical, forced lawyer without love for his profession will not, therefore, be a very good one." [25]

Thus, when she received her son's letter of 30 July 1830—in his estimation, the most important one he ever wrote or would write— Johanna Christiana Schumann cannot have been very surprised by its contents. He described his life as "a *twenty-year struggle* between poetry and prose," adding, as an afterthought, "or rather, between *music and law.*" Given his lack of the requisite financial means to ensure a lucrative law practice, his indifference to "petty legal details," and the humanistic thrust of his earlier education, Schumann announced his plan to carve out a career for himself in the musical world. Confident that "within six years, and under the guidance of a good teacher," he would be able to hold his own against any pianist, Schumann maintained, again to allay his mother's worries, that "piano playing, after all, is merely a matter of technical accomplishment." Only the precise emphasis of his musical studies remained to be settled. Careers in performance and composition were both possibilities, but since excellence could only be achieved in one area or the other, Schumann leaned toward a period of concentrated piano study under Wieck (who already knew his abilities) in preparation for a year in Vienna with Moscheles.[26]

Complying with Schumann's request that she ask Wieck's opinion of the plan, Johanna Christiana appealed to the Leipzig music master on 7 August as one parent to another. And indeed, her litany of reservations will ring true with any parent whose offspring has just determined to take up a precarious field: financial success in music is uncertain at best; her son may not be able to meet the demands of his chosen profession; his older brothers are unanimously opposed to the idea; embarking on a path he should have taken ten years ago, her youngest son will have a tremendous amount of catching up to do.[27] Wieck in turn replied two days later, suggesting strongly that Schumann depart from "warm" Heidelberg, which would "heat up his imagination all the more," and resettle in "dull, frigid Leipzig," where Wieck promised "to make Robert, within three years, into one of the greatest living pianists, who will play more warmly and ingeniously than Moscheles, and more grandly than Hummel." At the same time, the aspiring pianist would have to submit to five conditions: he must (1) strive for greater precision and accuracy, (2) take daily lessons with Wieck for a one-year period, (3) be prepared to supplement his income by giving private lessons, (4) study music theory—whose rules and regulations precluded the flights of fantasy in which Schumann loved to indulge—for two years with a teacher of Wieck's choice (named Weinlig), and (5) consent to a general review of his progress after a six-month trial period.[28] Wieck's response to Schumann's plan, laced as it was with a rhetoric of frigidity, displays the mixture of pompousness and pedantry that would, in the years to come, irritate the younger man no end. Still wary of the whole enterprise, but worn down and depressed by an enervating exchange of letters, Schumann's mother grudgingly approved her son's proposed course of action on 12 August.[29] At least one individual greeted Schumann's decision with genuine enthusiasm; his old teacher Kuntsch warmly applauded his former student's musical aspirations, prophesying that in time he would "count among the world's leading artists."[30] In any case, approval or no, the die was cast for music; as Schumann put it to Wieck, "I choose art, I will remain with her, I can and must."[31]

The creative projects Schumann either began or completed in Heidelberg reflect his increasing attention to the honing of his keyboard skills. The *Projektenbuch* for 1829 and 1830 makes reference both to etudes and to "shorter piano pieces," many of them now lost, or preserved in various states of incompletion, but in any event linked to Schumann's preparation for a performing career.[32] Among the earliest of these is a planned set of *6 Walzer*, material from three of which found its way into *Papillons*.[33] A product of the Schubert craze that set in during the summer of 1828 and motivated Schumann's composition of dances and variations for piano four hands, the *6 Walzer* may have been conceived shortly after he returned from the Swiss-Italian tour in the autumn of 1829. In a letter to Wieck of 6 November 1829, Schumann asks him to send "all of Schubert's [two-hand] waltzes (I believe there are ten to twelve volumes), Moscheles's G-minor Concerto [op. 60], Hummel's B-minor Concerto [op. 89] . . . [and] all of Schubert's compositions (that have appeared since Opus 100)."[34] While Schubert's waltzes would have served as models for his own (and also as suitable repertory for a young artist who was fast becoming the darling of Heidelberg's salons), the concerti of Moscheles and Hummel were no doubt intended as vehicles for projected public performances. In contrast, Schumann probably earmarked Schubert's more recent compositions—especially the String Quintet in C, D. 956, which he enjoined Wieck not to forget—for personal study.

Hence compositional activity, convivial music-making, virtuosity, and the disinterested contemplation of masterworks overlap and interpenetrate in Schumann's musical pursuits during his stay in Heidelberg. To be sure, the elements in the equation were often mixed in varying quantities and degrees. In one of the autobiographical sketches of 1840, Schumann alluded to Paganini, whom he had heard in April 1830, as "a most powerful stimulus for hard work."[35] This "hard work" took the dual form of concentrated practice and original composition: a set of piano variations on the *Campanella* theme from Paganini's Second Violin Concerto—unfinished, but subsequently tapped for the *Intermezzi*, op. 4, and the *Allegro*, op. 8[36]—is one among several documents attesting to Schumann's reception of the great virtuoso's wizardry. Eager to establish his credentials as a composing pianist in the tradition whose most recent representatives included Moscheles and Hummel, Schumann began composing a piano concerto in F during the spring or summer of 1830, an ambitious project that occupied him off and on for about two years. Indeed, the first movement—or, to be precise, the *solo* portions of the first movement—remained incomplete until the following summer in Leipzig, as indicated by a diary entry for mid-August 1831:

Probst and Zilia [Clara Wieck] like the second theme very much,
[Heinrich] Dorn the entire second solo, Master Raro [Wieck] the opening, the unknown student the first theme, [Julius] Knorr the entire last
solo, Lühe a couple of passages, Glock the Medical Muse [finds] much
[to his liking]. I can't expect a judgment on the whole, for the tuttis
aren't yet composed. Tomorrow I'll send the first solo to Hummel.[37]

A diary reference of 12 May 1831 to the inclusion of the slow movement
in his practice regimen suggests that Schumann may have worked on
both movements in tandem.[38] But while he began to draft a finale in
November 1831, the work was left unfinished: it appears in a list of
projects, dated August 1832, as "yet to be completed."[39] Even though
it remains a fragment, the concerto provides fascinating insights into
Schumann's absorption and transformation of the virtuosic keyboard
idiom inaugurated by Hummel and further developed by such figures
as Henri Herz.[40] All in all, Schumann was not displeased with the result.
The first movement of the concerto, he maintained in a diary entry of
14 August 1831, "appears to be the first thing in my style that leans
toward the romantic."[41]

When in August 1831 he approached Hummel as a possible teacher,
Schumann included, in accordance with the plan outlined in his diary,
the solo exposition of the concerto's first movement, noting that his
undertaking of such a challenging compositional enterprise was hardly
presumptuous, first because he had already written many pieces "large
and small," and second because "the concerto form, since it is quite free,
seems to me a simpler one than, e.g., the sonata form."[42] Schumann's
experiences with the actuality of concerto composition in the early
1830s and again in 1839, when plans for a D-minor piano concerto
were abandoned after the drafting of an opening movement, must have
led him to realize that the form was not such a simple one after all.

The earliest of Schumann's completed, extant works to demonstrate
his fascination with the virtuoso idiom to the fullest is the C-major
Toccata. Diary references to a "toccata" from late 1828 and early 1829—
the period, that is, when Schumann was principally occupied with his
C-minor Piano Quartet—may allude to the work finished in the spring
of 1830, reworked in the summer of 1832, and published in 1834 as the
Toccata, op. 7.[43] The two versions of 1830 and 1832 exhibit important
structural differences: the beginnings of both correspond, but the first
version continues in a monothematic vein, while the second displays
the contrasting themes typical of the classical sonata form. But paradoxically the second version is more compact, eliminating much of the neu-

tral, filler material that lends the earlier version a more etude-like character.[44]

In his 1834 review of the published version of the Toccata for the Leipzig *Komet,* Ernst Ortlepp detected in the work (and in Schumann's keyboard style in general) a manifestation of the same spirit that motivated Bach, Beethoven, and Paganini.[45] What may strike us at first as an inflated claim contains more than a grain of truth. Indeed, both versions of the Toccata represent an attempt to synthesize the historicist and virtuoso impulses personified, during the Heidelberg phase, by the twin configurations Thibaut/Handel on the one hand and Paganini/Ernst on the other. Only a pianist who possesses absolute digital independence will be able to execute the rapidly alternating double notes and glittering octaves in which the piece abounds, and which inspired its original title: *Etude fantastique en double-sons.* But the virtuoso idiom comes together with a characteristic element of the baroque toccata: a rhythmic drive that finds a fitting capstone in the coda (of the second version), where the rhythmic surge forces the metric accent one sixteenth "to the left." The prevalence of the opening figuration either as main event or as murmuring backdrop to contrasting material imparts unity to the classicizing, sonata-form frame of both versions. Structural subtleties, however, recede in favor of technical fireworks: the development section of the published version is given over largely to an A-major/minor episode featuring octaves in the right hand, while the coda provides the occasion for explosive virtuosic display. Hence in the Toccata, the spirit of Bach, Beethoven, and Paganini emerges through the interdependence of baroque rhythmic consistency, classicizing forms, and an up-to-the minute virtuoso idiom.

Virtuosity plays an equally significant role in the next major compositional project after the first version of the C-major Toccata. Though mentioned in a diary entry of 22 February 1830, the "Abegg" variations occupied Schumann mainly during July and August of the same year, and thus immediately followed his decision to pursue a musical career. Published in November 1831 under the imprint of Friedrich Kistner in Leipzig as *Thème sur le nom Abegg varié pour le pianoforte,* op. 1,[46] the work is situated at a crucial fault-line in Schumann's creative development. Identifying himself with his work, Schumann entered an effusive pronouncement in his diary on 7 November 1831, the day his variations appeared in print: "Today I come before the great world for the first time with my variations! May this event inaugurate a period of energy and inner betterment." Five days later he added: "Now the variations are out; it seems as if everything has more significance once published."[47]

Brimming with pride over having achieved a tangible measure of success in his chosen profession, he sent out copies of his first printed opus to over forty friends and relatives, including his mother (at the head of the list), his sisters-in law (but not his brothers), Dr. Carus, his friend Flechsig, his former teacher Kuntsch, Clara Wieck, and her father (who, in contrast to the aforementioned, received the "ordinary" and not the "deluxe" edition).[48]

In deciding to issue an opus 1, composers stake an important claim, and Schumann was no exception. Through the "Abegg" variations, he announced himself to the world as a virtuoso pianist-composer, a fact not lost on Ludwig Rellstab, who placed the work in line with others like it by Herz and Czerny in an 1832 review that the composer copied into his diary.[49] The composition owes just as much to Moscheles, whose "Alexander" variations—a staple of the young Schumann's repertory as a pianist—possibly provided a model for the projected orchestral version of the work.[50]

While not as unremittingly pyrotechnical as the Toccata, the "Abegg" variations make considerable demands on the performer, witness the cascading arpeggios and chromatic filigree in the first variation and the whirling triplets in the third. The most unusual of the work's effects, however—the release of one note at a time from the long-held V7 chord of F just before the coda, until only the upper-voice G remains—requires no particular technical prowess.[51] Throughout, the composition exudes the rarified air of the musical salon. The theme, an elegant waltz tune in octaves supported by pulsing chords, mimics the four-hand texture of the Schubertian dances of which Schumann had grown so fond in the preceding years. Even the overall form embodies elements of stylization. While apparently cast as a variation set, the work in fact aspires to a more rhapsodic, fantasy-like design: following on three variations come a *Cantabile* (a dreamy, highly ornamental cadenza based on the rising headmotif of the theme and taking off from the flat mediant, A♭) and an extended *Finale alla Fantasia* that together account for nearly half of the piece's duration.

Yet the most fantastic aspect of the piece resides in the theme itself, an idea generated from the surname of its purported dedicatee: Mademoiselle Pauline Comtesse d'Abegg (Example 2.1). Although Schumann related to Töpken that Mlle. Abegg hailed from Mannheim, and that she was the object of one of his other friend's admiration, Töpken was unaware of any close tie between Schumann and the young woman.[52] But whether or not Pauline d'Abegg was a sheer product of Schumann's imagination matters little; his chief interest lay in the musical encipher-

Example 2.1. *Abegg* Variations, op. 1, mm. 1–8.

ment of a *name* (recall the opening phrase of the work's full title: "Thème *sur le nom*") and not in the musical depiction of a person. In his review, Rellstab devoted considerable space to poking gentle fun at precisely this feature of the composition:

> I would like to set the talented composer even more complicated tasks to perform with so musical a name. And, once he got the hang of it, I would give him still other themes, such as—apart from the well-known *Bach* and *Fasch*—*Eis* ["ice," "ice-cream"], though obviously the theme would consist of just one note ["Eis" = E♯], *Caffé* ["coffee"] . . . *Fisch* ["fish"], *Hase* ["rabbit"], and *Schaaf* ["sheep"], so that a whole luncheon would be the result . . . Perhaps composers, who generally lack new ideas, would thereby come upon better themes [in using this cipher method] than when they sail about without any compass in the unbounded sea of emotion.[53]

To be sure, there is more than a little subversive playfulness in Schumann's employment of a technique usually reserved for contrapuntal *tours de force* in a frothy salon piece. (The generation of the second half of the theme from the ABEGG motive in retrograde should be viewed in this light). But as the piece progresses, Schumann seems less concerned with the musically enciphered name *per se* than with the two-note segment of the cipher (A-B♭) that sets the theme in motion. Specifically, the fourfold sequential repetition of the two-bar opening gesture produces a chain of half-steps—A-B♭, G♯-A, F♯-G, E-F—that ac-

quires greater significance than the cipher itself as the composition unfolds. These discreet chromatic touches in the theme are elaborated in
the omnipresent ascending and descending *appoggiatura* gestures of the
first variation, then in the arching chromatic ascent shared by treble and
bass in the second variation, and most impressively in the inner-voice
chromaticism of the Finale's opening gesture. And while the Finale does
make fleeting references to the ABEGG motive, it is all but displaced in
importance by the lilting chromatic gesture with which the concluding
section of the piece begins. Thus the musical cipher, itself an abstraction, is abstracted even further over the course of the work.

Still, Schumann's "Abegg" variations take as their point of departure
a determinate construct. In order to understand the point of the piece,
the gradual abstraction of a verbally derived musical unit, we must begin
by "reading" its opening gesture. The musical surface, in other words,
is conceived as a kind of text. This makes the composition a more than
appropriate opus 1 for a twenty-year-old artist who dreamt of "concen-
trating" his talent for poetry and music "into *a single* point." [54]

Schumann at Twenty-One

Schumann departed from Heidelberg in September 1830 and by 20 October had settled in Wieck's Leipzig home in the Grimmaschegasse. His
claim, in one of the 1840 autobiographical sketches, to have devoted at
least six or seven hours daily to piano practice, was probably no idle
exaggeration.[55] Indeed, it is supported by the marked decrease in his
compositional output in late 1830 (and probably during early 1831 as
well), the discontinuation of his diary (apart from travel notices) for
about a year, and also by the practice regimen recorded in the *Leipziger
Lebensbuch,* the new diary he began to keep in May 1831. At that time
we find him studying a rondo by John Field, Moscheles's etudes, Herz's
Variations, op. 48, and the slow movement of his own F-major Piano
Concerto.[56] In May 1831, and continuing until April of the following
year, he began to copy a series of difficult passages from a variety of
keyboard works into the sketchbook now preserved in the Bonn Universitätsbibliothek as Schumann 13. Since most of the passages are
dated, this portion of the first of the so-called "Wiede" Sketchbooks
amounts to a kind of *Übungtagebuch* or practice-diary.[57] Schumann's
study of the finger exercises from Hummel's *Anweisung zum Piano-Forte
Spiel* (1828), dutifully copied into the same sketchbook in both original
and transposed forms, no doubt also stems from the same period.[58]

To judge from the surviving documents, though, the aspiring virtuoso was less than enthralled with every aspect of Wieck's pedagogy. Already in a letter of 12 December 1830 to his mother, he reiterated his intention of moving elsewhere to study after the six-month trial period with Wieck had elapsed. But while in July of that year he had contemplated a year-long period with Moscheles in Vienna, now he planned on a visit to Weimar "for the sly purpose of being called one of Hummel's students."[59] For as he later explained, Hummel was a multi-faceted musician equally skilled as Kapellmeister, teacher, virtuoso, and composer, the latter two being the most likely career options for Schumann himself.[60] When he got wind of his student's plan, Wieck not surprisingly took offense; and although they were soon reconciled, the truce between teacher and pupil was an uneasy one: "You can have no conception of [Wieck's] enthusiasm, his judgment, and his insights into art," Schumann reported to his mother, "but when it comes to his or Clara's interest, he's like a wild boor."[61] When Schumann finally did approach Hummel formally in August 1831, he expressed his dissatisfaction with Wieck's instructional method in no uncertain terms. Careless in attending to his student's specific technical problems, and, if we read the subtext, more concerned with the furtherance of his daughter Clara's career, Wieck had grown curiously indifferent to Schumann's progress:

> How my old teacher had changed! Instead of weighing every note in the balance, and insisting that I study each piece conscientiously, page for page, he let me play through everything haphazardly, good and bad alike, and bothered to correct neither touch nor fingering. . . . Although [Wieck] wanted me to overcome a certain tense, mechanical, or overly studied quality in my playing, I realized that his technique for achieving this goal was better suited to his daughter than to me. . . .[62]

A year later, Schumann sketched a nasty portrait, made all the more disturbing by an anti-Semitic dig, of his one-time mentor in his diary: "Probst stands so much taller than Wieck, who gawks longingly at the Alps from which the former has already descended.—He tries to hide his stinginess, . . . [but] his greed has contaminated all his thoughts. Little by little, Jewishness has insinuated itself even into his facial features."[63]

But if by the spring of 1831 Schumann's relations with Wieck had begun their precipitous downward course, the period in and around his twenty-first birthday likewise marked the initiation of a pivotal phase in his development as an artist. His first and only formal studies in musical composition—with Heinrich Dorn, a conductor, theorist, and composer remembered today for his setting of the Nibelung saga and his humorous lieder—sparked a passion for counterpoint that remained with him until the end of his career. During his period as a law student in Leipzig and Heidelberg, Schumann revelled in Jean Paul and Schubert; now he complemented this duo with an equally unusual pairing: E. T. A. Hoffmann and Chopin. These stimuli brought Schumann closer to the goal toward which he had aspired since his youth: a dual career as a poetically inclined musician and a musically informed critic.

Shortly after settling in Leipzig in the fall of 1830, Schumann was introduced to Dorn, then conductor at the city theater, by his friend and collaborator on the "Tonwelt" essay, Willibald von der Lühe. It was not until mid-July of the following year, however, that lessons got under way with the "noble figured bass."[64] Although Schumann at first complained of his teacher's authoritarian manner ("I will never warm up to Dorn, for he has no feeling, and on top of that, there's his East-Prussian tone"), he soon came to realize that beneath the stiff exterior of this "highly clever, formidable, and ingenious man" lay an essentially kindhearted soul.[65] Likewise, Schumann initially chafed at the contrapuntal strictures to which he was being introduced for the first time in a systematic fashion: "Counterpoint is going pretty well," he wrote on 13 October 1831, "but the rules seem to run contrary; one rule negates the other."[66] Dorn in turn judged one of Schumann's first completed assignments, a chorale harmonization, to be "a model of irregular voice-leading." But perhaps taking to heart Wiedebein's sound advice, proffered several years before, on the necessity of tempering inspired fantasy with cool-headed understanding,[67] Schumann gradually submitted to the rigors of what he must have viewed earlier as a strangely restrictive sort of musical calculus. Indeed, Dorn described him to Wasielewski in a letter written a quarter-century later as an "indefatigible worker," relating an amusing anecdote as proof of his pupil's zeal. Having completed exercises in figured-bass realization, chorale harmonization, and canon, teacher and student moved on to double counterpoint. Intrigued by the mysteries of this discipline, and reluctant to tear himself away from his desk, Schumann once requested that his lesson take place in his own rooms. On arriving at Schumann's flat, Dorn found his student poring over a sheaf of papers, at his side an uncorked bottle of champagne, which they then jointly consumed as a means of "moistening the dry work at hand."[68]

Yet by late April 1832, lessons had been suspended, whether to accommodate Dorn's busy schedule or on account of Schumann's immersion in a series of compositional projects remains unclear (he was then working on the *Intermezzi*, the transcriptions of Paganini's Caprices published as opus 3, and perhaps a second, and now lost volume of *Papillons* as well).[69] In any event, the pair remained on good terms, their paths continuing to cross at the private musical gatherings that formed such an important part of the texture of Schumann's life in Leipzig. At one such event on 4 June 1832, Dorn reacted enthusiastically to his former student's opus 2, published in November of the year before: " 'Schumann, do you know that I like your *Papillons* very much?' "[70] At the same time, Schumann's study of counterpoint hardly came to a total halt; on the contrary, he continued to pursue the subject with unflagging vigor on his own. Having absorbed the precepts of Marpurg's *Abhandlung von der Fuge* (1753–54), largely as a result of personal initiative, he moved on to the examination of actual fugues. As indicated in a letter of 27 July 1832 to Kuntsch, Bach's *Wohltemperirte Clavier* had now become his "grammar," and he was "dissecting" its contents "down to their most minute particles." In the same letter, he asks his old teacher to lend him copies of "old Italian church music" for use in his study of score-reading and instrumentation.[71] Conforming to a pattern already established in his youthful reception of Jean Paul's and Schubert's works, Schumann found his best teacher in himself. Nonetheless, Dorn's role as a mentor should not be underestimated. In a sense, the Leipzig *Musikdirektor* played a part in Schumann's development comparable to that of Thibaut in Heidelberg. Their differences aside—Dorn, whose compositions for the most part evince an easy-going, Biedermeier quality, possessed little of Thibaut's antiquarian sensibility—both figures served as catalysts for their student's self-formation. Both, in a word, facilitated the process of *Bildung* that guided Schumann's passage from youth to maturity.

Just as he was bracing himself for a dip in the icy waters of strict counterpoint, Schumann found an outlet for his imaginative impulses in an area of world literature he had, as yet, only cursorily explored. E. T. A. Hoffmann's writings, though by no means terra incognita (three years before, they had figured in the aesthetic fragments of *Hottentottiana*), came in for particularly intense scrutiny at this time. A series of curt diary entries of 5 June 1831 speaks to the degree to which Schumann gave himself over to the author's mesmerizing spell: "Read that accursed E. T. A. Hoffmann in the evening. . . . One hardly dares to breathe while reading Hoffmann. . . . Continual reading of Hoffmann. New worlds."[72] At first horrified, then stunned, and finally enthralled by the writer's weird blend of reality and fantasy, Schumann responded to Hoffmann much as he had several years earlier to Jean Paul. Here too his encounter with a captivating author set his own poetic juices flowing, and with lightning swiftness: already in the 5 June diary entries he broaches the possibility of writing a "poetic biography" of Hoffmann and of reworking his "Bergwerke zu Falun" as an opera text.[73] (In October Schumann selected "Doge und Dogaressa" for operatic treatment, though he didn't actually draft a scenario until almost a decade later, when, in 1840, he intended to present Clara with an opera as a wedding gift). Even the *Leipziger Lebensuch* itself stands in the same relation to Hoffmann as *Hottentottiana* does to Jean Paul.

We can also assume that Hoffmann, like Jean Paul, was at once a source of gratification and disturbance for Schumann, and that it was precisely the troubling qualities in the writer's works that the impressionable young artist valued most. To put it bluntly: Schumann found in Hoffmann, as in Jean Paul, what he took to be a mirror of himself. But the mirror, if anything, was riddled with even more cracks than its Jean-Paulian counterpart. The terrors of the divided self or *Doppelgänger,* a favored theme for both authors, are ameliorated in Jean Paul's world by a generous dose of humor, the eerie moonlight of a novel such as *Siebenkäs* offset by the writer's inimitably jocular style. Hoffmann allows for few such concessions to the reader's sense of well-being. His is a shockingly contingent and mutable universe in which quotidian reality can turn, at any moment, into a terrifying fantasy world. Moreover, he links this contingency directly to the person of the artist, whose access to the darker side of being is more a curse than a blessing, for it can lead, in the most extreme cases, to madness.

Thus Schumann's preoccupation, during the spring of 1831, with the problem of the artist's relationship to the circumambient world was in all likelihood fueled by his avid reading of Hoffmann: on 27 May, he refers to a projected "Biographical Sketch" of Titian; by 5 June, he contemplates a specifically *poetic* biography of Hoffmann himself; but within a week his thoughts will turn to a more radical means of poeticizing the artist's experience in general and his own experience in particular.[74] Schumann at once articulates the problem and hints at the solution in a diary entry of 8 June 1831, his twenty-first birthday. "It sometimes seems to me," he writes, "as if my objective self wanted to separate itself completely from my subjective self, or as if I stood between my appearance and my actual being, between form and shadow." Intentionally or not, it is difficult to say, he moves toward a resolution of the dilemma by "objectifying" a series of "subjects," his closest associates: "From today forward, I'll give my friends more beautiful and more fitting names." Hence Wieck is dubbed "Meister Raro" ("Rare" or "Exceptional" Master), Clara becomes "Zilia" (a play on "Caecilia," the patron saint of music), Christel (Schumann's lover since at least a month before)[75] appears as "Charitas," Lühe as "Rentmeister Juvenal," Dorn as the "Musikdirektor," the law students Carl Semmel, Johann Renz, and Eduard Rascher, as "Justitiar Abrecher" (Magistrate for the Settling of Accounts), "Studiosus Varinas," and "Student Fust" respectively, Glock as the "Medicinische alte Muse" (Medical Muse), Probst as the "Alter Maestro," and Flechsig as "Jüngling Echomein." By according his friends "more beautiful and more fitting names," Schumann thus transforms them into a cast of fanciful characters, a congeries of poetic objects awaiting their master's command; this, at least, is the sense of his exhortation that they should "Come closer and behave romantically!"[76]

To "behave romantically" is to take one's place in a *Roman*, or novel, and a week later Schumann considered the possibility of situating some of his recently fabricated *dramatis personae*, along with other figures real and imagined, in just such a context:

> The idea for the *Wunderkinder [Child Prodigies]* recently came to me; characters and persons aren't lacking, only continuity and binding threads. Paganini must have a wondrous effect on Zilia. At the moment, the characters include Florestan the Improviser, Paganini, but under another name, Wieck, Clara (Zilia), Hummel as the pyrotechnical ideal, Music Master Faulhaber with his children Mara and Amadeus, Seraphine, [and] Paganini's wife. The ending will be set in Italy—the beginning in Germany—local interest perhaps in Milan—technical accomplishment as ideal—expression as ideal—union of both in Paganini—Clara's striving.[77]

Though never realized, the plan continued to occupy Schumann for some time. Under the heading "Plans for future hours" in a diary entry of 20 April 1832, he isolates the fundamental ideas of his "musical *Roman*" as the "purity of art and artists, technical mastery and irony." And on 1 May, he toys with the idea of according *Florestan* (the new title for the planned novel) a peculiarly Jean-Paulian twist: "Vult Harnisch [one of the twin-brother heroes from *Flegeljahre*] and the hornplayer Krümelchen will appear in the appendix."[78] "Der Davidsbündler," a tale probably drafted at this time, whose title will have important ramifications for Schumann's critical and compositional activities in the 1830s, employs many of the narrative strategies and themes associated with the *Wunderkinder*. Together with the Leipzig trombonist Carl Queisser, Clara and Friedrich Wieck appear as members of a fictive Band of David through which Schumann thematizes the necessity for the artist to strike a balance with the demands of the real world.[79]

Both the projected novel and the tale represent less an escape from the world than a means of giving poetic shape to the artist's refractory relationship to that world, though of course the artist in question is

none other than Schumann himself. His quest for a rapprochement between poetry and music, the motivating force behind nearly the whole
of his creative output, is neatly encapsulated in the notion of a "musical
Roman." Unlike Hoffmann's Johannes Kreisler, the tortured Kapellmeister who succumbs to madness, the Paganinian hero of Schumann's
novel will successfully mediate the conflicting elements that greet the
artist at every turn: technique and expression, ideality (or "purity") and
reality. On the one hand we might be tempted to write off the project
as an adolescent wish-fullfillment fantasy; but on the other, we should
acknowledge Schumann's attempt to hold lived experience—his enthrallment by Paganini's playing, his doubts over his own potential as a
performing artist, his uneasy suspension between musical and literary
careers—under an ironic and thus objectifying gaze. In the *Wunderkinder* and "Der Davidsbündler" as well, autobiography was to have
been chemically transformed through the reflective medium of art.

In this context, a diary entry of 1 July 1831 acquires new meaning:
"Completely new persons enter the diary from this day forward—two
of my best friends, whom I've nonetheless never seen before—they are
Florestan and Eusebius."[80] To be sure, the former was hardly the "completely new person" Schumann makes him out to be. As "Florestan the
Improviser" he was to have figured in the *Wunderkinder* project sketched
out less than a month before. Eusebius, however, does represent a new
addition to Schumann's band of prodigies, the source of the name having given rise to a fair amount of conjecture among specialists on the
composer's life and works. "Eusebius" might refer to any one of a number of churchmen and martyrs from the early Christian era, a period
with which Schumann might have occupied himself, as Peter Ostwald
suggests, in preparation for his projected dramatization of the celebrated
relationship between the twelfth-century French theologian Peter Abelard and his beloved Héloïse. Schumann's reference to the drama on 8
June 1831—in the same diary entry where he notes the cleft between his
subjective and objective selves, and perhaps as a consequence, decides to
give his friends "more beautiful" names—is striking indeed.[81] But within
the next several years, he had made a specific association between "his"
Eusebius and Saint Eusebius the Confessor (pope from 309 to 310, he
was exiled by the Emperor Maxentius as a result of his controversial
stance on the question of apostasy), whose feast day (14 August) is directly preceded by the name-days of "Clara" (12 August) and "Aurora"
(13 August). As Schumann put it to the real (and fictional) Clara in the
lyrical close of "Eusebius an Chiara," the first of four *Schwärmbriefe*
published in 1835: "Don't forget to check the calendar now and again,

where Aurora joins your name with mine."[82]

While it is difficult to know what precise connotations the name "Eusebius" might have had for Schumann in 1831, one thing is certain: both of his "best friends" were meant to be poetic self-projections. Florestan the rambunctious improviser, his persona a mixture of Paganinian virtuosity and Schumann's inclinations in the same direction, his name resonant with that of the hero of Beethoven's *Fidelio*, finds a striking complement in Eusebius the pensive cleric. And while Florestan displays the half-mad trappings of a character from one of Hoffmann's tales, the Jean-Paulian pedigree of Schumann's friends as a contrasting pair is unmistakable. Together they constitute the separate dimensions of the character of a *hoher Mensch* (such as Viktor in Jean Paul's *Hesperus* or Gustav in Schumann's own *Selene*) who proves himself as such by mediating between unbridled energy and thoughtful restraint. Schumann's "best friends" will figure not only as agents of confessional outpourings in his diary but also as critical voices in his activities as a journalist; they represent a poetic solution to the problem of the split self.

The birth of the child prodigies was likewise implicated with a purely musical stimulus: Schumann's discovery of a new idol in the person of Fryderyk Chopin. Sometime in May 1831, Schumann acquired the recently published Variations for Piano and Orchestra on Mozart's "Là ci darem la mano," op. 2 (composed 1827), and by late in the month had decided to review the work.[83] By 19 June he was "luxuriating" in Chopin ("Schwelgen in Chopin"), much as several years before he had revelled ("geschwärmt") in Schubert and Jean Paul. Determined to master the virtuoso turns in Chopin's composition, Schumann spent no less than eight hours at the keyboard on 1 July, the same day on which his "best friends" made their joint debut in his diary. His desire to present the variations to "Master Raro . . . in highest perfection as a reward" inspired him to embark on a renewed spate of intense practice. He outlines his self-imposed regimen in a diary entry of 9 July: from 7 to 10 A.M. he practices Chopin with "utmost relaxation of the hands"; then at 11 A.M. come Czerny's trill studies and Hummel's finger exercises; finally, he takes up Hummel's F♯-minor Sonata during the afternoon. "Don't be discouraged, dear Robert," Schumann adds, "if, as during the last eight days, things don't sparkle and ring; practice patiently, lift your fingers gently, hold your hand in a relaxed position, play slowly, and everything will get back on track." Frustrated by the sluggishness of his progress, and probably a little jealous of the ease with which Clara was able to toss off the variations, Schumann sketched a three-stage process for learning a piece in a diary entry of 18 July: first one is gripped by the "spirit and charm" of the composition and the fingers seem to move of their own accord; then comes a reflective phase, a period of "despair" when the reality of the piece's difficulties hit home; but if the player can overcome these obstacles, as Schumann had with the Hummel A-minor Concerto and the Moscheles "Alexander" Variations, he will reach a point where spirit and form, technique and fantasy, seem to flow into one another."[84]

Though Schumann's wish to "behold this paradise" was not fulfilled (on 30 July, he noted regretfully that his practice "goes and it doesn't go"), his study of Chopin's opus 2 would bear fruit nonetheless.[85] On 17 July, the same day on which he noted the "childlike simplicity" but brilliance with which Clara rendered the variations, he sketched, through his Eusebius persona, a narrative-dramatic account of the work that describes each of the variations as a reflection of the characters and events in Mozart's *Don Giovanni*. To underscore his awareness of the provisional quality of these quasi-programmatic musings, Schumann, again speaking through Eusebius, closed with a qualification: "No matter how subjective this all may be, and how little Chopin may have intended it, I nevertheless bow my head to his genius, his determined striving, his diligence, and his imagination!"[86] In somewhat revised form, the entire passage would serve as the focal point for Schumann's first published critical piece, the pathbreaking review of Chopin's opus 2, which appeared in the 7 December 1831 issue of the *Allgemeine musikalische Zeitung*.[87]

With Eusebius's famous phrase "Hats off, gentlemen, a genius!" Schumann announced the arrival of a brilliant newcomer on the musical scene, and he did so in a manner that music criticism had hardly known before. The singularity of his approach will be driven home by reading Schumann's review in tandem with the companion piece printed just after it in the *Allgemeine musikalische Zeitung*. The plodding style in this account by a "representative of the older school," who comments mainly on the technical challenges posed by Chopin's variations, claiming that "one is proportionately little rewarded" for having mastered them, pales in comparison to Schumann's verbal wizardry.[88] But it is even more important to recognize that the genesis of the review during the crucial period surrounding Schumann's twenty-first birthday marks the convergence of a number of diverse but densely interwoven strands. On the one hand, the review may be interpreted as a sublimation of Schumann's desire for fame and fortune as a keyboard virtuoso: displeased with his attempts to realize Chopin's opus 2 in sound (after starting on the work three times, he apparently gave up),[89] Schumann decided to recreate the variations through the medium of language. On the other hand, his poetic reading of Chopin's composition figures in the broader context of an issue already raised in his youthful diary, *Tage des Jüngling-lebens,* and in one of its principal relatives, the idyll entitled *Juniusabende und Julytage.* Situated midway between imaginative and critical prose, personal confession and public proclamation, Schumann's/Eusebius's reaction to Chopin's Variations highlights the reflective relationship between these terms. By focusing on a musical topic, Schumann attempts to negotiate the leap over the abyss separating word and tone, an issue raised in the "Tonwelt" essay of 1828. The "new" criticism toward which he was aspiring in the 1830s thus offered him a tentative solution to a problem of long standing: the mediation of music and poetry.

Outer circumstances contributed to Schumann's decision to devote himself heart and soul to this concern (and may have also been at the root of his inability to achieve technical mastery over Chopin's Variations). In a diary entry of 26 January 1830—dating, that is, from some months before his definitive choice of a career in music—Schumann alludes for the first time to his "numb" third finger.[90] Described variously as an "ever-worsening weakness" or "laming" of the right hand, the condition ultimately forced him to abandon his hopes of becoming a performing artist.[91] The cause of Schumann's complaint remains something of a mystery. While Ostwald has convincingly argued against the popular hypothesis linking the ailment with mercury treatments for syphilis, his own conjecture, according to which the stiffness in the middle finger of Schumann's right hand came about as a psychosomatic reaction to guilt over excessive masturbation, rests on slim evidence indeed.[92]

Whatever its cause, at least one thing is certain: the condition cannot have been ameliorated by Schumann's use of a chiroplast, a contraption championed by Johann Bernard Logier and recommended by no less a pedagogue and virtuoso pianist than Frédéric Kalkbrenner.[93] Players who wished to strengthen their fingers were required to insert them into this odd machine and pull them sharply toward the back of the hand. Although the earliest allusion to what Schumann called a "cigar mechanism" dates from May 1832, the reference to his "old hypochondriacal music mechanism," as well as Wieck's vociferous objections to its continued employment, a month later implies that he had been using the device for some time.[94] Equally certain is the gradual exacerbation of the malady over the course of Schumann's period of study with Wieck. By the autumn of 1831, it was already a source of "inner struggles."[95] While at work on the Paganini *Etudes,* op. 3, and the *Intermezzi* during the spring of the following year, Schumann detected some im-

provement (as the "weakness" in his right hand gave way, he recovered
a measure of independence in touch and attack), but relief was short-
lived; he noted on 22 May 1832: "the third [finger] seems really incorri-
gible"; on 14 June it had become "completely stiff." [96] Fearful that a
licensed doctor might declare the paralysis incurable, Schumann consulted with a Professor Kühl, who recommended a then popular but
grotesque remedy. The patient was to obtain the carcass of a freshly
slaughtered animal and insert his hand into its entrails, thereby absorbing healing warmth from a repellent mixture of blood, intestinal
slime, and fecal matter; he was also ordered to soak his hand for several
hours daily in a warm brandy fluid and wrap it in an herbally medicated
bandage during the evening. Schumann described his reaction to this
treatment with disarming nonchalance in a letter to his mother dated 9
August: "The cure is not the most charming, and I'm afraid that some
of the animal nature will seep into my own, but otherwise it's very
invigorating." [97]

The so-called "animal baths," however, had little effect. While Schumann had been led to expect at least partial recovery, though not before
a six-month period had elapsed, he soon recognized the futility of his
hopes. He emphasizes the point, again in correspondence with his
mother, on 6 November 1832: *for my part, I'm completely resigned* [to
my lame finger], and deem it incurable." Yet in the same letter, he con-
soles himself with the prospect of taking up the cello, "for which one
only needs the left hand, and which will be very useful for symphonic
composition." [98] Indeed, he was at this very time engaged in the composition of a symphony in G minor, his first purely orchestral project after
a four-year period of nearly exclusive concentration on keyboard music.
Thus, while Schumann was initially distraught over his hand condition—what aspiring pianist wouldn't be?—he soon reconciled himself
to its irreversibility. His acceptance of his fate went hand in hand with
a shift in self-outlook; to put it simply, Schumann began to view himself
primarily as a composer. And how better to register this shift than to
prove his mettle in the grandest of the absolute-musical genres, the symphony? If, in the "Abegg" variations, he proclaimed himself a pianist-
composer (and if, as we shall see, the *Papillons* represents the work of a
poet-composer), then the unfinished G-minor Symphony presents him
as a composer pure and simple. Schumann's new view of himself surfaces in a letter to his mother of 19 March 1834; he asks her not to
trouble over his impaired finger, for "I'm able to compose without it,
and I would hardly be happy as a travelling virtuoso. . . . It doesn't
prevent me from improvising, [and] has even renewed my courage to
improvise for an audience." [99]

Nonetheless, Schumann did not give up totally on finding a cure for the lameness in his right hand. We can surmise from a letter of June 1833 that shortly before he had submitted to some sort of "electrical" therapy, though the treatment apparently did more harm than good. Then, while under the care of Dr. Franz Hartmann in the summer of the same year, he held out some hope in a homeopathic remedy requiring strict attention to diet (coffee and beer were strictly forbidden) and the ingestion of a "tiny powder." [100] Nor did his regrets over the scuttling of his dream for a career as virtuoso completely subside. Writing to Clara from Vienna on 3 December 1838, he confided: "Sometimes I feel unhappy, especially since I have an ailing hand. And I'll let you in on a secret: it's getting worse . . . I can only play in a pinch, since one finger stumbles over the other." Yet he finds solace in a thought at once touching and prescient: "Now I have you as a right hand." [101]

The Papillons *Idea*

In November 1831, at the height of the "inner struggles" occasioned by the lameness of his right hand, Schumann's *Papillons* appeared in print as opus 2. While diminutive in scope, the pieces constituting the first of Schumann's poetic cycles for keyboard have been the object of more concentrated attention than perhaps any other of his works. In addition to generating a number of immediate offshoots (a lost second volume of presumably similar pieces, and the *Intermezzi*, op. 4), the *Papillons* will also have crucial implications for Schumann's development as a poetically motivated composer throughout the entire course of the 1830s. At the same time, the cycle is intimately bound up with the literary and musical tapestry whose threads were so tightly woven in the middle and later portion of 1831. As the central strand in the weave, *Papillons* shows us a young composer in the process of construing music as literature.

For such an outwardly unassuming composition, Schumann's opus 2 has a remarkably complicated history. And as the data pertinent to this history mount higher, so too do the questions surrounding it seem to multiply. When did Schumann decide to bring together several of his earlier miniatures, in revised form, amplify them with newly composed movements, and christen the whole as *Papillons?* When, in other words, was the *Papillons* idea conceived? When was it realized? How should we interpret the copious but often contradictory evidence regarding the work's relationship with Schumann's favorite among Jean Paul's novels, *Flegeljahre?* In what sense does *Papillons* embody a literary dimension? As Edward Lippman has rightly asserted, "there is no easy solution to the problem of the meaning of the *Papillons.*"[102] But while we cannot promise to provide definitive responses to these issues, we can at least review some of the available evidence and proffer some tentative conclusions.

Well over half of the dozen pieces comprising *Papillons* existed in some form already before Schumann's second move to Leipzig. On the basis of material culled from his *Projektenbuch,* an early *Kompositionsverzeichnis,* the Wiede sketchbooks, and the testimony of his friend Töpken, it is possible to place earlier versions of Nos. 1 through 9 in Heidelberg. Sketches for Nos. 4 through 6 of the projected *6 Walzer* from the Heidelberg period were realized as Nos. 6, 7, and 2, respectively, of the later cycle.[103] Moreover, Nos. 5 and 11 of the finished set draw liberally on Nos. 7 and 4, respectively, of the *VIII Polonaises* completed in the fall of 1828 during Schumann's first year as a law student in Leipzig.[104] *Papillons* was thus rooted in the easy-going milieu of the musical salons at which Schumann was a frequent guest in his earlier Leipzig and Heidelberg days, and in which the piano four-hand repertory figured prominently. But in *Papillons,* as in the "Abegg" variations, the convivial practice is refracted, so to speak, through a stylizing prism: the opening waltz of the cycle mimics the four-hand texture as if to call up a half-forgotten memory of music-making with friends.

Among the most telling documents relating to the genesis of *Papillons* are a series of overviews of its projected makeup transmitted in Wiede Sketchbook III, two of which indicate that the cycle, perhaps as originally conceived, was to have been limited to ten movements.[105] Through these outlines we can observe Schumann juggling the order of the pieces and ruminating over the contents of his cycle. While two of the overviews are confined to a listing of keys and meters, a third is composed of thematic incipits, thus allowing for close comparison with the final version. At this stage of the compositional process, the projected cycle included three pieces (Nos. 2, 7, and 10 in the overview) for which there are no equivalents in the published set; one of these (a ten-bar movement in B minor, labelled No. 2 in the overview) was even drafted complete.[106] Conversely, the same overview makes no reference to nearly half of the movements in the final version: the *Introduzione* and Nos. 2, 9, 10, 11, and 12. The absence of the last three is particularly telling, for it concords with the assertion of Julius Knorr, one of Schumann's fellow Davidsbündler, that the final piece was conceived after all the rest to round out the cycle, a bit of information not without significance, as we shall presently see, for the programmatic dimension of the work.

While these overviews and drafts were clearly intended for a cycle already entitled *Papillons* (or "Pappillons," as Schumann sometimes misspells it in his sketches), and thus attest to the subsumption of several early and more recently composed dances under a *Papillons* idea, it is difficult to know exactly when the idea began to influence Schumann's musical thinking.[107] To be sure, the butterfly—an emblem of metamorphosis, of the emergence of an elegant and beautiful being from a homely, larval state—had long been a potent image in the composer's poetic universe,[108] but during the late spring of 1831 it seemed to acquire renewed significance. In a diary entry of 14 May, for instance, we find: "Butterfly! Take away just a bit of your colored fragrance, and all that remains is a dull, lustreless skeleton."[109] Then on 8 June, Schumann began to draft a poetic cycle entitled "Schmetterlinge" (Butterflies), the first of its four verse fragments running: "Therefore do not rail against formative Nature! / What once crawled on the ground / Flits with divine lightness in the ether."[110] Hence the butterfly takes its place among the literary and musical discoveries—the child prodigies and Chopin's Variations, op. 2—clustered around Schumann's twenty-first birthday. It is possible that the musical realization of the *Papillons* idea likewise dates from the same time or shortly thereafter. If this is the case, then Schumann's creativity in the second half of 1831 followed a course similar to that already traced in the corresponding portion of 1828 (his first year in Leipzig and another extremely productive phase from a musical and a literary standpoint). Having "once crawled on the ground," he "flits," in both periods, "with divine lightness in the ether."

Not coincidentally, the image of the butterfly plays a significant role in Jean Paul's *Flegeljahre,* a novel to which Schumann turned again and again throughout the course of his life, and which he once described to Clara as "a book like the Bible in kind."[111] Costumed partly as a miner and partly as a wagoner for the masked ball scene that serves as the focal event of the novel's penultimate chapter (No. 63), Walt goes into a kind of rapturous trance as he is whisked onto the dance floor by his beloved (who of course does not recognize him): "He . . . believed himself to be flying after a summer aflutter with butterflies. Just as a youth touches the hand of a great and famous writer for the first time, so he gently touched—like butterfly wings, like auricula powder—Wina's back, and put himself into a position whereby he could best look into her life-breathing face."[112] Indeed, the butterfly is closely implicated with the principal metaphor of the chapter, the mask, the connection between the terms highlighted by the German *Larve*—literally "mask," but figuratively "larva" or "grub." The theme of metamorphosis, so crucial for

Schumann's *Papillons* idea, finds beautiful expression in a striking passage in which Jean Paul celebrates the ability of the mask to transform Walt and Wina into spirits bound by a mysterious communion: "From behind their dark masks they gazed at one another like foreign spirits from two distant planets, as if they were two stars in a solar eclipse, and each soul observed the other from a great distance, wanting thereby to appear all the more distinct."

Nor do we lack even more direct evidence for a link between novel and poetic cycle for keyboard. Writing to his mother on 17 April 1832, Schumann asks her to have "everyone read the final scene of Jean Paul's *Flegeljahre* as soon as possible, [and tell them] that *Papillons* actually transforms the masked ball into tones."[113] Two days later he similarly directs Ludwig Rellstab, editor of the journal *Iris*, to the novel's two concluding chapters, which he describes as the nearly invisible thread that binds his little pieces into a unity, noting further: "How often I turned over the last page [of *Flegeljahre*], since the ending seems to me a new beginning—almost unconsciously I was at the piano, and thus one *Papillon* after another came into being."[114] Then over two years later, he writes to his friend Henriette Voigt: "When you have a free minute, I suggest that you read the last chapter[s] of *Flegeljahre*, where everything appears in black on white right up to the giant boot in F♯ minor."[115]

To be sure, these comments come after the fact: they provide no information on the point at which Jean Paul's *Flegeljahre* may have exercised an influence on the musical realization of the *Papillons* idea. Schumann's diary does provide some clues, but even here the evidence is less than conclusive: an often-mentioned figure in *Hottentottiana*, Jean Paul makes relatively infrequent appearances in the *Leipziger Lebensbuch*. An isolated reference of 7 August 1831—"How different is Jean Paul [from Ludwig Anthom, author of *Ein Fragment aus einer Biographie*, a recently published work that had attracted Schumann's attention]; when his Walt is happy, he doesn't allow him to stumble . . ."[116]—perhaps indicates a renewed preoccupation with his favorite novel at this time. Taken together with the drafting of a series of "butterfly" poems two months earlier, the diary entry may speak to a convergence of poetic imagery, novelistic inspiration, and musical creativity during the summer of 1831, the result being *Papillons*.

Be this as it may, Schumann's apparently contradictory statements on the Jean-Paulian aspect of his musical cycle raise just as many questions as they answer. Were the final chapters of the novel a catalyst for musical creation, or did Schumann merely find in them a reflection, a literary analogue for what he had already conceived in largely musical terms? While his comments to his mother ("*Papillons* actually transforms the masked ball into tones") and also to Rellstab ("almost unconsciously I was at the piano, and thus one *Papillon* after another came into being") would seem to provide unequivocal evidence for the former point of view, Schumann's reaction to Rellstab's critique of *Papillons* suggests otherwise. To the critic's complaint that "even the key I have [to the meaning of *Papillons*] only tells half the story and leaves me with several thousand unsolved riddles," Schumann responds with the assertion that if Rellstab wants to know, "in black on white, where Vult flees and why—and where Jacobine is hiding," then he has most assuredly missed the point.[117] Jean Paul's scene, that is to say, should not be misconstrued as the programmatic basis for his musical cycle. Yet in his letter to Henriette Voigt, he employs the very same turn of phrase associated earlier with his repudiation of Rellstab's reading ("everything appears in black on white") in an implicit return to his first stance. Then in one final, maddening volte-face, he adds: "I will say only that I've underlaid the text to the music, and not the reverse—otherwise it would be a 'foolish beginning.' Only the last piece, which playful chance fashioned as a response to the first, was inspired by Jean Paul. One question more: isn't *Papillons* clear to you in itself? I'd be interested to know."[118]

Schumann's skittish turns from one position to another do, however, allow for a provisional explanation. Perhaps it is a mistake to frame the issue of the novel's ties to the musical cycle as an either/or proposition. Perhaps, in other words, *Flegeljahre* stands in a relationship to *Papillons* at once reflective *and* catalytic. On the one hand, Schumann's notations in his own copy of the novel, another source of much discussion, point to a reflective relationship. On the other hand, the later stages of the cycle's compositional history may well have been influenced by a rereading of the novel.

At some time while at work on *Papillons*—precisely when, it is impossible to say—Schumann underlined several passages in the penultimate chapter of *Flegeljahre*, numbering each in accordance with the supposedly corresponding movement from the musical cycle.[119] His notations are striking on several counts. First, he links the various passages in the masked ball scene with only ten movements. Second, there are some instances where the marked passage might plausibly be interpreted as a verbal analogue for the designated movement, but others where the relationship between text and music is tenuous at best. (The oddly accented main theme of No. 6, for instance, perhaps reflects Vult's gentle critique of Walt's less than elegant dancing: "For up to now—don't be offended—you've glided through the hall, horizontally as the wagoner and vertically as the miner, with good imitation waltzes."[120] But Schumann's association of the alternately melancholy and graceful No. 7 with Vult's impassioned entreaty that his brother consent to an exchange of costumes seems forced.[121]) And third, the passages associated with the sixth through the ninth pieces come out of narrative sequence, so that the following order results: Nos. 1, 2, 3, 4, 5, 8, 7, 9, 6, 10.

A more coherent picture begins to emerge when these features are considered together. Schumann's limitation of his numbering to ten movements suggests that he annotated the masked ball scene from *Flegeljahre* during the period when *Papillons* was conceived as a ten-movement cycle. As we have seen, Schumann experimented with both order and content at this stage. Hence, it may well be the case that the numbers in his copy of Jean Paul's novel do not refer to the movement-sequence in the published version of *Papillons,* but rather to the ordering of the cycle's contents in an earlier incarnation, either as transmitted in the overviews from the Wiede sketchbooks, or in other sources now lost. This, in any event, would account for the widely varying degrees of correspondence between musical and verbal texts.[122] Finally, the fact that Schumann's numbers, regardless of the pieces to which they might refer, occur "out of order," suggests strongly that his markings in the masked ball chapter refer to an already completed and provisionally ordered set of dances. This interpretation, in other words, bears out Schumann's claim, in his 1834 letter to Henriette Voigt, to have "underlaid the text to the music, and not the reverse," a procedure likewise in line with his practice as described in an often-quoted letter to Simonin de Sire of 15 March 1839: "The inscriptions for all of my compositions only come to me after the composition is complete."[123]

But just as Schumann recognized in a favored chapter from a favored novel a verbal reflection of a musical work-in-progress, so too he might have been motivated by a reading of that text to reconfigure, through amplifications and revisions, the compositional project at hand.[124] There is good reason to believe that this was precisely the case with *Papillons*. The masked ball scene from *Flegeljahre*—in which Walt's and Vult's rivalry for the affection of the beautiful Wina comes to a head—would have resonated with Schumann's own experience: four years before, in the *Tage des Jüngling-lebens,* he had expressed his love for Liddy Hempel in a poetic representation of the dance where the image of the butterfly takes primacy of place.[125] A large part of the final chapter of Jean Paul's novel is devoted to Walt's relating an "artfully constructed" *(künstlich-fügenden)* dream to his brother, a narrative in the author's irridescent, "moonlight" style that calls up many of the principal images dispersed throughout the book. In all likelihood, Schumann's rereading of *Flegeljahre* sometime after his twenty-first birthday inspired him to recast his most recent creative project as an artfully constructed, specifically *musical* dream-narrative of the masked ball. Thus it was probably owing to the influence of Jean Paul that Schumann decided to expand his musical cycle from ten to twelve movements and perhaps also to round out the work by alluding, in its final pages, to the opening waltz, the latter assumption supported by his remarks to Henriette Voigt: "Only the last piece, which playful chance fashioned as a response to the first, was inspired by Jean Paul." Likewise, his desire to "transform the masked ball into tones" no doubt lay behind his decision, at a relatively late stage in the compositional process, to add a distinctly programmatic touch to the Finale: six repeated A's evoke the striking of the tower clock that signals the dispersal of the maskers.[126]

While Jean Paul's *Flegeljahre* thus served as both a reflection of and a motivation for Schumann's *Papillons,* it would be a mistake to view the final chapters of the novel as a "program" for the musical cycle, at least in the crude sense of the term. On the contrary, *Papillons* brings into relief for the first time the many issues that will make the composer's relationship to program music such a complex one. While the repeated A's in the Finale provide a modicum of musical realism, other aspects of the compositional history of *Papillons* speak to Schumann's attempts to distance himself and his cycle from program music. The last sentence of the final chapter from *Flegeljahre,* for instance—"Walt, enraptured, listened to the fleeing tones [of Vult's flute] as they resounded up from the street, but he didn't realize that with them his brother too was fleeing"—originally stood at the head of the score. In eliminating the inscription from the published version of the work, Schumann covers his tracks so to speak. The same reticence to divulge too much probably accounts for the fact that his promise to share with Töpken the "key to the understanding of *Papillons*" remained unfulfilled.[127]

But, the apparent contradictions are perhaps not so contradictory after all. For what later polemicists lumped together under the general rubric of "program music" was subtly parsed by Schumann the critic into two distinct categories: "characteristic music," which reflects intimate "soul states" *(Seelenzustände),* on the one hand, and "pictorial music," which portrays external events *(Lebenszustände),* on the other.[128] Most of the time, he further maintains, "we find both intermingled," so that "characteristic" and "pictorial" music are not antithetical, but rather complementary. Yet of the two, the former is by far more "poetic," for through it we have access to the enigmatic language of the soul. If the restruck A's in the *Papillons* finale add a "pictorial" dimension to the music, Schumann's effacement of the prose inscription from *Flegeljahre*, like his reluctance to provide Töpken with a "key" to understanding, is an expression of his fear that the "soul-states" embodied in his musical cycle would only be minimized by verbal cues. An early reviewer of the work for the *Allgemeine musikalische Zeitung* came to a similar conclusion without the benefit of access to all of the pertinent documentary materials. Aware of the rootedness of Schumann's "jocular musical sketches" in his passion for Jean Paul, the critic goes on to suggest: "Perhaps the composer might have indicated those of the poet's passages that brought him to his *Papillons*." But ultimately he retracts his suggestion: "Let each listener attempt to catch the butterflies for himself, allowing their colorful play to glitter in a sunny hour." [129]

No doubt, the reviewer made a wise choice. Our consideration of the passages Schumann marked in the penultimate chapter of *Flegeljahre* has already underscored the imprudence of arguing for a one-to-one correspondence between poetic and musical texts. Furthermore, it is striking indeed that Schumann left the thematic center of the chapter— Walt's statement of the intermingling of Art and Life, poetry and prose, in the masked ball—unmarked:

> A masked ball is perhaps the highest means through which life is able to make a postlude to poetry's prelude. Just as all social stations and historical epochs are equal before the poet, and all external trappings a mere camouflage, but everything within is joy and resonance, so here people poeticize themselves and their lives—the most ancient fashions and customs are revived and take their place next to the most recent— the remotest savage, the finest and the coarsest classes alike, the mocking caricature, even different seasons and religions, the fiendish and the friendly—all these are rounded into *one* light and happy circle, and the circle is splendidly set into motion, as if through a metrical power, namely through music, that land of spirits, just like fancy-dress outfits are the land of bodies.

In this passage, Jean Paul sounds a mellifluous variation on one of the chief leitmotifs of his *oeuvre*: the notion that lived experience is a constellation of fragments awaiting the transfiguring touch of the poet, hence Siebenkäs's characterization of life as a "mosaic of minutes and specks," or Albano's perception of the landscape around the Roman Forum as "the heaped-up ashes out of the emptied urn of Time," or Walt's description of the quodlibet as "an anagram or an epigram of real life." To be sure, the fragment calls up a host of negatives: it is incomplete, detached, unfinished, isolated; it presupposes a perfectly shaped, but now broken or destroyed whole. Jean Paul and the Jena Romantics, however, recognized in the fragment a remarkably truthful cipher for human experience itself. Their work does not merely celebrate the phenomenon of incompletion; by pointing up the mysterious relationships between and among fragments, it gives poetic shape to an essentially fractured reality.

Schumann at once shared in this worldview and sought to accord it musico-poetic expression; nor did he need to affirm his stance by underlining a passage or two in Jean Paul's *Flegeljahre*. Evidence for his outlook is readily at hand in the musical fabric of *Papillons*, the first of his compositions to demonstrate an engagement with the phenomenology of the fragment. This quality is aptly projected by a wide variety of durational, tonal, thematic, and formal strategies. The second movement, no more than a dozen measures in length, begins with an extravagant flourish in E♭, only to break off after a capricious phrase in A♭. The tonally open-ended Nos. 4 and 7 waver just as fancifully between major and relative minor or minor and relative major. Nos. 6, 10, and 12 are in turn constructed as medleys of diminutive dances, the mosaic-like effect heightened in the Finale, where Schumann quotes from the *Grossvatertanz*, a tune associated with celebratory gatherings since the seventeenth century. What we first perceive as a beginning in Nos. 7 through 10 turns out not to be a beginning after all, but rather a kind of preparatory vamp for the real matter at hand. In No. 11, the truncated reprise of the movement's opening polonaise music creates a singularly striking impression: we imagine that a door has suddenly been opened and in waft the strains of a dance-tune from an adjacent room. Brevity, tonal dualism, stylized quodlibet, quotation, feigned openings, partial returns—all of these features contribute to the portrayal of a fragmented musical world in *Papillons*.[130]

No doubt it was precisely these qualities that made Schumann's cycle so difficult for its first listeners to fathom. When Clara played the work for a soireé at Wieck's in late May 1832, the assembled guests, "incapable of grasping the rapid alternation [of the pieces], looked at one another in amazement."[131] Christoph Sörgel, a student friend to whom Schumann had sent a copy of *Papillons* soon after it appeared in print, was equally bewildered: "So far we don't understand it."[132] And while generally impressed by the "Abegg" Variations and *Papillons*, Hummel was put off by Schumann's fondness for "overly abrupt harmonic shifts through which comprehensibility is endangered." A classicist in aesthetic matters, Hummel cautioned the young composer to desist in his pursuit of original and bizarre effects, for this tendency toward mannerism was "detrimental to the beauty, clarity, and unity of a well-regulated composition."[133] The first published reviews of *Papillons* likewise recognized, more often than not with disapproval, the challenges to comprehension posed by the work. The difficulties were seen to reside in the disposition of the work as a series of musical fragments, or "thought splinters," to quote Gottfried Weber's suggestive epithet.[134] According to the unsigned review in the 28 June 1832 issue of the *Allgemeine musikalische Anzeiger Wien*, Schumann "has created a new ideal world in which he mischievously revels, often with an original *bizarrerie*."[135] Indeed the bizarre, a not too distant cousin of the grotesque, becomes a touchstone of the early reception of Schumann's keyboard miniatures.[136] In large measure, this quality too is viewed as a function of the composer's penchant for the fragment. The critique in the *Allgemeine musikalische Anzeiger Wien*, for instance, locates the "bizarrerie" of the *Papillons* in its fanciful conception as a series of "twelve rhapsodic pieces, some shorter and some longer, in varying keys, tempi, and rhythms, but mainly teasing, flighty, and coquettish."[137] In all probability Schumann's critics found his *Papillons* (like its relatives in the years to come) so disconcerting precisely because of its reliance on unassuming, even popular materials: waltzes, polonaises, and well-known melodies such as the *Grossvatertanz*. But arranged in an eccentric sequence and projected through a fragmentary consciousness, these dance-based conceits emit a peculiar and at times disturbing aura. In a word, they are metamorphosed into emblems of incomprehension through the agency of the fragment.

Schumann was keenly aware of the radical nature of his cycle. Reluctant to concede that a well-wrought composition might require several hearings to make its point, he made an exception in the case of *Papillons*, for "the alternation is so swift, the colors so variegated, and the listener still has the previous page in his head while the player has already finished [a movement]."[138] To facilitate the listener's journey through this colorful but disorienting world of fragments, Schumann employs a number of tried-and-true harmonic and motivic strategies in the interest of cohesion. Organized around D major, the cycle makes frequent recourse to thematic recall: a quiet A-major episode from No. 6 recurs in a G-major context, *fortissimo*, in No. 10; the opening D-major waltz reappears in the same key during the Finale, interwoven with snippets of the *Grossvatertanz*.[139] But even these techniques are subjected to a process of defamiliarization. While *Papillons* begins and ends in D, it hardly articulates that tonality—or any other—in a conventional manner. No sooner has D been affirmed in the *Introduzione* and the first movement than it is immediately negated by the abrupt move to E♭ for No. 2. What Schumann called "self-annihilation" (*sich-selbst-vernichten*) operates within the cycle as well: the C major of No. 10 effectively cancels the third-based progression from F minor to D♭ over the course of Nos. 7 through 9. Similarly, the thematic recurrences form less a dense web than a gossamer tissue of premonitions and recollections. Often it is not even a question of thematic, but rather of topical recall: Nos. 4, 11, and 12, for instance, all share a horn-call motif, itself an emblem for distance in time and space. Hence, *Papillons* is animated by an odd sort of logic, the fanciful logic of the system of fragments.

While the content of Schumann's cycle resonates with the theme of fragmentation in the novels of Jean Paul, its structure resembles that of the literary-fragment collections of Novalis and the Schlegel brothers, a body of writings whose presentation likewise elicited an uncomprehending response from critics. Recognition of the elective affinities between these respectively musical and verbal constructs may even provide us with a further key to the understanding of the literary dimension of *Papillons*. As Philippe Lacoue-Labarthe and Jean-Luc Nancy have argued, the term "literature" acquired new connotations for the Jena Romantics. Previously construed as the body of classical texts that every educated person should know, literature was now seen to emerge at the point where creative formation and critical reflection intersect. By extending beyond the portrayal of the sensible to a representation of Kant's ideas of reason, literature was meant to offer a solution to the problem of the subject unrepresentable to itself. Thus the Romantics broadened the notion of literature to encompass all works of art through which the subject attempted to represent itself adequately.[140] Furthermore, the "absolute" of literature, for thinkers such as the Schlegel brothers and Novalis, arose less from the circumscribed art of poetry than from the activity of production itself.

Schumann was arguably the first composer to view his musical creations in this way—as literary products. This means neither that music should "tell stories" nor that it must depend on literary models to shore up its indeterminate meanings. It does suggest, however, that music should aspire to the same intellectual substance as the "lettered" arts: poetry and philosophy. While Friedrich Schlegel speculated that "pure instrumental music" was in some sense comparable to a "philosophical succession of ideas," and while Novalis frequently held up music as a metaphor for the autonomy he saw as the sine qua non of art, one still has the impression that the early Romantics (E. T. A. Hoffmann, and perhaps Tieck and Wackenroder, excepted) shared Kant's view: perhaps music was "more enjoyment than culture" after all. Schumann was probably of a different opinion. Convinced, like the Jena Romantics, that art was a self-reflective medium and that music was an agent for the transmission of transcendental ideas, he put his theory (as articulated in the "Tonwelt" essay and the aesthetic fragments of *Hottentottiana*) into practice for the first time in *Papillons*. Here the theme of metamorphosis, poetically figured through the twin images of the butterfly and the Jean-Paulian masked ball, is projected through the fragment, the part that points toward the fancifully conceived whole. The result is musically "absolute" (the relationships among the fragments in the system are purely musical), and yet, at the same time, it reaches beyond the absolute (the deciphering of the relationships within the system amounts to an act of reading). Hence Schumann was able, on the one hand, to think of his cycle as an autonomous creation—"Isn't *Papillons* clear to you in itself?" he asked Henriette Voigt—and on the other, to assert his independence from its autonomy—"in many a sleepless night I've seen a distant image, like a goal; during the composition of *Papillons* I actually felt as though a certain *independence* was trying to develop that criticism for the most part repudiates"—without thereby contradicting himself.[141] The paradox is the direct consequence of an outlook that views musical creation as a literary act.

By the time that his opus 2 was published in November 1831, Schumann was already contemplating a sequel; the first edition of *Papillons* was designated as *Liv. 1* (Book I), implying the appearance of a companion volume in the not too distant future. On 30 May 1832, the idea for a second collection occupied Schumann for the entire day, though the project probably did not get underway until late summer: a diary entry for August 1832 included *Papillons, Livr. 2* in a list of planned compositions and works-in-progress.[142] Finally, on 2 November 1832, he informed Breitkopf that he had recently completed "*XII Burlesken (Burle)* after the manner of *Papillons*."[143] While some of these pieces may have found their way into the *Albumblätter*, op. 124 (1854),[144] the set was never published, nor has it surfaced. This notwithstanding, the title alone of the lost volume has significant implications regarding the development of Schumann's musico-poetic thinking in the early 1830s, for it speaks to a metamorphosis in the *Papillons* idea itself. The concepts linked in the letter to Breitkopf, *Burleske* or *Burla* on the one hand, and *Papillons* on the other, were intimately bound up with one another in the composer's imagination: a fragmentary draft in Wiede Sketchbook III, for instance, is titled *Papillon sive Burla*.[145] At the same time, the notion of the *Burla*—translatable as joke, jest, or even parody—extends the original concept into the domain of the comic. Moreover, this outgrowth of the *Papillons* idea would continue to inform a number of Schumann's keyboard works in a wide spectrum of genres for several years to come: the sketch for a never completed work based on the bass theme of the *Impromptus,* op. 5 (1833), is labelled *Burla 1* or *Fandango;* the third movement of the F♯-minor Sonata, op. 11 (1832–1835), originally bore the indication *alla burla, ma pomposo; Burla* appears as a title for what would eventually become *Arlequin* from *Carnaval,* op. 9 (1834–1835); and finally, a manuscript devoted largely to preliminary materials for the *Etudes Symphoniques,* op. 13 (1834–1837) contains a fragmentary draft for a *Burla* in G minor (to which we shall presently return), one of whose counterthemes bears some resemblance to the main idea of opus 13.[146]

Hence, the *Papillons* idea and its derivatives colored much of Schumann's creativity throughout the course of the 1830s. *Florestan,* the sixth piece in *Carnaval,* quotes from *Papillons,* while the tenth piece in the same cycle is even titled *Papillons.* To cite another and perhaps the most revealing example: the composer once described his *Intermezzi,* op. 4— many of the sketches for which were even titled *Papillon*—as "longer *Papillons.*"[147] To be sure, the larger dimensions of the six pieces that constitute the cycle go hand in hand with an extension of topical range: in addition to the dance types familiar from the earlier cycle (best represented here by No. 5, a languid waltz), we now find mock-pompous and persistently cross-accented "Florestan" pieces (Nos. 1 and 2, respectively), alternately capricious and virtuosic scherzo types (Nos. 3 and 6), and even a lied-based composition (No. 4 draws on "Hirtenknabe," a song completed almost four years before). At one point conceived as a set of *Pièces phantastiques,* and completed between April and July 1832, the *Intermezzi* continue to explore the possibilities of the musical fragment first essayed in *Papillons.*[148] For instance, the second piece, a *Presto a capriccio* in E minor, features an oddly truncated recall of the opening music. Limited to the terminal phrases of the 62-measure A section, and prefacing a return of that section in its entirety, the fragmented reprise thus seems to imply that the "missing" music has been proceeding all the while, but from a location where we cannot hear it; the part, in other words, serves as an emblem for the absent whole. The middle section of the same movement begins with a simple song-melody to which Schumann underlaid the words of Gretchen's well-known lament from Goethe's *Faust,* "Mein Ruh' ist hin," so that the fragment appears in the guise of a citation that turns out not to be an actual citation after all. Schumann does, however, have recourse to genuine quotation, again as a cipher for an absent totality, in the sixth and final piece, where, just before its middle section, he cites the ABEGG theme at the same pitch level and supported by the same harmonies as at the opening of his opus 1. Similarly, the head-motif of the *Grossvatertanz* (in D major, just as in the *Papillons* finale) makes fleeting appearances in the opening and closing sections of No. 5. Much like Jean Paul's characters, Schumann's thematic materials often stray from work to work.

Nonetheless, it would be inaccurate to claim, as Rellstab did, that the *Intermezzi* were comprised of aphoristic utterances alone.[149] On the contrary, the cycle gives evidence of a complementary interest in motivic, formal, and tonal coherence on a larger scale. Conceived when Schumann was attempting to sort out the complexities of fugal composition on his own initiative, it is little wonder that contrapuntal strategies, primary means for ensuring thematic cohesiveness, play a significant role in the work; the imitative textures in No. 1, for instance, probably owe more than a little to the young composer's study of Marpurg's counterpoint treatise.[150] The motivic links within movements (the central sections, designated *Alternativo*, of Nos. 1, 3, 5, and 6 share material with or emerge logically from their respective A sections) are parallelled, at a higher level, by the *attacca* indications binding Nos. 2 through 5 into a continuous entity. The vacillation between third-related keys in No. 4 (C major and A minor) and No. 5 (F major and D minor) recalls the pairings that, in *Papillons*, extend the process of fragmentation into the tonal realm. Here, however, there are few signs of harmonic "annihilation": the motion from the A major of No. 1 to the B minor of No. 6 is realized through a logical series of fifth and third relationships. Far from celebrating the fragment for its own sake, the *Intermezzi* intensify its dialectical stance vis-à-vis the whole.

While the cultivation of the musico-poetic fragment may have been the dominant trend in Schumann's compositional approach during the early 1830s, it certainly was not the only trend. His interest in the larger, or "higher" forms as he would later call them, no doubt as vehicles for his own virtuoso pianism, found expression in the F-major Piano Concerto, on which he continued to work sporadically for over a year after returning to Leipzig in the fall of 1830, and also in a B-minor Piano Sonata. The latter project dates from 1831 and probably occupied Schumann during the second half of the year: a diary entry of 5 January 1832 indicates that by that point only the finale remained to be drafted.[151] Thus his interest in the venerable genre of the sonata roughly coincides with the inception and musical realization of the *Papillons* idea. As it turned out, only the first movement achieved fully finished form; published in 1835 as Allegro, op. 8, the work was surely intended as a showcase for the composer-pianist's virtuosity, witness the abundance of rhapsodic, cadenza-like passages, extravagant arpeggios, chromatic runs in thirds, and sparkling filigree textures in the upper reaches of the keyboard. The pyrotechnical display, however, is subsumed under a more serious concern first raised during the Heidelberg period in the first version of the Toccata: the mediation of virtuoso style and musical substance. Prefiguring a strategy employed much later in Brahms's concerti, Schumann solves the problem by integrating the flamboyant display passages with the formal argument of the work: in retrospect, the introductory "cadenza," for instance, is perceived to function as the first group of an expansive sonata form. Moreover, Schumann engages the "higher" form in an intriguing colloquy with the fragmentary utterance. The opening flourish of the movement settles on a powerful rhetorical gesture: three *fortissimo* pitches, B, C♯, and F♯, each marked with a fermata, and each fanned out through three octaves. This stark figure bears all the properties of a motto or citation; in a word, it is a kind of fragment. But as the movement unfolds, the initiatory, and fiercely shrunken motto displays far-reaching thematic consequences, serving in no less than five functionally differentiated capacities: as bass-line for the elaboration of the first group, melodic backbone for the opening of the lyric second theme, head-motif for the development, underpinning for the sequentially conceived retransition, and herald of the coda.

If the Allegro was torn from its original context in a larger, though unfinished work, then the fate of the Fandango in F♯ minor (subtitled *Fantaisie rhapsodique pour le pianoforte* and dedicated to Schumann's collaborator on the "Tonwelt" essay, Willibald von der Lühe) exhibits a reversal of this process. While at the piano in late May 1832, the composer was suddenly "overcome by Fandango thoughts." And not surprisingly, given its proximity to the drafting of the *Intermezzi*, the work was closely bound up with the images associated with the *Papillons* idea; as Schumann put it in his diary: the fandango "is a heavenly conceit, rich in divine figures, and even more pliant than the masked ball."[152] Though complete by August or September, the work was withheld from publication until 1836, when, in revised form and without its original title, it appeared as the principal, quick section of the first movement of the Piano Sonata in F♯ minor, op. 11. Thus both the Allegro and the Fandango adumbrate the dialectic between part and whole, fragment and "higher" form that hovers over Schumann's musical creativity throughout the middle and late 1830s, and even beyond.

Composing under the Spell of Paganini, Bach, and Beethoven

Just as the pivotal phase surrounding Schumann's twenty-first birthday was marked by a confluence of diverse influences and imaginative discoveries—a renewed interest in E. T. A. Hoffmann, an intense fascination with Chopin, the birth of the *Wunderkinder,* the emergence of the *Papillons* idea—so the corresponding period in the following year was rich in stimuli to creativity. During the spring and summer of 1832, Schumann fell under the spell of an unlikely trio: Paganini, Bach, and Beethoven, the three figures whose spirit the critic Ernst Ortlepp compared with that of Schumann himself. But if we consider that the respective members of the triumvirate served as emblems for rhapsodic virtuosity, contrapuntal density, and structural integrity—elements that Schumann later strove to synthesize in works such as the *Impromptus,* op. 5, *Kreisleriana,* op. 16, and the *Novelletten,* op. 21—then their joint influence at this stage of his career acquires a deepened significance.

As we have seen, Paganini first cast his spell over Schumann at an April 1830 concert in Frankfurt. Precisely two years later, just as work on the *Intermezzi* was about to get underway, he noted in his diary: "Paganini caprices made into studies for pianists who want to develop themselves further." [153] In less than two months, the first installment of the project was complete, arrangements of six caprices (Nos. 5, 9, 11 [limited to the introductory *Andante*], 13, 19, and 16 of Paganini's original twenty-four) published in the autumn of 1832 as *Etudes pour le pianoforte d'après les Caprices de Paganini,* op. 3. Schumann's encounter with the compositional products of the violinist's technical wizardry made a vivid, and at times terrifying effect on his imagination; in early June 1832, he saw "a picture that made a shocking impression—Paganini in a magic circle—the murdered wife—dancing skeletons and a train of dim, mesmerizing spirits . . . While making the arrangement of the G-minor *Presto* [Paganini Caprice No. 16/no. 6 in Schumann's set] the picture often hovered before me, and I think that the close [of the arrangement] reflects it." [154] To be sure, the final eight measures of the piece feature a striking texture: the steadily running sixteenths of Paganini's caprice plunge headlong into the bass register as full, *sforzando* chords sound in the right hand, the total effect complementing that at the beginning of the arrangement, where Schumann juxtaposes the *moto perpetuo* figuration of the original (here too in the bass) with a passionately accented countermelody. When during the next year Schumann arranged another half-dozen caprices—Nos. 12, 6, 10, 4, 2, and 3; published in 1835 as *VI Etudes de Concert . . . d'après des Ca-*

prices de Paganini, op. 10—he may have been visited yet again by a vision of Paganini "in a magic circle"; his treatment of the middle section of the B-minor Caprice (No. 2/op. 10, no. 5), another *perpetuum mobile,* recalls the strategy employed in the G-minor Caprice, op. 3, no. 6.

Schumann's interest in countermelodic textures might have been further stimulated by his counterpoint lessons with Dorn and his preoccupation with Bach. A diary entry of 14 May 1832 emphasizes the universality of the latter's genius: "Johann Sebastian Bach did everything—he was a human being through and through." Schumann amplifies this thought in a letter to his mother written in late July of the same year: "[Bach] did nothing by halves, there was nothing sickly about him, it's as if he wrote for eternity."[155] In doing "nothing by halves," Bach thus represents an antipode to the fragmentary consciousness characteristic of Schumann's and the immediately preceding generation; and by "Bach" Schumann certainly means the preludes and fugues of *Das wohltemperirte Clavier,* the collection that, by July 1832, had become his personal "grammar." Hence the "many contrapuntal studies" mentioned in the *Projektenbuch* for 1832[156] were perhaps intended not only to sharpen the composer's technical skills but also to nudge him toward the "wholeness" of which Bachian counterpoint was a supreme exemplar.

Schumann's attempt to elevate the fragment form through contrapuntal elaboration—no less than his youthful reception of Bach—is neatly reflected in a diminutive keyboard piece from this period, a G-minor *Burla* once part of a manuscript composed of sketch materials for the *Etudes Symphoniques* but now preserved as an independent sketch-leaf in the Moldenhauer Collection at the Library of Congress. This sixty-one-measure fragment (transcribed in Example 2.2) was probably not meant for inclusion in the sequel to *Papillons*—neither its key nor its meter can be matched with the entries in an overview of the projected *XII Burlesken*—but rather in a diptych of independent *Burle* mentioned in an August 1832 diary entry.[157] Situated midway between sketch and draft, the *Burla* falls into an ABA' scheme in which an opening section in G minor (mm. 1–24) gives way to a middle section in the parallel major (mm. 24–43), the whole rounded off by a varied reprise of the initial music (mm. 44–61). The fact that the sketchleaf is filled with music, taken together with the abrupt break after the first measure (m. 61) in what have been regular four-bar units, makes it unlikely that Schumann merely discontinued the piece at this point; what we have is almost surely the torso of a longer composition that was brought to completion in some form.

Example 2.2. Draft of *Burla* in G minor in Schumann's hand. (Moldenhauer Collection, Library of Congress, Washington, D.C.)

The simple tripartite scheme of the G-minor *Burla,* however, is considerably enriched by an array of contrapuntal strategies. The A section, for instance, unfolds as a series of variations based on the four-note motive (E♭-D-B♭-G) announced at the outset, but already in the first phrase (mm. 1–4), the motive gives rise to a three-voice stretto pattern, while in the second phrase (mm. 4–12) an extended form of the motive comes together with chromatic countermelodies. The third phrase (mm. 12–16) features a combination of the original motive with its retrograde, the former smoothed into a conjunct figure in the fourth phrase (mm. 16–24). Although the B section begins with an apparently new melody in the parallel major over a *Trommel* bass and a G pedal, the inner voice figuration clearly derives from the conjunct melodic patterns (mm. 16ff.) of the A section. What survives of the A' section introduces one last variant, the original motive serving as an undulating foil to a quasi-cantus-firmus in the bass. Thus the miniature is structurally ambiguous: on the surface a straightforward three-part form, it may in fact be viewed as a series of contrapuntal variations. Old and new, Bachian counterpoint and song-like melodic syntax intermingle in an eminently "modern" genre: the poetic character piece for piano.

Schumann's compositional horizons were similarly broadened by his close study of Beethoven's music in the spring of 1832. Fascinated by Beethoven's uncanny ability to make much out of little, Schumann mused on the relationship between musical form and melodic content in a diary entry of 12 May 1832: "[If] an idea is lacking, then try to make the form and structure of the parts interesting; if, however, a thought is at hand, then it won't require fancy harmonic attire, which in any case often does more harm than good. Here Beethoven will provide an incomparably fine model.[158]

Amplifying an analogy first touched upon in the musico-poetic aphorisms of *Hottentottiana,* Schumann proceeded, some weeks later, to draw a parallel between musical and poetic modes of elaboration: "If you have a beautiful thought, don't mangle and waste it until it's common and degraded, as many composers (like Dorn) do, and then call this 'development.' If you want to develop, then really make something out of a previously ordinary passage. . . . In this, Beethoven, like Jean Paul, offers a splendid ideal."[159] The compositions in which this ideal revealed itself most powerfully to the young Schumann were undoubtedly Beethoven's symphonic works. Evidence for this assumption is provided by Wiede Sketchbook IV (an important source for Schumann's tutelage under Dorn between summer 1831 and spring 1832), which includes unfinished piano reductions for a pair of Beethoven's orchestral

movements: the *Adagio* (mm. 1–24) of the Fourth Symphony, and the
Third "Leonore" overture (mm. 1–377).[160] Just as Schubert, Chopin,
Paganini, and Bach had inspired Schumann to original creation, so too
did Beethoven; a diary entry for 29 April 1832 makes reference, under
"plans," to *Acht Bilder, nach den Symphonien Beethovens, Florestaniana*.[161] While this project (which may have been a literary one) failed
to get off the ground,[162] Wiede Sketchbook IV transmits the drafts for
a Beethoven-related endeavor that did: a series of eleven *Etuden in Form
freier Variationen über ein Beethovensches Thema* for piano, the theme in
question being that of the second movement, Allegretto, of the Seventh
Symphony, op. 93. Schumann initially set great store by the work, for it
exists in no less than three versions, the other two preserved in manuscripts perhaps dating from 1833, each including some elements from
the previous incarnation of the piece together with newly composed
variations.[163] By November 1838, however, when he entered a synopsis
of his activities for the previous five years into his diary, Schumann had
written off the *Etuden* as an "ungrateful idea."[164] And indeed, only one
of the variations made its way into a published work: the fifth etude
from the second version—where Beethoven's solemn duple-time march
theme is transformed into a languid triple-meter dance generously
spiced with acciaccaturas—appears as the second piece, *Leides Ahnung*,
in the *Albumblätter*, op. 124. Nonetheless the *Etuden* as originally conceived mark an important turning point in Schumann's thinking on the
keyboard variation. The earlier virtuoso type as exemplified in the "Abegg" variations (and perhaps also in the lost sets on a theme by Prince
Louis Ferdinand [1828] and on an "original theme" in G [1831])[165]
gives way to the musically more substantive variety that found its first
mature expression in the *Impromptus*, op. 5.

In all probability, Beethoven's example likewise informed Schumann's undertaking of a major symphonic project in the autumn of
1832. Of course, his decision to turn away from the keyboard genres
that had occupied him almost exclusively for the past four years was
motivated by other factors as well. As we have already observed, by
November 1832 Schumann was completely resigned to the irreversibility
of the lameness in the third finger of his right hand. The G-minor symphony on which he set to work at the time[166] thus documents a shift
from "composing (and poetically inspired) pianist" to "pianistically
trained (though still poetically inspired) composer." Some of the material that ultimately found a place in the symphony is traceable to an
unlikely source: Schumann's desire to write an opera based on Shakespeare's *Hamlet*. The idea took hold several years after he first witnessed

the play on stage in the autumn of 1828, a period of intense musical and literary productivity.[167] On 12 December 1830 Schumann reported breathlessly to his mother: "the grand opera has been settled on; I'm all fire and flame, and rave the whole day long in sweet, marvelous tones. The opera will be called 'Hamlet'—the thought of fame and immortality gives me energy and inventiveness, while the bureaucrat in me recedes."[168] An eight-bar fragment in Wiede Sketchbook I datable to 1831 or 1832 and designated *Sinfonia per il Hamlet* was perhaps intended for the overture to the planned, but never realized grand opera. In two more extended symphonic sketches (of 58 and 65 measures, respectively) from Wiede Sketchbook III, the falling fifth motive from the eight-bar fragment is considerably elaborated, but the absence of any allusion to Shakespeare's play (the shorter of the two sketches is simply titled *Sinfonia*, while the longer bears no title whatever) may indicate that the original *Hamlet* idea had evolved into plans for an independent symphonic movement. Motives from the 65-bar sketch were in turn taken up in the second group and development section of the first movement of the G-minor Symphony.[169] The entire process thus presents a transformation through a series of interrelated genres: grand opera, concert overture, and symphony.

The genesis of the G-minor Symphony presents a fairly complicated picture. According to Schumann's account in one of his autobiographical sketches of 1840, the work was finished up to its final movement.[170] The first movement, probably begun in October 1832,[171] was ready in time for a performance in Zwickau on 18 November. Wieck, in attendance owing largely to Clara's participation in the same concert, gave the work a mixed review. While his daughter's rendition of Herz's "Bravura" Variations caused a sensation: "The first movement of Schumann's symphony was performed but not understood. It made too little of an impression, at least on the public; it is inventive and well elaborated, but too thinly orchestrated.[172]

Schumann soon thereafter thoroughly revised the movement, excising its slow introduction and expanding the already substantial Allegro molto. The movement in its newly revised form was then given in Schneeberg in mid-February 1833, but in the meantime, and perhaps before leaving for Schneeberg in January, Schumann set to work on the second and third movements.[173] While we have only lapidary sketches for the third movement, the second survives in two markedly different versions, one consisting of an Andantino quasi Allegretto only, the other (probably the later of the pair) contrasting an initial and concluding Andantino con moto with a central Intermezzo quasi Scherzo. The finale, which probably occupied Schumann between March and May,[174] never proceeded past a preliminary stage. Several of the surviving sketches are devoted to fugal elaborations of the motive G-C-D-G that, transposed down a fifth, would later serve as the bass counterfigure to the theme of the *Impromptus* (based on Clara's *Romance variée*, op. 3). According to a diary entry of about a year before, the motive had first come to Schumann while improvising late at night after a four-hand session with Clara devoted to the sightreading of six of Bach's fugues.[175] This intriguing tangle of influences and impressions reflects not only the confluence of personal experience, Bachian counterpoint, and Beethovenian symphonism in the G-minor Symphony,[176] but also the remarkable metamorphoses of the same elements in Schumann's creative thinking during much of the 1830s.

The spirit of Beethoven is a palpable presence in the opening movement of Schumann's G-minor Symphony, a triple-meter Allegro molto. The rhetorically pointed chordal flourishes with which it begins, the subsequently unfolding triadic theme in the first violins, the melodic descent (G-F-E) in the cellos and basses, even the syncopations in the violins at the striking turn to a diminished-seventh sonority in the fifth measure—all of these features point to the first movement of the "Eroica" symphony as a model.[177] Yet the ties between the works go deeper, for Schumann's opening idea, like many of those in Beethoven's middle-period compositions, is less a theme than a thematic configuration, a complex of brief but flexible motives capable of both linear development and contrapuntal combination (Example 2.3). Since it is not confined to a single voice but rather fanned out over the total range of the ensemble, the thematic configuration is genuinely symphonic, its employment here thus challenging the still commonly held view that Schumann's orchestral music often amounts to pianistic textures writ large.

Schumann likewise turned to Beethovenian sources for the second movement (in its presumably later version) of his symphony. The Andantino recalls the Allegretto of Beethoven's Seventh Symphony in both pace and character, while the conflation of slow movement and Scherzo at once resonates with the alternating Molto adagio and Andante sections in the *Heiliger Dankgesang* from the older composer's A-minor String Quartet, op. 132, and prefigures Brahms's practice in the middle movements of his F-major String Quintet, op. 88, and Second Violin Sonata, op. 100.

These allusions and premonitions aside, there are a number of elements, especially as regards form, that stamp the G-minor Symphony as distinctly Schumannian in conception. In the first movement, the

Example 2.3. Symphony in G Minor: first movement, mm. 1–8. (© 1972. Used by permission of C. F. Peters Corporation on behalf of H. Litolff's Verlag, Germany.)

recurrence of a significant lyrical idea in the closing stages of the development but not, as we would expect, in the recapitulation, betrays the rhapsodic attitude to extended structures that was Schumann's alone. Similarly, the second movement embodies the formal disruptiveness that will emerge as a hallmark of the larger keyboard works of the mid- and late 1830s. On the surface adhering to a straightforward tripartite scheme (ABA'), the movement in fact draws on several sonata-form traits: while the A section is constructed as a kind of exposition plus truncated development, A' functions as a compressed recapitulation. The middle section (Intermezzo quasi Scherzo) at once interrupts the surrounding sonata-form pattern and continues it; its principal motive, a boisterous idea in $\frac{6}{8}$ introduced by the strings, is derived from a figure in the flutes and oboe from the close of the immediately preceding A section. The total form cannot be subsumed under any of the canonical paradigms, yet it demonstrates a constructive logic nonetheless. As we shall see, Schumann fashions a similarly "fractured" sonata form in the opening movement of the C-major *Fantasie*, op. 17. In short, Schumann's first major essay in symphonic composition is marked by the same play of tradition and innovation that will characterize his response to the "higher" forms in the ensuing years.

The G-minor Symphony, the largest of the fragments of the early 1830s, brings our survey of Schumann's youthful works to a close, and with it a cycle that would play itself out over the entire span of the composer's career. In the space of a decade, he had either completed, drafted, begun, or contemplated works in practically all of the major musical genres: oratorio, lied, keyboard music in forms great and small (theme-and-variations, etude, contrapuntal study, character piece, sonata), chamber music, concerto, symphony, and even opera. It would be a mistake to pinpoint any one of these as indicative of the "true" Schumann; what counts is the totality of the system and its replication, over the course of the next two decades, on a grander scale. Of course, Schumann was hardly the first composer to undertake a regulated exploration of this sort; soon after arriving in Vienna in November 1792, Beethoven set out to establish his compositional credentials by making impressive contributions to a variety of musical genres in turn: piano trio, piano concerto, piano sonata, string trio, string quartet, symphony, and ballet. Yet Schumann's conquest of the genres was quieter (in it we sense little of Beethoven's imperious spirit), more systematic, more inclusive, and more durable: it occupied him up through his later years in Düsseldorf, when, hoping to crown his life's work, he turned to church music. Although none of the surviving lexical documents— letters, diaries, *Haushaltbücher*—tells us precisely when Schumann determined to stage such a conquest, a synoptic view of his *oeuvre* leaves little doubt as to his intent. And here too we may detect a poetic element: like Virgil, Milton, Shakespeare, and his beloved Jean Paul, Schumann aimed at no less than a charting of the expanses of an imaginative universe.

~3~

ℳusic Criticism
in a New Key

A Barrier against Convention

In March 1833 Schumann arrived in Leipzig after a four-month stay in Zwickau and nearby Schneeberg, the home of his brother Carl and sister-in-law Rosalie. As noted in the previous chapter, the first movement of his G-minor Symphony was performed at both locations: in Zwickau on 18 November 1832 and in Schneeberg in mid-February of the following year. On returning to Leipzig, Schumann took an apartment with Carl Günther, a law student, in Franz Riedel's Garten, an establishment on the outskirts of the city. He continued to work on his G-minor Symphony (certainly on the last movement, and perhaps also on the second and third as well), the first movement of which was rendered, but only with limited success, at Clara's "grand concert" of 29 April at the Gewandhaus. But at about the same time, which Schumann described as the beginning of his "richest and most active period," his thoughts turned to a project that would have tremendous consequences not only for his own career but also for the future course of music journalism: the founding of a new journal for music.[1]

Unfortunately, a thorough account of the initial stages of Schumann's "richest" phase is hampered by the suspension of his diary for much of the four-year period between March 1833 and October 1837.[2] Never again would he go for so long without maintaining some record of his daily activities. Hence, for documentary information on the composer's fortunes (and misfortunes) during the mid-1830s, we must rely

105

largely on letters and on the lapidary notices written in Vienna while he was "filled with melancholy" on the evening of 28 November 1838.[3]

Schumann's abandonment of his diary may be linked to his recent decision to pursue a full-time career as composer, and indeed, shortly after returning to Leipzig in March 1833 he embarked on a variety of compositional projects that no doubt absorbed much of his time and energy. In addition to his attempts to complete the G-minor Symphony, which according to an entry in his *Kompositions-Verzeichnis* occupied him until May, Schumann finished a second volume of Paganini transcriptions (*VI Etudes de Concert* after Paganini's Caprices, op. 10) between April and July, and drafted the *Impromptus,* op. 5, in the remarkably short space of five days in late May.[4] There is a good chance that many of the other works that were either begun (the Piano Sonata in F♯ minor, op. 11; the Piano Sonata in G minor, op. 22; the Variations on Schubert's *Sehnsuchtswalzer*) or completed (the second version of the *Etuden* or *Exercises* on the Allegretto theme from Beethoven's Seventh Symphony, the final revisions of the Toccata) in 1833 likewise date from the spring and early summer of that year; but as we shall see, it is unlikely that Schumann did much composing from July through early December.[5] If this is the case, it would mean that following on his only partially successful attempt to establish his credentials as a symphonist, Schumann undertook a systematic exploration of the keyboard genres. As a group, the works of 1833, both projected and realized, constitute a veritable compendium of forms and styles: Schumann's interest in cultivating the larger forms is exemplified by his preliminary work on the F♯-minor and G-minor sonatas; his conflation of variation and character piece by the variations (in free form) on themes of Beethoven and Schubert, and by the *Impromptus;* his fusion of virtuoso style and pedagogical intent by the Paganini transcriptions. Thus Schumann's turn to the keyboard as a vehicle for his creativity in mid-1833, and his almost total concentration on keyboard music for the remainder of the decade, can be interpreted from two points of view. On the one hand, it allowed him to shore up his compositional skills in the wake of his frustrated attempt at symphonic composition. On the other hand, the piano works of the 1830s comprise more than an episode, a stepping stone on the path toward the symphonies and chamber music of the 1840s;[6] ranging from the slightest of miniatures to the grandest of designs, they attest to the love of system that characterizes Schumann's creativity from the first to the last.

Probably the most fascinating of the compositions of mid-1833 are those in variation forms. We have already discussed the *Etuden/Exercises* in the context of Schumann's reception of Beethoven in the spring of

1832. The Variations on the *Sehnsuchtswalzer* in turn demonstrate a continued engagement with the musical idol of Schumann's youth: Franz Schubert. In "Der Psychometer" (1834), an extraordinary essay about a machine capable of responding to critical questions, Schumann divided waltzes into three categories: head-waltzes, foot-waltzes, and heart-waltzes. The third type "comprises [dances] in the visionary keys of D♭ and A♭, and its fathers appear to be the *Sehnsuchtswalzer*, evening flowers, twilight shapes, and memories of long-gone youth and a thousand loves."[7] Mistakenly attributed to Beethoven when it was published in 1826, the *Sehnsuchtswalzer* ("Yearning Waltz") combines Schubert's so-called *Trauerwalzer* in A♭ ("Sorrowful Waltz"; No. 2 of the *36 Originaltänze für Klavier*, op. 9/D. 365) and the second of three *Deutsche* for piano, D. 972. A sketch for the composition now in the Stiftung Preussischer Kulturbesitz in Berlin vividly demonstrates Schumann's rethinking of the variation form. Anxious to overcome the sectional nature of the traditional design, he links several of the variations with transitional ritornelli. Furthermore, the titles of the sketch as a whole, *Scenes musicales sur un thême connu*, and the draft for the fourth movement, Intermezzo, indicate that Schumann was nudging the variation in the direction of the character piece.[8] Thus it is hardly surprising that although these variations were never published, the opening two-dozen measures or so of the introductory movement to the set found their way into the *Préambule* of *Carnaval*.

In the *Impromptus sur une Romance de Clara Wieck*, composed between 26 and 30 May 1833, Schumann more fully realized his novel conception of the variation idea. In one of several autobiographical sketches, he even suggested that the work "might be seen as a new form of variation,"[9] a reference, perhaps, to the grounding of the *Impromptus* in not one, but two themes: the bass theme, a product of Schumann's contrapuntal study in the preceding years and the point of departure for an extended fugato in the unfinished finale of the G-minor Symphony, announced unadorned at the outset of the piece; and the slightly altered version of the melody from Clara's *Romance variée*, op. 3, with which the bass theme is combined immediately thereafter[10] (Example 3.1). But in a sense, Schumann's recourse to a kind of "double theme" is not so new after all. He would have found ample precedent for the technique in Beethoven's *Fünfzehn Variationen mit einer Fuge* for piano, op. 35, the so-called "Eroica" Variations of 1802. Even the outward designs of these pieces are similar: both begin with the bass theme alone (followed, in Beethoven's case, with three contrapuntal variations), proceed with the introduction of the melodic theme and an extended series of variations, and close with an impressive fugal finale.[11] Still, the more obviously

Example 3.1. Impromptus, op. 5 (first version): mm. 1–32.

Bachian pedigree of Schumann's variations distinguishes them from Beethoven's. As he wrote in the autobiographical sketch mentioned above,
the *Impromptus* were conceived "as a result of the stimulation" afforded
by a steady exposure to Bach's music in the early 1830s. This assertion
is further supported by a diary entry of 29 May 1832, where Schumann
maintains that the falling-fifth motive C-F-G-C, the opening gesture of
the *Impromptus'* bass theme, came to him after sightreading several of
Bach's fugues with Clara.[12] Moreover, the spirit of Bach extends past the
character of the bass theme and the contrapuntal gamesmanship of the
finale to encompass the body of the variations themselves, witness the
subtle use of invertible counterpoint in No. 3, and the treatment of
Clara's theme as a migrating cantus firmus in Nos. 4 and 8.

Yet the chief novelty of the variation form as rethought in the *Impromptus* probably lies elsewhere, in the subsumption of the allusions to Beethoven and Bach under an overriding poetic idea. The work, after all, is the first in a long and impressive series of "Clara" pieces, musical lyrics of personal experience intimately bound up with the young woman destined to play a crucial role in Schumann's life. Schumann summons up Clara's theme (in the second half of No. 1), elaborates it (Nos. 2–4), gradually converts it into a dreamy recollection (a process culminating in No. 11), effaces it (for the bulk of the Finale), and only at the last moment restores it as a fleeting reminiscence in the closing measures of the piece. The composition, in other words, turns on the transformation of Clara's melody into a memory.[13] Though Schumann draws on time-honored (Beethovenian), even archaic (Bachian) techniques, he places them within the eminently modern context of the cycle of character pieces. Thus the *Impromptus* certainly count as a musical realization of what we will soon encounter as the historical imperative of Schumann's criticism: the invocation of the past as an inspirational source for a "new poetic age."

After completing the *Impromptus,* Schumann both continued with works-in-progress (the second volume of Paganini transcriptions) and moved on to newer projects (the F♯-minor Sonata), but the events of summer 1833 brought his composing to a standstill. During July and August, he suffered from an attack of malarial fever, his recovery no doubt slowed by heavy and persistent drinking (the Vienna précis of 1838 refers to "champagne nights" before the onset of malaria and to a "dissolute life" shortly thereafter).[14] Then on 2 August his brother Julius (who, together with Eduard, had continued to manage the family book business in Zwickau) died at the age of twenty-eight from tuberculosis. But the death in mid-October of his favorite sister-in-law, Rosalie, a victim of the same disease from which Schumann was slowly recovering, took him over the edge. His first major neurotic spell, again as described in the Vienna précis, was characterized by the onslaught of anxiety and depression:

> The night of 17–18 October [1833]—the most frightful of my life—
>   Rosalie's death just before
> At this point, a crucial segment of my life begins.
> The tortures of the most dreadful melancholy from October until December—
> I was siezed by an *idée fixe:* the fear of going mad.[15]

Of the various accounts of Schumann's illness, the closest in time to the episode itself is a letter to his mother of 27 November. According to this document, the psychological symptoms detailed above were accompanied by a number of physical disturbances as well: "I felt like hardly more than a statue, without cold or warmth. . . . Violent congestion of the blood, unspeakable fear, loss of breath, [and] momentary loss of consciousness alternate rapidly, although now less so than in past days. If you had any inkling of this numbing of the spirit through melancholy, then you would forgive me for not writing." While Schumann noted some improvement in his condition at this time, he remained so "shy and timid" that he was afraid to fall asleep without someone else in his room (in September he had moved to a fifth-floor apartment at Burgstrasse 21, located near the center of town), and shared lodgings with his former roommate, the "fundamentally good-hearted" Günther; nor did he have the courage to travel alone to Zwickau, "for fear that *something might happen to me*." He adds a heartrending plea: "My mother, really love me! Because I'm often close to madness when I think of Julius and Rosalie. . . ."[16] A letter to Clara written a little over four years later sheds further light on the causes and nature of Schumann's disturbance. There he attributes the "gloom" that enveloped him in the latter half of 1833 not only to the deaths of his brother and sister-in-law, but also to the "disappointments experienced by every artist when things don't go as swiftly as he had imagined," to the realization, in other words, that the road to fame and fortune as a composer would be an arduous one. Indeed, the less than enthusiastic reception of the first movement of his G-minor Symphony would have fed into Schumann's recognition of this fact. Horrified by the thought that he might be losing his senses—"the most dreadful of heaven's punishments"—and fearful that this thought might lead him "to lay a hand" on his life, Schumann sought medical advice. His doctor, however, failed to acknowledge the seriousness of his patient's complaint, ascribing it to adolescent malaise and little more: "Find yourself a woman," Schumann was told, "she'll cure you in a flash."[17]

Although Schumann's bout with mental illness was triggered by the deaths of two of his closest relatives, it occurred at the culmination of a period marked by physical and emotional decline. Debilitated by malarial fever and over-indulgence in alcohol, and dejected by his failure to launch a brilliant career as composer, Schumann easily lapsed into a condition whose psychological symptoms comprised intense depression, fear of madness, generalized panic, and suicidal thoughts, and whose physical consequences involved inflammation ("congestion of the blood"), shortness of breath, and numbness in the limbs.[18] The first of three more-or-less evenly spaced and progressively worsening episodes (the others flared up in 1844 and 1854) Schumann's near breakdown in the autumn of 1833 should have set off a warning bell. Tragically, few were willing to listen, nor were those who did competent to act.

As Schumann indicated to his mother in November 1833, his "return to life came about only gradually, through hard work."[19] Much of this hard work centered around the "musikalische Zeitschrift" ("musical journal") that he listed in his diary under "Plans" as early as 8 March of the same year.[20] By late June, a group of like-minded individuals had clustered around Schumann, its members including the theologian and pianist Julius Knorr, Ernst Ferdinand Wenzel (then a philosophy student and fellow pupil of Wieck's), the deaf painter, journalist, and composer Johann Peter Lyser, the music critics Ernst August Ortlepp and Gustav Bergen, Schumann's old friend Willibald von der Lühe, the philosopher Johann Amadeus Wendt, and Ludwig Ferdinand Stolle, a writer for Karl Georg Herlosssohn's *Der Komet*.[21] During the early part of the summer, the group met at Friedrich Hofmeister's music shop, but by late in the year, it assembled for informal, weekly meetings at the Kaffeebaum, a pub owned and operated by Andreas Poppe, where Schumann was a regular customer. Gustav Jansen provides a colorful picture of Schumann's direction of the proceedings: "When he sat at his usual place at the head of the table, with the indispensable cigar in his mouth, he never had to ask for a fresh glass of beer; he had arranged that it would be brought to him without even a nod, as soon as the innkeeper or waiter noticed that his glass was empty."[22] United in their displeasure over the current musical scene that was dominated by the frivolous strains of Italian opera in the theatre, and by the facile but vapid stunts of virtuoso pianists such as Herz and Hünten in the concert hall and salon, Schumann and his friends determined to publish a journal whose "tone and coloring . . . would be more varied than that of similar enterprises." Above all, it was their highminded intention "to erect a barrier against convention," but, as Schumann wrote to his mother on 28 June 1833, the venture would also provide him with the "definite social standing" for which he, as an artist with an "undefined position," had long craved.[23] (The establishment of the journal in 1834 allowed Schumann to describe himself as a *Musikgelehrter* [musical scholar] on the new passport he acquired at that time).[24] Thus from the start, Schumann's career as a journalist was marked by a blend of idealism and practicality.

There can be little doubt that the preparatory work for the founding of the journal—and the moderation of his alcohol consumption—set Schumann on the path to recovery from the neurotic episode of late October and November 1833; immediately after sketching out the events of his traumatic autumn in the Vienna précis, he added: "Sobriety. Journalistic activities. The idea of the Davidsbündler further developed."[25] Moreover, Schumann associated his decisive "return to life" with one individual more than any other. The last entry for 1833 in the précis reads: "Then in December, *Ludwig Schunke*, like a star."[26] Soon this extraordinarily gifted young pianist became his most treasured companion. Schumann's description of his newly found confidant in a letter to his mother dated 19 March 1834 brims over with superlatives: "[Schunke] is a splendid fellow and friend, who always takes hearty pleasure in striving for and accomplishing the most beautiful and the best. A patch of blue often brings more pleasure than an entirely clear sky; I could do without all my friends for the sake of this one."[27] At about the same time, the pair decided to share an apartment, Schunke perhaps participating in the "frequently dissolute life style" into which Schumann again slipped in the spring of 1834.[28] Within months, however, the young artist was gravely ill; and although his doctor gave him "only one more winter to live," he didn't manage to survive for even that brief a period. Schunke died on 7 December 1834 at the age of twenty-four, a victim of tuberculosis.[29]

While Schumann's friendship with Schunke was cut painfully short, it was not without artistic consequences for both young men. Schunke's *Variations concertantes* on Schubert's *Trauerwalzer*, for example, were probably inspired by Schumann's variations on the *Sehnsuchtswalzer* (both works, incidentally, were dedicated to Henriette Voigt, the wife of a prominent Leipzig merchant, an excellent pianist, and a warm supporter of Schumann since late in 1833). In acknowledgment of his friend's superior gifts as a piano virtuoso, Schumann dedicated his Toccata in its final form to Schunke. The latter, in turn, dedicated his Sonata in G Minor, op. 3, whose first movement, like the Toccata, aims to mediate technical display and contrapuntal textures, to "son ami R. Schumann." Schumann closed this circle of homages with a review (actually more of a poetically colored eulogy) of the composition, culminating in the following account of Schunke's rendition of his sonata:

> Ludwig sat more or less in front of the piano, as if transported there by a cloud; without knowing quite how, we were drawn into the stream of this work, unknown to any of us—I still see everything before me, the fading light, the walls silent, as if listening, friends gathered round, hardly daring to breathe, Florestan's pale face, the Master [Raro] deep in thought, and Ludwig in the center, who like a sorcerer held us in a magical ring.

After Schunke had finished, Florestan offered words of high praise: "You are a master of your art, especially when you play. Verily, the

Davidsbündler would be proud to count such an artist as yourself among their number."[30]

When Schumann wrote this piece in 1835, the Davidsbund, his band of crusaders against philistinism in contemporary musical life, was still relatively new to the reading public. The group made its official debut in *Der Davidsbündler,* an article published in three installments in *Der Komet* between 7 December 1833 and 12 January 1834, during just the period, that is, that Schunke entered Schumann's life "like a star."[31] A fanciful blend of imaginative prose, critical commentary, and aphorisms attributed to Florestan, Eusebius, Raro, and other members of the Davidsbund (Hofmeister and Bergen), *Der Davidsbündler* brought together a cast of characters and a constellation of ideas about the nature of writing on art that had occupied Schumann for some time. To review what we have already detailed in Chapter 2: on 8 June 1831, his twenty-first birthday, Schumann decided to give his friends "more beautiful and fitting names"; a week later, many of these same friends appeared as characters in *Die Wunderkinder,* the projected "musical novel" in which Schumann intended to thematize the complex interplay of art and life; on 1 July of the same year, Florestan the Improviser, one of the protagonists in *Die Wunderkinder,* was joined by Eusebius; in a fragmentary tale possibly dating from the same time (like the later essay, titled *Der Davidsbündler*), Schumann and some of his "friends" from the 8 June diary entry took up the same theme broached in *Die Wunderkinder:* the need for the creative genius to recognize the fine line between ideality and reality; on 7 December, Florestan and Eusebius appeared in print for the first time as the two principal critical voices in Schumann's review of Chopin's Opus 2; and by May of the following year, *Die Wunderkinder* had been rechristened as *Florestan.*[32] To be sure, some of these strands appear to trail off into nothingness; Schumann's "musical novel," for instance, never materialized. But in the essay for *Der Komet* published in late 1833 and early 1834, personal confession, a poetic reshaping of reality, and critical awareness found a meeting point in the Davidsbündler idea.

By the mid-1830s, the notion of an artist-band primed to ward off philistinism was hardly new. As early as 1800, Friedrich Schlegel exhorted his colleagues to follow the example of the "medieval merchants" and "unite in a Hansa to defend themselves."[33] Similarly, at the heart of E. T. A. Hoffmann's "serapiontic" principle was a brotherhood of poetic individuals firm in their opposition to a world dominated by shallow tastes (it is probably no accident that Schumann had read Hoffmann's *Die Bergwerke zu Falun,* one of the tales in his *Serapionsbrüder,* less than a month before hitting upon the idea for *Die Wunderkinder*).[34] Nor were precedents lacking for actual artist associations united by this principle: witness the intellectual fraternity/sorority comprised of the Schlegel brothers and their wives, Novalis, and Schleiermacher, all of them contributors to the *Athenäum*, the short-lived journal (1798) whose contents represent the ideological core of early Romanticism; or, to cite a more specifically musical example, Carl Maria von Weber's Harmonische Verein, the statutes for which include the provision that "since the world is inundated with so many bad works, often upheld only by authorities and by wretched criticism, we are obliged to expose them and warn about them."[35] Groups such as the Ludlamshöhle in Vienna (founded 1817) and the satirically oriented and fancifully named Tunnel über der Spree in Berlin (founded 1827) counted both musicians and literati among their members and met regularly to discuss the latest happenings in the world of art. Clearly the *Litterarischer Verein* of Schumann's teenage years in Zwickau belongs to the same tradition. In Leipzig's Tunnel über der Pleisse, which met weekly and often sponsored literary and musical entertainments, Schumann would have found a direct model for his Davidsbund. Interestingly enough, several of the members of the Leipzig Tunnel—Wieck, Lühe, Lyser—became collaborators on or contributors to Schumann's *Neue Zeitschrift für Musik*.[36]

In all of these artist associations, we encounter precedents for the features that characterized Schumann's Davidsbund: the use of pseudonyms (Weber's Harmonische Verein, the Ludlamshöhle, the Leipzig Tunnel), the production of humorous essays or feuilletons (the Berlin Tunnel), the organization around a journal (the *Athenäum* group). Yet there is at least one important respect in which Schumann's Davidsbund differs from other comparable groups. If Hoffmann's Serapionsbrüder was a sheer product of the author's imagination, and if the Berlin and Leipzig Tunnels were firmly rooted in reality, then the Davidsbund came about at the juncture of *both* imagination and reality. It was this feature that Schumann had in mind when, in the Introduction to his collected writings (1854), he described the group as "more than a secret society." The Davidsbund, he went on to explain, "runs like a red thread through [my] journal, uniting poetry and truth ["Dichtung und Wahrheit"] in a humorous manner."[37] The group was not only the mouthpiece through which Schumann and his colleagues expressed their opinions on the state of the contemporary musical scene, it was, in addition, the central theme, the "red thread," around which their journalistic undertaking was organized. Moreover, Schumann's allusion to Goethe's autobiography, *Dichtung und Wahrheit*, points to the higher truth born of poetic expression toward which he and his associates aspired. The path to their goal led through fact and fantasy, realism and idealism, the poetry of an imagined utopia and the prose of everyday life. These oppositional pairs commingle at every level in the pages of the *Neue Zeitschrift*. Consider even the names of the "members" of the Davidsbund as they appear in the journal. Some are pseudonyms for actual individuals ("Walt"—the pianist Louis Rakemann; "Serpentinus"—the song composer and critic Carl Banck; "Fritz Friedrich"—J. P. Lyser; "Chiara," "Chiarina," or "Zilia"—Clara Wieck; "Juvenalis"—Willibald von der Lühe; "Sara"—Sophie Kaskel, a pianist and student of Adolph Henselt; "F. Meritis"— Mendelssohn; "Jeanquirit"—Stephen Heller; "St. Diamond"—Anton von Zuccalmaglio; and, of course, "Florestan-Eusebius-Raro" for Schumann's double nature and its synthesis into a single being);[38] others, in contrast, are at least partly fictional ("Hector," "Ambrosia," "Beda").[39] The procedure of assigning such pseudonyms stems directly from Schumann's decision, on his twenty-first birthday, to give his friends "more beautiful and more fitting names"; Lühe and Clara already appear at that point as "Rentmeister Juvenal" and "Cilia," respectively.[40] Thus through the medium of the Davidsbund, Schumann found a means of transforming this confessional practice into a critical one, of converting "poetry" into "truth."

Soon after the members of Schumann's band made their public debut in Herlosssohn's *Komet,* preparations for the appearance of the *Neue Zeitschrift* went into high gear. On 19 March 1834, Schumann announced confidently to his mother: "Apart from the advantages for my intellectual development, I believe a great success is in store." The contract establishing the journal was drafted exactly a week later. Titled the *Neue Leipziger Zeitschrift für Musik,* and thus emphasizing its origination in a city known throughout the German lands as a center for liberal thought,[41] the journal was slated to appear twice weekly. Its editorial board, in whose hands the contract vested chief control, was comprised of Knorr, Schumann, Schunke, and Wieck, while Christian Hartmann, a local book-dealer, served as publisher.[42] In addition, the document included stipulations for the payment of the editors (10 thalers for the first 500 copies sold), the annual subscription price (2 thalers), an honorarium for Julius Knorr, who at first acted as editor-in-chief (25 thalers quarterly), weekly meetings of the editorial staff, and the nullification of the contract if, after a year, 500 subscribers could not be found.[43]

On 3 April 1834, a little over a year after Schumann first seriously considered launching a musical journal, the first issue of the *Neue Zeitschrift* appeared. Its prospectus, printed as the lead item in the issue, promised much: "theoretical and practical articles," "belletristic pieces" (short tales on musical subjects), "critiques of the imaginative products of the present," "miscellanies" (passages on musical subjects culled from the writings of figures such as Goethe, Jean Paul, Heine, and Novalis), accounts of musical life by correspondents in the chief European musical centers, and a chronicle devoted to announcements of significant musical events. As time would tell, Schumann's journal by and large lived up to this promise. So too did it live up to its title as a fundamentally "new" journal for music. Not only did its independence from an established music-publishing firm (unlike the *Allgemeine musikalische Zeitung,* the *Berliner Allgemeine Musikzeitung, Cäcilia,* and *Iris,* the journalistic arms of Breitkopf und Härtel, Schlesinger, Schott, and Trautwein, respectively) ensure an impartial critique of the musical scene, it aimed at and often achieved an all-encompassing view of that scene. With representatives in Paris, London, Vienna, Berlin, St. Petersburg, and Naples (not to mention a healthy interest in the musical goings-on in Poland, Hungary, Belgium, and even the United States and South America), the journal provided a breadth of coverage unparalleled by any of its competitors. As Schumann wrote in the 1834 prospectus: "Whoever wants to investigate the artist should visit him in his workshop. It also seemed necessary to create a medium that would stimulate him to have an effect, beyond that of his direct sphere of influence, through the printed word."[44] Universal in content and scope, the *Neue Zeitschrift* did indeed provide just such a medium.

By Schumann's account, the project got off to an auspicious start; on 2 July he boasted to his mother that 300 of the requisite 500 subscribers had been found. But the same letter likewise makes clear that within months of the journal's founding, Schumann was shouldering most of the editorial responsibilities. "*I must dedicate my whole energy to the journal,*" he stated emphatically, "one can't depend on the others. Wieck is always on tour, Knorr is ill, [and] Schunke doesn't handle a pen very well."[45] What's more, strife had already broken out among the ranks; in a probable reference to late spring 1834, the Vienna précis alludes to "arguments with Wieck and the other editors." Further disagreements, coupled with Schunke's death in December, led to the "complete dissolution of the entire circle" by the end of the year.[46] The files of Heinrich Conrad Schleinitz, a lawyer retained by Hartmann late in 1834, help us to fill in some of the gaps regarding the near collapse of the venture. Hartmann took advantage of a dispute with Knorr (who wanted to print an infamatory declaration against Wieck in spite of the publisher's objections) to stage a kind of palace coup. Hoping to make the *Neue Zeitschrift* into a more conventional publication and thereby increase sales, Hartmann sought out legal counsel in an attempt to gain editorial control over the journal. His plans were foiled, however, by

Schumann's return to Leipzig in mid-December from a more than month-long stay in Zwickau and nearby Asch. By the day before Christmas, Schumann had negotiated a new contract (which he may have drafted himself), thereby acquiring sole ownership of the journal for 350 thalers payable to Hartmann. Within a week, he found a new publisher, the book-dealer Wilhelm Ambrosius Barth.[47] Alluding to his resolution of the crisis in the 1854 Introduction to his collected writings, Schumann spoke of the takeover of the journal by "the visionary of the group, who up to then had spent less of his time with books than in a dreamy reverie at the piano."[48] Yet Schumann's actions in December 1834 demonstrate that this visionary could be a shrewd businessman when the need arose, and also that he well knew how to put his spotty legal training to good use when the survival of his journal was at stake. Not surprisingly, the reorganization of the journal's directorship further exacerbated the already strained relations among some of the Davidsbündler. A particularly unpleasant episode ensued with Knorr, who threatened to take legal action over the payment of 25 thalers owed him for his (less than efficiently executed) editorial work in the last quarter of 1834. But on 20 July 1835, the day before he was scheduled to appear in court, Schumann settled the matter through Schleinitz.[49]

The first issue of the newly constituted journal appeared on 2 January 1835. While Schumann was certainly interested in preserving an image of continuity for his readers, subtle changes in focus indicate his equally strong desire both to broaden and to sharpen the original intent of the undertaking. Previously titled the *Neue Leipziger Zeitschrift für Musik,* the journal was henceforth issued simply as the *Neue Zeitschrift für Musik,* the elimination of *Leipziger* probably geared to ward off suspicions of parochialism. In the same spirit, Schumann added two cities, Prague and Weimar, to the list of centers whose musical activities would be regularly covered and struck the clause from the April 1834 prospectus concerning the journal's "special emphasis on reviews of piano compositions." And as we will see, Schumann's New Year's editorial for the January 1835 issue brought into relief the philosophical underpinnings of the Davidsbund's critical program.

While Schumann's activities in 1834 were dominated by his work for the *Neue Zeitschrift,* the same year brought important developments in his personal life. The founding of the journal in April roughly coincides with his meeting Ernestine von Fricken, a young woman from Asch (a village on the Bavarian-Bohemian border) whom the Wiecks had met after one of Clara's performances in Plauen, and who came to Leipzig for piano lessons with Wieck beginning on 21 April 1834. (Although Schumann did not know it at the time, she was the illegitimate daughter of Captain I. F. von Fricken, who adopted her only on 12 December 1834). According to the Vienna précis, Schumann's relationship with Ernestine intensified so rapidly over the course of the summer that by September they were engaged; visits to her hometown followed in October and December.[50]

Little wonder, then, given his all-consuming efforts on behalf of the *Neue Zeitschrift* and the complications in his private life, that Schumann's compositional productivity slackened considerably in 1834. A set of piano variations on Chopin's Nocturne, op. 15 no. 3 (preserved, in a fair copy, through the middle of the fifth variation) occupied him late in the year, but was never seen through to publication.[51] Intermittent work on the F♯-minor Sonata is likewise a possibility. The remainder of what little composing Schumann did manage was associated with Ernestine (the dedicatee of the Allegro, op. 8) and her father. While in Zwickau in December, he began on *Carnaval*, its celebrated three- and four-note "themes," or "Sphinxes," as Schumann called them, derived from the letters ASCH. At the same time, he set to work on the *Etudes Symphoniques*, an extended cycle of variations on a theme by Captain von Fricken.[52] But in the months before, the writerly side of Schumann's creativity surely had the upper hand.

History, Poetry, and Music Criticism

Writing in 1838, Schumann called the year 1834 "the most important in my life."[53] No doubt its importance was closely linked with the founding of the *Neue Zeitschrift*, the refinement of the Davidsbündler idea, and the cultivation of a brand of music criticism quite unlike that encountered in any of the other journals of the day. The designation of Schumann's writings, in the title of this chapter, as music criticism "in a new key" is justified by two features in particular. In the first place, although Schumann's knowledge of the facts of music history was quite limited, especially before 1840, he had already as a young law student in Heidelberg evolved a philosophy of history, a systematic framework for the evaluation of temporally discrete cultural phenomena.[54] This historical outlook pervades his writings at practically every turn. Second, Schumann was keenly aware of an obvious problem posed by the concept of music criticism itself, namely, its employment of a verbal medium to describe and evaluate tonal events. His highly idiosyncratic, but always engaging "poetic" criticism emerged as a response to this dilemma.

Nowhere did Schumann articulate his philosophy of music history more clearly than in his New Year's editorial for the 2 January 1835 issue of the *Neue Zeitschrift,* the lead essay in the first issue of the journal to appear under his sole editorship:

> In the short period of our activity, we have acquired a good deal of experience. Our fundamental attitude was established at the outset. It is simple, and runs as follows: to acknowledge the past and its creations, and to draw attention to the fact that new artistic beauties can only be strengthened by such a pure source; next, to oppose the recent past as an inartistic period, which has only a notable increase in mechanical dexterity to show for itself; and finally, to prepare for and facilitate the advent of a fresh, poetic future.[55]

According to this scheme, the past is a nurturing source for the present; the present a site of imperfection; and the future a poetic age toward which the imperfect present should aspire. Past, present, and future are not so much discrete categories as they are mutually interdependent phases in a teleological sequence. Schumann's care in designating these phases underscores the point. He does not refer to the past as *Vergangenheit,* a term implying definitive closure, finality, even death, but rather as *die alte Zeit* (the bygone age), thus implying that the past should continue to inform the present. It is rather the present, or at least those aspects of the musical present concerned with "mechanical dexterity" and little more, that Schumann designates as *die letzte Vergangenheit* (the recent past). Born under the star of death, the "inartistic" products of those who cater to the fad for empty virtuosity are doomed to oblivion. And to highlight the parallels between past and future, Schumann altered "junge, dichterische Zukunft" (fresh, poetic age) to read "neue, poetische Zeit" (new, poetic age) in the 1854 collected edition of his writings.[56] Only the past ("die alte Zeit") and the future are "ages," *Zeiten,* while the present is continually consumed by the fleeting moment.[57]

We may thus think of Schumann's view of music history as a "triadic" one. On 16 August 1828, he writes: "Love the past, act in the present, and fear the future. In this way a beautiful harmony, a powerful triad comes into being." Speaking through Eusebius in the *Denk- und Dichtbüchlein* of 1834, he takes the notion of temporal succession as harmonic construct a step further, and emphasizes the transitional function of the present: "Triad=[historical] epochs. The [interval of a] third, as present, mediates the past and future."[58] In this, Schumann's philosophy of history discloses an affinity with the outlook of the Jena Romantics in general and Friedrich Schlegel in particular. For Schlegel, too, criticism must be firmly grounded in a historical framework. And Schlegel's ideas, like Schumann's, derive their unity from the tripartition of this framework, which comprises a body of revered, "classical" texts, a critique of contemporary conditions, and a "redemptive" phase in the future.[59]

Schumann's tripartite scheme allowed him to view music history not as an undifferentiated continuum, but far more as a series of interlocking periods. Though he hardly subscribed to a rigid opposition of "classic" and "romantic" phases—much less to the crass notion that romanticism represented a reaction against classicism—he did, for instance, situate Beethoven's Ninth Symphony at the "turning point from a classical to a romantic period" in a letter of 18 August 1834 to Anton Töpken.[60] By the end of the decade, he had both refined and expanded his periodization of music history. Based largely on his reading of Wilhelm Christian Müller's *Ästhetisch-historische Einleitung in die Wissenschaft der Tonkunst* (Leipzig, 1830), Schumann's *Chronologischer Geschichte der Musik (Chronological History of Music)* includes twenty pages of tables and brief descriptions of the highlights in the development of musical genres, instruments, notation, and aesthetics. In a summary of the chief events in music history from 1200 B.C. (!) to the present, Schumann divides this three-thousand-year span into ten periods *(Zeiträume)*, each of the later phases an outgrowth of its predecessor. While the art of counterpoint entered a crisis phase in the fifteenth century, given the "overly artificial" approach of figures such as Ockeghem (Schumann writes "Ockenheim"), it attained a new and less mannered significance in the sixteenth century with Willaert and Lassus. Schumann in turn designates his seventh period, 1700–1750, as an era of "melodic counterpoint," its chief proponents including Porpora, Telemann, and of course, J. S. Bach. Then from 1775 to 1800 comes the "period of universality," the age of Haydn and Mozart, characterized by the "development of melody and melodic harmony," and the "unity of art, imagination, and thoughtful congeniality." Finally, the tenth period (1800 to the present) marks the "summit of musical art" in figures such as Beethoven and Schubert, whose works represent the fulfillment of the aspirations of previous ages.[61] Music history is thus construed not only as a succession of great men, but also as the logical progression of stylistic trends embodied in their works.

At the same time, music-historical progress, for Schumann, was not a purely continuous phenomenon. Its potential leaps and reversals come into play in his view of the relationship between Bach and the talented representatives of Schumann's own generation. "The profound combinatorial power, the poetry and the humor of modern music," he wrote to Gustav Keferestein on 31 January 1840, "have their origin mainly in Bach: Mendelssohn, [William Sterndale] Bennett, Chopin, Hiller, the whole of the so-called romantic school (of course I have the Germans in mind) are much closer than Mozart was to the music of Bach; indeed they all know his work thoroughly. I too make my daily confession to his lofty one, and strive to purify and strengthen myself through him." [62] Just as Schumann and his colleagues drew liberally on Bach's example, the latter's achievements were viewed as premonitions of the present and future. This mode of thought would allow Schumann to make the startling assertion that "most of Bach's fugues are character pieces of the highest kind; some of them are truly poetic creations, each of which requires its own expression, its own lights and shades." [63] As indicated in the letter to Keferstein, Mozart stands fundamentally apart from this line of influence. In an 1834 review of Hummel's *Studien,* op. 125, Schumann also maintained: "Cheerfulness, repose, grace, the characteristics of the artworks of antiquity, are also those of Mozart's school. Just as the Greeks gave their thundering Zeus a cheerful expression, so too does Mozart restrain his lightning bolts." [64] Hence Mozart's music partakes of the dialectical synthesis of opposites that Schumann, in a diary entry of 7 July 1831, associated with classical art and which he defined as: "the ingenious in the guise of the folk-like, the unfathomable in the guise of thrifty affluence, infinity of content in a beautifully rounded form, boundlessness in graceful limitation, the ponderous in the guise of the facile, darkness in luminous clarity, the corporeal inspirited, the real ennobled through the ideal." [65] In Schumann's estimation, then, the most promising trends in the musical present derive their inspiration less from the immediately preceding "period of universality" than from the blend of melody and counterpoint that dominates the music of the first half of the eighteenth century.

Schumann was similarly convinced that portions of Beethoven's output, like Bach's, would make their most profound impact only gradually. This was especially so of the late quartets, works "for whose greatness no words can be found," and which appeared to Schumann, "next to some of the choruses . . . of J. S. Bach, to represent the extreme limits that human art and imagination have yet reached." [66] Among his contemporaries, Schumann saw Hermann Hirschbach as one of the few who had seriously confronted this difficult music. Reviewing Hirschbach's *Lebensbilder in einem Cyklus von Quartetten,* op. 1, in 1842, Schumann asserted: "Beethoven's last quartets serve him as the starting point for a new poetic era."[67] True, Hirschbach's quartets have long since disappeared from the standard repertory, but the general thrust of Schumann's remarks on the reception of Beethoven's late quartets has been borne out by the passage of time: as sources of compositional inspiration, these works skipped not one but several generations.

Of course, Schumann's judgments of the artworks of the past frequently misfired. Domenico Scarlatti's keyboard sonatas, he wrote, occupied an important place in the repertory, but "how clumsy their form, how undeveloped their melody, how limited their modulation!"[68] And as for Haydn: "One can no longer learn anything new from him; he is like a familiar friend of the house who is always greeted with pleasure and respect, but is of no further interest for the present day."[69] But on the whole, Schumann's flexible view of music history as a process marked by continuities and discontinuities should strike us as remarkably prescient.

Just as intriguing as his conception of the relationships between past and future is Schumann's diagnosis of the present. No historicist, he remained firmly committed to the here-and-now and its special problems. He emphasized this stance in an aphorism from one of the 1834 issues of the *Neue Zeitschrift*: "*critics should engage themselves with the recent activity of the young creative spirits*, rather than dawdle over past love affairs. Fashionable withdrawal into the past or pedantic clinging to antiquated customs or dreaming about youthful infatuations is of no use. Time marches on, and we must march with it."[70]

On more than one occasion, Schumann appeared to contradict himself in evaluating the central term in his triadic historical scheme. In the 1835 New Year's editorial, for instance, he brands the present as an age of decline, but in the *Chronologischer Geschichte* drafted several years later, he designates it as the "summit of musical art." Yet Schumann had not made an abrupt volte-face in the intervening years. The apparent contradiction is far more a result of his recognition of the complexities and contradictions in current musical life. Indeed, the present as Schumann saw it was not characterized by a single, overriding trend, but by three distinct forces, each corresponding to one of the phases in his tripartition of historical time as a whole. The present thus reflects, in microcosm, the entire span of music history. (Just as Schumann's musical output enfolds smaller systems within larger ones, so too does his philosophy of history.) Schumann accords this view a decidedly political slant in "Der Psychometer" (1834), where he suggests that his contemporaries can be placed into three "parties": "classicists," "justemilieuists," and "romantics."[71] He elaborates on this division in a review of Johann Kalliwoda's overtures:

The present is characterized by its political parties. Like their political counterparts, musical parties can be divided into liberal, middle-of-the-road, and reactionary, or romantic, modern, and classic. On the right sit the old-timers, the contrapuntists, the anti-chromaticists, on the left the young newcomers, the Phrygian hotheads, those who scorn formal strictures, the impudent geniuses, among whom the Beethovenians are most conspicious. In the juste-milieu, old and young commingle. This group is responsible for most of the products of the age, the creations of the moment, brought forth here only to be destroyed.[72]

Both "classicists" and "juste-milieuists" belong to what Schumann called *die letzte Vergangenheit,* the recent, but moribund past. (The *Chronologische Geschichte* implicitly locates composers such as Czerny, Bellini, and F. W. Pixis in this category).[73] Only the romantics, those capable of transforming past practice into something fundamentally new, will at once survive the present and point the way toward the "new poetic age." To be sure, Schumann was circumspect in his employment of the term "romantic," probably because it was often used by his opponents (for example, Gottfried Fink, the editor of the rival *Allgemeine musikalische Zeitung*) as a term of derision for the very principles that the *Neue Zeitschrift* sought to promote.[74] Although by 1837 Schumann claimed to be "heartily sick of the word 'romantic'," he nonetheless found in it an apt designation for the younger generation of composers—Bennett, Chopin, Stephen Heller, Adolf Henselt, Ferdinand Hiller, Mendelssohn, Schunke, Wilhelm Taubert—who, like himself, combined an abiding respect for tradition with an equal commitment to the cause of musical progress.[75]

Given the flooding of the market with compositions of negligible worth, Schumann the critic was principally interested in the works of genuinely talented composers. Responding in the 1835 New Year's editorial to those who found his journal's editorial policy exclusionary, Schumann asserted that there were many items "that simply don't exist so far as criticism is concerned," and even proposed "stereotypical," prefabricated reviews for pieces by one of the three "archenemies" of art: the "untalented," the "cheap talents," and the "prolific scribblers."[76] Simply put, only art could supply an appropriate object for Schumann's criticism. This is the sense behind Florestan's exhortation for his cohorts to root out mediocrity in the cultural life of the present: "Assembled Davidsbündler, youths and men alike, prepare to slay the Philistines, musical and otherwise."[77] Yet it is important to bear in mind that he hardly viewed the artistic products of even the most gifted of his contemporaries—the young romantics—as embodiments of perfection: they lay claim to neither the impeccable craftmanship of Bach nor the Olym-

pian grace of Mozart. When asked to evaluate E. Güntz's recently published set of *Tänze* for piano, the psychometer offers a mixed review:
"Does he show outstanding talent?"—"I think so"; "Has he founded a
school?"—"no"; "Should he have withheld his work?"—"certainly"; "To
which party does he belong?"—"romantic." The fantastic machine goes
on to say: "[Güntz] feels deeply, but for the most part incorrectly—in
spite of isolated flashes of moonlight, he fumbles in the dark; while now
and again he seizes a flower, he also grasps at straw . . . his aim is
well-meaning, though like unpracticed marksmen, he fires with his eyes
closed." But still—and here we come to the crucial point—the psychometer would prefer to deal with a "scattershot, poetic hobgoblin"
such as this than with "a dozen dim-eyed, pointy-nosed pedants."[78]
Long forgotten today, Güntz is nonetheless representative of the ambivalent status of the "romantic school" as a whole: their works are imperfect but hold out much promise for the "new poetic age" to come. Even
those compositions that "distinguish themselves through only one tiny
felicitous trait," Schumann wrote in his 1835 editorial, would be considered for review.[79] In this too, Schumann's critical attitude bears comparison with that of the Jena Romantics. As Friedrich Schlegel maintained
in an essay entitled "On the Limits of the Beautiful" (1794): "Our failings themselves are our hopes, for they arise from the supremacy of
the understanding, whose perfection, while slow to come, knows no
bounds."[80]

Schumann recognized both the positive and negative aspects of the
music of his day, but the truly radical quality of his criticism lies in its
willingness to acknowledge that even the latter offered a measure of
hope for the future. For example, we may consider his reactions to three
of the most prominent characteristics of the recent compositional scene:
the surfeit of light, even "trivial" music, the tendency toward fragmentation, and the demise of the classical forms.

The waltzes of Johann Strauss (Senior) might not attain the same
heights as a Bach fugue, but it is still important for a young composer
to know them, for, as Schumann maintained, Strauss may well be the
most representative figure of his time. Schumann further prized Strauss's
dances for their naturalness, their lack of affectation, their easy-going
grace and charm, qualities toward which compositions in the more serious genres should aim. In an 1837 review of Mendelssohn's Preludes
and Fugues for Piano, op. 35, he expressed this thought in extreme
terms: "the best fugue will always be the one that the public mistakes
for a Strauss waltz, in other words, where the artistic roots are concealed
like those of a flower, so that we only perceive the blossom."[81] And just
as fugues should strive for the elegance of waltzes, so too can the waltz

and other dances, when infused with wit and irony, serve as the basis for the poetic character piece. Schumann's own *Papillons* and *Intermezzi* readily come to mind.

Schumann's ambivalent attitude toward the present—as an imperfect but perfectible age—is most apparent in his writings on the musical miniature. Speaking through his Florestan persona in 1834, he chides the philistines for "turning up their noses" at aphorisms, musical and otherwise, since after all, "isn't life itself patched together from half-torn pages?" But in the same year he cautions the pianist and composer Joseph Kessler against "seeking refuge in the miniature." Interestingly enough, Schumann's skepticism regarding the musical fragment intensified over the course of the 1830s, precisely when he was composing some of the most enduring keyboard miniatures of all time. In 1839 he exhorts Henselt to turn away from the smaller forms and toward the "higher genres" such as the sonata and concerto, but then, in an 1842 critique of Ludwig Berger's songs, returns to his earlier position: "One should not undervalue such short pieces. A certain breadth of foundation and a commodious structure . . . may elicit praise for an endeavor. But there are tone-poets who can say in minutes what others need hours to express."[82] As we will see in the following chapter, the dichotomy in Schumann's thinking on the fragment is reflected in the dialectic between smaller and larger forms played out in his own compositions of the 1830s.

The sorry state of the "classical" forms during the same period provided another cause for Schumann's anxiety as critic. The "most brilliant period of the variation," he feared, was drawing to a close; younger composers treated the sonata as a variety of academic exercise, while older composers avoided the genre altogether; the concerto was in serious danger of becoming obsolete; and composers of symphonies were, for the most part, content to write pale imitations of Beethoven.[83] But there was a positive side to this tale of decline, for Schumann recognized that while the older forms were on the wane, newer ones were emerging to take their place: the variation was giving way to the more freely conceived capriccio; the sonata to the fantasy and ballade; the three-movement concerto to a composite, one-movement form; and the traditional symphony to more rhapsodic conceptions, such as Berlioz's *Symphonie fantastique*.[84] Moreover, the alternation of decay and rebirth was a perfectly natural process. The sonata, Schumann noted in 1839, "has practically run out its life course, but this is indeed in the order of things, for rather than repeat the same forms for centuries, we should be intent on creating new ones instead."[85] The positive light in which Schumann casts the negative moments embedded in the music of his day underscores the teleological thrust of his thinking. As he put it in an aphorism from the *Denk- und Dichtbüchlein* (1833/34), "criticism should rush ahead of the sinking present and at the same time fight it off from the vantage-point of the future."[86] The critic who wages this battle is also a historian, "a prophet facing backward" in Friedrich Schlegel's suggestive formulation.[87]

In addition to its deep engagement with history, Schumann's criticism is notable for a poetic quality quite unlike that in any earlier writings on music. But what may first strike us as florid excess is in fact a solution to an acute problem: that of forging a specifically romantic music criticism. Like the Jena Romantics, Schumann displayed an antipathy toward the normative approach to criticism as often practiced in the eighteenth century. According to the early nineteenth-century view, the critic was neither a judge nor a dispenser of rigid, formal laws, but rather a kind of poet. As Friedrich Schlegel maintained, "the true critic is an author to the second power."[88] Insofar as "poetry can only be criticized by way of poetry," the critic ensures the continued growth of the literary canon itself.[89] Through criticism the romantic dreamer, who turns out to be not so dreamy after all, finds a means of putting his or her reflections to productive use. According to Novalis's even more radical presentation of the same conceit, the critic provides not just a complement but an actual completion of the literary artwork.[90] Untiring in his efforts to make musical journalism into an intellectually respectable enterprise, Schumann shared in these views. But at the same time, he recognized the obvious discrepancy between musical and verbal discourse. The principal objects of his attention were not literary texts but musical works whose "criticism" by way of other musical works was possible only in a metaphoric sense. Hence his crusade against philistinism takes up the tone, style, and even the form of early romantic literary-philosophical criticism, but derives its content from the musical phenomena under consideration. The result is the inimitably "poetic" criticism with which Schumann made his mark as a writer on music.

Two features more than any others account for the poetic quality of Schumann's criticism: its attempt to evoke the spirit of the musical work that called it forth and its reliance on a fanciful perspectival technique. In his articulation of the critical ideal in an 1835 review of Hiller's Etudes, op. 15, Schumann wrote: "we recognize the highest criticism as that which leaves an impression similar to the one evoked by the motivating original." On this view, the critic neither replicates, describes, nor passes judgment on the artwork, but rather responds to it with a "poetic counterpart" *(poetische Gegenstück)*, that is, with another artwork in its own right.[91] In 1828, Schumann had done just this in the closing portion of the "Tonwelt" essay, a prose poem titled "Beethoven," its high-flown language intended to call up the feelings inspired by the composer's music: "All my desires and cravings were quelled—a deep stillness, a great waveless ocean! Formless spirit shadows in clear white garments like distant sails pressed toward their homeland."[92] In Schumann's writings of the 1830s, Eusebius is largely responsible for effusions of this sort, though Florestan too can rise to poetic heights. On one occasion, Raro even praises him for offering, instead of a judgment, an "image" *(Bild)*, a metaphoric account "through which understanding is more easily attained than through technical-artistic expressions that remain incomprehensible to the musically uneducated."[93] Serving a similar purpose is Florestan's recounting of a "scenario" for Beethoven's Seventh Symphony he had read in *Cäcilia*, where the work is said to recall the "merriest of peasant weddings."[94]

Yet the critic must be more than a crafter of images, since metaphors, suggestive though they may be, function as only one means toward understanding. To accommodate other approaches, Schumann developed a wide array of perspectival techniques. In the Introduction to the 1854 collected edition of his writings, he provides a succinct rationale for the strategy: "In order to express different points of view on artistic matters, it seemed appropriate to invent contrasting artist-characters, of whom *Florestan* and *Eusebius* were the most important, with Master *Raro* occupying a mediating position between them."[95] Therefore Florestan and Eusebius, who constitute the flipsides of the double nature that Schumann hoped to resolve through a character like Raro, function as spokesmen for the diverse voices competing for attention within the critic himself.

We can observe the technique at work in an 1834 review of Dorn's *Bouquet musical,* op. 10, a set of three character pieces for piano, each named after a flower: the narcissus, the violet, and the hyacinth. Eusebius begins by relating a conversation among the flowers on which he has eavesdropped, their speeches taking the form of Jean-Paulian polymeters: "What then did the hyacinth say?—She said 'My life was as beautiful as my end, because the most beautiful Lord loved and destroyed me.' But from the ashes sprang a flower that might console you."[96] Eusebius is endowed with the power to comprehend the secret language of the flowers; like the poet, he transmits the mysterious utterances of Nature in a form understandable to ordinary mortals. Yet his poetic language likewise makes a significant critical point. Since the "ashes" emerging from the flower are an emblem for the musical composition itself, he suggests that the artwork arises from a mysterious transformation of the natural object that inspired it. Then Florestan continues in a more prosaic vein, gently chiding Dorn for "placing such German flowers into French pots" (that is, giving his pieces French titles), and commenting, not without irony, on the implications of descriptive titles for the possible content of the pieces: "Perhaps the flower is as fragrant for the deaf as the tone is sonorous for the blind. The language translated here is so congenial and finely differentiated that there can be no thought of 'tone-painting.' "[97] In this way, Schumann illuminates the object of his critical attention from different but complementary angles. The ideal critic, he implies, must be both poet and pragmatist, dreamer and realist, Florestan and Eusebius.

Furthermore, if music critics are to arrive at informed conclusions about the artworks under consideration, they must possess a deep understanding of the workings of a composition and also of the relationships among compositions. "In music everything depends on the contextual position of the whole," Schumann asserted in an 1835 review of Joseph Kessler's works, "and this applies to [the relations between] the small and large scale, to the isolated artwork as much as to the artist's entire output."[98] In order to effect the shuttling back and forth from part to whole associated with the hermeneutic method, critics must also be analysts, even if they don't flaunt their skills for a reading public who may not have much knowledge of or interest in the nuts and bolts of musical composition (recall Raro's words of praise for Florestan's avoidance of "technical-artistic expressions").[99] While in the nineteenth century detailed analyses were mainly the province of learned theoretical tracts, such as Gottfried Weber's *Versuch einer geordneten Theorie der Tonsetzkunst* (1832), a work Schumann knew well,[100] Schumann's interest in the "contextual position" of parts within wholes implies that, for him, analysis too had a place in critical discourse. Indeed, in his review of Dorn's *Bouquet musical*, he follows Eusebius's poetic reading and Florestan's ironic rejoinder with an analytical account of the first piece in the set by "Rohr," who illustrates his comments on thematic relationships and unusual harmonies with musical examples.[101]

Even in his 1831 review of Chopin's Variations on "Là ci darem la mano," often viewed as the example par excellence of Schumann's emulation of Jean Paul's quirky prose style, music-analytical issues play a significant role. His "musico-aesthetic Opus 1 of 'epoch-making' importance"[102] aims in part to present Chopin as an individual who nonetheless belongs to a tradition embracing both Beethoven and Schubert. Hence intermingled with Florestan's account of the Variations as a wordless drama are observations touching on musical structure (the connection, or rather lack of connection, between the slow introduction and the rest of the work) and the affective logic of the overall tonal plan (which moves from B♭ major to the parallel minor for Variation 5 and back to major for the Finale).[103]

But nowhere in Schumann's writings does analysis play such an extensive part as in his review of Berlioz's *Symphonie fantastique*. Published over six installments of the 1835 volume of the *Neue Zeitschrift*,[104] the review, by far Schumann's longest, falls into two parts: a "psychological" reading signed "Florestan" and a close analysis signed "R. Schumann." The former is a quasi-programmatic interpretation of the symphony as a reflection of the artist's life and his stormy relationship with his beloved, the latter, a consideration of form, "compositional fabric," the "specific idea" represented in the work, and "spirit." As in the Dorn review, though on a larger scale, the various perspectives complement one another. To take one example, Schumann's critique of Berlioz's program in the analytical portion of the essay resonates with Florestan's opening comments. In his discussion of the "specific idea" embodied in the *Symphonie fantastique*, Schumann argues that, on the one hand, programs are detrimental to the unfettered exercise of the listener's imagination while, on the other, people tend to worry too much about the capacity of music to represent thoughts and events: what counts is the intrinsic merit of the music. The second portion of the review, in other words, might be read as a gloss on the first, which, interestingly enough, Schumann omitted from the collected edition of his writings.

While the structure of the review, its bipartition into subjective/psychological and objective/analytical sections, recalls the similar division in E. T. A. Hoffmann's well-known account of Beethoven's Fifth Symphony,[105] Schumann's approach in the analytical portion recalls the strategies of the Jena Romantics. Just as Friedrich Schlegel, in his seminal critique of Goethe's *Wilhelm Meisters Lehrjahre*, had argued that the rhapsodic design of the novel was tempered by an artfully crafted web of topical relationships, so too does Schumann aim to demonstrate that the "formlessness" of the first movement of Berlioz's work is only an "apparent formlessness." While Berlioz seems to depart radically from the "older model" for opening movements, he merely reversed the order of themes in the reprise to produce a symmetrical and perfectly satisfying arch form.[106] Similarly, in the portion of his analysis devoted to "compositional fabric" (harmony, melody, continuity, workmanship, style), Schumann counters Fétis's disparaging appraisal of Berlioz's melodic and harmonic manner with a penetrating commentary on the work's harmonic freshness, syntactic freedom, and the logic of its thematic invention.[107] Thus, Schumann puts his analysis at the service of a higher goal: an argument for the grounding of Berlioz's work in a system of thoughtfully conceived musical relationships.[108]

The review culminates with a striking passage on the "spirit" that rules over form, matter (or "fabric"), and idea in Berlioz's *Symphonie fantastique.* Here Schumann synthesizes the psychological and analytical approaches developed thusfar, bringing them both together under the banner of his philosophy of history. The determination of the presence or lack of spirit in a musical composition is clearly a subjective activity, but given his objective look at the inner workings of Berlioz's symphony, Schumann is confident in asserting that it is indeed imbued with this quality. The work certainly has its flaws (Schumann reserves his harshest judgment for what he views as lapses of taste in the finale's representation of the witches' sabbath), but these flaws may well be inextricably linked to an age "that tolerates a burlesque of the *Dies irae.*"[109] On Schumann's view, burlesque, parody, and irony are very much a part of the texture of the present; moreover, all of these categories have been given poetic expression in the writings of Heine, Byron, and Hugo. To deny them to contemporary poets and composers would be tantamount to setting ourselves against the times—a futile and foolish exercise. As an artist living in an imperfect but perfectible age, Berlioz should not be too harshly criticized for what he has failed to do but rather praised for what he promises to accomplish in the future, in the "new poetic age" toward which Schumann looked forward.[110]

As we will see, Schumann eventually came to view his journalistic undertakings as a noisome drain on his time and energy. Just under a decade after assuming full editorial control of the *Neue Zeitschrift,* he sold his share in the journal to Franz Brendel, ostensibly to pursue his compositional projects undistracted. But in the mid-1830s, Schumann's work as critic answered to a real need: it provided him with a means of mediating a long-standing inner struggle between his dual inclination toward music and poetry, thus serving as yet another manifestation of his attempt to approach all creative activity as a form of literature. Moreover, there is a fascinating give-and-take between Schumann the critic and Schumann the composer throughout the middle and later 1830s. Often his comments on the triumphs and failings of other artists amount to veiled critiques of his own compositional endeavors. And if much of Schumann's criticism reads like "poetry", so too can much of his music be interpreted as a kind of critique in sound, a point to which we will return in the following chapter.

~4~

*M*usical Love Letters
in the Higher and
Smaller Forms

Reflections of a Turbulent Life

Art and life are perhaps more closely interwoven in Schumann's music than in that of any other composer of the nineteenth century. Nowhere is this phenomenon better represented than in his piano music of the middle and later 1830s, much of it bound up with the young woman with whom he fell passionately and irrevocably in love during the latter half of 1835: Clara Wieck. As he put it to his old counterpoint teacher, Heinrich Dorn, in a letter of 5 September 1839: "Certainly much in my music embodies, and indeed can only be understood against the background of the battles that Clara cost me. She was practically the sole motivation for the *Concert* [*sans Orchestre*, op. 14], the Sonata [op. 11], the *Davidsbündlertänze, Kreisleriana*, and the *Novelletten*."[1] The *Kinderscenen*, op. 15, and *Fantasie*, op. 17, belong in the same list. So too does a little piece in A major composed in December 1838 while Schumann was unsuccessfully attempting to gain a professional footing in Vienna. A nocturne in A major eventually published as the lead item in *Bunte Blätter*, op. 99, it was dedicated wishfully "To my beloved bride."

But while Schumann subscribed to the notion that music might reflect life, he was equally concerned that it make sense on its own terms—as an autonomous musical entity. This conviction lay behind his often-repeated claim to have added fanciful titles or programmatic inscriptions to his works only *after* the musical text was complete. When he explained to Moscheles the derivation of *Carnaval*'s germinal motivic cells from the letters ASCH (the name of his then-sweetheart Ernestine von Fricken's hometown), he not only assured him that the titles of the cycle's constituent pieces were afterthoughts, but also queried: "Don't you think the music speaks for itself?"[2] Thus in Schumann's compositions art and life continually engage in a kind of chemical process of transformation. "Biographical" subjects, ranging from place names to human beings, are converted into "aesthetic" subjects, musical materials, and then back again into more tangible, poetic designations.

From the spring of 1833 through the end of 1839 Schumann entrusted his confessional musings almost exclusively to music for the piano, producing in this six-year period many of the compositions for which he is best remembered today. As indicated in Table 4.1, an overview of Schumann's works from the second half of the decade, periods of relative inactivity give way to others characterized by intense productivity, their alternation often conditioned by external events. The dearth of compositional activity between the provisional completion of the Sonata in G Minor, op. 22, and the *Concert sans Orchestre,* in October 1835 and June 1836 respectively, can be coordinated with two factors: non-stop editorial work for the *Neue Zeitschrift* and emotional upheavals occasioned by the enforced separation of Robert and Clara just weeks after they declared their mutual love in December 1835. Conversely, the renewal of the lovers' bond in August 1837 no doubt sparked a productive phase extending into the early fall of 1838, when Schumann began in earnest to prepare for his trip to Vienna.

Several peculiarities of Schumann's approach to composition during the second half of the 1830s are worthy of our attention. In the first place, the creative process often involved a remarkably quick commitment of ideas to paper: Schumann claimed to have drafted the *Kreisleriana,* for instance, in no more than four days.[3] But as often as not, the initial white heat of inspiration gave way to a protracted reflective stage marked by revisions great and small, polishing, and much experimentation with the order of individual movements or the sections within them.[4] As we shall see, this interplay of inspiration and reflection makes for a complicated compositional history in works such as the *Fantasie,* op. 17. Second, a number of the compositions from this period were either conceived of or drafted in pairs—*Carnaval* and the *Etudes Symphoniques* in the winter of 1835; the *Fantasiestücke* and *Davidsbündler-*

Table 4.1. Schumann's Compositions from 1835 to April 1839

1835

January	*Winter:* fair copies of *Carnaval,* op. 9, and *Etudes Symphoniques,* op. 13 (begun December 1834)
February	
March	
April	
May	
June	
July	
August	Sonata, op. 11 (begun 1833)
September	
October	Sonata, op. 22 (provisionally completed; begun 1833) (?begins work on *Concert sans Orchestre,* op. 14)
November	
December	

1836

January	
February	
March	
April	
May	
June	*Concert sans Orchestre,* op. 14, completed completes one-movement *Fantaise/Ruines* (= first movement of *Fantasie,* op. 17)
July	
August	
September	idea for a "contribution to Beethoven" (work on second and third movements of *Fantasie,* op. 17) etudes (lost)
October	
November	
December	*Sonate für Beethoven* [*Fantasie,* op. 17] provisionally completed [Fourth] Sonata in F Minor, first movement (lost)

1837

January	[Fourth] Sonata in F Minor, last movement (lost)—entire sonata completed in some form by October 1837
February	
March	Sonata, op. 22 (work on end of first movement or last movement)
April	
May	
June	

Table 4.1. *(Continued)*

July	*Fantasiestücke,* op. 12
August	*Davidsbündlertänze,* op. 6 (completed September)
September	
October	
November	
December	
	(sometime during 1837, possibly October: scherzos and small piano pieces, polonaises among them [lost])

1838

January	*Novelletten,* op. 21 (January; February; March; April–provisionally completed)
	polishes *Fantasiestücke* and *Davidsbündlertänze*
	waltzes (lost)
	Etude in F# Minor (lost)
February	*Kinderscenen,* op. 15 (completed March)
March	*Dichtungen/Phantasien [Fantasie],* op. 17 *(Stichvorlage)*
April	*Kreisleriana,* op. 16 (provisionally completed May)
May	
June	
July	*Kreisleriana* (corrections)
August	*Novelletten* ("put in order")
September	*Kreisleriana* (completed)
October	
November	
December	Sonata, op. 22, new finale
	Scherzo, Gigue, Romanze und Fughette, op. 32, movements 1–3 (last movement completed September 1839)
	An C[lara] (later published as op. 99, no. 1)

1839

January	*Allegro* in C Minor (lost; begun December 1838)
	Guirlande (lost)
	Konzertsatz in D Minor, piano and orchestra
	Arabeske, op. 18 (begun before October 1838)
	Blumenstück, op. 19
February	
March	*by mid-March:*
	Humoreske, op. 20
	Faschingsschwank aus Wien, op. 25 (?sketch of entire work; completion of first movement; last movement completed summer 1839; entire work completed by May/June 1840)
April	*Nachtstücke,* op. 23 (begun March; polished, January 1840)

tänze in the summer of 1837; the *Novelletten* and *Kinderscenen* in the first four months of 1838; the *Humoreske* and *Faschingsschwank aus Wien* in early 1839—one member of each group tended toward greater breadth or seriousness either as a whole *(Etudes Symphoniques, Novelletten, Humoreske)* or in its parts *(Fantasiestücke).*

Another duality distinguishes Schumann's output between about 1835 and 1839: an initial focus on what he called the "higher" or "noble" forms, such as the sonata or fantasy,[5] was followed by a period devoted to the concantenation of "smaller" forms into poetic cycles of character pieces. Again, musical tendencies may be linked with biographical causes. Schumann's turn to the cycle of miniatures in the summer of 1837 with the *Fantasiestücke* and *Davidsbündlertänze* runs roughly parallel with the formalization of his engagement to Clara. The shift away from the higher forms was motivated by eminently practical considerations as well. His thoughts increasingly occupied with the financial obligations that married life would entail, Schumann hoped to earn larger profits from his compositions than had hitherto been the case, and knew that there was more of a market for attractive miniatures than for imposing sonatas and fantasies.

At the same time, Schumann in no way thought of the two genres (or familes of genres) as mutually exclusive. On the one hand, his essays in the higher forms frequently bear traces of the miniature; in the opening movement of the *Fantasie,* for instance, a self-contained character piece designated *Im Legendenton* intrudes upon an unusual, but still recognizable sonata-allegro design. On the other hand, some of the "miniatures" from the later 1830s aren't so miniature after all; a number of the *Novelletten,* to cite an example, attain to a length and breadth that belies the title's promise of "diminutive novellas." Higher and smaller forms thus stand in a dialectical relationship, interpenetrating to such a degree that one type is unthinkable without the other.

Schumann's own attitude toward the relative value of his efforts in the higher forms underwent a notable reversal within a short span of time. Writing on 8 February 1838 to his Belgian admirer Simonin de Sire, he predicted that this enthusiastic supporter of his music would find more "artistic merit" in the F♯-minor Sonata, the *Concert sans Orchestre,* and the *Fantasiestücke* than in the "short pieces" he already knew.[6] But by a little over a year later, Schumann's preference had tipped in the direction of his cycles of miniatures. Writing again to de Sire on 15 March 1839, he singled out *Kreisleriana* as the favorite among his recently published works.[7] In a revealing letter of 5 May 1843 to Karl Kossmaly, an associate from the Davidsbündler days who would soon publish a lengthy critique of Schumann's keyboard compositions, he cast a sharply critical eye on his earlier works, which he had come to view as the flawed products of youthful excess:

> With some hesitation I enclose a packet of my older compositions. You will easily see to what degree they are immature and lacking in finish. They are for the most part reflections of my turbulent earlier life when man and musician always strove to express themselves simultaneously; such is the case even now that I have learned to master myself and my art better. Your sympathetic heart will discover how many joys and sorrows lie buried together in these little bundles of notes.[8]

Thus Schumann implies that works such as *Papillons* and *Carnaval* count more as biographical documents, "reflections" of his "turbulent earlier life," than as art. But he is reluctant to write them off, for "even these earlier compositions will provide you with a portrait of my character, my striving; to be sure, many seeds of the future often lie in fledgling attempts. Therefore kindly accept them with all their weaknesses."[9] Interestingly enough, the four compositions from the 1830s that Schumann considered his best (and which, he apologizes, he could not lay his hands on to send along with his letter) are all constituted of "smaller" forms: *Kreisleriana, Fantasiestücke, Novelletten,* and *Romanzen* (op. 28). In part, Schumann's self-deprecating attitude toward many of the works for which he is best known today can be explained as a common-enough phenomenon among creative geniuses: their enthrallment by whatever project happens to be underway. When Schumann wrote to Kossmaly in 1843, he was close to finishing a draft of his oratorio *Das Paradies und die Peri,* next to which the likes of *Papillons* must have seemed insignificant indeed.[10] His list of aesthetically worthy keyboard cycles reveals much nonetheless, for in these works (the *Romanzen* perhaps excepted) Schumann makes noteworthy strides toward resolving the dialectic between higher and smaller forms that runs throughout his compositions of the second half of the 1830s with the persistence of a leitmotif.

If Schumann wavered in evaluating his earlier essays in the higher and smaller forms, there is one point on which he had no doubts: this music was difficult to understand. Writing to Clara on 15 April 1838, he attributed the difficulty to his music's "attachment to farflung interests" such as politics, literature, and people, to "everything" in fact "that goes on in the world."[11] Similarly, in his May 1843 letter to Kossmaly, Schumann explained that he was not better known as a composer because of the "difficulties in form and content" posed by his works.[12] Although his critics generally agreed with these assessments, they hardly approved. Again and again in the early literature on Schumann we stumble across adjectives such as "bizarre," "excessive," "eccentric," "capricious," and "arbitrary," all of them intended to describe what was perceived as a refractory, at times incomprehensible, musical language. Even sympathetic critics viewed this repertory with circumspection. Liszt was reluctant to program the *Fantasie,* a work dedicated to him, or *Kreisleriana* because "they are too difficult for the public to digest." [13] (Even Clara dropped the *Fantasie* from her repertoire after performing it once in public in 1867). Moscheles, author of an essentially positive review of the F♯-minor Sonata, wrote to his wife that the composition was "somewhat confused, but interesting." [14] These charges may strike us as parochial at best and downright muddle-headed at worst. But if nothing else, they serve to remind us that under the apparently well-behaved surface of much of Schumann's music lies an undeniably radical quality.

This radicality was not lost on Schumann's publishers, who despaired of its adverse effect on sales. When in 1848 Härtel rejected the *Album für die Jugend* for publication (a serious miscalculation: the *Album* became one of Schumann's bestsellers), he added by way of explanation: "the market for your compositions is, by and large, rather limited—more limited than you could believe. . . . [W]e have lost through the publication of your works a significant sum and there is at this point little prospect of recovering it." [15] Clara, at once a loyal supporter and a plain-spoken critic, implored Schumann on 4 April 1839 to write a composition geared to make an immediate effect on her audiences: "Listen Robert, couldn't you just once compose something brilliant, easily understandable, and without inscriptions—a completely coherent piece, not too long and not too short? I'd so much like to have something of yours to play that's specifically intended for the public. Obviously a genius will find this degrading, but politics demand it every now and again." [16] In fact, Schumann was already working along these lines in several compositions with which Clara was not yet familiar. Several of the works either completed or drafted during the winter of 1839 in Vienna, the *Arabeske, Blumenstück,* and *Faschingsschwank aus Wien* among them, evince a markedly less idiosyncratic style than the one he had cultivated up to that point.

Conscious that the formal and material difficulties of his music were impediments not only to comprehension but also to marketability, Schumann eventually began toying with the idea of reissuing his earlier works in versions more accessible to the music-loving public. In a letter of 5 November 1842 to the publisher Friedrich Hofmeister, he suggested replacing or amplifying the "mysterious" title of the *Davidsbündlertänze* with "Zwölf [sic] Charakterstücke" ("Twelve Character Pieces") as a means of making the work more appealing to the "dilettante circles" for which it was intended.[17] Indeed, by the early 1840s, Schumann was increasingly anxious to find a wider audience for music—his own—that he was unable to promote as a performer, that journalistic ethics forbade him from reviewing in his journal, and that was largely ignored by the musical press.[18] Then between 1850 and 1853 he reissued several of his earlier keyboard compositions, Opp. 5, 6, 13, 14, and 16, in versions specifically aimed at that wider audience. Some of Schumann's revisions appear, on first glance, to be purely cosmetic: the *Concert sans Orchestre*, for instance, was rechristened *Grande Sonate;* the *Etudes Symphoniques* became *Etudes en Forme de Variations.* Likewise the *Davidsbündlertänze*, in accordance with Schumann's suggestion to Hofmeister, became *Davidsbündler: Achtzehn Charakterstücke,* losing in the process its poetic motto ("In each and every age / Joy and sorrow are bound together: / So remain pious in your joy / And be ready to face sorrow with courage") and the ascription of the various pieces to "Florestan," "Eusebius," or both. Schumann added a number of repeats in the same cycle, presumably to facilitate the listener's comprehension of the rapid affective shifts within and between the pieces. Many of the changes in the other works were more substantive: entire movements, often the most rhapsodic or unusual, were excised from the *Impromptus* and the *Etudes Symphoniques* (conversely, when the *Concert sans Orchestre* became a *Grande Sonate* it gained a movement); the fifth piece from *Kreisleriana,* tonally open-ended in the first version, ends firmly on a tonic chord in the second.

The multiple editions of Schumann's earlier keyboard music raise a host of text-critical and aesthetic issues, none of them easily resolved. According to one especially provocative interpretation, the existence of differing but equally viable versions of the same composition may indicate that Schumann himself did not intend a single, definitive text for the works in question.[19] But however we decide to view the mutability of the Schumannian text, one thing is certain: whether great or slight, Schumann's alterations result in a considerably less fanciful, less "poetic" product than the original version. In an aphoristic dialogue from Raro's, Florestan's, and Eusebius's *Denk- und Dichtbüchlein,* Eusebius maintains: "Often two different readings of the same work can be of equal worth," to which Raro replies: "The original one is usually better."[20] I am inclined to think that Raro's pithy rejoinder holds in the case of Schumann's revised keyboard works. By the mid-1840s, and certainly by the early 1850s, he had simply lost interest in his earlier compositional efforts. Schumann was no less a musical poet (or a poetic musician) in the 1840s and 1850s; he was simply interested in exploring other means of imbuing music with a poetic dimension.

The differences between the various versions of Schumann's works resonate with a dialectic already in evidence at the height of the composer's "keyboard" period in the later 1830s. The tension between esotericism and accessibility which arises from a comparison of the earlier and later forms of the same piece is detectable in the gap between the technically and musically demanding *Novelletten* and the intentionally naïve *Kinderscenen*, for example. In some instances, the tension between high art and artlessness is embodied in one and the same composition. This dialectic in turn complements the others that we have considered thus far: art versus lived experience and "higher" versus "smaller" forms. Together these dualities constitute the principal themes of Schumann's creative life; and though they first come into focus in the latter half of the 1830s, they will continue to serve as the basis for many variations in the years to come. Moreover, all of them are regulated by Schumann's desire to imbue his musical works with the character of literary texts. We sense this above all in the witty play of motives in *Carnaval*, the digressive structure of the C-major *Fantasie*, the embedded or fragmented forms in the *Novelletten* and *Kreisleriana*, and the confluence of all these tendencies in the *Humoreske*. None of the keyboard works of the 1830s tells a story or elaborates a program, but the repertory as a whole constitutes a kind of literature.

These observations behind us, we may pick up the thread of Schumann's life where we left it in Chapter 3, with his proclamation of a "fresh, poetic future" in the early part of 1835.

1835: A Year of Important Consequences

Schumann completed two significant compositions in the winter months of 1835: *Carnaval*, op. 9; and the *Etudes Symphoniques*, op. 13. As we have seen, he began both works at roughly the same time, probably in December of the year before, and both were bound up with Ernestine von Fricken, one of two "glorious women" (the other was Emilie List, daughter of a diplomat, and eventually a great friend of Clara's) who entered Schumann's circle in the spring of 1834. Writing to his mother on 2 July of that year, he described Ernestine as "a splendidly pure, child-like spirit, tender and thoughtful, with the most heartfelt love for me and all things related to art—in short, all I could wish for in a wife."[21] Indeed, there was soon talk of marriage. But although this turn of events helped to firm Schumann's recovery from the neurotic episode he had experienced in the fall and winter of 1833, his idyll with Ernestine proved to be short-lived. In August of 1835, he learned of her illegitimate birth, an "unfortunate family matter" (as he eupemistically called it in a letter to Clara dated 11 February 1838) of which he had been previously unaware. His bourgeois sensibilities offended, and fearful that Ernestine's inability to earn much might force him to make his living "like a day-laborer," Schumann took steps to "loosen" their bond in the late summer and autumn of 1835. He put it a little coldly to Clara: "I talked over the matter with my mother, and we agreed that it would only lead to new worries on top of those already existing."[22]

While busily composing in the winter of 1834 and 1835, however, Schumann had only the warmest of feelings for the "tender and thoughtful" Ernestine. No doubt the upturn in his personal life spurred his creative energies after a nearly year-long period of only spotty compositional activity. *Carnaval* (its title, by Schumann's own account, a reflection of the work's completion around carnival season) beautifully demonstrates the process whereby a biographical subject is transformed into an aesthetic counterpart. As Schumann explained in a letter to Moscheles of 22 September 1837, most of the composition's twenty-one movements are based on the pitch equivalents of the letters "ASCH," the name of the village from which his "musical girlfriend" hailed, and also the only "musical" letters in Schumann's own name.[23] The letters yield three configurations of pitches, or "Sphinxes," as Schumann calls them, each laid out in long notes between the eighth and ninth pieces, *Replique* and *Papillons,* of the finished set: (1) S C H A = E♭ (the German pitch equivalent of S) C B (the German pitch equivalent of H) A; (2) As C H = A♭ C B; and (3) A S C H = A E♭ C B. Interestingly enough, the first Sphinx, derived from a reshuffling of the letters into the order in which they occur in Schumann's name, is not employed as generative material for any of the pieces in *Carnaval.* Schumann thus casts himself as an unseen presence, a master puppeteer regulating the motions of his creations from behind the scenes.

In a brief review of *Carnaval* that appeared in the *Hamburger musikalische Zeitung* on 11 October 1837, the anonymous critic described the work as "neither more nor less than a kind of potpourri," adding that while "it's certainly better than the usual sort, it can in no way lay claim to being called an artwork."[24] In a sense, the reviewer was right. Writing in 1840, Schumann himself characterized his cycle as a kind of musical "game" common enough since Bach's time.[25] This sportive quality was further emphasized in the work's original title, later dropped at Härtel's request: "Fasching:Schwänke auf vier Noten für Pianoforte von Florestan" (Carnival Pranks on Four Notes, for Piano, by Florestan). As indicated by the titles of its individual pieces, *Carnaval* is populated by a motley cast of characters who run the gamut from Schumann's Davidsbund (some of them "disguised" as *commedia dell'arte* figures such as *Arlequin,* or *Pantalone et Columbine*), to Clara and Ernestine (represented as *Chiarina* and *Estrella* respectively), to Chopin and Paganini. A fancy-dress ball provides them with an arena for their various pranks, the connection with the Jean-Paulian world of the masquerade confirmed by the quotation of the opening waltz from *Papillons* in the sixth piece, *Florestan.* The characters inhabit the realm of the fragment, a madcap world where nothing lasts for very long, and where every event is soon interrupted by another. (Some pieces, such as *Florestan, Coquette,* and *Replique,* in fact form mini-cycles of fragments within the larger set.) Conceived as a series of shocks, *Carnaval* teeters on the brink between playfulness and fright. Schumann himself recognized the dizzying effect that his composition would induce in its listeners: "the musical moods [in *Carnaval*] alternate too quickly for an audience to follow along without being startled at every moment."[26]

But at the same time, this "artless" world of carnival jests, strange disguises, and whirling fragments is held in check by an underlying "artful" construction, by two constructive modes, in fact, one providing for overt, the other for covert unity. The former involves the tonal organization of the cycle around A♭ and closely related keys (E♭, C minor, B♭), most of them implicit in the Sphinxes, and also the use of thematic recall: the concluding *Marche,* actually a waltz in which the masked Davidsbündler effectively rout the Philistines, represented musically by the *Grossvatertanz,* draws on the introductory *Préambule,* a boisterous variant of its coda neatly rounding off the whole work.[27] But Schumann ensures coherence through less palpable means as well. Responding to the charge that he was little understood, he explained to Clara that the "crowds" were more interested in "grace and charm" than in the "wittier" conceits featured in his music.[28] By *Witz* (wit), Schumann meant not only a talent for coining "witty" turns of phrase, but also the ability to perceive remote similarities between apparently unrelated terms and to construct a field in which they are allowed free play. A cornerstone of the aesthetics of Jean Paul and of the Jena Romantics as well,[29] the lightning flash of *Witz* is that element which can transform a series of disconnected fragments into a constellation of mysteriously related terms. Hence for the Romantics, *Witz* was considerably more than a function of sociable conversation. Indeed, they consciously sought to displace it from the salon and put it to work elsewhere: in works of art. This is precisely what Schumann does in *Carnaval,* where the Sphinxes serve as agents of a specifically musical *Witz.* Although Sphinxes 3 and

2 dominate the first and second halves of *Carnaval* respectively, there is hardly a single piece in which the generating Sphinx is coterminous with a motive, let alone a theme. Often a Sphinx will head off an opening idea, but its frequent compression into a tiny space makes it barely recognizable, as in *Papillons* and *A.S.C.H.—S.C.H.A. (Lettres Dansantes)*. In other instances the Sphinx is hidden in the bass or the middle of a phrase *(Pierrot)*, or it may be embedded in an ornamental melodic line *(Eusebius)*. In a word, the Sphinxes are everywhere and nowhere; they are the sources of the subcutaneous, "witty" connections that raise *Carnaval* above the level of run-of-the-mill salon pieces and that also transform a slice of life into a work of art.

The generating source for the simultaneously conceived *Etudes Symphoniques* was not a fanciful series of Sphinxes, but rather a more conventional melody articulated in two eight-bar phrases. According to Schumann himself, the tune stemmed from Ernestine's father, the Baron von Fricken, an amateur flutist who occasionally tried his hand at composition.[30] Originally titled "Etüden im Orchestercharakter . . . von Florestan und Eusebius," the *Etudes Symphoniques* unfold as a series of variations. (The proximity of variation and etude forms is implicit in Schumann's view that "in a broad sense, every piece of music is an etude"; in a narrower sense, however, an etude must have a determinate purpose: "it must develop technique or lead to the mastery of some particular difficulty.")[31] But while the C♯-minor theme is hardly out of the ordinary, the eleven variations upon it and their overall arrangement certainly are.

For Schumann, the variation form should comprise more than a chain of discrete entities, of fragments, that is; it should "organize itself into a whole whose focal point is the theme."[32] At first, an overall design for the work was probably intended to emerge from an alternation of Florestinian and Eusebian variations. However, the dreamier side of Schumann's personality is not much of a presence in the first published version of the *Etudes;* all but the first of the five variations that failed to make their way into the first edition betray Eusebius's workmanship.[33] In the first edition of the *Etudes Symphoniques,* Schumann fashions the whole as a symmetrical structure, its endpoints provided by the theme and an extended finale, and at dead center (Etude VI), a Florestinian variation in which a decorated version of the theme is restored to the treble register. Flanking the centerpiece are variations in a rich variety of styles. The migration of the theme into the bass in Etude II recalls Schumann's practice in the *Impromptus,* as do the contrapuntal textures in Etude IV, a march; Etude VIII, an evocation of the eighteenth-century French overture; and the Eusebian Etude XI. Perhaps most interesting

of all, however, are those variations in which Schumann departs significantly from the harmonic and melodic structure of the theme. These
"fantasy variations," as Brahms called them,[34] are four in number—
Etudes III (a study in contrasting *legato* and *staccato* articulations), V (a
delicate scherzo), VII (a propulsive character piece), and IX (another
scherzo, this time with shades of Paganini's *Campanella*)—and all of
them are arranged symetrically around the pivotal Etude VI. It is probably no accident that the pieces omitted from the second edition (1852)
of the *Etudes* were both fantasy variations: Etudes III and IX.

We know relatively little of Schumann's activities just after the completion of *Carnaval* and the *Etudes Symphoniques,* or of his activities
throughout much of the year 1835 for that matter. Bogged down by his
editorial responsibilities for the *Neue Zeitschrift,* he was not keeping a
diary, nor would he do so again until late July 1836. The lack of a daily
record of his comings and goings is doubly unfortunate, for in his summary account of the highpoints of his life for the period between March
1833 and October 1837 (written in Vienna on 28 November 1838), he
headed off the section devoted to the year 1835 with the comment:
"even more important in its consequences [than 1834]."[35] Among these
consequences was a broadening of his range of friends and acquaintances. On 27 September, he had the opportunity to meet, if only briefly,
with the virtuoso pianist and composer whom he had lionized in print
just a few years before and who was now passing through Leipzig on
his way to Karlsbad: Fryderyk Chopin. A more decisive meeting took
place a week later. On 4 October, the newly appointed director of the
Gewandhaus Orchestra, Felix Mendelssohn, made his official debut with
that group in a performance of his *Meeresstille und glückliche Fahrt*
Overture (op. 27) and Beethoven's Fourth Symphony. Henriette Voigt,
doyenne of Leipzig's musical elite and a confidante of Schumann's, introduced the two artists, and before long a close bond developed between
them. Founded on mutual respect, an abiding love for the German musical
tradition extending from Bach to Beethoven, a fascination with the writings of Jean Paul, and a shared passion for chess and billiards as well, their
friendship would last until Mendelssohn's untimely death in 1847.[36]

But the most significant of the consequences that Schumann must
have had in mind when he drafted the Vienna précis was the awakening
of his love for Clara Wieck. In the spring of 1835 and well before the
cooling of his relationship with Ernestine in the fall of the same year,
he had begun to take greater notice of Clara, who, at fifteen, was obviously no longer the little girl he had first met in 1828, but a blossoming
adolescent. When Schumann turned twenty-five on 8 June, Clara presented him with a watch chain, a suggestive token of the affection that

would soon develop into quite a bit more. Indeed, by November they had exchanged their "first kiss" on the steps outside Wieck's home, and a month later proclaimed their mutual love (Schumann writes "Vereinigung mit Clara" [Alliance with Clara] in the Vienna précis) in Zwickau where Clara, then on tour, found Robert waiting for her. If Schumann had had any lingering doubts about his relationship with Ernestine, none now remained: a complete break was in the offing. After returning to Leipzig, he and Clara continued to meet secretly at Wieck's home, but their "beautiful evening hours in [each other's] arms" soon came to an end. Having caught wind of these nocturnal trysts during the Christmas holidays, Wieck soon called them to an abrupt halt.[37]

In short, Schumann's personal life was in shambles, his world turned topsy-turvy: within the space of about a month he had acknowledged, and revelled in, his love for Clara, definitively severed his tie with Ernestine, incurred the wrath of his old teacher Wieck (a perfectly justifiable wrath from a father's point of view, given the near decade separating Schumann's age from Clara's), and now faced an indefinite period of separation from his beloved.

Just as the circumstances surrounding his infatuation with Ernestine had provided the biographical motivation for *Carnaval* (and to a lesser degree, the *Etudes Symphoniques*), so too was Clara implicated in the Piano Sonata in F♯ Minor, op. 11, the first of Schumann's major essays in the higher genres to achieve finished form. Completed by August 1835, the sonata had occupied Schumann intermittently since 1833; its roots go back farther still: the first movement draws liberally on the Fandango of 1832, and the second movement on his setting of the Kerner text "Nicht im Thale" *(An Anna)* dating from the summer of 1828.[38] The full title of the finished product eloquently reveals the depth of the work's association with Schumann's newly found love: *Pianoforte-Sonata. Clara zugeeignet von Florestan und Eusebius* ("Piano Sonata, Dedicated to Clara by Florestan and Eusebius"). And in a sense, the composition serves as the aesthetic analogue to the flirtatious exchanges in which Robert and Clara must have indulged during the summer of 1835. The Allegro vivace of its first movement develops a rocking, drum-like motive that Schumann culled from Clara's "Scène fantastique: Le Ballet des revenants" (op. 5, no. 4); no doubt he was thinking of this figure when he told Clara that his sonata "was a cry from my heart to yours in which your theme appears in every possible form."[39] At the same time, Clara had prefaced this cry with one of her own, for the middle section of her "Scène fantastique" alludes to the dactylic rhythm of Schumann's Fandango. (The relevant passage are reproduced for comparison in Examples 4.1a–c). Hence the "alliance" that the lovers

Example 4.1a. Sonata in F♯ Minor, op. 11: first movement, mm. 53–58.

Example 4.1b. Clara Wieck, *Scène Fantastique: Le Ballet des Revenants:* mm. 1–3.

Example 4.1c. Le Ballet des Revenants: mm. 44–48.

would proclaim in December 1835 was already beautifully etched in tones some months before.

As indicated in Schumann's dedication, the F♯-minor Sonata was the product of his alter egos, Florestan and Eusebius. And just as in the *Etudes Symphoniques*, the Florestinian side of his creativity has the upper hand, its presence clearly felt in the first movement's brooding *Introduzione*, its propulsive fandango rhythm, the oddly accented Scherzo, and the metrically unstable Finale. The dare-devil virtuosity of the last movement's coda serves as a reminder that Florestan was closely associated with Paganini as one of the main characters in Schumann's projected novel, *Die Wunderkinder*. Eusebius too makes notable contributions, above all in the reflective closing passages and transitions of the first movement and Finale, and of course in the second movement, designated Aria. Nor are the two personae merely juxtaposed. Already we find Schumann searching for a means of synthesizing the disparate aspects of his creative self into a cohesive whole, largely through the strategy of motivic recall and transformation. A phrase from Florestan's *Introduzione* (mm. 22–24), for instance, prefigures the opening idea of the Eusebian Aria. Conversely, the Aria includes a number of asides (lacking in the lied on which the movement draws) in the bass register that point back to the drummed motive from the Florestinian first movement. Moreover, Florestan and Eusebius make their debuts as composers in the higher forms with a work of impressive dimensions. Its imposing profile is a function of Schumann's attempt to overstep the generic boundaries of the sonata: the Aria points to opera, as does a lengthy recitative-like passage in the Scherzo; a portion of the latter marked "quasi Oboe" suggests the symphony, while the virtuoso coda of the Finale would not be out of place in a concerto.

The Sonata in G Minor, provisionally completed just two months after the F♯-minor Sonata in October 1835, is altogether smaller in scope. But like its outwardly more demanding counterpart, it has a long and involved compositional history. Begun in mid-1833, its slow movement derives from the song *Im Herbste* of 1828. While the opening movement was drafted in June 1833, Schumann was still tinkering with it as late as March 1838. Then in December of the same year he replaced the original finale (Presto: Passionato) with an entirely new one (Rondo: Presto). At long last, the work was published as Sonata No. II, op. 22 in September 1839, more than six years after it was first conceived.[40] Also redolent of the F♯-minor Sonata is the prominence of Florestan's voice in the somewhat later work. Often cited as one of Schumann's most classically structured efforts, the opening movement of the G-minor Sonata overflows with Florestinian pathos. Designated *So rasch wie möglich*

(As rapid as possible), it features an impassioned main theme supported by driving sixteenths and transitional passages shot through with cross accents and menacing chromaticism. Even the more lyric second idea discloses an underlying agitation resulting from persistent syncopations.[41]

While the G-minor Sonata is less obviously linked with Clara than the Sonata in F♯ Minor, the work in its final form owes much to her counsel. In a letter to Schumann of 3 March 1838, she remarked: "I love [the sonata] just as I love you; it expresses your whole being with such clarity, and at the same time it's not too incomprehensible." Then she asks him to simplify the "far too difficult" last movement, for "[even though] I already understand it and will play it if need be, other people, the public, even professional musicians—those for whom one composes—won't understand it at all."[42] Probably it was the rhythmic aspect that Clara viewed as the principal barrier to the movement's acceptance by listeners and performers alike. Indeed, the original, Passionato finale is a veritable encyclopedia of duple- versus triple-time effects, further complicated in some cases by syncopation. In complying with Clara's request, Schumann took extreme measures; as we have noted, he suppressed the original finale entirely, replacing it with a somewhat tamer Rondo. But in the process, a crucial element was lost. According to one writer, interpreters of Schumann's sonata movements often feel as if they were "climbing into a Formula One racecar and risking life and limb."[43] Breathlessness born of panic, a key feature of Schumann's sonata style, is what we miss in the new finale of the G-minor Piano Sonata.

Sad Times

It is little wonder that Schumann referred to 1836 as a "sad year" in the Vienna précis.[44] Furious at discovering what had been secretly transpiring right under his nose, Wieck packed Clara off to Dresden on 14 January. Undeterred even by the death of his mother on 4 February, Schumann set off for the Saxon capital, taking advantage of Wieck's absence to meet secretly with Clara during the following week. At the time he was still hopeful that Wieck could be persuaded to take a more sympathetic stance. As he wrote to Clara while en route to Zwickau on 13 February: "Perhaps your father will not refuse when I ask for his blessing. Obviously there is much to mull over and put in order. In the meantime, I'll trust in our guardian angel. We are fated for one another: this I knew for a long time, but I was not bold enough to tell you earlier."[45] As fate would have it, Schumann's hopes proved ill-founded;

in a letter to August Kahlert dated 1 March, he reported dejectedly that "[Wieck] is carrying on like a madman and forbids Clara and me to have contact under pain of death."[46] Schumann can hardly have imagined at the time that his enforced separation from Clara would extend until August of 1837.

Forbidden even to correspond (no doubt at Wieck's insistence, Clara eventually sent back all of Schumann's earlier letters and asked for hers in return), the lovers maintained the barest of contact through the reports of third parties or through fleeting glances exchanged at public concerts. After one such encounter, a Gewandhaus concert on 9 October 1836, Schumann marched directly to Poppe's to drown his sorrows in drink. A month-long period of heavy alcohol consumption culminated in a regular "champagne orgy" on 2 November.[47] Sorrow soon gave way to utter despair. In a letter to Clara of 2 January 1838, Schumann described the winter months of 1836 and 1837 as "the darkest of times, for I knew nothing of you and tried to force myself to forget you." During this phase, he sought consolation in sexual encounters, or as he put it more delicately to Clara: "I hurled myself to the ground and cried out—then I tried for a cure by compelling myself to fall in love with a woman who had already partially ensnared me."[48] The identity of this woman remains a mystery. Christel/Charitas reenters Schumann's diary on 8 October 1836, and we can assume that she and the composer met at least once more during this period. An entry in the Vienna précis for 1836—"Sought out Charitas and suffered the consequences in 1837"— has fueled speculation that Schumann may have contracted a venereal disease as a result of these encounters.[49] Still, it is unlikely that he would have felt threatened, "ensnared" by a young woman to whom he had turned for sexual gratification since resettling in Leipzig late in 1830. By mid-October 1836 Schumann had taken another mistress, identified in his diary under the code name "La Faneuse," literally, "a woman with whom one makes hay."[50] Perhaps it was through this relationship that Schumann made a desperate attempt to efface his memory of Clara.

In spite of his general dejection and the profligacy of his life-style, Schumann cultivated a number of fruitful artistic ties during the second half 1836. By the end of the summer, he was spending much time in the company of Ferdinand David, concertmaster of the Gewandhaus Orchestra and leader of a string quartet; the group's renditions of Beethoven's late quartets, often carried out at Schumann's new lodgings in the Rote Collegium on Ritterstrasse (since July 1835 he had lived at Hallesche Gasse 462), inspired him to try his hand at a piano quintet and piano trio, plans that apparently did not get very far.[51] Then on 9 September, Schumann had an unforgettable day with Chopin, who was passing through Leipzig and had brought along with him "heavenly new etudes, nocturnes, mazurkas, a new ballade [two ballades, in fact] . . . [he] played them all incomparably."[52] Schumann described the event in greater detail to Dorn in a letter that furthermore demonstrates the degree to which Clara provided the standard for all things great and good in piano playing:

> Just when I received your letter the day before yesterday and wanted to answer it, who came in?—Chopin. What a great joy! We had a beautiful day together, which I was still celebrating yesterday. . . . He gave me a copy of a recently composed ballade [in G minor, op. 23], which seems to me to be his most original if not his most ingenious work; I also told him it was my favorite of all his compositions. After reflecting for a while, he replied emphatically: 'I'm fond of it too, it's also my favorite.' . . . It's moving to observe him seated at the piano, . . . but Clara is a greater virtuoso and imbues Chopin's compositions with almost more meaning than he does.[53]

We can infer from a review written some time later that Chopin also treated Schumann and his friends to a rendition of his second ballade (op. 38), though in a form somewhat different from the published version. Commenting on this work in 1841, Schumann recalled that "when Chopin played the ballade here [in Leipzig], it ended in F major; now it closes in A minor."[54] Schumann's "beautiful day" with Chopin likewise fueled his creativity. Within a week of Chopin's departure, he was spending entire days at the piano, composing (no longer extant) etudes "with great joy and excitement."[55]

Late in the next month another significant figure entered Schumann's circle. On 29 October, the British pianist and composer William Sterndale Bennett arrived in Leipzig to further his studies with Mendelssohn, and within days his name was inscribed on the rolls of the Davidsbund. Resident in Leipzig until 12 June 1837, Bennett formed a warm and lasting attachment to Schumann, his "beautiful essence" (as Mendelssohn called it)[56] as man and artist earning him the dedication of the *Etudes Symphoniques*.

Throughout much of the "sad year," the salon of Henriette Voigt, Schumann's "A♭-major soul," served as a meeting place for the composer and his associates. The diary he again began keeping in July 1836, when read in conjunction with that of his hostess and friend, offers tantalizing glimpses into what was at once a convivial and an artistically stimulating atmosphere, a world in which like-minded spirits gathered for evenings of intense conversation (and gossip), plentiful food and drink, chamber music (with Mendelssohn equally at home at the keyboard or as one of the violinists in a string quartet), and readings from the classics of world literature (Jean Paul among them).[57] For his part, Schumann could often be found improvising into the wee morning hours, and in practically total darkness, apparently oblivious of his manual handicap. Gustav Jansen, author of one of the first major monographs on the composer, provides a colorful account of the special magic that Schumann's playing must have exuded at this time. Having secured an invitation to visit the composer's rooms at twilight, Jansen slipped into his studio unobserved. Only when Schumann paused to light one of his Havana cigars (according to Jansen, the remains of several others littered his music stand) did he become aware of his visitor's presence. His playing, Jansen reports, "sounded as if the pedal were always half down, so completely did the figurations melt into one another. But the melody was delicately set in relief. . . . [He] must have been a truly accomplished player at one time."[58] We can well imagine the mesmerizing effect that this approach must have had on the intimate group assembled at one of Henriette Voigt's soirées.

Schumann frequently tried out his latest creations at these musicales; we know, for example, that on 16 September 1836 he arrived at the Voigts' with his recently composed Concert sans Orchestre in hand.[59] Completed in early June of the "sad summer" of 1836, this work, like Schumann's other compositions in the higher forms dating from the 1830s, has a rather complicated history. Originally drafted as a five-movement piano sonata, it was issued in September 1836 as the three-movement Concert sans Orchestre, op. 14. Although the unusual title, specifically, the term "Concert," was perhaps suggested by Schumann's publisher Haslinger as a promotional ploy, it is not inappropriate for a three-movement composition bristling with technical difficulties. In the process of transformation from "sonata" to Concert, the original work lost both of its Scherzos, and also its original Finale, which Schumann replaced with a brand new one. Many years later, he subjected the first movement to considerable revision and restored the second of the two Scherzos (in D♭), reissuing the newly conceived work as a Grande Sonate in 1853.[60]

Only one portion of the Concert remained relatively fixed from the start: the penultimate movement, a set of four rhapsodic "fantasy" variations in F minor on an Andantino de Clara Wieck (Schumann's Quasi Variazioni may well capture in print the sort of improvising he did in private and at the Voigts' soirées).[61] Nor should the fixity of this movement in the scheme be surprising, for Clara's Andantino and Schumann's elaborations upon it form the emotional and musical center of the work. To cite the most obvious connection between the central variations and the surrounding movements: the languid opening gesture of the theme, a melodically filled-in fifth descending from dominant to tonic, is presented at the outset of the work in thundering octaves. While Clara's *Andantino* does not survive for comparison, there is a good chance that Schumann appropriated only a part of it. Indeed, the theme as presented in the *Concert* is peculiarly open-ended, both melodically and tonally. Although each of its three eight-bar strains features the same dirge-like rhythmic pattern (♩ ♩. ♪ ♩ ♩), the expected reprise of the opening idea is lacking. So too is tonal closure in F minor: the third phrase comes to rest on an equivocal half cadence. The ensuing elaborations not only vary the theme, they reconstrue it in two fundamental ways: first, by supplying the melodic return absent in the original subject (Variations 1 and 2); and second, by providing closure in the tonic (Variations 2, 3, 4). Hence Schumann's variations may be interpreted as a continuation or completion of what was only accorded fragmentary presentation in Clara's theme. (The movement would still have this effect even if it should turn out that Schumann did adopt Clara's *Andantino* in its entirety.) In other words, the *Quasi Variazioni* serve as a musical emblem for the composer's longed-after oneness with Clara. Denied this union in life, Schumann inscribed it into his art.

Of all of Schumann's keyboard essays in the higher forms, none plays so intriguingly at the border between life and art as the C-major *Fantasie*, op. 17. Nor is any other composition of the "sad year" more intimately linked with the image of Clara. "In order to understand the *Fantasie*," Schumann wrote to her on 22 April 1839, "you will have to transport yourself into the unhappy summer of 1836, when I renounced you."[62] Writing to her the year before on 19 March 1838, Schumann even referred to the first movement as "a deep lament for you."[63] In the same letter he claimed to have drafted the *Fantasie* "down to its last details" in June 1836, and thus close on the heels of the *Concert sans Orchestre*.[64] But as a result of the recent sleuthing of Nicholas Marston, it appears that by early summer 1836, Schumann had only completed the *first* movement of what was ultimately published as the *Fantasie*. Marston's careful reading of the title page of Schumann's autograph leads to the conclusion that this movement was conceived in June 1836 as an independent composition called *Ruines. Fantaisie pour le Pianoforte*.[65] Then in early September, Schumann and his friend Felix Günz made an excursion to the Leipzig suburb of Connewitz; his nap in a meadow rudely interrupted by a downpour, Schumann hit upon the idea for a "Beitrag f. Beethoven," that is, a contribution to the committee centered in Bonn, chaired by August Wilhelm Schlegel, and constituted for the express purpose of raising funds toward a Beethoven monument.⁶⁶ According to Marston's scenario, Schumann returned to his one-movement *Fantaisie,* his "deep lament" for Clara, added two movements by December, and planned to donate a portion of the proceeds from the newly completed work to the Beethoven committee. As he put it to Friedrich Kistner, a prospective publisher, in a letter of 19 December 1836: "Florestan and Eusebius would very much like to do something for Beethoven's monument and have written something to that end with the following title: 'Ruinen. Trophaeen. Palmen. Grosse Sonate f. d. Pianof. für Beethovens Denkmal.'"⁶⁷

The "Sonata for Beethoven's Monument" nearly ready for publication, Schumann set to work almost immediately on a now lost sonata in F minor.⁶⁸ But the genesis of the earlier work is far from over. Unable to interest a publisher in his contribution to the Beethoven committee, Schumann probably set it aside for a time. In all likelihood he subjected his sonata to revision in the early months of 1838 just prior to a hired copyist's preparation of an engraver's model *(Stichvorlage)* in March of that year. But the *Fantasie* as we know it today did not appear in print until March or April 1839, nearly three years after Schumann conceived his "deep lament" for Clara. Among the most remarkable features of the history of this remarkable work is the wide variety of titles associated with it between its inception in June 1836 and its publication in 1839. In addition to those already mentioned we should add: "Phantasien," "Fata Morgana" (a suggestive reference to the optical illusions of the sorceress Morgana, a figure from Sicilian folklore), and "Dichtungen: Ruinen, Siegesbogen, Sternbild."⁶⁹ Only in December 1838 was the designation on the engraver's model changed from "Dichtungen" ("Poems") to "Fantasie." Schumann's search for a fitting title issued from a conviction expressed in his review of Berlioz's *Symphonie fantastique:* "We are accustomed to judge a thing from the name it bears; we make certain demands upon a fantasy, others upon a sonata."⁷⁰ But it may well be that the most fitting title of all, at least for the first movement of the *Fantasie,* was the one Schumann ultimately rejected after having retained it for over two years: "Ruins." To be sure, his life was quite literally "in ruins" when he drafted the *Fantasie,* but the term would have had other connotations for Schumann and his generation. For them, a ruin was primarily a remnant of a bygone classical age and hence an object of veneration. Its complement was the "monument" (another term closely associated with the *Fantasie*), defined by Schumann himself as "a ruin pointing forward."⁷¹ Hence the "ruins" encoded in the first movement of the *Fantasie,* and perhaps in the work as a whole, hold out a strong measure of hope for the future.

As we have already observed, the *Fantasie* arose at the crucial inter-stice between lived experience and art. Indeed, the confessional and the more purely musical dimensions of the work are so densely interwoven that it is often impossible to untangle them. Here, as in the sonatas in F♯ Minor and G Minor, Schumann channels his own voice through those of Florestan and Eusebius, but in the *Fantasie* both figures are accorded more or less equal time. Florestan dominates in the second movement, a grand march culminating in a notoriously difficult coda where both hands leap in the opposite direction to the keyboard's ex-tremes. In contrast, Eusebius prevails in the hymnic third movement, perhaps Schumann's most poignant creation to date. The first move-ment represents a joint venture, Florestan supplying the principal, sonata-form argument (*Durchaus phantastisch und leidenschaftlich vor-zutragen* [To be played fantastically and passionately throughout]) and Eusebius the reflective character piece, *Im Legendenton,* that interrupts it. But Schumann is not content merely to juxtapose the utterances of his alter egos. On the contrary, he mediates them through the web of connections, apparent and "witty," that link the *Im Legendenton* with the surrounding music. The interpenetration of the contrasting voices is further signalled by the presence of a Eusebian second theme in Flo-restan's sonata form and a Florestinian climax in the *Im Legendenton.*

Moreover, these voices call toward Clara. Writing to her on 9 June 1839 about the poetic inscription for the work as a whole, the last qua-train of Friedrich Schlegel's *Die Gebüsche,* "Through all the tones in this colorful earthly dream, a quietly drawn-out tone sounds for one who listens furtively," Schumann asked: "Aren't *you* the 'tone' in the motto? I believe so."[72] The principal tone, or rather tones, toward which Clara should direct her attention come at the conclusion of the first move-ment in a lyric coda that many listeners have heard as an allusion to the final song in Beethoven's *An die ferne Geliebte.* Subtly prefigured in both the Florestinian and the Eusebian music preceding it, the lyrical close will sound like the inevitable outcome of all that has gone before to "one who listens furtively."[73]

These deeply personal aspects of the *Fantasie* interlock with broader, aesthetic concerns. In expanding his one-movement *Fantaisie* into a three-movement *Grosse Sonate* "for Beethoven's Monument," Schumann endeavored to situate himself, perhaps for the first time, in a definite relation to a tradition whose primary representative was Bee-thoven. He did this by maintaining a consistently elevated tone through-out and also by drawing liberally on the rhetoric and strategies of the sonata form. At the same time, he was equally firm in his belief that to

prove himself a worthy successor of Beethoven he would have to transform the models of the past into something fundamentally new. As
noted in the previous chapter, this conviction nurtured the tireless campaign for "new forms" waged in Schumann's critical writings. The experiments with large-scale design in several movements from the F#-
minor Sonata, G-minor Sonata, and the *Concert sans Orchestre*—in particular, the rethinking of the sonata-allegro as a symmetrical, parallel
form in which exposition and development correspond to recapitulation
and coda respectively[74]—aptly demonstrate Schumann's ability to put
his critical prescriptions into practice. In the *Fantasie,* however, the
search for new forms on both the large and the small scale reaches
stunning heights.

At the larger level, Schumann subverts the affective sequence normally associated with compositions in the higher forms by placing a
rousing, virtuoso "close" at the center of the *Fantasie* and an improvisatory reverie at its actual conclusion. At the local level, no component of
the work is more indebted to the aesthetic of new forms than the first
movement. Here the collaboration between Florestan and Eusebius does
no little violence to the time-honored sonata-allegro form. Inserted just
after the opening phrases of the recapitulation, the Eusebian *Im
Legendenton* literally slices the surrounding music in two, thereby offering a potent critique in sound of the ideology of harmonious unity that
underlies much nineteenth-century thinking on form.[75] Yet it is precisely this radical gesture that imparts to the first movement of the *Fantasie* its distinctive narrative quality. Schumann's placement of a self-
sufficient character piece *(Im Legendenton)* in the middle of a "higher"
form calls to mind the parentheses and gnarled clauses in the novels of
his beloved Jean Paul.[76] Called "arabesques" in Friedrich Schlegel's theory of the novel, these interpolations often function as textual mirrors,
microcosmic summations of or commentaries on the surrounding narrative. As such, they at once imbue a literary work with added depth
and allow the reader to distinguish essential from inessential details.
Schumann's *Im Legendenton* is a narrative embedding of just this sort;
in it we hear an essential strain of the deep lament that he claimed to
have uttered for Clara in the first movement of his *Fantasie.*[77] Hence an
aesthetic issue, the unusual form of the first movement of the *Fantasie,*
leads us back to a biographical fact: Schumann's dejection over his separation from Clara during the "sad year" 1836. It is certainly a token of
his rank as an artist that he was capable at this point in his career of
transforming biography into aesthetics without our being able to tell
exactly where one leaves off and the other begins.

Robert and Clara: United Forever

"Plans. Tears. Dreams, work, collapse. Reawakening." Thus Schumann summed up his emotional journey from abject despair to renewed hope in a diary entry of December 1836.[78] Having resigned himself to enduring an indefinite period of separation from Clara, he gathered his energies at the turn from the "sad year" to what would be its more auspicious successor. By late January and February 1837, he was "living well," that is, working diligently on the last movement of the (no longer extant) Piano Sonata in F Minor, contemplating a Symphony in E♭ (which "was never to be performed in Leipzig"), and reading avidly from Walter Scott, Rückert, and Shakespeare. During the same period, Schumann "completely laid aside old thoughts about La Faneuse," though he may have continued seeing her sporadically in the following months: shortly before August he refers cryptically to "unfortunate dealings with Faneuse—discovery in the cellar." Bach too played a key role in Schumann's reawakening; during February and March, he copied out the whole of the *Kunst der Fuge* and made a careful study of the organ chorale preludes.[79] Nor would this be the last time that the art of counterpoint helped ease him out of a depressive phase: his contrapuntal studies of early 1845 figured in his recovery from the acute neurotic episodes of the year before.

Schumann referred to the months between March and October 1837 as "the most important of all," but unfortunately he was less than meticulous in keeping up his diary during precisely this period. Regular entries resume only in early October, so that for the months before we must turn to the far from complete record in the Vienna précis and a rough summary of the highlights of the period written in the fall of 1837. After revisiting the G-minor Sonata in March, Schumann did little composing for some time. No doubt the editorial work for his "great journal" was making heavy demands on his time; moreover, negotiations were underway with a new publisher, Robert Friese, who assumed this position in July. Throughout the winter, spring, and early summer, Schumann heard next to nothing of Clara—even though she lived just a few blocks away from his apartment on Ritterstrasse. One bit of news, however, did manage to get through, and we can be sure that Schumann received it with great interest. As early as 1834, Wieck had begun to encourage friendly relations between Clara and Carl Banck, a local composer and voice teacher. But fearful that their relationship might become more than friendly, Wieck banished the young man from his house in May 1837.[80]

During the summer of that year a new person entered Schumann's life: Anna Robena Laidlaw, a gifted, young, and attractive British pianist who arrived in Leipzig in late June and performed elegantly at a matinee early in the next month. While we cannot be certain that Schumann and the "good Laidlaw" had an affair (his diary speaks of a "rapid agreement" and "parting with sadness"),[81] one fact is certain: like several young women before her (Agnes Carus, Ernestine von Fricken, and of course, Clara), she inspired Schumann to compose. After four months of little or no compositional activity, he drafted the "blissful" *Fantasiestücke* in July, publishing them in February 1838 as Opus 12, with a dedication to his new friend.

The *Fantasiestücke* occupy a pivotal position in Schumann's creative output during the second half of the 1830s. Composed just after his "reawakening" from the sadness of 1836, this cycle of eight character pieces (a ninth piece was deleted from the engraver's model) exudes a by-and-large light-hearted spirit generally absent from Schumann's music since the *Carnaval* of several years before. The shift in tone goes hand in hand with a shift in structure: relinquishing the "higher" forms that had hitherto claimed his attention, Schumann inaugurates, with the *Fantasiestücke*, the masterful series of poetic cycles that would occupy him until the end of the decade. The turn from higher to smaller forms is accompanied by the cultivation of a more specifically national art. In the *Fantasiestücke*, Schumann employs German titles and expressive indications almost exclusively, a practice maintained in the later cycles as well. The headings for the first two pieces include two of his favorite adjectives, *innig* and *rasch*, "intimate" and "impetuous," ciphers for his Eusebius and Florestan personae respectively. And indeed, the alternation of Eusebian inwardness and Florestinian impulsiveness governs the affective course of the *Fantasiestücke* from beginning to end. The title of the cycle in turn points to a figure whose characters are driven by mood swings of just this sort: E. T. A. Hoffmann. In Hoffmann's *Fantasiestücke in Callots Manier*, a collection of essays and fanciful tales named after the French draftsman and illustrator Jacques Callot, Schumann found a perfect literary analogue for his fanciful musical etchings.

The first of Schumann's "Hoffmann" cycles, however, differs in important respects from the cycles of musical fragments from the earlier 1830s. "In *Carnaval*, one piece interrupts the other, which some people find difficult to endure," he wrote to Clara on 24 January 1839, "but in the *Fantasiestücke* the listener can spread out more comfortably."[82] By this he was probably referring to the greater breadth of the pieces in the later set and also to their tendency toward formal and tonal self-sufficiency. Likewise, the cycle as a whole is governed by a more or less consistent pairing of third-related keys: D♭ and F. While Schumann had employed third-pairings *within* the movements of his works in the higher forms (in the first movement of the *Fantasie,* for instance, he consistently pairs C with E♭ and D minor with F), here he employs the strategy to ensure coherence over the span of an entire multi-movement composition. Perhaps for these reasons, the *Fantasiestücke* (along with the *Kinderscenen*) found public acceptance more readily than Schumann's more radically fragmented cycles.

At about the time he finished the *Fantasiestücke,* Schumann noticed a striking alteration in his psychological makeup: "from here on," he wrote in his diary, "a change in my essential nature and genuine desire for a wife."[83] At the age of twenty-seven, he had finally matured to the point where fidelity to one person seemed a realizable and not merely an ideal goal. Shortly thereafter, he experienced what he called "the most blissful and purest days" of his life. The jurist and amateur pianist Ernst Becker, acting on Clara's behalf, invited him to a morning concert on 13 August in which Clara played three of his *Etudes Symphoniques.*[84] On the same day, he sent off the letter that would mark the "dawn of a second alliance with Clara":

> Just write me a simple "yes" if you're willing to hand over a letter from me to your father on your birthday [in his letter to Wieck of 13 September Schumann writes "with trembling hand," beseeching the older man to give his blessing to a "spiritual bond" with Clara]. At the moment he's well disposed toward me and won't reject my plea if you intercede on my behalf.
>
> I'm writing on Aurora's day. Would that only one more sunrise separated us. Above all, be steadfast: our union will come to pass if we want it—Only don't tell anyone about this letter; otherwise all might be lost.[85]

Clara replied two days later on 15 August, and while she begins a little coyly, her closing words attest to the quiet but insuperable resolve that was perhaps the most remarkable aspect of her character:

> So all you desire is a simple "yes"? What a tiny word, but so important. Shouldn't a heart as full of inexpressible love as mine be able to utter this tiny word? I utter it, and my innermost being whispers it to you eternally. . . . Your plan seems risky to me, but a loving heart pays little heed to danger. Therefore, I say "yes" once again. Would God make my eighteenth birthday into a day of grief? . . . I'll show my father that a youthful heart can also be steadfast.[86]

Over the course of the next several days the lovers traded rings; henceforth they were "united forever," as Schumann put it in the final entry of the Vienna précis. To preserve the memory of these "blissful days," he and Clara designated 14 August, Eusebius's name day, as the anniversary of their engagement, celebrating the event until the very end of their life together.

Denied contact of any sort for an eighteen-month period, Robert and Clara began to exchange letters once again, but now with an almost obsessive intensity and heightened intimacy. (They first switched from the formal "Sie" to the familiar "du" form of address only after firming their engagement in August 1837.) By the end of 1839, their correspondence had grown to include about 275 items, many of them written over a period of several days and reaching sizable proportions: a letter to Clara drafted between 13 April and 9 May 1838, for instance, runs to 27 folios in the original.[87] Facilitated by the expert legwork of Clara's trusted maid Nanni, "a cunning accomplice who knows how to keep a secret," as Schumann described her,[88] this exchange provides us with an invaluable record of the lovers' joys and sorrows, plans and accomplishments, and thoughts on art and life. Each side of the correspondence, however, is characterized by its own distinctive tone; when Robert's flights of fancy threaten to send him spiraling into orbit, the considerably more practical Clara usually offers a rejoinder aimed to bring him back to earth.

The affirmation of a "second alliance" with Clara likewise served as a stimulus to Schumann's creativity. On 20 August, less than a week after receiving Clara's "yes," he set to work on the *Davidsbündlertänze,* a draft of which was complete by about the middle of the following month. "[I] composed blissfully as never before," he noted in his diary, "succeeding in all matters pertaining to form."[89] Here we encounter a derivative of a favorite adjective from this period—"blissful" *(selig)*— and there can be no doubt of its relationship to Schumann's hopes for an impending union with Clara. While putting the finishing touches on the *Davidsbündlertänze* in early January 1838, he wrote to her: "Many wedding thoughts are bound up with these dances, which came into being while I was in the most beautiful state of excitement I can recall."[90] Hence like the *Fantasie,* the *Davidsbündlertänze* mediate between lived experience and art, though the result in the latter case is a blissful kind of art indeed.

Schumann proclaims his debt to Clara's muse at the very outset of the new cycle with a quotation of the head-motive from her Mazurka in G, the fifth piece of a collection entitled *Soirées musicales* (1836). It is certainly no accident that Schumann's piece is also in G and that his cycle bears the same number as Clara's: Opus 6.[91] But at the same time, he was reluctant to accord the biographical subject of his *Davidsbündlertänze* too obvious a presence. After its initial appearance, the "Motto by

C[lara] W[ieck]" disappears for good. Even more telling is the fact that Schumann began to sketch a piece based on the motto, but left it incomplete.[92] These observations have an important bearing on a much-discussed topic: Schumann's encipherment of Clara's name in his music. Some writers have found evidence for a Clara cipher in the pitch configuration B-A♯-B-C♯-D, which appears, in one form or another, in several of the *Davidsbündlertänze* (Nos. 5, 6, 7, 11, and 13). But in order to read "Clara" out of the original sequence of pitches, we must run it backward (D-C♯-B-A♯-B), transpose it down a step (C-B-A-G♯-A), omit the second and fourth letters (C-A-A), and substitute, quite arbitrarily, "L" and "R" (C-L-A-R-A).[93] This widely accepted hypothesis simply requires too many leaps of faith. True, Schumann had a special fondness for mystifications of this type—witness the celebrated example of *Carnaval*—but he likewise tended to view them as frivolous exercises, as "games."[94] By August 1837, Clara Wieck was far too compelling a figure in Schumann's life to serve as the object of a game. She sets the *Davidsbündlertänze* in motion and then recedes into the background, an enchanted listener like the rest of us.

Of course, there is at least one respect in which the cycle shares in the madcap world of *Carnaval* and even *Papillons*. In the *Davidsbündlertänze*, Schumann returns to the fragmented manner characteristic of his earlier works; indeed, many of the cycle's eighteen pieces are intentionally left incomplete, either formally, tonally, or both (e.g., Nos. 7, 11, 12, 13, 16, 17). But Schumann likewise grants a modicum of order to the dizzying sequence of dances through an organizational principle already tested in the *Fantasiestücke*: the regular alternation of pieces "composed" by Florestan, Eusebius, or in some cases, by both figures (their initials appear as signs of authorship at the end of each dance in the first edition, but not the second). Tonal and motivic recurrences also contribute to coherence on the large scale, but in a typically idiosyncratic way. Schumann does not set up a correspondence between the first and last pieces, as we might expect (and as he does in *Papillons* and *Carnaval*); rather, he recalls the music of the second number (a plaintive Eusebian waltz in B minor, marked *Innig*) at the conclusion of the penultimate piece.[95] Eusebius then adds the last piece, a delicate waltz in C, "For no reason at all" according to the inscription; and in doing so, "much bliss streamed forth from his eyes." With a single dreamy gesture, Schumann's Eusebius persona transforms all that has gone before into a dream.

In the weeks and months following the composition of the *Davidsbündlertänze*, Schumann embarked on an emotional roller-coaster ride that would take him from the heights of bliss to the depths of despair.

The first blow came in mid-September, when his plea for Wieck's bless-ing—contained in a letter dated 13 September, Clara's birthday—met with a sharp rebuff. Schumann described his face-to-face exchange with the older man in a letter to Clara of 18 September: "The interview with your father was dreadful. Nothing but frigidity, bad will, confusion, and contradictions—he has devised a new brand of torture: he drives the blade *and* the hilt right into the heart." Wieck did, however, relent on two points: first, he sanctioned the lovers' meeting only in a public place (a concession Schumann found humiliating, for it would make him and Clara into a laughing-stock, a "spectacle" for one and all); and second, he agreed not to interfere with their correspondence, so long as they wrote only when Clara was away on tour. But Schumann could detect no higher purpose in Wieck's resistance to their union, no concern for the possibly adverse effects of an early engagement on Clara's career or on her tender years. So far as Schumann could tell, Wieck was only interested in "selling" his daughter: "Believe me, he'll throw you to the first suitor who comes along with a fortune and title. His highest aim is giving concerts and touring." Even at this early stage in his struggle for Clara, Schumann was prepared to take legal action as a last resort: "If [Wieck] forces us to take extreme measures, that is, if he won't consent to our union within a year-and-a-half or two, then we'll have to find a good lawyer. . . . A magistrate will certainly marry us. Heaven forbid that it should come to that."[96]

Nonetheless, Schumann was determined not to allow Wieck's recal-citrance to crush his spirit. He may have lost the first skirmish, but the war was hardly over. Hence the month of October began hopefully enough, with a "blissful meeting with Clara," and also with a firm re-solve to stay the course. Schumann's generally optimistic frame of mind shines through in the following diary entry: "New striving, new relation-ships, new bonds, old love, old heart, wild fantasies; believe in their constancy—How will it all end! Be modest, hard-working and sober. Believe in the grace of God."[97] At about the same time, Schumann made a conscious effort to put his house in order. In July 1837, he had started to keep careful track of the honoraria paid to the contributors to the *Neue Zeitschrift*; then, on 2 October, he began to maintain a daily record of his own expenditures. Schumann faithfully made entries in the *Haus-haltbücher* (household account books) until he was institutionalized in February 1854 (thereafter, Clara and the young Brahms kept them up to date through February 1856). These fascinating documents list Schu-mann's expenses on everything from cigars, trips to Poppe's cafe, beer, champagne, eau de cologne, soap, rent, clothing, and firewood, to manuscript paper, copyists, piano tuning, concert tickets, and journal subscriptions. Reading through them, we discover that the most mundane things are often the most revealing. That Schumann gave a thaler to "a poor devil" on 25 August 1838, for instance, is of some interest in itself;[98] more noteworthy still, however, is the obsession with detail that compelled him to record his act of generosity in the first place. As time went on, he confided more and more in the *Haushaltbücher*. After a couple of years or so, they include references to his compositional activities, his readings, and even the fluctuations in his physical and psychological condition. In other words, they begin to function as, and often substitute for, a kind of diary.

But regardless of these attempts to impose order on his outer life, Schumann's inner life was soon cast into a state of disarray, at first because of Wieck's "crackpot carryings on."[99] We can well understand the confusion occasioned by his old teacher's increasingly unpredictable behavior. When the two met by chance at Poppe's on 6 October 1837, Wieck's "disgusting politeness" and "crude demeanor" set Schumann off on a drinking binge; a week later, they bumped into one another at the same place, and Schumann found the older man "friendlier and more natural."[100] Gnawing doubts over Clara's steadfastness—and his own—likewise became a source of consternation. After a secret meeting on 10 October, Schumann noted: "Alas! A discord remains after every parting. . . . [Clara is] already wavering, she doesn't appear completely happy, she allows me to sense it, and worst of all, I begin to doubt my own feelings."[101] Slowly but surely, he was overtaken by melancholy, or, more precisely, by rapidly alternating phases of dejection over his uncertain future and elation triggered by a message from Clara. Thus he spent the evening of 14 October anxiously awaiting a few lines from his beloved and after having received them (through the good offices of Nanni's sister) noted in his diary: "How Clara's letter divinely inspired me with the energy to work. *The new life goes on.*"[102] This pattern repeated itself time and again in the weeks and months ahead, often with troubling variations. The day after Schumann pledged his commitment to a "new life," Clara embarked on a concert tour, accompanied as usual by Wieck, that would keep her away from Leipzig until May 1838. To judge from Schumann's diary, he spent much of the intervening period in nervous expectation of news from his distant beloved. Every day that passed without a letter brought him closer to despair: on 23 October, he cried out in the diary "Clara. Clara!"—then two days later he drowned his sorrows in alcohol, a mark of "dissolute living."[103] But even when the long-awaited letter arrived, the upturn in Schumann's mood was short-lived; sometimes the receipt of a missive from Clara would even plunge him more deeply into depression. Pained when he didn't hear from her and equally pained when he did, Schumann was caught in a vicious circle from which he only gradually extricated himself.

In the midst of this emotional turmoil, he sought an antidote in Jean Paul (on 16 October he started to reread *Siebenkäs*) and, for the second time that year, in the study of counterpoint. In late October he reviewed Marpurg's treatise on fugue and began a close analysis of Bach's organ fugues. At about the same time, he made some fitful attempts at composition, though he was "in an unpleasant, wild mood": on 23 October he felt the urge to write polonaises, and on the following evening he worked on a fugue, "but in vain."[104] Unable to make much headway on these compositions, Schumann returned to his contrapuntal studies. By 2 November he was in the throes of "fugal passion" (the same term, *Fugenpassion*, will appear in the *Haushaltbücher* in early 1845, during Schumann's period of recovery from the breakdown of the year before); two days later it had developed into a veritable "fugal frenzy" (*Fugenwuth*).[105] Most probably he assembled the results of his fugal passion into the manuscript known today as the *Fugengeschichte*. A sketchbook and instructional manual-in-one, this sixteen-page document includes drafts of fugal expositions (often with marginal comments in which Schumann critiques his own efforts), citations from key passages in Marpurg's treatise, and examples of fugal procedures culled from the works of Bach and Muffat.[106] Whether or not Schumann specifically intended the *Fugengeschichte* for Clara's edification, as has often been suggested, it certainly represents an early manifestation of a pedagogical impulse that would grow stronger over the years.

Although he may have succeeded in honing his contrapuntal skills at this time, and in spite of some other notable musical stimuli, Schumann had little success in warding off depression. On 11 November he heard Ferdinand David and the renowned violin virtuoso Henri Vieuxtemps in a rendition of Beethoven's C♯-minor String Quartet, op. 131, a work he knew well, but had never before experienced in live performance. Given his recent immersion in fugue, Schumann was certain to have been impressed by Beethoven's remarkably "modern" approach to the venerable genre in the quartet's first movement. But still he felt "sick, melancholy, and hung over," and his mood failed to improve in the company of his friends and the "very modest" Vieuxtemps, like himself an "artistic character" who "speaks little but absorbs much."[107] On the contrary, his psychological state took a dramatic turn for the worse within a short period. A "slight collapse" on 13 November left him incapable of doing much of anything for several days. "Blissful thoughts" of Clara on the evening of 17 November gave way to dismal spirits about a week later. The situation may have been complicated by

Christel, to whom Schumann probably turned for sensual fulfillment toward the end of the month.[108] A bout of heavy drinking between 29 November and 2 December led him to note in his diary: "Sad life—what should I think of myself!" Moreover, his sadness was compounded by guilt; although Clara had admonished him in a recent letter to moderate his alcohol consumption, he couldn't: "I know you've told me not to [drink], but nonetheless I do."[109]

December brought a disorienting series of emotional highs and lows. Early in the month, Schumann started to lead a "healthier life," listening to Beethoven at the Gewandhaus, reading Goethe, and playing billiards with his friend Dr. Reuter. Still, he continued to suffer from "a deep melancholy, but why, I don't know." Intense work for the *Neue Zeitschrift* precipitated "awful relapses" on 18 and 19 December, and then again, after a brief upswing coinciding with a visit from Friedrich Weber, an old friend from the Heidelberg days, on 22 December, when Schumann wrote in his diary: "Drank awfully much beer in the evening. How weak and pitiful I am!" Somewhat cheered by a pleasant Christmas eve spent in the company of the pianist Adolph Henselt (with whom he exchanged the first "du"), by news of his election to honorary membership in the Euterpe Society (one of Leipzig's leading concert-giving organizations), and by the convivial gathering at the Voigts' on Christmas day, he suddenly experienced a "horrid unhinging" on Christmas evening and made straight away for Poppe's: "I plunge into an infinite abyss—Oh-Oh!" His depression persisted through the end of the month, when at last a lengthy letter from Clara arrived: "It strikes midnight as I sit alone with sober thoughts about Clara. But with such a full heart I couldn't pray. . . . Why? Am I such a terrible sinner? What will you bring, 1838?"[110]

Although Schumann's description of his symptoms is less precise than we would like, there is little doubt that he was in a psychologically precarious state for over a two-month period. Exhausted from overwork, unable to curb his drinking, prone to anxiety attacks, and wracked by depressive episodes, his neurotic spell of late 1837 came close to approaching the proportions of the similar phase in late 1833. But somehow, by dint of sheer determination, he managed to recover: miraculously, the early part of 1838 brought a marked improvement in Schumann's condition. By the end of January, he had made a conscious effort to wean himself away from Poppe. In the weeks before, he tried his hand at composition, the results being a (now lost) group of waltzes and an Etude in F♯ Minor (also lost). Soon we find him "living and composing splendidly and industriously in a state of enchantment over my sweetheart."[111] Indeed, the period between late January and early

May 1838 produced a veritable spurt of compositional activity the results of which were three of Schumann's most masterful keyboard cycles:
Novelletten, Kinderscenen, and *Kreisleriana.* But even though each of
these works displays a markedly different profile, they converge on a
central point: an either obvious or oblique reference to Clara.

Begun in late January and early February "with genuine frenzy,"
and completely drafted by April, the *Novelleten* were finally "put in order" by August 1838 and published as Opus 21 in June or July 1839.[112]
When the draft of the cycle was nearly finished, Schumann turned again
to Bach, this time to *Das wohltemperirte Clavier* (which he had also
studied carefully in November of the previous year) and the organ chorales. "Fugues and the canonic spirit pervade all my fantasizing," he
wrote in early April while at work on the "peculiar *Novellette* in D and
B♭" (No. 5). One listens in vain, however, for either fugues or canons in
this boisterous polonaise. What we find instead are finely wrought imitative textures, especially in the piece's more subdued episodes and transitional passages. Schumann's investment in the study of counterpoint, in
other words, had begun to yield rich returns. Here and elsewhere in the
Novelletten we detect a deft internalization of the art of Bach and his
contemporaries. To be sure, Schumann delivers more in this, his most
ambitious keyboard cycle to date, than the title implies. The work is
less a series of "diminutive novellas" than of "extended, interconnected
adventure stories," to quote Schumann himself[113]—a collage of marches,
passionate Florestan pieces, elegant waltzes, rollicking polonaises, and
evocative songs without words, many conceived on the grandest scale.

In a high-spirited letter to Clara of 11 February 1838, Schumann
wrote: "For the past four weeks I've done practically nothing but compose . . . ; I sang along with the stream of ideas that came flowing
toward me, and for the most part have achieved success. I'm playing
with forms. . . ." The same letter includes a suggestive passage on his
favorite author: "I implore you to have a look every now and again at
Jean Paul's works, his *Flegeljahre* above all; at first you'll have to hack
your way through some fairly dense thickets—but then, what divine
waves of song will unfold before you!"[114]

And to be sure, Schumann's playful approach to form in the *Novelletten* owes much to the quirky narrative strategies of Jean Paul. In a
sense, the cycle is an encyclopedia of these strategies, witness the oddly
fragmented reprise of the opening music in No. 2, the embedding of
binary within ternary forms in No. 7, and the displacement, in Nos. 6
and 8, of the primary ideas by subsidiary materials that gradually usurp
the dominant role of the earlier music. Techniques such as these contribute to the palpable but elusive narrativity of the cycle, thereby confirm-

ing its status as a sequence of large-scale "adventure stories." As for the threads binding the disparate narrative strands into a totality, most are of the spiritual rather than the material sort. Avoiding overt thematic recall between pieces, Schumann imparts coherence to his musical tales through an almost obsessive emphasis on the D tonality from the second number forward and through his recourse to a generally jovial tone throughout. And just as in the *Fantasie,* Clara figures prominently in the establishment of that tone. While hard at work on the new cycle in early February 1838, Schumann wrote to her of his plan to call it "Novelletten, since your name is Clara, and Wiecketten doesn't sound very good."[115] In a letter to Clara written just after the cycle appeared in print, he claimed that she "appears in all possible places and situations in the Novelletten."[116] Clara's appearance is most vividly felt in No. 8, where a "Stimme aus der Ferne" quotes the long-breathed, Chopinesque *cantilena* of the *Notturno* from Clara's *Soirées musicales.* In fact, this "voice from the distance" functions as an agent of transformation in the last and most extended of the *Novelletten,* effecting the transition from the turbulent opening music to the good-humored series of dances with which the cycle closes. Here too a biographical subject, Clara's voice, becomes the medium for a formal-aesthetic strategy.

Between 12 and 17 February, well before the *Novelletten* had achieved their final form, Schumann channelled his compositional energies into another project, and by the end of the following month the new work, entitled *Kinderscenen,* was ready for publication. While the thirteen diminutive movements of *Kinderscenen,*[117] the first of Schumann's keyboard cycles to win something like popular recognition, appear to be worlds removed from the more ambitious *Novelletten,* the two cycles are in fact closely related. We learn from Schumann's letter to Raimund Härtel of 21 March 1838 that several of the pieces ultimately brought together as *Kinderscenen* were originally intended as a "beginning" *(Anfang)* for the *Novelletten.*[118] In other words, pieces eventually assigned to separate compositions were first conceived as part of a single project. Not surprisingly, the *Kinderscenen* feature many of the traits familiar to us from Schumann's earlier poetic cycles: a variety of topics (extending from stylized folksong and dance to lullaby, chorale, and recitative), tonal dualism (represented by the interplay of E minor and G in Nos. 11–13), and witty motivic connections (for example, between Nos. 1 and 4, or 2 and 6). Schumann wrote to Clara on 17 March that, as a result of his contrapuntal study, he "conceives almost everything canonically";[119] this tendency likewise shows through in *Kinderscenen,* for instance in the playful canonic duo between treble and bass in the fifth piece, *Glückes genug.* But here Schumann employs all of these techniques in a self-consciously naïve manner, so that art, a product of the grown-up world, and artlessness, the province of childhood, achieve a delicate balance.

It would be a mistake to conclude from its title and also from its character, however, that Schumann intended his cycle *for* children. On the contrary, he took pains to emphasize in a letter to Carl Reinecke dated 6 October 1848 that the pieces comprising *Kinderscenen* were "reflections of an adult for adults."[120] More specifically, they reflect an adult's ability to place himself or herself into a child's state of mind. Viewed in this light, the *Kinder* in the title are none other than Robert and Clara themselves. Writing to Clara on 17 March 1838, shortly after drafting *Glückes genug*, Schumann recalled a phrase she had once written to him: " 'I often appeared to you as a child.' "[121] United in late May and early June 1838 after a long separation, Robert and Clara "played like children—a happiness too great."[122] Clara's power to bring Schumann's childlike streak to the surface must have answered to a deeply felt need: the need to recover lost innocence. (All adults share in this desire to varying degrees; we are most ourselves, Schiller once observed, when at play). Thus in *Kinderscenen,* the composer's yearning for the world of childhood is embodied in an artful form.

While still at work on this cycle, Schumann embarked on another compositional project; perhaps inspired by Beethoven's String Quartet in C♯ Minor (op. 131), which he heard again in rehearsals of Ferdinand David's quartet, he made an attempt at writing a quartet of his own in late February or early March. According to a letter of 3 April 1838 to Joseph Fischhoff, he may even have drafted the work by that time, though no traces of it survive. Another quartet apparently begun (or at least contemplated) in June came to nothing.[123]

An important event in Clara's career may have provided the impetus for a composition that Schumann did, however, see through to completion: the eight character pieces assembled as *Kreisleriana,* op. 16. On 19 March Schumann learned that Clara, then at the height of her triumphant Viennese tour, had been named "kaiserlich-königliche Kammervirtuosin" (imperial-royal chamber virtuoso), a singluar honor which, at the time, was held by only six other artists, Thalberg, Paganini, and the celebrated prima donna Adelina Patti among them. Schumann recorded his telling reaction in his diary: "[The report] doesn't really bring me joy. Why not? Because I am so inconsequential next to this angel. Now there is much to do—and life shines through as never before. If old Wieck were really a good fellow, he'd realize that I too could bring honor to his name, that's for certain."[124] It is probably no accident that on the very same day he wrote to his brothers Eduard and Carl, informing them of his intention to set up house with Clara, after their marriage, in Vienna, where he hoped to find a broader "sphere of influence" for his journalistic and compositional endeavors. Nor is it pure happenstance that just three days later he asked his sister-in-law Therese to intercede on his behalf with her friend Gustav Hartenstein, a professor of philosophy at the University of Leipzig, who might be able to arrange, or so Schumann hoped, for the composer's receipt of an honorary doctorate from that institution. What we have in these maneuvres is an attempt to cope with a tension that would surface later in Schumann's marriage, the tension between Clara's renown as a keyboard virtuoso and his relative anonymity as a composer.

In part to prove himself in Clara's and Wieck's eyes—and his own as well—Schumann promptly set to work on his new keyboard cycle in late April 1838. Having completed a draft of *Kreisleriana* by early May, he returned to it some time later, in July and September, for polishing and final corrections. While Schumann exaggerated in claiming that he had finished the cycle in a mere four days, his allusion to the opening up of "completely new worlds" during its composition can more readily be taken at face value.[125] Like the *Fantasiestücke,* the eight pieces of *Kreisleriana* intersect with the poetic world of E. T. A. Hoffmann. Indeed, Schumann's title comes directly from the *Kreisleriana* section—thirteen items, including tales, music criticism, literary fragments, and satirical essays—of Hoffmann's *Fantasiestücke in Callots Manier.* Schumann further underscored the connection between his latest cycle and the earlier *Fantasiestücke* through a subtitle he eventually dropped: *Phantasiebilder für Pianoforte.*[126] But while it should be possible for the listener and the player to "spread out" rather "comfortably" in the *Fantasiestücke,* such is not the case in *Kreisleriana,* where Schumann comes face to face with Hoffmann's "eccentric, wild, and ingenious" Kapellmeister, Johannes Kreisler.[127] That the composer identified strongly with Hoffmann's fictional character is hardly surprising. Kreisler, much like Schumann himself, alternated between depressive phases and rapturous flights of fancy. Similarly, both figures, real and imaginary, were confirmed devotees of Bach.[128] (On 6 May, by which point the draft of *Kreisleriana* was nearly complete, Schumann made another pass through *Das wohltemperirte Clavier;* his *Kreisleriana,* in turn, abounds in Bachian touches: the prelude-like texture in the middle section of No. 1, the evocation of the two-part invention style in the first *Intermezzo* of No. 2, the close imitation in No. 5, the *siciliano* rhythms of No. 6, the driving fugato and pensive chorale in No. 7, and the gigue-like character of No. 8.) Thus Schumann's substitution of the Kreisler persona for the figures of Florestan and Eusebius marks a subtle but telling shift in his creativity: dualism now becomes a function of a *single* character. The "new worlds" revealed to him during the composition of the cycle emerge as a logical outgrowth of the old.

Schumann originally hoped to dedicate *Kreisleriana* to Clara, but word of his plans sent Wieck into a frenzy: "[he's] enraged by all my compositions" Schumann wrote in his diary on 17 August.[129] Within two weeks, the dedication had been withdrawn (it ultimately went to Chopin), much to Clara's relief. Her own initial reaction to the cycle fell far short of the enthusiastic response on which Schumann had counted. "Sometimes your music actually frightens me," she wrote to him on 30 July, "and I wonder: is it really true that the creator of such things is going to be my husband?"[130] Clara had good reason to take fright: panic, even terror, plays an essential role in her fiancé's most recent creation. Roland Barthes, a sensitive if eccentric critic of Schumann's music, sensed an underlying panic in the incessant rhythmic drive of many of the pieces in *Kreisleriana* (especially Nos. 1, 3, 5, 7, and 8).[131] Likewise, there is more than a passing element of terror in the stark contrasts between and within pieces. In No. 1, for instance, precipitously rising triplets against a syncopated bass give way to the most delicate of textures as a graceful melody soars atop an Aeolian-harp accompaniment. Partial returns and tonally open-ended utterances in Nos. 2, 5, and 7 produce fragmented forms geared to jolt the listener out of a state of complacency (in the second edition of 1850, Schumann eliminated the fragmentary quality in Nos. 2 and 5).

But as often as not, the "frightening" dimension of the cycle is grounded in eminently logical principles. Hence the abrupt mood-swings of the Kreisler persona frequently turn on a fixed tonal pairing: G minor for the character's "wilder" impulses, B♭, the relative major, for his reflective side (see, for example, Nos. 2, 3, 4, 5, 6, and 8). In subsequent works such as the *Humoreske* and *Faschingsschwank aus Wien,* we encounter the very same tonal pairing: in it, Schumann obviously found one means of providing a stabilizing element without which his music would fly apart at the seams. On the whole, though, the abrupt contrasts and the fragmented or episodic forms that prevail in *Kreisleriana* have an effect not unlike that produced by the similar strategies in the *Novelletten.* They imbue the music with an unmistakably narrative character, here modelled not only on the contingent assemblage of poetic sketches in Hoffmann's *Kreisleriana,* but also on the unusual organizational pattern of the same author's unfinished novel, *Lebensansichten des Katers Murrs,* where Murr the tomcat uses torn pages from Kreisler's "biography" as "backing and blotting paper" for his own memoirs.[132] What occasioned Clara's fright, in other words, was neither more nor less than a response to a creative imperative: Schumann's rethinking of music as literature.

After four months of generally good spirits, "orderly" living, and sustained creativity, Schumann took a turn for the worse after provisionally completing *Kreisleriana* in early May. Alternately agitated by the thought of Clara's return from a seven-month tour and depressed by his sudden inability to work, he downed a bottle of wine on 13 May and woke up to a mighty hangover the next day. On 15 May, the date of Clara's arrival in Leipzig, Schumann felt "sick and excited," his gloom intensifying over the following week: "Clara is here . . . I can neither sleep, eat, nor work . . . I thought I was more of a man—now give me energy, courage!"[133] Shaken to the core by the realization that Clara was physically nearer than she had been for over half a year, but for all intents and purposes untouchable, he succumbed to "utter despair" between 18 and 21 May. Then on 22 May, "the skies cleared," and for reasons that shed further light on the causes of Schumann's despair: "Wieck was at my place for the first time. In spite of it all, I love the old chap like my father!"[134] This line from the diary speaks volumes. Underlying Schumann's intense annoyance over Wieck's stubbornness was a kind a filial love. Indeed, winning the approbation of the individual whom he viewed, at some level, as a substitute for the real father he had lost over a decade before was almost as important as winning Clara's devotion. Wieck's refusal to sanction Schumann's union with his daughter was thus all the more hurtful a blow. By 9 June, relations between the two men had soured once again. Having learned that his secret meeting with Clara the day before nearly caused a major row, Schumann noted in his diary: "The old folks [Wieck and his second wife, Clementine; he had divorced Clara's mother, now Marianne Bargiel, in 1825] are incredibly stupid and narrow-minded—Clara must be gotten loose from such rabble."[135]

Within days, Schumann slipped back into a state of depression. While waiting for word from Vienna—on 10 June he wrote to Pietro Mechetti about the possibility of publishing the *Neue Zeitschrift* in the Austrian capital—he again turned to alcohol: "For several days I've been drinking too much beer," he wrote on 25 June, "Shame on you!" Feelings of guilt over lapsing into his old ways only exacerbated his melancholy: "Inwardly I'm often sad to the point of sinking—yesterday I thought 'Hardly, hardly can I bear it'."[136] Clara's departure in early July for a month-long stay in Dresden only made matters worse. Wieck, firmly resolved that "so long as [he] lives there will be no marriage," was eying his former student "like a cocked pistol." Although Schumann braced himself for action—"now get ready" he wrote on 5 July—his will was soon overwhelmed by profound melancholy. By the end of the month, he was drinking so heavily that he couldn't even drag himself to the Voigts'. Finally on 31 July he experienced a psychological crisis comparable in intensity to the neurotic episodes of October 1833 and of November and December 1837: "[I was] up the entire day and night, the most horrible in my life, thinking I might burn up with anxiety." A letter had just arrived from Clara, but even this failed to exercise the usually palliative effect: "Everything came together—the rapidly approaching separation, fear of being able to carry out my plans [to resettle in Vienna], the idea of staying alone in the great city—one moment more and I might not have endured it any longer—I couldn't sleep a wink amidst horrifying thoughts and eternally tormenting, tortuous music." [137] Most of the symptoms described here—anxiety, insomnia, suicidal thoughts—will be familiar to us from Schumann's earlier periods of nervous collapse. But with the reference to "eternally tormenting, tortuous music" we encounter yet another troubling complaint that will resurface in the mid-1840s and again in the severe breakdown of 1854.

As if by a miracle, Schumann's condition improved markedly within a day. His sister-in-law Therese, then visiting Leipzig, berated him for his "egotism," to which he responded with considerable pluck in his diary: "How can I be otherwise if I'm to succeed? So onward with God and good thoughts and a jolly mood. On 2 October I'm off [to Vienna]!" [138] This time Clara's return contributed greatly to the brightening of his spirits. The lovers met at Therese's lodgings on 8 August: "we were too happy; it had been years since we were alone and secure for so long." The next day, the faithful Nanni helped arrange a rendezvous; in the evening, Schumann "listened at the window, Nanni called, and I followed. Moments later Clara lay at my breast." She did likewise a week later on 14 August, Eusebius's day, the anniversary of their engagement. Nor could Wieck, who grew "more furious and impudent every day," dampen the lovers' mood. [139]

On 8 September, Clara played a concert at the Gewandhaus, including works by Chopin, Thalberg, Henselt, and her own Scherzo, op. 10. Sitting unobserved in the balcony, Schumann

> thought all was a dream. Clara looked so beautiful. Her engagement ring sparkled from afar. I was in a loge, unseen by anyone. She played splendidly, like a mature artist. I wrote to her beforehand, asking "whether I'd hear her as a child for the last time" [letter of 8 September 1838]. For the whole day I was anxious and quiet and happy and sad. God, when will you grant me peace? [140]

Inspired by Clara's masterful performance, Schumann quickly drafted a poem:

Vision at 9 in the evening
To Clara Wieck

An angel-child descended,
Now she sits at the piano, musing on old songs;
And when she touched the keys,
There appeared above,
Floating in a magic circle
    Figure upon figure
    Image upon image:
    The old Elfking
    And gentle Mignon,
    And defiant knights,
    Their lustrous weapons poised,
    And nuns on bended knee
    Lost in pious devotion.
Those who heard her raved,
Praising her as if she were a renowned prima donna;
But dismayed and feather-light
She vanished into her homeland.[141]

In the meantime, Schumann had begun to prepare in earnest for his exploratory trip to Vienna. On 5 September he acquired the obligatory passport. After celebrating Clara's birthday over champagne on 13 September, he got down to the tedious task of packing his books and other belongings. Unfortunately he would have to leave his piano behind: "the thought pains me" he wrote on 15 September. Several days later he and Clara exchanged their goodbyes—in Wieck's house, but secretly, of course—"revelling" in one another for a beautiful hour. Schumann then travelled to Zwickau on 22 September, but circled back to Leipzig for one last farewell meeting with Clara. At 5 P.M. on 27 September he headed for Vienna by mail coach, ready to take his "first step as a mature man."[142]

Schumann in Vienna

Travelling by way of Dresden, Maxen, Teplitz, and Prague, Schumann arrived in Vienna on 3 October 1838. According to his travel notes, he was in an unusually jolly mood after six days on the road, but more than a little dishevelled as well: "I lost my hat on the mail coach the other night, and thus got to Vienna hatless—tore my pants—unpleasant dust, after which *eau de cologne* is very refreshing."[143] As we have seen, Schumann's decision to relocate in the Austrian capital dates back to March 1838.[144] The plan went something like this: he would continue to edit the *Neue Zeitschrift* under the auspices of a Viennese publishing firm, augmenting his income through the profits on his compositions; Clara, for her part, would maintain her concert career and use her influence with the empress to obtain a teaching post at the Vienna Conservatory; once the necessary arrangements were complete, Schumann would call for Clara, hopefully no later than Easter 1840. The first order of business, therefore, required him to find a new publisher for his journal. During the summer before his departure, Schumann had broached the matter with the firms of Mechetti and Diabelli, but before there could be any serious talk of publication, he would have to obtain the requisite governmental approval for the venture. Hence, immediately on arriving in Vienna, he paid a visit to Count Joseph Sedlnitzky, Austrian chief of police and court censor. Two days later, he arranged for meetings with the publishers Diabelli and Haslinger, but made little headway on either front. Haslinger, a "cold but polite" man, emitted particularly mixed signals: "he wants to [take up the journal] and he doesn't want to." Moreover, Schumann attributed his equally cool reception in Diabelli's shop to Wieck's spiteful machinations. Within days he had the distinct impression that the authorities would rather he "went straight to the devil"—as indeed they did; by mid-October, Haslinger had probably written to the censor advising him to withhold approval of Schumann's request.[145]

Soon it became clear that the *Neue Zeitschrift* would not be issued from Vienna by the New Year, as Schumann had initially planned. Disappointed by his lack of success, he fell into an old pattern: melancholy induced him to drink, which only intensified his melancholy. On the evening of 4 November, he "consumed an incredible amount of alcohol, and this angers me—*so much*. Then I thought about my ardent love for Clara as never before . . . As for composing, it's out of the question."[146] Still, Schumann was far from giving up entirely; writing to Clara during this depressive episode, he reiterated his "firm decision" to make a life with her in Vienna.[147] Hence on 9 November, he obtained an interview with Katharina Cibbini, lady-in-waiting to the empress and an amateur pianist and composer, hoping that she might intercede at court on his behalf. Unfortunately, the meeting produced few tangible results. There was "embarrassment on both sides," Schumann wrote in his diary, "she's hardly even heard of me."[148] By the end of the month he had resigned himself to the fact that Leipzig would have to remain the home base of his journal.[149]

This setback notwithstanding, Schumann's first several months in Vienna were not without their brighter moments. Enchanted by the natural beauty of the city and its environs, he enjoyed strolling in the Prater or in the lush gardens around the imperial residence at Schönbrunn. And of course the capital also offered artistic stimuli of all sorts. Between his arrival in October and the Christmas holidays, Schumann paid regular visits to the opera and the theatre for productions of Rossini's *William Tell,* Donizetti's *L'elisir d'amore,* Meyerbeer's *Robert le Diable,* Mozart's *Marriage of Figaro,* and Schiller's *Fiesko.* The rendition of Haydn's *Die Jahreszeiten,* his last oratorio and one of his grandest works, at the Imperial Winter Riding School proved to be a memorable event. True, the Viennese approach to performance in general and to operatic performance in particular was not always to Schumann's liking: "Musicians here know little about the *piano* dynamic. Everything comes off with uncommon thickness, in accordance with the Italian style." On the whole, he was nonplused by the public's craze for this style. He remained for only the first half of Donizetti's *L'elisir,* even though the music was "agreeable in its own way; the Viennese are more enthralled by inanities than most people, but they're obviously excited by artistic figures." Nor did he feel comfortable with the city's cultural elite, whom he feared were "a bunch of gossips."[150] Still, the heavy dose of opera inspired Schumann to contemplate writing one of his own (a dream he would not realize for nearly a decade).[151] And among Vienna's generally gossipy musicians, he found at least one "unassuming, modest, and decorous" individual in the renowned piano virtuoso Sigismund Thalberg, who astounded Schumann with his ability to play the latter's *Kreisleriana* with "remarkable accomplishment and understanding," at sight.[152]

As much a mecca for a historically inclined musician in the late 1830s as it is today, Vienna offered Schumann the opportunity to commune with a great tradition at first hand. At a visit to Beethoven's grave during the first weeks of his stay, he found a steel pen that gave him "courage and good thoughts."[153] Then he "mixed up" the flowers he had plucked at this grave and Schubert's, a symbolic and prophetic gesture: within a few years he would attempt a synthesis of the two composers' styles in his own First Symphony (op. 38). Late in October he marvelled at the treasures in the library of the Gesellschaft der Musikfreunde, letters from Mozart and Beethoven among them. At about the same time, he examined the latter's sketches in the collection of the bibliophile Aloys Fuchs. Schumann made his most important find, however, during a series of visits to Schubert's brother Ferdinand. In a letter of 6 January 1839 to Raimund Härtel, he reported excitedly on the cache of unpublished and virtually unknown compositions he had viewed among Schubert's papers: "operas, four grand Masses, four or five symphonies, and much else."[154] Of all the works in this rich group, none impressed him as much as the "Great" C-major Symphony; before long, he had arranged for a premiere at the Gewandhaus under Mendelssohn (21 March 1839), and also for its publication by Härtel's venerable firm. In his celebrated review of Schubert's symphony, Schumann extolled the work's "heavenly length—like a thick novel in four volumes by Jean Paul."[155] And in another symbolic gesture, he wrote the review with the very pen he had earlier discovered on Beethoven's grave.

When Schumann realized that it would not be as easy as he had originally thought to find a new venue for the publication of his journal, he began devoting more of his time to literary pursuits, both critical and confessional. In the middle of November we find him occupied with a number of pieces for the *Neue Zeitschrift*. During the same period he set to work on a project of a far more personal nature: a *Brautbuch* or *Gedenkbuch* ("bridal book," "book of reminiscences") for Clara. (He had just received a troubling letter from her, in which she hinted that there was no rush to marry in 1840 and that they might have to put off their wedding date by a half year or so; seen in this context, the *Brautbuch* may have been undertaken to preserve the memory of what Schumann feared he might lose.) This fascinating document includes selected adages on married life, landmark dates in the lovers' relationship, a list of "difficult farewells," and intimate messages to Clara, thus prefiguring the role of the *Ehetagebuch* (marriage diary) of the years ahead.[156] "Full of melancholy" at the end of the month, Schumann also dashed off the précis of his life between 1833 and 1837, from which we have quoted on several occasions. This chronicle, taken together with the *Brautbuch*, speaks to a dual urge that pervades Schumann's critical writings (and his music as well): the urge to preserve the memory of the past as a means of coping with the present and preparing for the future.

Frustrated but undaunted by his setbacks with the authorities, Schumann did not waver from his plan to carve out a place for himself and Clara in Vienna. As late as March 1839, he remained convinced that they "would not find a city in all of Germany where one can live more respectably and more cheaply than in Vienna."[157] (The *Haushaltbücher*, however, do not bear out Schumann's claim, at least as far as rent is concerned: he paid nearly twice as much for lodgings in Vienna as in Leipzig.)[158] If he could not establish himself as a journalist in Vienna, then he would attempt to consolidate his position as a composer and even as a teacher (early in 1839 he took on a composition pupil named Rösle, "a hectic fellow without much talent"). Soon after his arrival, Schumann acquired a piano on loan from Graf's shop, and on 12 November, the same day on which he initiated the *Brautbuch*, he wrote a little piece for Clara titled "Fata Morgana" (later published as the fourteenth piece in the *Albumblätter*, op. 124). In the weeks ahead, he made fitful starts on a number of projects, but produced "nothing of consequence." After all, he was badly out of practice; in the past six months, his compositional activity amounted to little more than putting the finishing touches on *Kreisleriana* and the *Novelletten*, both of which had been "put in order" by September 1838. But by mid-December, he appears to have overcome this creative block, his imagination perhaps fired by an intense period of readings, including Goethe's *Tasso*, poems by Lenau and Heine, Mattheson's *Vollkommene Kapellmeister*, and Nissen's biography of Mozart. Whatever its cause, Schumann's renewed spate of composing proceeded at an unbelievably rapid rate. Soon a young runaway named Franz Jüllich was acting as his amanuensis; "a good-looking fellow with clear eyes and a pleasant face," Jüllich received free music lessons in exchange for running errands. The suspension of diary entries between 1 January and 20 March may likewise be linked to Schumann's nearly full-time immersion in creative work. And to be sure, before leaving Vienna in early April 1839, he had either made significant progress on or completed about a dozen pieces, some of them of considerable dimensions.

The compositions of this period exhibit a broad spectrum of tendencies. Works in the higher forms, sonata and concerto, appear side-by-side with character pieces and cycles or collections of miniatures. In many of the latter we sense the emergence of a more accessible strain in Schumann's art, a stylistic shift motivated in part by the composer's desire to cultivate a wider market for his music and to ensure him and his future bride a more stable income.[159] Not that Schumann relinquished his earlier esoteric manner entirely. In a work such as the *Humoreske*, one of the most impressive products of this phase, the quirky traits associated with the Davidsbündler pieces of the mid-1830s are much in evidence. Furthermore, accessible and esoteric tendencies not only coexist, they interpentrate. Hardly a single work conceived during Schumann's stay in Vienna was left untouched by this dialectic.

Schumann's creative outpouring began in mid-December, when, responding to Clara's request for a simplified version of the finale to the Second Piano Sonata, op. 22, he began to draft a completely new movement. The result, a G-minor Presto, is perhaps "simpler" than its predecessor in the rhythmic dimension, but in little else. Though designated a Rondo, the movement is in fact one of Schumann's idiosyncratic "parallel" forms. No less passionate than the earlier movement, it culminates in a gradually accelerating and technically challenging coda marked

Quasi Cadenza. In the following weeks Schumann composed two nocturnes, both of which were later published, though without titles, as the lead items in *Bunte Blätter*. He dedicated the first of these, an A-major song without words lasting a mere sixteen bars, "to my beloved bride for Christmas Eve 1838." Before the New Year, he may also have completed the first three pieces of the set published in March 1841 as *Scherzo, Gigue, Romanze und Fughette,* op. 32.[160] Here we can detect a continuation of the strategies and styles so brilliantly employed in *Kreisleriana,* though on a more modest scale. The duality between G minor and B♭ that grounds the tonal contrasts within and between the pieces of the larger cycle figures prominently in Opus 32 as well. The rhythmic displacements in the Scherzo, the sublimated contrapuntal textures in the Scherzo and Gigue, the mediation of agitation and calm through shared rhythmic figures in the Romanze—all of these traits resonate with the manner of Schumann's more celebrated Kreisler pieces (like the last piece in *Kreisleriana,* the Gigue and Fughetta are built around a persistently repeated dactylic motive). Schumann might have moderated his Hoffmannesque impulses, but he certainly did not forsake them.

At the turn to the New Year, Schumann lapsed briefly into melancholy. While pining away for Clara, he "attempted much, without having the energy to see things through to a conclusion." Among these attempts was "the beginning of a sonata or fantasy or etude or nothing at all in C minor." Listed in the *Projektenbuch* as an Allegro, this no longer extant composition may thus have been envisioned as a constituent part of a "higher form."[161] Another of the higher forms had occupied his thoughts during the month before. Just as he began to compose in December 1838, Schumann was busily writing an article on the piano concerto for the *Neue Zeitschrift.*[162] A letter to Clara of 24 January 1839 indicates that by then he had drafted his own contribution to a genre that he feared was in danger of becoming obselete. We will touch on this D-minor movement, his first foray into the genre since the unfinished F-major Concerto of 1830 and 1831, in our discussion of the Symphonic Year, 1841 (Chapter 6).

In the same letter to Clara in which he reported on the near completion of his concerto movement, Schumann also noted that he had recently finished a number of smaller works. One of these, now lost, he planned to call *Guirlande;* its disappearance is all the more unfortunate in light of his intriguing description of the work as "variations, but *not* on a theme." The letter also refers to "a *Rondolette* . . . and other small things, of which I have so many, and which I will chain together prettily under the title 'kleine Blumenstücke' ('little flower-pieces'), much like one might name a series of pictures."[163] As it turned out, Schumann did not fashion a cycle or collection of "kleine Blumenstücke," though he did call one of his "small things" a *Blumenstück,* issuing it somewhat later as Opus 19. Another diminutive piano piece, the *Arabeske,* Opus 18, was probably elaborated together with the *Blumenstück,* a hunch strengthened by their contiguous opus numbers, their joint publication in August 1839, and their dedication to his friend the Majorin Serre.[164]

Both compositions are likewise cast in the seemingly accessible style that becomes an increasing presence in the works of Schumann's Viennese period. It was perhaps with this stylistic quality in mind that he dismissed the *Arabeske* and *Blumenstück,* in a letter of 15 August 1839 to Ernst Becker, as "delicate—for ladies."[165] In Schumann's estimation, these pieces were charming but slight. They might find a place in the bourgeois salon, or even bring in a tidy profit, but neither could lay claim to being high art. Their titles say as much. In the visual arts, the term "arabesque" refers to the decorative filigree framing a portrait or landscape; likewise we would expect a "flower-piece" to be graceful and elegant, but little more. Neither composition, however, is as unassuming as it first appears. The *Arabeske* is cast as a little rondo (maybe it was the *Rondolette* of Schumann's 24 January letter to Clara), its six parts falling into an A-B-A-C-A-coda pattern. Yet the parts are subtly related: A and C share the same head motive, while the Eusebian transition between B and A serves as a basis for the evocative coda. The *Blumenstück* was crafted even more imaginatively as a rhapsodic double theme-and-variations form in which the primacy of the second theme only gradually makes itself felt. The piece therefore brings together the "fantasy-variation" techniques of the *Etudes Symphoniques* with the "evolving" forms characteristic of some of the *Novelletten.*

Schumann again alluded to the *Arabeske* and *Blumenstück* as a pair in a letter of 11 August 1839 to Henriette Voigt, describing them as "less important" than the recently published *Humoreske,* op. 20.[166] Probably completed between late January and mid-March of the same year, the *Humoreske* is among the least played of Schumann's piano works but in many ways the most impressive of them all. A veritable compendium of his earlier keyboard styles, its affective range runs the gamut from unbridled joy to profound sorrow in a mosaic-like array of character portraits. Its topics include the song without words, the free fantasy, and the Bachian invention, many of them bound by a deft web of thematic connections. Schumann did not exaggerate when, in a letter of 11 March

1839 to Clara, he referred to the work as his "grand" *Humoreske:* the kaleidoscopic succession of miniatures adds up to a satisfying if fantastically conceived totality.[167]

In a letter written four days later to Simonin de Sire, Schumann stressed that in order to understand the *Humoreske* one must have a feeling for *Humor,* a concept that "the French are incapable of comprehending. Unfortunately the French language has no truly appropriate equivalent at its disposal for *Humor,* a notion deeply rooted in the German national consciousness . . . [and] involving the happy union of easy-going cheerfulness and wit." It is probably no coincidence that two sentences later Schumann makes his often-quoted reference to Jean Paul as the figure from whom he "learned more counterpoint than from his music teacher," for *Humor* was the cornerstone of his favored author's poetics. In the *Vorschule der Ästhetik,* Jean Paul devotes no less than half a dozen chapters to *Humor,* which he variously defines as an "infinity of contrast" and a "setting of the small world beside the great" so that when we view them together, "a kind of laughter results which contains pain and greatness."[168] Schumann's *Humoreske* likewise embodies an "infinity of contrast," an interplay of dualistic traits infiltrating every parameter of the music: thematic content, affect, tonality, and structure. At the thematic-affective level, which we are apt to notice first, there is the alternation between dreamy, Eusebian passages (like the one at the very beginning) and the Kreisler-inspired antics that continually interrupt them. This contrast is in turn grounded by a tonal contrast present in *Kreisleriana:* the pairing of B♭ major with its relative minor, G. To this Schumann adds a dialectic between smaller and higher forms. As we have already noted, the *Humoreske* falls into a number of discrete sections, fifteen to be exact, not counting brief transitions or codas. Yet the fragmentary quality is balanced by the tendency of the sections to group themselves into larger movements, each of them unified by shared themes that recur, in a variety of guises, over the course of the entire piece.

Schumann once referred to the *Humoreske* as perhaps his "most melancholy composition."[169] This comment may strike us as odd, both in terms of the work's title and of the "easy-going cheerfulness" that pervades much of the music. At the same time, it is not difficult to locate the principal sites of melancholy, or at least of wistfulness, in the *Humoreske:* the G-minor section designated "Einfach und zart" (simple and delicate); the passage in the relative major coming not long thereafter, and bearing one of Schumann's favorite expressive indications, "Innig"; and most of the extended closing section ("Zum Beschluss"). Each of these is strategically placed, the first two heading off inner "movements," and the last comprising much of the "finale." Indeed, the melancholy passages of the *Humoreske* are all the more poignant precisely because they are embedded in otherwise cheerful music. We might also recall that the laughter occasioned by *Humor*—as Schumann would have understood the term—contains not only greatness, but pain as well.[170] Often the "best humorists," Jean Paul maintained, "come from a melancholy people."[171] After reflecting on the *Humoreske*, we can only agree.

Schumann's melancholy temper recedes into the background in another project conceived during the latter part of his stay in Vienna. According to a long diary entry of 20 March 1839, in which he summarizes his activities since the beginning of the year, Schumann began working on the *Faschingsschwank aus Wien* "happily enough," sketched out its five movements in some form, then "laid it aside" for elaboration at a later point.[172] Over the course of the ensuing year or so, he returned to the composition several times: by summer 1839 he had gotten as far as the last movement, which remained incomplete, however, even in late January 1840; the work was ready for publication by May or June of that year, but didn't actually appear in print until August 1841, almost three years after it was provisionally sketched.[173] Although the *Faschingsschwank* is hardly as emotionally, technically, or musically challenging as the *Humoreske*, the two works complement one another beautifully. Both reflect the dualisms that run through Schumann's Viennese period, accessibility versus esotericism, smaller versus higher forms, but each emphasizes a different side of the dialectical pairing. Whereas the *Humoreske* will be best appreciated by *cognoscenti*, the *Faschingsschwank* (in spite of its dedication to de Sire, an individual well attuned to the composer's esoteric art) is marked by a more consciously popular tone. Schumann's quotation of the *Marseillaise* in the first movement of the later work is only the most obvious sign of his attempt to strike a chord with a larger public. And if the *Humoreske* accommodates the rhetoric of the character piece to the structural demands of the higher forms, the *Faschingsschwank* does much the reverse. No doubt the sequence and number of its movements recall the outward pattern of a sonata.[174] But on closer inspection, the "sonata" turns out to be a cycle of character pieces in disguise. The titles of its inner movements, *Romanze, Scherzino,* and *Intermezzo,* are in line with designations frequently encountered in the miniatures of the 1830s. Furthermore, the spirit of the work clearly resonates with *Carnaval,* which was, after all, originally entitled *Fasching:Schwänke auf vier Noten.* This spirit is best in evidence in the first movement, a mock-heroic dance whose overall rondo design recalls similarly additive structures in Schumann's character pieces. Only the last movement adheres to a sonata-allegro pattern; but in reserving this time-honored paradigm for terminal placement and choosing to begin with a light-hearted rondo, Schumann effectively stands the sonata's traditional sequence of movements on its head. Acting in his role as musical humorist, he sets the "small world" beside the "great world," and in the *Faschingsschwank aus Wien*, it is the small world that looms larger.

Schumann's decision to set aside his latest composition, if only temporarily, in the late winter of 1839, was certainly related to the "sudden change in life-plan" to which he alluded in the long diary entry of 20 March: "In two weeks, I'd like to return to Leipzig." Disappointed over his failure to find regular employment in the last months and suffering from intermittent anxiety attacks, he still remained intent on establishing a sphere of influence in the city where he had lived and worked for almost half a year: "I've decided to bring Clara to Zwickau for the first year [of our marriage], but then we'll move to Vienna."[175] As events unfolded, Schumann would find himself in Zwickau sooner than he imagined. On 30 March he received an alarming letter in which his sister-in-law Therese informed him of the grave illness of his brother Eduard. He was convinced of the imminence of Eduard's demise, and indeed, a week later, he got word of Eduard's death while stopping over in Dresden en route to his family home. Suddenly, and mysteriously, he realized that he had somehow sensed the tragic turn in his brother's fortunes all along: "How strange are my presentiments—Eduard's leave-taking, his kindness toward me—all this became clear. How are such things revealed to me? That's my first question."[176] In yet another in a long line of attempts to capture lived experience in artistic form, he immediately set to work on a composition grimly entitled *Leichenphantasie* (Corpse Fantasy). Proceeding as he often had before, Schumann rapidly drafted the new cycle of four character pieces within about a week, but did not complete it until January 1840, at which time he contemplated naming its movements *Trauerzug* (Funeral March), *Kuriose Gesellschaft* (Strange Company), *Nächtliche Gelage* (Nocturnal Revels), and *Rundgesang mit Solostimmen* (Round with Solo Voices).[177] Finally, in June 1840, the work was published as *Nachtstücke*, op. 23, its title drawn directly from E. T. A. Hoffmann, who had issued a series of eight ghoulish tales under the same name. The cycle discloses other connections with Schumann's earlier preoccupations, and most unsuspected ones at that. The presence in the first piece of an obsessively repeated rhythmic pattern (a variant of which dominates the last piece as well) is hardly out of the ordinary: the pattern serves to evoke the somber tread of a funeral procession. It is striking, however, that a close relative of the same succession of rhythms underlies the opening melody of *Aus fremden Ländern und Menschen* (From Foreign Lands and Peo-

Example 4.2a. Nachtstücke, No. 1: mm. 1–2.

Example 4.2b. Kinderscenen, Von fremden Ländern und Menschen: mm. 1–4.

ple), the first piece in *Kinderscenen* (Examples 4.2a–b). The *Nachtstücke* transport us into a realm as inaccessible to the adult as the world of childhood, but one from which no travellers have returned to tell their tales.

On 4 April 1839, less than a week after he started on the new cycle, Schumann departed from Vienna. After passing through Prague and Dresden, and stopping briefly in Leipzig, he arrived in Zwickau on 9 April, by which time his brother Eduard had already been dead for three days. When he set foot in his hometown for the first time in over six months, Schumann had the dreary impression that the place "was now completely extinct."[178]

$\sim 5 \sim$

$\mathcal{F}$ierce Battles and Blissful Songs

"What Should Be United—Will Be United"

When he returned from Zwickau to Leipzig on 14 April 1839, Schumann must have felt as though his world was disintegrating around him. The two weeks before had brought one upheaval after another in rapid succession: word of his brother Eduard's illness, the hurried leave-taking of Vienna, then Eduard's death. For a time Schumann contemplated moving the *Neue Zeitschrift* to Zwickau and assuming responsibility for the family business; he may even have approached Friese, his journal's publisher for the last several years, to be a partner in the enterprise. These plans were dropped soon enough, though the book firm did, in a sense, remain in the family; it was eventually sold to Friedrich Fleischer, who married Eduard's widow Therese in November of the following year.[1]

But in the meantime, a storm of greater magnitude was brewing. Writing from Paris on 9 April, Clara informed Schumann of her discovery of a clandestine correspondence between her friend Emilie List and Wieck, who was threatening to disinherit her, confiscate her earnings, and initiate a lawsuit against the lovers unless Clara promised to break off all relations with Schumann.[2] By the end of the month, however, Wieck began to whistle a somewhat different tune, implying that his consent would be forthcoming contingent upon Schumann's ability to ensure Clara a "worry-free future" (which to Wieck meant an annual income of no less than 2,000 thalers). Clara fell immediately for what was surely intended as a ruse. On 1 May, she dashed off a letter to her

182

father, begging passionately for his approval of her marriage to "the best of men," and assuring him that her love for Schumann was hardly a passing whim: "Every man has his peculiarities; should one therefore reject him? . . . Don't you believe that I'm well aware of Robert's short-comings? Yet I also know his virtues." Even more important, she vowed not to proceed with wedding plans until they no longer "expected any worrisome days," that is, until Schumann could promise a sufficient yearly income (Clara proposed 1,000 thalers as a more realistic sum than Wieck's 2,000). She informed her fiancé of these developments the following day in a letter that understandably infuriated him: first, be-cause she suggested postponing their wedding well past Easter 1840, the date for which they had aimed; and second, because she alluded to plans for a concert tour of Belgium, Holland, and England to be undertaken that summer with her father (as she put it, "one is always better re-garded when accompanied by a man"). Although he was somewhat calmed by Clara's assurance, in her next letter of 13 May, that they would stick by their original intent to marry by spring 1840, Schumann remained uneasy: "I don't completely believe it," he noted laconically in his diary.[3]

Schumann's skepticism was well founded. Before the month of May was out, Wieck had imposed further—and, taken together, quite impos-sible—conditions on the couple's marriage plans: they were not to live in Saxony during his lifetime; for the next five years, Wieck planned to keep Clara's earnings, allowing her only 4 percent annual interest; Schu-mann was to provide Wieck with a legally validated statement of his income, but otherwise make no attempt to communicate with him; and last, Clara would have to forfeit all claims to her inheritance. Schumann summed up this state of affairs with devastating succinctness: "Unbeliev-ably vile behavior on Wieck's part. I could hate him to the point of madness."[4] Indeed, Wieck's actions fell into the pattern of attack, re-trenchment, and renewed attack with which Schumann was already painfully familiar. The older man had waged this kind of psychological warfare before, in the fall of 1837, probably hoping thereby to wear down his former student's resolve. Now he was up to his old tricks again, channelling them this time through his daughter.

But by late spring 1839, Schumann had clearly lost patience with what he earlier called Wieck's "crackpot nature." As a defensive measure he drafted a petition, dated 8 June, to the Royal Appeals Court in Leip-zig, requesting that it either order Wieck to give his paternal consent or, failing this, grant permission outright for the marriage with Clara to proceed. On the same day, his twenty-ninth birthday, he sent a grimly prophetic letter to Clara, sensing that "perhaps the greater part of my life is already behind me. In any event, I won't live to be very old; this I know for certain. Violent passions have raged within me, and worry on your account has also taken its toll." His melancholy tone, however, quickly gave way to unswerving confidence in a positive outcome of the upcoming struggle: "I'll hold you aloft like a trophy won in the fiercest of battles." With these words, Schumann girded himself for war, and he did not doubt for a moment that he would prevail.[5]

Soon after sending the petition to Paris for Clara's signature, Schumann turned to composition for the first time in two months. As noted in a diary entry for 9 June, he was "living in a very orderly and moderate fashion," spending much time with the *Neue Zeitschrift* and sketching out a string quartet in accordance with his plan, articulated in a letter to Hermann Hirschbach of about a week earlier, to devote the summer months to compositions in that genre. (The plan goes back farther still; in March 1838 he was "looking forward to writing string quartets, since the piano is getting too limited for me.") By 13 June 1839 he was able to report to Clara that he had actually begun two quartets, both of them "just as good as Haydn's," though his progress on the new works was impeded by external and internal pressures: "I lack time and inner peace; the quartets will not be completed in the near future." Within a few weeks, he was studying Beethoven's late quartets, no doubt an inspiration for his own efforts, but thereafter we hear nothing of quartet composition for some time to come.[6]

Other concerns now lay claim to Schumann's attention. On 24 June he made one last attempt to extend the olive branch to Wieck: "Clara writes that you yourself hope we might reach an agreement; I gladly offer my hand as a token of peace. Please inform me of your wishes, which I am ready to fulfill so far as my powers allow. If you do not respond to my inquiry in eight days, I will take it as a definite refusal of my offer." (It is probably not a coincidence that Schumann's "orderly living" was interrupted on the same day by a visit to Poppe's, the first since his return from Vienna). But Schumann cannot have been surprised when before the week was out he learned, in a curt message delivered through Wieck's wife Clementine, that the older man "wanted to have nothing to do with me."[7] Convinced of the inevitability of a court battle, Schumann sought legal counsel through the attorney Wilhelm Einert in a letter of 30 June. When the latter's attempt at an out-of-court settlement with Wieck failed a few days later, Schumann took the only course of action open to him: the petition he drafted nearly a month before had arrived with Clara's signature on 29 June; on 16 July, he submitted it to the Leipzig court, passing "dreadful hours, wondering whether I would survive the decision."[8] The battle, which would not be resolved for over a year, was in full swing.

In a sense, the outcome of this struggle, the nature of which had been transformed from a fight *for* Clara to a fight *between* the lovers on the one hand and a recalcitrant father on the other, was predetermined from the outset. Robert and Clara had done everything in their power to negotiate an amicable resolution; Wieck, for his part, had engaged (and would continue to engage) in subterfuge and avoidance tactics. Whether consciously or not, he must have thought it unlikely that they would actually press their claim in a court of law. In calling his bluff, they caught him hopelessly off guard. While Wieck flailed about with the pathetic rage of an inept Malvolio, Robert and Clara behaved with indomitable calm and deliberation, at least outwardly. In a wise first step, Schumann enlisted Clara's mother (Wieck's first wife, Marianne Bargiel) as an ally to their cause. The day before sending the fateful petition to the Leipzig court, he requested permission in a no longer extant letter for a meeting with her. She greeted him warmly in Berlin at the end of July and within a day or so had provided Clara with written consent for her marriage to Schumann.[9] Clara in turn cancelled the remainder of her Parisian concerts in order to attend the mediation session scheduled by the Leipzig court for 31 August.

Separated for almost a year, the couple met on 19 August in Altenburg, a little town just south of Leipzig. In a state of "anxious expectation," Schumann "went out on the road by which Clara would arrive. At 6 P.M. she was there—in my arms. If anything, my dear, lovely sweetheart had grown more dear and more lovely. For the first time in a long time we strolled arm in arm and gazed at the moon."[10] The pair spent an idyllic week as guests of Schumann's relatives in Zwickau and its environs (Clara stayed with Schumann's sister-in-law Emilie and her second husband, Johann Uhlmann, in Schneeberg), celebrating their reunion with extended periods of four-hand piano playing and much kissing besides.[11] But by the end of the month, they were both back in Leipzig, ready to get down to the serious business at hand.

On the morning of 31 August, Robert and Clara arrived at the chambers of Rudolf Richard Fischer, archdeacon at the Saint Nicholas Church and court-appointed mediator in their suit against Wieck. We can well imagine their astonishment and consternation in learning that Wieck, who was also summoned to appear by the court, had cancelled at the last moment, claiming that urgent business in Dresden called him away that very morning and would prevent his returning to Leipzig for up to a month. (Much to their chagrin, they also learned that Clara's father, in a personal interview with Fischer, vowed "never to give his consent to his daughter's union [with Schumann]," though their minds were somewhat put at ease by supportive words from Marianne Bargiel, who arrived from Berlin that afternoon.)[12] Wieck, it seems, had hit upon another maddening strategy to postpone the inevitable: fearful he might be beaten, he simply failed to show up for meetings at which his attendance was necessary. In the weeks ahead Wieck turned to all-too-familiar tactics. While in Berlin between 12 and 17 September for Clara's birthday, Schumann learned through Einert that a court hearing date had been set for 2 October. At about the same time, he received what appeared to be a conciliatory letter from Wieck. When the two met in Leipzig on the evening of 24 September, Schumann was filled with "gloomy forebodings" by the older man's "stupid suggestions": Clara's earnings for the last seven years were to revert to her half brothers, she would have to pay 1,000 thalers to repossess her piano and other items stored in Wieck's house, and Schumann was to set aside no less than 8,000 thalers so that, if the marriage failed, Clara could live on the interest from the sum.[13] Wieck's scheme was transparent enough. Here again was the old pattern of stubborn refusal, feigned conciliation, and extravagant demands, a last ditch effort to delay the formal hearing. "All will be lost forever if we don't appear on 2 October," Schumann wrote in the *Brautbuch*. "So for now be firm and strong, since the only thing [Wieck] fears is the trial. If he succeeds in thwarting us here, then he'll succeed in other things. I implore you, my little Clara, be on guard."[14] Then just a few days before the proceedings, Wieck submitted a written request for postponement on the incredible grounds that the mediation session with Fischer (for which he was not present) had not taken place. His petition denied, he failed to appear in court on 2 October, this time not even bothering to proffer an excuse. Given these circumstances, the Leipzig court ordered the case to be reported to the higher appeals body in Dresden and set a new hearing date for 18 December.

Schumann's reaction to all this was more complicated than might first be assumed. In one of his October diary entries, he makes reference to his "deeply sorrowful nature," while in others he complains of having "little energy to produce" (he tried to start a fugue, but "it went sour") and "always feeling weak in the head."[15] This onslaught of gloomy feelings is understandable enough: he must have experienced an immense letdown when the 2 October hearing resulted in yet another delay; Clara's departure with her mother for Berlin the next day deprived him of an important source of solace; and the death of Henriette Voigt, his "A♭ major soul," on 15 October, certainly came as a severe blow. At the end of the month another outlet of communication, this one with his own inner being, dried up when he suspended his diary, leaving it untouched except for a few brief notices until his wedding day nearly a year later. Yet Schumann was hardly about to surrender where either his personal struggles or his professional aspirations were concerned. He still hoped to have all "in order" on the legal front by Easter 1840, this in spite of the fact that "Wieck's vulgarity increases every day." One of his last diary entries for this difficult period speaks eloquently to his resolve: "What should be united—will be united; what doesn't belong together will be separated."[16]

Nor had his impulse to produce been completely expunged. Granted, Schumann's composing came to a near standstill after his return from Vienna and Zwickau in the spring of 1839. As we have seen, his plans to spend the summer writing string quartets had fizzled into nothing; and all he had to show for the summer months was a draft of the last movement of the *Faschingsschwank aus Wien*. But in light of the convulsions in his personal life (and the continued demand to bring out biweekly issues of the *Neue Zeitschrift*), the spottiness of his creative efforts is easily accounted for. Now in mid-October, however, the lull in the legal battle with Wieck afforded Schumann the opportunity (if not the energy) to return to composition. According to his diary, he started on several pieces and "thought about [composing] preludes"; writing to Clara on 10 October, he boasted of having begun about fifty new works.[17] The latter was perhaps an inflated claim: the only work completed during this period was the G-minor *Fughette* for piano (a realization of the neo-Bachian textures probably envisioned for the "preludes" mentioned in the diary entry), published in 1841 as the fourth and last piece in Opus 32.

But by 11 December Schumann had drafted a more substantial piece—actually, a cycle of three character pieces—and with it brought his rich outpouring of compositions for piano, initiated a decade before, to an auspicious close. The *Drei Romanzen,* issued in October 1840 as Opus 28, retained a special place in his heart. Indeed, the work appears as one of the four piano cycles (the others being the *Fantasiestücke, Kreisleriana,* and *Novelletten*) that he counted among his best in letters to Carl Kossmaly of 5 May 1843 and 25 January 1844.[18] Like so many of his keyboard works of the preceding years, this one is deeply influenced by Clara, who had herself composed a set of *Trois Romances* for piano early in 1839, while Schumann was still in Vienna. Published the following year with a dedication to her fiancé, these pieces may have spurred Schumann to make a contribution to the genre while he was again separated from Clara and anxiously awaiting the next round in the struggle with Wieck. The second of Clara's three character pieces, which alternates moderately paced and quicker episodes, was a particular favorite of her future husband. When she sent him a copy of this G-minor *Romance* in July 1839, asking for his opinion, he responded enthusiastically: "You complement me as a composer as I do you. Every one of your thoughts emanates from my soul, just as I have you to thank for all my music."[19] Schumann was probably struck by one aspect of this piece more than any other: the prominence of duet textures—between bass and alto, tenor and alto, soprano and alto, and soprano and bass registers—in its Andante sections. A similar textural play characterizes his second *Romanze,* the lyric gem of the set, cast in F♯ major and a lilting $\frac{6}{8}$ meter. The main tune unfolds as a duo in the tenor range around which rising arpeggios in the right hand and descending arpeggios in the left trace a delicate mirror image. In the middle section the pattern is reversed, the accompaniment now occupying the middle of the texture and the duo, between alto and bass, located at its extremes. Heard in tandem, these two compositions form the lyric strands in a duet carried on over the distance separating the lovers. And before long, Schumann would be writing bona fide vocal duets of his own.

After completing the *Drei Romanzen,* Schumann was again consumed by thoughts of the upcoming day in court. No doubt to calm his nerves, he made regular trips to Poppe's (whose establishment he had not visited for several months) during the week before the hearing scheduled for 18 December. At the same time, Wieck was hard at work on an eleven-page *Declaration* he planned to file with the court and in which he spelled out the reasons for his opposition to Clara's union with Schumann. Although neither came off well in this rambling document (Clara was judged unfit to run a household), Wieck's portrayal of the suitor for his daughter's hand bordered on the defamatory. According to the *Declaration,* Schumann was socially inept, badly brought up, and egotistical; he neither spoke clearly nor wrote legibly; he had injured his hand through his own stupidity; he had lied about his income; he wanted to exploit Clara for financial gain; and he was a shoddy musician, a mediocre journalist, and a drunkard to boot.[20]

When the "much feared day of judgment," 18 December, finally arrived, Wieck at last saw fit to attend the proceedings, but his erratic behavior seriously damaged his credibility in the eyes of the court. As Clara tells it in her diary, Schumann sat through the hearing with stoic calm, while Wieck's raving reached such a pitch that he had to be silenced several times. Profoundly embarrassed by the humiliation her father had brought upon himself, and "cut to the quick" each time one of his tirades was interrupted by the president of the court, she feared that "this day has parted us forever, or at least has severed the delicate bond between parent and child."[21] Clara's sympathetic reaction was grounded in perfectly natural feelings of filial devotion, but it showed insight into a character whose refractory psychological makeup is worthy of a study in its own right. Wieck, she realized in a way that Schumann understandably could not, was neither a villain nor a madman, but rather an obsessively stubborn individual who, once committed to a certain course of action, was prevented by hubris from yielding an inch. She realized as well that this tragic flaw would prove to be his undoing.

When the court delivered its decision on 4 January 1840, it acknowledged only one of Wieck's allegations as having any substantive bearing on the case: "the plaintiff's tendency to drink." Wieck, however, was held responsible for offering proof within six weeks. By now a master of procrastination, he managed to stretch these six weeks into six months. Within days he began circulating lithographed copies of his *Declaration* among music critics and concert managers, practicing a bit of "chicanery," as Schumann called it, directed at both Robert and Clara. On 13 January he formally contested the 4 January decision in a *Deduktionsschrift* presented to the court by the end of the month. Schumann countered on 13 February with a written refutation, claiming he would have no trouble coming up with 1,500 thalers yearly (the requisite amount cited in Wieck's *Deduktionsschrift*) to support Clara. (Here he exaggerated: two thirds of the sum was to accrue from the sales of his works, but it would be many years before Schumann earned anywhere near 1,500 thalers annually from his compositions). As for the charge of drunkenness, he threatened to sue Wieck for slander (which he did, successfully, in early June). Not until 28 March did the higher court in Dresden rule on this exchange. Although it upheld the Leipzig court's judgment of 4 January, Wieck was given another six weeks to substantiate his charge. Unable to do so by early May, he requested and received yet another extension. Thus it seemed that the case would drag on into the summer; Robert and Clara would obviously have to relinquish their long-standing plans for an Easter wedding.

But throughout this frustrating period, Schumann almost surely remained confident of his ultimate victory. Just days after the December 1839 hearing, Clara met privately with Johann Beck, president of the Leipzig court, who expressed his certainty that all would turn out well for the pair.[22] Writing to Gustav Keferstein on 31 January 1840, Schumann noted that although Wieck was doing all he could to scuttle the couple's union, he might postpone it but could not, in the end, prevent it. In the same letter, Schumann outlined a strategy to strengthen his hand further in the suit against Wieck. Already in February 1839, he had toyed with the idea of obtaining an academic position in England, possibly through the good offices of his friend Sterndale Bennett. Now with his legal battle well underway, he recognized the clear advantages that an academic title would bring to his case. Clara, he wrote to Keferstein, had by now attained an important standing as an artist, while his own position, "in the eyes of society," was somewhat lower. Then he came to the point: "Is it difficult to obtain a doctorate from the University of Jena [where Keferstein was deacon at the Garnisonkirche]? Will I have to take an exam, and if so, what kind?"[23] Schumann renewed his request a week later, indicating his willingness to demonstrate his scholarly abilities in a long essay "on Shakespeare's relationship to, his opinions and views on, music, and the manner in which he employs music in his dramas," a project that would of course require some time to complete, for he would have to read the playwright's entire output.[24] Much to his relief, this proved unnecessary: he needed only to submit a detailed résumé (the autobiographical sketches quoted in previous chapters were probably drafted to this end), some representative articles authored for the *Neue Zeitschrift,* a selection of testimonials to his compositional skills, and a letter of application to Ernst Reinhold, Dean of the Philosophical Faculty at the University. The latter document provides us with a rare glimpse into Schumann's views of his professional achievements at this important juncture in his life:

> Above all, I am conscious of my genuine veneration for tradition, for the past; no less have I also attempted to further the cause of present-day talents, whether they have drawn on the past (such as Mendelssohn has, at least in part), or invented something really new (Chopin, for instance). As a composer, I have perhaps taken a different path from all others, but it is best not to speak of these most confidential matters of the soul.[25]

Though Schumann stops short of a detailed personal assessment, it will not be difficult to provide the missing term. Grounding his observations in the triadic historical scheme that informs so much of his music criticism, he locates his interests at once in the past, the present, and the future. His accomplishments as a composer, the "different path" of which he is reluctant to speak, aimed at the union of all three. Dated 24 February and signed by Dean Reinhold and Rector Ferdinand Hand, the doctoral diploma arrived from Jena on 28 February. The next day, he proudly signed his letter of thanks to Keferstein "Dr. R. Schumann."[26]

The same month was notable in another regard. One of the entries in Schumann's sketchy summation of the period between the beginning of court proceedings and his wedding day reads: "In February [1840], a rich harvest of songs, through the composition of which I was able to forget everything else." And indeed, the *Liederjahr* ("Year of Song"), as he called it in his *Projektenbuch*, was off to a flying start.[27] By January of 1841, Schumann had completed upwards of 125 lieder, well over half his total output in the genre, setting the verses of dozens of poets in the process. And while most of these settings require solo voice and piano, other performing forces are represented as well: duets, choral partsongs, and even a patriotic lied for vocal soloist, chorus, and piano. We will explore the causes for this outburst of creativity at a later point in this chapter. For now, it will suffice to say that its initiation coincides with a protracted hiatus in the formal proceedings against Wieck, a period when Schumann again found himself without Clara's consoling presence (on 3 February she set off with her mother for a concert tour of Hamburg, Bremen, and Lübeck), but still retained a positive outlook on the successful resolution of their quest. Hence many, though by no means all, of the lieder may be viewed as musical missives to a distant beloved, much like the piano music of the middle and later 1830s. As a group, the songs function in part as confessions in tone, a substitute for the diary Schumann had suspended in the late fall of 1839. But as we will see, they were motivated by many other factors as well.

Schumann's *Liederjahr* officially began on 1 February 1840, the date on his draft of a witty setting of a Shakespearean text, the *Schlusslied des Narren* ("Fool's Farewell") from *Twelfth Night*.[28] According to his letters of 22–24 February to Clara and Breitkopf and Härtel, he had completed much more by the end of the month: the nine songs of the Heine *Liederkreis* (op. 24), an extended setting of Heine's ballad *Belsatzar* (op. 57), a group of four-part lieder (probably the *Sechs Lieder für vierstimmiger Männergesang*, op. 33), and several volumes on verses by Goethe, Heine, Byron, and Mosen. The new medium demanded a new working method: "As a rule I compose [songs] while standing or walking, not at the piano. Vocal music is quite different [from piano music]; it's much more direct and melodious, and does not come first through the fingers." Delighted with his newly won facility, he exclaimed to Clara: "How blissful it is to write for the voice!"[29] By 7 March, the volumes devoted to Goethe and the other poets just mentioned had become part of a projected "wedding present" for Clara. Titled *Myrthen* (Myrtles, after the blossom traditionally associated with marriage festivities), and expanded to include settings of lyrics by Rückert and Burns, the cycle was completed by early April, well before the August deadline Schumann initially set for himself.[30]

While busily composing songs, Schumann had begun to set his sights higher. He expressed his desire to write an opera in a letter of 18

February to Kistner, adding, however, that the undertaking would only be possible if he were released from his time-consuming editorial duties. Within a month, his plans had crystallized further. Writing to Clara on 13 March, he asked her to have a look at E. T. A. Hoffmann's *Doge und Dogaressa,* for which he had recently drafted an operatic scenario. Attracted by the novella's "nobility and naturalness," Schumann enlisted his friend Julius Becker as librettist, though their partnership soon ran aground. When Becker delivered a portion of the versified text some months later, the composer was far from satisfied. "Setting weak words is dreadful for me," he complained to Clara on 15 May. "I don't need great poets, but only wholesome language and sentiments. But I certainly won't abandon this beautiful plan, for I sense abundant dramatic talent within me." His confidence remained undiminished the following week, when he assured Clara that he would "stop writing so many small things and apply myself seriously to work on the opera."[31] Schumann's determination notwithstanding, the opera on Hoffmann's tale failed to progress past these preliminary stages. In fact, the entire episode embodies, in microcosm, the kinds of frustrations and reversals Schumann would face when he turned in earnest to operatic composition later in the decade.

For now, he would have to content himself with "small things," but even here there was a slackening off after the initial creative surge. On 16 March, he travelled to Dresden to hear Liszt in concert (the virtuoso "played divinely," Schumann jotted in the *Haushaltbücher*) and accompanied him to Leipzig the following day. The pair spent much time together in the next two weeks, a phase capped off by Liszt's performance of selections from *Carnaval* (to a less than enthusiastic audience) on 30 March, the day before his departure. While it is safe to assume that Schumann found little time for composition during this period, he did, by way of compensation, lay the groundwork for a contuining relationship with one of the major forces in nineteenth-century music. To be sure, this relationship was not without its tense moments. Though often warmly supportive of Schumann's compositional efforts, Liszt would have liked him to cultivate the "progressive" or cosmopolitan elements in his style more assiduously than he did; in one of music history's more famous back-handed compliments, Liszt praised Schumann's D-minor Piano Trio as less "Leipzigerisch" (Leipzig-like, that is, provincial) than his popular Piano Quintet. Schumann, for his part, was no less divided in his view of Liszt. On the one hand, he was captivated by his colleague's charisma, his worldliness, his irresistible, gregarious manner (all of them qualities noticeably lacking in Schumann's personal makeup). But on the other, Liszt must have represented a kind of forbidden fruit, a personification of the dangerous charms Schumann had experienced a decade before in Paganini's technical wizardry and in the seductive lyricism of Italian opera. He gave voice to this dichotomy in his pointed observation, made some years later, that Liszt's career was precariously suspended between apotheosis and scandal.

As noted above, Schumann put the finishing touches on *Myrthen* in early April, soon after Liszt's departure from Leipzig. Then he fell into something of a funk. Even Clara, who had returned to Leipzig with her mother for Liszt's last concert, was unable to effect much of an improvement. But fortunately, the episode was short lived. (Indeed, Schumann's lapses into melancholy during the final stages of his fight for Clara were surprisingly few and mercifully brief in duration; all told, he held up far better under the strain than we might assume from his past record.) By 14 April, he was feeling much better; three days later he was off to Berlin with Clara, where he remained until the beginning of May. Here it will be worth pausing over an entry in the *Haushaltbücher* for 16 April, in which Schumann notes an advance, repayable the next month, of 41 thalers to Clara. This was neither the first, the last, nor the largest of his loans to his fianceé: on 3 September 1839, he had given her 400 thalers "in trust"; early in July, he purchased her a piano for the same amount; between 15 and 18 July, she received 300 thalers from him in cash and 200 in government bonds; finally, on 5 August, he offered her another government bond, this one worth 100 thalers.[32] Her income from concertizing sharply curtailed, and for obvious reasons unable to enlist her father's aid, Clara found herself in a precarious position. While Schumann may have inflated his yearly earnings in his written refutation of Wieck's *Deduktionsschrift*, his willingness to provide Clara with generous support during troubled times speaks volumes to the depth of his commitment to her.

After returning to Leipzig on 1 May, Schumann again immersed himself in the composition of lieder. Within three weeks, he had essentially completed a *Liederkreis* to texts by Eichendorff (op. 39), his "most profoundly romantic" work to date, according to a letter to Clara of 22 May. In a letter written the week before, he described his compositional outpouring as "downright uncanny": "But I can't do otherwise; I'd like to sing myself to death, like a nightingale."[33] Nor did his singing abate with the Eichendorff *Liederkreis*. Practically before the ink was dry on the page, Schumann started another work. In two days he made vocal sketches for no less than eleven songs on texts from Heine's *Lyrisches Intermezzo*, and by 1 June the new cycle, *20 Lieder und Gesänge*, was complete. Several years later he excised four of the songs,[34] publishing the remainder in 1844 as *Dichterliebe*, op. 48.

On the same day that he finished the larger (and better known) of
his Heine cycles, Schumann turned to a considerably less pleasant matter: submission of a *Denunciation* to the Dresden court in which he
charged Wieck with defamation of character. (Although the court
moved favorably on Schumann's claim, sentencing Wieck to serve eighteen days in prison in April 1841, there is no record of the latter's incar-
ceration.)[35] The months of June and July 1840 proved unfortunate for
Wieck in other ways as well. In a *Declaration* filed with the Leipzig court
on 7 July, he conceded his lack of success in gathering evidence to support the contention that Schumann was a drunkard. Two of his wit-
nesses, he claimed, had simply disappeared. (In fact, this was only a half
truth: one witness, the pianist Louis Rakemann, had emigrated to
America in 1839; but the other, Clara's old flame Carl Banck, was giving
voice lessons in nearby Dresden). Still, Wieck stubbornly refused to give
his consent, his *Jawort*, to what was, according to his "innermost conviction," an "ill-founded union." If Schumann and his daughter wanted
official approval to marry, the legal authorities would have to supply it,
for he never would.[36] The court did just that in an *Erkenntniss* dated 18
July and issued publicly on 1 August. Allowed ten days to contest the
decision, Wieck responded with silence and nothing more. On 11 August, a little over a year after Schumann and Clara had officially initiated
their suit, it was all over. We can well imagine the feelings of relief that
accompanied the composer's entry for that date in his *Haushaltbücher*:
"happiest of days—end of the struggle."[37] With the posting of the banns
on 16 and 30 August, the way was finally clear for the wedding ceremony to take place.

Of course, the struggle had for all intents and purposes come to an
end at the beginning of the month before. When Schumann learned of
Wieck's *de facto* admission of defeat in the *Declaration* of 6 July, he
noted jubilantly in the *Haushaltbücher*: "Juchhe! Victoria!" (Hurrah!
Victory!).[38] By 8 July, he and Clara were apartment hunting (on 14 July,
they decided on a flat at Inselstrasse 5), and within days, Schumann was
composing lieder with a vengeance. On 2 July he had completed a set
of duos for soprano and tenor (*Vier Duette*, op. 34), but the news of
Wieck's concession unleashed the most powerful wave of creativity of
this incredibly productive year: on the afternoons of 11 and 12 July, he
drafted a setting of Chamisso's lyric cycle *Frauenliebe und Leben* (op.
42); three further Chamisso settings were finished in the next two days
(*Löwenbraut, Die Kartenlegerin,* and *Die rote Hanne,* op. 31); four lieder
on Hans Christian Andersen texts (rounded out with a Greek poem in
Chamisso's translation and published as Opus 40 in 1842), comprising
one of Schumann's most intriguing but sadly neglected cycles, followed

between 16 and 18 July; another cycle, this one on verses by Robert
Reinick, was begun less than a week later (issued as Opus 36 in 1842,
the set was completed on 22–23 August); then at the very end of the
month came two ensemble settings on Geibel texts (later published as
Opus 29, nos. 1 and 2). This richly creative surge, extending for a
twenty-day period during which Schumann produced just as many lieder, came to a temporary halt after 1 August, the date on which the
Leipzig court made public its consent, with a setting of Geibel's *Der
Hidalgo* (op. 30, no 3). The title character of the poem patrols the streets
of Seville at twilight, equally ready to serenade the elegant ladies of the
city as he is to fight a duel with his rivals for their affection. Courting
and duelling are not such different activities after all, the poet seems to
say, a point not lost on Schumann, who obviously identified with
Geibel's swashbuckling cavalier. Indeed, he effectively cast himself as the
poem's protagonist by alluding, in the pervasive bolero rhythm of the
piano part, to the eleventh piece from *Papillons*. "Composed on the day
of consent," he proudly wrote on the manuscript, confirming his role as
the *hidalgo*, prepared to fight to the finish for his lady love and triumphant in victory.

Although Schumann did manage to complete a few songs in the
weeks ahead—*Sehnsucht* (op. 51, no. 1), the remainder of the Reinick
cycle (op. 36) begun in July—composition definitely took second place
to preparations for the wedding. While Clara was away on a concert
tour that would take her to Jena, Gotha, Erfurt, and Weimar, he arranged for Carl August Wildenhahn, an old school friend from his
Zwickau days, to officiate at the ceremony. And in paying Einert his 52-
thaler fee for legal services, Schumann finally closed the books on a long
and enervating ordeal. On 4 September, he travelled to Weimar and on
the following day made a surprise appearance at Clara's second concert
in that city. From then on, they were "together for evermore," as he
noted in his diary. Back in Leipzig by 7 September, he paid for a lavishly
bound copy of *Myrthen*, its red velvet inscription reading: "To my beloved bride." Few brides, as Eric Sams notes, have ever laid claim to a
finer gift.[39] He spent 11 September in a whirlwind of activity, tending to
last-minute errands in preparation for the "great, good day": the purchase of gifts for Clara's birthday and of various items for himself (including a new pair of suspenders); arrangements for the transport of his
belongings to their new apartment. He capped off a day taken up by
"much running about and much dreaming" with a *Polterabend* (pre-
nuptial party) in the company of Julius Becker and other friends at
Poppe's. Then finally on 12 September, the day before Clara's twenty-
first birthday, fourteen months after the submission of their petition to

the courts, and nearly five years after the exchange of their first kiss, he and Clara were wed in the village church in Schönefeld, a little town near Leipzig. The simple ceremony began with a chorale and concluded with a brief but moving address from Pastor Wildenhahn. "It was a lovely day," Clara commented in her diary, "and even the sun, which had not shown itself for some time, cast its mild rays on us as we rode to the church in the morning, as if to consecrate our bond from above."[40]

Together at Last

Among the birthday presents that Clara received from Schumann on 13 September was a little book with "a very intimate meaning." Specifically, it was

> a diary for everything that touches us mutually in our household and our marriage; in it we will record our wishes and our hopes; it should also be a little book of requests directed at one another when speech is insufficient; and a book of mediation and reconciliation in case misunderstandings arise; in short, it should be our good and true friend, to whom we entrust everything, and before whom our hearts stand open.[41]

The Schumanns' *Ehetagebuch* (marriage diary), kept with varying degrees of regularity for about three-and-a-half years, is an invaluable source of information on the early phases of their life together. In many ways, it occupies a position at the intersection of confession, creativity, and even criticism. The rules and regulations Schumann laid down for its maintenance recall the similar prescriptions he had drafted many years before for the Zwickau *Litterarischer Verein:* he and Clara were to "exchange secretarial duties" every Sunday, preferably over morning coffee; at that time, they would read their entry (of no less than a page) for the last week, either aloud or silently depending on its contents; failure to submit an entry would result in the imposition of an unspecified penalty. At the same time, Schumann's outline of the subject matter appropriate for the diary—"critiques of our artistic accomplishments," character sketches of famous artists with whom the couple has come into contact—resonates with the aims of the *Neue Zeitschrift* as articulated in its first issue. Even the diarists' principal function—to keep a record of "all the joys and sorrows of married life as true history, [the reading of] which will give us joy in old age"—is informed by the kind of historical consciousness that had motivated Schumann's journalistic undertakings from the first. In the marriage diary, as in his critical writings and his music as well, the past is preserved as a nurturing source for the present and a safeguard for the future.

To be sure, the "true history" recorded in the diary is not without an unsavory side that should not be overlooked. Both Schumanns, for instance, disclose a troubling streak of anti-Semitism. After visiting the home of her friend Emma Meyer, Clara complained: "I found myself among a lot of Jews, which really makes me uncomfortable, even though one hardly notices the Meyers' Jewishness."[42] Or consider Schumann's reaction to Clara's recognition of subtle changes in his attitude toward Mendelssohn:

> I've certainly not changed [my opinion of him] as an artist—you know that—on the contrary, for years I've promoted his cause more than practically anybody else. Nevertheless—we shouldn't forget our own concerns. Jews remain Jews; only after seating themselves ten times will [they] offer a place to a Christian. Sometimes [the Jews] pelt us with the very stones we've carried to their Temple of Glory. So don't put yourself out for them too much—that's my opinion. We also have to accomplish things and work for ourselves. Above all, let us endeavor to approach more closely the beautiful and the true in art.

Clara seconded these views in her next entry, adding: "I will take your advice, and won't humble myself before Mendelssohn as much as I have in the past."[43] Schumann's anti-Semitic outburst may have been prompted by a desire to assert his artistic parity with one of the leading musicians of the day, but the form which the assertion assumes is disturbing nonetheless. Schumann trusted Mendelssohn as a confidant and respected him deeply as a colleague, but tainting these amicable feelings, if ever so slightly, was his need to remind Clara that his friend had been born a Jew.

To judge from the diary's account of their first months together, the Schumanns rapidly settled into Biedermeier coziness. "Our little establishment is very intimate indeed," Schumann noted on 15 September. Before long they were absorbed by a number of joint activities, both musical and literary. By the end of September the couple had embarked on a close examination of the fugues from Bach's *Wohltemperirte Clavier*. In mid-October they decided to suspend their Bach studies for a few weeks so that Schumann could return to a project first envisioned in connection with his pursuit of an academic degree: an investigation of Shakespeare's outlook on music. While her husband marked the relevant passages from the playwright's works, Clara copied them "into a nice book."[44] Clearly Schumann took the lead in these activities, aiming in part to enrich Clara's (in his view) spotty knowledge of the monuments of culture. As Clara reported on their fugal studies, "Robert indicates the places where the theme enters . . . and reproached me strongly because I had doubled one passage in octaves, thereby impermissably adding a fifth voice to the four-part texture."[45] Clara freely admitted the gaps in her education, but she was also quick to add a rationale: "I often feel downright oppressed by my ignorance of scholarship and my not being very well-read. But when should I read? I can't find the time as others do, and moreover I don't think I have the drive to read."[46] Late in October we find the couple reading Jean Paul, whose works Clara came to know for the first time. Her cursory description of these sessions perhaps indicates that she was less enthusiastic about the idiosyncratic writer than her husband. No doubt Walter Scott, whom she read "with great pleasure" early in December, was more to her taste.

We should not assume, however, that the early days of the Schumanns' marriage was a bourgeois idyll in every way. On the contrary, their diary speaks to all manner of tensions, great and small. Clara probably harbored a twinge of jealousy over Amalie Rieffel, one of her husband's piano students, "whom he prefers over me as an interpreter of his pieces—now this doesn't sit well at all!"[47] A subsequent quarrel over artistic license elicited a firm statement from Schumann: "You were incorrect, my little Clara. The composer alone knows how his pieces are to be played."[48] Disagreements of greater moment concerning the direction of Clara's career surfaced in the first month of marriage. Hoping to amass a tidy sum that would ensure the couple's future solvency, Clara was considering an extended concert tour of Russia. The thought filled Schumann, who, as mid-nineteenth century customs demanded, would have to accompany her, with nothing but dread: "To head up there, out of our warm little nest. Ugh! Still, we'll have to do it."[49] (And indeed they did, in the winter and spring of 1844, but with disastrous consequences.) After deciding to postpone the Russian tour, first because of a volatile political situation following on a war between Egypt and Turkey, and second because she would have to compete with Liszt, who was also planning a tour, Clara set her sights on Holland and Belgium for the next winter. Schumann was no more sanguine over this prospect, his reluctance prompting the following words from Clara: "It's awful that I can't put my talents to use for [Robert], now when I possess the greatest energy to do so. Think it over once again, dear husband! Let's make use of *just a couple* of winters [for touring]; anyway, I owe it to my reputation not to withdraw completely from the stage."[50] Not long after, she made a similar entreaty in connection with a projected trip to Denmark, promising that after a season or two she would "withdraw from public performance, live for my home, and give lessons. Then we will have a worry-free existence—think it over again very carefully, my dear husband."[51] As we will see, the question of Clara's touring would remain a point of contention in the years ahead.

Wieck, who had beaten a hasty retreat to Dresden in the weeks after the resolution of the court battle, was the source of "dreary impressions" during a week he spent in Leipzig in mid-October. A month later, Clara learned of his demand for 60 thalers, a sum she had already paid two years before, to cover moving expenses for her piano, a fine instrument presented to her by the famed maker Conrad Graf during her triumphant Viennese tour and now impounded in Dresden. Once again she and Schumann were compelled to seek legal counsel. As Clara summed up the affair: "There are moments of calm, when conciliatory sentiments toward my father rise within me, but they are often stifled by a nasty move or a shameful cabal."[52] Shortly after Wieck's departure, Clara fell into a bit of a depression because she felt "neither the energy nor desire to play. . . . It may have to do with a physical ailment, since I feel weary and anxious, and sometimes I'm gripped by terrible fear for my health, which has been precarious for the past year." Schumann himself had not been "entirely well" since the wedding, but Clara's remarks on her condition (which persisted into early December) indicate that he was not the only hypochondriac in the house.

Of the two of them, Clara definitely held up her end of the diaristic exchange better than Schumann. Her entries tend to be longer (an average of six or seven pages in the original as opposed to his two or three), richer in detail, and more pointed in their assessments of personalities, compositions, and performances: in Clara's view, Moscheles's playing had recently taken a turn for the worse, but after all: "He's getting old. Why do so many artists fail to realize that they've outlived themselves!"; Ferdinand David may have played his new violin concerto masterfully at an October Gewandhaus concert, but "the work is weak in invention—the man has absolutely no talent for composition"; Clara found the noted violin virtuoso Ole Bull, who had arrived in Leipzig with his "unpleasant, cold, and uncultured" wife in late November, to represent "a peculiar mixture of the artistic and the inartistic"; the choir of the Saint Thomas School, we read in a particularly amusing account of a concert on New Year's Day 1841, "didn't exactly cover itself with glory; its members sing so mechanically that one could scream."[53] Not even the great Mendelssohn, whose fugues struck Clara as "quite impoverished" compared to Bach's, escaped unscathed.[54] But she reserved her most stinging barbs for Sophie Schloss, a singer and rival of Clara's sensitive friend Elise List for the public's approbation. "Schloss is pro-

moting herself more and more," Clara noted after a November 1840
Gewandhaus concert, "it seems as though she's made the public, which
applauds her enthusiastically, forget how ugly she is." Or consider her
appraisal of the same singer's performance at a 4 December benefit concert: "Schloss has become more and more of a bore; indeed, she gave a
tedious rendition of an aria from [Mozart's *La Clemenza di*] *Tito*, which
we long ago grew tired of hearing."[55] After reading entries such as these,
we realize that just as Schumann was not the household's only hypochondriac, neither was he its only critic.

     If Schumann was less faithful than Clara in the fulfillment of their
"secretarial duties," he had good reason: in early October, he returned
to composition after a nearly two-month hiatus. His diary entry for 27
September through 4 October consisted only of "random jottings," for:
"Today everything is swimming in notes: I must get to the piano."[56]
Appropriately enough, his first completed works as a married man were
a set of vocal duets (*Drei zweistimmige Lieder,* op. 43), their sleek parallel
thirds and sixths a fitting emblem for connubial bliss. Soon thereafter
came the unusually scored *Zigeunerleben* for vocal quartet, piano, and
ad libitum triangle and tambourine (op. 29, no. 3). But between 13 and
17 October he spoke of "venturing into territory where not every first
step is successful" in a possible reference to sketches for a symphonic
movement in C minor. Preserved in the Universitätsbibliothek Bonn, the
sketches consist of a seven-measure introduction (its opening gesture, a
rising fifth motto, recalls the motto of Haydn's Symphony No. 104), a
continuation of about 150 bars, and a three-measure fragment designated Rondo.[57] Before long, though, Schumann returned to vocal composition, with settings of texts by Eichendorff (*Frühlingsfahrt,* op. 45,
no. 2) and J. G. Seidl (*Blondels Lied,* op. 53, no. 1).[58] On 2 November
he drafted a setting of August Becker's *Rheinlied, Sie sollen ihn nicht
haben* (published as *Der deutsche Rhein: Patriotisches Lied,* op. 27b and
WoO1) for solo voice, chorus, and piano. Inspired by the wave of patriotic fervor sweeping over the German-speaking lands in the wake of a
French threat to sieze the Rhine in July 1840, Becker's doggerel verses
were set by nearly two hundred other composers, including Conradin
Kreutzer, Heinrich Marschner, and Carl Loewe. Schumann's technically
irreproachable if aesthetically undistinguished setting became an instant
hit; indeed, within a month it was already in its fifth printing. Heartened
by this popular success, Schumann quickly rearranged his patriotic lied
for male chorus and also for mixed chorus and orchestra, entering the
latter in a "Rheinlied contest" (one of many that sprang up all over
Germany) to be held in the Leipzig Schützenhaus. (The prize went to
the little known Gustav Kunze; neither of Schumann's alternate settings

of Becker's *Rheinlied* survives). Here too we find a premonition of later developments in the composer's career. The easy-going "folkishness" and "accessibility" that Clara praised in her husband's most recent lied would resurface, though in an artistically richer guise, in the choral part-songs of the later 1840s. Early November also saw the completion of several isolated settings of lyrics by Eichendorff (*Der Schatzgräber*, op. 45, no. 1), Fröhlich (*Die Nonne*, op. 49, no. 3), and Clara's friend Lilly Bernhard (*Mädchen-Schwermuth* op. 142, no. 3), but by the end of the month Schumann was absorbed in a project of larger dimensions. On 20 November, he turned to the lyrics of Justinus Kerner, five of whose poems he had set as long ago as the summer of 1828. By around Christmas time he had completed fourteen settings, the bulk of which were brought together in a new cycle: *Zwölf Gedichte von Justinus Kerner, Eine Liederreihe für Singstimme mit Begleitung des Pianoforte*, op. 35 (published May 1841).

As Schumann put it in a diary entry for late November, his Kerner lieder brought Clara "both joy and pain, for she has had to endure my silence and invisibility."[59] But following on Schumann's example, and perhaps to console herself for his "silence and invisibility," she too tried her hand at vocal composition during this period. (To be sure, Clara was hardly a novice in this regard; as a girl, she had composed a number of songs, the majority of which are now lost.) When Schumann encouraged her to set a poem by Robert Burns in late September, she "didn't dare" at first, but her Christmas presents to her husband included not only a song to the Burns text *(Am Strande)*, but two others as well, both on lyrics by Heine: *Ihr Bildnis* ("Ich stand in dunklen Träumen") and *Volkslied* ("Es fiel ein Reif"). Although Clara wrote off these compositions as "*completely feeble attempts, of no worth at all*," we might best interpret her self-deprecatory remarks as an assurance that she did not intend to compete with Schumann on his own turf. In fact, she had no reason to be embarrassed about her compositional skills: her brooding setting of Heine's *Es fiel ein Reif*, which alternates deftly between declamatory and more lyrical styles, stands up very well against Schumann's far simpler treatment of the same text (the second lyric in the poet's *Tragödie*, a trilogy that Schumann set complete, probably in November 1841, and published as op. 64, no. 3).[60] Her settings of *Am Strande* and *Ihr Bildnis* are no less noteworthy, the former for its emotionally charged accompaniment, the latter for its suave vocal line.

Schumann readily acknowledged Clara's talent as a song composer. Delighted with her Christmas gift, he came up with the "cute idea" of weaving together some of her lieder with his own and having them issued as such.[61] The plan was realized the following year with the publication of *Zwölf Gedichte aus F. Rückerts Liebesfrühling* (Schumann's op. 37; Clara's op. 12), a cycle of solo songs and duets, nine pieces of which were composed by Schumann in January 1841 and the remaining three by Clara in June of the same year. In sheer beauty and immediacy of expression Clara's contributions to the set equal, or even surpass, those of her husband, witness the compelling transition from turbulence to calm in *Er ist gekommen*, the sumptuous but motivically economical setting of *Liebst du um Schönheit*, and the delicate blend of lullaby and chorale styles in *Warum willst du and're fragen?*

Apart from her composing, Clara offered Schumann other causes for joy in the last days of 1840. The couple spent Christmas day in the company of friends, eating, drinking, distributing gifts, and making music until the wee morning hours. For the past week, Clara had held out "beautiful hopes," and by the holiday she was certain of her pregnancy. Their first child, Marie, was born on 1 September 1841.

The Year of Song: "Embarking on Completely New Paths"

"If there is anything at all that Schumann has written which has become, and has deserved to become, world literature, it is surely his songs."[62] Many would no doubt agree with Grieg's assessment. But what motivated Schumann's incredible outburst of vocal composition early in 1840, and what sustained it for nearly a year thereafter? These questions, posed many times before, will not admit to easy answers. While Schumann's turn to song was swift and at times all-consuming, its sources were multi-faceted. The creative products of the *Liederjahr* emerged from a combination of pragmatic, personal, artistic, and critical factors.[63]

As we have seen, Schumann's deep engagement with the lied began in February 1840, just after the Leipzig court delivered its first judgment in the proceedings against Wieck. Although confident he would prevail, Schumann was also anxious to address an objection that Wieck had raised many times in the past years: his inability to secure Clara with the requisite financial support. Success as a composer of lieder, perhaps the most marketable of musical genres, would ensure just the sort of stability Wieck thought him incapable of providing. In early December 1840, he took obvious pride in reporting his annual earnings (actual and projected): 240 thalers received for compositions completed during that year, 330 thalers owed for manuscripts accepted by publishers, and 340 thalers expected for manuscripts still unspoken for. A keen financial manager when he set his mind to it, Schumann brought out the compositions of the *Liederjahr* incrementally, thereby guaranteeing profits in future years: between May 1840 and September 1841, the respective publication dates of the Heine *Liederkreis* and the Rückert lieder, he issued eight sets of songs, only about a third of his total output for 1840, the remainder appearing at intervals throughout the rest of his career (one set, the *Vier Gesänge*, op. 142, was published posthumously in 1858).

At the same time, Schumann viewed the composition of lieder as a profoundly personal activity and, like much of his earlier piano music, an activity densely interwoven with the image of his beloved Clara. "Much of you is embedded in my Eichendorff *Liederkreis*," he wrote to her on 22 May 1840.[64] The same could justly be said of the Heine *Liederkreis*, *Myrthen*, *Dichterliebe*, *Frauenliebe und Leben*, the Reinick lieder, op. 36, and the Kerner cycle, op. 35. In short order, Schumann was consumed by an unbridled (some might say obsessive) joy in writing for the voice. His letters and diaries speak to a building force that, once set in motion, threatened to spin out of control: the Heine *Liederkreis*, completed in February, was accompanied by "blissful" feelings in which laughter and tears intermingled;[65] while composing the Eichendorff *Liederkreis* in May, he expressed his desire to "sing himself to death, like a nightingale"; by November he had "written more than enough songs (over one hundred)—but it's difficult to stop."

Typically for Schumann, the line between the personal and the artistic is a fine one. Writing to the organist Wilhelm Rieffel on 11 June 1840, he mused wistfully: "Your remarks about my piano works have again given me pleasure. If only I could find more people who understand me as I intended; in my lieder I hope to succeed more easily."[66] The implications of these remarks are clear. Through the medium of vocal composition Schumann hoped to fulfill an aim only imperfectly met (at least according to some listeners) in his piano music: the embodiment of inner "states of the soul" in a palpable form.

Moreover, this transformative process neatly dovetails with another goal of long standing: the synthesis of the literary and musical sides of Schumann's creativity. In his earliest surviving autobiographical sketch, drafted when he was still in his mid-teens, he noted: "Poet and composer in one person (Lieder)." Or as he put it in the late summer of 1828, just after the completion of his first Kerner settings and during a period when he was absorbing the mainstays of the song literature (Beethoven's *An die ferne Geliebte*, ballads by Loewe, songs by Schubert and Marschner) at the home of his friends the Carus's: "Song unites the highest, word and tone."[67] A diary entry from the spring of 1833 mentioning "musical poems underlaid with Heine texts . . . dedicated to the poet" may refer to a projected series of character pieces for piano in which Heine's verses were to be notated but unspoken.[68] While this plan never materialized, something akin to it occurs in the piano sonatas op. 11 and op. 22, the slow movements of which are based on two of Schumann's youthful songs. The latent desire to fuse music and poetry in the keyboard music of the 1830s (consider also the underlaid text, "Mein Ruh' ist hin," in the second of the *Intermezzi*, op. 4; or the poetic mottos associated with the *Davidsbündlertänze* and the *Fantasie*, op. 17) thus rose to the surface in the lieder of 1840.

But if the art of song would provide a ready means for the realization of Schumann's quest to reconfigure music as a kind of literature, how are we to account for the apparent reversal in his outlook on song as articulated in an often quoted letter of 30 June 1839 to Hermann Hirschbach? "Have you composed more for voice lately," he asked his friend, "or are you perhaps of my opinion? For my whole life I've placed vocal composition *below* instrumental music, and have never considered it to be great art?"[69] In order to interpret Schumann's remarks fairly, we should consider them in the context of his professional aspirations at the time and also in the broader light of the contemporary musical scene he knew so well. In the early summer of 1839, he was determined to make his mark as a composer of string quartets, and to that end had turned for models to Beethoven's late works in that medium (works that, according to his letter to Hirschbach, he "was studying right down to the love and hate contained therein"). Furthermore, his experiences as a critic had convinced him that although many of his contemporaries had made valuable contributions to the song repertory, the market was in danger of being flooded by compositions of mediocre quality. A year after writing to Hirschbach, he would have to search through "fifty volumes of songs" to find "three good ones."[70] The reference to "vocal composition" in Schumann's letter was in all likelihood an allusion to the art as practiced by his less talented contemporaries; the "instrumental music" he had in mind was that of a giant in the field. The comparison, though unfair, is understandable given Schumann's preoccupations in June 1839. Viewed against this background, his subsequent turn to vocal music may be seen as yet another response to an imperative he pursued tirelessly as a critic: the refinement of imperfect but perfectible tendencies in contemporary art. In short, the will to song to which Schumann succumbed in early 1840 was informed by the same crusading spirit that motivated his critical writings.[71]

These writings in turn provide us with valuable insights into his aesthetic of song. While during his first years as editor of the *Neue*

Zeitschrift Schumann was little involved in reviewing the many collections of lieder that crossed his desk (he generally handed them over to Oswald Lorenz), the situation changed in 1836 with the appearance of half a dozen articles on the songs of his contemporaries. For the next several years Schumann maintained a lively critical interest in the lied, this fascination culminating in his own contributions to the genre. For Schumann the critic, the ideal lied would exude an aura of naturalness; as he put it in an 1836 review of Goethe and Uhland settings by Joseph Klein: "The poem should feel to the singer like a bride lying in his arms."[72] An analogue of what the early romantics called *Naturpoesie*, the lied must appear artless without thereby revoking its claims to art; it must mediate between the Scylla of simplicity and the Charybdis of pretension. If, as Schumann maintained in a review of 1843, "the lied is perhaps the only genre since Beethoven's day in which significant progress has been made,"[73] this was in large measure due to its sublimation of the musically enriched language of Bach and the Viennese classicists. In the works of the more sensitive songwriters of the day (among whom Schumann counted Marschner, Loewe, Norbert Burgmüller, Robert Franz, and Ludwig Berger), this tendency manifests itself in a subtle approach to structure and a rethinking of the relationship between vocal line and piano accompaniment. Strictly speaking, the piano part in an ideal lied will rise from the level of a merely decorative accompaniment to that of an equal partner in a shared discourse. (Schumann chides Theodor Kirchner, for instance, for writing vocal lines that seem to be "a quietly mumbled rendition of the words," and piano parts that take on the character of "self-sufficient instrumental pieces.")[74]

Moreover, the "significant progress" associated with lieder composition would be unthinkable without the rise of a new school of lyric poetry, whose chief lights included Eichendorff, Heine, Rückert, and Uhland. Indeed, a great poem is a necessary, if not a sufficient, condition for a great song: weak verses, Schumann argued, cannot but "take a toll" on the music they call forth, while a composer's musical talents will shine through best when setting the words of a worthy poet.[75] This prescription helps explain a curious feature of Schumann's outlook on the lied: the relatively limited role ascribed to Schubert's accomplishments in the genre.[76] While he revered Schubert as a master of instrumental composition and no doubt respected him as a composer of lieder (in 1828, he even took Marschner to task for not "valuing [Schubert] highly enough"), Schumann likewise felt that his great predecessor could have been more discriminating in his selection of texts for musical setting: "Telemann, who demanded that a respectable composer should be able to set a wall-poster to music, would have found his man in Schu-

bert."[77] He also feared that Schubert's sometimes persistent accompanimental figurations posed a threat "to the delicate life of the poem."[78]
Furthermore, it was the composer's central mission to preserve this "delicate life," not through mere imitation, but through a far subtler process
of re-creation. Not content to repeat what the poet has already stated
(although this, of course, must be his point of departure), the poetically
attuned musician seeks to "present it anew" ("wiedergeben"), and in "its
genuine depth."[79] Schumann articulated this thought most suggestively
in a review published in October 1840, at the height of the *Liederjahr*.
The lieder composer, he wrote, aims "to produce a resonant echo of the
poem and its smallest features by means of a refined musical content."
Such an artist will naturally be concerned with "truth," that is, with a
faithful rendering of the poetic thought in tone, but will also strive to
present it "in a beautiful garb."[80] This directive to idealize the truth
(and hence to represent it as something that is *not quite* and therefore
no longer the truth) obviously opens a tiny fissure through which the
composer is meant to enter, as poet.

In 1840, Schumann proved himself up to the task: the songs of the
Liederjahr more than rise to the standards prescribed in his critical writings. His effort to mediate art and artlessness, a *sine qua non* of success
as a lieder composer, is apparent at all levels. Consider, for instance,
his approach to form. Modified strophic and tripartite (ABA) designs
predominate in Schumann's lieder, both alternatives representing a
straightforward response to the relatively simple verse forms that characterize the majority of the texts he chose to set. At the same time, his
concern for continuity often led him to leave the opening strophe or
strophes harmonically open so that definitive closure was reserved for
the final moments of the lied. In *Morgens steh' ich auf und frage,* the
opening song of the Heine *Liederkreis,* op. 24, these qualities come together to produce a delicate interplay of folk-like simplicity and artful
intent.

In many songs, this interplay emerges in the relationship between
the melody and the accompaniment. The melodic line of *Der Nussbaum,*
the third song of *Myrthen,* is simplicity itself, but the diaphonous texture in the piano part (rolling arpeggios suggestive of the "gentle
breezes" wafting through the walnut tree) lends the whole an unmistakably dreamy, Eusebian atmosphere. The alternating presentation of melodic segments by voice and piano likewise contributes to the same effect. Indeed, the vocal and instrumental strands in this song engage as
co-equals in a finely wrought dialogue.

In some cases, the dialogue is an inner one, carried on at conscious
and unconscious levels represented by voice and piano, respectively. The

speaker in *Der Soldat,* the third of the Andersen *Lieder,* op. 40, is filled with grim forebodings of the death of his "best-loved friend in the world." The vocal line unfolds as a march tune, its mechanically repeated tones aptly portraying the numbness of the soldier fated to shoot his friend "right in the heart." The ominously repeated rhythmic figure in the piano part, a dull echo of the muffled drumbeats resounding in the speaker's psyche, imbues the song with the quality of a psychological thriller. Frequently the piano part completes a thought only partially articulated by the voice, a function usually fulfilled by the celebrated piano postludes of many of Schumann's lieder. In *Stille Thränen,* the tenth song of the Kerner *Liederreihe* and the lyric climax of the cycle, the newly awakened wanderer ventures out into a sunlit meadow at dawn. To underscore the speaker's longing for union with the great natural expanse surrounding him, Schumann elides the final melodic cadence in the vocal line (on the tonic, C) with a deceptive cadence in the piano. Instrumental melody, a cipher for awe-inspiring Nature, has the last word. But in spite of the richness of Schumann's piano parts, they only rarely overwhelm the voice. When they do, the effect is often intentional, as in *Die Löwenbraut* (op. 31, no. 1). The writing for piano in the closing portion of this setting of Chamisso's ballad features thick chords, sharply dotted rhythms, leaps from one registral extreme to the other, and heightened chromatic progressions bordering on the irrational. But after all, the passage comes just as the text describes the brutal murder of the lionkeeper's daughter: consumed by jealousy on learning of her imminent marriage, the lion tears her to pieces. Just as the raving lion (a figure whom Schumann must have associated with Wieck) goes berserk, so too does the music. Thus, even the composer's apparent affront to his poetic texts was grounded in a concern for the projection of an expressive message.

As we have noted, Schumann did not consider every poem equally worthy of musical realization: in his view, only the best would do. He by and large held to this standard throughout his career as a lieder composer, drawing again and again on the verses of the major lyric poets of the late eighteenth and early nineteenth centuries: Goethe, Eichendorff, Heine, Rückert (a particular favorite), Chamisso, Uhland, and Kerner. Nor did he limit himself to German poets alone. His many compelling settings of verses by Andersen, Burns, Byron, and Moore, albeit in German translation, attest to far wider tastes. Schumann was likewise drawn to the whole panoply of poetic forms and genres. While about half of his chosen texts may be classified as "lyric" in the strict sense of the word (that is, as inwardly directed utterances that we, as readers or listeners, chance to overhear), the other half is about evenly divided between balladic or narrative texts (where the speaker relates an event directly to his listeners in the name of the poet) and *Rollengedichte* or dramatic poems (where the speaker or speakers are portrayed as definite characters). Perhaps the most interesting cases are those in which one of the poetic modes—lyric, epic/narrative, or dramatic—is transformed into another. Andersen's *Der Spielmann* (op. 40, no. 4), for instance, shifts from a third-person, narrative account of a poor fiddler's collapse at his former sweetheart's wedding to a first-person plea for mercy, a startling twist signaling the narrator's terrifying realization that he has been describing himself all along. Schumann responded with a masterful projection of the dissociative state expressed in the poem. Conceived as a kind of mad dance, in which the left hand of the piano thumps out a waltz rhythm while the right hand and vocal line imitate the narrator's drunken turns on his fiddle, the song spins more and more out of control as the anguished fiddler's hair turns grey and he smashes his instrument "into a thousand pieces." Then, to articulate the wrenching shift in poetic mode during the final verses, the music abruptly switches into a prayerful tone when the speaker voices his entreaty for delivery from impending insanity (Example 5.1). Schumann's setting thus heightens the disturbing parallel that the poem draws between awakening to consciousness and madness.

To be sure, there are instances where Schumann was not as respectful of his texts as some critics would like. In the well-known *Du Ring an meinem Finger* from *Frauenliebe und Leben,* the repetition of the opening strophe at the end of the song serves a purely musical purpose: while the first statement of the text ends on a half cadence, the second provides closure in the tonic. But as often as not, Schumann's liberal treatment of his texts is poetically as well as musically justified. At the end of his setting of Geibel's *Der Knabe mit dem Wunderhorn* (op. 30, no. 1) he repeats the last line of text, "und grüssend vertönet das Horn" (and the horn, sounding its greeting, dies away), no less than four times, and at a progressively quieter dynamic, so that we literally hear the sound of the horn fade away as the merry lad in the poem gallops off into the distance.[81]

The topical range of Schumann's chosen texts covers a startlingly broad territory. Attracted for obvious reasons to poems dealing with love in all its shadings, the composer likewise set texts that took patriotism, wandering, death, isolation, and madness as their subject. Folksongs, dance-songs, and drinking songs appear side by side with lullabies, visions, and celebratory scenes of all sorts in the collections and cycles of the *Liederjahr.* The affective span of Schumann's music similarly runs the gamut from the infectious humor of *Räthsel,* op. 25, no.

Example 5.1. *Der Spielmann:* mm. 110–34.

16 (where the letter H, the solution to the "riddle" in the title and the
German equivalent of the pitch B, provides the opportunity for a fair
amount of musical punning) and the delicate wit of *Die Kartenlegerin,*
op. 31, no. 2 (with its elfin interludes for piano and patter-style vocal
writing) to the lyric ecstasy of *Stille Thränen* from the Kerner *Liederreihe.* In two of the most popular Heine settings from *Myrthen, Die
Lotosblume* and *Du bist wie eine Blume,* the music projects a subtle ten-

sion between contrasting affects; both songs begin with melodies whose
basic diatonicism is tinged with a hint of chromaticism, an emblem for
the ease with which innocence may give way to sensuality.[82]

It is no accident that this sort of affective contrast should come to
the fore in Schumann's settings of verses by Heine, for the resultant
tension may be viewed as a manifestation of the irony that is one of the
principal features of the poet's manner. Some writers have claimed that
Schumann was either curiously resistant to or blithely dismissive of the
ironic side of one of his favored poets. As Debussy bluntly put it: "Schumann understood nothing about Heinrich Heine, or at least, that's my
impression. He might be a great genius, but he could never capture that
fine spirit of irony that Heine embodies. Look at the *Dichterliebe*, for
example: he misses all the irony."[83] Later critics have voiced similar
opinions, if in less absolute terms.[84] Still, it is difficult to fathom that
one of the most poetically attuned composers of the nineteenth century
was insensitive to such an obvious characteristic of Heine's style. And as
it turns out, he was indeed not so insensitive after all. Consider, for

instance, Schumann's setting of *Lieb' Liebchen, leg's Händchen* from the Heine *Liederkreis,* where the poet's gruesome metaphor (he likens the pounding of his heart to the knocking of an "evil and spiteful" carpenter hammering together his coffin) calls forth a parody of the gentle accompanimental rhythm from the first song in the cycle, a remote modulation down a half-step, and eerie echoes of the piano part in the vocal line; or the posturing in *Ich grolle nicht* from *Dichterliebe,* where the mock-operatic style indicates that, despite his stubborn assertion to the contrary, the spurned lover certainly does "bear a grudge"; or the destruction of a heroic illusion in *Die beiden Grenadiere,* op. 49, no. 1, where the resolve of the patriotic soldier's closing speech (supported by the strains of the *Marseillaise*) is expunged by the piano's intoning of a solemn Requiem hymn as the French grenadier sinks, lifeless, to the ground. As Eichendorff once maintained, the irony in Heine's verses seems to say: "look here, all you good people, how pretty! But do not even for one moment think that I myself believe in these things! Almost every one of his beautiful poems ends with such a suicide."[85] In his setting of *Die beiden Grenadiere* and other texts like it (including *Belsatzar,* op. 57), Schumann proved himself more than willing to reflect this "suicide" in his music.

To be sure, the composer sometimes smoothed over Heine's mordant wit (the piano postlude to the last song in *Dichterliebe* has this effect), but in doing so he might have been thinking back on his first meeting with the poet during the spring of 1828 in Munich. Schumann had expected to find a "sullen, misanthropic" man, but to his surprise, Heine received him warmly and even spent several hours giving him a tour of the city: "A bitter, ironic smile played only at the corners of his mouth: at once a lofty smile over the trifles of life and a sneer over small-minded people; and it was precisely this bitter satire, which one so often observes in his *Reisebilder,* and this deep inner resentment over life . . . that made his conversation so compelling."[86] Heine's irony, Schumann realized as a young man of eighteen, may have sneered, but it also smiled; it was, in other words a *humanizing* irony, a profound realization of the complexities of the mixed blessing that we call the human condition.[87] In the course of the *Liederjahr,* he had many opportunities to encode those complexities in his music.

Schumann's softening of the irony in Heine's verses may also be interpreted as a response to the imperative, first articulated in his critical writings, whereby the lieder composer is enjoined to reflect the "truth" of the poem, but "in a beautiful garb." Viewed from this perspective, it represents just one of the many strategies through which Schumann assumed for himself the role of poet. And nowhere is this tendency more in evidence than in his fondness for the song cycle, a genre he cultivated more assiduously than any other nineteenth-century composer and for which he established the ideal type in such staples of the repertoire as the Eichendorff *Liederkreis, Dichterliebe,* and *Frauenliebe und Leben.* Responsible for the selection, arrangement, and setting of a group of texts so that together they constitute a coherent musical and literary whole, the composer of a song cycle functions no less as poet.

The nature of the whole, however, is not so easy to define. On the one hand, Schumann recognized a distinction between a collection, its contents comprised of self-sufficient parts bound by little more than their shared genre, and a cycle, the parts of which are subordinate to the effect of the whole. This distinction is implicit in a parenthetical comment on the specifically cyclic quality of the Heine *Liederkreis:* "In the last several days," he wrote to Clara on 24 February 1840, "I've completed a large cycle (interrelated ['zusammenhängend']) of Heine songs." [88] On the other hand, while he referred to some of his song cycles *as* cycles in his letters (to Clara and Kistner on the Heine *Liederkreis* and *Myrthen,* respectively), diaries (entry of early December 1840 on the Kerner *Liederreihe*), and drafts (for *Frauenliebe und Leben,*),[89] only one of them was designated as such in the title of its published version: *Dichterliebe—Liedercyclus aus dem Buche der Lieder von H. Heine.* Schumann's reluctance to draw public attention to the cyclic nature of these works probably reflects contemporary performing practices and even marketing strategies. At least until the late nineteenth century, the performance of song cycles in their entirety was the exception, not the rule. While in Prague with Clara in early 1847, Schumann heard a performance of selected lieder from the Eichendorff *Liederkreis* in which renditions of seven of the cycle's dozen songs (by a Herr Emminger) were interspersed with piano pieces by Bach and Mendelssohn; there is no indication that the composer objected.[90] Hence, had Schumann published his *Liederkreise* and *Liederreihen* as cycles per se (thus implying the need for singers to present all of the songs in a group),[91] he might well have discouraged sales—and if nothing else, songs were meant to sell.

Hence, if there is no recipe for the fabrication of a song cycle, the reasons for its creation are at least in part implied in the social and institutional qualities of the genre itself. But aesthetics too should be taken into account. In a review of Carl Helsted's *6 Gesänge,* op. 1, Schumann indicated that diversity was just as crucial as unity for the success of a set of songs: "Whereas other composers churn out miller songs and lullabies year after year, here we see what results from the choice of a varied group of poems: a varied array of musical colors."[92] Commenting on an even more obviously cyclic work, Loewe's *Esther, ein Liederkreis in Balladenform in fünf Abtheilungen,* Schumann noted the various means through which the composition attained textual and musical coherence—narrative consistency, large-scale tonal logic, and motivic recall—without insisting dogmatically that the presence of all these features is a necessary condition for cyclic construction.[93] By these criteria, nine sets of songs from the *Liederjahr* qualify as cycles. Listed in order of composition, they are: the Heine *Liederkreis,* op. 24; *Myrthen,* op. 25; the Eichendorff *Liederkreis,* op. 39; *Dichterliebe,* op. 48; *Frauenliebe und Leben,* op. 42; the Andersen *Lieder,* op. 40; the Reinick *Gedichte,* op. 36; the Kerner *Liederreihe,* op. 35; and the Rückert *Gedichte,* op. 37. All of these sets cohere both textually and musically, although no two of them cohere in quite the same way, and herein lies the point. Just before completing *Dichterliebe* in late May 1840, Schumann wrote to Clara: "Sometimes it seems as though I were embarking on completely new paths in music."[94] In his search for new solutions to the problem of ensuring textual and musical coherence on the large scale, the composer returns from his quest as a poet.

Of the three potentially contributing factors to a song cycle's coherence—narrativity, tonal logic, and motivic recurrence—the first is sometimes predetermined by the poetic source. In *Frauenliebe und Leben,* for instance, Schumann set all but the last of the poems in Chamisso's lyric cycle of the same name. The only one of his cycles to unfold a straightforward narrative, *Frauenliebe* takes its female protagonist from the blissful moments following on her first encounter with her future husband *(Seit ich ihn gesehen),* through courtship, marriage, and pregnancy, and finally to a pained but ultimately wistful reflection on her husband's death *(Nun hast du mir den ersten Schmerz gethan).*[95] In essence an inversion of the chivalric code, Chamisso's poems portray the man as the idolized object of a woman's veneration. The result is a kind of male wish-fulfillment fantasy that some nineteenth-century figures (the poet Eduard Mörike among them) found just as distasteful as their twentieth-century counterparts[96] and that is only redeemed as art through the irresistible grace, verve, and lyric intensity of Schumann's music. The first of his song cycles, the Heine *Liederkreis,* likewise draws on a pre-existent poetic cycle, in this case a series of nine poems, simply entitled *Lieder,* from the *Junge Leiden* (Youthful Sorrows) section of the poet's *Buch der Lieder.* While these verses hardly constitute a narrative in the usual sense of the term, they do trace an affective course that allows us to follow the speaker's progress from an initial state of mystification to an ultimate recognition of the ephemeral quality of love. Schumann mirrors this progress in traversing the distance from the folklike simplicity of the first song *(Morgens steh' ich auf)* to the reflective lyricism of the last *(Mit Myrthen und Rosen)*.

Like the Heine *Liederkreis, Dichterliebe* also takes demystification as its chief theme. But here Schumann asserts himself as poet to a greater degree than in either the earlier Heine cycle or *Frauenliebe*. In making a careful selection from the sixty-six poems of the *Lyrisches Intermezzo*, he intended, as Rufus Hallmark puts it, "to condense a drama from Heine's wide-ranging anthology of lyrics of frustrated and embittered love."[97] The resultant "drama," in other words, was largely of the composer's making. And although the song cycle was drafted in just a little over a week, its poetic, and even musical, content underwent several transformations during this period and in the years ahead. While Schumann's sketches reveal that he may have initially planned to set as many as twenty-nine poems from Heine's anthology, he soon settled on twenty (hence the original title: *20 Lieder und Gesänge*). Only after publication plans were well along with Peters in 1843 and 1844 did he decide to eliminate four of the songs *(Dein Angesicht, Lehn' deine Wang', Es leuchtet meine Liebe,* and *Mein Wagen rollet langsam,* originally positioned in pairs after Nos. 4 and 12, respectively, of the published set) and issue the streamlined cycle as *Dichterliebe*.[98] Schumann's play with number and order, no less than the temporal gap between initial inspiration and final conception, recalls a practice we have observed before in connection with the piano music of the previous decade. (Nor, as we will see, is this the only point of contact between Schumann's vocal and keyboard cycles).

The *Liederkreis,* op. 39, its texts culled from the lyric interpolations in three of Eichendorff's prose works *(Ahnung und Gegenwart, Dichter und ihre Gesellen,* and *Viel Lärmen um Nichts),* is characterized by a similar play with number and order. The high-spirited *Der Frohe Wandersmann,* which opened the cycle when it was first published in 1842, was replaced by the brooding *In der Fremde* when Schumann reissued the work in 1850. Each version of the cycle thus displays a markedly different affective trajectory. Whereas the later and more commonly performed edition describes a great arch from melancholic alienation to ecstatic union with the objects of the poet's longing (his beloved and Nature), the jaunty wandering song that heads off the first version, as Jon Finson has pointed out, was perhaps intended to cast this progression in an ironic light.[99] The compositional histories of *Myrthen* and the Rückert *Gedichte,* both of which focus on the theme of conjugal love, likewise speak to the depth of Schumann's (or Schumann's and Clara's, in the case of the Rückert cycle) concern for hitting upon an appropriate arrangement of his poetic texts.[100] They speak, that is, to the depth of his engagement as a poet.

Even the musically unifying elements in Schumann's song cycles, tonal coherence and motivic recall, disclose a poetic dimension. Almost without exception, adjacent songs demonstrate a close tonal bond, with relationships by third or fifth predominating, though in some instances, the bond is established by a simple shift in mode from major to minor or vice versa. Occasionally an inconclusive ending (like that of the first song in *Dichterliebe,* which fades away on a dominant seventh chord built on C♯) increases our sense for the necessity of a continuation. The cycles as a whole are either centered on a single key or, less often, they proceed logically from one tonality to another. While the former possibility affirms the circularity implicit in a genre designation such as *Liederkreis,* the latter is likewise employed toward the fulfillment of a poetic end. The large-scale motion from F♯ minor to the parallel major in the Eichendorff *Liederkreis* (second version), for instance, articulates the affective course of the texts from brooding melancholy to ecstatic embrace. Similarly, the progressive motion from D to F major in the Reinick *Gedichte* goes hand in hand with a peculiar feature of the narrative trajectory of the cycle's six poems. While the first three lyrics proceed in a logical sequence from a description of an idyllic life along the Rhine to an affirmation of bourgeois values in the poet's union with his sweetheart, the last three texts revert to a world of memories and reflections. The large-scale passage from D to F thus underscores the shift in the poetic landscape from reality to dreamworld.

The technique of motivic recall and transformation is deftly coordinated with poetic content in the later version of the Eichendorff *Liederkreis,* which, in sheer beauty and lyric intensity, is perhaps unsurpassed among Schumann's cycles. Determined to impart melodic coherence to the whole without threatening "the delicate life" of its constituent poems, the composer develops a tiny musical motive over the course of the cycle that is distinctive enough to be recognized upon its return, but hardly obtrusive enough to disturb the prevailing lyric tone. (It is, in other words, an agent of the "wit" we have noted in Schumann's poetic cycles for keyboard.) In the first song, *In der Fremde,* the motive takes the form of a rising and falling fifth in the right hand of the piano at the mention of the "quiet time" ("stille Zeit"), when the wanderer will be forgotten not only in his homeland but also in the lands to which he has journeyed. Here employed as an emblem of the poet's yearning for the ultimate peace of the grave, the motive recurs in subsequent songs in a variety of guises and is coupled with a broad array of expressive connotations. Its expansion to an octave in *Dein Bildnis wunderse-*

lig" (No. 2) meshes with the poet's expression of longing for his distant beloved. Transformed into a series of falling fourths and fifths in the evocatic soundscape of *Mondnacht* (No. 5), the motive is linked with the wanderer's desire for union with the great expanses of circumambient Nature. This descending form recurs in *Auf einer Burg,* where it is embedded in an imitative texture whose archaic flavor is a perfect emblem for distance in time. Unsurprisingly, variants of the initial motive figure in the two climactic songs of the *Liederkreis: Schöne Fremde* (No. 6), and *Frühlingsnacht* (No. 12). In the exhilarating third strophe of the former, it expands to a sixth to highlight the closing proclamation of impending joy: "Es redet trunken die Ferne wie von künftigem grossen Glück!" (The distance speaks, enraptured, of a great future happiness!). Then as the moon and stars and nightingales assure the wanderer that " 'She is yours, she is yours!' " in *Frühlingsnacht,* the cycle's last song, the piano line brings the characteristic motive in yet another transformation, its rhythmic pace quickened and its initial interval spanning a seventh (Examples 5.2a and b). The "great future happiness" prophesied in the sixth song, the music seems to say, is finally at hand.

Thematic recall on an even larger scale plays a decisive part in three other cycles. The last song of *Frauenliebe und Leben* closes with an extended piano postlude in which Schumann restates the music of the opening song. A voiceless, disembodied recurrence, it conjures up an image of the female protagonist, who has just chided her beloved for "sleeping the sleep of death," lost in a reverie of happier times. More to the point, it articulates the proximity of death and life and the eternal renewal of the latter through the medium of recollection. The final song of *Dichterliebe (Die alten, bösen Lieder)* begins on a bitter note, as the poet resolves to bury his love and his sorrow in a coffin cast out to sea. But again the piano serves as an agent of consolation in a postlude that elaborates on the evocative closing music of an earlier song (*Am leuchtenden Sommermorgen,* No. 12); at the same time, the B♭ major of the first presentation gives way to the D♭ major of the second. The last poem of the Kerner *Liederreihe* ends with the troubling thought that only an angel can awaken the dispirited wanderer from his "sad dream," but here too the music softens the blow. In setting this concluding lyric, Schumann recalled, practically note-for-note, the attenuated, ethereal folk-song that had provided the musical substance for the penultimate poem. Although his life may be a sad dream, the wanderer can thus take some comfort in the memory of the "old tune from the breast of a melancholy youth" with which the song cycle fades away. It is tempting to interpret these gestures, the reminiscence of bygone days in *Frauenliebe,* the murmuring arpeggios and evanescent lyricism at the conclu-

Example 5.2a. *Schöne Fremde:* mm. 18–25.

Example 5.2b. Frühlingsnacht: mm. 24–26.

sion of *Dichterliebe,* and the only slightly varied recall of a stylized folk
tune at the close of the Kerner *Liederreihe,* as musical day-dreams, each
of them signifying an embrace of the mystified states with which the
protagonists in the cycles wrestle from beginning to end. But in fact,
they all confirm the power of memory itself,[101] the theme that, perhaps
more than any other, brings us to the heart of Schumann's role as musical poet. Almost all of his song cycles hover at the border between
dream and reality, self-mystification and self-awareness, oblivion and
consciousness. In his musical embodiment of memory, the epic faculty
par excellence, Schumann discovered an ideal mediator for these antithetical terms. At the same time, he demonstrates the potential of music
for the transmission of ideas, its potential, in other words, as a literary
art.

The Year of Song and the "System" of Genres

There is no reason to believe that Schumann consciously determined, at
a specific point in his career, to exhaust the possibilities of the various

musical genres in turn. Yet when we stand back and view his output as a whole, its general outlines emerge with unmistakable clarity: the initial focus on piano music during the 1830s gives way, during the next decade, to song, symphony, chamber music, oratorio, and dramatic music, and finally, in the composer's last years, to a recapitulation of the entire scheme and the addition of church music. This is not to say that Schumann's accomplishments in one genre did not influence his outlook on the others, nor that he always concentrated on one genre at the expense of the others, but only to state the obvious.

Less obvious is the fact that the "system" answered to both artistic and psychological imperatives. To ensure parity with his esteemed predecessors—Bach and Mozart, Beethoven, and Schubert—Schumann felt compelled to establish his credentials in the whole spectrum of musical forms of expression. (As he put it in a review in the 9 August 1842 issue of the *Neue Zeitschrift,* the "masters of the German school" must "demonstrate their proficiency in all the forms and genres.") At the same time, his successive tackling of each of the genres finds a biographical parallel in the impulses that led him, as an adolescent, to devour the literary works of one writer after another, or even, as an adult, to keep track of his daily expenses down to the last penny in the *Haushaltbücher.* His obsession with lists (of everything from his current readings, to the female characters in Shakespeare's plays, to fugue subjects, to the contents of his correspondence), his passion for quotation (whether of a friend whose memorable phrase was recorded in one of the diaries, or of an author whose utterances on music were assembled in the *Dichtergarten*), his enthusiasm for the prospectus (whether it be for a new journal or for a musical or literary course of study)—all of these activities represent attempts on Schumann's part to keep the ever-threatening chaos of an uncertain future at bay. His exploration of the musical genres may be viewed in the same light.

The systematic character of Schumann's survey of the musical landscape was already recognized during his own lifetime, and quite early at that. According to an unsigned review in the *Blätter für Musik und Literatur* (Hamburg 1841), the composer had not only distinguished himself as an "original tone poet at the piano," but was now in the process of literally "graduating from" ("absolvieren") the genres of song and symphony.[102] Schumann's lieder occupy a pivotal position in his output, at once resonating with past accomplishments and pointing toward developments in the future. This too was observed by some contemporary critics. Franz Brendel, for instance, heard in the rich accompaniments of Schumann's lieder a continuation of the keyboard style of the 1830s, and in the "melodic distinctness" of their vocal lines a harbinger of the "objective" phase that the critic associated with Symphonies Nos. 1 and 2, the chamber music of 1842, and *Das Paradies und die Peri*.[103] Although Brendel was thinking primarily of individual songs, which he viewed as amplified piano pieces, we can refine his observations on the relationship between the *Liederjahr* and the immediately preceding phase by taking the song cycles into account as well. Like the earlier poetic cycles for keyboard, Schumann's *Liederkreise* and *Liederreihen* may be interpreted as constellations of lyric fragments. The constructive principle of both genres is fundamentally the same and can be summed up in a single word: montage. (Schumann's contemporaries took note of this quality too, though not always with approbation. While some critics felt that his song cycles created more of a "total impression" than the "tangled images" he assembled in his keyboard cycles, others were of a different opinion; levelling a by now familiar charge through a suggestive metaphor, an early reviewer of *Dichterliebe* complained that too many of the songs "rushed by skittishly, like butterflies," that is, like *papillons*.)[104] Even Schumann's experiments with the number and arrangement of the constituent parts of his song cycles parallel the similarly mosaic-like approach he often took in the composition of his keyboard cycles. Likewise, the composer's prolonged encounter with the lied would have clear repercussions in the future. His cultivation of a more plastic mode of expression not only prefigures the "objective" manner of the instrumental and vocal music of the early and mid-1840s, it also looks forward to developments at the end of the decade. The dialectic between accessibility and esotericism that surfaces in the *Hausmusik* of the later 1840s (whether for voice and piano, chorus, chamber ensemble, or keyboard) is directly grounded in the delicate balance Schumann strikes between popular song and art song in a lied such as *Du bist wie eine Blume* and many others like it. And as we have seen, the same dialectic can already be sensed in much of the piano music written during Schumann's earlier stay in Vienna. Hence the products of the *Liederjahr* stand at the meeting-point of some of the most important strands in the rich tapestry that constitutes his output as a whole.

Just as Schumann was of two minds about the aesthetic worth of the musical fragment in general, so was his outlook on the lied in particular complicated by a similar duality. On the one hand, a song was to be prized as a "concentrated composition" in which a "tone poet might say in minutes what others need hours to express." But on the other, "whoever has made an auspicious beginning [as a lieder composer] should not be surprised if the future makes even higher demands on him. Success in small genres often leads to one-sidedness, to mannerism.

May the young artist ward off this fault by embracing new artistic forms, by attempting to express his rich inner self through another medium besides the voice." [105] By the fall of 1840 Schumann himself was anxious to tackle "new artistic forms." (As we have seen, his thoughts had already turned to the string quartet and opera in the summer of 1839 and the winter of 1840, respectively). And although his attempt to draft a C-minor symphony in October 1840 cannot be called a success, he remained undaunted. Early in the next month, Clara raised the possibility of a Parisian tour, but Schumann would hear nothing of it until first completing a piano concerto and a symphony. [106] Within a year, he had made important contributions to both genres. As for the trip to Paris, it never took place.

～6～

*T*he Symphonic
Year: 1841

Settling into Marriage—and Symphonic Composition

On 11 December 1839, Schumann dispatched to his future wife a breathless account of a reading of Schubert's "Great" C-major Symphony he had heard just that day at the Leipzig Gewandhaus:

> Clara, today I was in seventh heaven. A symphony of Franz Schubert [the "Great" C-major] was played in the rehearsal [of the Gewandhaus orchestra]. It's beyond description; the instruments are made to sound like human voices—ingenious beyond measure—and this instrumentation despite Beethoven—and this length, this heavenly length like a novel in four volumes, longer than [Beethoven's] Ninth Symphony. I was totally happy, and wished only that you should be my wife and that I also could write such symphonies.[1]

In his last sentence, Schumann defines the poles between which the activities of his so-called Symphonic Year would be suspended: personal well-being and professional success in the form generally agreed to represent "the grandest species of musical creation."[2] Schumann's *Flegeljahre*, his "years of indiscretion," came to an end with his marriage to Clara Wieck on 12 September 1840. Not long thereafter he would embark on the composition of a series of works—the First Symphony, op. 38; the *Ouverture, Scherzo und Finale*, op. 52; the A-minor *Phantasie* for piano and orchestra (which would become the first movement of the Piano Concerto, op. 54, in 1845); and the D-minor Symphony (published in revised form as the Fourth Symphony, op. 120, in 1853)—

whose breadth and variety is practically unmatched. In the fall of 1840 and throughout much of 1841, Schumann's personal and professional concerns would indeed intersect. No doubt, his turn to orchestral composition issued in part from Clara's urging; consider the following exhortation from a letter of 7 January 1839: "Dear Robert, don't take it amiss if I tell you that I've been seized by the desire to encourage you to write for orchestra. Your imagination and your spirit are too great for the weak piano."[3] In addition, Schumann's turn to the grandest of the musical genres, a sure index of his hopes for widespread recognition, would usher in a more streamlined approach to the business of composing.

An excellent measure of the objectification that begins to affect Schumann's life and work is provided by the altered character and function of his diaries, specifically, of the marriage diary with alternating entries from Robert and Clara. Mendelssohn and his wife Cécile kept a similar diary, but discontinued the project after the first year of their marriage; in an entry for the week of 14–21 March 1841, Schumann registered his determination not to abandon his joint enterprise with Clara, to which she added: "Certainly not!"[4] Yet in spite of his professed commitment to the marriage diary, Schumann's entries became more prosaic and fewer as time went on; while at work on the First Symphony in January and February, he allowed five weeks to elapse without adding a single line. Not surprisingly, the diaries begin to lose their poetic flavor as their audience dwindles to include only the composer and his wife.

The domestication of Schumann's personal chronicle goes hand in hand with a gradual loss of interest in music-critical work. "Robert sits with his journal [the *Neue Zeitschrift*]," Clara noted in early March, "but it bores him horribly."[5] The composer himself would refer to the *Neue Zeitschrift* as a "vexatious stepchild"; twice in the *Haushaltbücher* he wrote of his grudging attention to the "damned journal."[6] Ever an avid reader, Schumann would nonetheless reduce his consumption of literary works during the Symphonic Year. Reading became a reward withheld until a major composition was more or less finished. Hence, a browse through Victor Hugo's *Notre Dame* would follow on the completion of the First Symphony; Jean Paul's *Unsichtbare Loge* figured after the drafting and scoring of the *Ouverture, Scherzo und Finale* and the *Phantasie;* Goethe's *Dichtung und Wahrheit* after the bulk of the sketching for the D-minor Symphony.[7]

To judge from the diaries, the first year of the Schumann's marriage passed with a relative minimum of emotional upset. Their hearts, Schumann wrote in April 1841, were "ever clear and bright and full of love . . . this too is inscribed in my music."[8] Only Clara's father, whose

libellous charges against his son-in-law earned him a sentence of eighteen days in prison, was a source of consternation. Wieck's visit with
Robert and Clara in May was therefore not without its awkward moments. Described by Schumann as "arrogant after the manner of Hans-
wurst," Wieck apparently offended the composer's sensibilities by dub-
bing the recently completed "Spring" Symphony (op. 38) as a
"Contradiction-symphony."[9]

All in all, Schumann cannot have been an easy individual with
whom to share one's life. While occupied with the scoring of his First
Symphony in late February, he noted in the *Haushaltbücher:* "cheerfully
revelled with Clara, joyous over the symphony."[10] But within a day or
so, he lapsed into the depression that typically plagued him in the wake
of intense work on a large project; by the end of the month, Clara found
him "in a vegetative state."[11] On Clara's side, we may observe a hint of
resentment over the fact that her practicing had to cease while her husband was at work: "Again I'll have to neglect my piano playing completely, as is always the case when Robert composes," she noted just as
Schumann began to sketch the D-minor Symphony in early June.[12] The
Schumanns, it would seem, were forced to cope with the eminently
modern problem of juggling the demands of a two-career family. Nor
did each of them derive an equal measure of support from the other. In
the next few years, Schumann's uneasiness over his spouse's professional
aspirations would come increasingly to the surface.

But at least during the Symphonic Year, the diaries served as a
means of assuaging these conflicts. By communicating through the medium of prose, the Schumanns managed to hold the tensions of their
relationship in check. In an October entry in the marriage diary, Schumann provides a rare example of humor. For the sake of preserving his
pun, the original German is appended to the translation: "[Belgian soprano Elisa] Meerti no longer pleases as she once did; one could say
that she's no longer what she used to be" (Die Meerti gefällt nicht so
wie früher; man sagt von ihr, sie wäre nicht mehr die (Meerti).[13] Clara
responds with a comparable rejoinder:

"[Eduard] Röckel played Oberon's Magic Horn [OBERONS
ZAUBERHORN, i.e., Hummel's *Fantasie* for horn and orchestra, op.
116] without much enchantment [ohne jedoch zu bezaubern], and after
that a fantasy of his own—a non plus ultra of fantasylessness [Fantasie-
losigkeit]."[14] But generally the exchanges held to a more serious tone.
Clara, for her part, often utilized the marriage diary to boost what must
have been a fragile ego. The following entry was certainly made for her
husband's sake, not for hers or posterity's: "daily I realize more what a
treasure of poetry [Robert] bears within him, and if I may say it once

again, daily I love him more—I can hardly treasure and honor him enough."[15] The difference in Robert's and Clara's respective "treasures" should not escape notice: his is poetry, hers is Robert.

Clara's comments on other musicians must frequently be read in this light, that is, as assurances that she "treasures" her husband before anything or anyone else. Though Mendelssohn was often the object of her unqualified praise, Clara did not shrink from making occasional but pointed digs: "But he [Mendelssohn] can also be a political operator," or "There was no dearth of 'bravos' [for Mendelssohn's conducting]; the ladies in particular took pleasure, sitting throughout the concert with their mouths agape as if they'd never seen a conductor before in all their lives; I certainly respect Mendelssohn highly, but this insipid idolatry I find unbearable."[16] Sensitive to having stolen the show at the December 1841 concert on which Schumann's *Ouverture, Scherzo und Finale* and D-minor Symphony were premiered, Clara soothed her husband's feelings by seconding his criticisms of her own playing. In the same diary entry, she offered a scathing account of Liszt, whose appearance on the program (for a performance of his *Hexameron* duo with Clara) had caused something of a sensation: "Liszt is ever the ingenious—if sometimes tasteless—pianist . . . but as for his compositions, one can only call them atrocious—a chaos of the harshest dissonances, an eternal rumbling in the lowest and highest registers at the same time, tedious preluding, etc.: as a composer I come close to hating him."[17] The subtext of Clara's appraisal is clear: Liszt's playing may have been dazzling, but his creative work fell far short of Schumann's in depth and substance.

Schumann, for his part, turned to the marriage diary to extend apologies that it must have been difficult for him to verbalize. We know from the *Haushaltbücher* that he could be irascible (on 6 March he noted "Sadness on account of an unkind word I let slip to Clara," and again on 17 October "very hot-tempered with Clara—how foolish of me"),[18] though the reasons for the outbursts remain unstated. Through the marriage diary, Schumann could assure Clara of his affection and at the same time assuage his guilty conscience: "[I] should be delighted to have such a wife and child [Marie, born 1 September 1841], and yet I often don't show it, which troubles my wife."[19]

It is clear from the diaries that the household was organized around Schumann's compositional workshop, to which Clara was granted admission but rarely. Even in the Schumanns' ostensibly joint projects, such as their collaboration on a song cycle on texts from Rückert's *Liebesfrühling* (begun in January and published as Opus 37 in September), Robert assumed the upper hand. As we have seen, Clara contributed only three settings (nos. 2, 4, and 11 in the final ordering), which, as she put it in a diary entry of early June, "were brought to light for my dear husband."[20] Their joint exercises in score-reading, undertaken during the spring and summer months, centered on Beethoven's symphonies (Nos. 2 and 4) and Mozart's overtures.[21] The project at once emanated from Schumann's preoccupation with orchestral composition and allowed him to devise a course of study for Clara. His plan to examine "old music" (the works of Lully, Schütz, Keiser, and Telemann)[22] with his wife served similar ends: a broadening of Clara's musical tastes and a refining of his own historical consciousness. In all these enterprises, Schumann took the lead, but as we shall see, he perhaps owed more to Clara's musical insights than he would admit either publicly or privately.

The Symphonic Challenge

"The main thing," Schumann wrote in July 1841, "is production itself,"[23] and produce he did, with amazing alacrity. Despite their rapid production, the compositional projects of the Symphonic Year radiate in multiple directions. As noted in our discussion of the *Liederjahr*, Schumann spent the first part of January 1841 with the nine Rückert settings for *Liebesfrühling*, op. 37. The opening rhythmic-melodic gestures of the first and last songs from the completed set *(Der Himmel hat eine Thräne geweint,* and *So wahr die Sonne scheinet)* find a parallel in the opening motto of the First Symphony. The fragmentary sketches of an opening movement and rondo for a C-minor symphony, probably conceived and abandoned just before Schumann set to work on the First Symphony in late January, also look toward the past and the future: the rising fifth of the introductory Un poco Andante simultaneously recalls Haydn's Symphony No. 104 and points toward Schumann's own Second Symphony, op. 61.[24] From 21 to 26 September, Schumann sketched all four movements of yet another C-minor symphony[25] that vividly demonstrates the confluence of pianistic and orchestral conception. Only the Scherzo would come to light in published form (and with minor alterations) as the thirteenth piece in the *Bunte Blätter,* op. 99 (1852), yet few listeners acquainted with the keyboard version might guess that the piece was originally intended for a symphony.[26] Having finished polishing his D-minor Symphony in early October, Schumann turned again to vocal composition with a setting of Heine's *Tragödie,* a miniature cycle for voices and orchestra.[27] In fact, vocal music had been on his mind since late summer: "How I long to write an opera," he noted in the marriage diary in early July.[28] Although Schumann first looked to Calderón as the possible source for a libretto, his interest in the Spanish playwright's works waned quickly. By early August, Thomas Moore's *Paradise and the Peri* had become a favored choice. Schumann's efforts to hammer out an opera text with poet Adolf Böttger were not wasted: an oratorio based on the tale of the Peri would form the centerpiece of his activities in 1843.[29]

Still, the core of Schumann's work during 1841 remained his symphonic projects. Nor would this be the first time in his career that he had concentrated on the symphony, witness the many symphonic attempts (including the fragmentary "Hamlet" Symphony and the piano reductions of Beethoven's Fourth Symphony and third *Leonore* Overture) recorded in the Wiede sketchbooks between 1829 and 1833,[30] and his work on a G-minor symphony in 1832 and 1833. What distinguishes Schumann's approach in 1841 is its thoroughness; the larger system, the composer's focus on song, symphony, chamber music, and oratorio in 1840, 1841, 1842, and 1843, respectively, enfolds a smaller one: a comprehensive exploration of practically all the possibilities afforded by the symphonic medium. Hence we find a representative of the grand symphony (after Beethoven's example) in the First Symphony. The more compact *Ouverture, Scherzo und Finale,* on the other hand, is less a symphony than a sinfonietta. The A-minor *Phantasie* for piano and orchestra mediates between free-wheeling rhapsody and concerto-allegro. The D-minor Symphony, given the prominence of thematic transformation across a series of movements that Schumann attempts to bind into a unity, is much like a tone poem in design. And finally, the reduced dimensions and modest scoring of the C-minor Symphony sketched in late September make it into a self-consciously "classical" work.

Like all the other composers who tried their hands at symphonic composition in the mid- and late-nineteenth century, Schumann had to confront the problem of coming to grips with the Beethovenian imperative—the "will to large-scale form" as Dahlhaus calls it[31]—in the face of essentially lyric materials. The challenge, as Schumann articulated it in his writings of the late 1830s, involved preserving the dynamism engendered by his great predecessor's works without at the same time descending into merely slavish imitation.[32] No doubt a way around the dilemma was to be had through Schubert, the composer who in Schumann's estimation had managed to preserve the spirit of Beethoven precisely by renouncing the latter's music as a model.[33] In Schubert's C-major "Wanderer" fantasy for piano (D. 760), E-flat major Piano Trio (D. 929)—both of them objects of Schumann's youthful admiration[34]—and "Great" C-major Symphony, Schumann found traces of a "will to

large-scale form" that manifested itself through technical means largely
independent of Beethoven: the obsessively repeated rhythmic patterns in
the outer movements of the symphony, the wholesale transposition of
large blocks of musical material in the opening movement of the piano
trio, the affective thematic transformations in the fantasy, tonal dualism
(that is, alternate presentations of the same melody in third-related
keys), and the prominence of parallel or strophic forms. Yet Schumann
hardly intended to copy Schubert any more than he did Beethoven. In
his hands, Schubert's leisurely processes of continuation—the generators
of "heavenly length"—would become agents of a Beethovenian teleology.
In the principal works of Schumann's Symphonic Year, Beethoven and
Schubert are omnipresent as spirits to be emulated, not models to be
imitated. But this dual appropriation of the Beethovenian and Schubertian legacies also contributes to the difficulties many listeners have
experienced in grasping Schumann's symphonic style. (Tovey was certainly right: "no orchestra ever earned its reputation by its interpretation
of Schumann.")[35] Beethoven may have been primarily a "dramatist" and
Schubert a "lyricist"; Schumann straddles both categories by treating his
fundamentally lyric themes with a dramatic urgency.

It is therefore fair to say that Schumann inaugurates a new tone
with his symphonic works. Up until the middle of the nineteenth century, the symphony answers to the demands of two complementary aesthetics: the Sublime and the Beautiful. It presents the solemn and grand
ideas suggestive of the former in the carefully balanced forms requisite
for the latter. Schumann adds a third dimension: the aesthetic of the
apparently banal, commonplace, or grotesque that the Schlegel brothers
would call the Characteristic. Even the aesthetically suspect has a role to
play in Schumann's symphonies, where it may take the form of an off-
kilter polonaise with one beat too many (in the finale of the First Symphony) or a bit of maudlin salon music (in the *Romanza*, originally
planned to include guitar accompaniment, of the D-minor Symphony).
When Spohr complained that the horn and flute cadenzas in the last
movement of the First Symphony were not "appropriate" for the
genre,[36] he unwittingly recognized the singular contribution of Schumann's much-derided orchestration to the new symphonic tone. G. W.
Fink, who reviewed the First Symphony's premiere, was equally offended
by the lapse of taste represented by the triangle in the opening movement;[37] apparently he did not appreciate Schumann's use of the instrument's distinctive timbre as a means of highlighting the movement's
chief rhythmic cell. And finally, the new tone derives in large measure
from Schumann's treatment of his themes much like mutable characters.
The gradual tightening of the thematic web from the First Symphony,

through the *Ouverture, Scherzo und Finale* and *Phantasie,* and culminating in the D-minor Symphony, is unmistakable. In a sense, then, the story of the Symphonic Year centers on a quest for ever more tangible methods of integration.

Two Symphonies, a "Symphonette," and a Phantasie

Schumann's First Symphony was the product of an incredible burst of creative energy. In the space of four days, the sketching was for all intents and purposes complete. The *Haushaltbücher* stenographically record the project's speedy unfolding:

> 23 January [1841]: The "Spring" Symphony begun.
> 24 January: The Adagio and Scherzo of the symphony completed.
> 25 January: Symphonic fire—sleepless nights—[work] on the last movement
> 26 January: Hooray! The symphony complete![38]

Even Schumann, when he returned to the marriage diary during the third week of February, couldn't help but marvel over the rapidity with which his symphony had taken shape. (Nor was his "symphonic fire" cooled by an annoying call to serve in Leipzig's Communal Guard; on 1 February he formally requested release from service on account of his "lame" right hand and a severe case of shortsightedness; after more than a year of wrangling, his petition was approved.)[39] And even though he made some important revisions in the following weeks and months—a coda for the first movement and a second Trio for the Scherzo added during the orchestration process, the shifting of the flute solo in the finale from introduction to retransition[40]—he would basically hold to the outlines of the symphony as laid down in the January sketches.

After the 31 March premiere, the composer justifiably noted: "this day has been one of the most important in my artistic life."[41] Indeed, with the First Symphony Schumann staked a claim, and for once the press agreed that he had done so successfully. What surprised the reviewers most was the fact that Schumann had been previously known, insofar as he was known at all, as a composer of miniatures, yet here in the First Symphony he proved his confident mastery of the largest dimensions and forces.[42] Although later commentators have faulted Schumann for the supposed pianism of his symphonic writing, there is little in the First Symphony to support the charge. When, in the finale's transition section, a woodwind phrase recalling the last of the *Kreisleriana* pieces is swept aside by the movement's chief motive in the strings, Schumann effectively says "O Freunde, nicht mehr diese Töne," with all the rhetorical force of Beethoven's baritone solo, to the keyboard music of the previous decade. Hence he comes into his own as a symphonist through an act of renunciation, but the gesture extends past his own earlier achievements to encompass those of his revered predecessors, Schubert and Beethoven. The echoes of Schubert are effectively neutralized by the emphatic trombone countermelody in the coda of the finale, where the trombone motive from the first movement of Schubert's "Great" C-major appears in inverted form (Examples 6.1a and b). And if the extra-musical touches of Schumann's First Symphony hark back to Beethoven's "Pastoral," Schumann allows for little of that work's idyllic expansiveness in his first major essay for orchestra.

In an apt turn of phrase, Ludwig Finscher has described Schumann's First Symphony as a work poised "between absolute and program music."[43] The composer's stance on what would become the chief sticking-point of nineteenth-century musical aesthetics was ambivalent at best. As early as 1835, Schumann asserted in his review of Berlioz's *Symphonie fantastique* that the poetic quality of a musical work increases in direct proportion to the quantity of "thoughts" and "pictures" suggested by the music.[44] Yet in a review of Spohr's "Weihe der Töne" Symphony of the same year, he raised the objection that programmatic titles might all too easily fetter the listener's imagination.[45] Similarly, it was all well and good for Mendelssohn to "murmur" of old legends and fairy tales in his *Melusine* overture, since an attempt to "represent" them would be doomed to failure.[46] Writing to Spohr on 23 November 1842, Schumann brought the same line of thinking to bear on his First Symphony: "I had no intention of painting or depicting."[47]

The dialectic between "suggestion" and "portrayal" (like that between absolute and program music) is vividly demonstrated in the genesis and character of the First Symphony. In late January Clara reported

Example 6.1a. Schubert, Symphony in C Major, D. 944: first movement, mm. 199–201.

Example 6.1b. Schumann, First Symphony: fourth movement, mm. 302–9.

in the marriage diary that the new orchestral work was to be called "Spring Symphony" (a fact confirmed by the *Haushaltbücher*), and further that the impulse for its creation was provided by a "spring poem" by Böttger. A year later Schumann would corroborate this account of the poetic source for his composition by sending Böttger his portrait inscribed with the symphony's opening motto and the following phrase: "Beginning of a symphony, occasioned by a poem by Adolph Böttger."[48] There can be little argument over the aptness of Schumann's original title; today we hear the same voices of "youthful energy" in the symphony that Clara heard in 1841. More tenuous, however, are the ties between the exuberant character of the symphony and the content of the poem, which has less to do with spring than with a despondent lover whose plight is made all the more poignant through its contrast with the season's arrival:

> You spirit of the clouds, cheerless and heavy,
> Coursing menacingly over land and sea,
> In an instant your gray veil cloaks the bright eye of Heaven,
> Your mist wanders from afar and night enshrouds the star of love:
> You spirit of the clouds, cheerless and damp,
> Why have you banished all my happiness,
> Why do you cover my face with tears and the light of my soul with
> shadows?
> Oh desist, desist from your present course—
> Spring blossoms in the valley![49]

Little wonder, then, that Schumann eventually effaced all outward connections with the poem in the published score of the symphony; gone were the reference to spring in the title and the figurative movement headings: "Beginning of Spring," "Evening," "Jolly Playmates," "Spring Replete." All that remains of the poem is an echo of its iambic tetrameter in the symphony's opening motto (Example 6.2, where the last couplet of Böttger's text is "underlaid" to Schumann's music). In the course of the first movement's slow introduction, Schumann proceeds to dismantle the rhythm of this emphatic "call to awakening"[50] before subjecting it to all manner of variations (involving both diminution and

Example 6.2. First Symphony: opening movement, motto.

fragmentation) throughout the ensuing Allegro molto vivace. But even here it might be questionable to speak of a wordless evocation of the poem. The opening rhythmic gesture of the First Symphony, after all, was one of Schumann's favorites. Reinhard Kapp locates it in no less than 163 works, where it is often coupled with the designation *Im Volks-ton.*[51] Thus, if the gesture "means" anything at all in the First Symphony, it probably aims less at a portrayal of spring than at a suggestion of the grandeur of nature.

However we choose to interpret the symphony's programmatic content, there can be little question of Schumann's arrival as a master of the larger forms, an arrival signalled by his profound rethinking of symphonic structure. The frequently repeated claim that, with the First Symphony, Schumann makes a regressive turn to classicism whereby new wine is poured into old bottles, simply will not hold up.[52] Among the most formally compelling (and unprecedented) moments in the symphony is the spot at the climax of the first movement's development section where the full orchestra jubilantly proclaims the opening brass motto. One of the sillier analytical wars in the Schumann literature has been waged over just this passage: given the tonic return, does the recurrence of the introductory motto mark the beginning of the recapitulation,[53] or are we still in the concluding phase of the development (the retransition), with the true reprise reserved for the Tempo I some 24 measures later?[54] Both questions miss the point, for the forcefulness of the opening fanfare's restatement is such that the categories of traditional formal analysis (development, retransition, recapitulation) are effectively suspended. The power of the motto is sufficient to occasion the omission of the opening Allegro material (itself based on the motto), thus causing the music at Tempo I to function as a point of recovery from a tremendous shock wave. The reprise of the motto, then, might be described as a moment of "breakthrough," an overcharged gesture whose threat to the balance of the movement exposes the fiction that music must proceed as a seamless, logical discourse. (The intentionally fragmented forms of Schumann's earlier keyboard works make much the same point.) Schumann's sketches graphically reveal the cleft in the musical flow; as shown in Example 6.3, the motto is literally lifted out of its surroundings: metrically (by the shift from $\frac{2}{4}$ to common time), visually (by the double bars), and affectively (by the designation "Un poco [maestoso]").[55] By way of the "breakthrough," Schumann lodges a protest against the conventions of symphonic form.

No less profound is Schumann's rethinking of the symphony as a genre. Though barely longer than Mozart's last symphonies, Schumann's First already discloses the traits of a musical epic. Closed forms give way

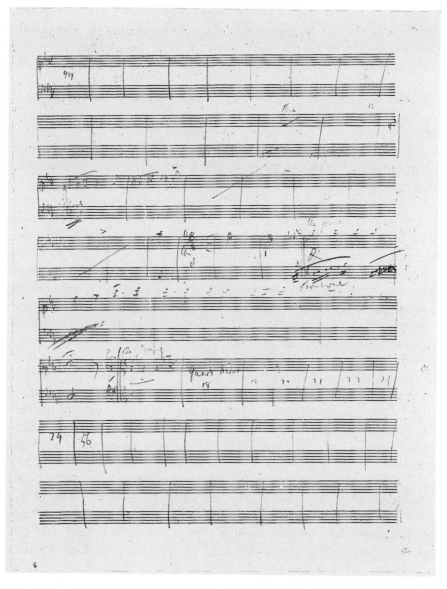

Example 6.3. First Symphony: from the continuity draft for the first movement, p. 5. (Library of Congress, Washington, D.C.)

to contingent, episodic structures whose outcome is difficult to predict: in the coda of the first movement, for instance, a chorale (stated first by the strings, then amplified with winds) appears long after we expect any new music. The symphony, in Schumann's hands, becomes inclusive enough to admit seemingly pedestrian material, its presence justified by its monumental treatment. The finale provides a good example. Its focal point is the second-group chorale, a counterpart to the worldly dance that functions as the movement's first theme. Though hymnic in tone (due to its scoring for clarinets and bassoons, and second-species partwriting), there is nothing particularly distinguished about Schumann's second subject. What raises it above the workaday is its placement in a web of developing variations: the same rhythmic cell (𝄴 ♩ ♩ | ♩ ♩ ♩ | ♩ ♩ | 𝅝 |) informs the movement's introductory flourish, the string retorts of the transition, the second-subject chorale, the development's fugatos, the preface to the horn and flute cadenzas, and the apotheotic strains of the coda.

In several of his reviews of 1835, Schumann observed the tendency of recent composers to imbue their symphonies, sonatas, and concertos with "historical interest" by elaborating the same ideas across the whole span of a work, or by linking its movements with transitions.[56] Both techniques contribute to the epic quality of Schumann's First Symphony. The trombone chorale at the conclusion of the slow movement, for example, generates the principal idea of the ensuing Scherzo. Schumann ensures the practically unbroken continuity of the whole through a series of other strategies as well: the Larghetto ends indecisively on the dominant of G in preparation for the Scherzo; the latter in turn concludes with an unexpectedly quiet gesture. As Alfred Dörffel noted in his chronicle of the Gewandhaus concerts, Schumann thus saw to it that the customary applause would not interrupt the course of his First Symphony.[57] In this work the composer put himself on a par with Beethoven and Schubert by redrawing the boundaries of the symphonic tradition.

The First Symphony was one of the small number of Schumann's symphonic works to achieve a lasting success during his lifetime. According to a review of 1848, it virtually "electrified its audience."[58] Few of Schumann's later works—another symphony, the "Rhenish" (op. 97), among them—would garner this kind of approbation. Yet it would be inaccurate to say that his next major orchestral work, the *Ouverture, Scherzo und Finale,* op. 52, a composition rarely heard in concerts today, gathered dust on the shelf after its first Leipzig performance on 6 December 1841. Dörffel's statistics for the Gewandhaus concerts from 1781 to 1881 indicate that while its seventeen performances during that period could not rival the First Symphony's thirty, they nonetheless compare respectably with the figures for well-known favorites such as Beethoven's *Egmont* and *Fidelio* overtures (with fifteen and ten performances, respectively, for the period from 1840 to 1880).[59]

To judge from the *Haushaltbücher,* the new composition was conceived in the same fever heat that brought forth the First Symphony: within three days (12–14 April) the *Ouverture* was sketched and scored; the sketching of the remaining two movements occupied Schumann for a similarly brief period a week later.[60] The only matter to give him pause was an overall title. In the course of the next weeks, he would refer to the work variously as a "Suite" or "Symphonette";[61] on the slip attached to a letter to Friedrich Hofmeister of 5 November 1842, the title reads: "Second Symphony (Overture, Scherzo, and Finale) for orchestra."[62] Schumann's rejection of all these possibilities for the published version might well be taken as an index of the work's generic singularity.

The relatively tepid reaction of the early critics, who complained of "sketchiness" and a lack of easily memorable motives,[63] has been ascribed to a variety of sources. Schumann himself blamed the critics' coolness on Mendelssohn's absence from the podium at the premiere, and on the audience's inability to absorb so much of his music at one sitting (the D-minor Symphony also appeared on the same program).[64] More recent writers have suggested that Schumann's attempt to please just about every taste in symphonic music ran aground owing to the work's failure to conform to any particular generic tradition.[65] But perhaps Clara came closest to the heart of the problem in a diary entry written after Schumann had sketched the *Ouverture*. She noted that although her husband derived the greatest pleasure from immersion in his work, "he is in no way unreceptive to the praise of the crowd, that simply isn't the case—and certainly there exists no artist who is indifferent to the applause of the public."[66] This dialectic between artistic aspirations and popular success manifests itself as a play of esoteric and exoteric elements in the *Ouverture, Scherzo und Finale*. The uneasy balance that results may have been a source of puzzlement for Schumann's listeners, both in 1841 and in the present.

To be sure, it is difficult to miss the "delicate," "jolly," and "bewitching" effects that Clara heard in the *Ouverture*.[67] Its elfin orchestration hearkens to the sonic world of Weber's *Oberon*, just as its lack of complex developmental passages recalls the easy-going manner of the Rossinian overture. The Scherzo proceeds with the feather-light pace of the best of Schumann's "Florestan" pieces. The boisterous conclusion of the FINALE is geared to generate the applause that, according to Clara, no artist can do without. Yet these undeniably popularizing elements may not satisfy the astute listener's questioning response to the anomalies of the work: where, in the *Ouverture*, is the customary second group? why is there no slow movement? why does the second group of the *Finale*, flouting one of the time-honored rules of textbook sonata form, appear in the dominant in exposition and recapitulation alike?

The tension between exoteric and esoteric features further plays itself out in the nature of the thematic web. Compared with the First Symphony, intra-movement recurrences in the *Ouverture, Scherzo und Finale* are both more densely woven and, as exemplified in the muted echoes of the *Ouverture's* Allegro in the coda of the Scherzo, more obvious. While motivic recall of this sort was not uncommon in the mid-nineteenth century, we might keep in mind that the device was initially viewed with some skepticism. A reviewer of Schumann's First Symphony cautioned that overt similarities between motives in different movements might lead to monotony; Spohr could find "no good reason" for the thematic links between the middle movements of the same work.[68] In the *Ouverture, Scherzo und Finale,* however, Schumann subjects his recurrent material to a number of functional shifts. The first movement's coda theme, transformed into an impish $\frac{6}{8}$ meter, resurfaces as the main theme of the Scherzo (Examples 6.4a and b). The course of the two-bar motive heading the slow introduction of the *Ouverture* is equally varied: it figures next in the bridge section and coda of the ensuing Allegro before making a final (and surreptitious) appearance in the development of the last movement.

Not surprisingly, issues of large-scale coherence were similarly approached and resolved in Schumann's next major composition, the A-minor *Phantasie*, whose genesis was closely bound up with its predecessor's; as Schumann set to work on his first successfully completed work for piano and orchestra in early May 1841, he was simultaneously occupied with the orchestration of the op. 52 FINALE.[69] By the end of the month the new work, known to us as an early version of the first movement of the ever-popular Piano Concerto, op. 54, was completely scored, though it would have to wait until mid-August for a trial performance with Ferdinand David conducting the Gewandhaus orchestra and Clara at the keyboard.[70] "The piano and orchestral parts are interwoven to the highest degree," Clara wrote shortly thereafter, "one can't imagine

Example 6.4a. Ouverture: coda (opening).

Example 6.4b. Scherzo: opening.

one without the other."[71] No doubt, Schumann's projection of a finely wrought partnership between piano and orchestra has done much to ensure the favored status of the concerto of which it would eventually form a part, even if this ideal was a long time in coming. A decade earlier Schumann had begun to draft a piano concerto in F; in January 1839, while investigating new venues for his musical career in Vienna, he would come close to finishing the first movement of a D-minor concerto for piano and orchestra. A look at the recently published reconstruction of the work (completed by Jozef de Beenhouwer and edited by Joachim Draheim) allows us to appreciate the extent to which it foreshadows the preoccupations of the later *Phantasie:* here too is a nearly obsessive use of a limited amount of thematic material, a notable freedom in formal design (the movement unfolds as an arch pattern), and a self-conscious withholding of virtuosic display.

Schumann's description of the projected D-minor work as a cross ("Mittelding") between grand sonata, symphony, and concerto accords well with the realization of this synthesis in the *Phantasie.*[72] While the outlines of sonata form are audible enough, just as noteworthy is Schumann's reconfiguration of the traditional form as a sequence of character pieces. Each of the principal sections, first group and transition, second group, development, reprise, cadenza, and coda, elaborates the same motive (or motivic group), but each presents this material in a different mood through a technique of thematic transformation akin to that in the *Ouverture, Scherzo und Finale.* The symphonic argument issues not only from the thoughtful interplay of soloist and orchestra, but also from the teleological drive of harmonic areas consistently propelled by thirds and the fashioning of the cadenza as a developmental site. Although the *Phantasie* proceeds with the sweep of a single movement, the Eusebian Andante espressivo before the development section proper and the quickly paced concluding march (Allegro molto) lend to the whole the characteristic fast-slow-fast disposition of a three-movement concerto.

Thus the *Phantasie* looks forward to the compressed four-movements-in-one-form of the D-minor Symphony at the same time that it hearkens back to the compactness of Weber's and Spohr's similarly experimental concerto forms.[73] Even Clara may have provided an important but unacknowledged model for the work. Her own A-minor Piano Concerto, op. 7, completed between 1832 and 1835 under the watchful eyes of her father and her future husband, contains many features that resonate with Schumann's later composition: the overall A-minor tonic;[74] the extended episode in A-flat in the first movement (comparable to the central Andante, also in A-flat, in the *Phantasie*);

the monomotivicism of the outer movements; the punctuating melodic descent (D-C-B-A) of the finale's coda (a gesture taken up in Schumann's march-coda). None of these elements counts for much in isolation, but taken together they strengthen the case for viewing Clara's concerto as a source of inspiration for her husband's.[75]

Unfortunately, neither she nor Schumann left any documentary evidence to support the notion of a creative exchange in this instance. Though he orchestrated the finale of Clara's concerto in late 1833 and early 1834,[76] Schumann's diaries are conspicuously lacking in references to the project. He of course had much to say about Clara as an individual and as a performing artist, but as for her efforts as a composer, we have far less evidence.[77] Clara, on the other hand, tended to denigrate her compositional ability, in part to remove any threat it may have posed to Schumann's own aspirations: "I have absolutely no talent for composition," she stated flatly in an entry of 16 January 1841 in the marriage diary.[78]

But perhaps the near silence on Schumann's part and the self-denigration on Clara's constitute negative evidence for the claim that, during the Symphonic Year, Schumann's acts of appropriation embraced not only the achievements of the classical symphonists but also those of his own wife. (Schumann's proprietary feelings toward Clara emerge in a diary entry relative to the concert of March 1841 on which the First Symphony was premiered: not the least of his joys was Clara's appearance, for the first time, as Clara *Schumann*).[79] Just as Schumann encouraged Clara, as a performer, to cultivate the "classics" of the piano repertory (Bach and Beethoven as opposed to Herz and Henselt), so might Clara have furnished her husband with an obliquely complementary course of study in the form of her youthful virtuoso concerto.

The image of Clara and the notion of the orchestral fantasy intertwine in the last major work completed by Schumann during 1841, the D-minor Symphony. The "symphonic fire" that attended the rapid sketching of the First Symphony smoldered somewhat longer in the case of that work's minor-key counterpart. "Sometimes I hear D-minor strains resounding wildly from the distance," Clara noted in the marriage diary at the end of May.[80] But while she reported on the completion of the sketches in mid-June, the scoring of the symphony was interrupted by a vacation in the environs of Dresden during the first part of July. Further work on the symphony proceeded intermittently over the course of the next several months, with periods of intense labor clustered around late July and early August, and late August and early September. On 1 September, soon before Clara's twenty-second birthday, the household routine was altered by a singular and joyous event: the birth of the couple's first child, Marie. Finally, by early October Schumann was able to record, in the *Haushaltbücher,* that he had finished polishing his latest composition.[81] His satisfaction on the occasion of the symphony's 4 December rehearsal (two days before its premiere with Ferdinand David leading the Gewandhaus orchestra) thus owed just as much to his arrival at the final stage of a project spread over half a year's time as to the orchestra's spirited reading.[82] Yet as it turned out, this was not to be the final stage after all. Unable to find a publisher, Schumann allowed his symphony to lie fallow for a decade before subjecting it to a thorough revision (involving major changes in orchestration and alterations in thematic content) from 12 to 19 December 1851.[83]

Why was the D-minor Symphony so long in the making, and why did it await publication for a dozen years? Although we will limit ourselves here to the form that the work took in late 1841, the answer to both questions probably stems from the same source: Schumann's radical approach to symphonic structure. In a sense, the D-minor Symphony is hardly a "symphony" in the traditional mold, but rather an orchestral "fantasy" on several themes, at least insofar as Czerny defined the latter genre as one in which several thematically related sections proceed without pause.[84] Indeed, Schumann referred to the 1851 revision alternately as a "Symphonie" and a "Phantasie"; its title page even bears the designation: "Symphonistische Phantasie für grösses Orchester."[85] The same dialectic between multi-movement symphony and multi-sectional fantasy held in 1841, as attested by Clara's comments in the marriage diary just after Schumann began the sketching process: "yesterday [Robert] started on a new symphony, which will consist of one movement and yet contain an Adagio and Finale."[86] Thus, it is clear that the earlier version, like the later one, was to proceed in a continuous sweep, a fact obscured by the placement of double bars at the end of the first two movements in Franz Wüllner's and Brahms's 1891 edition of the 1841 version. As noted in the 9 December 1841 review in the *Leipziger Allgemeine Zeitung,* "the five parts of the symphony form a whole, but without the customary pauses between individual movements."[87]

Hence the D-minor Symphony confronts head-on both aspects of a problem articulated at several points in Schumann's critical writings: how, on the one hand, to preserve the highest possible degree of coherence in an extended composition without, on the other hand, resorting to the contrivance of exact thematic recall. To be sure, Schumann was not alone among his contemporaries in grappling with the conflicting demands of unity and variety. Just after the first performance of the D-minor Symphony, a reviewer observed that Mendelssohn's *Lobgesang*, op. 52, was likewise distinguished by transitional passages intended to temper the potential diffuseness of the composition's ten-movement design.[88] The four movements of Mendelssohn's "Scottish" Symphony, op. 56, completed a year after Schumann's work, are similarly linked. But Schumann goes considerably farther than his illustrious colleague. The radicality of his D-minor Symphony lies in its systematic application of the techniques of thematic variation and transformation, techniques that Schumann had first encountered in Schubert's "Wanderer" Fantasy, to the orchestral medium. As such, Schumann's symphony bridges the gap between the keyboard fantasies of the earlier part of the century and the later tone poems of Liszt.

The D-minor Symphony, like the two orchestral works directly preceding it, makes do with remarkably little material. The languid cantabile of its slow introduction recurs as a subsidiary melody in the *Romanza*, whose middle section (like that of the subsequent Scherzo) brings similar music in major to ground the sumptuous violin figuration (Examples 6.5a–c). The main idea of the first movement's Allegro di molto, one of Schumann's more propulsive conceits, informs first group, transition, second group, and development alike. The gradually strengthening references to the same motive in the Largo transition between the last two movements usher in the triumphant D-major fanfare that serves as the finale's main theme, itself first evolved in the development of the first movement.

The tautness of the thematic web affects the shape of the parts no less than that of the whole. When an early reviewer complained of the

Example 6.5a. D-Minor Symphony: slow introduction.

Example 6.5b. D-Minor Symphony: *Romanza*, mm. 12–14.

Example 6.5c. D-Minor Symphony: *Romanza*, mm. 26–28.

symphony's lack of "outward finish,"[89] was he perhaps reacting to the fact that the first movement eschews the expected recapitulation, substituting in its stead the breakthrough of an apparently new lyrical idea in D major? If so, then the incompleteness of the opening sonata-allegro may be viewed as a consequence of Schumann's attempt to impose an overarching sonata-form design on the symphony as a whole. According to this reading, the initiatory Andante con moto and ensuing Allegro di molto exposition constitute an "introduction" at the larger level; the transpositionally related segments of the development provide the larger-level "exposition" (replete with customary repetitions); the *Romanza* and Scherzo (given their dependence on the material of the first movement) function as "development"; and the apotheotic recall of the first-movement fanfare in the finale marks the point of "recapitulation." A more complete synthesis of detail and large-scale design is hardly thinkable.

If Schumann was indeed referring to the D-minor Symphony when, in a diary entry of March 1841 he wrote: "Really, my next symphony will be called 'Clara' and I will portray her with flutes, oboes, and harps,"[90] then it is conceivable that traces of the portrait are to be detected less in the hidden "Clara" ciphers whose discovery is the favored pastime of many writers than in the elective affinities between the Schumanns' creative products. In the D-minor Symphony, as in the *Phantasie*, we again hear echoes of Clara's Piano Concerto, whose overall "fantasy" form (with each movement leading directly into its successor) and rhapsodic developments (in the first movement especially) foreshadow similar traits in Schumann's work. A few days after Clara's twenty-second birthday Schumann queried: "What might I offer her apart from my own artistic endeavors?" and then went on to list them: the publication of the Rückert lieder (op. 37), the appearance of the printed parts for his First Symphony, and the completion of the D-minor Symphony.[91] The last-named of Schumann's birthday gifts turns out to be a dual-natured offering, its gestures of emulation countered by a desire to outdo Clara in the area of motivic integration. Is it too much to suggest that Schumann felt compelled to clear imaginative space for himself not only in relation to Beethoven, Schubert, and Mendelssohn, but also as regards his composer-pianist wife?

～7～

The Chamber Music
Year: 1842

The Poetry and Prose of Artist-Marriages

The first major crisis of Schumann's married life occurred in 1842, the year during which he would extend his conquest of the principal musical genres into the realm of chamber music. The precariously maintained checks and balances between personal and professional concerns that nurtured Schumann's productivity during the previous year threatened to come undone in the months preceding the composition of the String Quartets, op. 41, nos. 1–3, the Piano Quintet, op. 44, the Piano Quartet, op. 47, and the *Phantasiestücke*, op. 88, for piano trio. The crisis of 1842 was precipitated by a concert tour on which Schumann and Clara embarked on 18 February. Intended primarily to showcase Clara's pianism (although Schumann's First Symphony figured on several programs), the tour thrust the couple into a veritable whirlwind of rehearsals, soirées, public performances, and social calls in Bremen, Oldenburg, and Hamburg. But in the weeks just before departing, Schumann complained of feeling "very ill," "always sick and melancholy"; for several days he was not even well enough to leave home.[1] As documented in Schumann's *Reisenotizen* (travel notes), later filled out as a discursive account, the composer was in a "horrible state of health" by the time that he and Clara arrived in Hamburg in early March. The last straw came on 9 March: "We had a terrible night. . . . In the pub beneath us (we stayed on the first floor) there was an awful racket and bellowing until 4 A.M."[2] The following day, Schumann headed back to

Leipzig, ostensibly because he couldn't leave the *Neue Zeitschrift* unattended any longer. He was not reunited with Clara, who went on to concertize in Copenhagen, accompanied by Marie Garlich, a young girl from a respected Bremen family, until 25 April in Magdeburg.[3]

The causes underlying Schumann's abrupt withdrawal from the North German tour were just as much personal and psychological as they were physical or professional. On 25 February, Clara gave a concert in Oldenburg after which Schumann was excluded from a gathering at court in his wife's honor. This "rude impropriety," together with Clara's decision to attend the event alone, no doubt contributed to his "miserable mood" in the following days.[4] The episode is emblematic of a problem he confided to the marriage diary shortly after arriving home in March: "This separation [from Clara] has once again made clear to me our particularly difficult situation. Should I neglect my talent in order to serve as your travelling companion? And conversely, should you let your talent go to waste simply because I happen to be chained to the journal and the piano? Now when you're young and full of energy?"[5] It may come as a surprise to learn that as a possible remedy for this dilemma Schumann contemplated a two-year stint in America for Clara and himself that would ensure them of financial security for the rest of their lives.[6]

In short, Schumann was torn by two conflicting outlooks on Clara's career. On the one hand, he greatly admired her artistry: "I was so beside myself," he wrote concerning her rendition of one of Mendelssohn's keyboard fugues at a Bremen soirée (28 February), "that I applauded vigorously over Clara's so very beautiful playing."[7] But on the other hand, the thought of his "undignified situation . . . hardly gives rise to joy."[8] Now and again Schumann experienced a twinge of guilt that his need for undisturbed quiet while composing necessarily limited Clara's practicing.[9] Once he even commented, with uncharacteristic self-deprecation, on his regrets over hindering Clara's compositional efforts: "But children and a continually day-dreaming husband just aren't conducive to composing."[10]

But on the whole, it is difficult to escape the conclusion that Schumann's guilty feelings were overridden by wounded pride and even jealousy. Nor were matters helped by Clara's apparent reluctance to program her husband's pieces. The bulk of Clara's repertory for the tour was made up of pieces by Bach, Weber, Henselt, Mendelssohn, and Liszt; Schumann was represented by a single movement from his *Novelletten*, op. 21.[11] When asked to play one of Schumann's works while the couple vacationed in Bohemia later in the year (6–22 August), Clara maintained, much to her husband's chagrin, that she didn't know any.[12] Sev-

eral days before this incident, the Schumanns had gone mountain-
climbing near Teplitz: "Today Clara was more vigorous than I, which
both pleased and angered me, because a husband doesn't like to be left
twenty paces behind his wife."[13] While this statement may be taken as
a metaphor for Schumann's view of Clara's professional activities, several
diary entries from the ensuing months drive home the point in no uncertain terms. "Clara understands that I must attend to my own talent,"
Schumann wrote in October, "that I'm at the peak of my energies, and
that I must take advantage of my youth. So it goes with artist-
marriages."[14] Absent is the equivocation of the March diary entry
quoted above; Schumann has settled the first crisis of his life with Clara
in favor of his own needs. By February of the following year, he was able
to assert confidently that "Clara herself surely recognizes motherhood as
her primary vocation."[15] Schumann's stance was hardly unusual for its
time (perhaps, in some quarters, even for our time). A passage from the
De l'Allemagne (published 1813) of Germaine de Staël, herself a woman
of no mean accomplishment, comes to mind: "It is right to exclude
women from politics and civil affairs: anything that puts women in
competition with men goes against their natural vocation. Fame itself is
only a brilliant way to bury the happiness of a woman."[16] So it goes,
apparently, with artist-wives as well.

That the Schumanns struggled to preserve some kind of equilibrium between their private and public lives is less surprising than the
fact that their relationship survived as well as it did; the marriage diary
served as an important palliative. After his precipitous return to Leipzig
in mid-March, Schumann elaborated his travel notes in order to "banish
melancholy" through "recollection of the last weeks spent with Clara."[17]
And Clara, for her part, would turn to the marriage diary in late May
with a lengthy account of the anguish she suffered while forced to continue her tour without Schumann at her side. Clara's rhetoric of sorrow—"Thursday March 10 was the most miserable day of our marriage
up to now; we parted, and it seemed to me that I would never see him
again"[18]—probably served as a gentle reproach to Schumann for having
abandoned his wife, if only temporarily.

The melancholy that Schumann attempted to banish through recollection surfaced again and again throughout the year. During the weeks
spent in Leipzig apart from Clara ("Trübsinnzeit," or "gloomy time"
runs the laconic entry in the *Haushaltbücher* for 29 March),[19] Schumann
occupied himself with exercises in counterpoint and fugue, but was unable to do any serious composing. And although the references to a
"miserable" or "horrid life" (and to over-indulgence in alcohol) abated
after his reunion with Clara in April, the *Haushaltbücher* indicate that

Schumann's mood had darkened again in late May ("a sinful life") and June ("turbid melancholy"), by which time he was already at work on his second string quartet.[20] Thus the notion that Schumann alternated depressive, inactive phases with more ebullient, productive phases is an oversimplification. By 8 October, three days after he had begun sketching the Piano Quintet, depression had returned; and during the second half of the month, he suffered from insomnia as a result of the intensity of his recent compositional activities: the completion of the Piano Quintet and the drafting of the Piano Quartet.[21] Progress on the *Phantasiestücke* was likewise hindered by "nervous irritation" (*"Nervenschwäche"*).[22] While Schumann did manage to finish the composition on 28 December, the tone of his entries in the *Haushaltbücher* from about the same time (16 December: "Worked on the Trio—too much—feeling unwell in the evening"; and 17–18 December: "Unwell")[23] makes it clear that he had strained himself to the limit of his powers.

While Schumann occupied himself more and more with composition from midyear onward, the task of maintaining the marriage diary fell increasingly to Clara. In fact, her entries throughout the course of the year tend to be lengthier than those of her preoccupied husband. If Schumann's contributions serve as a source of consolation from gloom, then Clara's are notable for the vitality and incisiveness of their characterization of a broad range of individuals. "A young coquette is bad enough, but an old one," like Arnoldine Lose, (the widow of the music publisher Carl Lose), whom Clara had met in Copenhagen, "is completely unbearable."[24] We learn that Hans Christian Andersen, whose acquaintance Clara had also made while touring in Copenhagen, "possesses a poetic, childlike nature, is still somewhat young, but very ugly, and also frightfully vain and egotistic."[25] No less sharply drawn are her appraisals of contemporary musicians. Heinrich Marschner's music (like his character) exudes "raw passion," but too often degenerates into the "commonplace" and trivial. In Clara's opinion, this master of *Schaueroper* "should have stopped composing after his *Templer, Vampyr,* and *Heiling.*"[26] But she saves her most cutting remarks (with which Schumann agreed) for Bellini and Donizetti: "[their] appeal to a lay-person is understandable, but not to someone who wants to be recognized as a musician."[27] (During the course of their Bohemian holiday in August, Schumann and Clara were granted a brief audience with Metternich in Königswart. But when he expressed his fondness for Donizetti's *Linda di Chamounix,* it is unlikely that the Schumanns, who stood in awe of the notorious diplomat, had the nerve to contradict him.)[28] We even get a sense of Clara's reactions to what might have been an early attempt at historically informed performance: "For the first time I played some sonatas of Bach with [Ferdinand] David. I can't yet pass judgment because one must play these things often in order to appreciate them. I was struck by David's *staccato* rendition of all the running figures—could Bach have wanted it so?"[29]

But the most telling of Clara's diary entries dates from November. Obviously she and Schumann were having differences over the financial management of their household: "The thought that you should have to work for money is most repugnant to me, because this can't make you happy, and yet I see no other way around it if you don't allow me to work, if you cut off all means for me to earn something."[30] But in spite of Clara's mollifying rhetoric—she lives only for Robert (whom she loves infinitely), she regrets having to "tear [him] away from his beautiful dreams,"[31] her entry is a shrewdly but gently phrased reminder that artist couples must tend to the practical side of their relationship. If Schumann sometimes lost himself in fanciful reveries, Clara was on hand with the Goethean admonition that married life has its prose as well as its poetry.

Tradition, Innovation, and Social Character

Schumann's prolonged engagement with chamber music in 1842 was not his first. As we have seen in Chapter 1, one of his earliest major essays in the larger forms was the C-minor Piano Quartet of 1828–29, a work that, while clearly indebted to Schubert, nonetheless held out much promise for the future. Sketches and drafts for quartets (possibly piano quartets) in A and B date from about the same time.[32] Nearly a decade later, in March of 1838, Schumann wrote to Clara of the satisfaction he felt in beginning to compose string quartets, for "the piano has become too restrictive for me."[33] By the beginning of the next month, one of the quartets, of which no trace survives, was finished, even if Schumann would describe it to Fischhof as only an "attempt."[34] In the course of the same year, Schumann's lodgings provided the setting for a series of private "quartet-mornings" at which Ferdinand David and some of his colleagues from the Leipzig Gewandhaus Orchestra gathered for the express purpose of reading through the latest string quartets. These sessions, devoted to works by established masters (Spohr and Cherubini) and younger talents (Johann Verhulst, Leopold Fuchs, and Hermann Hirschbach among them), in turn served as Schumann's point of departure for a series of five brief but colorful essays, his first serious critical appraisals of the string quartet repertory.[35] And as we have seen

Robert Schumann,
charcoal drawing by Eduard Bendemann, early 1850s.
Robert-Schumann-Haus, Zwickau.

Jean Paul.

Clara and Marie Schumann, daguerreotype, circa 1850–51.
Robert-Schumann-Haus, Zwickau.

Neue
Zeitschrift für Musik.

Im Vereine
mit mehren Künstlern und Kunstfreunden
herausgegeben unter Verantwortlichkeit von R. Schumann.

Jahrgang 1835.   **№ 1.**   Den 2. Januar.

Die allein,
Die nur ein lustig Spiel, Geräusch der Tartschen.
Zu hören kommen, oder einen Mann
Im bunten Rock, mit Gold verbrämt, zu sehen,
Die irren sich.
         Shakspeare.

Diese Zeitschrift wird Folgendes liefern:

Theoretische und historische Aufsätze, kunstästhetische, grammatische, pädagogische, biographische, akustische, sodann Nekrologe, Beiträge zur Bildungsgeschichte berühmter Künstler, Berichte über neue Erfindungen oder Verbesserungen, Beurtheilungen ausgezeichneter Virtuosenleistungen, Operndarstellungen; unter der Aufschrift: Zeitgenossen, Skizzen mehr oder weniger berühmter Künstler, unter der Rubrik: Journalschau, Nachrichten über das Wirken anderer kritischen Blätter, Bemerkungen über Recensionen in ihnen, Zusammenstellungen verschiedener Beurtheilungen über dieselbe Sache, eigne Resultate darüber, auch Antikritiken der Künstler selbst, sodann Auszüge aus ausländischen, Interessantes aus älteren musikalischen Zeitungen.

Belletristisches, kürzere musikalische Erzählungen, Phantasiestücke, Scenen aus dem Leben, Humoristisches, Gedichte, die sich vorzugsweise zur Composition eignen.

Kritiken über alle bemerkenswerthe Geisteserzeugnisse der Gegenwart. Auf frühere schätzbare, übergangene oder vergessene Werke wird aufmerksam gemacht, wie auch auf eingesandte Manuscripte talentvoller unbekannter Componisten, die Aufmunterung verdienen. Zu derselben Gattung gehörige Compositionen werden öfter zusammengestellt, gegen einander verglichen, besonders interessante doppelt beurtheilt.

Kunstbemerkungen (in weitem Sinn), literarische Notizen, Musikalisches aus Goethe, Jean Paul, Heinse, Hoffmann, Novalis, Rochlitz u. A. m.

Correspondenzartikel, vorzüglich dann, wenn sie eigentlichstes Musikleben abschildern. Wir stehen in Verbindung mit Paris, London, Wien, Berlin, Petersburg, Neapel, Frankfurt, Hamburg, Riga, München, Dresden, Prag, Weimar, Stuttgart, Cassel u. a. Städten. Artikel, welche blosse Vorfälle berichten, kommen in die folgende Abtheilung.

Chronik, Musikaufführungen, Concertanzeigen u. s. w. — Es wird keine Mühe gescheut, diese Chronik vollständig zu machen, um die Namen der Künstler oft in Erinnerung zu bringen.

Vermischtes, Notizen über Reisen, Aufenthalt der Künstler, Beförderungen, Anekdoten, überhaupt kurzes Musikbezügliches.

Prospectus of the first issue of the *Neue Zeitschrift für Musik*
to appear under Schumann's sole editorship.

"Hausmusik," engraving by Ludwig Richter. Archiv für Kunst und Geschichte, Berlin.

The Schumanns' townhouse in Düsseldorf, 1032 Bilkerstrasse. Robert-Schumann-Haus, Zwickau.

in Chapter 5, Schumann started on a pair of quartets, in E♭ and D—
which he thought were "as good as Haydn"—in the early summer of
1839.[36]

Hence, his turn to chamber music in 1842 was far from abrupt.
We are reminded again that Schumann's creativity often unfolded in
overlapping phases: tendencies first nurtured while he was still primarily
a composer of piano music came into full bloom only later. After a
period of compositional inactivity in the first half of 1842, the "continual quartet-thoughts" that Schumann noted in the *Haushaltbücher* (on
14 February, just before the North German tour) and that informed his
reviews of quartets by Schapler, Hirschbach, and Verhulst for several of
the May issues of the *Neue Zeitschrift,* were musically realized with a
vengeance. The "quartet-thoughts" apparently poured out fast and furious, for after rapidly sketching the A-minor Quartet (op. 41, no. 1) in
early June, Schumann immediately sketched a second quartet in F before
elaborating both of the sketches in turn, each part of the process taking
about a week. The pair of quartets were then joined by a third, in A
major, sketched and elaborated from 8 to 22 July.[37] After a brief hiatus
(taken up partly by the Schumanns' pleasant Bohemian excursion in
August), the Piano Quintet in E♭, op. 44, followed (23 September–12
October), and then the Piano Quartet, op. 47, also in E♭ (25 October–
26 November). By three days after Christmas, the *Phantasiestücke,* op. 88
had been completed, this in spite of the nervous irritation that impeded
Schumann's progress on the work.[38] Thus, within a mere six months,
Schumann produced just as many significant compositions: an impressive achievement by any standard.

Schumann's exploration of the musical genres—lied, symphonic
music, chamber music, oratorio—from 1840 to 1843 contains within it
yet further systems. His efforts during the Symphonic Year, for instance,
resulted not only in the cultivation of the "grand" symphony, but also
of the more popularizing overture and the virtuoso concerto. A similarly
varied range of subgenres informs the products of the Chamber Music
Year. The "pure," delicately etched chamber style of the string quartets
gives way to the broader gestures of the Piano Quintet and Piano Quartet. Intimacy is restored in the *Phantasiestücke,* only here the esoteric
qualities of the string quartets recede in favor of a decidedly bourgeois
flavor that foreshadows, in some ways, the *Hausmusik* of the later 1840s.

According to one writer, the string quartet represented a "stimulating novelty" for Schumann, but not an "essential thread."[39] In all likelihood, the composer himself would have flinched at this appraisal. As he
put it to Raimund Härtel in a letter of 3 December 1847: "My quartets,
which you published, have taken on a special meaning for me through

the death of Mendelssohn, to whom they're dedicated. I still view them as the best works of my earlier period, and Mendelssohn often expressed a similar opinion to me."[40] Schumann's own critical writings on the string quartet as a genre might afford us a means of getting at the "special meaning" he had in mind.

Two aspects in particular of Schumann's aesthetic of the string quartet were essential for his thinking. In the first place, the quartet should remain within certain strictly delimited boundaries that, in other genres, it is permissable to cross. Operas might perforce employ symphonic effects, just as symphonies might draw on the techniques of chamber music. The composer of string quartets, however, must be careful to avoid "symphonic furor."[41] To Schumann's ear, the persistent "orchestral" syncopations of K. G. Reissger's A-major Quartet, op. 111, no. 1, betrayed the composer's unease with a genre that was still relatively new to him. The frequent eighth-note figures in the middle voices of the same work likewise struck Schumann as more appropriate for a piano piece or lied accompaniment. The "operatic, overladen," qualities of Cherubini's E♭-major Quartet seemed no less out of place.[42] For Schumann, "everyone has something to say" in a "proper string quartet": it is a "by turns beautiful and even abstrusely woven conversation among four people."[43] The string quartet, in other words, is more than a mere entertainment for amateurs. The "proper" quartet style includes the self-sufficiency of the individual voices and the contrapuntal integrity of the whole. (Yet Schumann had little interest in the perfunctory counterpoint of, for instance, the development section of the finale of W. H. Veit's E-major quartet, op. 5: the few imitative parries on the movement's main theme served no higher purpose, in Schumann's view, than to elicit the awe of easily-impressed dilettantes.)[44]

In the second place, the quartet is a "venerable" but "difficult" genre. The two qualifications are interdependent. Schumann believed strongly that the prospective composer of string quartets must possess a deep understanding of the genre's history, and for Schumann this history embraced, not surprisingly, the quartets of Haydn, Mozart, Beethoven, and his great contemporary, Mendelssohn. (Although he gave high marks to the "Death and the Maiden" Quartet, Schumann's historical scheme by-passed Schubert, most of whose quartets would not have been available to him in published form).[45] But while an awareness of history was more crucial for the composition of string quartets than for any other genre, Schumann maintained with equal conviction that slavish imitation of older models was to be avoided, and here lay the difficulty that figures such as Hirschbach and Verhulst did not always successfully overcome.[46]

In sum, composers of string quartets were faced with a singular challenge. They had to fashion contrapuntally integrated structures in which every member of the ensemble had something of substance to contribute. At the same time, they were expected to demonstrate a keen awareness of tradition without overtly copying their predecessors. Both aspects of this ideal were aptly realized in the three quartets of Schumann's Opus 41.

As noted earlier, Schumann turned seriously to the study of counterpoint and fugue during the "gloomy time" of his separation from Clara in March and April of 1842. After the couple's reunion, Clara too was drawn into Schumann's self-designed course in fugue.[47] The results of this contrapuntal study are obvious in all three quartets that Schumann would soon complete. Indeed, the first movement of Opus 41, no. 1 begins with a slow introduction in which nearly every measure features the same plaintive sixteenth-note motive, first treated in fugato and then as a countermelody to a rhythmically differentiated idea (Example 7.1). In the ensuing Allegro, the transition to the second group is likewise initiated by a fugato on the principal music of the first group (we encounter a similar strategy at the corresponding spot in the first movement of Opus 41, no. 2); the playful duos from later on in the transition in turn serve as the basis for the densely imitative central section of the development. The whole of the second variation in the second movement (Assai agitato) of Opus 41, no. 3 is conceived as a fugato on a persistently driving figure. The self-consciously contrapuntal spots in the quartets thus function in a variety of ways: either as modes of presentation, development, or varied repetition. The three principal functions associated with the sonata form, in other words, are enriched through the medium of counterpoint.

In his review of the first of Hirschbach's *Lebensbilder in einem Zyklus von Quartetten*, Schumann acknowledged that, while the daring forms of Beethoven's last period should no doubt serve as the principal examples for the aspiring composer, "heavily laden trees are also to be found in the fruit-gardens of Haydn and Mozart."[48] Both of the latter figured prominently in Schumann's self-imposed course of study during the Chamber Music Year. In late January, we find him deeply absorbed in Mozart's symphonies. While Clara toured in Copenhagen, Schumann pored over the scores of Haydn's and Mozart's string quartets. And after Clara's return, the couple read through many of these scores at the piano.[49]

In a sense, there is a built-in affinity between Haydn's and Schumann's styles, especially as regards their respective approaches to the sonata form. Both were exceptionally economical composers, remark-

Example 7.1. String Quartet in A Minor, op. 41 no. 1: first movement, mm. 1–15.

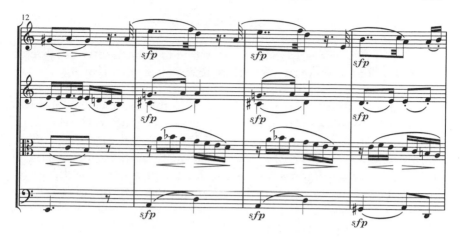

ably adept at deriving the most from a limited amount of musical material. Hence, the monomotivicism of the first movement of Opus 41, no.
1 (its first and second groups draw on the same motivic ideas) readily
bears comparison with that of any number of Haydn's quartet movements. Similarly, Haydn's teleological sonata forms (which frequently
withhold a solid confirmation of the dominant until the very last moments of the exposition) find a counterpart in the delayed articulation
of the dominant that characterizes the expositions of the first and last
movements of Schumann's Opus 41, no. 2. Moreover, Haydn's fondness
for "hybrid" forms combining variation, rondo, or ternary elements[50]
has an analogue in Schumann's blend of the Scherzo's traditional ABA
form with variation principles in the second movement of Opus 41,
no. 3.

Schumann's debt to Mozart is perhaps less obvious but no less
noteworthy, and again the chief link resides in the handling of sonata
form. In several of Mozart's sonata-style movements (examples from the
string quartets include the finales of K. 428 in E♭ and K. 575 in D), the
exposition proceeds immediately to a restatement of the first group, in
whole or in part, in the tonic, much like a rondo. The opening music is
then followed by an expanded or elaborated version of the earlier transition leading to a return of the second group in the tonic. Sometimes
described as a sonata form with "displaced development," this design is
probably better construed as a sonata form in which development and
recapitulation have in fact been interwoven or conflated.[51] Schumann
opts for just this kind of pattern in the finale of his Opus 41, no. 1 and
the opening movement of Opus 41, no. 3. In doing so, he attains a kind
of concision that the textbook sonata form does not so easily allow and

at the same time belies the charge of schematicism that has been levelled
more than once at his quartets.[52]

"I love *Mozart* dearly," Schumann wrote in a diary entry of November 1842, "but Beethoven I worship like a god who remains forever
apart, who will never become one with us."[53] To be sure, the most
powerful model for Schumann's approach to the chamber medium was
furnished by Beethoven, whose string quartets he studied closely, along
with those of Haydn and Mozart, during the period of his separation
from Clara.[54] And we can be just as certain that Schumann looked to
the quartets of Beethoven's last period for his principal models, not to
imitate, but rather to emulate. The E♭ major Quartet, op. 127, and the
C♯ minor Quartet, op. 131, he noted several years before, were works
"for whose greatness no words can be found."[55] Unfortunately, Schumann held to his promise: he offered more details in the course of his
career as a music critic on the quartets of a forgotten figure like Leopold
Fuchs than he did on Beethoven's masterful but enigmatic works. Still,
it is possible to derive some idea, from scattered remarks in the critical
writings, of the features that Schumann especially prized in Beethoven's
late string quartets: their avoidance of stereotypical forms, their "romantic humor" (that is, striking contrasts), and their conception as large-
scale unities.[56]

Not surprisingly then, echoes of late Beethoven abound in Schumann's string quartets. But of greater moment than the obvious allusions (the head-motive of the hymnic slow movement of Opus 41, no.
1, as many writers have pointed out, recalls the corresponding gesture
in the slow movement of Beethoven's Ninth Symphony) are the more
oblique references to Beethoven's last quartets. The slow movement of
Schumann's Opus 41, no. 2 adopts the tone, if not the thematic substance, of the slow movement of Beethoven's Opus 127, with which it
shares the same form (variations), tonality (A♭), and meter $\frac{12}{8}$. The imitative slow introduction of Opus 41, no. 1 conflates the detached character
(and A-minor tonality) of the opening Assai sostenuto of Beethoven's
Opus 132 with the fugal texture of the first movement of Opus 131. The
unusual tonal argument of the first movement of Schumann's Opus 41,
no. 1—its introductory Andante espressivo, in A minor, prefaces a full-
fledged sonata-allegro in F—may likewise be viewed in terms of a Beethovenian example: F major is the unexpected counterpole to the tonic,
A minor, in the first-movement exposition of Beethoven's Opus 132. Of
the three quartets in Schumann's set, the first displays the most palpable
inter-movement connections: the F major of the first movement recurs
as the key of the slow movement (Adagio) and again as an important
tonal station in the finale's development section; the Scherzo's main

theme serves as the basis for the shape of a significant countermelody in the Adagio; the bassline for the beginning of the "chorale" in the coda of the finale (mm. 264–67) recalls the descending fourths of the main theme of the Adagio. Thus, Schumann's attempt to make of his quartet an over-arching, but delicately woven unity, bears comparison with Beethoven's similar attempt in his C♯-minor Quartet, op. 131. Yet in none of these examples does Schumann merely copy from a model. What we have instead is an imaginative encounter with the spirit of late Beethoven.

When it came to his contemporaries, Schumann reserved his highest praise for Mendelssohn, whose string quartets (along with those of George Onslow) counted among the few recent efforts worthy of late Beethoven.[57] As indicated in a long diary entry of October 1842, Schumann was heartened by his colleague's warm praise for his own newly composed quartets as rendered on 29 September by Ferdinand David and other members of the Gewandhaus orchestra, "for Mendelssohn is a formidable critic; of all living musicians, he has the sharpest eye."[58] Schumann's dedication of the quartets "to his friend Felix Mendelssohn-Bartholdy with heartfelt respect" may thus be taken as an outward sign of his deep admiration for a composer whose approbation he avidly sought. Inward signs are readily apparent in the fabric of the musical works themselves. The second movement of Opus 41, no. 1, for instance, exhibits many of the earmarks of Mendelssohn's elfin Scherzos. (So too does the second movement of the Piano Quartet, composed later in the year.) The slow movements of Opus 41, nos. 1 and 3 replicate the hymnic tone of the Andante espressivo from Mendelssohn's E♭-major Quartet, op. 12, whose contrapuntally textured finale finds notable parallels in the last movements of Opus 41, nos. 1 and 2.

At the same time, Schumann's quartets amount to more than the cluster of influences that possibly went into their making. Unmistakably Schumannian is the continuation of the quest for "new forms" that animated so many of his keyboard works of the 1830s. The strophic variation form of the slow movements of Opus 41, nos. 1 and 3, to take an example, is practically without precedent in the string quartet literature before Schumann. So too is the design of the Opus 41, no. 3 finale, whose mosaic-like succession of miniature character portraits (after the manner of the *Novelletten*) is given shape by an overarching "parallel" form (the music of mm. 112–84 recalls that of mm. 1–72, for the most part a minor third higher)—an idiosyncratic sonata-form variant that, as Linda Roesner has shown, plays a significant role in Schumann's earlier piano sonatas and *Fantasie*.[59]

Likewise, it is possible to gauge the individuality of Schumann's quartet style by recognizing its *distance* from the style of his contemporaries' works in general and Mendelssohn's in particular. Their similarities aside, Schumann and Mendelssohn present us with radically differing approaches to moment-by-moment pacing and long-range structure. The leisurely unfolding designs of the opening movements of Mendelssohn's Opus 44, no. 1 (D major) and no. 2 (E minor) stand in sharp contrast to the more compact mode of utterance in Schumann's Opus 41 quartets. So too do Mendelssohn's means of achieving overall unity. The clear-cut thematic links that bind the movements of his Opus 12 (like the overt references to Beethoven's Opus 132 in Mendelssohn's own A-minor Quartet, op. 13) are qualitatively different from Schumann's less tangible allusions.

As any practiced quartet-player will confirm, Mendelssohn's quartets are eminently more "readable" that Schumann's. Mendelssohn's figurations lie well under the fingers; his rich textures are geared to resonate without undue effort on the part of the executants. With the possible exception of the F-minor Quartet, op. 80, his quartets are written for the delectation of the talented amateur. Not so Schumann's quartets. Even the most seasoned professionals will be challenged by the rhythmic displacements and skittish arpeggios of the C-minor Scherzo from Opus 41, no. 2. Yet paradoxically, Schumann may well have been truer to the conversational but agonistic ideals of the quartet style.

We should keep in mind that both Schumann and Mendelssohn reached maturity as composers during a period in which chamber music had come to occupy an intermediary position between private and public entertainment. One of the earliest formal performances of Schumann's A-minor Quartet occurred on 8 January 1843, as part of a *Musikalische Morgenunterhaltung* (literally, "musical morning-entertainment or conversation") at the Leipzig Gewandhaus that also featured his Piano Quintet, several of his (and Clara's) lieder, Beethoven's A-major Piano Sonata (op. 101), a prelude and fugue by Bach, and the same composer's celebrated *Ciaccona* for solo violin (played by David).[60] The private character (like the aristocratic roots) of the occasion was emphasized by its exclusivity: only those especially invited could attend. (The reviewer of an 1847 rendition of Schumann's Piano Quintet at a soirée held in Copenhagen's Hôtel d'Angleterre felt compelled to "remain silent about the performance" given the secretive nature of such gatherings).[61] But at the same time, the audience for chamber music, which, strictly speaking, should be limited to the players themselves,[62] was growing ever larger. During the Schumanns' Russian tour of 1844, a performance of the Piano Quintet at a private soirée drew thirty to forty listeners.[63] The violinist Henri Vieuxtemps's quartet-matinées generally involved audiences of between 100 and 150.[64]

The split between private and public concerns manifests itself in the decidedly orchestral textures that encroach more and more on the nineteenth-century string quartet. One thinks of the pulsating tremolos and restless syncopations that support the soloistic flights of the first violin in the openings of Mendelssohn's D-major and E-minor quartets, respectively. Yet it is precisely this kind of "symphonic furor" (or concertante display) that Schumann generally eschews in his string quartets, except when it is understandably employed to effect a ringing close (as in the final bars of Opus 41, no. 1). And while Schumann does have recourse to conventional, "noodling" accompaniments in the inner parts from time to time (see, for example, the beginning of Opus 41, no. 2), the general impression one derives from listening to and playing his quartets is that of a discourse, "by turns beautiful and abstrusely woven," among equals. There is no better evidence for the esoteric quality of the motivic web in these pieces than Schumann's insistence that players study them from the full score.[65] Schumann's quartets, in short, may number among the last representatives of the true chamber idiom where players and listeners are one.

In a review of piano trios by B. E. Philipp, Karl Seyler, Alexander Fesca, and Mendelssohn, Schumann articulated an ideal for the composition of chamber music involving piano and strings that concords in some points with his aesthetic of the string quartet. Here too the appropriate style will result when "no instrument dominates, and each has something to say."[66] But even though this repertory shares its social space with the quartet (Schumann's chamber music with piano was heard in the same soirées, matinées, and semi-private *Morgenunterhaltungen* that featured his string quartets), it evinces a markedly divergent social character. Schumann hinted at this difference in his critique of Mendelssohn's Piano Trio in D Minor, op. 49, a work he singled out for special praise because of the equilibrium it achieved between musical substance and virtuosity.[67] The string parts of Mendelssohn's trio (like those in most other piano trios from this and earlier periods) remain within the technical capabilities of musically adept amateurs; the concertante piano part, however, will only receive its due from an artist at home on the concert stage. The balance between musically substantive qualities and virtuoso display that Schumann locates in Mendelssohn's D-minor Piano Trio thus goes hand in hand with a dialectic of private and public characters.

A similar interplay informs the works for piano and strings of

Schumann's Chamber Music Year. It is particularly evident in the Piano Quintet and Piano Quartet, of which the former remains one of Schumann's most enduringly popular compositions. Rendered for enthusiastic audiences on the Russian tour of 1844,[68] the Piano Quintet was hailed in Berlin, where Clara appeared during the 1846–1847 season of the Singakademie, as "one of the most important works of its kind since Beethoven."[69] Though Liszt found it too "Leipzig-like," Wagner, never a whole-hearted fan of Schumann's compositions, had kind words for its first two movements.[70]

Although Schumann's string quartets were subjected to revision (on matters of phrasing, dynamics, and the distribution of motives among the parts) just prior to publication,[71] these alterations pale in comparison to the many changes undergone by the Piano Quintet on its way to a definitive form. The preliminary drafts show that the work was originally conceived in five movements: the middle movement was to have been a *Scena* in G minor, but after sketching about two dozen bars of introductory figuration and the beginnings of a cello melody, Schumann apparently gave up on the idea.[72] In addition, the slow movement was first imagined along considerably broader lines than it would ultimately take: at Mendelssohn's suggestion, Schumann excised a complete statement of the main funeral-march theme and an additional Trio in A♭.[73] Thus, the original form—A B A^1 [Trio A^2] C A^3 B^1 A^4—was rethought as a more concise A B A^1 C A^3 B^1 A^4. Yet all the tinkering apparently paid off, for with the Piano Quintet Schumann attained the kind of popular success that often eluded him in the future. According to one early reviewer, the work definitively healed the "cleft between poetic and purely musical demands" that sometimes marred the composer's earlier works.[74]

While the dialectic between tradition and innovation that we have noted in the string quartets is discernible in the Piano Quintet, the immense popularity of the latter work stems more directly from its nearly ideal mediation of an alternate pair of qualities. The unusual position of nineteenth-century chamber music, suspended midway between private and public spheres, leaves its imprint on Schumann's quintet in the form of a play between quasi-symphonic and more properly chamber-like elements. Their mediation manifests itself first in the work's distinctive tone color, which will be best appreciated in neither the bourgeois drawing room (traditionally considered the ideal location for chamber music) nor the grand concert hall, but rather in a space proportioned somewhere between the two. Tovey was among the earliest critics to recognize the aptness of the quintet's scoring: "every note tells, and the instruments are vividly characterized in spite of the preponderance of the pianoforte throughout."[75] Indeed, the doublings for which this work (like Schumann's orchestral compositions) has been frequently criticized are often calibrated to make an almost impressionistic effect: in the first episode (C major) of the slow movement the triplet quarter-notes in the piano, against rippling eighths in the second violin and viola, delicately color the sustained *cantilena* in the first violin and cello, (Example 7.2); in the first Trio of the Scherzo the piano's steady eighths shadow the canon between first violin and viola.

The finely wrought web of contrapuntal lines that distinguishes the quartets gives way, in the Piano Quintet, to a more extroverted, "public" counterpoint, most obviously at the peroration of the last movement: after an emphatic arrival on the dominant, the opening theme of the first movement, in augmented note values, is combined with the finale's main theme (Example 7.3) in a brilliantly effective double-fugue exposition. This feature complements Schumann's altered approach to motivic reminiscence. If the intermovement connections in the A-minor String Quartet tend toward the subtly elusive, then in the Piano Quintet they proclaim themselves openly. While one is likely to overlook (or even question the presence of) the oblique allusions that run through the quartet, there is no missing the recall of the quintet's opening idea in the finale.[76]

Thus, with the Piano Quintet Schumann returned to a question that he had confronted first in the *Fantasie,* op. 17 and next in several of the symphonic works of 1841: how is it possible to shape the finale of a multi-movement work so that it is not only complete in itself but also lends closure to the entire work of which it forms but a part? The solution he hit upon in the finale of the Piano Quintet led him to fashion a movement that begins to unfold as a "parallel" form (the material of mm. 1–85 is elaborated, a half-step higher and a major third lower, in mm. 136–220),[77] but evolves, ineluctably, into something quite different: an apotheotic form culminating in a climactic restatement of the first movement's opening motto in augmentation.[78] Indeed, the closing pages of the quintet offer far more than a straightforward instance of thematic recall. As Schumann noted in a review of B. E. Philipp's Piano Trio: "There is a danger in so-called 'retrospective passages' [Rück-blicken]; unless they occur as a result of the freest flight of the imagination (as in, e.g., the finale of [Beethoven's] C-minor Symphony, where the Scherzo reappears), so that we must say: it can only be thus—then these passages can too easily seem forced and contrived."[79] Schumann avoided both force and contrivance in the quintet finale by strategically motivating the climactic, contrapuntally enhanced return of the opening theme from the first movement: first, the melodic shape of its third and

Example 7.2. Piano Quintet: second movement, mm. 29–37.

Example 7.3. Piano Quintet: last movement, mm. 319–26.

fourth measures is approximated in the corresponding bars of the finale's main theme; and second, the contrapuntal texture at the finale's
climax is prepared by the slightly earlier fugato on the movement's main
theme.

Schumann's solution to the problem of long-range closure turned
out to be remarkably prescient: the design of the quintet finale prefigures the similarly "evolving" form of the last movement of the Second
Symphony, op. 61 (1845–1846), where the goal is again the opening idea
of the first movement, a solemn but genial chorale. Hence, the public
character of the Piano Quintet derives less from Schumann's occasionally scrubby writing for the strings than from his serious engagement
with a structural problem more readily associated with that most public
of musical genres, the symphony. As such, the quintet occupies a pivotal
position in the composer's development as a cultivator of the larger
instrumental forms, reminding us that the products of the Chamber
Music Year resonate with other aspects of Schumann's conquest of the
genres.

In many ways, the Piano Quartet, op. 47, may be interpreted as a
creative double to the quintet. Both works are cast in E♭. Both bring
together the piano and a complement of strings. In the Piano Quartet,
Schumann again addresses the issue of thematic recall and in so doing
provides one of his most magical responses to the question of large-
scale coherence. The fact that the opening gesture of the finale takes up
a three-note figure first introduced in the coda of the immediately pre-

ceding slow movement is hardly remarkable in itself. What *is* remarkable is the spiralling series of transpositions (melodically upward by fourth, harmonically down by fifth) to which the figure is subjected in the slow-movement coda. The resultant sense of harmonic dislocation, grounded by the low B♭ pedal that cellists are required to produce by tuning their C-string a step lower, beautifully softens the effect of what otherwise would have been a straightforward (and somewhat crass) instance of motivic linkage. The finale in turn discloses several telling points of contact with its counterpart in the quintet. It too is cast as a "parallel" form (with exposition and development answered by a recapitulation and an elaboration of the earlier development, the latter largely at the lower fifth). Once again, the finale rehearses (if less ostentatiously than in the quintet) many of the principal gestures presented earlier in the work: the beginning of the second group recalls a dreamily syncopated idea from the slow movement (mm. 31ff.); the development gets under-way with references to the slow movement's coda; and the digressive arabesque (in essence, a binary-form character piece in A♭) that inter-rupts the course of the recapitulation looks back to the descending me-lodic lines of the first Trio from the Scherzo.

But in spite of the similarities between the largest of Schumann's works for piano and strings from the Chamber Music Year, we would err in viewing them as twins. While they both display the extroverted, exuberant side of the composer's creative genius (particularly in their respective opening and closing movements), the presence of one less violin in the later work makes for a more intimate sound world whose most obvious emblem comes with the sumptuous cello solo at the out-set of the Andante cantabile. (The passage was certainly not lost on Brahms, who likewise initiated the slow movement of his C-minor Piano Quartet, op. 60, with a cello solo of comparable sumptuousness). Even more significantly, the individuality of the Piano Quartet derives from a neo-classic tone largely absent in the quintet. The hymnic quality of the introduction (Sostenuto assai) to the first movement, no less than the figural, abstract character of much of the material from the ensuing Allegro ma non troppo, bears comparison with the tone struck by Bee-thoven in his "Harp" Quartet, op. 74, and "Archduke" Trio, op. 97. (Carl Dahlhaus's conjecture—that the works of the "transitional" phase be-tween Beethoven's heroic and late periods were more important for the generation of Schumann and Mendelssohn than is generally recog-nized—turns out to be right on the mark).[80] Schumann's decision to begin the last movement with a spirited fugato places his Piano Quartet in line with a tradition extending back through Beethoven (finale of the

C-major String Quartet, op. 59, no. 3) to Mozart (finale of the G-major String Quartet, K. 387).[81]

The essence of the Romantic artwork, according to Friedrich Schlegel, lay in its presentation of a "sentimental theme in a fantastic form."[82] This concise definition seems ready-made for the slow movement of Schumann's Piano Quartet, given its frankly "sentimental" cello melody and the rhapsodic, "fantastic" unfolding of this theme. On reflection, however, it will become clear that the "fantastic" form amounts to a conflation of variation and tripartite designs:

	Cello Melody		B♭	m. 1
A	Variation 1	quasi-canon: violin and cello	B♭	17
	Variation 2	duo: piano and viola	B♭	32
B	Episode	chorale texture	G♭	48
A¹	Variation 3	duo: viola and violin (figuration)	B♭	73
	Variation 4	quasi-canon: violin and viola	B♭	88
	Variation 5	cello solo	B♭	102
CODA		finale prefigured	B♭	117–30

The ultra-expressivity of the movement's thematic material is thus balanced by a "hybrid" variation form that, as we have seen in our discussion of Schumann's string quartets, may owe something to Haydnesque models. If, in the Piano Quintet, the mediation of "private" and "public" characters is tipped toward the latter, then it is probably safe to say that the Piano Quartet, given its neo-classic tone and its close ties with the string quartet tradition, tends more toward the former.

On 3 December 1842, just before he set to work on the *Phantasiestücke* for piano trio, op. 88, Schumann jotted "Trio by Mendelssohn" in the *Haushaltbücher*.[83] But although Mendelssohn's D-minor trio might have been the catalyst for Schumann's first essay in the piano-trio medium, the two works have little in common. In a letter to Verhulst of 19 June 1843, Schumann set the *Phantasiestücke* apart from his own earlier works for piano and strings by calling attention to its "much more delicate . . . nature."[84] An important signifier for this delicacy is Schumann's employment of German tempo- and character-designations as opposed to their internationally recognized Italian equivalents. This small but telling feature aptly complements a turn from the sonata-style forms of the Piano Quintet and Quartet toward the more intimately etched designs of the keyboard miniature. And indeed, the four movements of the *Phantasiestücke* are designated as character pieces: *Romanze, Humoreske, Duett,* and *Finale: Im Marschtempo.*

In his 1840 critique of recently composed piano trios, Schumann contrasts enduring artworks with more ephemeral creations like Karl Seyler's trio, a composition at once "modern, pleasant, [and] bourgeois."[85] Unfortunately, history has consigned the *Phantasiestücke* to the same realm as Seyler's work: Schumann's earliest piano trio is seldom heard; the 1987–1988 rendition by the Göbel-Trio Berlin is one of the few available on CD. This is not to say that the *Phantasiestücke* can be written off as "modern, pleasant, bourgeois," and nothing more. On the contrary, the last two movements of the work embody the esoteric dimension requisite for the chamber style in the form of a refined contrapuntal sensibility. The violin heads off the middle section (mm. 15ff.) of the *Duett,* for instance, with an inversion of the cello's opening melody. The first episode of the *Finale* (mm. 25–40; Example 7.4), its diminutive proportions notwithstanding, is a contrapuntal tour de force featuring the combination of a four-note figure with its inversion. The mirroring techniques intensify in the episode's second half (mm. 33ff.), which commences with the inversion of the initial figure and freely reverses the order of the voices' subsequent entries (cf. mm. 25–26: bass-alto/tenor-soprano; and mm. 33–35: soprano-alto-tenor-bass).

Still, it is difficult to deny that the underlying seriousness of purpose in the string quartets, Piano Quintet, and Piano Quartet is simply not a decisive factor in the *Phantasiestücke.* Schumann's turn to a more easy-going, "bourgeois" style is evident in his more relaxed approach to musical structure. The *Humoreske,* for example, proceeds as a medley of quasi-independent miniatures, all of them in binary form. First comes a march in F, then another march (which recasts the opening idea of the first movement in dotted rhythms) in A minor. A third march (F major) gives way to a fourth (D minor), which derives its characteristic rhythm (featuring a heavily accentuated second beat) from the preceding miniature. Restatements of the third march (B♭) and the first round off a design that, in spite of all the thematic cross-references, seems oddly random. It is as if the complex medley forms of the *Novelletten* had been pared down for popular consumption. But in a sense, Schumann's Opus 88 is no less pivotal a work than the Piano Quintet: at the same time that it hearkens to the earlier keyboard miniatures it looks forward to the *Hausmusik* of the later 1840s.

Example 7.4. Phantasiestücke, op. 88: *Finale,* mm. 25–40.

Toward a Poetic Chamber Music

For Franz Brendel, writing in the mid-1840s, Schumann's creative development proceeded from a youthful, "subjective" phase that reached its highpoint in "poetic" collections such as the *Davidsbündlertänze* and *Kreisleriana* to a more sober, "objective" phase whose artistic products bore the imprint of the composer's intense study of counterpoint.[86] On the surface, it appears as though the works of the Chamber Music Year should naturally occupy a place on the objective end of the continuum. Conspicuously absent in the five major compositions of 1842 are the fanciful titles and poetic inscriptions encountered so frequently in the earlier keyboard works. There are no "Clara" quartets to stand beside the "Clara" symphony (in D minor) of the previous year; nor have any motivating verses (as in the first symphony) come to light as possible sources of inspiration for the chamber music of 1842. To judge from the documentary evidence, Schumann even seems to have lost something of his voracious appetite for literature; according to the *Haushaltbücher,* his reading during this period was limited to Byron's *Don Juan* and Schiller's *Don Carlos.*[87]

Recognition of the apparently abstract turn of Schumann's thought has not prevented scholars from attempting to locate a poetic basis for some of the compositions of the Chamber Music Year. Akio Mayeda, for example, finds this basis in the "speech-quality" of the musical mottos that head the first movements of the A-major String Quartet, the Piano Quintet, and the Piano Quartet. Mayeda rightly points out that the spoken quality of Schumann's mottos (the falling fifth of the A-major quartet, the chorale-like opening gesture of the Piano Quartet) is a function of their susceptibility to transformation (both mottos are first presented in a slow introduction, and then elaborated in the ensuing Allegro); but he perhaps goes too far in underlaying "Cla-ra" to the falling fifth of the String Quartet.[88]

Hans Kohlhase, who has written extensively and insightfully on Schumann's chamber works, goes even farther. For him, the poetry of this music resides chiefly in its allusions, both to Schumann's own works and to those of others. The slow movement of the Piano Quintet, in his view, is raised from a generalized symbol of sorrow to a wordless tragedy by its allusion (just before the central Agitato) to the melodic shape of the opening idea of "Es ist vollbracht" from Bach's *St. John Passion*.[89] Likewise, the falling fifths of the first Trio from the Quintet's Scherzo recall Schumann's bassline to the theme by Clara that served as the point of departure for the *Impromptus,* op. 5. Kohlhase links the same gesture with several passages from the last of the *Faust* scenes, where it is associated with the notion of union with the divine.[90] But although Kohlhase is certainly justified in attempting to refute those critics who descry only an empty formalism in Schumann's chamber music, many of his observations seem farfetched. The descending line from the Piano Quintet figures not only in Bach's *St. John,* but in hundreds of other pieces as well. The Quintet's allusions to Clara on the one hand and Goethe's Eternal-Feminine on the other too easily dissolve into so many castles in the air.

Moreover, this sort of approach directly violates Schumann's own aesthetic of originality. Time and again he upbraided young composers for making overly obvious allusions to earlier masterworks. Verhulst's reference to the finale of the "Eroica" Symphony in the finale of his own D-minor String Quartet (op. 6, no. 2) evoked the following pair of rhetorical questions from Schumann: "Did this [allusion] escape the attention of the composer? If not, why did he let it stand?"[91] Similarly, he felt that the echoes of Beethoven's "Moonlight" Sonata in the finale of B. E. Philipp's Piano Trio "detracted from the overall effect."[92] To be sure, Schumann's chamber music is not without allusions to the works of others, but the most significant of these references, as we have seen, are those that present an earlier compositional technique or strategy in a new light. The mere imitation of an earlier thematic idea, for Schumann the critic and practicing composer, was a sure symptom of weakness in invention.

If the poetry of Schumann's chamber music does not lie principally in its allusiveness, where can it be situated? Again, the composer's critical writings provide a clue. In his review of Hermann Hirschbach's first string quartet, op. 1, Schumann links the late music of Beethoven with the beginnings of a "new poetic era" marked by the cultivation of striking and unusual musical forms. His remarks warrant quotation in full:

"He [Hirschbach] hopes to merit the title of 'poet' through his avoid-ance of stereotypical forms; in this, Beethoven's last quartets serve as the starting-point for the new poetic era in which he plans to distinguish himself."[93] Shortly after writing this review, Schumann too would ex-tend his quest for new forms to the domain of chamber music, most notably in the hymnic slow movements of Opus 41, nos. 1 and 3, the quirky last movement of Opus 41, no. 3, and the rhapsodic but logically conceived finales of the Piano Quintet and Piano Quartet. These works engage listeners and players (as they had the composer) in an imagina-tive dialogue with the tradition from which Schumann inherited the special problems and concerns he addressed in the Chamber Music Year.

~8~

The Oratorio
Year: 1843

"Absorbed in Peri Thoughts"

Late in June 1843, Schumann noted in the marriage diary: "Now Clara
is putting her *lieder* and several piano pieces in order. She wants to press
forward [with composition]; but *Marie* is tugging at her dress, Elise
[born just two months before] is keeping her busy, and her husband
sits absorbed in Peri thoughts."[1] Apparently Schumann's self-indulgent
cogitation paid off; shortly before making the diary entry, he completed
his most sustained effort in a larger musical form to date, the secular
oratorio *Das Paradies und die Peri,* op. 50. The result of four months of
almost steady labor, Schumann's latest composition would belie a suspicion he had voiced in a review of 1841, namely that a few notable
exceptions aside (such as Mendelssohn's *St. Paul*), the oratorio was in
danger of becoming extinct.[2] Not only would the *Peri* contribute to the
revivification of a languishing genre, it would establish Schumann in
contemporary opinion as one of the undisputed masters of his time.
The *Peri,* a work heard all too infrequently today, marks a watershed in
Schumann's career. And if we linger over this composition, it will not
only be because of its historical importance for the unfolding of Schumann's artistic life; the oratorio merits a closer look on strictly aesthetic
grounds.

But before considering the *Peri* in closer detail, we should introduce
a qualification. The parsing of Schumann's creative activities between
1840 and 1843 into "Song," "Symphony," "Chamber Music," and "Orato-

rio" years does some violence to the facts, which sometimes resist the neat compartmentalization that, after all, is no more than a convenience for biographers. Schumann's exploration of the various musical genres discloses an overarching system, but the system is often characterized by overlaps, retrenchments, and unexpected turns.

Clearly enough, the *Andante and Variations* in B♭ for two pianos, two cellos, and horn, drafted with Schumann's usual speed between 26 January and 7 February 1843,[3] represents a completion of the previous year's activities. As we have seen, the products of the Chamber Music Year are situated at the meeting point of contrary tendencies: innovation and tradition come together in the string quartets; the Piano Quintet and Quartet mediate the demands of symphonism and the chamber idiom; the *Phantasiestücke*, op. 88, provide a foretaste of the dialectic between high art and Biedermeier sensibility that will inform the *Hausmusik* of the later 1840s. Like the *Phantasiestücke*, the "Quintet Variations" (as Schumann called them) of 1843 recall the manner of the earlier keyboard miniatures, now colored by a chamber setting—and a remarkable setting at that. (Owing to the ensemble difficulties posed by the work in its original scoring, Schumann rearranged the Variations, at Mendelssohn's suggestion, for two pianos; while the later version appeared in print, as Opus 46, by late 1843, the first version was not published until 1893).[4] Schumann spelled out the link between his newest work and the compositions of the previous decade in a letter of 7 September 1843 to Breitkopf and Härtel, where he compared the *Andante and Variations* to "a somewhat delicate plant," and requested that the print be fitted out similarly to the *Kinderscenen*.[5] The theme of the set resonates with the main idea of *Kreisleriana* No. 2 (also in B♭), just as the alternation of boisterous (and technically demanding) "Florestan" variations and more subdued "Eusebius" variations recalls the similar patterning in the *Davidsbündlertänze* and the *Fantasiestücke*, op. 12. But, as Eduard Hanslick said of the *Peri*, "Master Florestan is getting a bit older."[6] In the *Andante and Variations*, Schumann's Jean Paulian rhapsodizing is tempered by a nearly symmetrical disposition of the "Eusebius" pieces, three of which are strategically placed at the opening (the theme), the midpoint (Variation 6), and near the close (the thematic return in the Coda) of the cycle.

In contrast to his practice in the *Phantasiestücke*, op. 88, Schumann caters little if at all to popular taste in his "Quintet Variations." Clara, who collaborated with Mendelssohn for the first public rendition of the two-piano version on 19 August 1843, attributed its lukewarm reception to the audience's having "somewhat lost its musical frame of mind and composure because of the fire alarm" that interrupted the concert. Furthermore, Schumann's "profoundly genial" piece probably failed to make a strong impression due to its coupling with "the endless coloratura, which in any event isn't really music," of mezzo-soprano Pauline Viardot-Garcia, the featured soloist on the program.[7] According to Hermann Schellenberg, author of a brief review for the *Allgemeine musikalische Zeitung*, the *Andante and Variations* attempted to "say much with little ado" (in contrast to virtuoso music, which "says little with much ado"), and hence would demand repeated hearings to create the proper effect. In this instance, at least, Schumann's economical handling of his materials, a compositional strategy refined in the symphonic and chamber works of 1841 and 1842, was perceived as a hindrance to comprehensibility.[8]

Another of Schumann's ensemble works, the Piano Quintet conceived at the height of the Chamber Music Year, may have played a small but significant role in the composer's rapprochement with his father-in-law, Friedrich Wieck. A frequent (and sometimes disruptive) guest at the Schumanns' Leipzig flat, Wieck proffered the olive branch in a letter dated 16 December 1843, in which the older man expressed his willingness, if only for Clara's sake, to set aside his past differences with his son-in-law.[9] In all likelihood, Wieck's change of heart was encouraged by Schumann's improved standing in the official musical world. Clara reported that after hearing the Piano Quintet (which was encored, from beginning to end, at a soireé of 14 February), her father suddenly became "wildly enthusiastic about Robert's compositions."[10] It is probably not a coincidence that Schumann received Wieck's formal letter of reconciliation shortly after the first spectacularly successful performances of the *Peri*. Indeed, Wieck must have realized that "Master Florestan" was tempering his earlier (and wilder) ways.

Schumann's pedagogical activities constitute a further sign of the composer's settling into maturity. In a diary entry of 17 February 1843, he expressed his enthusiasm for Mendelssohn's plans to organize a conservatory in Leipzig, its faculty to include Moritz Hauptmann (harmony and counterpoint), Ferdinand David (violin), and Ferdinand Becker (organ). Mendelssohn himself, in addition to serving as director, would teach voice, instrumental performance, and composition. Schumann was to provide three hours of instruction per week in composition, score-reading, and piano.[11] Although it was hoped that Clara too would participate (she eventually did), she seems at first to have been mystified by the latest practices in musical pedagogy. As she wrote in early April, shortly after Schumann first met with his young charges: "I have no idea how one can teach six students at once."[12] By midsummer, Schumann was bemoaning the fact that of the academy's forty to fifty enrollees, few were talented in composition.[13] Still, the conservatory would have offered him an institutional framework for the realization of his pedagogical ideas. Among the most fascinating of these is a plan, transmitted in a series of notebook jottings now at the Robert-Schumann-Haus in Zwickau, for a historical course of study. Schumann's outline is worth quoting in full:

> To use for study:
>   From the first period:
>   Bach, Scarlatti, Handel, Couperin, C. P. E. Bach
>
>   From the second [period]:
>   Haydn, Mozart, Beethoven, Clementi, Cramer, Prince Louis [Ferdinand]
>
>   From the third [period]:
>   Hummel, Moscheles, [Ludwig] Berger, [Christoph] Weyse, Schubert
>
>   From the fourth [period]:
>   Mendelssohn, Chopin, Bennett, Henselt[14]

Just as telling as the names on the list is Schumann's decision to omit some of his most prominent contemporaries. Clara was perhaps echoing her husband's opinions when she wrote of Niels Gade, whom we would expect to find under the "fourth period," and whose First Symphony was performed at the Gewandhaus in March 1843: "I think that *Gade* is just about finished; his talent appears to extend only to a certain genre the possibilities of which he will soon exhaust, because the Nordic national character (the genre in question) quickly becomes *monotonous,* like all national music in general."[15] Wagner, like Liszt and Berlioz, is conspicuously absent, and again Clara offers a vivid (and none too flattering) portrait with which Schumann would not have disagreed. In February 1843, *Rienzi* was "making the whole of Dresden crazy"; but as for Clara, then visiting with her father: "My entire feeling was one of *displeasure;* more I can't say. The same feeling returned when I met Wagner—a man who never ceases to talk about himself, is very arrogant, and laughs continually in a whining tone."[16]

Clara's trip to Dresden fell in the middle of the Leipzig visit of one of the contemporary musical world's most colorful and controversial personalities, Hector Berlioz, whose German tour brought him to Saxony between 29 January and 1 March. It is clear from the diaries and the *Haushaltbücher* that Schumann took in with great interest his concerts of 4 and 23 February that featured the composer's own renditions of the Offertorium from his Requiem, the *King Lear* Overture, and the

Symphonie fantastique.[17] (As Berlioz related in his *Memoirs,* Schumann was deeply impressed by the movement from the Requiem. "At the rehearsal, Schumann, breaking his habitual silence, exclaimed: 'That Offertorium beats everything.'")[18] Nonetheless, Schumann's attitude toward the French composer's music had cooled somewhat in the eight years separating the celebrated review of the *Symphonie fantastique* and the performances of 1843. "There is much unbearable stuff in his music," Schumann wrote in a lively account dated 17 February, "but certainly also much that's extraordinarily ingenious and original. Often he seems to me like the powerless King Lear himself. . . . Now he travels with a certain Mlle. *Rezio* [Marie Récio, the interpreter of the romance "L'absence" for the Leipzig concerts, and ultimately Berlioz's second wife], who is certainly more than his performance partner. Unfortunately he spoke no German, so we couldn't converse much. I had imagined him as a wilder and more animated man. His laughter is hearty; otherwise he's a real Frenchman, drinks watered-down wine, and eats compote." Schumann went on to indicate, if only obliquely, the source of his reservations concerning Berlioz's compositions. Hermann Hirschbach's music, he claimed "is lacking in too many of the foundational properties of art; in this he is similar to Berlioz."[19] The music of Berlioz (and no doubt Wagner as well) was certainly "interesting" in the sense that Schiller and the Schlegel brothers used the term, but was hardly to be taken as a model by young composers, hence its omission from Schumann's historical curriculum. More experienced composers, however, may draw their sustenance from a wider variety of sources, some of them suspect from a pedagogical point of view. Schumann affords proof of this supposition in his *Peri,* some of whose orchestral effects, as we shall see, show traces of Berlioz's influence.

Berlioz's visit overlapped with the beginning of Schumann's sustained work on the music for the *Peri,* although the roots of the project extended back over two years into the past. In a December 1840 entry in his *Projektenbuch,* Schumann listed three of the four tales from Thomas Moore's epic in verse, the *Lalla Rookh* (published 1817; literally, "Princess Tulip-cheeks"), under the rubric "Texts suitable for concert pieces": "Paradies und die Peri" (Paradise and the Peri), "Der falsche Prophet" (The False Prophet), and "Das Rosenfest/Das Licht des Harams" (The Light of the Harem). That the first two were further designated as "opera materials" is notable though hardly surprising; during the course of the *Liederjahr,* Schumann entertained the possibility of setting a variety of operatic subjects, ranging from E. T. A. Hoffmann's *Doge und Dogaressa* to Byron's *Sardanapal.*"[20] By early September 1842, when Immermann's *Tristan und Isolde* came under consideration, the thought of writing an opera was Schumann's "morning and evening artist-prayer."[21] And at the end of 1843, he noted in the marriage diary: "An opera will be my next work, and I'm fired up to proceed."[22] Given this context, it is understandable that the *Peri*, as it finally took shape, bore the imprint of Schumann's preoccupation with dramatic music. At the same time, it would be a mistake to think of the *Peri* as an ersatz-opera. On the contrary, Schumann emphasized its distance from that genre in a letter to Kossmaly written several weeks before the completion of the sketches for the oratorio: "At the moment I'm involved in a large project, the largest I've yet undertaken—it's not an opera—I believe it's well-nigh a new genre for the concert hall. I plan to put all my energy into it and hope to have finished it within the year."[23]

In early August 1841, at the height of the Symphonic Year (the D-minor Symphony and A-minor *Phantasie* for piano and orchestra were both more or less complete), Schumann's boyhood friend Emil Flechsig rekindled the composer's interest in Moore's tale of the Peri's quest for a place in paradise. To be sure, there is a good chance that Schumann's first encounter with the poem came well before his *Projektenbuch* entry of December 1840: J. L. Witthaus's translation, published by the Verlag Gebrüder Schumann in 1822, would have been available to the composer in his teenage years. Drawing on Flechsig's translation of Moore's original and also on Theodor Oelckers' translation of 1839, Schumann immediately set to work on a libretto, completed in its essential outline by early January 1842. Adolf Böttger, author of the lyric that served as a poetic impetus for the First Symphony, was likewise consulted, probably on the finer points of versification, as the text took shape in the previous months. This scenario is supported not only by the *Haushaltbücher*, but also by Flechsig's report to Wasielewski of 7 May 1857, according to which Schumann "in part retained, and in part shortened, improved, or altered" his friend's translation.[24] Among the most significant of Schumann's alterations were a series of additions to the original poem, including the Peri's "Wo find ich sie?" (No. 4 in the oratorio), and the choruses of Nile genies (No. 11), Houris (No. 18), and Peris (No. 22, quartet of solo voices), all of which afforded him the opportunity to compose some of his most picturesque and delicately wrought music.

Having a suitably refashioned poem in hand, Schumann was in a position to proceed with the musical setting. Oddly enough, however, he seems to have left his text untouched for over a year.[25] But when he returned to the project early in 1843 (the entry in the *Haushaltbücher* for 23 February reads: "A step forward in the *Peri*"),[26] he pressed forward at full throttle. By 30 March the whole of Part I had been sketched and scored. The obsessive singlemindedness of Schumann's efforts was a source of some concern for Clara, who wrote in the marriage diary:

> [Robert] has already played me the First Part [of the oratorio] from the sketch, and I think it's the most splendid thing he's done so far; but he's working with his whole body and soul, and with such intensity that I sometimes worry he might become ill; nonetheless [his work] also makes me happy, for I think it must be pleasing to Heaven for a human being to create something so noble, and therefore [I hope] that my Robert will be kept from harm!"[27]

After the drafting of Part II between 6 and 17 April there followed a month-long hiatus, no doubt occasioned by three factors: first, the "annoying journal," which kept Schumann from doing much of anything else, second, the birth of a second daughter, Elise, on 25 April, and third, the hubbub surrounding the firing of the Schumanns' "malicious and insolent" cook, who made off with fifty bottles from her employers' wine cellar.[28] But on 17 May he was back at work on Part III, the sketch for which was completed by May 25. (Clara was just as delighted as her husband that the end was in sight; earlier in the month she made a plea at once touching and amusing: "Our poor diary would be so pleased if you would soon finish the *Peri*, because it's not at all interesting when you don't write something.")[29] Three days later Schumann set to work on the orchestration of the oratorio's third and final part, so that by June 16 the entire composition was essentially complete.[30]

The intense work on the *Peri* obviously took its toll. Indeed, the *Haushaltbücher* contain many references to Schumann's "exhaustion" and "melancholy," references that belie the popularly held (and simplistic) notion that the composer teetered back and forth from inactive and gloomy to hyperactive and high-spirited phases.[31] The documentary evidence suggests that hyperactivity and depression might well go hand in hand. Nonetheless, Schumann came to the end of his labors with considerable relief. As he put it in the marriage diary:

> On 16 June my "Peri" was completed after several days of strenuous work. What a great joy for the Schumann couple! Except for a few oratorios by Loewe, which are basically didactic, I don't know of anything similar in the musical repertory. I don't like to write or speak about my own works; my wish is that they will have a good effect on the world and secure for me the loving memory of my children.[32]

Schumann's high hopes for his oratorio were soon fulfilled. Mid-nineteenth-century critics were almost unanimous in viewing the *Peri* as the work in which the composer demonstrated his absolute mastery of the largest musical forces.[33] The positive reception of the musical press was closely bound up with the nature and quality of the first performances, on 4 and 11 December, at the Leipzig Gewandhaus. No doubt there were mishaps, both probable and real. Reports vary, for instance, regarding Schumann's effectiveness on the podium. Clara praised her husband's "beautiful" conducting and "calm demeanor."[34] But Livia Frege, who sang the title role, found Schumann's demeanor too calm; in her opinion, a truly able conductor needed to call more attention to himself.[35] Then, too, the success of the first performance was jeopardized by the temperamental tenor soloist, Heinrich Schmidt, who at the last minute decided not to go on. Fortunately, the Viennese tenor Johann Vesque von Püttlingen, who happened to be present at the concert, stepped in to sing at sight the scene for the plague-stricken youth in Part II.[36] This unexpected turn of events aside, two months of careful rehearsing and Livia Frege's stunning rendition of the Peri contributed to a premiere so successful that a second performance had to be arranged for the following week. (According to Clara, the applause was great at the first performance, but even more enthusiastic at the second, where Schumann was recalled after each of the oratorio's three parts). One listener, the poetaster Hermann Stähnisch, felt compelled to pen some embarrassingly sentimental verses in the composer's honor: "Oh, how bleak it has become / Since the Peri was redeemed! / And now the gates to heaven are closed [a reference to No. 26] / *Only she has earned a place in Eden,* / And we are left behind, here on earth, / Gazing up at her happiness . . ."[37] Within the next five years, the *Peri* played in most of the chief German musical centers; during the same period, it began to make its way throughout continental Europe with performances in Utrecht (1844/1845), Amsterdam, Prague, Riga (1845/1846), Zurich and The Hague (1846/1847).[38] Late in 1847, Schumann was surprised to learn that the American Musical Institute in New York was planning a rendition for its 1848 season.[39] In short, the *Peri* was the work that made Schumann into an international, as opposed to a merely German, phenomenon.[40] Not only was Master Florestan getting older; he was poised to develop into a cosmopolitan figure.

Das Paradies und die Peri: An Overview

It may surprise some modern-day devotees of Schumann's works to learn that the composition which secured his international reputation was not a symphony, a song cycle, a chamber work, or a poetic cycle of keyboard miniatures, but rather an oratorio. Yet according to Carl Dahlhaus, it was precisely in genres such as the dramatic cantata, the choral ballad and ode, and the secular oratorio that "the nineteenth century recognized itself."[41] (Schumann too recognized himself in the *Peri*. "My life's blood is bound up with this work," he wrote to Brendel in 1847.)[42] And even if these genres have not been so completely forgotten in our century as Dahlhaus claims, still it is undeniable that the institutional support for their cultivation has diminished. Schumann's *Peri* was the product of an age in which Handel's oratorios were practically as popular as Beethoven's symphonies, and in which the Gesangverein, the Singakademie, the Liedertafel, and the Männerchor, manifestations in equal measure of late eighteenth-century humanitarianism and the incipient nationalism of the early nineteenth century, were very much a part of musical culture. Keeping this context in mind, we can well understand Schumann's keen devotion to choral music in the last dozen years of his career. Liszt was right on the mark in viewing the secular oratorio, along with the keyboard miniature, as one of the central genres of Schumann's oeuvre.[43]

The principal figure of Schumann's first oratorio derives from Persian mythology. According to the definition in Herlosssohn's *Damen Conversations Lexikon* (1837), to which Flechsig directed Schumann in a letter of 8 August 1841, Peris were heavenly beings, but they belonged

> more to the field of Romanticism than to religious faith. [They] were thought to be completely ethereal in nature and satisfied their hunger on the aroma of blossoms [similarly, Moore's Peri feasts on the scent of perfumes]; their beauty, namely that of the female Peris, is so unearthly that no description is capable of doing it justice. Their essence is angelic; they are elfin in lightness and airiness, and yet they are far more sublime in nature than elves. One might compare them with fairies if the latter . . . didn't represent but a shadow of the complete concept of a Peri.[44]

Indescribable beauty is difficult if not impossible to portray unequivocally in musical terms. All the same, Schumann wonderfully captured the elfin quality of these strange creatures in the solo quartet from No. 22, "Peri, ist's wahr," one of the lightest and airiest passages in the oratorio, just as the hymnic quality of much of the music for the Peri herself (consider especially the finale of Part II: No. 17, "Schlaf' nun und ruh") aptly suggests an angelic essence.

Descended from the union of a fallen angel and a mortal, the Peri, much to her chagrin, is excluded from paradise. But the Peri of Moore's poem has been promised admission to heaven if she can only find a suitable gift. This challenge in turn supplies the motivation for each of the three tableaux of Schumann's oratorio. In Part I, the Peri hopes to have discovered her gift in the blood of a young warrior killed by the cruel tyrant, Gazna. Since the guardian of the heavenly gates is unimpressed with this offering, the Peri spends the remainder of Part II in search of a second gift: the sighs of a maiden who dies in the arms of her plague-stricken beloved. Predictably, this offering too is found wanting at the beginning of Part III. Only through the presentation of the tears of a viscious criminal, moved by the sight of a boy at prayer, is the Peri assured a place in paradise at the triumphant conclusion of the oratorio. The quest romance, a familiar plot-archetype of nineteenth-century literature, is thus given a decidedly christological slant: Paradise (a cipher for originary innocence) gives way before the Fall (a state of sin) only to be regained through an act of redemption.

History has not been kind to Moore's poetry. Our postmodern sensibility finds it difficult to embrace the unlikely notion that innocence, once lost, can be recovered. As one specialist on Moore's poetry writes: "Reading [the *Lalla Rookh*] today is a task, not a pleasure. It is long, drawn-out, florid, bathetic, and occasionally absurd."[45] Yet for Schumann, echoing the views of his friend Flechsig, Moore's *Peri* was "as if intended for music from the start. The overall idea was so poetic that it enraptured me completely."[46] Likewise, many of the first reviewers of Schumann's oratorio agreed that the "charming poem" contributed substantially to the work's success.[47]

Indeed, Schumann certainly found more in the poem than an opportunity to contribute to the fad for oriental literature that had been sweeping Europe since the early days of the nineteenth century. In addition to the secular theology of its plot, the tale offered a mediation of sacred and profane realms in the figure of the Peri herself. An ethereal creature half-human and half-divine, the Peri is arguably an emblem for Schumann's outlook on the oratorio as a genre. Although he emphasized, in a letter to Eduard Krüger of 3 June 1843, the secular character of his latest work—"The subject is Das Paradies und die Peri of Th. Moore, an oratorio, though not for the chapel [Betsaal], but rather for "cheerful" [heitre] folk"[48]—Schumann's statement does not gainsay the presence of a distinctly religious element in his composition. It only suggests that the *Peri* was not conceived as a sacred work in the narrower sense. Similarly, the "concert hall" for which Schumann intended his "new genre" was not an exclusively secular space. Drawing on a Romantic *topos* that would recur in the writings of Liszt and Wagner, Schumann imagined it as an ideal, sanctified realm, a meeting ground for art and religion over which the composer officiates.[49] No less than the "new genre for the concert hall," the artist, a quasi-human, quasi-divine agent of redemption, finds a striking poetic counterpart in the figure of the Peri.[50]

The positive reception of what may strike us as an improbable and excessively sentimental tale represents less a lapse of taste on the part of Schumann and his contemporaries than a difference in outlook. Through its passion for the Orient, helped along by Napoleon's campaigns in Egypt and Britain's incursions into India, the early nineteenth century indulged in a fantastic play with distance, the poetic and philosophical fruits of which blossomed in Goethe's *West-Östlicher Divan* (1819) and Friedrich Schlegel's *Über die Sprache und Weisheit der Inder* (1819). In Moore's verses, distance in space becomes a metaphor for distance in time. Indeed, the theological scheme of the Peri tale—Originary bliss-Fall-Paradise regained—readily maps onto the historical scheme—classical antiquity-contemporary critique-redemptive future—articulated in the fragments and essays of the early framers of Romanticism, Novalis and the Schlegel brothers among them. Schumann too subscribed to this tripartite philosophy of history. As noted in Chapter 3, the *Neue Zeitschrift für Musik* rested on a critical foundation in which preservation of the past, recognition of deficiencies in the present, and hope in the future interlock and mutually support one another. In the *Peri*, Schumann seized on the opportunity to present a theological variant of this interplay. Thus our embarrassment over the Peri's sentimental quest should probably recede in favor of the realization that only in the work of art can utopian schemes become actuality.

Just as important as the broadly cultural sources for Schumann's work are its more specifically musical sources. Between 1840 and 1842 his thoughts turned increasingly to the oratorio in a series of reviews for the *Neue Zeitschrift* of new works by Marschner, Hiller, Sobolewski, and Loewe.[51] To judge from his comments, Schumann was much taken by the continuous flow from one movement to the next in Marschner's *Klänge aus Osten* (a feature he would adopt in the *Peri*) and by Loewe's attempt to mediate opera and sacred oratorio in his *Johann Huss*. Echoes of the Offertorium from Berlioz's Requiem take the form of prominent passages for ophicleide in Nos. 6, 7, and 23 of the *Peri*. Early in February 1843, Schumann attended the dress rehearsal and premiere of the final version of Mendelssohn's secular cantata on Goethe's ballad, *Die erste Walpurgisnacht*, op. 60, a work whose expressive *ariosi* and colorful choruses likewise left their mark on the *Peri*.[52] Weber counts as another important influence. The chorus of Nile Genies (No. 11) recalls the chorus of elves, mermaids, nymphs, fairies, sylphs, and spirits of the air from the Act 2 Finale of *Oberon*, just as the Peri's triumphant aria with chorus, "Freud', ew'ge Freude, mein Werk ist gethan" (No. 26; Finale of

Part III) echoes the heroic tone of Weber's *Euryanthe* (specifically, the heroine's aria with chorus, "Zu ihm! O weilet nicht" [No. 21]). Hence, the richness of Schumann's *Peri* derives, in part, from the multiplicity of genres upon which it drew: secular and sacred oratorio, secular cantata, Requiem, fairy-tale opera, and grand opera.

As we have seen, Schumann divided his *Peri* into three parts or tableaux. Each of these in turn divides neatly into two large scene-complexes: the first centered on the Peri's various exchanges at the heavenly gates, and the second on her search for an acceptable gift. Likewise, the clearly differentiated vocal forces—narrating tenor and alto, picturesque choruses of warriors and spirits, the Peri and the other specifically named characters—submit to an underlying order, each entity corresponding to the epic, lyric, and dramatic principle, respectively. And while the epic and lyric modes prevail throughout, it is eminently sensible that the dramatic principle, in the form of brief dialogues for the Indians and Conquerors (No. 6), Gazna and the young warrior (No. 7), and the maiden and her beloved (Nos. 15–16), should emerge in those portions of the work given over to the Peri's quest. Of the nineteenth century's larger creations for vocal and orchestral forces, only Wagner's *Parsifal* equals the *Peri* in dispositional logic and symmetry.

Much of this logic derives from Schumann's handling of tonality. To be sure, we would undermine the variety and freedom of his conception by attempting to ascribe a single key to the work, and it does not progress ineluctably from the E major of the opening scene at the heavenly gates to the G major of the Peri's ultimate admission into paradise.[53] But in spite of Schumann's fluid approach to harmonic organization, it is important to recognize the role of tonal pairing, usually by third, on both the small and large scale. At the level of the individual number, the progressive motion from minor to relative major becomes a musical cipher for yearning (for example, the Peri's "Wie glücklich sie wandeln" [No. 2] and "Verstossen!" [No. 20]). At the level of the scene, the same directional thrust accompanies the Peri's attainment of her long-sought goal (Nos. 23–26).

Progressive tonal schemes combine with motivic recurrence to ensure coherence over relatively extended spans. The Peri's rejoinders to the Nile Genies in No. 11, for instance, recall her lied, "Wie glücklich sie wandeln" (No. 2) (Examples 8.1 and 8.2). Consider also the scene for Gazna, his retainers, and the young warrior from Part I (Nos. 6–8). The recurrence, at the same pitch level, of the orchestral prelude to No. 6 as support for the Chorus of Conquerors in No. 7 imparts continuity to the first half of the scene, while the transfigured return of the flowing accompaniment to the tenor solo ("Und einsam steht ein Jüngling

Example 8.1. Das Paradies und die Peri: No. 2, mm. 1–8.

noch," No. 7) in the ensuing Chorus of lamentation ("Weh', Weh'," No. 8) functions similarly for the scene's conclusion. Owing to the interlocking motivic relationships and the overriding descent in thirds (Db[= C♯] = A = F♯ minor), three nominally independent numbers are perceived as a unit. Strategies of this sort were basic to Schumann's notion of a "new genre for the concert hall." In his 1840 review of Marschner's *Klänge aus Osten,* Schumann lauded his colleague for having made a beginning, a first attempt, "which others have only to develop further in order to enrich the concert hall with a new musical genre." [54] Specifically, the most notable aspect of Marschner's oratorio was the disposition of its individual movements in a continuous, uninterrupted sequence; in a letter to Brendel written seven years later, Schumann would even cite the same characteristic as one of the outstanding features of his *Peri.* [55] Thus the notion of a "new genre" was intimately tied to the question of musical continuity.

Unity and continuity, however, are complemented by variety throughout this most highly differentiated of Schumann's larger works. Each of the Peri's principal solos, to take a case in point, unfolds as a distinct song-type: three-strophe lied (No. 2), recitative, lied, and arioso

Example 8.2. Das Paradies und die Peri: No. 11, mm. 36–44.

(No. 4), binary-form lullaby (No. 17), recitative and aria (No. 20), imitatively accompanied arioso (No. 25), and rondo-aria with chorus (No.
26). The gradual progression from lied forms to quasi-operatic arias
(the closing movement would not sound out of place at the culmination
of a rescue opera) thus mirrors the Peri's path from unreflecting inno-

cence to redemption through grace. In a sense, the mediating forms, those poised between recitation and lyricism, are the most telling of all. In fact, they represent a solution to the problem Schumann posed for himself in the *Peri:* namely, how best to avoid a merely formulaic setting for the lengthy narrative portions of the text—how, in other words, to treat the epic portions of the poem in a musically substantive manner. This is of course the same dilemma that Wagner would face as he set about composing *The Ring*.[56] But whereas Wagner's solution entailed the creation of a leitmotivic web (and a concomitant break with traditional musical syntax), Schumann's was bound up with a continuum of melodic styles. From the start, he thought in terms of a carefully graduated range of vocal idioms; his structural plan for the oratorio, superimposed on the manuscript copy of Flechsig's translation, labels the projected movements variously as "Rezitativ," "Rezitativischer Gesang," "Gesang," "Lied," and "Arie."[57] In the published score, only the designation "Rezitativ" survives, all the other movements (the choruses, of course, excepted) being marked with the neutral "Solo." Still, the notion of the "Rezitativischer Gesang," a syntactically flexible vocal line supported by a motivically rich orchestral texture, appropriately describes the writing in a large number of the oratorio's movements (for example, sections of Nos. 1, 3–5, 7, 9–12, 14, 16, 19, 20, and 25). More significantly, the declamatory style associated with this melodic category answers to the composer's search for a musically substantive means of coping with the epic dimension of his text.

Some of the most impressive moments in the score come in the three finales (Nos. 9, 17, and 26). The Part I finale, for example, is dominated by a fugal chorus of Handelian power. Not surprisingly, Schumann is hardly content to write a staid, textbook fugue: the more or less regular exposition ("Denn heilig ist das Blut") and subsequent stretto dissolve into a leaner texture at "Für die Freiheit verspritzt," where the original fugue subject serves as countermelody to a new, rhythmically driving idea. Furthermore, the climax of the finale comes not with a statement of the subject, but rather with a grand homphonic setting of "Denn heilig ist das Blut." The movement, in other words, traces a directed course from fugue to homophony, from the sacred (for which the fugue is a compelling musical metaphor) to the profane. The conflation of secular quest romance and eschatology that characterizes the Peri tale as a whole is thus encoded in the musical fabric. On first hearing, the finale to Part II appears to be simplicity itself: a binary-form lied, modulating from tonic to dominant and back to tonic again, first presented by the Peri, and then, with ethereal string tremolos, by the Peri and chorus. The only touches of "art" in this otherwise "artless" setting come with a brief tonicization of the minor mediant, in the first half of the lied, and the punctuating hemiolas near the close of each half. Yet this finale, no less than that of Part I, occupies a place at the intersection of sacred and profane tendencies: the Peri's lied is at once a lullaby for a pair of expiring lovers and a prayer for their eternal salvation. With the finale to Part III, Schumann demonstrated that he knew very well how to bring an audience to its feet. But here too, the idea of the movement resides in its contrast and mediation of secular and sacred topics, represented by the Peri's operatic rondo-refrain ("O ewige Freude mein Werk ist gethan") and the chorale-textured music of the chorus, respectively. Schumann makes the point best when we expect one topic (the rondo tune, just after the third orchestral tutti arrives emphatically on the dominant) but get the other (the chorale, "Ja giebt es ein Opfer"). Aria and chorale interpenetrate in the closing stages of the movement, where the Peri's soaring descent in long note values, coupled with sustained harmonies in the chorus (all this over an intensifying dominant pedal in the orchestra) makes for a kind of Schumannian endless melody.

If the deferred climaxes and arching melismas of the Part III finale aspire to the "heavenly length" that Schumann found so attractive in Schubert's last symphony, then much of the *Peri* evinces another "heavenly" category from his critical vocabulary. In a review of 1838, Schumann alluded to the "heavenly airiness" ("himmlische Leichtigkeit") of Mozart's and Beethoven's piano sonatas, a quality just as important as the "profound revelations" for which those works are more often prized.[58] The "heavenly lightness" of the *Peri* manifests itself in a delicate and varied pallette of orchestral and vocal colors, most notably in the string-quartet texture at the very beginning of the work (where the chamber style figures as a symbol of purity), the quartet of solo voices, "O süsses Land!" from No. 5 (which hearkens to similar textures in Mozart's *Zauberflöte*), the deftly wrought Janissary scoring of No. 11 (Chorus of Nile Genies, "Hervor aus den Wässern") and No. 18 (Chorus of Houris, "Schmücket die Stufen"), the horn choir and shimmering strings of the Part II finale, and the subtle touches of color from the upper winds in the modally tinged No. 21, "Jetzt sank des Abends gold'-ner Schein." Hence, even those portions of the score that do not involve the Peri herself are pervaded by the angelic essence that, as Schumann learned from Flechsig, is required for the "complete concept of a Peri."

All in all, the listener cannot help but be impressed by the oratorio's lyric richness. For Brendel, an astute if tendentious critic of Schumann's works, it was precisely in this quality—melodic freedom—that the composer fulfilled the historical moment's demand for an unimpeded progress of the spirit toward subjectivity.[59] Whether or not we agree with Brendel's Hegelian assessment, there can be little doubt that Schumann rose to the task for which many of the critics of his keyboard miniatures and lieder questioned his fitness: in the *Peri*, he found a means of sustaining what were essentially lyric materials over protracted temporal expanses.[60] At the same time, Schumann demonstrated that it was possible for a mid-nineteenth-century composer to conceive a work whose serious message was not a hindrance to its popular appeal. The balance between accessibility and artistry in the *Peri* puts it in touch with other "universal" works such as Haydn's *Creation* and the finale of Beethoven's Ninth Symphony. The success of Schumann's venture secured for him a position as perhaps the last representative of musical Classicism.

Moreover, the *Peri* occupies a pivotal spot in Schumann's oeuvre. Having the benefit of hindsight, we can recognize that the teleology of his career was directed toward the "literary operas" of the 1840s and early 1850s, *Genoveva, Manfred,* and the *Faust* scenes prominent among them.[61] The *Peri* discloses important links with these works. The notion of redemption, to take the most frequently cited example, is central to all of them.[62] Even more telling is the unusual but fitting genre designation transmitted in the published score of the *Peri*. The work is called neither an oratorio, a religious opera, nor a secular cantata, but rather a *Dichtung,* a poem. The music for the *Peri*, in other words, is more than just music: it aspires to the intellectual status of poetry, of literature in the highest sense.

Of course, Schumann's systematic cultivation of the principal musical genres did not come to an end with the literary operas of the Dresden years; the process arguably culminated in the church music of 1852 and 1853: the Mass, op. 147, and the Requiem, op. 148, both composed in Düsseldorf. The *Peri* therefore mediates the fantastic, "profane" works of the 1830s and the darkly hued, sacred works of the final years. It is, to draw on one of Walter Benjamin's critical categories, a "dialectical sounding image," perhaps the most significant such image from the composer's output.

~9~

*S*chumann's
New Way

Off to the World's Wonder-Cities:
The Russian Tour of 1844

Notwithstanding the challenges of the period from 1841 to 1843, these years represented a relatively stable phase in Schumann's often unstable life. Now he could look back with justifiable pride, had he wanted to, on a not insignificant series of accomplishments, both personal and professional. The victor in a messy legal dispute over the woman he loved, and the father of two children, he was well on the way toward achieving bourgeois respectability. A staple of Leipzig's musical life, his reputation as a composer, consolidated through the symphonic and chamber works of 1841 and 1842, would soon spread far and wide in the wake of the *Peri*'s successes; Schumann was within striking distance of the artistic renown he had dreamed of for over a decade. But lives seldom if ever hold to an undisturbed course; the artist-life in particular is more apt to be rent by turmoil, frustrated by reversals, and besieged by psychological trauma. Such was the case with Robert Schumann in 1844.

Sounding a familiar theme, Clara noted in the marriage diary the previous summer: "I trouble about our future, and would like, now that we're young, to assemble a small capital, although Robert is of another opinion. . . . Nonetheless he's pacified me with the promise that next winter we'll undertake something grand." [1] That "something grand" materialized as a concert tour of Russia's cities great and small, which would keep the Schumanns away from home for four months. Seldom sanguine over enterprises of this sort, Schumann was eventually won over to the merits of the idea thanks to some gentle prodding from Mendelssohn.[2] On 13 December 1843 he entered the laconic "Decisions about Russia" in the *Haushaltbücher;*[3] a little over a month later (on 25 January 1844) he and Clara set off, not to return to Leipzig until late May.

"My greatest happiness," as Clara told Schumann through the marriage diary, "consists in the thought of your being able to live solely for your art and without any mundane cares."[4] Ostensibly planned with this aim in view, the Russian tour was very much Clara's from start to finish. She and Schumann made their way, often under miserable conditions, through Königsberg (Kaliningrad), Riga, Mitau (Jelgava, in Latvia), and Dorpat (Tartu, in Estonia), where Clara gave trial run-throughs of the repertory for her performances in major centers such as St. Petersburg and Moscow.[5] In spite of the vexatious and sometimes life-threatening adversities to which an artist touring in the 1840s was apt to be exposed—the brutal chill of the Russian winter ("it's as if your face were being cut in two by the tip of a knife," Clara wrote of a windy sleighride on the river Daugava),[6] gloomy, filth-ridden hotels,[7] the last-minute unavailability of concert halls,[8] all-night carriage rides on practically impassable roads, fierce sea-storms on the return journey—Clara seemed to triumph over it all with unflappable resilience. Her receipt of an honorary membership in St. Petersburg's male-dominated Philharmonic Society, to cite just one of the several accolades bestowed upon her, may be taken as a sign of the critical acclaim she garnered.[9] And financially, the venture was an unqualified success. All told, Clara's earnings amounted to about six thousand thalers, half of which was pure profit.[10]

On their journey toward the Russian interior the Schumanns were greeted by strange and wonderful sights to which they responded with childlike awe. St. Petersburg's splendid triumphal gate granted them entry to what Schumann called "this most wondrous of the world's cities," site of the czar's Winter Palace, with its magnificent collection of rare artworks (including a whole roomful of Rembrandts) and precious jewels, and its "fairyland garden."[11] Arriving at the Petrovski Castle on the outskirts of Moscow, the Schumanns imagined themselves "transported into the *Thousand and One Nights.*"[12] Once in Moscow itself, they were ineluctably drawn by the Kremlin and the "indescribable" view it afforded of the surroundings: "it seemed as if we were in Constantinople, so completely and peculiarly oriental is this city with its many towers."[13] Indeed, the couple made almost daily excursions to the Kremlin, "which always re-awakened Robert's imagination and always offered new charms for our eyes,"[14] Schumann's enchantment inspiring him to write four long poems on the great bell of Ivan Velikii. Both Robert and Clara were struck by the "Asiatic" character of the crowd milling about in the nearby bazaar, the men in ankle-length coats belted at the waist, the women in silken jackets trimmed in fur.[15] During their third week in Moscow, the Schumanns paid a visit to its large and efficiently administered Home for Foundlings, whose residents Clara treated to a brief recital. Instituted and subsidized by Czarina Catherine, the home served as a temporary refuge for between seven and eight thousand orphans per year; most of the boys were eventually placed with foster families in the country, while the girls were trained for positions as governesses. A three-hour tour of the facility made for an experience that Clara would not soon forget.

Schumann's copious travel notes, fleshed out by Clara after returning to Leipzig, are rich in observations of what surely seemed an unusual society and its customs. But the idiosyncratic manners of the Schumanns' acquaintances did not always strike an agreeable chord. Riga's elite were judged a "stiff and tedious" lot, a "bunch of uncultured instigators." Moreover, when the Rigans "spoke of the Czar, they acted as if spies were standing behind them with a whip"; Robert and Clara became so fearful that they "hardly dared to utter a candid word," even in their hotel room.[16] The czar's indomitable power even influenced the behavior of celebrated visitors; his distaste for long hair caused Liszt, a darling of Russia's musical elite, to make frequent trips to the barber.[17] Although Schumann gladly indulged in after-dinner cigars and billiards with his hosts and their other male guests, both he and Clara were nonplused by the custom of separating men and women at meals, a practice that "can hardly encourage conversation."[18] Nor were either of them particularly impressed with Russian cuisine.[19] The prohibitive cost of transportation, in St. Petersburg and especially in Moscow (where one could not accomplish much on foot) was another cause for consternation; and much to the Schumanns' bemusement, when a Russian coachmen was unsure of the way to his destination, he simply drove straight ahead.[20]

The indigenous musical culture likewise held many surprises for the couple. Their first exposure to Russian choral singing (at a rehearsal of the imperial court choir, directed by Alexei Lvov, in St. Petersburg) did not fail to make a deep impression: the resonance of the basses called to mind the organ's deepest register; the all-male discants produced an "otherworldly" sound, "more beautiful than the loveliest female voices"; and the choir's renditions of an admittedly mediocre repertory (in the Schumanns' opinion) were characterized by subtle nuances and shadings worked out to the smallest detail.[21] Robert and

Clara were considerably less enthusiastic over the liturgical choral singing they heard in Moscow. According to Clara's report, the droning of
hollow-voiced monks in fifths and octaves drove Robert, who endured
"two hours of this torture," right out of the Simonov Monastery.[22] For
her part, Clara found the Orthodox liturgy even more "excessive" than
the Catholic Mass, what with the congregation "throwing themselves
to the ground every minute," and "crossing themselves a thousand
times."[23]

A typical day in St. Petersburg or Moscow saw the Schumanns
thrust into a whirlwind of social calls to journalists, instrument-makers,
and aristocrats. The latter group included many musically enlightened
individuals, such as Prince Peter von Oldenburg, Director of St. Petersburg's Law School, who required his students to supplement their legal
studies with instruction in music so that, as Clara explained, they would
have a useful occupation for their leisure hours.[24] But the Schumanns
found their most loyal and knowing supporters in Count Matvei Wielhorski, a talented amateur cellist (according to the marriage diary, he
played Mendelssohn's cello sonatas "like an artist"),[25] and his brother
Michail, a composer. Avid patrons of the arts, the Wielhorskis regularly
hosted musical soirées at their mansion in St. Petersburg. At one such
event, Robert and Clara enjoyed string quartets by Beethoven and Spohr
(with the noted virtuoso Bernhard Molique playing first violin) until
the wee hours of the morning;[26] another musicale included Glinka—
according to Schumann, a "gentleman" through and through—among
the guests.[27] (A Moscow performance of Glinka's *Life for the Czar* elicited only lukewarm praise from Schumann, who criticized its brassy
orchestration and found its last two acts "lame in every respect").[28]

Unfortunately, the Wielhorskis' refined sensibility and cultivated
musical taste were not characteristic of the Russian upper class as a
whole. Much to Clara's annoyance, tea was served while she played her
first piece for a soirée at the home of Julius Behrens, a Rigan pianist
and composer.[29] The Schumanns were even more scandalized by the
deportment of the audience at one of Pauline Viardot's concerts in St.
Petersburg. While the listeners greeted the simplest of Russian folksongs
with hearty applause and sat in rapt attention for Viardot's rendition of
a set of "boring" Italian opera arias, they blithely chattered away during
the "better" music, Beethoven's *Egmont* Overture.[30] Clara's astonishment
over the Russian craze for Italian music turned to vexation when she
realized that the opera was the cause of the spotty attendance at her
second concert in St. Petersburg.[31] Likewise, the experiences leading up
to Clara's audience with the imperial family did little to improve her
opinion of the ways of the Russian nobility. Heinrich Stöckhardt, one of

St. Petersburg's most respected legal scholars, had arranged an evening for Clara at the home of the czarina's secretary, Ivan Chambeau. As it turned out, she had to play "on an old rattletrap" for the secretary's daughter and wife, who had the impertinence to suggest that Clara should request a letter of introduction from Chambeau. Her pride wounded, Clara decided instead to attract the court's attention by giving an extra concert. This strategy apparently worked, for the following day she was granted a long-sought entree into the imperial apartments. The czarina herself took a place on the piano bench next to Clara, who was asked to encore Mendelssohn's *Frühlingslied* (among the *Lieder ohne Worte* dedicated to her) no less than twice.[32]

The indifference of the greater part of Russia's musical establishment to Schumann's artistry was responsible for the composer's only modest successes while on tour. True, his Piano Quintet was enthusiastically received at one of the Wielhorskis' soirées (where Anton Rubinstein was among the guests), and made an "extraordinary" impression, to quote Clara, at the third of her St. Petersburg concerts.[33] But when the violinist Karl Kudelski helped to assemble a group for a performance of the work in Moscow, the best cellist he could come up with "barely knew what music was"; worse yet, the cellist, who "scratched mightily" at the first rehearsal, demanded payment for his mediocre services.[34] And although Schumann's First Symphony was performed to general approbation for a private gathering at the Wielhorskis' home, he had no luck organizing a similar event in Moscow. The pianist Ivan Reinhardt, one of the Schumanns' Muscovite friends, offered various explanations for the composer's inability to put together an orchestra: a local music director, Johannes, like the cellist Schmidt, was offended that Schumann had not paid him a personal call; another cellist, Charles Marcou, had hurt his finger. Clara, seldom one to mince words, responded tartly to these excuses: "It's scandalous to call such people as Johannes and Schmidt 'artist'—they're merely artisans, and uncultured artisans at that."[35]

Reversals of this sort can only have exacerbated for Schumann what, by the end of the Russian tour, had developed into a debilitated physical and psychological state. Already by late February, while in Dorpat, Schumann suffered an attack of "nervous fever" severe enough to keep him in bed—and away from Clara's concerts—for the better part of a week and to warrant consultations with two doctors (the first, a Dr. Walther, made so little of the illness that another physician had to be brought in). But even as Schumann gradually regained his strength, his "dreadful, melancholy state" lingered on.[36] A few weeks later in St. Petersburg he was again feeling weak, so weak in fact that he was unable to accompany Clara on her daily rounds. Since it was unthinkable for a woman, even an independent-minded individual like Clara, to make her way alone in Russian society, the good-hearted but "insufferably pedantic" Adolph Henselt, a German pianist and composer resident in St. Petersburg, stepped in to perform the requisite duties as escort.[37] By mid-April Schumann was again seeking medical advice, this time from a "Dr. Nov" (like Reinhardt, a former piano pupil of John Field), for now he was suffering from a new symptom. Returning to his Moscow hotel on the evening of 15 April, he experienced a dizzy spell so acute that his vision was temporarily impaired. Later a friend ascribed the attack, erroneously as it turned out, to the effects of the potent local beer that Robert and Clara drank daily.[38] Indeed, Schumann's condition would remain precarious up through the end of the tour; in an entry for 23 April in the marriage diary, Clara alluded to "Robert's persistent unwellness"; sounding a theme that recurred in many guises during the weeks and months ahead; Schumann's entry for 15 May reads: "Indisposition, physical and mental."[39] Confiding in her own diary after the return to Leipzig, Clara wrote of the difficulties both she and Schumann had in readjusting to their former routine, which now seemed so "desolate" and "empty"; moreover, they had to cope with "Robert's persistent illness, which actually lasted the whole journey, but which was always held in check."[40]

For all its colorful details, the marriage diary offers little in the way of firm evidence concerning Schumann's increasingly complicated and increasingly tortured inner life while on tour. The most telling description of the composer was penned by an outsider, J. K. Arnold, a guest at a soirée held on 19 March at the home of Alexei Lvov:

> As usual, Schumann was silent and taciturn the whole evening. He spoke only very little, murmuring incomprehensibly to the questions of Count Wielhorski and the host, A. F. Lvov. Something like a conversation ensued with the famous violinist Molique, who had arrived in St. Petersburg just a few days before, but it was carried on in hushed tones, without life or spirit. For the most part, Schumann sat in a corner by the piano (music stands for the players in Mendelssohn's Octet [op. 20] had been set up in the middle of the room); there he remained with his head sunken and his hair hanging in his face; his face bore an intensely pensive expression; it seemed as though he were about to whistle to himself. As I observed him that night, Schumann precisely resembled the life-size statue by Donndorf [the sculptor who did the monument for the composer's tomb]. Clara Schumann was a bit more talkative; she answered all the questions for her husband. In

her piano playing, she proved to be a great artist with masculine energy
and feminine instinct in interpretation and execution, although she was
only twenty-five or twenty-six years old [in fact, she was twenty-three].
However one could hardly characterize her as a gracious or sympathetic
woman. They both spoke French with a Saxon accent and German like
real Leipzigers.[41]

Neither of the Schumanns comes off particularly well in this account.
Clara takes the role of the talented but brash and unsophisticated provincial. Likewise, it is perhaps too easy to conclude that Schumann—
incommunicative, mumbling distractedly, preoccupied—was already in
the grip of the all-consuming illness to which he would succumb a decade later. The rhetoric of Arnold's account points toward impending
madness and, more powerfully still, to death: Schumann is practically
mute; his speech is lifeless; his head bowed, his body verging on petre-
faction, he attends only to his inner voices. It would be a mistake, however, to overlook the elements of exaggeration in this one-sided description. If, to take one example, Schumann looked as if "he were about to
whistle to himself" (the subtext reads: "He was gradually losing touch
with reality"), we should recall that almost every surviving pictorial representation of the composer, from adolescence onward, shows him with
pursed lips. And if Schumann seemed dejected at Lvov's soirée, he had
good reason to be: the performance of his Piano Quintet that evening,
as Clara relates, went miserably.[42]

This is not to minimize the accuracy of Arnold's report, but rather
to place it in perspective. For Schumann clearly had begun to exhibit
the depressive tendencies that would continue to plague him, in varying
degrees of intensity, in the ensuing months. And here Arnold alludes
obliquely, if not to a cause of Schumann's condition, then to a factor
that no doubt aggravated it: his position vis-à-vis Clara. A mixture of
"masculine energy and feminine instincts" characterized not just Clara's
playing but her entire personality. Consider her diverse roles on the
Russian tour: as artist, impresario, agent, and manager all wrapped into
one, she became a symbol of the physical and psychological strength of
which her husband felt himself slowly sapped. Moreover, the fact that
while on tour she held center stage, literally and figuratively, must have
been a source of annoyance to Schumann, whose notation in the marriage diary only a year before—"Clara . . . recognizes motherhood as
her primary vocation"[43]—proved to be a bit of wishful thinking. (As
Germaine de Staël wrote with some irony: "It would no doubt be generally preferable for women to devote themselves entirely to the domestic
virtues," but, oddly enough, men "are much likelier to forgive women

for neglecting these duties than for attracting attention by unusual talent.")[44] Although Schumann shared in Clara's triumphs, her professional success at the same time threatened his fragile sense of self. On 19 April, the day before Clara's first public appearance in Moscow, Schumann noted: "Hardly bearable insults and Clara's behavior thereby."[45] Clara provides a gloss: "I didn't know what [Robert] could mean, but now it appears to me, on reading through his travel notes, that I've often aroused his indignation—certainly not with bad intentions, but only through brusqueness and lack of quick thinking."[46] Yet Schumann's travel notes up through mid-April contain no specific references to Clara's having aroused his indignation. They read more like jottings for a travel and adventure novel with Clara as the principal character. And she was perspicacious enough to realize, if only in retrospect, that it was precisely her role as herione in what Schumann viewed as *his* story that disturbed her husband's sensibilities.

As a consequence of his discomfort on tour, Schumann's ability to make any headway with his compositional projects was seriously impaired. While confined to his bed in Dorpat, he read portions of Goethe's *Faust,* but with effort, and even considered treating *Wilhelm Meister* as an operatic subject.[47] A few weeks later in St. Petersburg he managed to begin sketching a scene from the second part of *Faust,* but otherwise made little headway on what soon developed into a decade-long endeavor.[48]

Interestingly enough, Schumann's primary creative efforts during the early spring of 1844 took a literary, not a musical, turn. Rekindling impulses that had lain dormant for over a decade, he wrote a series of five extended poems, all but the last inspired directly by the great bell tower to Ivan Velikii.[49] Each is notable for a rather complicated poetic structure, featuring free verse, irregular rhyme schemes, and strophes of varying length as pendants to an underlying message, or complex of messages, of equal richness. For Peter Ostwald, these verses reflect Schumann's "morbid preoccupations" while in Moscow; the image in the second poem of the huge bell pulling its supporting cupola deeper into the earth he interprets as a masochistic allusion to the composer's burdensome effect on Clara's artistic development.[50] While autobiographical elements such as these undeniably fed into Schumann's verses, the resonance of the Ivan Velikii poems derives in equal measure from their transcendence of personal by way of universal themes. Specifically, the set invites interpretation as an allegory for the problem of creative artistry.

The first poem, largely devoted to an account of the casting of the great bell, reflects the notion of artistic toil, depicting in vivid detail the intense labor required to transform an inchoate lump of matter into a coherent and beautiful shape:

> How the work [i.e., the bell] lives from within,
> How it strives toward perfection!
> The master creates by day and night,
> Embracing the rigid mass
> With the loving warmth of artistic truth.[51]

Only through persistent acts of force are the raw materials of nature made to submit to the artist's will: "It takes time to tame the resistant metal; / Drops of sweat run from the master's brow."[52] The final step in the bell-caster's endeavor, the moment when, surrounded by a curious throng of onlookers, he oversees the hoisting of "the incredible weight from the depths into the airy heights,"[53] becomes a metaphor for the process whereby the impulse for the artwork is summoned up from the psychological depths of its creator. But in the end, the caster's hopes are dashed; as the bell is slowly lifted out of the mold, a portion breaks off and remains lodged therein: "Horror seizes the people and the master . . . / The face of a mother who beholds her stillborn child / Could not be more full of suffering . . ."[54] And as a man from the crowd explains, it was the artist's hubris that occasioned this cruel trick: "You have attempted something you shouldn't have, / Lacquered over a lowly purpose with a divine one: / It is not God whom you want to serve, / You have become a slave to vanity . . ."[55] The second poem points the way out of the dilemma, for the czar, on hearing of the artist's great but flawed undertaking, orders that: "The striving of the artist who envisioned the highest / Shall be sanctified / Whether or not the deed was fulfilled."[56] In a word, Promethean hubris finds redemption through Faustian striving.

The same interlocking themes—the tortuous process of creation, the artist's overweening pride, redemption through striving—are accorded a historico-political slant in the second pair of poems. Here Schumann compares the bell-founder's lot with that of another master whose identity, though undisclosed in the third poem, is not difficult to determine. Like the caster of the great bell, Napoleon has triumphed over seemingly insuperable forces, his conquests symbolized by a heap of corpses gathered at his feet. He too is plagued by the nagging suspicion that his achievements have been motivated by personal ambition, by self-aggrandizing urges, and not by a desire to serve God and humanity. The emperor-general's hubris will not go unpunished: the misfiring of his ill-starred Moscow campaign bears comparison with the bell-founder's cruel misfortune. But even if Napoleon's striving was driven by worldly impulses, he strove nonetheless and suffered mightily to boot. Introducing a new theme in the fourth poem, Schumann invokes the fallen conqueror's exile and death as metaphors for the artist's isolation and mortality. Napoleon pays the ultimate price for his sins, but wins in death a measure of immortality for his deeds that could never attach to his physical being. The artist's works and not his fragile self, Schumann seems to say, are destined to endure.[57]

More than merely registering his depressed psychological state, Schumann's Ivan Velikii poems testify to a profound shift in the makeup of his poetic cosmos, a shift from a Jean-Paulian to a Goethean sensibility. The attempt at a musical realization of this new ideal would involve Schumann in his most ambitious project to date: the setting of portions of Goethe's *Faust*, which he undertook in earnest after returning from Russia. But like the bell-caster and the conquering general he would pay dearly for his hubris.

Crisis

The Russian tour marked a kind of fault-line in Schumann's life. In its wake came a series of seismic shocks, the greatest of them bringing a nearly total physical and mental collapse, but even the lesser ones signalling profound changes in the rhythm of his existence. For one thing, entries in the marriage diary, initiated over three years earlier as an expression of conjugal bliss, came to a halt. While Clara would maintain a private journal of her own, Schumann's diaristic activities were limited to sporadic travel notes and, of course, to the faithfully kept *Haushaltbücher*. By far the less conscientious partner in the joint diary enterprise, Schumann now withdrew from it completely. Only two years later, during a period of relief from the recurrent symptoms associated with his illness, would he indulge in a confessional enterprise. The so-called *Kurztagebuch* (Short Diary), many of its entries clustered in March and April of 1846, was intended to serve as a repository of notes for a projected autobiography.[58] This fascinating document, to which we shall presently return, brings together materials of many types and on a wide variety of subjects: maxims, accounts of visits with Mendelssohn, Jenny Lind, and Friedrich Hebbel, thoughts on the visual arts, and comments on the process of composition.[59] But following a series of severe dizzy spells in mid-April 1846, the entries in the *Kurztagebuch* became less frequent. Though Schumann returned to the diary in 1847 and again in 1850, his plans to write an autobiography came to naught.

Schumann's ever more apparent reserve likewise manifested itself in the suspension of his activities in music criticism. For some time he had viewed his editorship of the *Neue Zeitschrift* as a burdensome task that diverted his attention from the business of composing. The decision to sell the journal, recorded in the *Haushaltbücher* on 24 June 1844, not surprisingly coincides with the beginning of Schumann's work on the *Faust* music[60] and also with a resurgence (or continuation) of the illness that had clouded the Russian tour. By 20 November the deal had been closed, the *Neue Zeitschrift* sold to Franz Brendel for the relatively modest sum of 500 thalers.[61] As Ostwald suggests, Schumann's severance of his ties with the journal was probably a mistake. Ostensibly a means of allowing for increased concentration on compositional projects, it turned out to be a cipher for withdrawal.[62]

Yet the sale of the journal hardly represented a definitive cessation of the composer's critical or literary interests. In the course of the next several years, Schumann's fascination with world literature would continue unabated, witness his reading of Dante's *Divine Comedy*, Fielding's *Tom Jones*, Goethe's *Hermann und Dorothea* (for the tenth time), and Homer's *Odyssey*. Within a couple of months of relinquishing the *Neue Zeitschrift* we find him assembling a list, in the *Lektürebüchlein* (Little Book of Readings) begun January 1845 in Dresden, of "Journal material for a later time," potential topics including the nature of music conservatories, the state of contemporary musical criticism, recent editions of Handel's works, and a projected *Gesamtausgabe* of Bach's works.[63] And although he declined an offer to assume the editorship of the *Allgemeine musikalische Zeitung* in April 1846, later in the same year, just after returning from a holiday on the East Frisian island of Norderney, Schumann contemplated founding a new "Monatsschrift f.[ür] Musik," and may even have broached the subject with a visitor from Leipzig who would soon establish himself as a major critical voice: Eduard Hanslick.[64] The plan did not come to fruition, though Schumann did, during the next year, begin to document Dresden's rich music-dramatic culture in a series of brief essays on the operas of Boieldieu (*Jean de Paris*), Marschner (*Der Templer und die Jüdin*), Gluck (*Iphigénie en Aulide*), and others.[65] But never again would Schumann's music-critical activity occupy him as it had during the Davidsbündler days.

Another significant rift in the texture of the Schumanns' lives came with their move to Dresden in December of 1844. What was originally intended as a winter getaway for the exhausted couple became their home for the next five years. Why the sudden uprooting from their longtime home in Leipzig? Schumann provides insight on this point in a letter to Eduard Krüger begun before the move but completed shortly thereafter.

In the first place, the Schumanns' departure from Leipzig represented a statement of their dissatisfaction with its musical establishment. Schumann alludes to this factor obliquely in his letter to Krüger: "since Mendelssohn has left Leipzig [for Berlin], perhaps it won't suit us musically."[66] But left unmentioned is his intense disappointment over being snubbed as Mendelssohn's successor at the Gewandhaus, a position he coveted and which ultimately went to Niels Gade.[67] In contrast, Dresden's flourishing operatic culture might afford Schumann fertile ground for the cultivation of his own operatic ambitions. Numerous entries in the *Haushaltbücher* attest to his regular presence at performances of works ranging from such classics as Mozart's *Entführung* to the latest of Wagner's extravaganzas. And it was Dresden that provided Schumann with his first real taste of this operatic dynamo—as composer and personality. His attendance at the 19 October 1845 premiere of Wagner's *Tannhäuser* resulted in a heated discussion the following day with the composer and conductor Ferdinand Hiller, one of the mainstays of Dresden's musical life. Following a performance of a somewhat revised version of the same work in late November and a day of musing on what certainly struck him as a most extraordinary creation, Schumann met with Wagner himself.[68] (The laconic Schumann's description of his loquacious colleague in the *Kurztagebuch* whets our appetite for details on this and subsequent interchanges between these two very different personalities: "Wagner possesses an enormous gift of gab, crammed full of overwhelming thoughts; one can't listen to him for long.")[69]

The stimulation of Dresden's operatic life notwithstanding, Schumann's heart remained in the city where he had spent the last fourteen years; as he put it to Krüger: "Leipzig remains the most important city for music, and I would recommend that every young talent go there, for one can hear so much good music."[70] Both he and Clara were frustrated by their inability to find a circle of cultured and musical friends comparable to the group they had known in Leipzig. Hiller, according to an entry in Clara's diary, was "the only one here with whom one can have a decent conversation about music."[71] Friedrich Wieck did little to satisfy their understandable need for intellectually stimulating company. Schumann's April 1845 reference to the old Wieck's "coarseness" is but one of many similar allusions to the father-in-law with whom he had reached an uneasy truce.[72] As we will see, the most compelling reason for the Schumanns' removal to Dresden lay with the composer's precarious physical and mental state. As he wrote in the first part (dating from October 1844) of the letter to Krüger: "Perhaps you don't know how ill I've been from a general nervous ailment [Nervenleiden] that afflicted me for about a quarter of a year," and in the second part (written five weeks later): "We've moved to Dresden for the winter. The doctor advised it. . . ."[73]

Eleven years before, between October and December of 1833, Schumann had weathered a phase of intense psychological disturbance, its symptoms including pervasive melancholy and an obsessive fear of succumbing to madness. By some reports he even contemplated suicide.[74] In the spring and summer of 1844 Schumann again came perilously close to total nervous collapse, but with an important difference: his illness of 1833 endured for the more or less circumscribed period of several months; now, however, it lingered as a series of episodes of varying intensity spread over more than a year.

Several days of "feeling horrid" in early June 1844 were a mere prelude to the real crisis that set in later in the summer. By August Schumann was suffering from "ever persistent illness," a situation only exacerbated by overindulgence in drink. For three consecutive days (14–16 August), an attack of colic, perhaps the result of nervous anxiety, forced him to stay at home. And although the disturbance soon appeared to moderate a bit, "wretched melancholy" and "a dreadful state of health" would return by the end of the month.[75] In late September, after a brief trip to the Harz mountain district, Schumann experienced his worst bout of illness yet. Practically confined to his bed, he "could hardly cross the room without the greatest effort," according to the account in Clara's diary."[76] The entry for 26 September in the *Haushalt-bücher* reads simply: "spent nothing"; even a visit to Poppe's café, an obligatory stop on Schumann's daily Leipzig rounds, was out of the question. On 1 October Dr. Moritz Wilhelm Müller, a practitioner of homoeopathic medicine, was called in, but the effectiveness of his ministrations is difficult to gauge: the regular entries in the *Haushaltbücher* give way to a record of weekly amounts spent on an exploratory trip to Dresden. The first part of Schumann's previously quoted letter to Krüger nonetheless gives us a sense of the acuteness of his condition: "ailing and dejected," frequently too weak even for a walk, Schumann found that he "couldn't listen to music at all; it cut into my nerves as if with knives."[77] By late December and into the beginning of the new year, Schumann's state reached something of a nadir. Within days of completing a draft of the closing scene of *Faust,* he succumbed to a "violent nervous attack" coupled, in the next weeks, with eye strain and "intense weakness in the limbs."[78]

But after what had amounted to at least half a year of illness, a gradual improvement set in. Schumann's turn for the better coincided with an important juncture in his musical life: the initiation on 23 January, with Clara as a willing accomplice, of a self-designed course of

contrapuntal study.[79] The results, on Clara's part, took shape as a series
of six fugues on themes by Schumann and J. S. Bach and three preludes
with accompanying fugues on the former's themes, and on Schumann's
part as the *Vier Fugen*, op. 72, the *Sechs Fugen . . . über B-A-C-H*, op.
60, and the *Sechs Studien für den Pedalflügel*, op. 56. Indeed, Schumann
appears to have turned a significant corner on his illness by early March.
While intently focused on the Opus 72 fugues, he jotted in the *Haushaltbücher* for the first time in many, many months: "feeling cheerful."[80]

Unfortunately, Schumann's newly won high spirits did not sustain
themselves consistently. For most of the immediately ensuing months
the *Haushaltbücher* in fact make reference to at least a couple of bad
days, and at times these devolved into a bad week or more. On 6 July
1845, for instance, Schumann made note of an invitation he had received to participate in a Beethoven festival scheduled for 10–12 August
in Bonn; its participants including Liszt and Spohr, the festival was to
culminate in the unveiling and dedication of a monument to the master.[81] But while he and Clara duly set out for Bonn by way of Leipzig
and Weimar on 31 July, their travel plans were soon aborted. The following day Schumann suffered an attack of "anxiety and dizziness," the
intensity and persistence of which led the couple to forego the trip to
Bonn and remain in Thuringia (for what turned out to be a therapeutic
visit with Schumann's relatives in Zwickau) instead.[82] Another relapse
in February and March of 1846 would slow Schumann's progress on the
instrumentation of his Second Symphony, bringing with it, in addition
to the usual melancholy, headaches, and dizziness, "a peculiar distortion
[Verstimmung] of the faculty of hearing."[83] Only in the spring of 1847,
after returning from a four-month concert tour that took him and Clara
to Vienna and Berlin, would he enter on a relatively protracted phase of
physical and mental well-being, a phase ushered in by an intense wave
of creative activity.

Despite all the references to illness in Schumann's travel notes, correspondence, and in the *Haushaltbücher*, it is still difficult to form a
coherent picture of the composer's symptoms. Frequently he referred to
his malady in the most general of terms as "unwellness," "feeling horrible," or simply "my condition." Then too, both Robert and Clara had
more than a bit of the hypochondriac about them. Schumann acknowledged this tendency on more than one occasion. Writing in March 1845,
he ascribed a sleepless night to sickness "half imaginary, half real."[84]
And while vacationing in Norderney during the summer of the following year, he alluded, with some irony, to the "hypochondria of a married
couple."[85]

Nonetheless, two descriptions, both dating from this period, offer us a fairly detailed picture of Schumann's condition during the second major depressive phase of his life. One comes from Dr. Carl Helbig, who treated him throughout his five-year residence in Dresden. Recommended by Dr. Carl Gustav Carus (a relative of Ernst August Carus, to whom Schumann had gone for medical advice in Leipzig), Helbig first met with Schumann shortly after the latter's arrival in Dresden in October 1844. His report, presumably written later in the same year or early in the next, describes a depressed and physically debilitated patient whose complaints ranged from insomnia, general weakness, auditory disturbances, tremors, and chills in the feet, to a whole range of phobias. Indeed, the objects of Schumann's fearful anxiety make for a peculiar list including death, metal items such as keys, medicines, poisonous substances, mountain heights, and tall buildings.[86] Many of the same symptoms figure in Schumann's own description of an attack he suffered on the aborted journey to the Beethoven Festival: "Saturday, 2 August [1845].—Tendency toward dizziness. Fear and unrest, namely in the hands and feet—Jerking in the limbs—not much appetite—pulse weak, easily excitable—Pains at various spots in the head—not severe, but alarming—"[87] The results of one of Schumann's more peculiar undertakings, a phrenological examination to which he submitted in the summer of 1846, may have convinced him that his illness was an obligatory burden he would have to bear in the light of his sensitive and "poetic" nature. The final entry in the *Kurztagebuch* recounts a certain R. R. Noël's reading of the furrows in Schumann's skull as follows: "Particularly strong development of the organs of foresight—of anxiety, that might even interfere with my happiness—of music, of poetic power— of noble striving—of great artistic but noble ambition—of great love for truth—of great sincerity—of great benevolence—'spirit through and through'—sense for form—modesty—constancy—"[88]

Schumann sought relief from his ailments through many remedies—daily walks, travel, mineral baths, even mesmerism—but none of them produced lasting results. The September 1844 trip to the Harz Mountains, for instance, was intended as a diversion from the quotidian stresses that probably fed the depressive episode of the month before. Although the fog and drizzle of early autumn did little to bolster Schumann's gloomy spirits—"the melancholy weather makes our stay even more melancholy," he wrote in his travel diary[89]—his mood gradually improved under the influence of the impressively romantic landscapes that stimulated his poetic sensibility. The Baumannshöhle, a stalactite cave on the river Bode, with its "gruesome, unusual darkness [and] dead silence, interrupted only by dripping water," reminded him of passages from Schiller's celebrated ballad *Der Taucher*.[90] The rocky crags of the surrounding region called up a verse from the Walpurgis Night scene in Part I of Goethe's *Faust:* "how they snore, how they resound."[91] And in all likelihood, Schumann recognized in the strange rock formations of the "wild Bode valley" a tangible image of the "mountain gorges" that form the backdrop for the closing scene of Goethe's drama, the setting of which had occupied him in the preceding months. But just after a pleasant foot journey through the Ilse river valley that triggered cheerful memories of his student days in Heidelberg, Schumann reverted to his earlier morbid state on reading a brief piece in one of the local newspapers: an account of two poets, both "victims of madness." One of them, the son of a bookdealer, slit his wrists; the other had been confined to an asylum in Aachen.[92]

For centuries hydrotherapy in one of its many forms was employed as a treatment for psychic complaints.[93] Schumann's first known attempt at a water cure is recorded for 30 August 1844 after nearly a month of alternately poor and improved health. Immersion seems to have had a positive effect on this occasion, for by the following day Schumann was feeling considerably better.[94] Later in the same year or early in the next, Dr. Helbig prescribed cold baths, perhaps as a last resort given Schumann's persistent refusal to ingest medicinal substances. (In January 1845 Helbig resorted to "magnetizing" or hypnosis as a possible remedy; Schumann's 20 January reference to the "application of an amulet" probably alludes to this short-lived and obviously ineffective encounter with mesmerism).[95] Again the hydrotherapeutic treatment had a beneficial effect: Helbig noted that within a short time Schumann's condition had improved sufficiently to allow him to resume his composing.[96] Indeed, the relocation to Dresden was probably deemed particularly attractive because of the many mineral baths near the city. During the summer of 1845, Schumann was a regular visitor at such spots.[97] A five-week stay on the island resort of Norderney between 15 July and 21 August 1846 was also motivated by an opportunity to indulge in the many bathing facilities at the popular spa. On the journey from Dresden, Schumann was plagued by depression and, after departing by steamship from Hamburg, by seasickness as well, his state no doubt made all the worse when "the news that 'Clara Wieck' is supposed to be on board" renewed anxieties he had not felt since the Russian tour.[98] All in all, the Schumanns' holiday turned out to be less pleasant than they had hoped. On 20 July, Schumann noted, much to his chagrin, his "certainty over Clara's pregnancy." A week later, however, she miscarried. And although this "alteration in Clara's condition" was originally a source of "joy," the Schumanns' relief would turn to worry when Clara's temporary illness after her miscarriage necessitated consultation with a

Dr. Bluhm.[99] The therapeutic effects of Schumann's twenty-five visits to Norderney's mineral springs were mixed. The Jean-Paulian entries in the *Haushaltbücher* for 14 and 15 August—"Eusebius's Day" and "the butterfly and its emergence from the cocoon"—suggest that the high-spirited Schumann of the Davidsbündler days was attempting to make a comeback. But his notes on the palliative effects of bathing are intermingled with references to a persistent head-cold, anxiety, discomfort in the face of oppressive heat, overall exhaustion, and, by the end of the trip, insufferable boredom.[100]

What was the effect of Schumann's fluctuating health on his compositional routine? In some cases, Schumann's work may have been, if not the actual cause of illness, then at least a powerful irritant. Hence, according to Helbig's report, the setting of the final scene from Goethe's *Faust,* Part II, especially its closing section, strained the composer to such an extent during the summer and fall of 1844 that he fell into a state of psychological torpor and physical exhaustion; Schumann too confirmed this diagnosis in his letter to Krüger.[101] And while Helbig's suggestion that Schumann should turn to other, non-musical pursuits came to nothing (after a brief flirtation with natural history and physics he found himself ineluctably drawn back to music), on recovering from a relapse in March 1846 he did admit that "complete mental rest sometimes helps."[102] On other occasions, however, Schumann's compositional activity served an undeniably therapeutic function. His self-imposed contrapuntal course of study, for instance, probably contributed to the gradual recovery during the spring of 1845. At times Schumann's work was neither cause nor cure, but rather a cover for underlying unrest, a view supported by those instances where illness and inactivity followed on the heels of a sustained period of productivity. The pattern would repeat itself with some regularity: in late March 1845, after the completion of the Opus 72 fugues and a period of high spirits; in June 1845, when "weakness in the eyes, as in Moscow" resurfaced two days after Schumann finished the Opus 56 *Studien;*[103] and in mid-July 1845, when, just after putting the final touches on the Piano Concerto, he suffered from exhaustion and anxiety, symptoms that intensified sufficiently to preclude his attendance at the Beethoven Festival in Bonn planned for the next month.

The shifting relationships between Schumann's illness and his working habits should caution us against arriving at hastily drawn conclusions regarding the effects of this illness on the actual substance of his works. Yet it is precisely in the compositions stemming from the second major depressive phase in Schumann's life (1844–46) that many commentators have heard the first signs of a fatal condition. Dieter

Schnebel, for instance, senses something peculiarly "out of control" in the "meandering," "contourless" lines of the Opus 72 fugues.[104] Likewise, Georg Dadelsen points to Schumann's failure to find his own voice and his lapse into an "alarming monotony" in the Opus 60 fugues on B-A-C-H.[105] Stephen Walsh detects in the same works an oddly "impersonal quality" marking them as the products of a "sick man," prefigurations of the "declining powers" of Schumann's last decade as a composer.[106] Not even a generally acknowledged masterpiece such as the Second Symphony is exempt from this sort of dubious conflation of life and artwork. How is it that the works of Schumann's earlier depressive phases (especially those from 1833 and 1834) have escaped from charges of diminished capacity? Why has the quality of some compositions from the mid-1840s been thrown into doubt by psychobiographers, while that of others, notably the final two movements of the Piano Concerto, has remained unquestioned? Did the quality of Schumann's efforts begin to vary as widely as many writers have suggested? We will return to some of these questions in the context of our consideration of the Second Symphony. For now it will suffice to say that the presence of works unremittingly optimistic in affect and undeniably masterful in their handling of compositional challenges should, if nothing else, give us pause.

"A Completely New Manner of Composing"

The documents pertaining to Schumann's life in the troubled period from 1844 to 1846 are peppered with metaphors for disruption. Among the most striking of these is the image of the knife, a signifier, for Clara, of the ferocious Russian wind, and for Schumann, of the grating effect that music could have on his frazzled nerves. A biographer considering the fate of Schumann's march through the musical genres is apt to draw on the same image: the composer's progress toward the fulfillment of his operatic ambitions, steadily prepared in the Years of Song, Symphony, Chamber Music, and Oratorio, seems to have been summarily interrupted, sundered in twain, by the psychological traumas of 1844 and 1845.

But on reflection; the cleft in the fabric of Schumann's creative development may not have been as severe as it first seems. The will to opera in fact runs through the mid-1840s like an alternately overt and covert ostinato. Part of the summer of 1844 was devoted to work on *Faust* and a setting of Byron's *Corsar* (reworked as an opera libretto by Oswald Marbach), though the latter project was abandoned after only a couple of scenes were drafted.[107] Music-dramatic compositions thus loomed large in the "plans, musical and otherwise" to which Schumann alluded on 9 June.[108] First mentioned as a "beautiful opera text" in January 1845, August Bürck's *König Artus (King Arthur)* was a serious contender for dramatic treatment until later the same year, when Schumann learned of Wagner's preoccupation with a similar subject and was even among those present at his colleague's reading of the *Lohengrin* text on 17 December.[109] Nor was this the only time that the two composers' interests converged. While on holiday in Norderney during the summer of 1846, Schumann had in his portmanteau a copy of Immermann's *Tristan und Isolde* (described in the *Lektürebüchlein* as "a most delectable gem"), a gift from Mendelssohn.[110] Several dramatic projects first envisioned at about this time would bear fruit only later in Schumann's career. Goethe's *Hermann und Dorothea,* for instance, considered "with great excitement" in March 1845 and again in March 1846 for treatment as an opera or *Singspiel,*[111] served as the programmatic impulse for the overture of the same name, Opus 136, completed in 1851. Just after finishing the Opus 72 fugues, likewise in March 1845, Schumann hit on the novel idea of combining spoken verse with piano accompaniment, thus prefiguring the "declamation ballads" on texts by Hebbel and Shelley (*Schön Hedwig,* op. 106; *Ballade vom Haidenknabe* and *Die Flüchtlinge,* op. 122, nos. 1 and 2) of 1849, 1852, and 1853.[112] Nothing came of an opera text solicited from F. Winkler in June 1845, nor of a possible setting of Eichendorff's *Glücksritter* considered in April 1846, but Robert Reinick, called upon that spring perhaps in connection with the Eichendorff text, would soon collaborate with Schumann on his one and only completed opera, *Genoveva.*

Of course, the single dramatic project from the mid-1840s to achieve something approaching completed form did not, strictly speaking, involve an operatic text at all. For Schumann, cobbling together a libretto out of an undisputed masterwork of world literature such as Goethe's *Faust* would have been tantamount to blasphemy; hence he opted for the (at the time) much more radical solution of setting portions of the text unaltered. Schumann's prophetic foray into *Literaturoper,* or "literary opera," an endeavor that colored much of his work for nearly a decade and that came close to providing the capstone on his conquest of the musical genres, will occupy us at greater length in the following chapter. At the moment we will have to make do with a brief sketch of the inception of what proved to be the composer's most monumental undertaking.

Although Schumann had made some fitful attempts at setting the *Faust* material during the earlier phases of the Russian tour, it was only in June 1844, when the *Haushaltbücher* make reference to "Goethe's

Faust," "musical beginnings," and "Faust beginnings," that he set to work in earnest on the closing scene of Part II.[113] Doggedly persisting with his sketching and drafting throughout the summer and into the fall, Schumann found himself unable to maintain his usually rapid compositional pace, distracted as he was by Byron's *Corsar* (late June and early July), news of Clara's pregnancy (at about the same time), a serious depressive episode (August), the trip to the Harz (10–18 September), another flareup of illness (late September), and an exploratory trip to Dresden. By 26 July he had gotten far enough with his sketches to begin the orchestration; but not until 23 December could he write "Faust completed, with effort."[114] (Actually his work was hardly over: the conclusion of the Chorus mysticus, "Das Ewig-Weibliche zieht uns hinan," though probably sketched in 1844, was further elaborated in April 1847, and an entirely new version was completed in July of the same year; then in May and June 1848 Schumann added a rousing coda to the central chorus, "Gerettet ist das edle Glied.")[115]

After having earmarked Goethe's drama as a possible opera text in his *Projekentbuch* for 1844, Schumann soon came to realize, no doubt under the influence of his experience with the closing scene, that conventional operatic treatment would fail to do justice to the poetic material. As he put it to Krüger in December: "I'm still much occupied with Faust. What would you think about treating the entire material as an oratorio? Isn't this a clever and beautiful idea?"[116] An oratorical approach would place into relief the textual points of contact between the Faust story, transfigured by Goethe into a drama of redemption, and Schumann's own oratorio of redemption from the year before, *Das Paradies und die Peri*. Writing to Friedrich Whistling on 26 June 1848, the day after a performance of his setting of the final scene from *Faust,* Schumann acknowledged the shared poetic themes of the two works, whose main characters "attain to heaven after much straying and striving." *Literaturoper* and oratorio complement one another: in the composer's view, *Faust* is to the *Peri* as "the occident to the orient."[117] Not surprisingly, then, the Faust music is replete with echoes of the earlier oratorio, the most stunning of which comes at the climax of the Chorus mysticus, where the soprano's soaring descent from a high C recalls similar passages in the finales of Parts I and III of the *Peri*. And as we have seen, the notion of Faustian striving is prominent in another of the creative products of Schumann's "crisis" years, the cycle of poems to the great bell of Ivan Velikii.

At the same time, the *Faust* setting of 1844 points decisively toward Schumann's musical future. The theme of redemption, reconfigured in "absolute" musical terms, will surface again in the crowning chorale of the Second Symphony. Another pre-echo of the Second Symphony, this time of a crucial motivic element in the second group of its first movement, comes in the moving paean to Nature of Pater Profundus, where a rising chromatic figure helps to firm the point that even the wildest of natural forces—crashing torrents, fierce thunderbolts—are a function of "almighty love." Likewise, Schumann's deft handling of the art of thematic combination in the closing chorus resonates with the renewed interest in contrapuntal issues that flowered during the period of recovery from illness in the spring and summer of 1845. And last, the sustained encounter with Goethe's poetry prompted a shift in the tone of Schumann's musical language that is just as noticeable as it is difficult to describe. In the opening chorus, "Waldung, sie schwankt heran," and even more powerfully in the ensuing solos for tenor and bass, we sense that the Jean-Paulian fantasy and humor, not to mention the Hoffmannesque grotesquerie, of much of Schumann's earlier music is giving way to a sobriety redolent of Friedrich Hölderlin's mature poetry. If nothing else, the composer's subtly changing attitude to musical Romanticism reminds us that Romanticism was a multifaceted thing indeed.

The music for the early phase of the Faust project is poised at a significant juncture in Schumann's compositional development. A manifestation of the will to musical drama that will inform his work for several years to come, it echoes the achievements of the previous years and prefigures, in technique and tone, the "New Way" upon which he would soon embark. A fascinating entry in the *Kurztagebuch* documents Schumann's awareness of this shift. The passage, dating from sometime after July 1846, deserves quotation in full:

> I used to write most, practically all of my shorter pieces in [the heat of] inspiration; many compositions [were completed] with unbelievable swiftness, for instance, my First Symphony in B♭ major [was written] in four days, as was a *Liederkreis* of twenty pieces *[Dichterliebe]*; the *Peri* too was composed in a relatively short time. Only from the year 1845 on, when I began to invent and work out everything in my head, did a completely new manner of composing begin to develop.[118]

Prior to 1845, which saw the completion of a rich array of contrapuntal works, the last two movements of the Piano Concerto, and the sketches for the Second Symphony, Schumann had depended heavily on his not inconsiderable skills as an improviser at the keyboard for creative inspiration.[119] In many cases, it is almost impossible to draw a firm line between pre-compositional planning (this in spite of Schumann's practice of making continuity drafts from the First Symphony onward) and compositional elaboration: both were inextricably linked to the same process. In contrast, the "completely new manner of composing" that set in during 1845 gives primacy of place to the act of reflection, to a more sober attitude toward the business of putting notes to paper.

To be sure, Schumann's diary entry addresses the issue of compositional process, not musical style. For Schumann, however, the "new manner of composing" did indeed result in a complex of stylistic realignments that, taken together, justify the designation of this phase of his career as the initiation of a "New Way." Greater reflectivity in compositional planning finds a parallel in a more refined approach to the art of transition, a trait particularly in evidence in the outer movements of the Second Symphony. More important, a fanciful (sometimes hectic) play of musical affects, one of the defining characteristics of Schumann's approach to large-scale structure during the 1830s, gives way definitively, in a work like the completed Piano Concerto, to a carefully graduated progress of moods, a feature analogous to the "alternation of tones" articulated in Hölderlin's poetics. But most significant of all, Schumann's compositions of 1845 speak to a profound change in his notion of what constitutes a musical idea. Simply put, the linear development of a melodic entity begins to recede in favor of a rich web of simultaneously elaborated motivic combinations. And as this process was set in motion by the products of Schumann's contrapuntal studies in the spring and summer of 1845, it is to those works that we should now turn.

"Fugenpassion"

Between January and November 1845 Schumann devoted himself for the third time in his career to a rigorous study of counterpoint. If the results of his tutelage under Heinrich Dorn in 1831 and 1832 had amounted largely to exercises and preliminary sketches, and if his contrapuntal interests between 1836 and 1838 led to the drafting of a *Fugengeschichte* and to the textural enrichment noticeable in works such as *Kreisleriana*, then his activities of 1845 would conflate all of these tendencies. Now he wrote, for the first time, compositions in strict contrapuntal forms intended not as pedagogical exercises, but as substantial concert pieces in their own right: the *Vier Fugen*, op. 72, the *Sechs Fugen* for organ on B-A-C-H, op. 60, and the *Sechs Studien* for pedal-piano (*Pedalflügel*) or piano 3–4 hands "in canonic form," op. 56. The *Vier Skizzen* for pedal-piano or piano four hands, op. 58, though neither fugal nor canonic, date from the same period, and, as we shall see, share in the same neo-Baroque tendencies.

On 21 February and again on 15 March Schumann jotted down "Fugenpassion" in the *Haushaltbücher*—an apt designation considering the intensity with which he threw himself into his work.[120] After nearly a year of frustrated or interrupted attempts at composition, he seems once again to have found his stride. The *Vier Fugen,* begun on 25 February, were completed in a little less than a month. This was a happy period in the Schumann household; the composer's references to "good" or "cheerful" feelings go hand in hand with a series of pleasant experiences, personal and professional, all of them bespeaking a state of restored well-being: the birth of a third daughter, Julie, on 11 March; the couple's assembly of an album of their most valued correspondence;[121] and the appearance, on 17 March, of Brendel's important (and in many ways flattering) article on Schumann's music, its historical position, and its relationship to Mendelssohn's output. The *Vier Fugen* behind him, Schumann (with Clara at his side) delved into Cherubini's *Cours de contrepoint et de fugue* (1835) on 7 April, the same day on which he finished the first of the B-A-C-H fugues for organ. But soon after the completion of a second fugue on 18 April, this, the most ambitious project of the Contrapuntal Year, was interrupted by a singular event: the arrival of a rented pedal-piano at the Schumann residence.

Equipped with a pedalboard like that of an organ, instruments of this type first appeared in the eighteenth century. Schumann's interest was clearly piqued, for on 27 April he noted in the *Haushaltbücher:* "Idea to compose for the pedal-piano."[122] In the next week or so he worked steadily at the *Vier Skizzen,* the intensity of his labors now a possible cause of the "nervous troubles" and "very anxious [condition]" recorded in the *Haushaltbücher* for 2 and 6 May.[123] These by now familiar complaints notwithstanding, he was able to put the finishing touches on the *Sechs Studien* by 7 June, the day before his thirty-fifth birthday. For most of the remainder of the summer, Schumann called a halt to his contrapuntal activities, understandably enough, given the other projects that commanded his attention: work on the final two movements of the Piano Concerto, and the (derailed) journey to the Beethoven Festival in Bonn. While he returned to Cherubini's treatise on 19 August, his progress on the B-A-C-H fugues was hampered again by a recurrent bout of illness and by several meetings, with Hiller, Wieck, and Julius Becker, a local music teacher and composer, regarding a projected series of orchestral concerts in Dresden. Three more fugues were drafted by the end of September, but then came another interruption (this time occasioned by revisions of the *Finale* of Opus 521), a period of intermittent illness for both Robert and Clara, and preparations for the first subscription concert on 11 November, the program including Mendelssohn's Violin Concerto played by the fourteen-year-old prodigy Joseph Joachim.[124] The set was finally completed by late November.[125]

Inspired partially by Mendelssohn's Preludes and Fugues for piano and organ, opp. 35 and 37 (1837), Schumann's fugal works of 1845 have not fared well with many commentators. While some view them as part of an obligatory rite of passage to the late style, others hear symptoms in these compositions of the disintegrative tendencies that several writers detect in the composer's last works.[126] Similarly, most critics view the canonic *Studien,* like the *Vier Skizzen,* as an odd byway but little more. Troping on Brendel's division of Schumann's career into "subjective" and "objective" phases, writers have pointed to the emergence of an ultra-rational, even impersonal quality in this music, made doubly disturbing by memories of the unbridled fantasy of the earlier keyboard music. In short, the conventional wisdom maintains that Schumann's imaginative impulses, if not fully extinguished, were at least seriously dimmed in the fugues and canons of the Contrapuntal Year.

Schumann, however, set great store by his contrapuntal accomplishments of 1845. Writing to Whistling in March 1846, he even predicted (wrongly, as it turned out) that the B-A-C-H fugues would be judged by later generations as among his greatest creations: "I worked on this set for the whole of last year in order to make it somewhat worthy of the exalted name it bears; [it is] a work that will, I believe, long outlive my other works."[127] Is it possible that later critics have been simply unattuned to the poetry of Schumann's fugal art? In an often quoted review of 1838, he had written that "most of Bach's fugues are character pieces of the highest kind; in part truly poetic creations."[128] At about the same time, the dialectic between rationality and caprice could be heard in the subtly woven lines of the *Novelletten* and the imitative textures of the *Kreisleriana.* But whereas in 1838 this dialectic had played itself out through the agency of the character piece, in 1845 it emerges as an aspect of fugal and canonic writing per se.

Both the Opus 72 and the Opus 60 sets aspire to the condition of character pieces; hence, both draw on the techniques Schumann had perfected in the poetic cycles of the 1830s. Each set, for instance, is conceived as a tonal unity, the *Vier Fugen* progressing from D minor to its relative major, F, the B-A-C-H fugues circling around B♭. Likewise, inter-movement motivic connections play a significant role in both collections. In the *Vier Fugen,* a counterfigure from Fugues 2 (mm. 6ff.) and 3 (mm. 19ff.) points toward the subject of Fugue 4 (which itself recalls the second-movement fugue subject of Bach's Third Sonata for unaccompanied violin). The progressively simpler homophonic realizations of this melody throughout the course of the final fugue in turn provide a fitting close for the entire set. The use of the B-A-C-H motive of course ensures a measure of built-in motivic coherence for the Opus 60 fugues, but here it is important to distinguish between two very different approaches: in some cases (for example, Fugue 1) the motive parallels the fugue's main theme, while in others (such as the gigue-fugue, No. 5; Example 9.1) it is merely a starting point for a more extended line. In the latter case, Schumann's employment of a motivic cell as abstract building material readily calls to mind his elaboration of the Sphinxes, both as foreground themes and subliminal motives, in *Carnaval.* The final fugue of the set, like the corresponding piece in Opus 72, progresses from dense counterpoint to massive homophony. Culminating in a chordal peroration on the B-A-C-H theme, the fugue's coda at the same time prefigures a climactic passage in the Finale (mm. 343ff.) of the Second Symphony. If the essence of a fugue is a fixed subject, then that of the character piece is the transformation of an eloquent motive. It is a transformative process of precisely this sort that informs the fugues of Opus 72: in Fugue 2, the full subject gives way just past the midpoint of the piece to compressed variants of the original idea; in the middle section *(Etwas belebter)* of Fugue 4, a derivative of the subject is given over to imitative treatment. The overall planning no less than the motivicism of both sets of fugues reveals that they are cycles of character pieces in disguise.

"The best fugue," Schumann wrote in an 1837 review of Mendelssohn's Preludes and Fugues, op. 35, "will always be the one that the public takes—for a Strauss waltz; in other words, where the artistic roots are covered as are those of a flower, so that we only perceive the blossom."[129] Schumann's provocative statement on the relationship between concealed artifice and manifest artlessness, though directed at fugue, resonates with his own approach to the technique of canon. The fussy tile of his Opus 56, *Studien für den Pedalflügel . . . Sechs Stücke in can-*

Example 9.1. Sechs Fugen for organ, op. 60: Fugue 5, mm. 1–4.

onischer Form, is misleading, for there is as much poetry in these pieces as in the earlier cycles of keyboard miniatures. The set easily lends itself to interpretation as a succession of character pieces, many of them taking off from baroque topics: a figural prelude à la Bach, a siciliano (reminiscent of *Kreisleriana,* No. 6), two *Lieder ohne Worte,* an elfin scherzo, and a chorale. In none of the pieces, however, does the canonic underpinning call attention to itself; on the contrary, Schumann aims to make the contrapuntal artifice as inconspicuous as possible. Hence, the canon at the octave in No. 1 seems to dissolve into long stretches of parallel sixths. The frequent rests in No. 3 create the illusion that *dux* and *comes* form a single, gracefully contoured cantilena. The same device, coupled with constant shifts in the temporal interval between the two canonic voices, contributes to the dreamy lyricism of No. 4. In the last two pieces, both of which employ canons at the octave, the contrapuntal technique is concealed by predominantly chordal textures. Throughout the set, in other words, the accent falls on the "blossom" and not the "artistic roots."

Neo-Baroque topics figure prominently in the Opus 58 *Skizzen* as well, witness the sarabande rhythms in Nos. 1 and 2, the spicy acciaccaturas, again in No. 1, and the chromatic lament bass in No. 3. The general absence of overtly contrapuntal devices brings these pieces even closer to the style of the miniatures from the decade before. So too do Schumann's various strategies for achieving tonal and motivic coherence. In Nos. 2–4, for instance, the subsidiary key in one piece turns up as the tonic of its successor, a practice hearkening to the *Fantasiestücke* (op. 12) and the *Kreisleriana.* The technique of affective pairing, again a mainstay of Schumann's approach to structure in compositions such as the *Davidsbündlertänze* or *Carnaval,* likewise has a part to play: No. 2 can be heard as a variation of No. 1; the principal theme of No. 4 echoes, in varied guise, the main idea of the middle section of No. 3.

The keyboard collections of the Contrapuntal Year may therefore represent more than a mere diversion in Schumann's compositional masterplan. Aesthetically suspect for some writers, these pieces arguably strive for a rich synthesis of the dissimilar elements that criss-cross in the composer's musical cosmos: unabashed lyricism, romantic wistfulness, Jean-Paulian rhapsodizing, Baroque affect, and Bachian counterpoint. That Schumann had penetrated to the essence of Bach's art is borne out by more than one spot in the Opus 72 and Opus 60 fugues. For Bach, fugal technique amounts to more than the superficial concept of one thematic entrance chasing after another. As Schoenberg was fond of pointing out, Bach's fugues have far more to do with the vertical combination of distinct motives than with the horizontal unfolding of a single motivic idea. This is not to say that Bach merely had a penchant for countersubjects, but rather that he was apt to make flexible and subtle use of his countermaterial.[130] In Fugues 17 (A♭ major) and 23 (B major) from Book I of *Das wohltemperirte Clavier,* for instance, the withdrawal and resoration of the original countersubject, together with a tonic return, imparts a tripartite shape to what might have easily been a mere alternation of expositions, episodes, and developments. Schumann employs a comparable tactic in the third fugue (G minor) from his Opus 60 set.[131] The subject, on its first presentation, is coupled with a pair of two-bar countermelodies *(a* and *b)* that, during subsequent statements of the main theme or its answer, are gradually dismantled. The answer in mm. 5-8, to take an example, brings only countermelody *b* and a fragment of *a* in the bass (Example 9.2). But as the fugue proceeds past its midpoint, the original four-bar countersubject (or segments thereof) is just as gradually reconstituted to articulate important stations in the tonal trajectory of the piece: cadences in C minor, E♭, and finally, the tonic, G minor. Thus the fragmentation and reassembly of the initial countermaterial is coordinated with harmonic considerations to lend shape and direction to the fugue. Much the same could be said of the second of the *Vier Fugen,* where the notion of a strict countersubject is actually displaced by an array of flexible counterfigures, each associated with a different portion of the subject.[132]

Example 9.2. Sechs Fugen for organ, Fugue 3: mm. 1–8.

Schumann's deft approach to the *ars combinatoria* is thus more than a regressive act of homage to a composer who had been dead for almost a century. On the contrary, it betokens a penetrating reformulation of what in fact constitutes the material basis of a composition. As we will see, this shift in the nature of the musical idea, from melodic to combinative entity, will have profound consequences for the Second Symphony of 1845–1847 and the piano trios of 1847, the works in which Schumann's New Way comes into full flower.

"Symphoniaca"

In the four years since its completion, Schumann had little luck in placing the A-minor *Phantasie* for piano and orchestra with a publisher. When he submitted it to Breitkopf und Härtel in December 1843 as a *Concert-Allegro für Pianoforte mit Begleitung des Orchesters,* no offer of publication was forthcoming.[133] Frustrated by his lack of success, he added two movements to the *Phantasie* in the summer of 1845; in the more marketable form of a traditional three-movement concerto, the work elicited some interest from Kistner in Leipzig, though it was ultimately placed, in January 1846, with Breitkopf und Härtel.[134]

We learn from entries in the *Haushaltbücher* that Schumann made the unusual decision to proceed in reverse movement-order. Between 14 June (the day before Clara announced her suspicions of a fourth pregnancy) and 12 July, he was occupied with the drafting and orchestration of the finale, designated in the *Haushaltbücher* as a Rondo in A.[135] In four days' time, he was "very happy" over having completed the slow movement, and by the end of the month, he had made a final pass through the first movement.[136]

With the Piano Concerto, Schumann not only picked up a thread left suspended since 1841, but also initiated a symphonic strand in the New Way that would include the thoroughly revised Opus 52 *Finale* (taken up in October 1845) and the Second Symphony (begun later the same year). In part, Schumann's revisitation of earlier symphonic projects, like his turn to newer ones, was motivated by a desire to enrich Dresden's concert life; his efforts, along with Hiller and Becker, to launch an orchestral series, emanated from the same impulse. The Piano Concerto was given a private premiere on 4 December 1845 at the Hôtel de Saxe with Clara as soloist and Hiller, the work's eventual dedicatee, leading the Dresden orchestra in a program that also included the revised *Ouverture, Scherzo und Finale.* Oddly enough, in light of its subsequent popularity even among listeners who do not count themselves as

Schumann enthusiasts, the concerto was never performed in public during the composer's lifetime.

Tovey, an early and perceptive apologist for Schumann's idiosyncratic symphonism, wrote of the concerto: "There is a depth and a breadth in Schumann's lyric vein which already shows that it was no mistaken ambition that led him to turn from it to larger designs."[137] Tovey's remark resonates most strongly with the two movements conceived in 1845. Put another way, Schumann's technique had developed to the point where he could dare to adopt a strategy largely avoided during the Symphonic Year: the fusion of the character piece and the symphonic work. This is not to say that the final movements of the Piano Concerto actually reworked previously composed keyboard miniatures. Moreover, we have already seen in Chapter 6 how the opening movement itself unfolds as a series of affectively differentiated but thematically unified character portraits. But in the slow movement in particular, the dialectic between miniaturism and long-breathed symphonism is resolved with a simplicity and economy of utterance that bespeaks mastery. The opening section of this straightforward ABA form, a kind of Eusebian *Fantasiestück* replete with orchestral accompaniment, gives way to a middle section dominated by a soaring, passionate tune first introduced by the cellos. But as it turns out, this sweeping melody derives from a casually introduced, ornamental flourish in the piano's opening "character piece" (Example 9.3). With a single unobtrusive gesture Schumann closes the gap between symphonic breadth and lyric containment.

A similar dialectic informs the finale, only here it is the dance topic, long a favorite for Schumann, that regulates the symphonic argument. Alfred Dörffel, in an otherwise glowing review of the concerto, claimed that the finale was not on the same level as the other movements, since

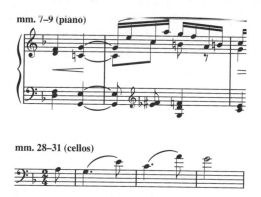

Example 9.3. Piano Concerto, op. 54: second movement.

its main theme was somehow "not meaningful enough."[138] Yet Schumann's expansive treatment of his materials more than compensates for their light-hearted, dance-like character. The fanciful hemiolas of the second group, no less than its luxuriant harmonic digressions, the imaginatively conceived variations during the development, the broadly but gracefully unfolding coda—all of these features serve to legitimize the dance-like material as a vehicle for symphonic elaboration.

The issue of large-scale coherence, already a paramount concern in the single-movement *Phantasie* of 1841, loomed large in Schumann's conception of the added movements in 1845. For Clara, her husband's efforts spelled unmitigated success: "What a beautifully interrelated *[zusammenhängend]* whole," she wrote of the concerto.[139] In a letter to Mendelssohn, Schumann resorted to similar (if less exuberant) rhetoric; his concerto, he wrote, consisted of "Allegro affetuoso, Andantino and Rondo—the last two movements interrelated *[zusammenhängend]*."[140] The specific relation Schumann probably had in mind was the celebrated six-bar link between the slow movement and finale. To judge from the layers of revision in the autograph, this transition gave Schumann considerable trouble; no fewer than five different versions of the passage can be reconstructed from the manuscript. According to Bernhard Appel, who has carefully examined the autograph emendations, the transition in its final form allowed Schumann to counterbalance the weightier first movement with a composite and tangibly linked two-movement structure. As Appel rightly points out, the transition makes such a powerful effect because it yokes together gestures of reminiscence and anticipation in a very short space: the winds recall the head-motif of the first movement's main theme while the rushing scale in the strings propels us into the finale.[141] Moreover, these gestures transform what would have otherwise been a discrete sequence of movements into a tightly wrought "alternation of tones." In the poetics of Friedrich Hölderlin, the apparently rhapsodic surface of a well-made poem is in fact controlled by a systematic rotation of "tones" or moods. Potentially infinite in number, the tones are limited, in Hölderlin's theory, to three: an ideal tone associated with fantasy and reflection, a naïve tone characterized by lyric expressivity, and a heroic tone exuding energy and suggestive of striving. The poet moves from one to the other by way of deft transitions that mediate the striking contrasts between and among the various tones.[142] This is precisely what happens in the six-bar link in Schumann's Piano Concerto. Situated between the "naïve" slow movement and the "heroic" finale, it plays largely on a motive from the "ideal" first movement. The motive, supported by horn fifths, wavers between the minor mode of the first movement and the major mode of the last. The dance-like opening gesture of the finale in turn retains the horn fifths but inverts the direction of the motive. With the utmost economy, Schumann redirects the reflectivity of the first movement and the naïveté of the second toward the heroism of the finale. In less than a dozen bars, the "alternation of tones" is complete, the disparate characters of the concerto bound together as an "interrelated whole."

Buoyed by the completion of the Piano Concerto, the B-A-C-H fugues, and the revision of the *Ouverture, Scherzo und Finale*, Schumann set to work on an even more ambitious project in December of 1845. The first reference to what was published as the Second Symphony, op. 61, came in a letter to Mendelssohn written earlier the same fall: "For several days there's been much trumpeting and drumming within me (trumpet in C); I don't know what will come of it."[143] On 6 and 9 December, Schumann attended a rehearsal and performance of Schubert's Ninth Symphony with the Dresden orchestra under Hiller. Within several days, he noted his own "symphonic thoughts" in the *Haushaltbücher*. The references to "Symphoniaca" on 14 and 15 December may indicate that preliminary compositional work was already underway at that time.[144] And although Schumann did not keep to the same feverish schedule that had allowed him to sketch the First Symphony in a mere four days, still the sketches for the C-major Symphony were assembled in record time; three days after Christmas, he could write: "Almost finished with the symphony."[145]

Yet at this point, Schumann's labors took a sluggish turn. The orchestration of the First Symphony took up about a month; continued work on the Second Symphony, in contrast, was spread over the better part of a year. In fact, apart from the two volumes of choral partsongs composed in late January and early February (*Fünf Lieder von Robert Burns*, op. 55; and *Vier Gesänge*, op. 59) and final revisions of the B-A-C-H fugues in March, the elaboration of the Second Symphony turned out to be Schumann's single major compositional project for 1846. By late February, several weeks after the birth of a fourth child and first son, Emil, he had made "only minimal progress" with the instrumentation of the symphony.[146] Following on almost a month of poor health—it was during this period that Schumann registered his alarm over a "peculiar distortion of the auditory organ"—he returned to the symphony in April, only to suspend his work after orchestrating the first movement because of severe dizziness and debilitating weakness. Not until September, shortly after a six-week holiday in Norderney, did he take up the orchestration of the final three movements. His work was completed on 19 October, but it took its toll on his mental and physical constitution; according to entries in the *Haushaltbücher*, he suffered from nervous tension, anxiety, and exhaustion during the final weeks of labor on the symphony.[147]

The first performance on 5 November, with the Leipzig Gewandhaus Orchestra under Mendelssohn's direction, did not bring the resounding success for which Schumann had hoped. Though Mendelssohn approached the work with his usual sensitivity, and in spite of Ferdinand David's special care in drilling the violins on the treacherous passages in the middle movements, the work as a whole fell flat, in part because it appeared on the second half of an already overly long program. Much to the annoyance of Schumann and his supporters, Mendelssohn encored Rossini's *William Tell* Overture before the intermission, so that the audience already had too much of a good thing before the orchestra even took up the symphony.[148] Perhaps as a result of the work's tepid reception, Schumann set about tightening several spots in the next week (in an unsigned review of the second performance, Brendel noted that the first movement and finale were somewhat shortened). His efforts were rewarded at a repeat performance on 16 November, again with Mendelssohn conducting, when the symphony was more warmly applauded.

If the public reaction to his latest symphony was mixed, Schumann was probably heartened by the response of the professional critics, many of whom agreed that with the Second Symphony he had reached a watershed in his compositional development. For Dörffel, glossing on Brendel's thesis that Schumann's oeuvre can be divided into "objective" and "subjective" phases, the dialectic between these elements is very nearly resolved in the Second Symphony. The slow movement, in Dörffel's interpretation, comes close to realizing this goal, while the finale (in its earlier form) promises no less than a synthesis of the spirit of Mozart's "Jupiter" Symphony and Beethoven's Fifth.[149] Similarly, Ernst Gottschald devoted a major part of his review of the work to a demonstration of its proximity to the manner and tone of Beethoven's Ninth Symphony. His detailed critique of the relationship between Schumann's symphonism and that of the major representative of the genre leaves no doubt over the willingness of the composer's contemporaries to admit at least this symphonic effort into the canon. In Gottschald's view, Schumann even manages to outdo Beethoven: the respective finales of his Second Symphony and Beethoven's Ninth are both "artistic representations of universal love"; but Schumann's achievement is all the more impressive because he makes his point without the aid of voices.[150] Brendel, in an 1846 review of a performance of the Second Symphony in Leipzig, was delighted to discover that the "objective" elements characteristic of Schumann's "second creative epoch"—clearly profiled melodic ideas and contrapuntal density—were complemented by a resurgence of "subjective" tendencies in the symphony's middle movements. The Scherzo, for instance, afforded a place for "fantastic humor," a touchstone of Schumann's earlier (and for Brendel, more characteristic) compositional style.[151] Whether they happened to praise the humor of the second movement, the pathos of the Adagio, or the sublimity of the Finale, the critics were unanimous in locating Schumann's latest orchestral work at a creative highpoint.

Though impossible to validate empirically, it is probably safe to say that for Schumann's devotees, the Second is the symphony of symphonies. Armed with the deepened technical sensibilities of the New Way— an assured contrapuntal technique, a sophisticated sense for large-scale unity, and a finely developed strategy for manipulating musical "tones" or moods—Schumann transported the genre from a profane into a quasi-religious realm. The new tone, solemn but uplifting, is evident from the start of the slow introduction to the first movement and maintains its position of dominance at key points throughout the symphony by way of Schumann's subtle and varied approach to the *ars combinatoria*. The celebrated opening motto, a rising fifth from C to G in horns, trumpets, and trombones, first appeared in a sketch (now in the Bonn University Library) dating from late 1840 or early 1841 and can thus be associated with the preoccupations of the Symphonic Year.[152] Frequently heard as a reference to the opening gesture of Haydn's Symphony No. 104, a nurturing source for the secular symphonic tradition,[153] the motto here gives rise to a full-blown chorale tune. Set against a flowing counterpoint in the strings, the more slowly paced chorale melody unfolds leisurely in six phrases, each largely a variant of an initial four-bar unit. But as illustrated in Example 9.4, the chorale tune *(a)* and its countermelody *(b)* engage in an interesting repartee whereby the first two bars of the latter are continually displaced in relation to the metric disposition of the former: they initially support mm. 1–2 of the principal melody, then straddle the closing and opening bars of its first and second phrases respectively, and finally serve as an accompaniment to the cadential gesture in the third chorale phrase. Hence, the three squarely articulated phrases of the chorale are bound into one overarching entity. Contrapuntal thinking is thus not only a contributing factor to the quasi-religious tone of the symphony's opening, it also becomes an agent of syntactic flexibility and melodic continuity.

Each of the subsequent movements draws in varying degrees on similar textures. The second trio of the Scherzo, for instance, brings a (new) chorale melody with two variations, the first playing on the con-

Example 9.4. Second Symphony, op. 61: reduction of first movement, mm. 1–14.

trast between sustained theme and staccato countermelody, and the second hearkening to the mellow brass sonority of the opening movement's introduction. As if to affirm the Bachian pedigree of his materials, Schumann weaves an allusion to the B-A-C-H motive itself into the transition between the variations.[154] The retransition to the recapitulation in the Adagio features an equally suggestive allusion, this time to the contrapuntal variations in the scene with the armored men from the Act

II Finale of Mozart's *Die Zauberflöte*, similarly geared to enhance the symphony's reverential tone. In the Finale, the closing variations on yet another chorale melody (and its integration with the first-movement chorale) crown Schumann's symphonic celebration of the *ars combinatoria*.[155]

Of course, Schumann's Second was not the first symphony to make prominent use of the chorale topic. The introductory pages of his work find a parallel in the corresponding passage from Schubert's Ninth Symphony, which, as noted earlier, Schumann heard just days before being overtaken by "symphonic thoughts" of his own. (The "three-key-exposition" of Schumann's first movement, articulating C, E♭, and G, likewise recalls a typically Schubertian procedure). The hymnic quality of Beethoven's setting of Schiller's *An die Freude* in his Ninth Symphony/Finale would have provided Schumann with another model. But what distinguishes Schumann's strategy in his Second Symphony is the thoroughness with which the chorale topic determines and is in turn interwoven with a network of tonal and motivic relationships spanning the entire work.

Practically the whole of the first movement's exposition, to cite an example at the local level, derives its substance from the preceding chorale-introduction, though less from the motto theme itself than from its countermelodies, subsidiary phrases, and episodic asides. Hence, the cadentially driven closing group (mm. 92ff.) gives the opening counterline, now in the dominant G major, to violins and 'cellos/basses. Only with the coda is the principal chorale theme, withheld during the body of the Allegro, triumphantly restored. At the global level, the first movement sets in motion a web of thematic relationships whose strands are finally knit together in the closing paragraphs of the last movement: the skittish principal idea of the Scherzo (a not-too-distant relative of the main theme of *Kreisleriana*, No. 7) takes off from a passage in the opening movement's coda; the Scherzo's raucous coda in turn recalls the opening gesture of the first movement's chorale at a point where we least expect it. The doleful opening theme of the Adagio, a musical symbol of supplication reminiscent of the main idea of "Erbarme dich" from Bach's *St. Matthew Passion*, recurs in the major mode, surrounded by cascading eighths, as the second group of the Finale (and in inversion during its development section). And lastly, the first-movement chorale, again in a luminous C major, returns to round off the symphony as a whole. Equally significant for the work's large-scale coherence are the reverberations of the first movement's tonal plan. The motion from C to E♭, the initial gambit in its three-key exposition, is replicated in the initial stages of the second movement and in the exposition of the third. In complementary fashion, the chorale variations in the finale reverse the process, taking off from E♭ and ultimately arriving at C major.

In his 1848 review of the Second Symphony, Krüger praised the Finale for its grandeur, its rich abundance of themes, and its clearly delineated sections; at the same time, he found "much that is peculiar and capricious, that one will find astounding, and over which one will not know whether to question or to be angry."[156] To this day, the Finale is viewed as among the most impressive, if problematic, of Schumann's symphonic movements.[157] One thing is certain: it represents at once a summation and culmination of the arguments preceding it.[158] Yet Schumann's realization of these goals led him into wholly original territory; the "alternation of tones" that previously regulated the direction of multi-movement works (and continues to do so in the Second Symphony) is coordinated here with the evolving course of a single movement. Specifically, the jubilant march of the movement's opening gives way to the quasi-religious chorale of its close. Prefiguring a pattern familiar from Mahler's symphonies, Schumann's movement traces a path from the mundane to the divine, the secular to the sacred. Little wonder then that the sonata-form categories traditionally associated with weighty symphonic movements were for all intents and purposes abrogated. Although the opening march and the ensuing major-mode presentation of the main idea from the slow movement relate as first and second group respectively, and although the material of this "exposition" is subsequently developed at some length, the raison d'etre of the development resides in its evolution of a lyrical idea whose even tread, block-chord harmonization, and graceful melodic curve foreshadow the "new" idea in E♭ that will in turn set off the concluding chorale variations. In the finale of Schumann's Second Symphony, form is less a matter of symmetrically disposed parts than of transformational process.[159]

This transformative impulse continues unabated within the chorale variations themselves. The initial chorale in E♭ (Example 9.5) is eventually displaced by a variant in C (Example 9.6) that, as many listeners have observed, invites comparison with the final song of Beethoven's *An die ferne Geliebte* (a favorite allusive source for Schumann at least since

Example 9.5. Second Symphony: Finale, mm. 280–83 (oboe).

Example 9.6. Second Symphony: Finale, mm. 394–97 (violin I).

the composition of the C-major *Fantasie,* op. 17). The chorale, in its new guise as lied-melody, is then integrated with an abbreviated but broadly serene restatement of the first-movement chorale, its opening fifth, as we have already observed, a cipher for the symphonic tradition extending back to Haydn. Through the agency of the *ars combinatoria,* song and symphony are consecrated at a stroke. And how better to seal the ritual act of sanctification than with the expansive plagal cadence at the very end of the symphony? Recalling an eminently Goethean theme, Schumann "redeems" the secular musical genres, the symphonic-instrumental and the lyric-vocal, on a quasi-religious plane.

To judge from the documentary evidence, art and life commingle in the Second Symphony to a degree matched by only a few of Schumann's other compositions. But paradoxically, the work places in sharp relief the hazards of assuming that creativity and biography proceed in lockstep. Schumann's own words take us to the heart of the dilemma. Writing to J. C. Lobe, to whom he had sent the score of his recently completed symphony in November 1846, the composer maintained: "it will tell *[erzählen]* you of many joys and sorrows."[160] Schumann provides more details on his narrative *(Erzählung)* in tones in a letter of April 1849 to D. G. Otten: "I wrote the [C-major] symphony in December 1845 [while] still half sick; it seems to me that one must hear this. Only in the last movement did I begin to feel like myself; I became really well again [only] after completing the entire work. But otherwise . . . it reminds me of a dark time."[161] Apparently an invitation to interpret his symphony as a reflection of lived experience, Schumann's letter raises as many questions as it settles. As we have seen, he did indeed *sketch* the symphony in mid- to late December 1845, but did not bring it to completion until nearly a year later. Did Schumann then "begin to feel like himself" around Christmas 1845, while orchestrating and elaborating it? One would tend to guess the latter, but the *Haushalt-bücher* tell a different story; the entry for 28 September 1846 (the day after he noted "always occupied with the last movement of the symphony") reads: "nervous agitation all day long."[162] The letter to Otten does, however, direct us to a spot in the symphony where Schumann probably "heard" his "half-sickness": the "melancholy bassoon [line] in the Adagio." But oddly enough, he retained a "special fondness" for just this passage, in spite of its association with the "dark time" during which the symphony was conceived.

Taking their cue from Schumann's account, many critics interpret the symphony as a steady progression from pain to triumph, sorrow to joy, suffering to health.[163] These hypothetical narratives may speak to the affective trajectory of the Adagio and Finale, but they have little to do with the Jean-Paulian highjinks of the Scherzo, let alone the over-whelmingly affirmative tone of the first movement. Viewed from the perspective of a Hölderlinian "alternation of tones", the opening move-ment links a "sublime" introduction with a "heroic" Allegro, the exuber-ant effect of the latter a function of its incredible rhythmic vitality and the persistent repetitions of its main rhythmic figure: (indeed, Schumann's motive, given its accentuated second beat, restores the sara-band to its historical origins as a propulsive, breathless dance-type). As tempting as it may be to read Schumann's depressive tendencies into his music, the exercise, in this case, simply will not square with aural reality.

"Trio Thoughts"

Alfred Dörffel, sounding a theme held in common with other mid-nineteenth-century critics, sensed in the D-minor Piano Trio, op. 63, a continuation of Schumann's exploration of the "new ground" broken in the Second Symphony. In the trio's first movement he heard particularly strong intimations of a new *Sturm und Drang,* an artistic awakening powerful enough to break the spell of what had been "a long romantic dream."[164] The D-minor Trio and its companion piece, the Piano Trio in F Major, op. 80, came on the heels of a flurry of creative activity in the spring of 1847. Following on the return to Dresden, in late March, from a four-month tour that took the Schumanns to Vienna and Berlin, the composer tackled a variety of projects, both old and new, with a vengeance. The most far-reaching of these, his preliminary work on the long-projected opera, will occupy us at greater length in the next chap-ter. Here let it suffice to say that by 1 April Schumann had decided on an operatic treatment of Friedrich Hebbel's *Genoveva* and that during the next weeks he would sketch the Overture and, in consultation with Hebbel and Robert Reinick, begin the task of adapting the text for his purposes. But there was also unfinished business to attend to: the four-hand piano arrangements of the Second Symphony (a joint effort with Clara) and of the *Finale* from Opus 52; the piano-vocal score of the completed portion of *Faust* (here too Clara took a leading role), along with its orchestration and an alternate closing chorus (for "Das Ewig-Weibliche zieht uns hinan"). If Schumann's creative energies ebbed in 1846, they flowed with irrepressible vigor in 1847.

Schumann's plans to write a second piano trio (at the time, he thought of the as yet unpublished *Phantasiestücke,* op. 88, of 1842 as his first) may have dated back to March 1846, when he wrote of his promise to provide the Hamburg publisher Schuberth with such a work.[165] Thus the "trio thoughts" to which he referred in early June 1847 had been spinning about in the Schumann household for some time; indeed, Clara completed her own Piano Trio in G minor (op. 17) between May and September of the previous year.[166] Schumann's "trio thoughts" soon took shape as a D-minor trio, sketched with typical alacrity between 9 and 16 June, though not elaborated until September and October. For in the interim, further "trio thoughts" (noted in the *Haushaltbücher* for 11 August) resulted in the partial sketching of yet another work, in F, for the same medium. Just like the first two string quartets of the Opus 41 set, the piano trios of 1847 were thus conceived as a unit,[167] the first ready for a private performance held on Clara's birthday, 13 September, the second complete by 1 November.

At least in part, Schumann's D-minor and F-major trios were composed in response to Clara's Piano Trio of the year before. Here again we find a manifestation of the personal and artistic interchange that informed the marriage diary, the settings from Rückert's *Liebesfrühling* of 1841, and the couple's joint contrapuntal studies. Not surprisingly, Clara's Piano Trio, her most ambitious composition (though she wrote it off as "effeminate and sentimental"),[168] was frequently paired with Schumann's D-minor Trio in nineteenth-century performances, a practice that began even before his F-major Trio was complete.[169] Yet there is an unmistakable element of one-upmanship in both of Schumann's trios. His blurring of the interface between development and recapitulation in the first and last movements of Opus 80 recalls Clara's subtle employment of the same strategy in the finale of her trio. Likewise, the fugato in the development section of Clara's finale, an impressive passage praised even by Mendelssohn, finds parallels in the prominent contrapuntal textures in both of Schumann's trios.

Indeed, it is largely through their refined approach to the *ars combinatoria* that Schumann's trios distinguish themselves as products of the New Way. The dark-hued opening movement of the D-minor Trio (*Mit Energie und Leidenschaft*) proves to be a masterpiece in this regard. Dörffel was correct in asserting that the most noteworthy aspect of the movement resided neither in its rich harmonies nor its expansive form, but rather in its novel thematic combinations.[170] More specifically, each

of the main formal divisions in the exposition is articulated by a contrapuntal duo. The opening theme, for instance, is an outgrowth of the
gestural complex presented in the first measure: a cadential figure in the
violin (*a* in Example 9.7) and a turning figure in the bass *(b)*; the second
measure then subjects the initial complex, slightly varied, to voice exchange, so that what we at first perceive as linear entities (the two-
measure motives in violin and bass) emerge, on reflection, as byproducts
of a vertically conceived unit. The new dotted motive heading the transition is in turn drawn into a series of imitative parries between piano
and strings. The hints of imitation in the first four bars of the second
group give way to full-fledged canon between melody and bass in the
varied response to the phrase. And finally, the closing group conjoins a
variant of the lyrical second theme with the movement's opening idea.
(Performers who fail to take the first ending and repeat will miss the
point of the exposition: the presentation, withdrawal, and gradual resti-
tution of a motivic combination). It would be no exaggeration to say
that with this movement Schumann effects a telling shift in what consti-

Example 9.7. Piano Trio in D Minor, op. 63: mm. 1–2.

tutes a musical "idea": no longer conceived as a leisurely unfolding lyrical entity, the musical idea is reconfigured as a terse combinative unit.
In addition, this process attests to the internalization of techniques first
tested in the fugal works of 1845.

The *ars combinatoria* also contributes to the textural richness and
complements the motivic economy of the trio's subsequent movements.
Thus the nervously dotted main theme of the second movement is
smoothed out, in the middle section, as a gracefully rising figure that
soon combines with a freely inverted variant.[171] The third movement
offers one of the most remarkable mixtures of constructive rigor and
unbridled fantasy in Schumann's oeuvre. Specifically, this blend issues
from the employment of contrapuntal artifice on the one hand (the
violin's opening arioso functions as a countermelodic foil to the subsequent phrase in the cello) and variation techniques (consider the piano's
highly altered delivery of the arioso near the end of the movement) on
the other. The initial paragraphs of the finale strike a considerably
lighter tone. The drone-like accompaniments to the squarely cut opening tune and transitional theme lend them a decidedly pastoral flavor,
while the sweeping second theme is one of those bittersweet conceits
that bear Schumann's unmistakable stamp. But neither the sunny first
theme nor the wistful second give any hint of the contrapuntal machinations of the development section, where the transitional theme acts as a
kind of cantus firmus and portions of the first theme, in original and
inverted forms, are treated in fugato. If, in the Second Symphony, the
ars combinatoria is associated largely with the chorale, over the course
of the D-minor Piano Trio it affects the whole spectrum of the work's
materials: a compact motive (first movement), a lyrical scale fragment
(second movement), an arioso (slow movement), and a full-blown cantilena (Finale).

In Schumann's view, the D-minor Trio (together with the Second
Symphony and the works for pedal-piano) belonged to a "time of
gloomy moods."[172] But with the F-major Trio he seems to have banished
melancholy once and for all. The later trio, again according to Schumann, "is of a completely different character than [the Trio] in D—it
makes a friendlier and breezier effect. I'm particularly pleased with the
beginning of the Adagio and the Allegretto."[173] No doubt, the two compositions diverge widely in mood and character, the second providing
the satyr play to the tragedy of the first. (One thinks of other antitheti-
cally paired works such as Brahms's *Academic Festival Overture* and
Tragic Overture). But their surface differences aside, the trios have much
in common. It is probably not a coincidence that Schumann took particular pleasure in just those movements from the F-major Trio in which

the *ars combinatoria*, developed to such a high level in the earlier composition, come to the fore: the opening five bars of the slow movement feature a canon at the fifth between the cello and the piano left hand; and the principal section of the Allegretto, a siciliano marked *In mässiger Bewegung*, unfolds as a canon in which all instruments take part. Although the finale eschews strict canons or *fugatos*, its pervasive play on the combinative possibilities afforded by a limited number of motivic cells makes for a finely wrought contrapuntal mosaic. Similarly, both trios include moments of what may be called "sublime removal," the obverse of the impassioned "breakthroughs" in more public works like the First Symphony. In the D-minor Trio, such a passage occurs early on in the first movement's development section, where pianissimo triplets in the upper reaches of the piano color an ethereal chorale, the numinous effect enhanced by the *sul ponticello* in the strings and a modulation from F to A♭.[174] At a nearly corresponding spot in the first movement of the F-major Trio, the moment of sublime removal comes with an extended quotation of the second song from the Eichendorff *Liederkreis*, op. 39, *Dein Bildnis wunderselig*, its text a reverie on the poet's contemplation of the portrait of a lost love. Relatives of the digressive arabesques and dreamy asides in Schumann's early keyboard music, these passages introduce voices as if from afar, incursions into the "real" time of the piece from distant realms. Although it contains no intrusive voices, the slow movement of the F-major Trio is remarkable for its musical evocations of distance: both spatial (the canonic writing makes for a marvelous echo effect) and temporal (the opening violin melody recalls the slow movement of Beethoven's Piano and Violin Sonata, op. 30 no. 2; the modally tinged second theme reaches back even farther in music-historical time).[175] For all its sophisticated motivicism and contrapuntal gamesmanship, Schumann's music of the mid-1840s still reveals a markedly poetic dimension.

Just days after completing the F-major Trio, Schumann learned, through a letter from Dr. Moritz Reuter, of the death of Mendelssohn on 4 November. While Niels Gade had told him of his friend's serious illness on 31 October, we can well imagine that Schumann was shaken to the very core by the report of the demise of the one fellow composer with whom he had formed a close spiritual bond. Soon after returning from the funeral ceremony in Leipzig, Schumann began collecting materials for a memoir of his great contemporary. And even though his reminiscences remained in the form of fragmentary jottings, these notes, covering the period from the composers' first meeting in 1835, reveal much about Mendelssohn and, not surprisingly, about Schumann himself.

Just as the early Romantics practiced what Novalis and the Schlegel brothers called "symphilosophy" (a kind of collaborative or even communal philosophy), so Schumann and Mendelssohn shared an aesthetic whose elements included a guarded outlook on the worth of the keyboard miniature, a distaste for fantasies on operatic themes, a suspicion of Meyerbeerian grand opera, an intensely self-critical attitude, an undying faith in the neccessity to produce, an abiding love for the masterpices of world literature (Goethe and Jean Paul loomed large for both composers), and a deep reverence for Bach and the musical tradition he inaugurated.[176] Schumann's account of Mendelssohn's reaction to a recently invented telescope offers us a brief but tantalizing glimpse into the nature of the conversations between them: "When I told him about the great telescope and about a remark I read somewhere that to the inhabitants of distant planets we would appear, when viewed through the telescope, somewhat like mites on a piece of cheese—[he said] 'Yes, but *Das wohltemperirte Clavier* would still inpire them with respect'."[177] Schumann's notes also shed light on an issue, perhaps the central issue, over which every biographer of a nineteenth-century artist will have to ponder long and hard: the relationship between lived experience and creative product. When he maintains that "His [Mendelssohn's] life [was] an artwork: perfect," Schumann tells us that in his friend the process of *Bildung* (self-cultivation, self-formation) had reached an apogee (Mendelssohn succeeded, in other words, where the bell-caster of the Ivan Velikii poems failed) and implies conversely that if his work reflected his life, this was the case simply because his work *was* his life.

Schumann's musical *Hommage à Mendelssohn* is the simple but delightful *Erinnerung* (No. 28) from the *Album für die Jugend*, op. 68. Interestingly enough, the main theme of the little piece alludes clearly, both melodically and tonally, to *Dein Bildnis wunderselig*, the song that resounds like a voice from afar in the first movement of the F-major Piano Trio. In addition, the evocative violin melody at the beginning of the trio's slow movement alludes not only to a Beethovenian source, but also to the main theme of the slow movement of Mendelssohn's D-minor Piano Trio, op. 49, a work that Schumann deeply admired (Examples 9.8a and b). True, he inverts (and transposes) Mendelssohn's

Example 9.8a. Mendelssohn, Piano Trio in D Minor, op. 49: slow movement, opening gesture (piano).

Example 9.8b. Schumann, Piano Trio in F, op. 80: second movement, mm. 1–3 (violin).

theme; but still, the resemblance between the melodies may not have been fortuitous. In retrospect, then, the slow movement of Schumann's trio, the expressive center of the work, turns out to be a requiem, but before the fact.

~10~

The Musical Dramatist

Toward a Literary Opera

With the possible exception of the choral partsongs and the late works, sacred and secular, for soloists, chorus, and orchestra, Schumann's dramatic music constitutes the least explored area of his output. His opera *Genoveva,* the only one of the major dramatic compositions to have acquired something of a critical tradition, is little known and rarely performed; the first complete recording of the work was made as recently as October 1976.[1] Likewise, the other dramatic essays of the Dresden years have fared poorly in contemporary concert life: only the Overture to *Manfred* has secured a place in the standard repertory; selections from the *Scenen aus Göthe's Faust* (WoO 3) are only infrequently accorded a spot on concert programs.

Conventional wisdom has it that Schumann possessed neither the temperament nor the talent necessary for a successful career in the theatre. A born lyricist with an ill-developed sense for characterization, or so we are told, Schumann could not but fail as a dramatist.[2] In a word, Schumann's dramatic music has been deemed undramatic. If by "dramatic" we mean "stagey," then there is no doubt some truth to the charge. Critics who take their bearings from Aristotle's *Poetics* might justifiably complain of too much *dianoia* ("thought") and far too little *opsis* ("spectacle") in Schumann's approach to drama. Successful dramatists often have a bit of the trickster, even the charlatan about them (among musicians, Wagner was exemplary in this regard), while Schu-

mann, who tended more and more toward a seriousness of purpose and
a sobriety of idiom throughout his career, knew little of either persona.
But is it possible that the models against which we measure the success
or failure of a Singspiel, a grand opera, or a music drama are simply
not appropriate for the evaluation of Schumann's efforts? Writing to
J. B. Laurens on 11 August 1850, shortly after the first performances of
Genoveva in Leipzig, Schumann expressed the wish that "in time, my
endeavors in this, the dramatic field, will be accorded a just assessment."[3] If we concede that he was attempting something fundamentally
different from his predecessors, and that the nature of his departure
from the operatic mainstream has yet to be carefully analyzed, then the
absence of a "just assessment" of Schumann's endeavors in the dramatic
field should come as no surprise.

Dramatic music formed the core of Schumann's output during the
second half of his residence in Dresden. As such, it represents a continuation of his systematic march through the musical genres, its progress
suspended in part due to the psychological crises of 1844–1846. But
even more important—and herein lies the decisive factor in Schumann's
attitude toward the conjunction of music and drama—the dramatic music brings to a highpoint his lifelong effort to raise music to the level of
literary culture. Liszt, whose penchant for hyperbole often makes him a
less than reliable critic, was nonetheless right on the mark in his assertion that Schumann's desire "to appropriate the most beautiful trophies
of poetry for himself and to link his name with the likes of Goethe,
Schiller, Uhland, [and] Moore" approached fulfillment in the dramatic
and oratorical works of the Dresden years.[4] In *Genoveva*, the *Manfred*
music, and the *Faust* scenes, Schumann moved ever closer to his goal:
the reconfiguration of music as literature.

The path toward a literary opera was an arduous one. Of the fifty
subjects Schumann considered at various points, only one, the legend
of Saint Geneviève, as dramatized by Friedrich Hebbel and Ludwig
Tieck, bore fruit. His search began early. Not yet out of his teens, and
inspired by performances at La Scala in Milan, Schumann looked forward to writing a *Hamlet* opera with "fire and flame."[5] (He employed a
similar metaphor over a dozen years later when, shortly before the premiere of the *Peri*, he noted in the marriage diary: "An opera will be my
next work, and I'm fired up to proceed.")[6] Schumann's operatic ambitions intensified in the early 1840s. During the *Liederjahr*, he managed
to draft a scenario based on E. T. A. Hoffmann's *Doge und Dogaressa*, a
tale that had first attracted his attention about a decade before and that
he subsequently hoped to elaborate in operatic form as a wedding gift
for Clara. In 1842, disappointed by the uneven quality of the recent

dramatic works he was reviewing for the *Neue Zeitschrift*, he would proclaim: "We are so wanting in a German opera."[7] But again, his "morning and evening artist prayer" for a viable German opera produced little by way of tangible results. Though Immermann's *Tristan und Isolde* was earmarked for operatic treatment in 1842 and again in 1846, when Schumann approached Robert Reinick (a key player, as we shall see, in the genesis of *Genoveva*) for a libretto, nothing came of the project.[8] Plans for an opera on Shakespeare's *Tempest*, the subject of discussions between Schumann and Reinick in June 1846, suffered a similar fate.[9]

What is immediately striking about most of the texts Schumann alternately took up and rejected is their inherent literary worth. Indeed, he seems to have been just as interested in the poetic quality of his materials as in their embodiment of those traits usually deemed essential for an effective piece of musical theatre: powerful situations and memorable images. To put it in Aristotelian terms: Whereas most opera composers are chiefly concerned with the *mythos* (plot) of a potential text and the possibilities it holds out for *opsis* (spectacle), Schumann placed equal weight on *lexis* (verbal texture or diction) and *dianoia* (thought). This will be clear from his approach to Byron's *Corsair,* the only one of the operatic projects from the first half of the 1840s for which musical fragments have been preserved. Like Manfred and Golo (the villain in *Genoveva*), Conrad, the central figure of Byron's verse epic, is a misanthrope, a nobleman-robber whose withdrawal from society was motivated by injustices suffered during his youth. Not only did Schumann intend to follow the course of Byron's plot with minimal alterations, a feature demonstrated by his draft scenario,[10] he also planned to adopt much of Byron's text (in translation) intact, witness the opening Chorus of Corsairs, for which a complete musical setting survives. Schumann's recourse to melodrama, his first use of a technique that figures prominently in *Manfred,* in the transitional passage between the opening chorus and the ensuing fragment of an aria for Conrad is the extreme consequence of an attitude that gives primacy of place to the comprehensibility of a poetic text. The *Corsair* project, though dropped shortly after it was undertaken in the summer of 1844, affords us a telling premonition of the shape a "literary opera" might take.

Although Schumann did not produce an extensive body of writings on dramatic music—and although he remained profoundly suspicious of theoretical treatments of the subject, this in spite of his having read Wagner's *Oper und Drama* with keen interest,[11]—it is still possible to piece together a coherent aesthetic from the handful of opera reviews written between 1837 and 1842, from the brief notices in the *Theaterbüchlein* (1847–1850), and from comments in the correspondence.[12]

For Schumann, both the text and the music of an opera must aspire to an elevated style. (Little wonder, then, that his own dramatic works contain so many echoes of church music). "We want an overarching style for the whole," he noted in an 1842 review of Karl Reissiger's *Adele de Foix,* "a pervasively noble conception, an artist-heart beating ever vigorously."[13] According to Schumann's ideal, an ideal markedly at odds with contemporary practice, an opera should edify before it entertains. Indeed he felt that "in their intention to please the public" recent composers had actually hindered the operatic cause.[14] Given this context, it is hardly surprising that Schumann found Meyerbeer's latest extravaganzas so offensive. *Les Huguenots,* he wrote in a scathing review of 1837, plays "alternately in the brothel and in church." He pithily (and a little malevolently) summed up Meyerbeer's grand opera in three words: "debauchery, murder, and prayer."[15] But it was not Meyerbeer's sometimes shocking realism that occasioned Schumann's critical ire. On the contrary, debauchery, murder, and prayer all figure in his own *Genoveva.* Moreover, Schumann's comments on the affective intent of his only opera indicate a willingness to sacrifice surface beauty for the sake of dramatic truth and vivid representation.[16] Yet in Schumann's view, Meyerbeer's attraction to realistic themes and his fondness for striking effects were not motivated by a quest for dramatic truth, but merely by the desire to shock a sensation-hungry public. The result was a stylistic shallowness that Schumann found abhorrent. Distasteful subject matter, he seems to say, is one thing, distasteful poetry and music, quite another.

No less than his emphasis on the ethical aspect of opera, Schumann's conception of operatic melody sets him apart from most of his contemporaries, or more particularly, from his Italian (and some of his French) contemporaries, for here a nationalistic streak shows through as nowhere else in his critical writings. The popular notion of melody, Schumann argues, has been conditioned by the public's love for Italian opera. But what passes for melody among the Italians is in fact little more than "running passages, scraps of song-melodies, singly selected notes (easily sung, and perhaps pleasing) for isolated words."[17] In contrast, a "true" melodic style will unite "profundity and facility, significance and grace."[18] Thus for Schumann, melody is less a technical than an aesthetic category: "There is more melody in the first two chords of the *Eroica* Symphony . . . than in ten melodies of Bellini."[19] As this remark strongly suggests, Schumann looked to musical profundity and eloquence, and not singability, as the critical features of a truly melodic style.

In this, Schumann's outlook closely approximates Wagner's. Wagner too distinguished between the formulaic, tuneful conceits of the Italians and the eloquent musical ideas of the Germans. And like Schumann, he held up Beethoven's symphonies as works in which one "can recognize melodic significance in every note in the harmony, indeed, in every rhythmic pause."[20] But beyond this point, the composers' approaches to dramatic composition diverge sharply. Aristotle's categories can be invoked again to measure the chief differences between them. To put it simply, the gap separating Schumann's and Wagner's conception of musical drama is inscribed in the varying weight they attached to *opsis* and *dianoia*, spectacle and thought (if we understand Schumann's insistence on the technical correctness of an operatic score as a species of purely musical thought). This attitude lies behind Schumann's initially negative reaction to Wagner's *Tannhäuser*, about which he wrote to Mendelssohn shortly after its Dresden premiere on 19 October 1845:

> "Wagner has just completed an opera—he's certainly an ingenious fellow, full of the most extravagant ideas and immeasurably audacious, but believe me, he can hardly set down and think out four measures either beautifully or correctly. Precisely when it comes to voice-leading and four-part chorale harmonization, he's entirely deficient. . . . And now that the whole score lies nicely printed before us—with all its parallel fifths and octaves to boot—he would probably like to correct and erase them—but it's too late!"[21]

About a month later, after having attended a second performance of *Tannhäuser* on 22 November 1845, and perhaps swayed by Wagner's own arguments,[22] Schumann tempered his original judgment. As he put it to Mendelssohn: "Perhaps soon I'll be able to talk to you in person about *Tannhäuser;* I will have to retract much of what I wrote after merely looking at the score; from the stage everything appears quite differently. I was completely struck by much of it."[23] Although some writers have vented their frustration over this apparently contradictory stance,[24] Schumann in fact maintained a remarkable consistency in his appraisal of Wagner and his work. Writing to Heinrich Dorn on 7 January 1846, he predicted that Wagner "could become of great significance for the stage," and praised *Tannhäuser* for its "depth and originality," while at the same time conceding "certainly [the opera] contains much that's musically trivial."[25] Schumann returned to the same ideas in a letter of 8 May 1853 to Carl van Bruyck, though in this case he accented the negative: "[Wagner], if I may put it bluntly, is not a good musician; he has no sense for form or euphony. But you shouldn't judge his works from piano scores. One can't help but be deeply stimulated by many passages in his operas when heard from the stage."[26] The contradiction, in other words, resides not in Schumann's views, but in Wagner's works.

The "flaws" in their musical fabric might be sublimated in, or might even contribute to, the total theatrical effect, but in Schumann's estimation they remained flaws nonetheless. The irreconcilable cleft that Schumann located between purely musical thought and visible action or spectacle in Wagner's *Tannhäuser* may thus be viewed as one of the problems whose solution lay in the literary operas of the later Dresden years.

"Literary opera" may be a makeshift expression, but it at least captures the central tenet in Schumann's aesthetic of musical drama: the conviction that the subject matter for a musico-dramatic composition should be drawn from world literature. "Choose your material from history or from the imaginative world of poetry," he advised Carl Wettig in a letter of 8 October 1848. "Only thus can the problem be solved. Take up Shakespeare, Calderón, perhaps Boccaccio, arrange the material musically and theatrically, and then seek out a poet who will put it into verse for you!"[27] Here too Schumann's general approach varied little throughout his career: Shakespeare's *Hamlet* was to have served as the basis for his first major operatic endeavor; at about the time of the *Genoveva* premiere in the spring of 1850 he drafted a scenario for a *Romeo and Juliet* opera.[28] To be sure, Schumann was not alone in deriving inspiration from the major figures of world literature; any number of nineteenth-century opera composers (Verdi, for instance) and their librettists did likewise. What distinguishes Schumann as a musical dramatist is his additional concern for fidelity to the poetic source. His scenarios for operas based on Hoffmann's *Doge und Dogaressa*, Byron's *Corsair*, and Shakespeare's *Romeo and Juliet* retain much more of the poetic originals than would have been the norm for composers and librettists of his generation. In *Genoveva*, *Manfred*, and the *Faust* scenes, Schumann's fidelity to his poets emerges in his retention of their actual words.

The aesthetic of Schumann's literary opera thus resonates with the Hegelian philosophy of music history promulgated in Liszt's essay of 1855 on Berlioz's *Harold en Italie*.[29] From Liszt's perspective, musical genres follow an evolutionary course comparable to that of biological life-forms. Hence, these genres are historically conditioned, temporally specific entities, and not the timeless, transcendental forms that neo-classical criticism makes them out to be. The eighteenth-century oratorio, given its focus on heroes and their deeds, aptly reflected the epic spirit of the age, but for Liszt, who modelled his argument on nineteenth-century literary theory, the historical moment for the epic had passed. The music of his day demanded a genre that could "realize in a modern sense" the "meaning" of the monumental genres of earlier ages. Specifically, music was in need of an equivalent for the *modern epic*, the "philosophical epopoeia" as Liszt called it, a literary type in which bold heroes give way to brooding anti-heroes, stirring deeds to inner psychological impulses. The emphasis on Goethe's *Faust* and Byron's *Manfred* as prime examples of the modern epic is telling, for it suggests that Schumann's literary operas had just as much impact on Liszt's theorizing as Berlioz's *Harold*, the nominal subject of the essay.[30]

No doubt, there are significant differences between Liszt's and Schumann's conception of a modern musical epic. According to Liszt, the psychic workings of the characters in a philosophical epopoeia are better portrayed through the "sounding inwardness" of instrumental music (that is, through the programmatic symphony) than through a stage presentation. Yet the stage serves as the medium for two of Schumann's musico-philosophical epopoeias, *Genoveva* and *Manfred*, while the third, the *Faust* scenes, though not intended for the theatre, contains many overtly dramatic qualities. Still, Liszt's famous dictum—"Music in its masterpieces tends more and more to appropriate the masterpieces of literature"[31]—invites interpretation as a theoretical echo of Schumann's realization of the ideals of a literary opera in *Genoveva, Manfred*, and *Faust*.

The prescience of Schumann's literary operas extends from theory to practice. Indeed, my decision to subsume Schumann's dramatic works of 1848–1850 under the expression "literary opera" was motivated in part by a desire to stress their proximity to the *Literaturoper* of the early twentieth century, a genre represented by Debussy's *Pelléas et Mélisande*, Richard Strauss's *Salome*, and Berg's *Wozzeck* and *Lulu*. The texts of these work are, of course, not traditional opera libretti, but rather self-sufficient literary creations, a fact that in turn greatly influenced their musical realization as *Literaturopern*. Hence, to understand the dramaturgy of the *Literaturopern* of Debussy, Strauss, and Berg, we must first understand the dramaturgy of the plays—by Maeterlinck, Wilde, Büchner, and Wedekind, respectively—on which their operas were based. Carl Dahlhaus, who makes this point eloquently in one of the few essays devoted to this fascinating genre, traces the roots of the *Literaturoper* to Wagner's mature works. In the Wagnerian music drama, he finds the whole complex of interrelated elements that come together in the twentieth-century *Literaturoper*: a text of literary substance, a reflective musical discourse in which practically every event points to what precedes and what follows, the replacement of four-square syntax with a freely unfolding "musical prose," and the abrogation of closed forms such as arias and duets in favor of monologues and dialogues.[32] As we will see, the dramaturgy of Schumann's *Genoveva, Manfred*, and *Faust* is closely bound up with that of the poetic material on which each work draws. Likewise, the musical preconditions for *Literaturoper*—reflectivity, musical prose, open forms—are just as prominent in Schumann's dramatic compositions as in Wagner's, though they understandably assume different forms in each composer's works.

Schumann's literary operas form a tightly knit group by virtue of their many shared preoccupations. Common to them all are misanthropic, brooding, or self-centered principals: Golo in *Genoveva*, Manfred and Faust in the works bearing their names. As the notion of redemption looms large in all three literary operas, they represent a clear continuation of the thematic tendencies first essayed in the *Peri*. But most important, each work demonstrates a varied solution to the problems that ensue when music aims to appropriate a poetic model. *Genoveva* remains an obscure work in part because of the obscurity of the literary genre, the *Trauerspiel* or "play of mourning," that Schumann subjects to operatic treatment. In *Manfred*, Schumann confronts the decidedly anti-dramatic turn taken by a modern drama for which inner action is of greater moment than external event. And in the *Faust* scenes, he attempts no less than a portrayal of the circumambient world, thus providing a musical analogue for the novelistic aspects of Goethe's all-inclusive drama. Whether or not we agree with Liszt, who saw in the *Faust* settings the highpoint of Schumann's entire oeuvre, there can be little doubt that the last completed of the literary operas most nearly realizes its composer's goal: the elevation of music to the level of literary culture.

Genoveva: *From* Trauerspiel *to* Hagiographic Drama

On the evening of 25 March 1847, the Schumanns—Robert, Clara, and their two oldest children, Marie and Elise—returned to Dresden from a four-month concert tour that had taken them to Vienna, Brünn, Prague, and (after a brief respite in Dresden) Berlin. Looking back over their experiences of the past months, the artist couple would not have called the tour an extraordinary success. Wieck, who arrived in Vienna on 12 December 1846 with his foster daughter, the singer Minna Schulz, was certainly a source of annoyance. Robert and Clara suspected his hand in a snide notice placed in a January issue of Leipzig's *Signale für die musikalische Welt:* "In nine years much has changed: the artist who was deified as Clara Wieck is ignored as Clara Schumann."[33] While Clara frequently played to bored audiences, Schumann found little by way of an audience for his works at all. A performance of his First Symphony and Piano Concerto at the Gesellschaft der Musikfreunde in Vienna on New Year's Day 1847 was poorly attended, barely publicized, and, to complete the dreary picture, coolly received. According to Hanslick's eyewitness report, Clara was inconsolable: "Then Schumann spoke those unforgettable words: 'Calm yourself, Clara dear; in ten years it will all be different'. "[34] Not surprisingly, most of the Schumanns' Viennese concerts were a financial disaster (the couple in fact had to cover the 100-gulden loss incurred at the ill-fated New Year's Day concert); profits in Berlin were only modest.[35] The snags leading up to the central event of the Berlin leg of the tour, a performance of the *Peri* on 17 February 1847 by the Singakademie under Schumann's direction, also took their toll. In the first place, neither of the organization's chief directors, Mssrs. Grell and Rungenhagen (described by Clara as "kind-hearted men, but genuine old fogies"),[36] were sympathetic to what struck them as a difficult and "modern" work. Next came endless troubles with the ill-prepared vocal soloists: when it appeared as though Madame Tuczek wouldn't take the role of the Peri, the Schumanns engaged another soprano (Madame Burkhardt), only to discover that Tuczek had decided to sing after all. Then at a rehearsal two days before the concert, Grell and another of his colleagues publicly humiliated Schumann by proffering unsolicited advice on how to conduct. Miraculously, the actual performance (which Schumann had threatened to cancel) came off well enough to generate talk of scheduling a second. Still, the 17 February rendition of Schumann's oratorio left much to be desired: Parts I and II went quite well, but in Part III, three of the soloists became so hopelessly lost that Grell had to peck out their lines on the piano.[37] None of this can have worked to the benefit of Schumann's precarious recovery from the physical and psychological turmoil of the preceding years. Indeed, the composer had already fallen ill in Vienna and suffered from "great anxiety" for a day or two in Prague; similarly, anxiety resulting from the unsettling events surrounding the performance of the *Peri* landed Schumann in bed; and during the last weeks in Berlin, most of his old symptoms recurred in full force: insomnia, dizziness, exhaustion, and "nervous weakness."[38]

Nonetheless, there was one undeniably positive aspect of the Vienna-Berlin tour: it afforded Schumann a steady diet of opera and operatic culture. In early January 1847, both Schumanns fell under the sway of the famed Jenny Lind, the "lovely, splendid artist" (as Schumann described her) whose arrival in Vienna on 31 December 1846 was something of a godsend. Lind's participation in Clara's 10 January concert at the Gesellschaft der Musikfreunde helped provide a success to counter-

balance the fiasco on New Year's Day. Schumann delighted in the singer's sensitive rendition of his *Der Nussbaum* (the third song in *Myrthen*)
and likewise marvelled over her uncanny ability to grasp, practically at
sight, the interplay between text and music in his lieder; never before
had he witnessed such a "simple, natural, and deep interpretation on
seeing a composition for the first time."[39] Beginning in early January,
when they heard Lind as Marie in Donizetti's *La fille du régiment,* Robert
and Clara regularly attended both operatic and theatrical performances.
In the course of their subsequent travels to Prague and Berlin, they
witnessed a wide range of productions, including Rossini's *Barbiere* (28
January, 21 February), Meyerbeer's *Les Huguenots* (16 February, 23
March), Halévy's *La Juive* (7 March), Flotow's *Stradella* (9 March), and
Shakespeare's *King John* (12 March).[40] We can well imagine that much
of this, especially the latest French fare, was not to either Schumann's
taste. Clara, who attended the February performance of *Les Huguenots*
alone, offered a highly unflattering, if brief description of Meyerbeer:
"[he is] an unpleasant, obsequious and toadying courtier who knows
full well his power over people."[41] Schumann summed up his reaction
to the 23 March performance of Meyerbeer's opera (he could endure no
more than a single act) in two words: "insipid music."[42] Still, it seems
likely that his steady patronage of the theatre provided Schumann with
the impetus to fulfill at long last his own operatic aspirations. On 15
March, he wrote in his travel diary: "desire to write operas—plans."[43]
In short order, his desire would become an actuality.

Immediately after returning to Dresden in late March, Schumann's
thoughts turned toward dramatic music. At first he considered Byron's
Mazeppa for operatic treatment, enlisting Robert Reinick, his would-be
collaborator on the projected *Tempest* and *Tristan* operas of the year
before, as librettist. But soon his plans took a quick and decisive turn
in another direction. During the first week of April, Schumann settled
on Friedrich Hebbel's *Genoveva* as the basis for his opera, sketched an
Overture over a three-day period, completed his own scenario for the
text (which, unfortunately, does not survive), and again approached Reinick to fashion a libretto. In the ensuing month he kept in close touch
with his poet friend, at the same time immersing himself in Homer's
Odyssey, Hebbel's other dramas, including *Judith, Der Diamant,* and *Maria Magdalena,* and, perhaps at Reinick's prompting, he also read Tieck's
dramatization of the Genoveva legend.

But while the new project got off to an auspicious start, its progress
soon slackened. The text proved to be a major stumbling block; already
by 11 April, Schumann entertained the possibility of completing it himself. According to Wasielewski, Reinick, unlike Schumann, wanted to

retain a portion of the legend that figured in Tieck's drama but of which only a vestige remained in Hebbel's: the exiled Genoveva's wandering in the wilderness with her child.[44] This disagreement between composer and librettist highlights a fundamental difference in their points of view. From the start, Schumann's imagination was fired more by Hebbel's "extraordinarily powerful" drama than by the content of the popular legend on which it was based.[45] Reinick, understandably enough, intended only to provide a serviceable libretto. Yet this was precisely what the composer did *not* want. Schumann made the point with unimpeachable clarity when, dissatisfied with Reinick's efforts on the first two acts of the opera, he solicited the advice of Hebbel himself in a letter of 14 May 1847: "above all, [the completed portion of the text] is lacking in power—and conventional opera libretti are now repugnant to me; I wouldn't know how to, nor would I want to find music for such tirades."[46] Schumann's well-meaning collaborator, in other words, proceeded as if a mere opera were at stake, while Schumann envisioned a specifically *literary* opera as his ultimate goal. He emphasized, in his letter to Hebbel, that he was not asking the poet to rework his drama "operawise" ("opernhaft") but to offer guidance, for after all: "Isn't your own child asking for your protection? And should it later appear before you clad in music, I very much hope you might say 'even so I love you still'."[47]

Work on the text continued piecemeal throughout the remainder of the spring, summer, and fall of 1847, its completion interrupted by other musical projects (*Beim Abschied zu singen,* op. 84, for chorus and winds, in May and June; the first two songs published in the *Romanzen und Balladen,* op. 64, in late May; and the piano trios, opp. 63 and 80, from June through November), and also, in all likelihood, by grief over the deaths of Fanny Mendelssohn (14 May) and, on 22 June, the eighteen-month-old Emil, the Schumanns' firstborn son. Although Schumann kept in sporadic touch with Reinick during this period, the composer had clearly assumed major responsibility for shaping the *Genoveva* text, probably retaining his erstwhile librettist as an advisor on the finer points of versification. Reinick, who bore Schumann no ill will for what a more sensitive individual would have taken as a snub, further acknowledged the composer's singular role in the drafting of *Genoveva's* idiosyncratic text: "[Schumann] has reworked the text so strangely, and often adapted it so quixotically, that I can no longer recognize my little child, and must disavow it publicly. Without blaming him, I can't lend my name to the text . . . [which] is by Schumann, after Tieck and Hebbel, with at most a few verses by me."[48]

By late in 1847, the text was apparently in good enough order to allow Schumann concentrated work on the music for his opera. Between 17 and 26 December he orchestrated the sketch for the Overture, presumably left untouched since its rapid drafting in April, hence departing from the practice, common among eighteenth- and early nineteenth-century opera composers, of tackling the overture (or instrumental prelude) only after the body of the opera was written. But this unusual procedure means neither that Schumann was unaware of the "proper" method of approaching the art of operatic composition, nor that music counted for more than drama in his conception of the whole. On first reading Hebbel's *Genoveva*, he was struck by how "musically alive" its poetry was, an impression that only increased as he studied the play more carefully.[49] Schumann's sketching of the overture represented an attempt to capture something of this impression in tones, or more precisely, to provide a hint of the transformation of Hebbel's psychological thriller into a drama of redemption. In the long run, Schumann's inversion of the customary compositional practice worked to the advantage of the finished opera; the overture foreshadows its general affective thrust, moving from dejection to triumph, but by no means discloses all of its secrets.

Once he had orchestrated the overture, Schumann soon fell into a routine that carried him through the completion of the entire opera. After finishing the continuity draft for an act, generally consisting of the vocal part(s) and a skeletal piano score, he would orchestrate it, the first part of the process usually requiring no more than a week or two, the second taking up to a month. Beginning with the second act, he prefaced these activities with another step: a fairly extended period during which he brought the text for the given act into order. In essence, though, the basically two-pronged compositional process resembles the method Schumann had employed throughout the decade for his large-scale works. Considering the scope of the project and also the fact that it was, after all, his first sustained effort on an opera, the whole took shape in a relatively short time. Apart from a brief spell of "stupid hypochondria" that kept him from his work in early February 1848, and interruptions in May and June caused by preparations for the first performance of his music for the *Schlussszene* (final scene) of *Faust,* Schumann kept religiously to a regular schedule of work on his opera.[50] (While at work on Act II in February and March of 1848, Schumann began to record some of the events that shook Europe during that incredible year of revolutions: the fall of the July Monarchy in France, the Bundestag's declaration of freedom of the press, Metternich's resignation, and the Milan uprising. His concentration apparently undisturbed, Schumann pressed on with his *Genoveva.*) On 4 August 1848, he was able to write in the *Haushaltbücher:* "*Genoveva* finished, [to my] great joy, and also Clara's."[51] Clearly buoyed by the near completion of the project that had occupied him for sixteen months (and by the fulfillment of a dream extending back almost two decades), Schumann was already planning his next major work: on 29 July he read Byron's *Manfred* in the translation of Karl Adolf Suckow.

But if he thought he was finally getting into his stride as a composer of dramatic music, Schumann could not have foretold what headaches were in store for him so far as *Genoveva* was concerned. The long and frustrating tale of the attempts to find a performance venue for the opera was just about to unfold. As a resident of Dresden, its reputation as a distinguished operatic center long established, Schumann naturally hoped for a premiere at the city's Court Theatre. But his hopes for staging *Genoveva* in the Saxon capital were soon scuttled by the intrigues of the Hofkapellmeister, Carl Gottlieb Reissiger, who according to a letter of 15 November 1848 from Schumann to Christian Schmidt (the theatre's chief Regisseur) had "characterized [the opera] as highly boring."[52] Negotiations to mount the opera in other centers—Frankfurt, Berlin (where his old teacher, Heinrich Dorn, had just been appointed Royal Kapellmeister), and Weimar (where Liszt eventually did direct a performance, but not until April 1855)—likewise failed to produce immediate results. A letter to Ferdinand David dated just a week after the completion of the *Genoveva* score indicates that Schumann had already been in touch with Julius Rietz, the recently named conductor at the Leipzig Opera, concerning the possibility of a performance in his adopted hometown.[53] And while Leipzig indeed proved to be the site of the premiere, Schumann would have to endure a series of maddening and seemingly endless postponements before the production actually took place. Schumann hoped for a performance at the Leipzig Opera no later than February 1849, since "by the time the flowers start blossoming in April, no one is interested in going to the theatre."[54] But the flowers had been in bloom for some time by 23 June, when Schumann was summoned to Leipzig for rehearsals, though he remained in Dresden to see Clara through her approaching confinement; and they had long withered by November, when Schumann was promised a January 1850 performance by the new theatre directorship. January came and went, and with it the possibility of a winter premiere, for yet another administrative shift had thrown the theatre's schedule of events into disarray. Exasperated by what he took as a flagrant violation of a long-standing agreement and on the verge of calling in an attorney, Schumann vented his anger in a letter to Hermann Härtel: "I no longer have the breath to be taken for a fool."[55] His sense of betrayal reached fever pitch when in

February he learned that *Genoveva* was to be temporarily postponed in favor of, of all things, Meyerbeer's *Le Prophète*. (Schumann's entry for this work in his *Theaterbüchlein*, a blank space, speaks volumes).

Perhaps heartened by the warm reception accorded the opera's Overture on February and March concerts of the Gewandhaus Orchestra and the Hamburg Philharmonic and otherwise occupied with the fifth and sixth of the *Faust* scenes later in the spring, Schumann held his anger in check. Finally on 18 May 1850 he headed toward Leipzig for the long delayed rehearsals and production of *Genoveva*, which the composer himself would direct. But his joy over the first sessions with the singers quickly turned to consternation when the orchestral rehearsals began, making for a particularly tense atmosphere on opening night.[56] Schumann, an uneven conductor at best, was no doubt skittish about holding together such a motley throng as an operatic troupe; in addition he had to endure the scrutiny of the eager and curious members of the musical elite who had assembled for the event, a group including Spohr, Hiller, Gade, and Liszt. As recorded in Schumann's travel notes, the 25 June premiere went smoothly until "the great error" in Act III, when Carl Widemann, the singer playing Golo, forgot to produce the all-important letter (a crucial bit of evidence against the falsely charged Genoveva), thus throwing much of the cast into a protracted state of confusion.[57]

But in spite of the more assured renditions at the subsequent pair of performances (on 28 and 30 June) and the generally positive reaction from the Leipzig audience, *Genoveva* hardly scored the major triumph for which Schumann had hoped. The miniscule profits from the first performance, a mere 27 thalers, provide a telling emblem of the opera's fate. So too does Schumann's failed attempt, initiated just after the premiere, to secure a commitment from Spohr for a production in Kassel, even though the eminent Kapellmeister was not unimpressed by the opera.[58] To be sure, *Genoveva* eventually made the rounds of the principal Austro-German centers—Vienna, Berlin, Hamburg, Dresden, Weimar—and by the first decade of the twentieth century had been staged at least once in many of the major European capitals, such as London, Paris, St. Petersburg, and Prague. But by the First World War, the opera, a "work cherished with so much love" as Schumann put it to Spohr, all but disappeared from the repertory.[59]

Schumann's *Genoveva*, it would seem, has gone the way of many another *succès d'estime*. Little more than a name even to an avid operagoer, it has led a shadowy half-life in the writings of a handful of scholars and critics. What is more, the outline of a critical tradition that began to form around the work in the second half of the nineteenth century is marked by opposing stances themselves lacking in internal consistency. Caught in the crossfire between Wagner's adherents and detractors, *Genoveva* has suffered at the hands of both groups.

For a self-proclaimed progressive like Brendel, author of the first major review of the opera, Schumann's *Genoveva* is notable less for what it actually achieves than for the "surety" it holds out for a "better future."[60] Specifically, Brendel applauds Schumann's response to the formal imperative whereby an "entire opera, that is, each of its acts, *must proceed with the uninterrupted flow of a Finale*."[61] Yet measured against this standard, *Genoveva* is sure to come up short. Schumann's linking of one number to the next was by no means a novelty in 1850; almost three decades earlier Weber had done much the same in *Euryanthe*. In fact, *Genoveva* is neither a number opera nor a continuously unfolding music drama, but more properly a "scene opera." Therefore it occupies a position between "no longer" and "not yet": a dangerous position indeed when viewed by a teleologically oriented critic who takes his philosophical bearings from Hegel. In Brendel's view, Schumann may have taken a decisive "first step" toward an operatic ideal in both form and content, but Wagner, in *Tannhäuser* and even more clearly in *Lohengrin*, was travelling much farther down the same path.[62]

Thus the foundation was prepared for critics to posit an outright connection between Schumann's *Genoveva* and Wagner's principles. For Hanslick, Schumann's recourse to declamatory vocal writing, motivically dense orchestral textures, and open forms demonstrated an unmistakable gravitation toward the Wagnerian style.[63] But this tendency did not meet with the Viennese critic's approval: instead of "passionate melodies," Hanslick heard only "murky twilight and declamatory zigzag" in the music for the principals.[64] Thus the very features that would have won the approval of critics attuned to the "music of the future" occasioned nothing but censure from writers, such as Hanslick, of a more conservative stamp. Still, *Genoveva*'s detractors hardly maintained a unified front. Consider, for instance, the question of the work's melodic style. Krüger, Schumann's harshest critic on this point, characterized the opera as "a continuous recitative," tedious and incomprehensible to the average listener and the trained specialist alike.[65] In contrast, J. C. Lobe described each act as "an extended, through-composed lied."[66] Again, the discrepancies between the critical voices cancel each other out.

But perhaps no other feature of Schumann's *Genoveva* has been so widely disparaged as its text. Brendel, for instance, looked askance at the use of a ghost as the agent of the denouement in an otherwise realistic plot. Nor could he muster much enthusiasm for the principals: Genoveva aroused only compassion, the villains he found abhorrent, and

Siegfried proved to be an utter "Dummkopf" of a husband.[67] Hence Brendel would have probably concurred with George Bernard Shaw's pointed dismissal of the *Genoveva* text as "nakedly silly" from the start and "pure bosh" from the Act I Finale.[68]

Not even ardent proponents of Schumann's music would delude themselves into predicting *Genoveva*'s eventual acceptance into the standard operatic canon. Like many of the characters that populate Schumann's dramatic works, the opera will ever remain an outsider. Yet the causes for its exclusion from the repertory are arguably just as deeply rooted in the unfruitful strategies adopted by the opera's early critics as they are in the supposed deficiencies of the work itself. *Genoveva* is no more a proto-Wagnerian music drama than it is a continuous recitative, a continuous lied, or a botched adaptation of a popular legend. The contradictions and inconsistencies in the critical tradition emanate from a lack of sensitivity to what the work in fact *is:* a literary opera.

The chief distinguishing feature of literary opera is its retention, in whole or in part, of the words of its poetic source. This aspect of Schumann's conception, more so than any disagreements over the course of his opera's plot, undoubtedly motivated his gradual withdrawal from the collaboration with Reinick. Shortly after perusing Tieck's *Genoveva* in April 1847 and finding much that could be taken over without alteration, Schumann wrote somewhat disingenuously to his librettist: "If *I* serve as arranger [Bearbeiter] of the text, no one would blame me, a musician, for using [verbatim] the material at hand; you however, to preserve your good name, would have to guard against direct allusions [to already written dramas], and therefore I, as the composer, would have to forfeit much that two poets [Tieck/Hebbel] created so effectively."[69] Schumann would underscore his near elimination of a mediating hand between poetic original and operatic text in his subtitle for the published score of *Genoveva*: "*Oper in vier Acten nach Tieck und F. Hebbel.*"

But poetry not originally intended for musical setting may present challenges that the straightforward verse forms of conventional libretti are meant to circumvent. At the opening of the Act III Finale of *Genoveva*, a marvelously spooky scene in which Margaretha summons up images of the past from her magic mirror, Schumann draws liberally on the text from Act IV, scene 6 of Hebbel's play. Much of the poet's description of the weird apparatuses cluttering the witch's den is even replicated in Schumann's stage directions. To establish an appropriately eerie mood for Margaretha's narrative of her dream vision of the child she once drowned, Schumann employs in his orchestral introduction a panoply of effects from the contemporary horror opera: a chromatically meandering figure in the lower strings, tense tremoli, ominous pizzicati, and piercing shrieks from the winds. The text of Margaretha's monologue, which Schumann took over almost verbatim from the opening and close of her twenty-seven-line speech in Hebbel's play, likewise demanded special musical treatment. Although the verses proceed throughout in iambic pentameter, their metric regularity is obscured by a number of factors: the absence of rhyme, the curt, fragmented units from which the opening lines are built up, and the prominence of enjambement toward the end of the monologue. Schumann, in other words, was faced with the problem of fashioning a musically coherent realization of a poetic text that was, for all intents and purposes, prose. In response to the dilemma he cast Margaretha's vocal line in the arioso style of the *Rezitativischer Gesang*, a melodic category developed for the *Peri*, while the music of the orchestral introduction, first restated, then varied, provided motivic support (Example 10.1). Margaretha's line, which faithfully imitates the short-breathed phrases of the text, is imparted syntactic sense by a series of regularly alternating two-measure units in the orchestra (and an overall AAB, or bar form). The resultant "musical prose" is no "declamatory zigzag" (as Hanslick might have called it), but a calculated reaction to the demands of literary opera.

The modified retention of a poetic text is but one aspect, however, of a broader issue: the reflection, in a literary opera, of the dramaturgical qualities of the poetic source. Schumann compounded his difficulties by conflating *two* sources, Hebbel's *Genoveva* (1841) and Tieck's *Leben und Tod der heiligen Genoveva* (1799), and also compounded ours by fastening on what is today a little-known genre: the *Trauerspiel*, a drama whose primary aim is the display of human misery, wretchedness, and suffering. Martin Opitz, writing when the genre came into its own in the mid-seventeenth century, relates that the *Trauerspiel* "deals only with the commands of kings, killings, despair, infanticide and patricide, conflagration, incest, war and commotion, lamentation, weeping, sighing, and suchlike."[70] This litany of woes resonates more powerfully with Hebbel's than with Tieck's dramatization, this in spite of the fact that the earlier and not the later play is specifically designated as a *Trauerspiel*. Indeed, Hebbel's *Genoveva* touches on most of the themes in Opitz's list; only patricide and incest are omitted. His drama focuses on the tragic predicament of the steward Golo: torn between loyalty to his master, Siegfried, and sensual desire for his mistress, Genoveva, he ultimately takes his own life. Genoveva, falsely accused of adultery and forced into exile, likewise perishes before her husband can save her. In

Example 10.1. Genoveva: Act III Finale, opening.

contrast, Tieck is less concerned with the psychology of forbidden passions than with painting a sympathetic portrait of his long-suffering
heroine; as in Hebbel's play, Genoveva dies in the end, but in the arms
of her husband, and only after having attained to a kind of saintliness.
In conflating these two sources, Schumann gradually shifts the center of
gravity from Golo to Genoveva. The dramaturgical shape of his text is
thus transformational. (That Schumann allows Genoveva to survive beyond her reunion with Siegfried is not the sentimental legerdemain that
some critics have made it out to be; the decisive point is for the drama
to achieve closure, and this it does with Genoveva's salvation through
the mystical powers of the Cross.) To put it succinctly, Schumann's *Gen-*

oveva begins as a *Trauerspiel,* a play of mourning, and ends as a hagiographic drama of redemption. The passage from one to the other determines the large-scale design of this literary opera.

Hence, although Schumann's *Genoveva* invokes a number of specifically operatic genres—grand opera (in the Act II Finale, where Genoveva is taunted by an angry mob), horror opera (in the scene with Margaretha's magic mirror), and rescue opera (at the close of the work)—it relies heavily on the traditions of the spoken theatre.[71] Its obscurity is arguably a function of the obscurity of the *Trauerspiel,* the genre whose dramaturgy colors much of the opera and which Schumann knew not only through its modern offshoots in the plays of Tieck and Hebbel, but also in its original seventeenth-century form. Long viewed as little more than a bizarre and ill-conceived precursor of eighteenth-century neoclassical drama, the *Trauerspiel* was salvaged for criticism by Walter Benjamin's difficult but brilliant study, *Ursprung des deutschen Trauerspiels* (1925). While a detailed account of this still controversial book would be out of place here, it will be helpful to review some of the chief features of the *Trauerspiel* as articulated by Benjamin, all of which, as we will see, are reflected both dramatically and musically in Schumann's *Genoveva.*

In contrast to the tragedy, which is grounded in myth and reënacts the fall of a hero who is ethically superior to the gods, the *Trauerspiel* is firmly grounded in history and thus portrays the transience of mundane existence. Its central character is either a tyrant, who arouses fear, or a martyr, who arouses pity, both characters sharing an important trait: as earthly representatives of the godhead, they embody the dialectic between human and divine qualities that distinguishes Christ. Moreover, the genre's highly developed allegorical code, in Benjamin's interpretation, emerges as a further manifestation of the fundamentally dialectical nature of the Christian Savior.[72] While there is little evidence that Schumann knew the grim dramas of Lohenstein, Gryphius, and Hartmann, the principal seventeenth-century German proponents of the genre, he had expressed since his youth a lively interest in the works of Calderón,[73] the figure who, for Benjamin, brought the "play of mourning" to its perfect form.[74] Whereas the works of the German baroque playwrights are "taken up entirely with the hopelessness of the earthly condition," Calderón's dramas often culminate with the restoration of order through an act of grace.[75] Thus it was perhaps from Calderón (especially his *Life is a Dream*) that Schumann derived a model for the positive ending in *Genoveva.*[76]

In fact, Schumann's literary opera replicates the entire complex of dramaturgical features that Benjamin associated with the *Trauerspiel.*

When Schumann, in a letter to Dorn of 6 November 1849, referred to his *Genoveva* as a *Lebensgeschichte*, he was not, as some writers have assumed, alluding to its purportedly autobiographical overtones,[77] but rather contrasting its historical realism with the mythological tone of "the old sentimental tale."[78] Temporally situated in the eighth century, the action of *Genoveva* unfolds in the wake of the journey of Siegfried, Count Palatine and commander of Charles Martel's army, to do battle with the Moorish infidels who have entered France from Spain. In this context, the modally tinged chorale that consecrates his departure at the beginning of the opera and celebrates his reunion with Genoveva at its close not only frames the work with a patina of religiosity, but also serves as an emblem for removal into the distant past.[79] Schumann's placement of a sixteenth- or seventeenth-century chorale into the mouths of an eighth-century Catholic community is no doubt both anachronistic and naturalistically suspect, but these incongruities hardly interfere with the melody's function as an agent of historicity.

Of the two principal types of *Trauerspiel*, the tyrant drama and the martyr drama, *Genoveva* clearly belongs to the latter category, where, according to G. P. Harsdörffer's definition of 1648: "The hero [or heroine] must be the perfect embodiment of all virtues and must be afflicted by the faithlessness of friends and enemies; and yet in such a way that he [or she] shows magnanimity in all circumstances and courageously overcomes the pain which causes sighing, loud cries, and much lamentation."[80] If, as Benjamin put it, the male tyrant restores order in a state of *political* emergency, then the female martyr puts down *moral* emergencies by maintaining her chastity in situations where the emotions of others threaten to spin out of control.[81] Hence the plot of the martyr drama will often hinge on the loss of the heroine's honor through deception wrought by scheming courtiers and its reinstatement through an act of grace.[82] In Schumann's *Genoveva*, the conniving Margaretha and the lust-driven Golo act as dual agents of intrigue; the theme of deception is employed as a logically organizing force for much of the action. The four acts of the opera each fall into two scene-complexes,[83] and of the resultant tableaux, fully half turn on a deceptive ploy: in the Act I Finale, Golo is taken in by Margaretha's trickery; in the second scene-complex of Act II, Drago, the faithful courtier, is in turn duped by Golo; in Act III, Siegfried falls first under Golo's sway, then Margaretha's. It is only fitting that Golo, the central tragic character, should be at once deceiver and deceived.

Brendel was merely the first of several critics to fault Schumann for the many apparently unmotivated twists in the action of his *Genoveva* text.[84] But as it turns out, the rapid-fire shift from one state of affairs to another (Golo's passionate love for Genoveva, to take an example from Act II, turns to hatred in a flash) is fundamental to the dramaturgy of the *Trauerspiel*, bringing together the themes of history's contingency and shock born of deception. The seemingly arbitrary maneuvres of the characters thus highlight their helplessness in the face of the unpredictable whims of history. (As Benjamin expressed it with the aid of a particularly colorful metaphor: the desperate human figures in the *Trauerspiel* "sway about like torn and flapping banners").[85] Schumann even encodes the shock principle into the musical fabric: the discovery, capture, and murder of Drago in Genoveva's bedchamber (Act II Finale) all transpire in a mere seven bars.

As we have noted, the principal characters in the *Trauerspiel* may be viewed as representatives of the figure of Christ insofar as they embody his dual essence, at once human and divine. For Benjamin, the dialectic between these qualities is irreconcilable, yet it pervades the seventeenth-century *Trauerspiel* at practically every level in the form of allegory, the significative mode wherein signifier and signified, like the human and divine aspects of Christ's earthly counterparts, are separated by an unbridgable gap. Indeed, Benjamin devoted a substantial portion of his study to the *Trauerspiel*'s emblematic code and its decipherment.[86] In Schumann's *Genoveva* text, the emblems have been reduced to a minimum: the magic mirror from which Margaretha conjures up false images of the past (Act III Finale), the sword and ring that Golo displays to Genoveva as proof of Siegfried's resolve to see her punished (Act IV, No. 17), and the Cross that ensures the heroine's salvation (Act IV, Nos. 16, 18). The emblematic quality of Schumann's *Genoveva* manifests itself more clearly still in the musical fabric, through the interplay of referential motives and timbres.

But here we should introduce an important qualification. Many critics, following the lead of those early commentators who detected a Wagnerian stratum in Schumann's work, have argued for the existence of a leitmotivic system in Schumann's opera—a highly questionable claim. Judged against Wagner's leitmotif technique, Schumann's is certain to seem deficient. Often taking on a life of their own, Schumann's "leitmotifs" frequently appear either curiously out of synch with the perspectives of the characters they supposedly represent or decidedly lacking in individuality. Consider, for instance, the motive usually associated with Genoveva. It first appears in the Overture, buried in the transitional passage linking first and second groups (Example 10.2a). Shorn of its continuation, it heads off the close of the duet of parting (No. 3) for Siegfried and Genoveva (Example 10.2b). A further variant, markedly different from the original in character if not in shape, plays

Example 10.2a. Genoveva, Overture: "Genoveva" motive.

Der   dich   mir   gab

Example 10.2b. from *Genoveva*, No. 3.

an important role in the music for Margaretha in the Act I Finale (Example 10.2c). Missing both its characteristic octave leap and its continuation, the motive sounds in the orchestra as Genoveva prepares to retire in No. 10 (Example 10.2d) and insinuates itself into her vocal line as she attempts to prove her innocence in the Act II Finale (Example 10.2e). But in fact the motives given as Examples 2a, b, d, and e are not really leitmotifs at all: 2a is without referential specificity; 2b is too briefly elaborated to make much of an impression; 2d takes the original motivic shape too far afield; 2e embeds the characteristic intervals of the first motive in a relatively neutral vocal phrase. Only 2c, which is much more Margaretha's property than Genoveva's, is accorded the gestural profile, the elaborative extension, and the referential fixity required of a leitmotif, or more precisely, of a musical emblem of deception. To

Example 10.2c. from *Genoveva*, No. 7 (Act I Finale).

Example 10.2d. from *Genoveva*, No. 10.

O   nehmt Euch mei - ner an!

Example 10.2e. from *Genoveva*, No. 12 (Act II Finale).

be sure, its employment in Nos. 7, 8, and 15 makes it just as much a part of Margaretha's evil world as the accoutrements of her witch's den. (As we shall see, Schumann also makes prominent use of a very similar melodic idea in the *Faust* scenes as a signature motive for a complex of related conceits: deception, evil, guilt, and lust.) In addition, Margaretha is associated throughout much of the score with distinctive gestural and timbral effects as well: impish phrases for flute and piccolo, disjointed pizzicato fragments, all of them ciphers for the grotesque.

Golo, as Margaretha's accomplice in crime, understandably enough partakes of her musical-emblematic world. The opening idea of the Act I Finale (Example 10.3), a motive first presaged in the Overture, generates a number of variants shared by both intriguers in the mock triumphant conclusion of No. 7 (Act I Finale), and also in Nos. 8, 9, and 10. Golo also lays claim to a pair of motives more specifically his own: a rising and falling figure of narrow compass whose low registral placement and ominous trill suggest little more than a rumble (Example 10.4; heard in the Overture and Nos. 9, 17, and 18); and a more extended, ascending idea, in essence a free inversion of Margaretha's signature motive, its faltering rise tinged with chromaticism (Example 10.5; prominent in Nos. 7, 8, 14, and 15). An ambivalent partner in the plot to slander Genoveva, Golo is at once bound to and differentiated from his co-conspirator. While Margaretha's music is marked by spiky articulations and piercing timbres, Golo's motives are more often coupled with broad legatos and the somber colors of the low strings. The chief dialec-

Example 10.3. *Genoveva*, No. 7, opening.

Example 10.4. *Genoveva*, Overture, mm. 4–5.

Example 10.5. from *Genoveva*, No. 7.

tic in this conflicted character—his inability to balance the claims of emotions born of rampant power on the one hand and chivalric devotion on the other[87]—is further reflected in his voice type: unlike the typical operatic villain (which he certainly is not), Golo is not cast as a baritone or bass but as a lyric tenor.

The almost total lack of an emblematic dimension in the music for Genoveva should not be interpreted as a sign of Schumann's inadequacies as a dramatist. On the contrary, his decision to deny the heroine a complex of referential motives and timbres is intentionally bound up with the dualistic nature of his poetic text. For Genoveva, while a descendant of the martyr in the Baroque *Trauerspiel*, is at the same time the medium through which the genre is transcended. Schumann encodes this transcendance musically in the primarily lyric tone of Genoveva's utterances. Her lack of fixed musical emblems is thus a function of her role in a literary opera that evolves from a *Trauerspiel* into a hagiographic drama of redemption.

The passage from one dramatic type to the other, however, is mediated by a specifically operatic genre. In the Act III Finale, where the intriguers' plans are foiled by Drago's emergence from Margaretha's magic mirror, Schumann invokes the dark and eerie stock-in-trade of the horror opera. While Marschner's *Hans Heiling* or *Der Templer und die Jüdin* may have provided models for Margaretha's dream narrative at the beginning of the Finale,[88] the Wolfs' Glen scene (especially the portion devoted to the casting of the magic bullets) from Weber's *Der Freischütz* was almost certainly the source for the central incantation episode, one of the most memorable passages in the entire work. With a wickedly hortatory "Erscheint!", Margaretha summons up three deceptive images from her magic mirror (Schumann was obviously not averse to the spectacular side of the music dramatist's art, so long as the situation demanded it), each intended to offer Siegfried increasingly vivid evidence of Genoveva's adulterous affair with Drago. Linked with music of a pastoral quality—mellifluous offstage sopranos answered by graceful wind figures and supported by a rocking accompaniment in the strings—the first image places Genoveva and her supposed lover in a quiet evening landscape. The pace quickens for the second image, a representation of Genoveva and Drago intimately chatting in a bower by moonlight. And just as the vocal texture is amplified by the addition of two tenors, so the pastoral gives way to a decidedly chivalric tone, the rising figures in the horns at once emblems for distance, courtly pomp, and forbidden love. With the third image, in which Genoveva welcomes Drago into her chamber, the intensification is complete: at breakneck speed the full chorus breathlessly delivers a jaunty tune whose text is as crudely suggestive as its music is purposefully banal. But in the end, Margaretha's trickery turns against her, for through the shards of the magic mirror, smashed by Siegfried in a fit of anger, steps the ghost of Drago himself. An emissary of divine forces, Drago's spirit precipitates a definitive reversal in the intriguers' fortunes; the stage is set for the unfolding of the hagiographic drama in Act IV.

Indeed, the decisive move from the gloomy atmosphere of the *Trauerspiel* to the hopeful tone of the quasi-religious drama comes in the remarkable scene-complex that opens and occupies well over half of the final act. Again, Schumann alludes unmistakably to Weber, in this case to the opening scene-complex of the final act of *Euryanthe.*[89] Weber situates his falsely accused heroine in a barren ravine by moonlight, where her erstwhile beloved, Adolar, plans to put her to death; likewise, the unjustly slandered Genoveva is lead into a wild and rocky region by the heartless retainers Caspar and Balthasar, her desperate plight mirrored by increasing darkness at the approach of a storm. Musically, both scenes present a flexible mixture of brief but suggestive orchestral tone-portraits, rhetorically profiled ariosos, song-like episodes, and dramatically charged dialogues. Likewise, both evolve as expansive tableaux internally unified by a network of motivic and textural recurrences.[90] At the same time, there is a crucial difference between the scenes. Weber's culminates in a powerful, decalmatory arioso in which Euryanthe invokes the heavely hosts to protect Adolar in his battle with a fierce serpent. In contrast, at the heart of Schumann's scene (and of the opera as a whole) is a bipartite aria for Genoveva that builds to one of the composer's most impressive passages of sustained lyricism. The aria begins as a lament, the heroine's nervous desperation aptly conveyed by an often chromatic vocal line, anxiously shifting harmonies, and undulating figures in the strings. But when Genoveva catches sight of the glowing Cross on which she also descries a picture of the Virgin—a moment underscored by two long-held dominant-sevenths of B♭ in the winds— the character of her music alters drastically. As Genoveva kneels in rapt adoration of the heavenly image, lament gives way to prayer, a sumptuously lyrical invocation unfolding in three stages: a songful opening that blends melodic simplicity (a cipher for Genoveva's childlike awe) with a supple phrase syntax; a central section of growing intensity in which the magical harmonic shifts, quietly intoning off-stage chorus, and climactic entreaty to "Almightly God" go hand in hand with the heroine's envelopment in the rosy light emanating from the Cross; and a gradual dissolution of the music of the opening lied. The decisive turn to lyricism in

Genoveva's heavenly vision thus articulates the crucial shift from deception to religious transcendence in the theme of Schumann's literary opera.

According to Benjamin, the seventeenth-century *Trauerspiel*, like the age it reflects, knows no eschatology: "The religious man of the baroque era clings so tightly to the world because of the feeling that he is being driven along to a cataract with it."[91] An element of this bleak outlook even holds in the more optimistic plays of Calderón, where grace is bestowed by a king who emerges as "a *secularized* redemptive power."[92] But Benjamin likewise stressed the rootedness of the baroque *Trauerspiel* in a dramatic genre with clear religious overtones: its immediate precursor was not the tragedy of classical antiquity but the Passion Play of the Middle Ages.[93] Similarly, in *Genoveva* Schumann can be said to have restored a transcendental dimension to what had been, since the seventeenth century, a primarily earthbound genre. Nowhere is this clearer than in the work's most striking image. If the various emblems in the *Trauerspiel* group themselves about the corpse,[94] the emblematic focus of Schumann's literary opera, the image that inspired the luminous music for Genoveva's prayer in the final act, is the Cross.

Manfred *and the Modern Drama*

On 29 July 1848, a week before completing *Genoveva*, Schumann noted in the *Haushaltbücher*. "Busy—Byron's Manfred."[95] This was not his first encounter with what Byron himself, in a March 1817 letter to Thomas Moore, referred to as a "sort of mad Drama" or "Bedlam tragedy;"[96] nearly two decades earlier, it cost Schumann a restful night's sleep.[97] But in 1848, the idiosyncratic work evoked a comparably idiosyncratic response from the composer: a condensed adaptation of Byron's (translated) text in which spoken dialogue alternates with fifteen brief instrumental pieces, vocal solos and ensembles, choruses, and melodramas, the whole prefaced by an overture of imposing proportions.

"Never have I devoted myself to a composition with such love and energy as to Manfred," Schumann confided to Wasielewski.[98] And to be sure, the second of his literary operas took shape in a remarkably short time. The very day after finishing *Genoveva* he was occupied with a draft of the text. While much of September was devoted to the *Album für die Jugend*, Schumann returned in mid-October to *Manfred*, sketching and scoring the overture by the end of the month. If anything, his pace accelerated as he set to work on the body of the drama. The sketch for the first of its three parts was completed in a single day (6 November), the orchestrated version in two. The second and third parts achieved their finished form by 17 and 23 November, respectively. The music for the entire drama, in other words, required just over a month of fairly concentrated labor.[99]

Writing to Carl Montag shortly after the Weimar premiere of the work under Liszt in June 1852, Clara noted that *Manfred* "won't have much effect on the general public; the whole will leave a poetic impression . . . only on more cultured listeners."[100] By and large, her prediction has proven accurate. Only the overture has gained something of a place in the standard repertory. Most listeners would have to agree with the composer's assessment of this impressive tone portrait as one of his "most powerful children."[101] Indeed, the persistently dark-hued and unremittingly passionate overture (cast in the unusual key of E♭ minor) demonstrates brilliantly that the lessons of the "New Way" had hardly been forgotten: instead of themes, Schumann employs a web of motivic particles brought into ever new relationships through the dual workings of developing variation and the *ars combinatoria*. While it has become an analytical cliché to maintain that a well-wrought composition grows from its first few bars, the truism accurately describes the musical events in this case. The introduction to the overture opens with three interrelated ideas (Example 10.6): *a*, three syncopated chords delivered in quick tempo *(Rasch)* by the full orchestra; then, after an abrupt shift to slow tempo *(Langsam)*, *b*, a painfully slow chromatic ascent from A through B♭ to C♭ (supported by the bassline of *a*, sequenced up a third); and *c*, a complementary descent to E♭ accompanied by richly chromatic harmonies. The last two ideas then serve as a generating source for almost the whole of the ensuing music. In mm. 6 and 7, *b* is coupled with a countermelody that, at *In leidenschaftlichem Tempo*, provides the point of departure for the principal idea *(d)* of the main, sonata-form portion of the overture (Example 10.7). The latter is in turn elaborated, through developing variation, in the course of the second group and with even more striking consequences in the development. Likewise, the unstable harmonies of *c* undergird a new melodic idea *(e)* first presented during the transition from first to second group and subsequently discussed at some length during the second group and in the coda (Example 10.8). Contrapuntal manipulation and thorough-going motivicism come together in a work where everything is related to nearly everything else.

At the same time, this apparently abstract play of musical ideas can be said to serve a poetic end. According to Hugo Wolf, an enthusiastic apologist for the *Manfred* overture, Schumann's music "has brought the essence, the focal point of the drama to plastic expression with the simplest strokes." Less justifiable is his claim to the effect that "Schumann's

Example 10.6. Manfred, Overture, mm. 1–8.

Example 10.7. Manfred, Overture, motive *d*.

Overture tells us just as much as Byron's three-act dramatic poem."[102] What it *does* convey, however, is a sense for the character of Byron's grim anti-hero. Consider, for instance, the closing paragraphs of the overture, where Schumann subtly weaves together a whole complex of ideas: a somber brass chorale (presaged in the development), the initial melody of the second group, and the transitional figure *e*. A gradual process of liquidation begins as the headmotif (f^1 in Example 10.9) of the second-group melody is detached from its continuation and repeated hypnotically as a foil to the receding strains of the chorale. A melodically compressed variant (f^2) in turn replicates the intervallic shape and actual pitch content of motive *b* from the slow introduction, so that the return of the introductory music itself to round out the overture appears as a logical consequence of what has gone before. The recapitulation of the introductory music of course ensures closure, but more important, it signals defeat. The widely ranging shapes of the ideas developed out of the germinal figures of the introduction collapse, exhausted, into their original forms. The masterfully handled liquidation in the coda emerges as a cipher for the inwardness, the destructive solipsism of the central character in Byron's "mad drama."

Much of the music for the body of the drama is of a diametrically opposite character, its gossamer lightness in marked contrast to the somber ethos of the overture. While the full textures of the latter resonate with the symphonic products of the New Way, the deft treatment of the instrumental forces in the music for the drama itself recalls a lighter tone redolent of the *Peri*. In No. 1, for instance, the first of the four spirits "of the unbounded universe" (Air, Water, Earth, and Fire) summoned to quell Manfred's unrest is accompanied by a disembodied orchestral texture featuring a cantilena in the muted solo violin and impish triplet figures for two violas. The melodrama for Manfred and the Chamois Hunter (No. 4) involves only the English horn as instrumental support, the striking combination of speech and unaccompanied woodwind tone no doubt a reaction to the "natural music" of the shepherd's pipe sounding in the distance. Schumann responded to Manfred's invocation of the Witch of the Alps ("Rufung der Alpenfee," No. 6), who appears under a rainbow spanning a mountain stream, with an exquisite sonic mixture: a scurrying line in the upper register of the muted first violins, delicate melodic snippets in the winds, and repeated C♯ harmonics in the harp. The most beautiful passage in the score—the music accompanying Manfred's encounter with Astarte—is at the same time

Example 10.8. Manfred, Overture, motive *e*.

Example 10.9. Manfred, Overture, motives f^1 and f^2.

built from the simplest elements. As Manfred pleads with the spirit of his beloved to let him hear "the voice which was my music," a continuous melodic stream begins to unfold in the orchestra. The tender scoring—wisps of melodies shared by violins and winds, murmuring eighths in the violas—provides an otherworldly backdrop for Manfred's opening speech. And Astarte's first utterance, "Manfred!" takes on a magical aura through the third-related harmonic shift from the dominant of E to the dominant of C. In short, the music that Byron's spirits elicited from Schumann is as evanescent as the spirits themselves.[103]

Still, it is not difficult to understand why commentators have found less to recommend in the music for the body of the drama than in the overture: there seems to be so little of it, and what there is seems curiously insubstantial.[104] But to consider the music somehow independently of the text is precisely to miss the point, for in the second of his literary operas Schumann effects a radical reversal in the traditional relationship between word and tone. If, in the overture, the poetic subject, Manfred's solipsism, is practically swallowed up by the density of the musical elaboration, then in the presentation of the drama itself, music all but retreats into the background, where it serves as the disembodied voice against which the action (an inner action, but an action nonetheless) plays itself out.

Schumann's title underscores the pre-eminence of the text in his conception: *Manfred: Dramatisches Gedicht in drei Abtheilungen von Lord Byron mit Musik von Robert Schumann*. He stressed the same point in a letter to Liszt concerning the possibility of a Weimar performance of the work: "*[Manfred]* should not be advertised to the public as opera, Singspiel, or melodrama, but as a 'dramatic poem with music.'—That would be completely new and unprecedented."[105] Although Schumann viewed his *Manfred* as a sui generis creation, we will do little violence to his conception by placing the work under the rubric "literary opera," so long as the phrase is taken to refer to a musico-dramatic work that not only draws liberally on the words of its poetic source but also endeavors to reproduce its dramaturgy.

There is, of course, one aspect in which Schumann's outlook on *Manfred* apparently departs from Byron's. The composer's comments to Liszt speak to his desire for an at least partially staged performance: "I am convinced that the appearances of the spirits must naturally be given physical representation."[106] Byron, on the other hand, was altogether more ambivalent on the theatrical dimension of his work. In a letter to John Murray, he described it as both "a kind of Poem in dialogue (in blank verse) or drama" and as "*quite impossible* for the stage."[107] Yet the two artists were perhaps not so far apart after all. Byron's notion of an unstageable drama finds a parallel in the fusion of dramatic ostentation and lyric inwardness in Schumann's genre designation *(Dramatisches Gedicht).*

So far as the text is concerned, Schumann is more faithful to Byron than he was to either Hebbel or Tieck in *Genoveva.* Of the 1,336 verses of the original drama, he retained 975, almost without altering a word in Suckow's translation. In trimming the original down to size, Schumann systematically dispensed with Byron's allusions to predestination and classical antiquity (and also softened the oblique references to Manfred's incestuous relationship with Astarte, an understandable cause of the central character's guilt).[108] A logical outcome of Schumann's desire to place the poetic text in the foreground is his extensive reliance on melodrama, the conjunction of unadorned speech and accompanying, sometimes illustrative instrumental music. This technique, frequently employed as a special effect in the horror opera, figures in no less than ten of the drama's fifteen musical numbers. In deference to his concern for verisimilitude, Schumann generally allows only the inhabitants of the spirit world to sing, while the human figures, Manfred, the Chamois Hunter, and the Abbot, are accorded melodramatic treatment. In fact, Manfred's expressly stated inability to sing makes him into a cipher for *logos,* just as his lost spirituality is allegorized through Astarte, the "voice" that was his music. At the same time, Manfred wishes that he *were* music: "A bodiless enjoyment—born and dying / With the blest tone which made me." The delicate wash of sounds in which his words are bathed thus functions as a constant reminder to us, the listeners, of the spiritualized, disembodied state, the original condition of harmony, that he yearns to recapture.

If Schumann's Manfred is less pessimistic, less vehemently anticlerical, and less resistant to salvation than Byron's, the composer nonetheless demonstrated a deep understanding for the problem of the poet's eminently modern drama. According to the critic Peter Szondi, the drama of the last century or so has had to confront a crisis, namely, a form at odds with a peculiarly undramatic content. Beginning with the ancient tragedians, drama has aimed to represent interpersonal relationships through the medium of dialogue. Its focus, therefore, is very much a present in which every moment contains the seeds of the moment to follow. But in the plays of Ibsen, Hauptmann, Chekhov, and Strindberg, dialogue gives way to monologue, or to monologic responses framed as conversation, for the simple reason that the content of the drama is no longer the present but the past. Given this context, the present becomes little more than an occasion for conjuring up forgotten or repressed events. As a consequence of its obsession with the past, the modern

drama thus becomes more and more susceptible to the incursion of
epic elements, whose appropriateness for the dramatic genre has been
questioned since Aristotle's time.[109]

Already in the early nineteenth century, we see this problem fully
expressed in Byron's *Manfred*. A chronic sufferer from ennui, misan-
thropy, melancholy, and remorse, its central character finds himself incapable of forging lasting interpersonal relationships. In spite of its outwardly dialogic form, Byron's drama is in essence a protracted
monologue for its brooding anti-hero. Many of the other figures with
whom he comes into contact are little more than self-projections. What
little action the drama can claim centers on an attempt to cope with a
past that the chief character would sooner obliterate than face. Hence it
is for good reason that Byron leaves the cause of Manfred's remorse—
his incestuous affair with Astarte—half unexplained. The memory of
forbidden love becomes a cipher for the past from which the title character seeks, with increasing urgency, to extricate himself.

Schumann's music provides palpable evidence that the composer
firmly grasped the central dilemma of Byron's drama. In the opening
scene, Manfred asks the spirits for release from the tortures of a secret
that even he can barely recall. Schumann projects this dialectic between
forgetfulness and memory through a delicate tissue of understated reminiscences, musical ciphers for a vaguely remembered past. Manfred's
attempt to clutch the beautiful female shape of which he has a vision in
No. 2 brings with it a reference to the sinuous continuation of the second theme (motive *e*) from the Overture. The pastoral scenes straddling
Parts I and II (Nos. 4, 5, and 6) likewise share a number of ideas:
echoes of the jaunty shepherd's tune from the "Alpenkuhreigen," No. 4,
infiltrate the middle section of No. 5. The closing gesture of the latter
(a relative of the descending triadic figure already employed at the end
of the Overture) in turn prefaces Manfred's invocation of the Witch of
the Alps in No. 6. The drama's pivotal scene-complex (Nos. 7–11), Manfred's appearance in the Hall of Arimanes, the underworld spirit whom
he convinces to summon the dead, likewise features a network of thematic recurrences binding the five numbers to one another and to the
surrounding music as well. As Nemesis conjures up Astarte's spirit (No.
10), the violins present an eerie, winding melody whose headmotif recalls the brief figure shared by Nos. 5 and 6 and the close of the overture. A variant of the incantational melody from No. 10 accompanies
Manfred's plea for the silent Astarte to speak at the opening of No. 11.
(The resonance of this initiatory phrase extends beyond the *Manfred*
music to the orchestral prelude to the *Peri*, with which it shares the
same key, texture, and melodic shape. For Schumann, Byron's brooding

anti-hero and the Peri are both seekers in a quest for redemption.) The disappearance of Astarte's image near the conclusion of the same scene provides the occasion for two melodic reminiscences: first, a reference to the sinuous motive *e* from the Overture and No. 2 (its role as a musical symbol for Astarte now firmed), and second, an allusion in the winds to the rising fourth figure associated with the last two spirits in No. 1. The music for this scene-complex not only looks to the past but also prefigures the coming denouement. Hence, an important strand in the densely woven contrapuntal texture of No. 12, a gracefully arpeggiated dominant seventh chord followed by a melodic appoggiatura, recalls the tender affect of the music supporting Manfred's all-too-brief exchange with Astarte in No. 11. In addition, Manfred takes leave of the setting sun in No. 13 to the same music that had articulated Astarte's first utterance—"Manfred!"—in their earlier exchange. It is no accident that Schumann's *Manfred* makes more consistent use of motivic recall than any of his other literary operas. His recourse to a fundamentally epic technique goes a long way toward resolving the inherent contradiction in a modern drama whose focus on the past is stubbornly resistant to dramatic treatment.

This fact may help us to place a much-disputed aspect of Schumann's *Manfred* in its proper perspective. Byron's drama ends on an equivocal note. The dying Manfred, unmoved by the Abbot's entreaty that he make his peace with the heavenly powers, asks for the older man's hand:

> ABBOT: Cold—cold—even to the heart—
> But yet one prayer—Alas! how fares it with thee?
> MANFRED: Old man! 'tis not so difficult to die
> [MANFRED expires]
> ABBOT: He's gone—his soul hath ta'en its earthless flight;
> Whither? I dread to think—but he is gone.

In Schumann's work, there is less doubt over the destination of the "earthless flight" of Manfred's soul. The solemn intoning of the Introit from the Requiem Mass to the accompaniment of the organ, the jubilant turn from minor to major for the setting of "Et lux perpetua" after Manfred's death, the brief allusion to the "Astarte" theme, the hopeful plagal cadence at the very close, all this suggests that Schumann's Manfred attains to heavenly grace (this in spite of his scorn for the church and its dogmas) through the agency of his departed beloved. Nietzsche, for one, had little sympathy for the religious and sentimental overtones implicit in Schumann's decision to redeem Byron's heroic nihilist: "his Manfred music is a mistake and misunderstanding to the point of an injustice."[110]

Yet regardless of Schumann's undeniable swerve from Byron's intentions, it is equally mistaken to view his ending ("Klostergesang," No. 15) as inherently religious, sentimental, or both. The initially somber setting of the Requiem text, a contrapuntal tour de force consisting of two double fugatos, the themes of the second related by inversion, has nothing to do with conventional religiosity; on the contrary, the music functions as an emblem for Death, its grim spectre providing the backdrop for the terminal exchange between Manfred and the Abbot. Schumann's treatment of Manfred's actual passing is without any trace of bathos, involving instead a masterful transition from sound to silence, substance to nothingness: first the four-part choral texture gives way to a single, long-held B♭; then the very last words between the Abbot and Manfred (including, of course, the chilling "So schwer ist's nicht zu sterben" [" 'tis not so difficult to die"]) are delivered without any instrumental support whatever; and finally, absolute silence. Likewise, the subsequent appearance of the Astarte theme should not be interpreted as a signifier for Manfred's sentimental union with his beloved in the beyond, but rather as a Goethean gesture of redemption through the mediating power of the "Eternally-feminine."

But while Schumann deviates from the content of his poetic source, he remains essentially true to its spirit, and more important, to the central feature of its dramaturgy: the focus on the past. Indeed, Schumann's final scene can be fully understood only in relation to its specifically *musical* past. The E♭ minor of the Requiem setting resonates with the tonality of the Overture, only here it gives way, in the moments after Manfred's death, to a triumphant E♭ major. Thematic particles from the Overture—motive *b* and Astarte's theme—are likewise caught up in this progression from murky darkness to heavenly light. The crucial point, however, is this: Manfred's redemption of the past occurs not in the here-and-now, but in the hereafter. The transfigured recall of earlier motives, like the turn from minor to major, occurs only *after* he expires. Up to the end, Manfred is denied what he desperately seeks: solace *in the present*. Thus Schumann's ending, despite its consoling tone, is fundamentally tragic. In this too the composer remained true to the spirit of Byron's "modern" drama.

Faust *as Musical Novel*

Schumann's allusion to the Eternally-feminine at the conclusion of *Manfred* is not the only point of contact between his second literary opera and Goethe's *Faust*. The family likeness shared by Byron's misanthropic anti-hero and Goethe's brooding protagonist is too obvious to discount, even though the author of *Manfred* downplayed it. The similarities extend to individual scenes of the respective dramas. Just as Faust summons Mephistopheles into his study, so Manfred, weary of the meager results of his scientific and philosophical pursuits, receives the Spirits of the Universe in his Gothic gallery. Manfred's diagnosis of humankind's tragic condition, "half dust, half deity," would not sound out of place on Faust's lips. These relationships were not lost on Schumann, whose settings attest to a sensitivity to even less obvious relationships. The similarities between the "Gesang der Geister" (No. 1) in his *Manfred* and the opening of the Mitternacht episode (No. 5) from the *Faust* scenes—both are in B minor and both feature a delicate scoring dominated by high wind sonorities—forge a link between Byron's four spirits and Goethe's gray hags: Want, Debt, Care, and Need.

As the project that occupied him off and on between 1844 and 1853, the setting of seven scenes from Goethe's *Faust*, prefaced by an orchestral overture, colors the whole of Schumann's later period. The work at once acts as the capstone of his literary operas and nearly serves in the same capacity vis-à-vis his conquest of the musical genres. For the sake of the subsequent discussion, it will be useful here to provide an overview of the contents of Schumann's work. The location of each scene in Goethe's drama is provided in brackets:

Overture

Erste Abtheilung

    No. 1. Scene im Garten [Part I; from "Garten" and "Ein Gartenhauschen"]

    No. 2. Gretchen vor dem Bild der Mater dolorosa [Part I; "Zwinger"]

    No. 3. Scene im Dom [Part I; "Dom"]

Zweite Abtheilung

    No. 4. Ariel. Sonnenaufgang [Part II; Act I, "Anmutige Gegend"]

    No. 5. Mitternacht [Part II; Act V, "Mitternacht"]

    No. 6. Faust's Tod [Part II; Act V, "Grosser Vorhof des Palasts"]

Dritte Abtheilung

    No. 7. Faust's Verklärung [Part II; Act V, "Bergschluchten"]

        i. Chor. "Waldung, sie schwankt heran"

        ii. Tenor-Solo. "Ewiger Wonnebrand"

        iii. Bass-Solo (+ baritone solo, chorus). "Wie Felsen-Abgrund mir zu Füssen"

        iv. Chor (+ soprano solo). "Gerettet ist das edle Glied"

     v. Bass-Solo. "Hier ist die Aussicht frei"
    vi. Bass-Solo. Chor (+ vocal solos/ensembles). "Dir, der Un-
        berührbaren"
   vii. Chorus mysticus. "Alles Vergängliche ist nur ein
        Gleichnis" (2 versions of the *Schlusschor,* "Das Ewig-
        Weibliche zieht uns hinan")

    Originally considered as the basis for an opera, Goethe's *Faust* came
in for treatment as an oratorio when Schumann turned to its final scene
after the Russian tour of 1844. As we have already summarized Schumann's work on this phase of the project in Chapter 9, it will not be
necessary to traverse the same ground here.[111] Suffice it to say that Schumann was not satisfied with his preliminary attempt to realize Goethe's
verses in music. "The scene from Faust rests on my desk," he wrote to
Mendelssohn on 24 September 1845. "I'm downright afraid to look at
it again. Only because the sublime poetry of precisely this closing scene
grips me so would I venture [to resume] work; I don't know whether
I'll ever publish it."[112] Four points emerge from Schumann's letter: first,
he did not regard his work thusfar as a fully polished artistic product;
second, he was clearly daunted by the drama that would soon become
something of a Bible of nineteenth-century German literature; third,
there is no mention at this point of his earlier thought, raised in a letter
of December 1844 to Krüger, to treat "the entire [Faust] material as an
oratorio";[113] and fourth, the project was viewed as a deeply personal
one.
    For about a year-and-a-half we hear nothing of the Faust music.
But in the spring of 1847, perhaps motivated by the settings he had
recently heard in Berlin by Anton Heinrich von Radziwill, an aristocratic
dilettante, Schumann returned to his music for the *Schlussszene* of
Goethe's drama.[114] On 19 April, he was "busy with the Finale," probably
a reference to the concluding portion of the Chorus mysticus, "Das
Ewig-Weibliche zieht uns hinan," the portion that, according to a letter
to Whistling, nearly "drove the composer to desperation on several occasions."[115] But even after orchestrating this revised version of the closing
chorus on 23 April,[116] Schumann had not fully exhausted the possibilities of Goethe's richly symbolic verses. By 22 May he had set to work
on "another SCHLUSSCHOR ('Das Ewig-Weibliche') for Faust," its
sketching, elaboration, and orchestration complete by 28 July. Once
again, however, the Faust scene rested basically untouched on Schumann's desk, apart from a 23 February 1848 reading of selected portions
by his Dresden Chorverein,[117] this time for just under a year. Then in
May and June 1848, he added a rousing choral conclusion in B♭ to the

central number of the *Schlussszene,* "Gerettet ist das edle Glied." Finally satisfied with his labors, Schumann directed a private performance of the entire scene (in which his Chorverein participated) for invited guests on 25 June. Not until over a year later did the work receive its first public renderings, among them a lively performance of 29 August 1849, when it figured as part of the Dresden festivities surrounding Goethe's 100th-birthday jubilee.[118]

But in the meantime, the scope of the Faust project had expanded considerably. Between 13 and 24 July 1849, Schumann drafted and scored the whole of Abtheilung I.[119] Just days before the Dresden performance of the *Schlussszene,* he brought the opening scene of Abtheilung II (No. 4) to completion. And a year later, in late April and early May 1850, he finished the remaining two scenes of Abtheilung II (Nos. 5 and 6) with equal alacrity. On 10 May he was able to write with palpable relief in the *Haushaltbücher:* "Completed Faust, with joy."[120] Yet his work was not quite done: in mid-August 1853, he crowned the whole with an instrumental overture. On 17 August, after practically a decade of intermittent labor, the massive undertaking was finally over.

As will have been apparent from this summary, the genesis of the *Faust* scenes was no haphazard affair. After completing the *Schlussszene,* in many ways, a musico-poetic world unto itself, Schumann returned to the earlier stages of Goethe's work, selecting those scenes that, for him, captured the essence of the farflung action and setting them in the order in which they appear in the original drama. The body of the work thus complete, Schumann took up the overture last in a gesture redolent of contemporary operatic practice. Hence, even though the *Faust* scenes were composed in fits and starts over a protracted period, their conception was directed by an overriding sense for the whole.

How odd, then, that the work, perhaps Schumann's grandest in form and most highly differentiated in content, has garnered so little in the way of critical attention. Like *Genoveva,* the *Faust* scenes were a casualty of the partisan battles between Wagnerians and anti-Wagnerians. Krüger put it trenchantly in a review of 1862: "[Schumann] has received the same honor as Sebastian Bach, namely that of being revered by high conservatives and red radicals alike and having his name inscribed on the flags of both."[121] Liszt was practically alone among Schumann's contemporaries in according the *Faust* scenes unqualified praise. And to be sure, he was particularly enthusiastic over the treatment of the poetic source, for so far as he knew, Schumann was the first composer "to set *entire sections* of a tragedy, the most imposing work of our time, *Faust, without in any way modifying or adapting the text.*"[122] (Liszt himself concluded his *Faust-Symphonie* with a setting of the

Chorus mysticus, although this music owes less to Schumann than the Grail scenes from Wagner's *Parsifal* owe to Liszt.) No doubt, Liszt exaggerated: while Schumann leaves Goethe's verses basically untouched in Nos. 2, 5, and 6, elsewhere he does both modify and adapt the text for his own purposes. In No. 1, he conflates the last quarter or so of Goethe's garden scene with the middle portion of the very brief scene that follows. At several points in Nos. 3, 4, and 7, he either alters, omits, or repeats individual words or phrases and occasionally adds an interjection of his own.[123] Nonetheless, we are more apt to be struck by what Schumann retains than by what he varies. Thus Liszt put his finger on a qualitative distinction separating Schumann's approach to the Faust material from that of, say, Spohr, Berlioz, Wagner, or Liszt himself. Schumann takes neither the attitude of the run-of-the-mill opera composer or librettist (in whose finished work the poetic original will be barely recognizable), nor that of the tone poet (whose music will immerse its poetic subject in a wash of pure instrumental sonority). His textual materials become the basis for a literary opera in which not only the content but also the language of the poetic source is situated in the foreground.

Moreover, Schumann strove in his musical settings to approximate the dramaturgy of Goethe's *Faust*. Of course, to impute a single dramaturgical condition to Goethe's sprawling creation, much less to call it a drama, will require some qualification. For Schumann, ever the sensitive student of world literature, must have realized that at bottom the bipartite "Tragedy" was hardly a drama at all: its outward recourse to the dialogic form, no less than the apparently dramatic thrust of its First Part, does not conceal a pervasive reflective spirit that has far more to do with the inwardness of the *Roman*, the novel, than with the teleology of the drama. Schumann betrays his attitude in ways great and small. Consider, for instance, his approach, in No. 4, to the key line in the opening scene of Goethe's Part II (the centerpiece of both the composer's and the poet's *Faust*): "Am farb'gen Abglanz haben wir das Leben."[124] To establish the atmosphere for Faust's assertion that "In the many-hued splendor of reflection we find life," Schumann suspends the heroic gestures prevalent up to that point, offering in their stead a mysterious series of sustained, chromatically shifting harmonies in the winds. The ethereal effect continues right up through the first half of the verse, "Am farb'gen Abglanz," only to swing back just as decisively to the heroic tone, and a solidly grounded E major, at "haben wir das Leben." Schumann's decision to underscore the central term ("Abglanz," that is, splendid reflection) was no accident. As we will see, the novelistic principle of reflectivity animates not just the part but even more important, the whole of his final literary opera.

An understanding of the tension between part and whole, and its mediation through reflection, may bring us closer to a resolution of the question regarding the large-scale coherence of Schumann's *Faust* scenes. For many critics, the composer's settings do not in any way comprise a unity.[125] Support for the notion that the *Faust* settings amount to little more than a loose assemblage of disparate entities derives from Schumann himself, who, during the course of a conversation with Wasielewski in Düsseldorf, said of Parts I and II: "In composing them, I thought primarily that they might perhaps serve to round out concert programs, since there are hardly any small-scale compositions like these for soli and chorus."[126] Indeed, he maintained that his Faust music "should not be performed in toto on a single evening, since too many things of a grand and colossal nature would thereby follow one after the other; at best it might be done as a curiosity."[127] Although the latter statement is often adduced as evidence for the discontinuous, contingent quality of the *Faust* scenes, it speaks more to the limitations of Schumann's audience than to the inner nature of the work, for his comments on the Overture provide compelling testimony for an overall vision extending past the individual detail to the larger whole: "I have often given some thought to writing an overture for the Faust scenes, but I am also convinced that this task, which I view as most difficult, hardly admits to a satisfactory solution; there are simply too many—and too gigantic—elements to overcome. Nonetheless, it will be necessary for me to preface the Faust music with an orchestral introduction, otherwise the whole will not be rounded off, and also, the various moods must be prepared for."[128] In one sense, Schumann's settings undeniably create the impression of a series of discrete fragments, but so too does the drama that occupied Goethe intermittently from 1770 until 1831, the year before his death. Adorno's concise description of *Faust* as a "Stück in Stücken" (literally, a piece in pieces) not only resonates with Eckermann's view of the play as a series of "little independent worlds," each acting upon the other (a view sanctioned by Goethe),[129] it also aptly addresses the dialectic between part and whole that animates Schumann's work. In this too, the *Faust* scenes disclose an affinity with the novel, the genre whose "wholeness" is not that of the harmonious unity, but rather that of the heterogeneous totality.[130]

One aspect of Schumann's *Faust* scenes more than any other lends credence to the notion that the work rises above the level of a sequence of isolated fragments: the presence of symmetries on the small and large scale. The seven scenes are divided into three Abtheilungen, the first two containing three scenes, the third falling into three principal sections (movements i–iii, iv, v–vii).[131] The sevenfold division of the whole is mirrorred in the seven movements of Abtheilung III, whose relative lengths roughly duplicate the proportions of the seven scenes. The heartpiece of both the whole and the *Schlussszene* comes at dead center: Nos. 4 and 7/iv respectively. The first of these movements, situated at the opening of Abtheilung II, displays further symmetries. The scene is comprised of four sections: Ariel's invocation of the spirits, a chorus of spirits, Ariel's greeting of the sun, and Faust's monologue. The second and fourth sections are likewise articulated by a four-strophe structure. Even the tonal plan turns on a symmetrical progression in minor thirds: Bb-G-E. Early nineteenth-century novelists, Jean Paul and Novalis among them, were fond of placing a "mirror in the text," a condensed summation of the total narrative.[132] The fourth of Schumann's *Faust* scenes is just such a textual mirror. Located at the center of a larger reflective network, it articulates one of the central poetic themes of Goethe's drama: the notion that the divine is only accessible through the reflective medium of art. This is the ultimate message of the verse that Schumann obviously understood well: "Am fest'gen Abglanz haben wir das Leben."

In addition to the many, but essentially inaudible symmetries, Schumann employs other, more palpable means toward the end of ensuring the large-scale coherence of the *Faust* scenes. While it can hardly be said that the work is "in" any single key, or even that it progresses ineluctably from its opening to its closing tonality, it is still clear that the two terms in the D-minor/F-major pair dominate the tonal idiom from start to finish: D minor, often associated with gloomy but grand spaces in Schumann's later works,[133] is the key of the Overture, the grim cathedral scene (No. 3), and the initial portion of the scene of Faust's death (No. 6); the pastoral F major, on the other hand, serves as the governing tonality of Abtheilung III, "Faust's Transfiguration," in its entirety. And while recurrent musical materials play only a limited role in the *Faust* scenes,[134] there is nonetheless one idea that emerges as a kind of signature motive at key points throughout. First intimated during the second group of the Overture, the motive, a sequential chain of descending fourths, only takes on determinate meaning in No. 1, where it at once announces Mephistopheles and casts Faust's expansive declaration of love for Gretchen in an ironic light (Example 10.10). The signature motive is, of course, a close relative of one of the chief musical emblems of Margaretha's black-magical world in *Genoveva* (Example 10.2c). Although the motive figures as a musical metaphor for otherworldly ma-

Example 10.10. Faust scenes, from No. 1.

levolence in both works, it takes on an even wider range of connotations
in the *Faust* scenes. During the cathedral scene (No. 3) it serves to portray the Evil Spirit, a personification of Gretchen's guilty conscience. In
No. 5 ("Mitternacht"), the motive is associated with Care, the allegorical
being who relates to Faust as the Evil Spirit does to Gretchen. It accrues
further layers of meaning in the closing scene (movements ii, vi, vii),
where it is linked first with Pater Ecstaticus and the bittersweet pangs of
his intense love for the divinity, then with the three Penitent Women,
who, like Gretchen, are guilty of sins of the flesh, and finally, in the
concluding chorus, with the yearning for mystical union with the godhead. Thus, the signature motive underscores the dialectic between car-
nal and divinely transfigured passion and, at the same time, lends an
epic dimension to the work as a whole.[135]

In one of his conversations with Goethe, Eckermann characterized
Faust as an artistic representation of "a manifold world." Schumann's
Faust settings likewise constitute a manifold musico-poetic world, one
that deserves a monograph of its own, but that will have to settle for a
brief overview here.

The Overture, like so many of Schumann's late instrumental works
in the larger forms, is notable for its intense economy. The cellular technique, already masterfully deployed in the *Manfred* Overture, is here
taken to its extreme limit. To be sure, almost all the ideas of the overture's principal, sonata-form portion derive either directly or indirectly
from two motivic cells presented in the slow introduction: a chromatic
encircling of A from above and below (a cousin of the halting half-step
rise from the beginning of the *Manfred* Overture); and a diatonic expansion of the same figure. (The baroque quality of both is striking; a
seventeenth-century musical rhetorician like Joachim Burmeister would
have called the first a *pathopoeia*, the second a *circulatio*). Yet Schumann's designation of the piece as an "overture" is something of a mis-
nomer in light of its relationship to the ensuing scenes. If Goethe's *Faust*
presents four manifestations of its protagonist's striving, toward sensual
love, classical beauty, entrepeneurial action, and transcendence, then
Schumann's settings treat all but one of these: the tragic consequences
of his affair with Gretchen provide the content for Abtheilung I; his

career as a land developer figures in Abtheilung II; and his redemption comes at the conclusion of Abtheilung III. The Overture, however, prefigures only two of these themes. The dusky, ominous tone of its opening and the sentimental lyricism of its second group both point to various aspects of the Gretchen tragedy as it unfolds in Nos. 1 and 3. The triumphant D-major peroration in the coda, its character lying somewhere between that of a march and a chorale, looks forward to the close of No. 5, where Faust, apparently oblivious to his blindness, vows to press on with his grand land-reclamation project. Hence, Schumann's reference, in conversation with Wasielewski, to a projected "orchestral introduction" ("Instrumental-Einleitung") for the *Faust* scenes supplies a fitting designation for the piece as it ultimately took shape. The Overture prepares us for Abtheilungen I and II, but contains not even a hint of the mystical transcendence with which Abtheilung III will culminate.

As we have seen, Schumann completed the whole of Abtheilung I in a little over a week. The genesis of a work, its pre-history, so to speak, often tells us less about the finished product than we would like. But in this case, Schumann's working method impinges directly on a significant aspect of Abtheilung I in its final form. The constituent scenes were conceived as a unit, all three having been sketched first, and only then scored. Not surprisingly, they form a tightly knit group, both dramaturgically and musically. Together the three scenes articulate the three principal stages in the tragic tale of Gretchen, the hapless object of Faust's striving for sensual love, who moves from innocence in No. 1, to despair in No. 2, only to teeter on the brink of madness in No. 3. The relatedness of these seemingly disparate affects is underlined by a logically progressive tonal scheme moving from F major, to A minor, and finally to a grim D minor.

In No. 1, the garden scene, Schumann perfectly captures Gretchen's psychological upheaval in the face of burgeoning emotions whose course she cannot control. From a technical point of view, his setting of the text in phrases of irregular length goes hand in hand with a conversational melodic idiom that effectively dissolves Goethe's verse into prose; but in terms of the drama, Gretchen's breathless delivery of her lines aptly conveys the conflicting mix of embarrassment, anxiety, and hopefulness that comes with growing passion. Indeed, the music is remarkable for its suggestiveness of the principle dialectic of the scene: that between innocence and ardor. The brief orchestral prelude, with its leisurely $\frac{12}{8}$ meter, pulsing eighths, gracefully rising figures tossed from cello to violin, and delicate off-beat sighs, has the air of a pastoral. But in the course of the scene's pivotal episode, as Gretchen plucks a flower to determine whether "he loves me" or "he loves me not," the innocent idyll is transformed under the influence of Eros. Schumann prefaces the episode with the sighs from the opening pastoral, but at its climax these formerly gentle figures evolve into rapturous gestures for Gretchen's "Er liebt mich" and Faust's complementary "Er liebt dich." The music, in other words, speaks to the proximity of schoolgirlish flirtation and full-blown passion.

A variant of the same sigh gesture occurs in No. 2, where Gretchen gives voice to her growing despair before a representation of the Mater Dolorosa set into a niche in the city wall. Although this image of a supplicant poised before a religious icon finds a parallel in the final act of *Genoveva,* Gretchen is hardly the beneficiary, at this point, of the consoling grace that showers forth on the heroine of Schumann's opera. Her invocation takes the form, not of a luminous aria, but of a plangent *Rezitativischer Gesang,* the coherence of the largely declamatory setting ensured by a subtle employment of the technique of strophic variation. To articulate the arrival at the second stage of the Gretchen tragedy, Schumann recalls the sighs from the garden scene, only here they suggest neither innocence nor ardor. On the contrary, they appear as the anxious appoggiaturas, often in the lower range of the viola, that pervade the opening and closing of Gretchen's plaint. The plagal coloration of the final cadence to A both emphasizes the prayerful tone of No. 2 and foreshadows the D-minor tonality of No. 3, where Gretchen is a cowering, terrified onlooker at the celebration of a Requiem Mass (either for her mother, dead from an overdose of the sleeping draft administered by Gretchen to facilitate her trysts with Faust; or for her brother Valentin, victim of a duel in which Faust's victory was won with the aid of Mephistopheles' magic). By this point, the poor girl's mind has practically come unhinged from guilt and grief, and to drive home the point, Schumann imbues the scene with all the qualities of a hallucination. The Evil Spirit, who at times takes up and expands Gretchen's anxiously delivered phrases, is nothing more than a projection of her guilty conscience. Likewise, we hear the choral intonation of the Dies irae as Gretchen hears it, that is, as a frenzied distortion, a frantic parody of the solemn strains that the other attendees at the service "really" hear. While Schumann gave no indication that he intended his *Faust* music to be staged (this in spite of his retention of many of Goethe's stage directions), one can easily imagine a scene such as this in the theatre. To be sure, it would not sound at all out of place in a contemporary horror opera.

At the same time, the cathedral scene turns on a dialectic between the sacred and the profane, the archaic and the modern. If, in No. 1, Schumann portrays the convergence of innocent and fatal attractions, here he demonstrates the close bond between horror (allegorized through the Evil Spirit) and religious revelation (figured through the quasi-liturgical intoning of the Dies irae, not coincidentally, perhaps, in D minor, the key of Mozart's Requiem), both of which are functions of the numinous. Consider, for instance, the very opening of the scene. For his gripping representation of terror, Schumann draws on the rhetoric of the horror opera: a darkly-hued orchestral texture dominated by the overpowering sonority of horns and trumpets, longheld, but curiously syncopated chords, and cascading statements of the signature motive in bassoons, violas, and cellos. But these theatrical effects are supported by a device that lends an undeniably hieratic quality to the whole. The orchestral introduction, like the initial stages of the ensuing dialogue for Gretchen and the Evil Spirit, is grounded by a typically baroque gesture: the descending minor tetrachord. Employed in the seventeenth and eighteenth centuries as an emblem for lament, it serves here not only to project that affect, but also to establish a ritualistic aura for the scene. In Schumann's hands, the archaic gesture sounds unmistakably new; indeed, it mediates the principal generic tension in the scene: that between horror opera on the one hand and church music on the other.

In Abtheilung II, the focus shifts from Gretchen to Faust. Schumann selected three key scenes from Part II of Goethe's drama, each of them marking a significant moment in the course of the protagonist's fortunes: his awakening to a higher consciousness (No. 4), his blinding (ironically interpreted, in No. 5, as a heightened ability to "see"), and finally, in No. 6, his death, a variant on the theme of removal from light treated in the previous scene. In addition, the poetic coherence of Abtheilung II derives from another feature of which Schumann was certainly aware: the allusion of each of the three scenes to a Shakespearean source. Ariel, the spirit of the air from *The Tempest*, looms large in No. 4; the four gray hags from No. 5 recall the witches in *Macbeth*; and in No. 6, the Lemures, spirits of the evil dead, set to work preparing for Faust's burial with a saucy lyric modelled on the gravediggers' song in the final act of *Hamlet*. Thus, while Schumann's plans for operas based on *Hamlet* and *Romeo and Juliet* came to naught, camouflaged fragments of a Shakespearean drama are embedded in the middle portion of the *Faust* scenes.

As noted earlier, No. 4 occupies the center of the work, its text (and music) articulating one of the drama's most profound themes: the reflective relationships between and among Life, Art, Nature, and the Divine. Schumann's setting abounds in wonderful touches. It opens with an orchestral evocation of the spirit world as luminous as the previous scene was gruesome. The soaring violin melody, its expansiveness a function of flexibly alternating $\frac{3}{4}$ bars and broad hemiolas, no less than the supporting instrumental texture—divisi strings, delicately punctuating harp and wind chords—beautifully projects in tones the essence of Goethe's heading: "Charming landscape. Faust reclining on a lawn with flowers, trying to sleep. Twilight. Circle of spirits—charming little figures—hovering above." Ariel's ensuing invocation of the spirits, proceeding from stylized declamation to a lyrically extended final cadence, ushers in a series of choral lieder for the spirits themselves, each corresponding to one of the four vigils of the night. In his manuscript for the scene, Goethe even labelled each of the strophes as follows: "Sérénade" [evening song], "Notturno" [night song], "Mattutino" [morning song], and "Réveille" [call to awaken]. A gradual intensification of pace and tone characterizes Schumann's setting, which begins with a muted lullaby for the restless Faust and concludes with an exuberant $\frac{6}{8}$ dance celebrating the dawning day. But the decisive event, the arrival of the sun, is left for Ariel to proclaim. According to Goethe's stage directions (omitted in Schumann's score), the sun approaches with a "stupendous clangor," and in Ariel's monologue, the dawn is similarly described as an audible event, a deafening tumult shot through with the clattering of Phoebus's wheels, and "trumpeting" and "tromboning" all around. Schumann clearly took great delight in representing, musically, the abundant sound-images in Goethe's text. He cast Ariel's exhortatory speech as a *Rezitativischer Gesang* of singular power, the declamatory vocal line supported by shimmering harmonic turns (of which the most breathtaking is an expressive shift from B major to the tonic, B♭) and alternating with fanfares in the brass.

But the most impressive, and the most extended portion of the scene is its fourth and final part: a monologue for the awakened Faust. A mirror of the scene as a whole, the protagonist's speech falls into four parts. The first reflects his turn to Nature as the object of his striving; the second shows him backing down in a confrontation with Nature's overpowering forces; in the third, he ponders his dilemma; the fourth centers around the image of the rainbow, a symbol for the reflective medium, Art, through which alone the Sublime in Nature is made accessible to humankind. Schumann in turn links each of these parts with a specific vocal genre: Faust's awakening to Nature with a lied introduced by a cantabile for solo cello, his retreat from the Sublime with a *Rezitativischer Gesang*, his resignation to defeat with a propulsive arioso, and his reawakening to reflective consciousness with a heroic aria. In lending special emphasis to the second and fourth of these sections, Schumann demonstrates the depth of his understanding of the chief problem of the monologue, humankind's inability to grasp directly the Divine in

Nature, and its resolution through reflection. Hence, in Faust's *Rezitativischer Gesang*, the awesome sight of the sun's rays illuminating a steep mountainside comes together with an orchestral texture of incredible power. Pitted against a syncopated, chromatically ascending figure in the bass, a series of rising fifth "calls," emblems for Faustian striving, fans out through the entire wind and brass section. Taking off from B♭, the spiralling fifth progression reaches its upper limit, D, at just the point where Faust attempts to confront the sun in all its blinding force. But at this climactic point, the harmony comes curiously unhinged: D major, heard as a dominant, does not resolve to the expected tonic, G, but is rather deflected to the subdominant, C. The intractability of the progression (which Schumann repeats several times for emphasis) simply but brilliantly mirrors the intractability of the forces of Nature. The passage finds a parallel in the concluding portion of the monologue, where Faust pauses to muse on the mysterious significance of the rainbow. But there the shifting chromatic harmonies in the winds move toward a firmly grounded E major as Faust penetrates to the deeper meaning of the rainbow and thereby resolves the conflict in his relationship with the sublime: "Am farb'gem Abglanz haben wir das Leben."

With No. 5, we plummet from the overwhelming brightness of the previous scene to the murky darkness of midnight. Yet the images are not merely juxtaposed, for the light of No. 4 is, after all, a potentially *blinding* light. Here, in No. 5, this potential becomes reality as Faust is struck blind by Care, a counterforce to the activity of the creative spirit, who exercises her black-magical powers on the protagonist as punishment for his role in the death of the innocent couple, Philemon and Baucis. Faust's downfall, symbolized by his blinding at the hands of Care, is precipitated by a primarily ethical failure, and as such can be viewed as a complement to the Gretchen tragedy from Part I of Goethe's drama. Sensitive to this relationship, Schumann casts the scene as a pendant to the cathedral scene (No. 3) in Abtheilung I. Just as the signature motive set the stage for the appearance of the Evil Spirit in No. 3, so here it figures prominently in the music for Care and her grim companions. More important still, both scenes turn on a similar dialectic of genre. The midnight scene, like its counterpart in Abtheilung I, derives its characteristic profile from the tension between the shocking effects of horror opera and the elevated tone of a quasi-liturgical, oratorio style. The bewitching sing-song of Care's incantational lied in her central exchange with Faust may well have been inspired by the demonic characters in one of Marschner's horror operas; Faust's responses, in constrast, have all the solemn dignity of an oratorio baritone. Yet the two styles are mediated by a figure introduced at the beginning of the scene and elaborated at various points throughout. The four gray hags enter to a nervously scrambling variant of the signature motive in the strings over which hovers a slow-moving line in the winds, its eeriness highlighted by the piercing tone of the piccolo. At the close of the scene, the same line recurs in the monologue that Faust delivers just after his blinding. Only here it plunges into the bass register of a densely imitative texture. In essence treated as a migrating cantus firmus, the figure makes a musical and a dramatic point. It not only binds together the opening and closing of the scene in abstract musical terms, but also, in traversing the space from the "light," upper reaches to the "dark," lower reaches of the texture, mirrors the paradox in the closing text: through murky blindness Faust imagines himself to have attained to a new light. It is precisely through this ironic conceit that the scene reveals its Shakespearean essence. Nor was Schumann unaware of the irony underlying Faust's determination to press forward with his grand plan to reclaim land from the sea. His setting culminates in a mock-triumphant march replete with dotted rhythms, raucous fanfares, and a crass, wind-dominated scoring. This none-too-subtle allusion to the Meyerbeerian style that Schumann found so detestable points up the irony between the "light" of which Faust assumes he is the beneficiary and his imminent demise.

In Goethe's drama, Faust's death scene follows immediately on the midnight scene. Schumann too conceived both scenes as a unit; returning to the working method he had employed in Abtheilung I, he sketched Nos. 5 and 6 together, and only then proceeded to score them. Shakespearean irony is just as prevalent in No. 6 as in the preceding scene; indeed, the textual contrast between low comedy and high tragedy, like that between the demonic forces that now control Faust's realm and the protagonist's utopian vision of an ideal society, finds a musical analogue in the disparity between the grotesque tone of the saucy march tunes associated with Mephistopheles and the Lemures at the beginning of the scene, and the sublime tone of Faust's monologue and the ensuing orchestral obsequies at its conclusion.[136] But at the same time, Schumann mediates the contrast between grotesquerie and sublimity through a sophisticated process of motivic evolution that encompasses much of the scene. The second of the Lemures' mocking lieder, "Wie jung ich war," is supported by a mechanically repeated *Trommelbass*. Just as Faust enters, a new figure appears over the bass; announced by the horns in thirds, it consists of no more than a falling and a rising sixth (Example 10.11). Although the figure as initially presented seems to hold out little promise for further elaboration, it takes on an increasingly significant role as the scene unfolds, providing the motivic backdrop, in the orchestra, for Faust's dialogue with Mephistopheles and his ensuing soliloquy.

Example 10.11. Faust scenes, from No. 6.

Moreover, it serves as the headmotif for the concluding orchestral chorale (Example 10.12), the final stages of which transport the rising-sixth
portion of the figure from the bottom to the top of the texture. The
close of the death scene resonates powerfully with two earlier moments
in the *Faust* settings: the closes of the Overture and No. 4, where Schumann also brings a gesture spanning the major sixth from scale-degree
5 upward to scale-degree 3, no doubt as an emblem for Faustian striving. Of course, the orchestral close of the death scene has none of the
affirmative confidence of the corresponding spots in the Overture and
No. 4, but its meaning is still clear: Faust's days of earthly striving have
come to an end.

Schumann's title for Abtheilung III, "Faust's Verklärung" (Faust's
Transfiguration), though without precedent in Goethe's drama, neatly
encapsulates the essence of the scene in which Faust is saved through
the intervention of a transcendent power: the Eternally-feminine. Although it was completed before the two preceding parts of the work,
there is no jarring break in compositional idiom. On the contrary, the
solemnly rising octaves that preface the opening chorus of the *Schlussszene* ("Waldung, sie schwankt heran") appear to take off directly from
the rising sixths at the close of No. 6, thus mediating the more outwardly dramatic stages of the work and what Schumann described as its
"serene and deeply peaceful" conclusion.[137] And while there may be
room for doubt on Schumann's thoughts regarding the overall unity of
the *Faust* scenes, he clearly intended the *Schlussszene* as a unified capstone for the whole: "The scene has in its total configuration a closing
character; the single parts are not finished in themselves; everything
must mesh together swiftly and completely in order to reach the high-

Example 10.12. Faust scenes, from No. 6.

point, which seems to me to come with the first statement of the words 'Das Ewig-Weibliche . . .' (shortly before the beginning of the lively concluding chorus)."[138]

Goethe drew on two principal pictorial and literary models for the scene that, owing to its rich and often arcance symbolism, poses greater interpretive challenges than practically any other in the drama: a fourteenth-century Pisan fresco depicting Holy Anchorites (hermits of the early Christian era who practiced self-mortification in order to achieve union with the Divinity) poised high above a surging stream in the wilderness; and Dante's mystical approach to the Divinity in the final cantos of the *Paradiso*. If scholars still complain that Faust's salvation is hardly a logical outcome of the previous action in Part II of the drama, just as they still dispute the precise meaning of the enigmatic turns of phrase that abound in the closing scene ("das Ewig-Weibliche" is the most celebrated of any number of examples), then it is precisely because Goethe, like the Pisan artist and Dante before him, was attempting to give utterance to something that admits to neither logic nor determinate meaning: the ultimate mystery of transcendence. Schumann too sought to capture this mystery, but in musical terms, through the fusion of the sacred and the profane on a scale grander than anything since the Finale of Beethoven's Ninth Symphony, and not to be equalled in scope until Mahler's Eighth Symphony.

In this context, the widely spaced octaves at the beginning of the opening chorus not only resonate with the contemplative orchestral chorale at the conclusion of the previous scene, but, even more important, they, together with the echoing exchanges between upper and lower voices in the chorus, create a sense of immense space, an aural metaphor for the vast, untamed landscape, "Mountain Gorges, Forest, Rock, Widlerness," in which the final act of redemption will play itself out. The opening chorus, in other words, creates an aura: an awe-inspiring space for the unfolding of a transcendental mystery. Just as Goethe's Pater Ecstaticus floats "to and fro," so too is Schumann's arioso for the first of the Holy Anchorites (No. 7/ii) dominated by the sinuous twists and turns of the signature motive in the solo cello. According to Christian lore, each of the Anchorite Fathers, Patres Ecstaticus, Profundus, Seraphicus, and Marianus, represents an ascending degree of divine knowledge. Schumann beautifully thematizes this rise in No. 7/iii, where we proceed from the deep baritone register of Pater Profundus, his opening recitative supported by the mellow tones of the trombone choir, to the lyric baritone of Pater Seraphicus, and finally to the pure soprano tone of the Blessed Boys (unbaptized children who died just after birth, and who, once released from the eyes of Pater Seraphicus, do their joyous ring-dances in an upper realm free from the untamed forces of earthly Nature). To be sure, ascent is no more than a metaphor for increasing sanctity or purification, a conceit that Schumann figures musically through a turn from profane to sacred musical genres. The operatic tone of the opening monologue for Pater Profundus is therefore displaced by the simple, hymnic quality of the closing music for Pater Seraphicus and the Blessed Boys, the purity of the latter further emphasized by its almost total diatonicism.

" 'Wer immer strebend sich bemüht, Den können wir erlösen' " (Whoever endeavors to strive, to him may we grant redemption)—these justly celebrated lines (which Goethe emphasized by placing in quotation marks, though so far as we know he was not quoting at all) are accorded an appropriately dignified chordal setting near the beginning of No. 7/iv, the central choral complex of the *Schlussszene*. But it is important to keep in mind that Faust's redemption is not ensured by his striving alone. As Goethe's text makes clear, love from on high, personified here by the host of saving angels sent by the Mater Gloriosa at Gretchen's behest, must intercede on Faust's behalf. Hence Schumann's setting continues the theme of ascent through a series of soli and choruses, one as vividly characterized as the next: a solemn presentation of the opening lines ("Gerettet ist das edle Glied"), a lighthearted lied for solo soprano and responding chorus ("Jene Rosen, aus den Händen"), a propulsive fugato ("Nebelnd um Felsenhöh' spür' ich soeben' ") on a *stile antico* subject whose dance-like treatment is far from antique,[139] and a passage of singular beauty, conceived as an allusion to the Palestrina style, for the Blessed Boys who receive Faust's spirit "im Puppenstand" ("in pupal form"). Then comes a move apt to offend a poetic purist: a repetition of the opening text, set here as a jubilant fugal chorus on an upwardly surging, fanfare-like motive. As noted earlier, Schumann first decided to round out No. 7/iv with this powerful evocation of the Handelian oratorio style in the spring of 1848, nearly four years after the *Schlussszene* had been provisionally completed. Yet the new chorus provided Schumann with more than the mere opportunity to put to creative use his thorough study of Handel's oratorios from the year before.[140] His recall of the earlier text, but with music of a markedly different character, allowed him to make a poetic point. For if, in the first chorus, the crucial line, "Wer immer strebend sich bemüht," is set to a rather neutral, descending line, then in the new closing chorus, it is coupled with a confidently rising figure that ushers in the return of the principal fugue subject, both gestures thus imparting a markedly triumphant turn to the overall poetic theme of ascent.

The central choral complex of the *Schlussszene* is also notable for the increasing density of its allusions to the surrounding music in the scene a a whole. The interjections of the Younger Angels ("Jauchzet auf, es ist gelungen!"), for instance, point back to the striking exhortation of Pater Seraphicus, "Steigt hinan zu höh'rem Kreise," from No. 7/iii. In complementary fashion, an important melodic strand in the chorus of Blessed Boys (at "Lösen die Flocken los") looks forward to one of the lyric highpoints of the score: the monologue for Dr. Marianus, "Hier ist die Aussicht frei," No. 7/v. The monologue falls into three sections: a brief *Rezitativischer Gesang* by way of introduction, a central "aria" whose pervasive lyricism and sumptuously wrought orchestral texture— featuring solo oboe, muted strings, and harp[141]—aptly portray Dr. Marianus's "enraptured" delivery of his hymn to the Mater Gloriosa, and a concise postlude in arioso style whose turn from G major to minor and open-ended final cadence prepare for the subsequent movement. To bridge the gap between declamatory and lyric styles, Schumann derives the principal motive of the "aria," presented in its basic form by the oboe in mm. 18–19, but soon elaborated by other instruments and the voice as well, from what at first appears to be a neutral, declamatory gesture in the introductory *Rezitativischer Gesang* (Example 10.13). This gesture, in turn, proves to be none other than an allusion to the music for the Blessed Boys' command, in No. 7/iv, that Faust's spirit shed its "flaky coccoon" ("Löset die Flocken los") (Example 10.14). Just as Goethe's Dr. Marianus, poised "in the highest, purest cell," serves as a foil to Faust brooding in his study at the beginning of the drama, so Schumann firms the connection between the two figures with a concise, but suggestive musical gesture.

It would not be an exaggeration to maintain that Schumann found a means of creating an "associative magic" (Thomas Mann's term for the web of relationships in Wagnerian music drama) every bit as compelling as Wagner's, but largely independent of leitmotivic syntax. In No. 7/vi, a multi-partite movement involving vocal soli, solo ensembles, and chorus, the Mater Gloriosa "hovers into view" to music that closely parallels Schumann's depiction of the dawning day's "stupendous clangor" in No. 4. To be sure, both passages share the same tonality ($B\flat$), shimmering chromaticism, and orchestral color (string tremoli, sustained chords in the winds, brass fanfares). The poetic point of the allusion is obvious: the Virgin, in the person of the Mater Gloriosa, serves to infuse Faust's spirit with "light." Moreover, the movement resonates with an even earlier stage in the drama: Gretchen's prayer to the Mater Dolorosa in Abtheilung I. Compare her desperate entreaty in No. 2,

Example 10.13. Faust scenes, No. 7/v, mm. 1–21.

"Ach neige, du Schmerzenreiche," with the plea of the Penitent ("formerly called Gretchen") to the Mater Gloriosa on Faust's behalf: "Neige, neige, du Ohnegleiche." Schumann's music subtly mirrors the textual parallel *and* the affective disparity between the two spots: the A minor of No. 2 is answered by the A major of the passage in No. 7/vi; the supplicative headmotif and drooping vocal line of the former give way, in No. 7/vi, to the opposite configuration: the two initial melodic descents preface an expressively arched gesture on "Ohnegleiche" (Example 10.15a & b). The movement culminates with the Mater Gloriosa's command "Komm! hebe dich zu höhern Sphären" ("Come! Lift yourself into higher spheres") set to music that both recalls the sunrise episode in No. 4 and underscores the theme of ascent. The shifting harmonies supporting the Mater Gloriosa's declamatory phrase effect an upward move from A major to B♭, while Dr. Marianus, "prostrate, adoring," continues the process with two parallel phrases nudging the tonality higher still, from B♭ to B, then to C, each stage in the progression articulated by a

Example 10.14. Faust scenes, from No. 7/iv.

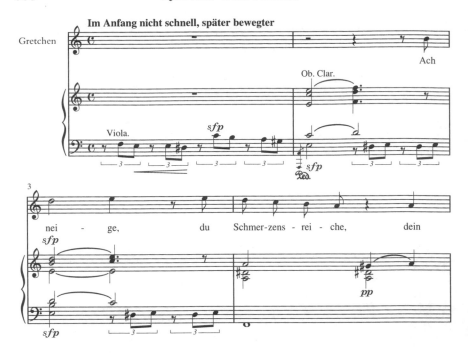

Example 10.15a. Faust scenes, No. 2, mm. 1–4.

Example 10.15b. Faust scenes, from No. 7/vi.

fanfare from the horns and trumpets. Schumann's music, no less than Faust's spirit, lifts itself into higher spheres.

Writing in 1849, shortly after its first public performance, Brendel heard in Schumann's music for the *Schlussszene* elements of a "church music of the future" ("Kirchenmusik der Zukunft").[142] Nowhere is this epithet more suggestive than in the concluding *Chorus mysticus,* Schumann's setting of Goethe's celebrated but inscrutable verses:

Alles Vergängliche
Ist nur ein Gleichnis;
Das Unzulängliche,
Hier wird's Ereignis;
Das Unbeschreibliche,
Hier ist's getan;
Das Ewig-Weibliche
Zieht uns hinan.

[All that is transitory
Is only an allegory;
Here the inaccessible
Becomes actuality;
Here the indescribable
Is accomplished;
The Eternally-feminine
Draws us forward.]

To be sure, Schumann initially responds to this text with music whose progressive thrust is deeply implicated in, but ultimately transcends, its archaic surface. He begins with a fugal chorus whose *alla breve* notation, staid subject—a formulaic interlocking of two descending fifths and no more—and thorougoing reliance on contrapuntal feints of every imaginable kind—stretto, triple counterpoint, inversion—make for a deliberate allusion to the *stile antico* (Example 10.16). Yet there is little antiquated about the actual sound of Schumann's music, its newness inscribed in the tonal ambivalence of the opening (the subject suggests D minor, but its harmonization takes off from F, then hovers between A minor and C), the pungent chromaticism of the body of the fugue, and the dramatic surge to the quicker second section of the Chorus mysticus. Not since the great C♯-minor fugue from Book I of Bach's *Das wohltemperirte Clavier* have the old and the new come together so powerfully.

The second portion of the chorus (which "several times drove the composer to desperation,"[143] and which he invariably referred to as the "Schlusschor") presents the tension between archaicism and modernity as a dialectic between the sacred and the profane. In the first version,

Example 10.16. Faust scenes, No. 7/vii (*Chorus mysticus*), opening fugue subject.

the turn to *Lebhaft* has about it the gestural quality of an operatic
stretta. Likewise, the principal theme of the *Schlusschor*, which recurs
twice more in the manner of a triumphant refrain, wouldn't be at all
out of place in a chorus of jubilation at the conclusion of a rescue opera.
At the same time, the employment of the *ars combinatoria* in its central
section, where an episodic idea from the *Schlusschor* converges with the
fugue subject from the opening of the Chorus mysticus, imparts a hieratic tone to the proceedings. The two styles, one redolent of opera, the
other of church music, are magnificently fused at the climax of the
movement, where the soprano solo, descending from a high C, soars
above the final statement of the refrain theme in the chorus. The gesture, a variant of the similar conceit in the closing moments of the *Peri*,
is frankly operatic, but likewise discloses a contrapuntal dimension: the
soprano's line inverts one of the countersubjects from the *stile antico*
section of the Chorus mysticus.

The second version of the *Schlusschor*, which Schumann viewed as
the more successful of the two,[144] embodies the same dialectic, if less
obviously. For here the balance is tipped in the direction of the quasi-
sacred in a lengthy central development, a veritable tour de force of
contrapuntal manipulation where a new fugue subject is treated in
stretto, combined with itself in augmentation, and linked with a countersubject and its inversion.[145] Nonetheless, both versions describe a
roughly comparable shape that works up to a stunning central climax
and dissolves into a subdued close in which any residual elements of
Faustian striving are effectively transcended.

Goethe's closing verses have been the object of a long-standing debate. For Walter Kaufman, they are an expression of the poet's "Diony-
sian tolerance," his willingness to grant his protagonist, in heaven, the
redemptive light he failed to achieve on earth.[146] In Hans Eichner's
equally sensible view, the conclusion of *Faust* represents a synthesis of
the active and contemplative principles that functioned as the count-
erpoles of Goethe's ethical system.[147] According to this line of argument,
Goethe was faced with the Fichtean dilemma of mediating between the
"practical," but potentially destructive drive toward self-assertion on the
one hand, and the "theoretical" or "reflective," but potentially paralyzing
drive toward self-examination on the other. Schumann arguably approached Goethe's *Faust* from the same philosophical standpoint. Indeed, his reaction to the entire drama was perhaps conditioned by one
word more than any other in the enigmatic concluding lines:
"Gleichnis." In that context, the term can be translated as "allegory," the
hollow form of which disintegrates into nothingness with the passage of
time. But it embraces a variety of other connotations as well: symbol,

likeness, image, and reflection. Taken in the latter sense, the term resonates not only with the "farb'gen Abglanz" of No. 4, but also with the
Faust settings as a whole, where Schumann solves the Fichtean dilemma
of mediating between unbridled force and enervating solipsism through
an artful reflection of the manifold world, or more precisely, of the
manifold musical world. His *Faust* scenes bring together an encyclopedic
array of genres: church music, oratorio, horror opera, grand opera, lied,
symphony. The result, as intimated earlier, is not a harmonious unity,
but a heterogeneous totality, a system of musico-poetic fragments—a
musical novel.

In Schumann's *Faust* scenes, we therefore encounter a mature realization of the novelizing tendencies that animated Schumann's artistry
practically from the start. In the 1840s, the poetic impulse may have
shifted from Jean Paul (whose novels Schumann continued to read and
whose birthday he continued to note in the *Haushaltbücher*) to Goethe,
but the inner nature of that impulse remained fundamentally the same.
The path to the "New Poetic Age" lead through the musical novel.

~11~

*U*nbounded
Creativity

The Most Fruitful Year

Writing to Hiller on 10 April 1849, Schumann vividly juxtaposed the incredible surge in his own rate of production with the equally incredible upheavals then sweeping though western and central Europe: "For some time now I've been very busy—it's been my most fruitful year—it seemed as if the outer storms impelled people to turn inward, and only therein did I find a counterforce against the forces breaking in so frightfully from without."[1] At the end of the next month, safely ensconced in Bad Kreischa, the village where he and his family had temporarily repaired following on the outbreak of revolution in Dresden, Schumann again boasted of his productivity in a letter to Liszt: "Recently and in the whole preceding year I've been incessantly active—quite a bit, large and small, will soon appear."[2] During the months ahead, Schumann continued to compose with Mozartean fluency. In 1849 alone, he would complete nearly forty works, many of them cycles, collections, or multi-movement compositions of considerable dimensions. If the period from mid-1848 to mid-1849 marked his most fruitful year to date, the stretch from the beginning to the end of 1849 proved to be more fruitful still. Apparently unruffled by the outward storminess of world events, Schumann appears to have put those "recent times of gloomy moods" (to which he counted the Second Symphony, the canonic *Studien* for pedal piano, and portions of the D-minor Piano Trio) definitively behind him. Since then, as he put it to Louis Ehlert

388

late in 1849, "I've made my way into other spheres, of which the recently published Christmas-Album [*Album für die Jugend,* op. 68], *Spanisches Liederspiel,* and Liederalbum [*Lieder-Album für die Jugend,* op. 79] will give you an idea—much else from this happy time rests in my portfolio."[3] To be sure, there were the usual bad days here and there, the occasional flareup of "stupid hypochondria" or relapse into "dumb melancholy."[4] But on the whole, the amazingly fruitful phase between mid-1848 and the end of 1849 was also a period of emotional and psychological calm.

As we have already seen in the previous chapter, the later Dresden years in general and the year 1848 in particular were colored by Schumann's foray into literary opera. But already toward the end of 1848, new directions in his creative trajectory are noticeable. In September and October, taking a breather after the completion of *Genoveva,* Schumann drafted the over forty delightful keyboard miniatures that comprise the *Album für die Jugend.* Keyboard music occupied him again in December, when, after putting the finishing touches on the *Manfred* music, he finished the *Bilder aus Osten,* op. 66, for piano four-hands, and set to work on the *Waldscenen,* op. 82. The *Adventlied,* op. 71, for chorus, soloists, and orchestra, drafted simultaneously with the *Bilder aus Osten,* represents a turn toward a quasi-religious genre that would have far-reaching repercussions in Schumann's last years.

Then in 1849, the floodgates of creativity burst open with practically unprecedented force. As indicated in Table 11.1, the works of Schumann's most fruitful year embrace almost the entire range of musical genres, from unassuming choral *Romanzen* in a folkish idiom to high-minded literary opera, from little pieces for the fledgling pianist to concertante works for the virtuoso. And within several of these categories, Schumann explores nearly every conceivable combination of performing forces. The choral works, for instance, include compositions for mixed chorus (SATB), double chorus, women's voices, men's voices, double men's chorus, and chorus and orchestra. There is, in addition, a kind of chronological progression in Schumann's unbounded creativity that allowed him to focus alternately on instrumental chamber music and concert pieces (February–March), unaccompanied choral works (March), solo and ensemble lieder (March–June), literary opera (July–August), pedagogical and concertante keyboard music (September), and finally, ceremonial, quasi-religious music for chorus and orchestra (November–December).

Of the major genres, only purely orchestral music is not represented, but Schumann's development of a number of arguably "new" genres—the choral ballad, the dramatic song cycle, the "spiritual poem"

Table 11.1. Schumann's Works of 1849

Instrumental Chamber Music

Fantasiestücke [originally *Soiréestücke*] for clarinet (ad libitum violin or cello) and piano, op. 73 (February)

Adagio [originally *Romanze*] *und Allegro* for horn (ad libitum violin or cello) and piano, op. 70 (February)

Fünf Stücke im Volkston for cello (ad libitum violin) and piano, op. 102 (April)

[Drei Romanzen] for oboe (ad libitum violin) and piano, op. 94 (December)

Concertante Works

Concertstück for 4 horns *(Ventilhörner)* and orchestra, op. 86 (February–March)

Introduction und Allegro appassionato. Concertstück for piano and orchestra, op. 92 (September)

Choral Works (unaccompanied or with ad libitum instrumental accompaniment)

Romanzen und Balladen for mixed chorus, Heft I, op. 67 (March)

Romanzen und Balladen for mixed chorus, Heft II, op. 75 (March)

from *Romanzen und Balladen* for mixed chorus, Heft III, op. 145: Nos. 1, 4, 5 (March, August)

Romanzen und Balladen for mixed chorus, Heft IV, op. 146 (March, September)

Romanzen for women's voices (SSAA), Heft I, op. 69 (March/May)

Romanzen for women's voices (SSAA), Heft II, op. 91 (March/May)

Fünf Gesänge aus H. Laubes Jagdbrevier for men's voices (TTBB) and 4 horns ad libitum, op. 137 (May)

Verzweifle nicht im Schmerzenstal, motet ("religiöser Gesang") for double men's chorus and organ ad libitum, op. 93 (May; orchestrated 1852)

Vier doppelchörige Gesänge für grössere Gesangvereine, op. 141 (October)

Liederspiele

Spanisches Liederspiel (Geibel), op. 74 (March)

Spanische Liebeslieder (Geibel), op. 138 (March–April, November)

Minnespiel (Rückert), op. 101 (June)

Vocal Ensemble Music with Piano

from *Drei Lieder* for 3 women's voices, op. 114, Nos. 1 and 3 (May)

Vier Duette (ST), op. 78 (August, September)

Sommerruh (2 voices and piano), WoO 9 (November)

Lieder

Lieder-Album für die Jugend, op. 79 (April–June–July)

Lieder und Gesänge aus Wilhelm Meister, op. 98a (May–June–July)

Dir zu eröffnen mein Herz (Goethe), published as No. 5 of *Lieder und Gesänge*, op. 51 (October)

Gesänge aus Lord Byrons "Hebräischen Gesänge" op. 95 (December)

Dramatic Works/Literary Opera

Scenen aus Göthe's Faust, Nos. 1 *(Scene im Garten),* 2 *(Gretchen vor dem Bild der Mater Dolorosa),* 3 *(Scene im Dom),* 4 *(Ariel. Sonnenaufgang)* (July, August)

Keyboard Works

Waldscenen, op. 82 (December 1848–January 1849)
IV Märsche, op. 76 (June)
12 vierhändige Klavierstücke für kleine und grosse Kinder, op. 85 (September)
Polonaise for piano four-hands [=No. 2 of *Ball-Scenen,* op. 109] (October)

Works for Chorus, Soli, and Orchestra

Requiem für Mignon, op. 98b (July, September)
Nachtlied (Hebbel), op. 108 (November)
Neujahrslied (Rückert), op. 144 (December 1849–January 1850; orchestrated September 1850)

Declamation Ballad

Schön Hedwig (Hebbel), declamation and piano, op. 106 (December)

---

for chorus and orchestra, the declamation ballad—more than makes up for its absence. Indeed, Schumann's correspondence makes frequent reference to the novelty of many of the works from this period. He described the *Concertstück* for four horns and orchestra, for instance, as "something completely unusual," and the *Spanisches Liederspiel* as "quite original in form." The declamation ballad, *Schön Hedwig,* he maintained, was "a kind of composition that didn't previously exist."[5]

In this context, an often-told anecdote involving Schumann and Liszt takes on added meaning. In June 1848, the Schumanns arranged a soirée at their flat specifically for the great virtuoso, who had expressed an interest in hearing Schumann's D-minor Piano Trio. But much to his hosts' annoyance, the guest of honor appeared several hours late, and although he gave his stamp of approval to the Piano Trio, he dismissed another chamber work given on the same evening, the E♭-major Piano Quintet, as too "Leipzigerisch." Thereafter Liszt played several selections from *Carnaval,* but very sloppily, and, adding insult to injury, he then ventured an unflattering appraisal of Mendelssohn which prompted the usually taciturn Schumann to retort "Sir, who are you to make such remarks about a master like Mendelssohn!" After the incensed Schumann left the room, Liszt turned to Clara and said: "Please tell your husband that there is only *one* person in the world from whom I would take such words calmly."[6] A year later, Schumann was still smarting from the unfortunate episode. Responding in a letter of 31 May 1849 to

Liszt's interest in his setting of the *Schlussszene* of *Faust,* he queried: "But dear friend, wouldn't the composition be 'too *Leipzigerisch*' for you?" The continuation of Schumann's reply indicates that it was not the charge of provincialism that offended him most, the intimation that, as Nietzsche would later maintain, he was "a merely *German* event in music, no longer a European one,"[7] but rather the suggestion that he and other composers associated with Leipzig (Mendelssohn, Hiller, Bennett) shared a common style and were therefore "unoriginal": "If you examine my compositions more closely, you will certainly find a variety of perspectives therein, for I have always endeavored to bring to light something new in all my works, and not only as regards form. . . . And if our works [those of the 'Leipzig' composers] share many musical traits, you may call the phenomenon philistinism or what you will—but all the various artistic periods exhibit it as well: Bach, Handel, Gluck, and later Mozart, Haydn, and Beethoven can be mistaken for one another. . . . *No one is completely original.*"[8] The works of Schumann's last years in the Saxon capital go a long way toward demonstrating that he was hardly too "Leipzigerisch."

At the same time, Schumann's compositions from the latter part of 1848 through the end of the following year raise a whole complex of knotty questions regarding the relationship between style and style periods. Unlike, say, Beethoven's output, Schumann's simply does not lend itself to a parsing into more or less distinct stylistic phases. (Scholars may disagree over the number of Beethoven's style periods, current opinions ranging from three to five, but they generally subscribe to the usefulness and validity of some sort of periodic division. Wilhelm von Lenz's tripartition of Beethoven's oeuvre, in *Beethoven et ses trois styles* (1852–1853) has been refined but not totally rejected.) Nonetheless, recent commentators on Schumann's music are at one on several points relating to the works of the later 1840s. Many agree, for instance, that they are characterized by a turn to a more conventional, accessible and commercially successful style. Not without justification, Wolfgang Boetticher speaks of a "Biedermeier" phase initiated by the eminently accessible *Album für die Jugend,* one of the enduring bestsellers among Schumann's collections of keyboard miniatures.[9] What was the reason for the apparently abrupt about-face (at least in the keyboard genre), the shift from an esoteric idiom to the charming but far tamer manner associated with *Hausmusik,* a genre specifically intended for domestic entertainment and edification? According to Anthony Newcomb, Schumann merely decided "to stop beating his head against the wall" when he realized that the sophisticated style he had hitherto cultivated would not bring him the public acceptance and commercial success he deserved.[10]

For Arnfried Edler, one of our most sensitive commentators on Schumann's artistry, the compositions of this period in general inaugurate the decisive shift from an "optimistic," "poetic" outlook (consistent with the liberal ideals of the literary movement known as "Junges Deutschland") to a more "resigned," "prosaic" phase. By the late 1840s, he writes, the ideals of the Davidsbündler "had gone up in smoke."[11] And with resignation came withdrawal and retreat; even those compositions inspired by the mid-century revolutions, Edler maintains, speak less to active engagement than to "the echoing reverberation of a distant, inner realm."[12]

Thus, many of the current attempts to sketch out a periodic division of Schumann's output result in a series of binary oppositions: esotericism versus accessibility, poetry versus prose, engagement versus withdrawal. And while there is a measure of truth in all of them, it is equally evident that the rhetoric of these oppositions harbors a value judgment: the second term in each pair speaks implicitly to a creative decline.[13] Simply put, for most writers, Schumann's later works just are not as good as his earlier ones. (This fact is also reflected in contemporary concert life. Recordings of *Dichterliebe* flood the market, while performances of the *Meister* lieder are few and far between. Every major pianist has the Piano Concerto under his or her fingers, but many of the same artists have not even heard of, much less played, the *Introduction und Allegro appassionato,* op. 92.) Each of the binary oppositions, however, is easily called into question. The whimsical and complex keyboard style that, according to some, was abandoned after the *Novelletten,* op. 21, resurfaces in the G-minor Piano Trio, op. 110, the *Fantasiestücke,* op. 111, and the *Gesänge der Frühe,* op. 133, all from the Düsseldorf years.[14] The *Waldscenen* and the *Meister* lieder are arguably as rich in "poetic" content as the *Davidsbündlertänze* and the Eichendorff *Liederkreis.* The *Neujahrslied,* conceived after the suppression of the revolt in Dresden that is supposed to have occasioned Schumann's disillusionment with the liberal ideals of the mid-century revolutions, is one of his most uplifting and affectively optimistic pieces.

Hence, representations of Schumann's later music through a single term in a binary opposition will hardly do it justice. The apparent simplicity of the musical language in the *Waldscenen* and the convivial function of the *Spanisches Liederspiel* bring both works in line with certain aspects of the Biedermeier sensibility, but the creative essence of neither is exhausted by a single, overarching rubric. Nor is it really possible to say that the Biedermeier quality alone provides the underlying impetus for Schumann's creativity in his later Dresden years. We may have to settle for the less tidy notion that the composer's output during this period is characterized by a delicate web of overlapping, criss-crossing stylistic tendencies. At several points in his most fruitful years, Schumann worked more or less simultaneously on music for *Kenner* (professionals, virtuosi) on the one hand and *Liebhaber* (amateurs, consumers of *Hausmusik*) on the other. Within a week of completing the intimate *Fantasiestücke* for clarinet and piano in February 1849, he drafted the *Concertstück* for four horns and orchestra, still a major challenge even for seasoned players. From April through July, he worked alternately on the self-consciously naïve songs comprising the *Lieder-Album für die Jugend* and the emotionally gripping settings of the lyrics from Goethe's *Wilhelm Meister*. Almost immediately after orchestrating his sublime setting of the opening scene of *Faust*, Part II (No. 4 of the *Faust* scenes), he wrote the delightful choral miniature, *Der Schmied* (published as No. 1 of the *Romanzen und Balladen*, op. 145) and the equally charming *Tanzlied* that heads off the *Vier Duette* for soprano and tenor, op. 78. Both the *Introduction und Allegro appassionato* for piano and orchestra, op. 92, and the *12 vierhändige Klavierstücke*, op. 85, date from September, but the former was intended as a vehicle for Clara's artistry, while the latter was within the modest technical grasp of the seven-year-old Marie Schumann.

The continual shuttling between accessible and esoteric or virtuosic pieces (we will encounter a similar pattern in Düsseldorf) suggests a conscious strategy no doubt partially motivated by commercial exigencies. Writing in August 1851 to C. F. Peters and clearly troubled by the poor sales of the *Genoveva* score, Schumann promised a more financially viable composition in the near future.[15] But in terms of the logic of Schumann's creative trajectory, the dialectic between pieces for *Kenner* and *Liebhaber* that characterizes the years 1848 and 1849 attests to a fascinating play of depth and surface: what may be latent at one point in his career becomes manifest at others. The supposedly abrupt turn to *Hausmusik* represented in the keyboard genre by the *Album für die Jugend* and in the chamber idiom by the *Fantasiestücke* for clarinet and piano, was in fact presaged by the *Arabeske* and the *Blumenstück* of the late 1830s, and the *Phantasiestücke* for piano trio, op. 88, of 1842. Likewise, the *Concertstücke* of 1849 further explore tendencies first essayed during the Symphonic Year, 1841, and the New Way of the mid-1840s. Its variegated surface notwithstanding, Schumann's oeuvre is all of a piece.

The dialectic between esotericism and accessibility is further complemented by the tension between inner calm and outer storms to which Schumann alluded in proclaiming his most fruitful year in the April 1849 letter to Hiller. Indeed, the outward, public impulse in Schumann's art during this period manifests itself in the conviviality of the music for vocal ensemble and piano four hands, the pedagogical thrust of much of the keyboard and vocal music, the republican overtones of the works for male chorus, and the virtuoso display of the *Concertstücke*. In contrast, the intimacy of the *Waldscenen* and the *Fantasiestücke*, like the ultra-expressivity of the *Meister* lieder, emanates from a subjective, highly personal, inner realm. Yet Schumann was not content simply to alternate pieces for *Kenner* with others for *Liebhaber*, inwardly directed confessions with outer, public proclamations. Almost every composition of the later 1840s conflates *both* aspects to varying degrees. The *Requiem für Mignon*, to take an example, projects a personal, quasi-religious message in universal, humanistic terms.

In sum, Schumann's music of the fruitful period extending from mid-1848 through the end of 1849 exhibits a rich variety of tendencies: Biedermeier accessibility, republican fervor, virtuoso display, humanist religiosity. But while one or the other tendency may appear to dominate in a given instance, practically all the works of the period play on the interpenetration of esoteric and exoteric qualities, of inner and outer realms. Uniting them is an unflinching faith in the ideal that Schumann had already set for himself as a youth: the possibility of a poetic music.

Schumann and the Biedermeier Sensibility

In the mid- and late 1850s, Adolf Kussmaul and Ludwig Eichrodt began to publish in the pages of the satirical journal *Fliegende Blätter* some of the recently discovered verses of Samuel Friedrich Sauter, an obscure village schoolmaster. Kussmaul and Eichrodt presented Sauter's laughably sentimental poems as the work of one "Gottlieb Biedermaier," the fictitious surname bringing together an adjective meaning "honest but ordinary" ("bieder") and an exceedingly common German name, "Maier" or "Meier." It was not long before Papa Biedermeier had lent his name to both an age—the period in German history between the Wars of Liberation and the onset of revolution in 1848—and a concept, a restrictive world-view to which nostalgia, domestic tranquility, and indifference to political upheavals contributed in equal measure. As one writer puts it, the Biedermeier sensibility is "a curious and unique configuration of time-honoured habits, rich meals, ancient or at least old-fashioned furniture, solid broadcloth and solid moral maxims."[16] Biedermeier culture is thus profoundly conservative: centered around the home (the living room, in particular) over which the eldest male presides, obsessed with order, repelled by the erotic aspects of life, and secure in a naïve religious faith, it represents in many ways the exact obverse of the Romantic aesthetic. According to the historian James Sheehan, the Biedermeier outlook actually "took the fear and torment out of Romanticism, leaving in its place only some vaguely menacing motifs and exciting titillation."[17]

Music too played a significant role in Biedermeier culture. If Papa Biedermeier went to the opera, it was probably to hear Lortzing's *Zar und Zimmermann* or Otto Nicolai's *Die lustigen Weiber von Windsor*. If he wanted to impress his friends with his knowledge of high art music, he might whistle a tune from a Spohr string quartet or a Loewe ballad. His own musical activities were probably centered on the weekly rehearsals of the local Liedertafel (men's chorus) or Chorverein. A small but not insignificant part of his household budget went to the purchase of the *Hausmusik* produced in ever greater quantities by the *Kleinmeister* of the 1830s and 1840s, its style marked by technical simplicity but harboring pretensions to cultural breeding. Here too the Biedermeier sensibility differentiates itself from its Romantic counterpart. If Romantic music tends toward an esotericism that drives composers and their public ever farther apart, then the music of Biedermeier culture is sustained by a variety of institutions, the choral society and the choral festival chief among them, in which the gap between producer and consumer is considerably narrower.

Schumann undoubtedly partook of and contributed to this complex of phenomena, though, as we have already suggested, it would be a mistake to conclude that his music of the later 1840s represents a wholehearted embrace of the Biedermeier sensibility. Here Carl Dahlhaus's analysis of that sensibility may help us to assess Schumann's ties with it. For Dahlhaus, Biedermeier culture combines conviviality, bourgeois self-display, and an educational function, all of which are in turn projected in actual musical technique. The tunefulness of Lortzing's opera melodies, for instance, lends a convivial dimension to these works, just as the stylistic eclecticism of Spohr's chamber music represents the kind of "even-handed justice" prized by the liberal bourgeoisie. Likewise, the interplay of melodic simplicity and syntactic sophistication in Loewe's ballads would have appealed to the tastes of educated music-lovers. All three elements contribute to an unmistakably Biedermeier "tone" shared by Lortzing, Spohr, and Loewe alike.[18] To be sure, Dahlhaus's explication is not without its problems. Specifically, "conviviality" and "bourgeois self-display" are probably too closely intertwined to allow for their independent use in a meaningful analysis. Nonetheless, the twin concepts of conviviality and education, or more properly, *Bildung,* that peculiarly nineteenth-century German conflation of nature and self-cultivation, may serve as a useful framework for a discussion of Schumann's relationship to the Biedermeier sensibility; they respectively correspond to the outer and inner realms that interpenetrate in his music of 1848 and 1849.

The convivial side of Schumann's art during this period is clearly reflected in his assiduous cultivation of unaccompanied choral music and his active engagement with the institutions that sustained it. Soon after Hiller decided to assume the post of municipal music director in Düsseldorf in late October 1847, Schumann stepped in as conductor of the Dresden Liedertafel previously under his colleague's direction. According to a letter written some time later, the post afforded him "renewed confidence in my directing powers, which, due to nervous hypochondria, I thought had been completely shattered."[19] It also provided the impetus for a trio of collections for male chorus: the *Ritornelle in canonischen Weisen*, op. 65, seven pieces on Rückert texts (October 1847);[20] the *Drei Gesänge*, op. 62, for chorus and ad libitum winds (December 1847); and the pieces published much later as *Drei Freiheitsgesänge*, WoO 13–15 (April 1848).[21] While the latter two collections feature the patriotic texts, simple melodies, basically syllabic settings, and TTBB scoring typical for Liedertafel fare since early in the nineteenth century, the seven *Ritornelle* (Schumann's first foray into the male choral medium since the *Sechs Lieder*, op. 33, of 1840) display a more unusual profile. His handling of the conventional verses—a mix of Volkslieder, drinking songs, and sledding songs—is remarkable, first of all, for its textural variety, with combinations extending from three parts (BBB) in Nos. 2 and 4 to full choir and soloists (TTT) in No. 3. More striking still is the range of contrapuntal techniques employed: straightforward canon (Nos. 2 and 4), canons embedded in freely contrapuntal textures (No. 1), and canonic voices disposed in Josquin-like imitative pairs (No. 5 and the perpetual canon, No. 7). The eminently convivial medium, it would seem, was hardly immune to a strong dose of compositional artifice.

Nonetheless, Schumann's interest in the activities of the Liedertafel soon waned; by October 1848, less than a year after his first rehearsal with the group, he had resigned as director in favor of Julius Otto. Although Schumann found the members of the organization to be a pleasant enough lot, the musical side of his duties proved less than fulfilling. The Liedertafel, he explained to Hiller, simply "offered too little in the way of actual musical inspiration." Or as he put it to Verhulst: "After devoting the whole day to musical activities, it was difficult to relish the eternal $\frac{6}{4}$ chords of the male-choral style."[22] His two works for men's chorus of 1849, the *Fünf Gesänge aus H. Laubes Jagdbrevier* for voices and ad libitum horns, op. 137, and the motet for double men's chorus and organ ad libitum, *Verzweifle nicht im Schmerzenstal,* op. 93 (orchestrated in 1852), would be his last.

In the meantime, Schumann had found another, more musically rewarding outlet for his interests in convivial choral music. On 29 November 1847, only a week after his first rehearsal with the Dresden Liedertafel, he noted in the *Haushaltbücher:* "Idea for a choral society [Chorverein]."[23] Originally dubbed a "Caecilienverein," the Verein für Chorgesang first met on 5 January 1848 and occupied an important place in the composer's musical life until he and his family took up residence in Düsseldorf in September 1850. (The organization continued to thrive after Schumann's departure; in 1898 it celebrated its fiftieth anniversary as the Robert Schumann'sche Singakademie.) The group, whose size had swelled to between sixty and seventy members within about six months, obviously flourished under Schumann's leadership. Schumann, in turn, took genuine pleasure in his directorship: "My Chorverein," he wrote to Hiller in April 1849, "is a source of much joy, for I can try out, to my great delight, all the music I love."[24] This included, to judge from the group's performances in the spring of 1848, a varied repertory encompassing the works of both older and contemporary masters: Bach (selections from the *St. John Passion*), Beethoven (the Kyrie from the *Missa Solemnis*), Gade, and Mendelssohn. Palestrina's representation on the 26 March program demonstrates that Schumann's historical consciousness, nurtured during his student days in Heidelberg, heightened during his period as a music critic, and further reflected in his draft curriculum for the Leipzig Conservatory,[25] had, if anything, deepened over the years. (Schumann's sense for "early" music also exercised an abiding effect on the young protégé of his last years, Johannes Brahms.) In the mid-nineteenth century, it was only in organizations such as Schumann's Chorverein (and the scores of others like it) that the distant past and the immediate present met on equal terms. In this, the choral institutions of the day fostered not only conviviality, but *Bildung* as well.

Schumann's own works, large and small, likewise figured in the repertory of the Chorverein, which quickly became a kind of laboratory or testing ground for the composer's latest creations. With Clara at his side as assistant director and rehearsal pianist, he tried out portions of the *Schlussszene* from *Faust* beginning in February 1848. It was perhaps as a result of these trial rehearsals, which would have accorded Schumann the first palpable impressions of the actual sound of his imposing choral setting, that he decided in May 1848 to amplify the central chorus, "Gerettet ist das edle Glied," with a rousing, Handelian epilogue.

Similarly, the *Requiem für Mignon* was treated to a preliminary runthrough at a rehearsal of 19 September 1849. Of course, the success of the Chorverein (like that of any large performing organization) derived from the mutual benefits reaped by conductor and membership alike. If Schumann's singers proved remarkably receptive to their quirky director's grander projects, he responded in kind with a wide array of pieces at once convivial in tone and educational in function. In early 1846, Schumann had composed two charming sets of choral partsongs, the *Fünf Lieder* on Burns texts, op. 55 (from which the Chorverein performed selections in March 1848), and the *Vier Gesänge*, op. 59, but his regular contact with the Dresden Chorverein had as its consequence in 1849 a veritable spate of unaccompanied choral works for all manner of combinations: four volumes of *Romanzen und Balladen* for mixed chorus, eventually published as opp. 67, 75, 145, and 146;[26] two volumes of *Romanzen* for women's voices (SSAA), opp. 69 and 91; and a set of *Vier doppelchörige Gesänge für grössere Gesangvereine*, op. 141.

Echoing views shared by his contemporaries, one mid-nineteenth-century critic, A. F. Riccius, counted "elegance" and "sweetness," folk-like melody, absolute agreement of text and tone, and technical accessibility as the chief stylistic desiderata of the choral partsong.[27] Schumann's unaccompanied choral lieder beautifully embody these ideals. The first volume of *Romanzen und Balladen*, op. 67, may be taken as representative of the repertory as a whole. As indicated in the title, the texts upon which Schumann drew fall into two types: lyric verses centered on the expression of a single emotional state and ballads involving the narration of a striking event to an imaginary audience. Schumann had already brought together settings of both poetic types in his four volumes of *Romanzen und Balladen* for voice and piano of 1840 (opp. 45, 49, and 53) and 1847 (op. 64). Yet it is precisely in the transference of the literary *Romanze* and ballad to the choral medium that the originality and the compositional challenge of the Opus 67 set resides. The assignment of a personalized message or a bardic pronouncement to a collective body would, after all, appear to entail a contradiction. But Schumann convincingly transforms the lyric-epic "I" into a lyric-epic "we" through those apparently artless qualities, folkish melodies, straightforward harmonies, simple forms, syllabic settings, that together constitute the ideal for convivial choral music. Simply put, the stylized naïveté of the partsongs universalizes what the text presents as an individualized statement.

At the same time, the Opus 67 partsongs abound in subtle touches. In his setting of Goethe's famous poetic account of the dying king who takes a last draught from a golden goblet, *Der König von Thule*, Schumann evokes a dim, distant past through his recourse to a modally flavored melodic-harmonic idiom and a texture redolent of the sixteenth-century *Tenorlied*, the archaicisms thereby lending the choral ballad an ineffable, "once-upon-a-time" quality. Schumann articulates the shifts from narration to dialogue in Mörike's *Schön Rostraut* (which, intentionally or not, begins with a major-mode variant of the headmotif from the previous piece) through a graceful alternation of the full chorus and smaller groupings within it. He highlights the text even more directly by breaking out of the simple strophic form at the point where the king's daughter boldly asks for a kiss. The inner-voice chromaticism in *Heidenröslein* reminds us that the rose in Goethe's celebrated lyric is a metaphor for sensuality and that the young boy who catches sight of it is about to experience his first taste of love; the sensuousness of the harmonies belie the innocence of the folk-like tone of the text. Chamisso's *Ungewitter,* like Mörike's *Schön Rostraut,* employs both narrative and dialogue, features to which Schumann responds with a through-composed setting and an alternation of declamatory and lyrical vocal styles for the troubled king and his consoling beloved, respectively.

The artless surface of the *Romanzen und Balladen* is therefore deceptive, the naïve tone of the set a "second" naïveté, a projection of self-conscious innocence tinged with reflection. Nowhere is this more apparent than in the last partsong, arguably the finest gem of the collection, a setting of Burns's *John Anderson* in German translation. Based on an eighteenth-century folk poem, Burns's lyric (presented below in the original English) centers on the theme of reflection, figured through an aging wife's recollection of the past, when her John Anderson's "locks were like the raven," her sudden move into the present, where those same locks have become "like the snaw," and her premonition of future happiness beyond the grave:

> John Anderson, my jo, John
> when we were first acquent
> your locks were like the raven,
> your bonie brow was brent.
>
> But now your brow is beld,
> your locks are like the snaw,
> But blessings on your frosty paw
> John Anderson, my jo.

Schumann's dignified, hymn-like music lends a religious aura to a text that must have struck a personal chord, for two days after setting it on 13 March 1849 he took it up again. The 15 March version (published as Opus 145, no. 4) is remarkable for the extraordinary dissonances that Schumann couples with the invocations of "John Anderson." At the first of these, a dominant (B) in the bass rubs against a subdominant (A) chord in the upper voices, as if to imbue the name of the lyric's title character with an almost magical quality (Example 11.1). Moreover, the grace note (in the soprano) and the hairpin dynamic inflection (in all voices) seem to lift the little word "mein" right out of the opening phrase, thus underscoring the tender, personal quality of the speaker's words. Indeed, details such as these count for everything in the lapidary art of the choral partsong, for it was through the deftly handled melodic turn, the subtle play with formal convention, the piquant touch of chromaticism, the carefully chosen harmonic conceit, or the quiet highlighting of a single word that Schumann elevated an artless idiom to the level of an artform.[28] The convivial function of the genre was thus

Example 11.1. John Anderson, op. 145, no. 4: mm. 1–2.

linked to an educative one: the *Romanzen und Balladen* offered the musical enthusiast with little formal training a first-rate introduction to the world of art music.

Schumann's music for one-on-a-part vocal ensembles and piano was cultivated by the same institutions that supported his choral partsongs. Vocal duets from his Opp. 29 and 43 (1840) figured on the same program of the Chorverein in April 1848 that also featured selections from Bach's *St. John Passion* and Beethoven's *Missa Solemnis*.[29] In 1849, Schumann approached the genre with renewed vigor, his *Vier Duette* for soprano, tenor, and piano representing a marvelous contribution to a repertory intended for the educated music lover and the professional alike. The texts for this set, like those of the *Romanzen und Balladen*, are of two basic types: subjective lyrics and dramatic dialogues. The second type naturally lends itself to the duet medium, witness the opening *Tanzlied*, where Schumann brillianatly evokes the ballroom scene described in Rückert's text through an elegant waltz-accompaniment over which soprano and tenor interweave freely, the shift from one breathless dancer to the other often signalled by a third-related modulation. In setting the texts of the lyric type, Schumann confronted the same problem that had already arisen in the choral partsongs: the justification of his conversion of an "I" statement into a "we" statement. Although the duet medium obviously transforms the single lover in Goethe's *Ich denke dein* into a pair, the subjective essence of the poem remains untouched. The voices proceed in parallel sixths and thirds almost throughout, as if to signify the melding of the individual lovers into a higher unity. Schumann's assignment of the lyric "I" to soprano and tenor voices moving largely in parallel motion in his setting of Hebbel's *Wiegenlied am Lager eines kranken Kindes*, the most deeply felt lied in the set, is poetically justifiable insofar as it summons up the image of man and wife, united in grief, lulling their sick child to sleep. And finally, Schumann mediates both poetic types, subjective and dialogic, by alternating lyric statements for male and female personas and then allowing them to join harmoniously in *Er und Sie*. The lovers in Kerner's poem, like the young woman in *Frauenliebe und Leben*, see each other wherever they look; hence it is probably no accident that Schumann's setting of the line "Blick ich nur auf eine" (I fix my gaze on only one) employs the appoggiatura gesture associated with the phrase "Seh' ich ihn allein" (I see him alone) in the earlier cycle.

The dialectic between lyric and drama, emblems for personal and interpersonal expression, respectively, recurs on a larger scale in the three *Liederspiele* of 1849: the *Spanisches Liederspiel*, op. 74, the *Spanische Liebeslieder*, op. 138 (both on texts translated from the Spanish by

Emanuel Geibel) and the *Minnespiel,* op. 101, on a series of Rückert poems. In its early nineteenth-century incarnation through the practically single-handed efforts of J. F. Reichardt, the *Liederspiel* was a musico-dramatic entertainment in which songs, often on widely known texts, were introduced into plays. But by the 1820s the genre as Reichardt knew it, with scenery and spoken dialogue, had all but died out, Mendelssohn's *Heimkehr aus der Fremde* of 1829 being among the last of a dwindling number of examples. Thus with his three *Liederspiele* of 1849 Schumann can be said to have revived a languishing genre.

These works differentiate themselves from their early nineteenth-century counterparts in one respect above all: the absence of spoken dialogue. Yet they are by no means lacking in a dramatic component. On the contrary, Schumann's concern for precisely this dimension occasioned the following remarks, written the day after a performance of the *Spanisches Liederspiel:* "I am convinced now (as I was already after the dress rehearsal), that for the sake of the concentrated effect of the whole, two of the slower songs should be omitted, namely No. 4, a lied for alto, and No. 6 for baritone [both were indeed struck from the published version]. By themselves they don't fail to make a charming effect, but as I've implied, they impede the dramatic flow of the *Liederspiel*—thus I'll have to sacrifice them. Moreover, *Der Contrabandiste* [*Ich bin der Contrabandiste* for solo bass, published as an appendix] isn't, strictly speaking, part of the action."[30] And to be sure, it is not difficult to intuit the dramatic progression around which the nine lieder of the *Spanisches Liederspiel* weave a lyric commentary: from the first meeting of the lovers to the burgeoning of their love in the form of grief, from their fear that neither returns the other's feelings to union in mutual bliss.

Although Schumann proudly described the work as "quite original in form,"[31] some writers have detected a note of exaggeration in the composer's claim.[32] Still, it is arguable that given his conflation of tendencies culled from a broad spectrum of musical types—vocal duet, song cycle, opera—Schumann not only enriched a nearly moribund genre, but actually reinvented it. The pair of lovers in the *Spanisches Liederspiel* appear in two distinct guises: first as individuals (in the solo lieder, Nos. 6 and 7), and second, hearkening to the manner of the vocal duet and even the choral partsong, as universal types (in Nos. 1, 3, 8, and 9, where soprano and alto simultaneously project the part of the maiden; and in Nos. 2 and 9, where tenor and bass represent the youth). At the same time, Schumann's conception of the work as a tonal unity (in A minor-major) and his recourse to a subtle network of referential gestures and topics (for instance, the recurrence of the anxious accom-

panimental heartbeats from No. 1 in No. 9 and the shared Bolero
rhythms of Nos. 5 and 8), unmistakably recall the techniques whereby
a group of lyric fragments are unified as a cycle. Furthermore, the ultra-
expressive melodic leaps and alternation of declamatory and cantabile
styles impart a decidedly operatic tone to No. 3, a solo lied in which the
maiden bemoans her fate as an unrequited lover.

In drawing together a colorful bouquet of generic strands, Schumann created a work delicately suspended between private and public
spheres. On the one hand, there is much in the *Spanisches Liederspiel*
that would have spoken directly to the convivial impulses of the more
talented members of the Dresden Liedertafel and Chorverein. The eu-
phonious thirds and sixths of the "we"-statement lyrics, the rollicking
Bolero rhythms of the central solo quartet and the penultimate duet,
the sense that everyone, even the humble accompanist, will have his or
her moment in the sun: all of these traits seem perfectly geared to promote sociability among music-loving amateurs. On the other hand, the
performance history of the work demonstrates that its appeal readily
extended beyond the confines of the bourgeois drawing room: it was
rendered by professional singers (joined by that consummate professional, Clara Schumann, at the keyboard) at a 29 April 1849 matinée of
the Harmoniegesellschaft;[33] similarly, Peter Cornelius reported on an
enthusiastically received public performance of the work (again by
trained singers) at an 1867 convocation of the Allgemeine deutsche
Musikverein in Meiningen.[34] Similar in this regard to the instrumental
chamber music of 1842, the *Spanisches Liederspiel* bridged the gap between the private and public sectors of the musical world.

While the accent in Schumann's choral partsongs, ensemble lieder,
and Liederspiele still rests on their convivial function, the other key
element of the Biedermeier sensibility, an educative or pedagogical intent, lies at the heart of much of the keyboard, solo vocal, and even
instrumental chamber music of the later Dresden years. No doubt Schumann and his contemporaries would have subsumed this repertory under the heading of *Hausmusik*, the term having gained general currency
in the years immediately following the publication, between 1837 and
1839, of a multipartite article in the *Neue Zeitschrift* by C. F. Becker
entitled "Zur Geschichte der Hausmusik in früheren Jahrhunderten." Although Becker's largely historical account equated *Hausmusik* with the
entire range of instrumental and vocal genres intended for performance
in the home as opposed to the concert hall, the contemporary press was
quick to employ the term to designate a category distinct from concert
music (symphonies, concerts), church music, and dramatic music on
the one hand, and *Unterhaltungsmusik* ("entertainment music," a sub-

category comprised mainly of salon pieces for piano) and music for Gesangvereine on the other.[35]

As a repertory cultivated in the privacy of the bourgeois home, intended (at least ideally) as a means of heightening the cultural awareness of its practitioners, *Hausmusik* amounts to a quintessentially Biedermeier phenomenon. One image more than any other from the midnineteenth century captures the essence of the practice: Ludwig Richter's engraving for the frontispiece of Wilhelm Heinrich Riehl's *Hausmusik. Fünfzig Lieder deutscher Dichter* (1855), a collection comprising "only unpretentious, honorable music for the German home. . . . If one sang these pieces in the salon, the songs would be thereby profaned and the guests at the salon would be bored. Only in the sanctity of the home and in the company of friends will these songs make their proper effect, for they are not at all intended for the shimmer and glare of a public performance."[36] Richter in turn portrays a cozy domestic scene: a table set for dinner occupies the background; at the left foreground, a bent old woman (probably the grandmother of the family) warms her hands at the hearth; on the right, the pater familias presides at the keyboard while his wife, holding a baby, and daughter look on; one of two small children in the center enthusiastically joins in the music-making. Richter's illustration lends visual immediacy to a central Biedermeier theme: withdrawal from the outer tumult (whose looming presence we sense precisely because it is *not* depicted in the engraving) into that most hallowed of spaces, the domestic interior, its security ensured by generational and cultural ties. Interestingly enough, Schumann's music is directly implicated in the creation of this image. In his *Lebenserinnerungen eines deutschen Malers*, Richter, who heard Clara perform selections from the *Album für die Jugend* with her husband at her side, related the composer's comments on *Winterzeit. II*, the thirty-ninth piece in the collection: "The surrounding forests and field are covered in snow; thick snow blankets the streets of the city. It is dusk. A light snow begins to fall. Inside in the cozy room the old people sit by the fire and watch the joyful frolicking of the children with their dolls."[37] Both the illustration and the verbal description that probably inspired it thus speak to the motion from an outer world to the inner world where *Hausmusik* has its place.

But while Schumann's *Hausmusik* belongs to an inner, private sphere of activity, it is at the same time closely bound up with the outer circumstances of his life. The *Album für die Jugend*, he maintained in a letter of 6 October 1848 to Reinecke, "grew directly out of my family life . . . I wrote the first several pieces in the album as a birthday gift for our oldest child, and before I knew it, one [piece] followed on an-

other."[38] Nor did Schumann complain when what began as a humble
set of training pieces for his daughter Marie eventually proved to be a
best-selling item: "the Jugendalbum," he wrote to Brendel in September
1849, "has found a market like few if any works of recent years—I hear
this from the publisher himself."[39] For after all, by the end of the 1840s
the composer had become quite the pater familias himself. What with
an ever-growing brood to support (five of six children survived through
the end of the decade) and the gradual levelling-off of Clara's professional engagements, he would understandably savor his newly garnered
financial success: within a year, the intake from Schumann's compositions leapt from 314 thalers (in 1848) to 1275 (in 1849), reaching a level
that was even surpassed in the Düsseldorf period.[40] Pedagogical, practical, and artistic factors likewise interlock in Schumann's (and Clara's)
activities as private instructor during the later Dresden years. Beginning
in November 1847, he augmented his income by giving weekly and
sometimes bi-weekly composition lessons to Carl Ritter; a year thereafter
he began tutoring Heinrich Richter. One of the tangible results of these
activities was the *Lehrbuch der Fugenkomposition* completed in September 1848 (a pendant to the *Fugengeschichte* of 1837), in which Schumann amplified the canonical precepts of Marpurg and Cherubini with
insights of his own into the arcana of the fugal art.[41]

Given these circumstances, Schumann's turn to *Hausmusik* late in
1848 and throughout much of 1849 represents less an act of withdrawal
from the world than a sign of active engagement. Indeed, a crusading
impulse reminiscent of the Davidsbündler spirit informs the composer's
desire to make a contribution, at once educationally useful and aesthetically substantive, to a repertory that was veering further and further
from its original ideals.[42] The result was a grand pedagogical project
unequalled in scope since the days of J. S. Bach. Completed during August and September of 1848, the *Album für die Jugend,* a latter-day
equivalent of the *Clavier-Büchlein* for W. F. Bach, formed the keystone
of the enterprise. As indicated in the sketches and drafts for the collection, it was originally to have included a representative sampling of
works by great composers past and present, including Bach, Handel,
Gluck, Mozart, Haydn, Beethoven, and Weber. In the final version, these
were displaced by a pair of *Hommages* to Mendelssohn, *Erinnerung* (No.
28), and Gade, *Nordisches Lied* (No. 41), in the second of which the
composer's name is enciphered in the melody. Ludwig Richter, who provided the illustration for the frontispiece, an arabesque in the style of
Otto Philipp Runge on familial themes, was also supposed to have supplied illustrations for selected pieces. And as Schumann first envisioned

his pedagogical *Gesamtkunstwerk*, aphorisms from the *Musikalische Haus- und Lebensregeln* would have been interspersed throughout.[43] Published instead as an *Extrabeilage* to the 1850 volumes of the *Neue Zeitschrift* (though they appeared as an appendix to many subsequent editions of the *Album für die Jugend*), the *Lebensregeln* offer invaluable insights into Schumann's views on the foundational aspects of the art of music. Strictly speaking, the collection is not comprised of aphorisms at all, but rather of prescriptive maxims, pithy directives aimed at the fledgling musician, whom the composer addresses in the familiar *du* form on a broad range of topics: sensible practice habits, the development of basic musical skills, the acquisition of taste, the cultivation of a literary sensibility, advice on compositional method, and the formation of sound critical judgments. Yet the diverse content of the *Lebensregeln* is unified by an overriding idea: "There is no end to learning."[44] Between April and June 1849, the composer produced a vocal counterpart to the *Album für die Jugend* in the twenty-eight songs, most of them for solo voice and piano, of the *Lieder-Album für die Jugend*. And finally, he returned to the keyboard medium in September with the *12 vierhändige Klavierstücke für kleine und grosse Kinder*, thus bringing to a provisional conclusion the "grand pedagogical project" he had begun a little over a year before. (Similar impulses were rekindled in Düsseldorf, where in 1853 he composed the *Drei Klaviersonaten für die Jugend*, op. 118, and the *Kinderball* for piano four-hands, op. 130).

To be sure, the *Album für die Jugend* remains the locus classicus of Schumann's pedagogically conceived *Hausmusik* of the later 1840s. Divided into two parts, the eighteen pieces of the first intended "für Kleinere" and the remaining twenty-five pieces of the second "für Erwachsene" (more-grown-up children), the *Album* takes the young player, in carefully graded fashion, from the simplest of melody-and-accompaniment styles to contrapuntal textures of some complexity.[45] In between come a whole range of topics, including marches, chorales, Lieder ohne Worte, stylized folksongs, medleys, musettes, comic pieces, and representations of the hunt. Both parts are further organized around a governing key, C major and A minor-major, respectively, with adjacent pieces either sharing the same tonal center or exhibiting third- or fifth-based relationships. In addition, many of the pieces group themselves into pairs through shared motivic, gestural, or affective ties (for example, Nos. 7-8, 9-10, 27-28, 38-39, 41-42). Thus, the pedagogical plan of the collection is complemented by a web of musically unifying features.

Critics have long heard echoes in the *Album für die Jugend* of the tone struck earlier in the *Kinderscenen*. Indeed, both volumes provide compelling testimony of Schumann's affinity for the "happy days of childhood," and of his ability to recapture them—for himself and his listeners—through the medium of art.[46] Anticipating the comparisons that would be drawn between the two sets, Schumann made a fascinating distinction between them in a letter to Reinecke of 6 October 1848: "Although you will detect signs of my old humor here and there [in the *Album für die Jugend*], these pieces are completely different from the *Kinderscenen*. The latter are the reflections ["Rückspiegelungen"] of an adult for other adults, while the *Album* is rather made up of foretellings ["Vorspiegelungen"] and premonitions for children."[47] But while Schumann's distinction certainly holds for the earlier pieces in the *Album* ("für Kleinere"), many of the later ones ("für Erwachsene") are just as reflective in tone as the poetic miniatures of the 1830s. All three of the pieces headed only by three stars arranged in a triangular pattern (Nos. 21, 26, and 30), for instance, are pure emanations of Schumann's Eusebian persona. The closing cadence of the first of these alludes subtly to the coda of the first movement of the C-major *Fantasie*, op. 17, itself a dreamy evocation of the final song of Beethoven's *An die ferne Geliebte*. The reflectivity of the later pieces in the *Album* also emerges in their employment of a sophisticated array of textural, harmonic, and formal techniques: imitation enlivens the A section of *Fremder Mann* (No. 29), its central trio infiltrated by references to the macabre march tune of the opening; imitation likewise plays a role in *Thema* (No. 34), a miniature otherwise characterized by pervasive appoggiaturas and side-slipping chromaticism; the first two measures of *Sheherazade* (No. 32) recur at the very end of the piece, lending the whole a circular, infinitely continuable form marvelously suggestive of the princess's weaving of one tale after another.

　　Reflectivity and naiveté come together in *Winterzeit. II* (No. 39), the miniature that, as we have seen, may have inspired the best-known pictorial representation of the practice of *Hausmusik*. We can, without much difficulty, match the various sections of the piece with portions of Schumann's "program" as transmitted in Richter's *Lebenserinnerungen:* the languid motive of the opening C-minor segment captures the mood of the snow-covered scene outside; the more rapid figuration at the turn to G minor calls up images of children at play; the old people gathered around the fire are represented by the subsequent allusions to the *Grossvatertanz*. But at the same time, the little medley derives its aesthetic sense from a purely musical relationship, for, as shown in Examples 11.2 a and b, the descending motive of the opening section turns out to be a minor-mode premonition of the the C-major *Nachtanz* to

Example 11.2a. Winterzeit. II, mm. 1–2.

Example 11.2b. Winterzeit. II, mm. 50–52.

the *Grossvatertanz.*[48] Hence, the naïveté of the materials, and their naïve relationship to the "program," is countered by the subtlety with which they are manipulated.

Schumann's musical representation of a typically Biedermeier scene further reveals a broadly poetic but specifically Jean-Paulian dimension. In an essay on the "natural magic of the imagination" appended to *Quintus Fixlein,* the composer's favorite author voiced his desire to mediate the outer and inner worlds by bathing the quotidian "realities of the pastor's life" in "idealizing moonshine."[49] Schumann does much the same in the coda to *Winterzeit. II,* where fleeting references to all of the piece's principal motives dissolve in a C-major wash of sound over an open-fifth pedal. Even Schumann's program resonates with Jean Paul's novel, which abounds in scenes marked by an identical contrast: "the frost and snow outside; within, the stove and the coffee, the poodle and the pipe."[50] At a stroke, Schumann's music transforms Biedermeier homeliness into the stuff of a romantic idyll. "Even the fledgling pianist," Dörffel wrote of the *Album,* "is offered poetry."[51]

In the *Bilder aus Osten,* op. 66 (his first composition for piano four-hands since the youthful *VIII Polonaises* and the lost variations on a theme by Prince Louis Ferdinand) and the *Waldscenen,* op. 82, both conceived within a short space of each other in December 1848 and January 1849, Schumann returned even more obviously to the poetic ideals of the cycles from the decade before. In that he intended the first work as a Christmas gift for Clara, and considering its scoring for the most convivial of keyboard media (piano four-hands), it can be said to have sprung no less directly out of family life than the *Album für die Jugend.* But given the technical challenges posed by several pieces in the set, the sociability it aimed to promote was clearly that between artists of the first rank. According to the composer's own prefatory note to the

1849 Kistner edition of the *Bilder aus Osten*, the work was inspired by the *Makamen des Hariri*, Rückert's translation from the Arabic of a medieval epic dealing with the adventures of Abu Seid and his friend Hareth.[52] The cycle represents a further manifestation of the same enthusiasm for oriental topics that had kindled Schumann's interest in Moore's *Peri* some eight years earlier. But here, as in the poetically inspired cycles of the 1830s, the programmatic subject is swallowed up by a purely musical set of relationships. In his note to the 1849 edition, Schumann attributed the "unusual character" of some of the pieces to the fact that he couldn't keep the images of Abu Seid and Hareth "out of his head" while working. Yet he also emphasized that only the sixth and last of the pieces could be viewed as a direct response to a specific *maqam* (or disquisition), the one "in which we see the hero, rueful and repentant, approach the end of his life." Therefore we might well interpret the "unusual character" of the fourth piece, manifested in the Aeolian flavor of its principal melody, as a reaction to the exotic images of Abu Said and Hareth, no doubt Florestan and Eusebius in oriental garb. The recurrence of the same melody at the end of the cycle, however, not only serves as an emblem for the expiring hero's "rueful and repentant" memories, but also as a means of binding the individual parts into what Schumann called "a very intimate whole,"[53] a quality further ensured by the set's overall organization around a B♭-minor tonic.

Programmatic and musical subjects likewise overlap in the *Waldscenen*, where we are transported from the cozy trappings of the bourgeois interior to the wondrous world of the romantic forest. Schumann lavished great care on this cycle, an indication of its personal significance within his oeuvre. Though he brought his score to a provisional conclusion with typical speed between 24 December 1848 and 6 January 1849, he continued to polish and refine it off and on for almost two years until finally, in September 1850, the composition reached its final form.[54] Chief among the objects of Schumann's attention was the literary dimension of the cycle, as represented by the fanciful titles and mottos for its constituent pieces that he alternately adopted, altered, and in some cases rejected. At one point, all but three of the nine pieces were to have been headed by verses drawn from a variety of sources, including Gustav Pfarrius's *Waldlieder* and Heinrich Laube's *Jagdbrevier*.[55] Of course, neither the titles nor the mottos constitute a motivating program for the cycle. Indeed, some of the latter could only have been added after the pieces were composed,[56] and in the end, Schumann retained only the motto for "Verrufene Stelle" (No. 4), a pair of morbid stanzas from Hebbel's *Waldbildern*:

The flowers growing here so tall
Are pale as death;
Only one stands dark red,
There in the middle.

But its color comes not from the sun,
Whose glow it has never met,
But rather from the earth,
From drinking human blood.

The sinister imagery of the poem reminds us that the marvels of the romantic wood could take a decidedly weird form, a conceit encoded in the music through a complex of Baroque gestures—French-overture rhythms, fussy ornaments, imitative parries on a variety of doleful motives—suggestive of removal into a temporally distant and unfamiliar world.

For the most part, then, listeners are left to intuit for themselves the poetic meanings of the pieces from the topical content with which Schumann imbues his music in rich abundance. The musical evocation of the romantic forest in *Waldscenen* resounds with the mellow strains of the horn choir (*Eintritt*, No. 1; *Vogel als Prophet*, No. 7), raucous horn calls (*Jäger auf dem Lauer*, No. 2; *Jagdlied*, No. 8), tuneful folk melodies (*Herberge*, No. 6), eerie birdsongs (*Vogel als Prophet*), and expressive lieder (*Abschied*, No. 9). In addition, this multiplicity of characters is imparted a unifying shape by the organization of the cycle around a B♭-major tonic (together with its nearest relatives) and an alternation between pieces dominated by naïve affects on the one hand and bizarre affects on the other, a throwback to the alternating Florestan and Eusebius qualities in earlier cycles such as the *Davidsbündlertänze* and the *Fantasiestücke*, op. 12. A delicate web of thematic reminiscences binds together the miniatures of the first type no less than those of the second. The closing flourish of *Verrufene Stelle*, for instance, provides the shape for the principal motive of *Vogel als Prophet*, the most enigmatic miniature in the set, incorporated as an afterthought to the original group of eight.[57] The "naïve" pieces are linked by a considerably denser network of relationships. The middle section of *Herberge* echoes the opening of *Freundliche Landschaft* (No. 5), while the opening, folklike tune of the former is in turn echoed in *Abschied*, overtly in the broadly conceived principal melody, and covertly in an inner voice near the conclusion of the piece. The final miniature of the cycle likewise resonates with allusions to the remaining naïvely-toned pieces: the delicious rubbing of B♭ and B in *Einsame Blumen*, No. 3 (a product of the imitative partwriting) recurs in the course of a sequential passage in *Abschied* (m. 17), while the closing gesture of *Eintritt,* in slightly varied form, serves to round off the cycle as a whole. The network of reminiscences, some attentuated, some immediately perceivable, with which Schumann colors his encounter with the sylvan world tinges the apparently artless pieces of the cycle with a discernible measure of reflection.[58] Thus the dialectic between naïveté and reflectivity that informs some of the later pieces in the *Album für die Jugend* also lies at the heart of the musical poetry of the *Waldscenen.*

A similar interplay characterizes the poetic *Hausmusik* for various solo instruments and piano that occupied Schumann intermittently throughout 1849: the *Fantasiestücke* for clarinet, op. 73; the *Adagio und Allegro* for horn, op. 70; the *Fünf Stücke im Volkston* for cello, op. 102; and the *Drei Romanzen* for oboe, op. 94. Together, these compositions, along with the *Märchenbilder* for viola and piano, op. 113 (1851), and the *Märchenerzählungen* for clarinet, viola, and piano, op. 132 (1853), constitute a systematic exploration of the coloristic possibilities of the few-voiced instrumental chamber idiom, situating Schumann in the center of a tradition bounded by J. S. Bach on one end and Hindemith on the other.

With the exception of the *Adagio und Allegro* for horn, all of the instrumental chamber works of 1849 were conceived as cycles of poetic miniatures, each unified, like the *Bilder aus Osten* and *Waldscenen,* by a central tonic (interestingly enough, all three cycles were cast in A minor/major) and an overall affective profile. The close relationship among the three pieces comprising the *Fantasiestücke* is further underscored by the *attacca* indications linking each of the movements and, more important, by a web of thematic connections. The overlapping third chains of the principal melody of No. 2 derive from the counterline to the opening idea of No. 1. No. 3 recalls material from both of the preceding pieces: the allusion, in its A section, to the main idea of No. 1 is so deftly woven into the melodic fabric that one is apt to miss it on first hearing (Examples 11.3 a and b); the coda then recalls the opening of No. 2 (at first *piano, dolce*), which, as we have noted, is traceable to the very beginning of the cycle. Yet in no way do the various reminiscences overtly call attention to themselves; Schumann's refined technique of lyric recall rather makes for a delicate tracery of fleeting allusions, half-remembered ideas. One mid-nineteenth-century critic who was particularly struck by the intimate unity of these pieces came to essentially the same conclusion in describing the cycle as the refraction of a single mood (*Stimmung*) into diverse psychological moments, all of them beautifully captured in sound.[59]

Common to all the chamber cycles is an incredible melodic flexi-

Example 11.3a. Fantasiestücke, op. 73: No. 1, mm. 1–3.

bility characterized by the fluid passing of brief ideas from one instrument to the other, resulting in a lyric-coloristic composite shared by solo instrument and piano alike. Yet the apparent simplicity of the ideas themselves is often in subtle conflict with the unusual manner in which they are conjoined. This dialectic between naïve lyricism and esoteric syntax is prominent in the *Fünf Stücke im Volkston,* where four-square phrase groupings are often enlivened by irregular inner divisions, or conversely, where irregular phrase lengths are regularized through repetition. In the first piece, for instance, the *Humor* of the overall expressive indication manifests itself in the metrically irregular groupings—1½ + 1½ + 1—within the four-bar phrases of the main idea, an outwardly jaunty, folkish tune (Example 11.4). The second piece, a lullaby, falls into a simple ABA + coda form, its sections contrasting both tonally (F major versus F minor) and melodically. Yet the contrasting parts are bound together by an identical and quite unusual phrase structure wherein seven-bar units are first divided in a 3 + 4, then a 4 + 3 pattern. Thus the technique of variation, usually a function of melodic, harmonic, or harmonic-rhythmic manipulation, is here applied to an irregular hypermeter. The opening six-bar idea of the third piece divides into two phrases of 2½ and 3½ bars respectively, its speech-quality enhanced by the discrepancy between the arching melody in the cello and the

Example 11.3b. Fantasiestücke, op. 73: No. 3, mm. 9–15.

punctuating chordal asides in the piano. And while the fourth piece maintains a generally straightforward metric profile, the rondo theme of the fifth features a skittish interplay of 5-, 6-, 2-, and 4-bar units.

In each case, the metric irregularities serve as a means of imparting to the music the character of a spoken utterance. And in this, the *Fünf Stücke im Volkston,* along with the other sets of miniatures for chamber ensemble, partake of a broader concern shared by all of Schumann's poetic *Hausmusik,* including the pieces "für Erwachsene" in the *Album für die Jugend* and the poetic cycles for piano and piano four hands. The entire repertory projects an ineffable "once-upon-a-time" quality, a sense that a narrative is under way, even though no determinate content

Example 11.4. Fünf Stücke im Volkston, op. 102: No. 1, mm. 1–4.

is being narrated. Schumann's cultivation of this quality during the central years of the nineteenth century—years of intense social, economic, and political turmoil—is telling indeed. For the composer and his contemporaries, to state their problem in terms employed by the critic Walter Benjamin, were witnessing a breakdown in time-honored modes of perception: the enduring experience or *Erfahrung,* a product of accumulated wisdom passed down from one generation to its successor, was giving way to momentary experiences or *Erlebnisse,* striking but ephemeral disturbances on the temporal continuum. Writing in 1852, Eduard Krüger feared that precisely this situation would have disastrous implications for the fostering of art; concert life in the larger cities, he maintained, was no longer animated by the chief requirement for the production of great music, namely, "the continual preservation of the after-echoes of that which has been experienced."[60] Art, in other words, thrives best in those societies whose members have retained the ability to exchange experiences, to tell stories. And it is just this that Schumann does with such consummate skill in the poetic *Hausmusik* of 1848 and 1849. He assumes the role of the storyteller, a persona we will meet again in the composer's Düsseldorf period, as a means of preserving continuity with tradition in a world where experience, as *Erfahrung,* was becoming ever more of a rarity.

Concertante Experiments

As we have already noted, the products of Schumann's most fruitful years, 1848 and 1849, display a variety of coexistent and at times interpenetrating trends. The two principal concerted works of 1849, the *Concertstück* for four horns and orchestra, op. 86, and the *Concertstück (Introduction und Allegro appassionato)* for piano and orchestra, op. 92, represent a continuation and refinement of some of the tendencies associated with the New Way of the mid-1840s. At the same time, they draw liberally on features first essayed in a seldom heard but intriguing work: the *Adagio und Allegro* for horn and piano, op. 70.

Conceived in mid-February 1849, the *Adagio und Allegro* forms part of the series of works just discussed, in which Schumann furthered the aims of a poetic *Hausmusik* for chamber ensemble. But in a sense, the *Adagio und Allegro* hardly belongs under the rubric of *Hausmusik* at all. Only the consummate professional will want to tackle this work, the first substantial solo piece to exploit the full capabilities of the valve horn. Although the instrument had been invented around 1818, and began to appear in orchestras, especially in France, during the 1830s, it was slow to gain official acceptance. (At the Paris Conservatoire, instruction on the valve horn was suspended between 1864, when the only professor retired, and 1896; it became the officially recognized variety of horn at that institution only in 1903). Hence Schumann's little piece, poised midway between the bourgeois music-room and the concert stage, makes an important contribution to a repertory that even today is far from large. The first of the work's two sections begins with an expressive idea (Example 11.5) whose immediate recourse to half-step motion unmistakably stamps the composition as the property of the valve horn. The ensuing Allegro falls into a rondo form (ABACAB'A), both of its episodes drawing on the opening four-note gesture of the Adagio. As we will discover shortly, Schumann continued to investigate ever more subtle means of linking introductory or slow movements with complementary quick movements in the larger concerted works from later in the year.

Obviously pleased with his first essay for the valve horn, Schumann quickly drafted and elaborated what counts among the most unusually, but effectively scored works in the symphonic repertory: the *Concertstück* for four horns and orchestra.[61] The piece is just as impressive from a visual as from an aural standpoint: the sight of four horns ranged in front of an orchestra creates an image not easily forgotten. Its title, however, is somewhat misleading: the *Concerstück* is in fact a full-fledged three-movement concerto (Schumann himself sometimes referred to the work as his "Hornconcert"),[62] its last two movements linked after the fashion of the Piano Concerto, op. 54. Yet the published genre designation may also be interpreted as a reflection of an underlying dialectic between a unitary *Stück* and the several movements (*Lebhaft, Romanze,* and *Sehr lebhaft*) into which it is articulated. The entire work is bound together by a complex of features, the most obvious of

Example 11.5. Adagio und Allegro for horn and piano, op. 70: mm. 1–4 (horn melody).

which involve the last two movements. The middle section of the *Romanze* is given over to a sumptuous melody (with hemiolas supplying breadth) first stated by the orchestra and then by the full horn choir over cello pizzicatos. The same idea then recurs in the finale as a moment of sublime removal, a lyric episode in the midst of the scurrying motivic play of the development section. The immediate precedent for the technique derives from the linking of lyric introduction and ensuing quick movement in the *Adagio und Allegro,* though its roots extend back even farther to the episodic asides prominent in Schumann's keyboard works of the 1830s.

In composing the Opus 86 *Concertstück,* Schumann was faced with two chief problems: how was he to shape the characteristic gestures associated with the horn into sufficiently eloquent motivic ideas? and how should he balance his unwieldy concertante group, both internally and in its relationship to the orchestra? He tackled the first problem at the outset of the first movement, when after two stirring hammer-strokes from the full orchestra, the soloists, as if to assert their dominance without further ado, present a basic idea that welds together two highly differentiated characters: a triplet fanfare and an accented legato continuation (Example 11.6a). As the movement proceeds, the first component of the idea is often treated as a quasi-independent, developmentally malleable gesture. The fanfare (or its derivatives) pervades the transition to the second group, the rousing close of the exposition, and the entire second half of the development. The orchestral rejoinder to the basic

Example 11.6a. Concertstück for 4 horns and orchestra, op. 86: first movement, mm. 2–4.

idea will have even more striking consequences: the figure first stated in m. 6 (Example 11.6b) next appears at the close of the brief tutti; the first horn then takes up the figure's rhythm, but freely inverts its shape (Example 11.6c); soon thereafter, a transitional theme evolves a completely new melodic shape while retaining the original rhythmic pattern; and finally, the opening of the second group offers a rhythmic variant of the initial idea (Example 11.6d). Diastematic and rhythmic elements are treated independently in a stunning example of the technique of developing variation. Thus a compositional strategy associated with the Symphonic Year and the New Way was brought to bear on the challenge of writing an extended work for an unusually constituted ensemble.

Schumann's response to the second problem demonstrates a real sensitivity not only to the coloristic possibilities of the concertante group but also to the interdependence of color, form, and function. In the exposition of the first movement, the full horn choir is employed to articulate the chief ideas of both first and second groups. In contrast, transitional and bravura closing sections are characterized by a playful exchange of brief motivic particles, the orchestra often joining in the repartee among the soloists. The principle idea of the slow movement unfolds in a genuinely contrapuntal texture: a canon at the unison for first and second horns. But the most dazzling treatment of the instrumental forces comes in the finale, an exuberant movement driven largely by a propulsive dactylic motive. Hardly a single idea is sustained for long in any given voice: the scoring of the movement is rather character-

Example 11.6b. Opus 86: first movement, mm. 4–6 (violins, winds).

Example 11.6c. Opus 86: first movement, mm. 15–17 (horn I).

Example 11.6d. Opus 86: first movement, mm. 42–44 (horn I).

ized by a textural mosaic in which motivic fragments are capriciously tossed about, both within the concertante group, and between soloists and orchestra. In an 1847 entry in his *Projektenbuch,* Schumann entered Bach's Concerto for "4 Klaviere mit Begl.[eitung] d.[es] Quartetts" (the Concerto in A Minor for Four Harpsichords, Strings, and Continuo, BWV 1065, after Vivaldi's Opus 3, no. 10), under the heading "compositions for study."[63] No doubt Schumann's interest in the Baroque concerto grosso fueled his desire to write one of his own. And in the *Concertstück* for four horns and orchestra, he fashioned a response to the time-honored genre that more than lives up to its eighteenth-century models.

Several of the issues explored in the *Adagio und Romanze* and the Opus 86 *Concertstück* resurface as well in the *Introduction und Allegro appassionato* for piano and orchestra. Composed between 18 and 26 September 1849 as a vehicle for Clara, the soloist for its less than resoundingly successful premiere on 14 February 1850 at the Leipzig Gewandhaus, Schumann's second *Concertstück* remains, in spite of its many compelling features, one of his most sadly neglected works.[64] In the late 1830s, Schumann the critic had bemoaned the paucity of recently composed concerted works of substance, suggesting as an alternative to the "serious and worthy" form of the traditional three-movement concerto a more compact one-movement design in which the various "characters" of the older form—introductory, lyric, bravura—were nonetheless maintained.[65] To be sure, elements of this prescription inform both the A-minor Piano Concerto and the Opus 86 *Concertstück.* But in the *Introduction und Allegro appassionato* Schumann transformed the design of the concerto in a manner that reflected a common mid-nineteenth-century practice of piano virtuosos, who often programmed only the final two movements of a three-movement concerto.[66] By shaping his Opus 92 as an extended introductory *Langsam* followed by an imposing Allegro, Schumann inscribed a performing practice into the very fabric of the music.

No doubt echoes of the Opus 86 *Concertstück,* and even of the Opus 70 *Adagio und Allegro,* reverberated in Schumann's ears as he set to work on the *Concertstück* for piano and orchestra.[67] The mellow tone of the horn is a significant presence practically throughout; nor is the instrument limited to a coloristic role. Consider, for example, the evocative idea that heads off the *Introduction.* Over murmuring arpeggios in the piano, the clarinet presents a four-bar lyric fragment—on first hearing, it appears to emanate magically from the piano figuration—to which the horn appends a two-bar call (Example 11.7). The horncall, much like the corresponding figure in the first movement of the Opus

Example 11.7. *Concertstück* for piano and orchestra, op. 92: mm. 1–7 (clarinet and horn).

86 *Concertstück,* subsequently insinuates itself into practically all of the form-parts of the ensuing *Allegro;* during the second group, development, and coda, it is even appropriated by the soloist. Yet Introduction and Allegro are bound together not only by motivic ties, as in the *Adagio und Allegro,* but also by an all-embracing tonal scheme. The G major of the *Introduction* is displaced by the E minor of the *Allegro's* first group, its reinstatement in the expansive coda the outcome of a protracted argument spread over much of the piece. Motivic and tonal cross-references function interdependently in Schumann's treatment of the opening clarinet phrase. This music recurs as a dreamy aside (for winds supported by pizzicato strings) first during the development, in B major, and next near the outset of the coda, in B♭. Only in the closing peroration for the soloist is the idea restored to the tonic, G major, and brought into line with the exuberant affect of the *Allegro.* An obvious relative of the moment of sublime removal that linked the *Romanze* and finale in the Opus 86 *Concertstück,* the comparable strategy in the *Introduction und Allegro appassionato* goes a long way toward recasting the conventional tonal-thematic polarity of the sonata style into a contrast between distance (as represented by the evocative introductory music) and presence (as asserted in the martial first theme of the *Allegro*). Likewise, it is not difficult to detect the voices of Schumann's Eusebius and Florestan personas in these musically contrasting inner and outer worlds. Just as in the poetic *Hausmusik,* the Davidsbündler spirit continued to animate Schumann's concertante experiments of the late 1840s.

Storms Within and Without

"I am not a prophet and I don't know what will happen, but I am an old physician and can distinguish between temporary and fatal diseases. We now face one of the latter."[68] Metternich's grim diagnosis, offered to a visiting diplomat in the spring of 1847, proved to be correct. Fueled by a variety of social and economic ills on the one hand, and demands for legal and constitutional reform on the other, the first in a series of mid-century revolutions broke out in Palermo on 12 January of the following year. By late in February, anti-governmental demonstrations in Paris occasioned King Louis Philippe's flight from the French capital. Unrest quickly spread into the southwestern German states, with insurgents there, as elsewhere, demanding political reform, social justice, and deliverance from servitude. Soon after the capitulation of the Viennese government on 13 March 1848, Metternich, that "old physician" of European politics, sought refuge as an exile in England. Later in the month, King Friedrich Wilhelm's promises to allow a Prussian constitution and abolish censorship raised the hopes of moderate reformers, but all was thrown into confusion when royalist troops fired into a crowd assembled before the Royal Palace in Berlin, killing several innocent citizens. The violent collapse of an old order, it seemed, was definitely at hand.

Students of Schumann's life and work have long grappled with the questions surrounding his relationship, as man and artist, to the bloody events of 1848 and 1849. These questions do not admit to easy solutions: the evidence, both documentary and musical, is rife with contradictions. As we have already seen, Schumann wrote to Hiller in April 1849 that an inward turn to musical creativity provided him with a counterforce to the "outer storms" of revolution.[69] At the same time, he insisted that this inward turn was not to be equated with a retreat from reality. On the contrary, it afforded him a means of chronicling, in tone, the world events surging around him. As he put it to Brendel on 17 June 1849: "Ah yes—to tell, in music, of the sorrows and joys that motivate the times—this, I feel, has fallen to me more than to many others. And that you maintain how strongly my music is rooted in the present and aims for more than mere euphony and pleasant entertainment—this pleases me so much and inspires me to strive all the more."[70]

Schumann's attitude as a private citizen was marked by a tension between high-minded ideals and an intense distaste for brute force, a tension likewise reflected in the tug-of-war between inner and outer realms played out in his work as an artist. As a teenager, he subscribed to a utopian ideal in which art drew sustenance from democratic ideals. According to a diary entry from early 1827, "Political freedom is perhaps the actual wet nurse of poetry; it is necessary above all for the unfolding of poetic blossoms; genuine poetry (that is, poetry which enters into public life enthusiastically and passionately) can never thrive in a land where serfdom and slavery prevail."[71] And as an adult, he held fast to the view that the republic, not the constitutional monarchy favored by political moderates, remained the best form of government.[72] Throughout the revolutionary period itself, both Schumann and Clara followed the course of the central- and western-European struggles with keen

interest, often engaging in spirited debates with their small circle of
Dresden friends.[73] In addition, the composer dutifully noted the major
advances and reversals in the republican cause in the *Haushaltbücher,*
including the upheavals of February 1848 leading to the fall of the July
Monarchy, the "enormous political excitement" generated by the Bundestag's declaration of freedom of the press in early March, Metternich's
resignation, the Prussian king's initial concessions to demands for reform, and reports of uprisings and calls for independence in Schleswig
and Milan.[74] Indeed, Schumann claimed to have read "more newspapers
than books" during the "great revolutionary years," 1848 and 1849.[75]

The "dreadful happenings of the time"[76] were at first a source of
shock and dismay, but these feelings soon mingled with fear when, in
early May 1849, the revolution that the Schumanns had heretofore observed from a distance became an awful presence in Dresden. In April
1849 the Saxon Landtag attempted to convince the government to accept
the constitution for a German Confederation recently ratified by dele-
gates, assembled in Frankfurt, from the twenty-nine smaller German
states. But the Saxon king, Friedrich Augustus II, confident of Prussian
military backing, responded by simply dissolving the Landtag. Open re-
bellion subsequently broke out when royal troops fired at demonstrators
gathered at the Dresden Arsenal. Before long, the entire city had become
a stage for the enactment of a gruesome and terrifying drama.

The Schumanns, no less than their fellow Dresdeners, were caught
up in the pandemonium, their reaction to the general state of turmoil
vividly described in Clara's diary. On 3 May, shortly after enjoying a
pleasant meal at the Plauenschen Grunde, they heard the tocsin sound
from the city towers and gunshots ringing in the distance: "the revolution is here," Schumann jotted in the *Haushaltbücher.*[77] The night passed
calmly, but when, on the next day, the couple ventured into the city,
they discovered that barricades had been erected in the streets. "Everywhere the greatest lawlessness ruled," Clara wrote, just barely sup-
pressing her horror at the dreadful sight she and her husband had witnessed: fourteen dead bodies, casualties of a skirmish between royalists
and republicans, on public display in the courtyard of the hospital.[78]

But matters truly came to a head for the family on 5 May when
members of a neighborhood security brigade, intent on enlisting every
able-bodied man into their number, came knocking on the Schumanns'
door. Clara managed to fend them off twice, but when they threatened
to search the flat, she, Robert, and their eldest daughter Marie fled
through the garden gate and headed post-haste for the train station. By
1 P.M. they were on their way to the suburb of Mügeln, while the three
other children, Elise, Julie, and Ludwig, presumably remained in the

hands of the Schumanns' maid. "I was very upset that we hadn't at least brought Elise along," but, as Clara went on to explain, "we departed just as we were, so there wasn't time to fetch all the children, and Robert thought that we'd be back by evening."[79] From Mügeln, they went on foot to Dohna, and then, after hearing from the passengers in the next train that the situation in Dresden remained perilous, on to Maxen. When the Schumanns realized that their stay at the estate of their friend Major Serre might be a protracted one, Clara desperately wanted to return for the children, but was unable to do so without first finding someone to accompany her. Robert, she explained, simply could not re-enter the city, for the insurgents had made it clear that the male citizenry would be forced to participate in the uprising.

Thus far in the tale, neither of the elder Schumanns comes off very well. It seems unconscionable that they would have left three children—the youngest, Ludwig, was only a little over a year old—basically unattended. (The maid Henrietta, who had been ill on the day of the family's escape, proved an ineffectual guardian.) Robert's behavior was at worst cowardly—compared, for example, with that of Wagner, who on the day of the Schumanns' flight did lookout duty for the insurgents from the Kreuzkirche, the highest vantage point in the city—and at best passively acquiescent to the escape plan of an overly protective wife. Schumann's entries in the *Haushaltbücher* for May 5 and 6 tell us the amount of money he took along to the train station (55 thaler), provide brief references to the crisis described at greater length in Clara's account ("the search party—our escape"), and record the results of his compositional activity (the hubbub on 5 May did not preclude the completion of the delightful duet on a Fallersleben text, *Frühlings Ankunft,* for the *Lieder-Album für die Jugend*), but disconcertingly enough, they make no mention of the children.[80]

In the next days, however, Clara would more than redeem herself. Playing Leonora to her husband's Eusebius, she and a Frau von Berg (the daughter of Serre's steward) set off for Dresden in the wee morning hours of 7 May. Traveling part of the way unaccompanied and on foot, Clara, then seven months' pregnant, "proceeded amidst continuous cannonading" as she reached the outskirts of the city, at one point even coming up against forty scythe-armed soldiers. Undeterred, she pressed on toward the embattled city, found her children sleeping quietly, tore them out of bed, dressed them, and packed in short order. Within an hour she and her young charges were in the fields outside of town; before noon they arrived in Maxen, where "my poor Robert had also spent many anxious hours and was therefore doubly happy [to see us]."[81] Clara's account of the ordeal reads like the scenario for a rescue opera; Schumann's, in contrast, is oddly detached, even for the generally laconic style of the *Haushaltbücher:* "Clara departs at 3 A.M.—I wait with Marie—Clara and the children arrive at 11."[82]

Whatever victories the Dresden insurgents could claim were painfully shortlived, for by 9 May, the royalists had recaptured the city (with the help of Prussian troops) and sent the provisional government packing to Freiberg. The Schumanns later learned from their landlady of the "horrid atrocities" committed by the king's forces in the name of the restoration of order: twenty-six students had been shot, and countless rebels were bodily hurled from third- and fourth-floor windows. "It is too horrible to have to experience such things," Clara fulminated. "So this is the price that people have to pay in order to gain a bit of freedom for themselves! When will the time come when everyone will have the same rights?"[83] Nonetheless, things seem to have calmed sufficiently for the Schumanns to venture back to Dresden, if only to gather up enough belongings to tide them over during their temporary exile, on the afternoon of 10 May. (Schumann, who apparently forgot to bring along his re-entry permit, at first only travelled as far as the suburb of Strehla). The couple wandered through the city streets, amazed at the devastation wrought since their departure: homes riddled with bullet-marks, crumbling walls everywhere, the old opera house a burnt ruin. Schumann's entry for the day in the *Haushaltbücher* expresses at once amazement and fear: "Image of a horrible revolution."[84]

Schumann's pained reaction to the rapid and bloody squelching of the republican cause notwithstanding, he suggested on the return journey to Maxen that the family take refuge in nearby Bad Kreischa, a little resort town nestled in a lovely valley not far from the Serre estate. Here they lived until 12 June in "cozy stillness," and in an atmosphere where, as Schumann put it to Liszt, "the desire to work, even though the great world events lay claim to our thoughts, will rather grow than subside."[85] And grow it did. While in Kreischa, Schumann either completed or made considerable headway on an amazingly diverse array of compositions: the *Lieder-Album für die Jugend;* a pair of Mignon lieder (*Kennst du das Land* and *Nur wer die Sehnsucht kennt,* the former published both as the last song of the *Lieder-Album* and the first of the *Meister* lieder, op. 98a); several lieder for three women's voices and piano (published as Opus 114, nos. 1 and 3); the piano accompaniments for the *Romanzen* for women's chorus, opp. 69 and 91; the *Fünf Gesänge* (initially called *Jagdlieder*) for men's chorus, op. 137; the first version of the motet for double men's chorus, *Verzweifle nicht im Schmerzenstal,* op. 93; and the *Minnespiel,* op. 101. Clara was perhaps the first of many to observe the disparity between the untroubled surface of much of this music and the highly troubled state into which the contemporary world had been thrown. Commenting on the *Lieder-Album für die Jugend,* she wrote: "I find it remarkable that the terrible events from without awaken [Robert's] inner poetic feelings in such a diametrically opposite manner. A breath of the highest tranquility hovers over all these songs; laughing like blossoms, they seem to me like harbingers of spring."[86]

Clara's remarks articulate the dialectic between inner and outer realms that runs like a leitmotif through Schumann's most fruitful years. Yet it would be a mistake to assume that the composer completely sealed himself off from reality in Kreischa, withdrawing, as one writer puts it, "into a strange dissociative rapture that allowed him to go right ahead with his creative work."[87] The trip to Kreischa was motivated less by a desire to seek hermetic concealment than by the Schumanns' distaste for the anti-republican sentiments expressed by the aristocrats camped in Serre's home. While in the little resort town, the couple closely followed the rapidly breaking news of the revolution, subscribing immediately to the *Augsburger allgemeine Zeitung* for that purpose. The "cozy stillness" of the place was frequently interrupted by the antics of the younger members of the family. Indeed, Schumann wrote to Härtel in late June that he composed *Kennst du das Land,* "amidst a veritable children's uproar."[88] The natural beauty of the surrounding countryside lent itself to one of Schumann's favored activities: long hikes with his children; on one of these excursions he, Marie, and Elise, to their mutual surprise and consternation, came upon families of snakes and toads.[89]

Stimulated by the idyllic, holiday atmosphere, Schumann's creativity flowed unchecked. And although many of the artistic products of this happy phase are characterized by the "tranquility" that Clara observed in the *Lieder-Album für die Jugend,* not all of them echoed the carefree laughter of the burgeoning springtime blossoms. On the same day that Schumann and his children made their unexpected find in the countryside, he began to draft the motet for double men's chorus and organ ad libitum, *Verzweifle nicht im Schmerzenstal,* a work conceived in "response to the world events without."[90] Here the easy-going *Volkstümlichkeit* of much of the vocal music from this period gives way to wrenching chromaticism, finely woven contrapuntal lines, and by the end of the work, a prayerful but confident tone. In this "religiöser Gesang," as the work is designated in the *Projektenbuch,*[91] Schumann proclaims inner faith as a bulwark against outer turmoil, his recourse to a contemplative idiom emerging as a subtle commentary on a political theme. Nor is it mere happenstance that the motet was cast for a male choral ensemble. Flourishing institutions since the liberation of the German states from Napoleonic domination in 1813, the male Gesangvereine and Liedertafel often acted as pockets of liberalism during the *Vormärz* period, the decade or so leading up to the mid-century revolutions. (The potential for song to serve as an agent of political reform is among the themes explored in *Des Sängers Fluch,* the second of the late choral-orchestral ballades.) The same upsurge of patriotic sentiment that caused Schumann in 1840 to join the scores of German composers who set Nicolaus Becker's Rheinlied, "Sie sollen ihn nicht haben," informs the male chorus works on nationalist-democratic texts of 1847 and 1848: the *Drei Gesänge,* op. 62 (referred to as "patriotic songs" in the *Haushaltbücher*),[92] and the *Drei Freiheitsgesänge,* WoO 13–15. The folkish melodic style and basically syllabic approach to text-setting typical for these collections likewise distinguish the *Fünf Gesänge* on texts from Laube's *Jagdbrevier,* op. 137, composed at Kreischa. In *Verzweifle nicht im Schmerzenstal,* however, the overtly nationalist tone seems to have been sublimated, directed toward an interior realm.[93]

Soon after returning to Dresden in mid-June, Schumann was seized by a veritable "Marschfeuer" that resulted in the *IV Märsche,* op. 76.[94] As he pointed out in a letter of 17 June to Whistling, the pieces were not "of the old, Dessau [march] type, but rather republican in spirit. I couldn't think of a better way to channel my excitement—they were written with genuine ardor."[95] But here, too, the composer sublimated his republican sentiment in a cycle of four character sketches for piano. Binding the pieces into a coherent whole hardly posed a significant problem, for the march topic provides a ready-made focal point. Likewise, the affective unity of the set is complemented by an overall organization around an E♭ tonic and an interlocking tonal scheme, wherein the key of one piece is echoed in the central section of its successor, a device employed earlier in *Kreisleriana* and the *Fantasiestücke,* op. 12. The challenge lay in finding a means of ensuring a satisfactory degree of variety and also in avoiding the metric and rhythmic monotony that might naturally result from a quarter of an hour of march music. Schumann solved the first problem easily enough by alternating the principal march sections with lyrical Trios. He addressed the second by fashioning themes notable for their rhythmic differentiation and hypermetric irregularity. The first march, for instance, opens with a three-bar idea in which each measure presents a different rhythmic idea (Example 11.8). A condensed variant of mm. 1–3 then follows in mm. 4–5, while m. 6 compresses the previous two-bar pattern into a single bar. The hypermetric diminution creates an overall $3 + 2 + 1$ grouping that imparts a striking sense of forward drive (a reflection of the *Energie* in the expressive indication) to the entire six-bar phrase. Republican fervor apparently did not preclude artful syntax.

Example 11.8. IV Märsche, op. 76: No. 1, mm. 1–6.

If in the *Vier Märsche* Schumann tells of the "joys that motivate the times," he tells of their sorrows in the *Lieder und Gesänge aus Goethes Wilhelm Meister*, published as the *Erste Abtheilung* of Opus 98. To be sure, the inwardness through which the composer sought a counterforce against the frightful happenings of the day frequently has the upper hand in this work. But at the same time, the tension between withdrawal and engagement colors the entire cycle, settings of all but one of the lyrics for Mignon, the Harper, and Philine, from Goethe's celebrated *Bildungsroman*:

1. *Kennst du das Land*—Mignon (from Book III, Chapter 1)
2. *Ballade des Harfners: Was hör' ich draussen vor dem Thor?*—Harper (from Book II, Chapter 11)
3. *Nur wer die Sehnsucht kennt*—Mignon (from Book IV, Chapter 11)
4. *Wer nie sein Brot mit Thränen ass*—Harper (from Book II, Chapter 13)
5. *Heiss' mich nicht reden, heiss' mich schweigen*—Mignon (from Book V, Chapter 16)
6. *Wer sich der Einsamkeit ergiebt*—Harper (from Book II, Chapter 13)
7. *Singet nicht in Trauertönen*—Philine (from Book V, Chapter 10)
8. *An die Thüren will ich schleichen*—Harper (from Book V, Chapter 15)
9. *So lasst mich scheinen, bis ich werde*—Mignon (from Book VIII, Chapter 2)

Schumann composed the *Meister* lieder between 12 May and 7 July 1849, his work overlapping with the settings of the first four *Faust* scenes in July and August of the same year. Thus within a relatively short time, he fashioned a musical response to the "two poetic schemes" that, as Wagner put it, run through Goethe's output like "two main arteries."[96]

While the early Romantics were struck by Goethe's treatment of the conflict between the bourgeois sensibility and a career devoted to art—according to Friedrich Schlegel, *Wilhelm Meisters Lehrjahre*, the French Revolution, and Fichte's *Wissenschaftslehre* together comprised the three "greatest tendencies of the age"[97]—some were disappointed by the novel's largely mundane subject matter. Novalis, for one, concluded that *Wilhelm Meister* was "actually a *Candide* directed against poetry."[98] Little wonder then that several generations of composers, from Beethoven, Schubert, and Loewe to Wolf, Tchaikovsky, and Medtner, were drawn precisely to those fantastic figures who serve as emblems of poetry in an otherwise prosaic world: Mignon, whose "strange personality . . . consists almost entirely of a strange sort of yearning,"[99] and the Harper, veering ever nearer to madness and consumed by guilt over an affair with a woman whom he later discovered to be his sister (we eventually learn, though the Harper never does, that Mignon was the product of their union). What distinguishes Schumann's treatment of the interpolated verses for these figures is the breadth of his conception. Schubert, in addition to setting several of the individual poems as freestanding entities, also grouped most of the lyrics for the Harper and Mignon into mini-cycles of three songs each (D. 478 and D. 877, respectively). Wolf prominently positioned his settings of all ten *Meister* poems at the opening of his lyric compendium, *Gedichte von J. W. v. Goethe*. But only Schumann fashioned the lyrics, practically in their entirety, into a unified cycle.[100]

The *Meister* lieder no doubt number among Schumann's most powerful and affectively gripping creations, yet they have been neglected by all but a handful of performers and critics. The cycle seems to have succumbed to the same caprices of reception history as *Genoveva*: too "Wagnerian" for those purists who argued that lyric poetry demands only lyrical realizations in tone and overly constrained by the laws of "absolute music" for the *Zukunftmusiker*, the work has often been judged a failed experiment.[101] Many critics have remained insensitive to the fact that it is precisely in the dialectic between obviously lied-like qualities (cantabile melodic writing, foursquare syntax, strophic forms, discreet but expressive accompaniments) and dramatic, even operatic qualities (declamatory vocal lines, prose-like syntax, through-composed forms, quasi-orchestral accompaniments) that the raison d'être of the

cycle resides. The interplay between lyricism and drama reflects the tension between the inner world of the soul and the outer world of action
so powerfully presented in Goethe's novel. No less than the literary operas of the late 1840s, Schumann's most emotionally charged song cycle
is animated by a crucial theme of its literary source.

A cursory glance at the contents of the cycle (listed above) seems
to suggest that Schumann has thoroughly jumbled the order of the lyrics
in relation to their original position in Goethe's novel. If we consider
the Mignon lieder alone, however, it is clear that they do indeed appear
in the same order as the lyrics in the novel. The same holds true for the
settings of the Harper poems. Schumann, in other words, interleaved
the two mini-cycles (Philine's saucy account of the pleasures of night
lends a bit of comic relief to the otherwise serious proceedings) to form
a coherent but dramatically differentiated whole. The genesis of the cycle
further supports this view. Schumann tackled the Mignon poems first,
setting *Kennst du das Land* and *Nur wer die Sehnsucht kennt* shortly after
arriving in Kreischa in mid-May 1849. *Heiss' mich nicht reden* and *So
lasst mich scheinen* followed on 20 and 21 June, respectively, after the
Schumanns' return to Dresden. The Harper songs, or more exactly, the
final three (Nos. 4, 6, and 8), were likewise composed as a group,
the Ballade *(Was hör' ich draussen vor dem Thor?)* completed on 30 June,
and the mini-cycle proper, consisting of *Wer nie sein Brot mit Thränen
ass, Wer sich der Einsamkeit ergiebt,* and *An die Thüren will ich schleichen,*
drafted on 6 and 7 July.[102]

The two simultaneously unfolding inner dramas are at once unified, through an overarching tonal plan centered around G minor-major,
and contrasted, most obviously through the alternation of female and
male voices. Each of the constitutent mini-cycles in turn forms a tightly-
knit group. Mignon's four lieder traverse an affective arc extending from
bittersweet longing and anxious yearning to awestruck mystery and
transfigurative calm. Writing to Emanuel Klitsch in December 1849,
Schumann maintained that in *Kennst du das Land* Mignon directs "her
sight presciently toward a more active life of the soul."[103] And to be
sure, he could easily have said the same of her other lyrics as well. But
the intensity of Mignon's inwardness, at least as Schumann envisioned
it, is such that her lieder are often on the verge of transforming themselves into operatic scenes. Each of the strophes of *Kennst du das Land,*
for instance, is cast as a miniature recitative and aria. The essentially
through-composed *Heiss' mich nicht reden* is unified by a complex of
motivic particles (quasi-leitmotifs) shared by voice and piano, its declamatory opening giving way to a cantabile setting of the second and
third strophes that wells up to a powerful climax (at "allein ein Schwur

drückt mir die Lippen zu" [only an oath seals my lips]) and then dissolves into a varied reprise of the introductory recitative. The tension between lied and aria, lyricism and drama, is already latent in the opening vocal gesture of Mignon's first song, an intervallically expanded variant of which begins her second (Examples 11.9a and b). The recitational quality of the idea in *Kennst du das Land* is displaced, in *Nur wer die Sehnsucht kennt*, by an affectively charged lyricism. Yet in both cases, the upwardly surging gesture aptly conveys a sense for the "strange sort of yearning" that distinguishes Mignon's mysterious nature. Her yearning is likewise tinged with melancholy, or so Schumann seems to say through his frequent recourse to the chromatically descending tetrachord, the venerable emblem for lament that undergirds the sinuous figuration in the piano prelude to *Kennst du das Land*, the opening phrase of *Nur wer die Sehnsucht kennt* (Examples 11.9 a and b), and the dissolution of the climactic phrase in *Heiss' mich nicht reden*. Only in the piano postlude of *So lasst mich scheinen* is a major-mode variant of the figure employed as a serene expression of longing for peace in death. Hence Mignon's intense yearning, whether for an exotic land "where the lemon blossoms bloom" or for sensual fullfillment, is effectively quelled in her final song.

Example 11.9a. Kennst du das Land, mm. 1–7.

Example 11.9b. Nur wer die Sehnsucht kennt, mm. 1–4.

The last three Harper songs (Nos. 4, 6, and 8) are no less closely related. We follow this singularly odd character—his bald head "wreathed by a few grey hairs," his long white beard leaving "his kindly mouth uncovered," his slender body "clothed from head to foot in a dark brown garment"[104]—on an emotional journey that takes him from frustration born of pain, through yearning for the solitude of the grave, and finally to abject resignation. Like Mignon's songs, his too are bound together as an affective unit by a variety of musical figures. Tortuous chromaticism in both the melody and accompaniment serves as an emblem for pain in all its manifold guises: the pain of guilt in *Wer nie sein Brot mit Thränen ass,* the pain that creeps toward the Harper like a furtive lover by night in *Wer sich der Einsamkeit ergiebt,* and the pain of the compassionate onlookers who shed tears over the pitiable character's plight in *An die Thüren will ich schleichen.* Not surprisingly, the songs are punctuated by all manner of harp-like effects. The extravagantly cascading arpeggios of *Wer nie sein Brot* underscore the Harper's angry invocation of those heavenly powers who sentence the poor human to an unending pattern of guilt and atonement. The gently rolled chords of the closing chorale in *Wer sich der Einsamkeit ergiebt* lend poignancy to the plea for release from earthly torture in death. The harp is all but silenced in *An die Thüren will ich schleichen,* a wandering song for the Harper, now a holy fool benumbed to his pain: the luxurious arpeggios of the earlier songs give way to a series of hypnotically repeated Gs in the piano's opening representation of the Harper's measured tread. And as if to firm the inner bond between Mignon's melancholy yearning and the Harper's all-consuming pain, Schumann closes the latter's final song with a postlude in which the lament tetrachord, in its minor-mode form, but ultimately coming to rest over a C-major chord, appears in the right hand of the piano.

The first of the Harper songs, the ballade *Was hör' ich draussen vor dem Thor,* stands somewhat apart from the rest, and indeed from the other songs in the cycle. Here, in the most extended and most operatically conceived song of the set, we encounter the Harper in his public guise as a voluble bard. The poem, no less than its musical realization, sheds some light on the problematic relationship between Schumann's *Meister* lieder and the tumultuous world events surrounding their composition. Many writers, whether they react positively or negatively to the cycle as a whole, hear in these songs distinct echoes of the turbulence and uncertainty of the revolutionary years. For some, the pervasive chromaticism reflects Schumann's anguish over the abortive Dresden uprising; for others, the tragic ethos of the Harper songs is consistent with Schumann's own desolation in the face of the destruction wrought by the revolution, while Mignon's doleful yearning for an unattainable land resonates with the composer's resignation over the collapse of his dreams for a political utopia.[105] There is no doubt a modicum of truth in all these suppositions: if it fell to Schumann to sing of the sorrows of the time, he never did so more eloquently than in the *Meister* lieder. At the same time, it would be a mistake to view the songs, or, for that matter, any other works of the revolutionary years, as unmediated representations of the outer world. The suspicion remains that Schumann's settings might have more to do with his abiding admiration for Goethe than with contemporary politics, that the revolution of which he sang was a largely musico-poetic event. As Jean Paul once said: "Let each improve and revolutionize, instead of his age, his self."[106]

This reading is consistent with the message of *Was hör' ich draussen vor dem Thor,* a poem cast in the form of an allegory of the artist's problematic place in bourgeois society. The Harper reminds us that creative geniuses are forced to practice their most private of arts for the delectation of the public, yet they find their reward not in the "golden chain" offered them by princes and nobles, but rather in "a draught . . . of the best wine," that is, in the act of creation itself. The reflectivity of this "poem-about-a-poem" is compounded by the rich layering of voices—those of the narrator, king, and bard—in its musical realization. The composer "sings" through the words of the poet, Goethe, who "speaks" through the Harper, who in turn assumes the roles of the narrator, king, and bard. Schumann responds to each of these roles with corresponding shifts in musical style, moving flexibly from declamation, recitative, and arioso, to fullblown cantabile for his setting of *Ich singe wie der Vogel singt* (I sing like the bird sings). Here the Ballade reaches its lyric climax when, supported by gentled rolling arpeggios (one of many evocations of the harp), the vocal line brings an allusion to *Dein Bildnis wunderselig*, the second song in the Eichendorff *Liederkreis*, op. 39. At this magical moment, we realize that Goethe's poem-about-a-poem has been transformed into a song-about-a-song.

To conclude that the musico-poetic content of the Harper's song counts for more than its possible reflection of contemporary events is not, however, to empty the song of social meaning. On the contrary, embedded in our reading is a social message of real importance. Goethe's poem, first of all, is a ballad: it tells a story. As such, it embodies a mode of experience that was no less endangered during the mid-century revolutions than in the aftermath of the French Revolution, when Goethe wrote his *Bildungsroman*. Schumann's increased interest in the musical possibilities of the narrative mode, as manifested in the "declamation" ballads of 1849 and 1852–53, the choral-orchestral ballades of 1851–53, and even, as I have suggested, in the instrumental cycles of 1848 and 1849, stems from a similar urge to preserve the art of storytelling. The Harper's *Ballade*, the melodramatic rendering of Hebbel's text in *Schön Hedwig*, the resplendent portrayal of the restoration of the blind singer's sight in *Der Königssohn*: all became sites for the preservation of experience as *Erfahrung*. These pieces remind us that there are some activities, such as the telling of tales or the singing of songs, that are worth cultivating even during—or precisely during—times of trouble. Schumann, like the bard in *Was hör' ich draussen vor dem Thor*, engages most profoundly in the issues of his day when he appears to withdraw from them.

The Formative Power

Schumann's works for chorus and orchestra fill four hefty volumes of the Breitkopf collected edition, but a few exceptions aside, such as an occasional unearthing of the *Peri* or an excerpt from the *Faust* scenes, this repertory is seldom aired publicly today. Schumann, however, set great store by this aspect of his compositional activity. In the *Musikalische Haus- und Lebensregeln* he even directed the young musician to "keep in mind . . . that the highest in musical expression is achieved through the chorus and orchestra."[107]

The expressive range of Schumann's compositions for combined orchestral and choral forces is estimable indeed. At one end of the spectrum come those works on Latin texts with unmistakable religious connotations: the Mass, op. 147, and Requiem, op. 148. At the other end are a group of compositions falling squarely in the secular sphere: the first six of the *Faust* scenes, or the late choral-orchestral ballades on texts either by or adapted from Uhland and Geibel. Many works, however, lie somewhere between the two extremes. In the *Peri, Der Rose Pilgerfahrt,* and the *Schlussszene* of *Faust,* the theme of redemption—like the musical styles employed to reflect it—lends a religious quality to a genre, the oratorio, otherwise intended for the concert hall. Yet another group, the one that will occupy us here, is even more difficult to define. In a number of the choral-orchestral works either completed or begun during the late 1840s—*Beim Abschied zu singen,* op. 84 (1847), *Adventlied,* op. 71 (1848), *Requiem für Mignon,* op. 98b (1849), *Nachtlied,* op. 108 (1849), and *Neujahrslied,* op. 144 (1849–50)—religious, political, ethical, and humanistic themes are intertwined so closely that it is often impossible to separate them.

The interpenetration of sacred and secular spheres is already much in evidence in the unassuming *Beim Abschied zu singen,* a brief setting of a Feuchtersleben text for chorus and winds or piano. On the one hand, the choral writing hearkens to the easy-going, tuneful manner of the convivial *Romanzen* and *Balladen,* while on the other, the wind sonority and quasi-chorale style imbue the text, whose moralizing message stresses the necessity of resignation in the face of loss, with a religious aura.

The difficulties Schumann encountered in finding an appropriate title for the *Adventlied,* the first of the lieder for chorus, soloists, and orchestra, place into relief the hybrid nature of the arguably new genre for which it serves as a paradigm. While at work on this setting of a Rückert text in November and December of 1848, Schumann referred to it in the *Haushaltbücher* as a "cantata."[108] But in a letter to Härtel of 2 May 1849, he objected to this designation as a "somewhat misused word."[109] Elsewhere in his correspondence he called the work, whose text deals with Christ's entry into Jerusalem (a traditional liturgical theme during Advent), a "Kirchenstück" or "Motette,"[110] although to add to the confusion, he also expressed his doubts over the title "Adventlied" in the May 1849 letter to Härtel, since it might unduly limit the performance of the piece to a specific time of the year.[111] Ultimately, Schumann even rejected what was perhaps the most compelling title of all, "Geistliches Gedicht" (spiritual poem),[112] a designation that places the *Adventlied* in line with *Manfred* (a *Dramatisches Gedicht*) and the *Peri* (a *Dichtung*) as their more specifically sacred counterpart.

In all fairness, though, Schumann's apparent indecision is less a sign of confusion than an indication of the inability of the tried-and-true musical labels to capture the essence of a genre at once spiritual but neither liturgical nor denominational. The "religion" celebrated in the choral-orchestral lieder is the humanist religion—that "original way of looking at infinity," as Friedrich Schlegel put it[113]—promulgated by the early Romantics. In this context, the *Adventlied* can be said to occur at a significant fault line in Schumann's output: as his first major essay on a spiritual theme, the work prefigures the final phase in the composer's march through the genres. Cast in seven (by and large) seamlessly connected and tonally related movements, the *Adventlied* alternates broad orchestral preludes and interludes, vocal solos (either for soprano or quartet), and sonorous choruses, the grandest of which is the closing "Und lösch' der Zwietracht." Yet the central placement of the chorale-like "O Herr von grosser Huld und Treue" lends added emphasis to the "religious" ethos of the whole.

The sacred quality is somewhat more muted in the *Nachtlied*, a setting of a Hebbel text in which the poet beautifully portrays the feelings overtaking the spirit in its passage from wakefulness to the dream state, a metaphor for the passage from life to death. Schumann's concise setting of the tripartite lyric—comprising invocations to "Quellende, schwellende Nacht" (welling, swelling night), "Steigendes, neigendes Leben" (waxing, waning life), and finally to approaching slumber, which casts its magic spell over "the paltry flame" (dürftige Flamme) of consciousness—likewise falls into three sections: a fantastically hushed opening, a surge to the climactic representation of "Steigendes Leben," and a gradual dissolution suggestive of the soul's graceful descent into sleep.[114]

With the *Neujahrslied*, Schumann returned to the structurally broader model already employed in the *Adventlied*. Like the earlier work, and again on a Rückert text, it is comprised of seven continuously linked movements, some of them further bound by thematic cross-references, and all of them characterized by a distinctive vocal type or style: *Rezitativischer Gesang* (No. 1), "convivial" duet (No. 2), Handelian choral homophony enlivened by imitation (Nos. 6 and 7), simple recitative (No. 4), fugato (No. 5), and chorale (Nos. 6 and 7). Yet the character of the two works is markedly different, the humanist-religious quality of the

Adventlied displaced by a political-religious tone in the *Neujahrslied.* Indeed, Rückert's paean to the newly born year can be read as a barely veiled allegory for the enlightened rule of a newly crowned monarch. Hence the text, in holding out the possibility for a rapprochement between king and populace, proclaims a frankly liberal message. Schumann in turn suggests that it is precisely through a democratic-religious sensibility that a brotherhood among men (or a reconcialiation between ruler and ruled) can and will be attained, a point confirmed by the chorale-like "O Fürst, auf dem Throne" (No. 6) and the quotation of an actual chorale, *Nun danket alle Gott,* at the conclusion of the work. The *Neujahrslied,* we should keep in mind, was drafted in late 1849 and early 1850, well after the suppression of the Dresden uprising. Its unabashedly optimistic tone provides striking testimony to the composer's continued hope for a future in which art and democratic ideals will enter into a mutually nurturing relationship.

The general thrust of the *Requiem für Mignon,* perhaps the most moving of the choral-orchestral lieder and by far the best known, is directed less toward politics than toward a kind of religious humanism. Drawn from the final book of Goethe's *Meister,* the text readily lends itself to musical treatment. A sizable group of guests have been summoned to the sumptuously decorated Hall of the Past in Lothario's castle for Mignon's funeral rites:

> Huge wax candles were burning in the four big candelabras at the corners of the room, and others of appropriate size in the four smaller ones surrounding the sarcophagus in the center. Four boys were standing beside the bier, dressed in silver and blue, fanning with sheaves of ostrich feathers a figure that lay on top of the sarcophagus. The assembled company all took their seats, and two invisible choruses intoned in gentle strains: "Whom do you bring to our quiet company?" [115]

With this question, the exequies begin, the ritualistic alternation of boys and invisible spirits elaborated by Schumann as six interrelated movements for orchestra, chorus, and soloists in various combinations.

Not surprisingly, the *Requiem für Mignon* discloses a number of points of contact with the *Meister* lieder of mid-1849. Drafted on 2–3 July, before the composition of the mini-cycle of Harper songs, the *Requiem* was orchestrated in July and September, after the completion of the lieder cycle as a whole.[116] It then appeared as the *Zweite Abtheilung* of a publication whose title emphasizes the close relationship between the two parts of the *Meister* project: *Lieder, Gesänge und Requiem für Mignon aus Goethe's Wilhelm Meister,* op. 98. Indeed, the yearning quality of Mignon's lieder colors the earlier stages of the *Requiem* as well:

the C-minor tonality, anxious accompanimental figuration, sinuous vocal lines, and restless chromaticism of its first two movements specifically recall *Heiss' mich nicht reden,* though the histrionics of the lied have been replaced by an air of dignified mourning.[117] Moreover, the work makes several striking allusions to the *Faust* scenes (Nos. 1 through 4 of which Schumann had completed just before orchestrating the *Requiem*), thus pointing to the inner unity of the entire Goethe project. Embedded in the opening choral setting of "Wen bringt ihr uns zur stillen Gesellschaft?" (Whom do you bring to our quiet company?), for instance, is the signature motive that, in *Faust,* was associated with a number of affects ranging from sensual yearning to divine rapture (Example 11.10). The music for "Ach! wie ungern brachten wir ihn her" (Oh! with what sadness have we brought the child here) in the second movement recalls Gretchen's plaintive invocation to the Mater Dolorosa, "Wohin ich immer gehe, wie wehe wird mir im Busen hier" (Wherever I go, my breast is torn by grief) from the second *Faust* scene. The refractory dominant-to-subdominant progression at "Schaut mit den Augen des Geistes hinan" (Behold the spirit with your eyes) in the third movement resonates unmistakably with Faust's approach to the rising sun in the central movement (No. 4) of the *Faust* scenes. And finally, the subdued F-major close of the *Requiem* parallels the corresponding moment in the *Schlussszene* from *Faust.* The last of these allusions makes explicit what is implicit in the rest: Mignon, like Gretchen and Faust, finds redemption only in the hereafter.

The *Requiem für Mignon* maintains a tone of noble simplicity from beginning to end. In fashioning the music for the four boys (represented here by soprano and alto solos), Schumann may have even turned directly to the luminous passages for the Drei Knaben in Mozart's *Die Zauberflöte* as models. Likewise, he projects the fundamental message of the text with the simplest but most effective of means. Chief among the work's topics are the funeral march with which it opens and the chorale style that dominates its final three movements—and in a sense, the composition is about the passage from one topic to the other. The transition takes place with marvelous fluency in the third movement, where the anxious entreaties of the boys alternate with increasingly affirmative gestures in the full chorus, and where, to highlight the otherworldly beauty

Example 11.10. Requiem für Mignon, op. 98b: No. 1, mm. 3–6 (choral sopranos).

of Mignon's repose ("Seht die schöne, würdige Ruh'!"), Schumann creates a truly magical effect as the dynamic drops from *forte* to *piano*, the harmony shifts from C major to a suspenseful half-diminished chord, and the harp enters with extravagant arpeggios.

The fourth movement then opens with the central message of Goethe's text, a powerful exhortation to the still fretting boys and to us: "In euch lebe die bildende Kraft" (May the formative power dwell in you). It is the business of the living, that is, to go on living their lives to the fullest rather than losing themselves in maudlin lamentation. Specifically, we are conjoined in no uncertain terms to cultivate the process of self-formation that alone makes life worth living. To drive home the point, Schumann introduces a pure chorale texture for the first time in his setting, thereby imparting to this profoundly humanistic message the weight of religious truth.

The *Requiem für Mignon* thus turns on the notion of *Bildung,* already a key element in the teenage Schumann's notion of a "hoher Mensch" and a term that, perhaps more than any other, knits the many and varied strands of the composer's most fruitful years into a coherent whole. What Thomas Mann wrote of the man of letters (the "gebildeter Mensch" in his highest incarnation) applies with equal force to the *musical* man of letters Schumann aspired to be: "[He is] an educator who has himself been strangely educated, and in his own case education always goes hand in hand with his own inner battle; here we have an interweaving of the inner and outer self, a simultaneous wrestling with the ego and with the outer world."[118] On the surface, the little pieces of the *Album für die Jugend,* the tortuous musical utterances of the Harper in *Wer nie sein Brot mit Thränen ass,* and the transcendent choral exhortations of the *Requiem für Mignon* seem to have little in common. But on reflection, we realize that they are all artistic documents of just such a battle between inner and outer worlds and that they are all animated by the formative power of *Bildung.*

~12~

The Final
Phase

Municipal Music Director in Düsseldorf

In mid-November 1849, Schumann received an invitation from Ferdinand Hiller, who had just accepted a post in Cologne, to assume the latter's old position as municipal music director in Düsseldorf. The offer was tempting, especially since Schumann had been hoping for a salaried position for some time: in July 1847 he expressed interest in the directorship of the Vienna Conservatory; during the summer of 1849 he set his sights on the directorship of the Leipzig Gewandhaus concerts and even allowed some of the members of his Chorverein to make inquiries on his behalf regarding Wagner's vacant post at the Dresden Hoftheater. Still, he was reluctant to make a hasty decision on Hiller's offer, and his reservations were compounded by memories of Mendelssohn's unfortunate experiences as music director in the capital of the Rhine Province, working with an odd assortment of professionals and dilettantes.[1] In a letter to Hiller of 19 November 1849, Schumann requested further details on salary, cost of living, moving expenses, the size of the chorus and orchestra, flexibility in the arrangement of his schedule, and last, an appropriate sphere of activity for Clara: "You know her; she can't be unoccupied." In any event, he could not take up residence in Düsseldorf until Easter of the following year owing to the Leipzig premiere of *Genoveva* in the winter of 1850 (as we know, the production was postponed until June).[2] By 3 December 1949, Hiller had allayed all Schumann's

439

fears but one: his recent discovery, in an old geography book, of an insane asulym in the environs of Düsseldorf.[3]

The first part of the new year was taken up with sketches for the *Neujahrslied* and by two successful performances of the *Peri*. Then in early February, Schumann and Clara travelled to Leipzig, ostensibly for the *Genoveva* premiere. Mightily annoyed to learn of its postponement in favor of Meyerbeer's *Prophète*, Schumann took some consolation during his month-long stay in the warm reception accorded several of his pieces, including the *Genoveva* Overture and the *Concertstück* for four horns. He and Clara spent 3–9 March in Bremen giving more concerts (featuring his *Andante and Variations*, op. 46, and the F-major Piano Trio, op. 80), and on 10 March headed for Hamburg, where two concerts presented later in the month with Jenny Lind turned a handsome profit of 800 thalers. After a brief visit with Clara's relatives in Berlin (25–29 March), the couple returned to Dresden. Two days later, Schumann wrote to the executive committee of the Allgemeiner Musikverein in Düsseldorf, officially accepting the post of municipal music director.

Having passed nearly two months on the road, Schumann found little time for composing. But now came a veritable outburst of vocal composition that would extend, with one interruption, well into the summer. Between 30 March and 2 April he completed the *Drei Gesänge*, op. 83, and on 12 April the song *Aufträge* (op. 77 no. 5). Later in the month he returned to the *Faust* project, finishing Scenes 5 *(Mitternacht)* and 6 *(Fausts Tod)* by 10 May. During the next week he returned to song with the *Sechs Gesänge*, op. 89, on texts by Wilfried von der Neun. Composition understandably took a back seat between 18 May and 10 July, spent in Leipzig for the long-delayed first performances of *Genoveva*, but once resettled in Dresden, Schumann resumed his songwriting activities. Before the month was out, he had completed the *Lieder und Gesänge*, op. 96, three songs subsequently published as Opus 125 nos. 2, 4, and 5, and two more issued as Opus 77 nos. 2 and 3. August began with *Mein altes Ross* (op. 127 no. 4) and with the work that in many ways represents the crown jewel of Schumann's second Year of Song: *Sechs Gedichte von N. Lenau und Requiem (altkatholisches Gedicht)*, op. 90. He set the last item in the cycle (a translation of a lament for Abelard, traditionally ascribed to his beloved Heloïse) on 5 August under the mistaken impression that Lenau had died. When he learned, on 25 August, that the poet had in fact died on 22 August (in an insane asylum near Vienna), he wrote, bemused at his prescience, to Friedrich Kistner: "Without knowing it, [I] had sung an elegy to the poet's memory."[4] On the same day, the *Requiem* was given for the first time at a private gathering at the home of his friend, Eduard Bendemann. The better part of the month, however, was consumed by preparations for the move to Düsseldorf, culminating in a farewell dinner at Brühl's Terasse. According to Eduard Devrient, Schumann was not on his best behavior. Dissatisfied with the performance of some of his choral partsongs, he demanded to conduct himself, but the pieces went worse than before; and after sampling some wine sent along by Bendemann, he rudely announced that it was not to his taste.[5]

On 1 September the Schumanns departed from Dresden. Passing through Leipzig to bid their old friends farewell, they arrived in Düsseldorf at 6 P.M. on the following day and were given a festive welcome that included a serenade later in the evening by some of the local musicians. Members of the town orchestra serenaded them again on the evening of 4 September, and three days later came the highpoint of the celebrations marking the arrival of the new music director and his family: a concert devoted to Schumann's music (including the *Genoveva* Overture, Part Two of the *Peri,* and several lieder), followed by a supper and ball. Schumann found the whole experience overwhelming. Exhausted by the steady round of concerts and parties, and feeling ill at ease in the family's temporary lodgings, he remained uncomfortable even after settling into their new apartment at the corner of Allee- and Grabenstrasse on 10 September. Four days later, he complained of rheumatism in his foot (a recurrent malady during the next years); by the end of the month, he was so vexed by the dreadful street racket that he and Clara thought of moving (within the next two years, they would change addresses no less than three times).

But before long Schumann was caught up in a whirl of professional duties and creative projects. Indeed, he was about to embark on one of the busiest and most productive phases of his career. As municipal music director, he was expected to conduct the orchestral subscription concerts of the Allgemeiner Musikverein and direct the weekly rehearsals of the choral society (Gesang-Musikverein), which often performed jointly with the orchestra. He was also charged with the direction of performances on major feast days at Düsseldorf's two principal Catholic churches: Saint Lambertus and the Maximiliankirche. During Schumann's tenure as music director, the Musikverein gave from eight to ten concerts (each preceded by two, or at most three rehearsals) in seasons extending from October to May. One of these programs, sometimes an evening of chamber music, was usually a benefit, for which Schumann received 100 thalers on top of his annual base salary of 648 thalers. Every season likewise featured at least one large-scale oratorical work; during the three years of his directorship, Schumann led performances of Handel's *Israel and Egypt* and *Joshua,* Bach's *Saint John Passion* and

Saint Matthew Passion, and Haydn's *Seasons.* The other concerts tended to be longish affairs, consisting of one or more overtures, a concerto, aria or opera scene, a number of smaller pieces for the featured soloist, a choral-orchestral work, and at the end of the program, a symphony. The program of the 21 November 1850 subscription concert (the second under Schumann's direction) is fairly typical: the overture to Cherubini's *Faniska,* a concert aria by Weber *(Non paventar mia vita),* Mendelssohn's Violin Concerto (with Wasielewski, Schumann's handpicked concertmaster, as soloist), the overture to Gluck's *Iphigénie in Aulis,* the public premiere of Schumann's *Requiem für Mignon,* and Beethoven's Seventh Symphony. Schumann prepared for these events with great care. His conducting score of Beethoven's A-major Symphony, for instance, is peppered with markings: in it he made orthographical corrections, added rehearsal letters, circled important entrances and articulations, and underscored significant thematic lines.[6] By all accounts, this approach paid off during the earlier part of Schumann's directorship. According to Hiller, who was present at the 24 October 1850 concert, Schumann's debut performance proceeded without a hitch; his conducting, a major point of contention in the years ahead, was at once secure and composed. "The Düsseldorfers are now very happy," Hiller wrote, "and I think the present arrangement will work out for the best."[7] As we will see, the Düsseldorfers would not remain happy for long.

Not surprisingly, Schumann had little opportunity to compose during his first month in Düsseldorf: his creative work was limited to scoring the *Neujahrslied* in late September and early October. Within a short time, however, he was motivated to compose with a vengeance, his focus on the larger forms of symphonic and oratorical composition a natural consequence of his new position. Between 11 and 24 October he completed a draft of the Cello Concerto, op. 129 (although he "read it through" with Christian Reimers, the principal cellist of his orchestra, on 23 March 1851, the work was never given publicly during his lifetime). His next major project, the Third Symphony, op. 97 (the fourth of Schumann's symphonies in order of composition, popularly known as the "Rhenish")[8], was probably inspired by an earlier event. As Wasielewski tells it, the sight of Cologne's magnificent cathedral, which Schumann viewed on a day trip in late September, provided the initial impetus for the symphony, although work on the first movement did not get underway until 2 November.[9] His sketching interrupted by a second trip to Cologne between 4 and 6 November, during which he took a tour of the cathedral, Schumann learned, shortly after returning to Düsseldorf, of the elevation of Cologne's Archbishop von Geissel to cardinal. This news, again according to Wasielewski, led him to alter the traditional symphonic plan by placing an additional movement just before the finale. Originally designated "Im Charakter der Begleitung einer feierlichen Zeremonie" (In the character of a procession for a solemn ceremony), this movement presents a marvelous evocation of the *stile antico*, its masterful employment of contrapuntal manipulations of all sorts a sure sign that the lessons of the New Way had not been forgotten. Completed by 9 December, the Third Symphony proved to be an immensely popular success. Indeed, it made such an impression at its premiere on 6 February 1851 (the sixth Düsseldorf subscription concert) that it had to be encored on 13 March.

In late December 1850, Schumann took up a more modest project: the gathering together of several piano pieces composed between 1832 and 1849. Though he initially wanted to issue the collection as "Spreu" (a suggestive title meaning "chaff"), the idea didn't meet with the approval of his publisher Friedrich Arnold; hence, the pieces ultimately appeared as *Bunte Blätter,* op. 99, and *Albumblätter,* op. 124. Between 29 December 1850 and 12 January 1851, Schumann was back at orchestral composition with the overture to Schiller's *Braut von Messina,* op. 100. The review of the work's premiere on the 13 March 1851 subscription concert contains the first hint of an intensifying problem: the critic blames the orchestra's sloppy rendition of the overture and the public's tepid reception on Schumann's idiosyncratic conducting. (Hiller provides us with a vivid description of his manner on the podium: "[Schumann's] direction of his own pieces was most unusual. With his head buried in the score, he would give the performers . . . an indication of the tempo—it was obvious that he heard his work principally with his inner ear.")[10] After setting several texts by Mörike and other poets in late January and early February (published as Opus 107, nos. 1–3, 6; and Opus 125, no. 3), Schumann completed an overture to Shakespeare's *Julius Caesar* (op. 128), like its predecessor a darkly hued work imbued with a spirit of tragic grandeur from start to finish.

Clearly, Schumann's compositional habits had begun to fall into a pattern. Larger works intended for public performance with his orchestra alternated with projects centered on the smaller genres. Personal, professional, and commercial motives intersect in the process, for while Schumann could count on the marketability of his lieder and short piano pieces, his efforts in the larger forms would both enhance his position as music director and answer to a compositional imperative set in motion in the early 1840s. Thus it is hardly surprising that in early February he drafted a scenario for an oratorio with Martin Luther as its subject and soon thereafter enlisted the poet and critic Richard Pohl as a collaborator. Although their correspondence continued off and on throughout the year—even by the end of 1852 Schumann was still con-templating the Luther project—the composer's plans for a "thoroughly folk-like" oratorio, understandable by "peasants and burghers" alike, were never realized.[11] But after devoting most of March 1851 to works in the smaller genres—the delightful *Märchenbilder*, op. 113, for viola and piano, and *Vier Husarenlieder*, op. 117, on texts by Lenau—Schu-mann took up an oratorical project that did come to fruition: a setting of Moritz Horn's *Der Rose Pilgerfahrt* (The Pilgrimage of the Rose) for vocal soloists, chorus, and piano (op. 112). Before completing this *musi-kalisches Märchen*, or "musical fairy tale," he began to set Ludwig Uh-land's *Der Königssohn*, a chivalric ballad replete with fierce storms and shipwrecks, a wild horse, a fire-breathing dragon, and a blind minstrel whose sight is miraculously restored. The result was a form very much of the composer's making: the ballade for soloists, chorus, and orches-tra.[12] This genre, arguably an embodiment of the same ideals that in-formed the "literary operas" of the late 1840s, though on a smaller scale, held a real fascination for Schumann; indeed, by early in 1853, he had made three more contributions to what remains one of the most un-justly neglected components of his output. For some time he worked concurrently on both *Der Rose Pilgerfahrt* and *Der Königssohn*, finishing the former in late May and the orchestration of the latter by the end of June.

Even after the last subscription concert of the 1850–51 season on 18 May, Schumann's compositional activities continued unabated, though his focus shifted to smaller forms. On 28 May (the day after completing *Der Königssohn*) he set Uhland's *Der Sänger* as a choral part-song (Opus 145 no. 3), and then between 30 May and 1 June came settings of eleven lyrics by Elisabeth Kulmann, a remarkable talent who may have written nearly 1,000 poems before her untimely death in 1825 at the age of seventeen.[13] Four of these deceptively simple settings ap-peared as *Mädchenlieder*, op. 103, for vocal duet and piano, the remain-der as one of Schumann's most haunting (but infrequently performed) solo cycles: *Sieben Lieder*, op. 104. Mid-June was given over to *Haus-musik* in the form of nine miniatures for piano four hands, the collec-tion issued as *Ball-Scenen*, op. 109 (Schumann reserved the original title, *Kinderball*, for a later publication).

Unable to endure the noise from the busy intersection just outside their flat, the Schumanns moved to a building on the Kastanienallee on 2 July. Four days later, they christened their new lodgings with a perfor-mance of *Der Rose Pilgerfahrt* featuring twenty-four specially selected singers from the Gesangverein and Clara at the keyboard. Then Schu-mann took a much-deserved break from the creative work that had proceeded relentlessly since the previous October. Indeed, one of the most common entries for this period in the *Haushaltbücher* reads: "Immer fleissig" (Always busy). On 19 July, Schumann and Clara embarked on a pleasure trip that the composer would remember as the most idyllic journey of their life together. Travelling down the Rhine, they decided while in the village of Rudesheim to head toward Switzerland. After spending a day in Heidelberg (where Schumann took pleasure in revisiting the old haunts of his university days), the couple passed through Basel, Neuchâtel, Lausanne, Genf, and Freibourg, marveling over the sublimity of the landscape all the while. By 5 August they were back in Düsseldorf, remaining long enough for Schumann to complete the first two of the *Drei Fantasiestücke*, op. 111 (the third followed at the end of the month), but on 16 August they journeyed to Antwerp, where Schumann served as one of the judges in a competition for male choruses. While they much enjoyed viewing the rich art treasures in Antwerp, Brussels, Liège, and Aachen, their brief trip was marred by illness: Clara suffered from a nagging toothache and Schumann from a bad attack of dizziness, one of many that would plague him in the months and years ahead.

The couple returned to Düsseldorf on 21 August, just in time for Schumann to prepare for the upcoming concert season. But while the first year of his directorship was by and large a success, his second got off to a shaky start. On 25 August he apparently lost his temper at a conference with members of the Gesangverein. Clara offers further details on the sort of behavior that occasioned the outburst: "Several movements of Bach's B-minor Mass are supposed to be sung [by the Gesangverein], but the ladies and gentlemen don't show up for rehearsals, they aren't interested in learning anything, no, they only want to amuse themselves, and they make no secret of their aversion to hard work. The people here respect neither art nor conductors!" Never one to mince words, she summed up the situation in no uncertain terms in a diary entry of 6 September: "The choral society is falling apart, there's no enthusiasm, no love for the thing, and the orchestra is not even fully manned." On the same day, Schumann had a "stormy confrontation" with Deputy Mayor Wilhelm Wortmann (a ranking member of the executive committee of the Allgemeiner Musikverein), presumably over the selection of repertoire and artists for the winter concert season.[14] The first skirmish in the battle between dilettantism and professionalism, a battle that would ultimately contribute to Schumann's downfall, ended in a kind of stalemate. Although he registered his "grave considerations about the future" in the *Haushaltbücher*, he decided to stay the course, at least for the time being (in June 1852 he did, however, correspond with Gottfried Hermann regarding a post as Hofkapellmeister in Sondershausen).

In fact, Schumann appeared to renew his commitment to enriching Düsseldorf's musical life in the autumn of 1851. At about the same time as his acrimonious exchange with Wortmann, he organized a Singekränzchen, a private musical club devoted to the singing of early polyphony (by Palestrina, Lassus, and Bach) that met weekly in the homes of its members. Then in November he founded a complementary group, a Quartettkränzchen whose reading sessions focused on the instrumental chamber repertory. Although both organizations were short-lived, they attest to the importance Schumann continued to place on musical *Bildung,* on edification through the medium of music. Similarly, while he did not compose anything specifically for either of the Kränzchen, his compositional activity at this time may be viewed as a corollary to the repertory cultivated by these groups: vocal and instrumental music for small ensembles. Once again, professional and private concerns go hand in hand. On 16 September Schumann completed an A-minor Sonata for Piano and Violin (op. 105), a work intended as a vehicle for his concertmaster Wasielewski. Later in the month came the *Drei Gedichte aus den Waldliedern von Pfarrius,* op. 119. Then on 2 October he had "trio thoughts," thoughts no doubt inspired by the excellent resident trio comprised of Wasielewski, Reimers, and Schumann's deputy, Julius Tausch, that took shape as the G-minor Piano Trio, op. 110, which he completed by the end of the month. Immediately afterward he set to work on another composition for violin and piano. Finished in early November, the *2te Grosse Sonata* (Second Grand Sonata), op. 121, was probably also conceived with Wasielewski in mind, though the dedication went to Ferdinand David.

After this burst of chamber music activity, Schumann conformed to a by now familiar pattern in turning to larger media, specifically, to a number of orchestration projects. Between 7 and 27 November he drafted an orchestral version of *Der Rose Pilgerfahrt.* On 1 December (the same day that Clara gave birth to their seventh child and fourth daughter, Eugenie), he orchestrated the *Scherzo* of Norbert Burgmüller's (unfinished) Second Symphony. And finally, on 12 December he began to rescore the "old" D-minor symphony, the first version of which had been completed a decade before, but subsequently shelved. In the process of orchestration, however, he made a number of rhythmic and structural revisions as well, recasting the transitions into the opening and closing quick movements, and tightening the motivic argument in the finale. These changes are reflected in his plan to retitle the newly configured work, which the composer viewed as the definitive version, a *Symphonistische Phantasie*.[15] (The scoring of Schumann's later works, an issue to which we shall return, has been the object of much negative criticism. For now, it will suffice to say that the character of his orchestrations is not as unremittingly dreary as many detractors have made out: while there is only a measure or two in the 1851 version of the D-minor Symphony where the melodic lines in the strings are not doubled, the version of *Der Rose Pilgerfahrt* with orchestra is as deftly scored as anything in Mendelssohn or Weber.) Having completed what was later published as his Fourth Symphony (op. 120) on 19 December, Schumann quickly drafted the overture to *Hermann und Dorothea*, op. 136, a work he may have considered as a kind of trial run for an opera or Singspiel on Goethe's play; to be sure, his interest in dramatic music had been rekindled in late November through his study of Wagner's manifesto of operatic reform, *Oper und Drama*, a book whose importance he stressed in a letter to Liszt.[16]

Schumann's creative projects during the first half of 1852 represent the continuation of a significant thread from the spring of the year before: the composition of large-scale works for chorus and orchestra. In January he provisionally completed *Des Sängers Fluch*, op. 139, the second of the choral-orchestral ballades, plans for which dated back to late June 1851, when Schumann asked Pohl to mold Uhland's text "into a musical form." We discover from the correspondence between composer and librettist that the latter found this to be a frustrating assignment; after many "squabbles . . . concerning its realization," the text was finally hammered into shape, but the experience taught Pohl "that it was not easy to work with Schumann."[17] During the next month Schumann tackled the genre he had described in a letter to August Strackerjahn as a composer's "highest ideal": church music.[18] Much of February was taken up by work on the C-minor Mass (though designated *Missa sacra* in the partly autograph full score, it was posthumously published in 1862 as *Messe*, op. 147), which Schumann may have envisioned for performance at either Saint Lambertus or the Maximiliankirche. Still, it should be emphasized that the Mass was not meant to fulfill a strictly liturgical function; as Schumann pointed out in a letter of 10 December 1852 to the publisher Schott, the work was intended "for the church service as well as for concert use."[19]

Work on the orchestration of the Mass was interrupted by a trip to Leipzig between 5 and 22 March for a series of concerts devoted to Schumann's music. Held on 14, 18, and 21 March, these programs featured a broad sample of his compositions, including *Der Rose Pilgerfahrt*, the *Manfred* Overture, the Third Symphony, the A-minor Violin Sonata, and the G-minor Piano Trio (the last two works rendered by

Clara, Ferdinand David, and Johann Grabau), and were given for large and generally enthusiastic audiences. Now in his early forties, Schumann was at last gaining public recognition as a major force on the compositional scene. (His success is further reflected in the higher sums he demanded for his works and in his ever-growing income from their publication: 1,584 thalers in 1850, 1,439 in 1851, 1,717 in 1852, and 1,925 in 1853).[20]

After returning to Düsseldorf on 22 March, Schumann immersed himself in preparations for the upcoming subscription concert (a performance of Bach's *Saint Matthew Passion* on 4 April) and in the completion of his Mass. The latter task provisionally completed by 30 March, the work was given its first reading at a meeting of the Singekränzchen on 18 April. Although the family's move to Herzogstrasse in early April temporarily disrupted Schumann's creative work, he continued his foray into church music with sketches for a Requiem between 27 April and 8 May. Before scoring the new work, he wrote an orchestral accompaniment to *Verzweifle nicht im Schmerzenstal,* the double-chorus motet of 1849 on a devotional text by Rückert. By 23 May, he had orchestrated the Requiem (posthumously published as Opus 148 in 1864), which, like the Mass, is best viewed as straddling sacred and secular, church and concert hall. With this work, Schumann's exploration of the possibilities of church music, the final stage in a process begun years earlier, came to an end.

Throughout the late spring of 1852, Schumann also kept busy with two projects of a literary nature. The first of these, begun on 11 April, marks a return to a venture undertaken jointly with Clara during the early days of their marriage: the excerpting of passages on music from Shakespeare's plays. But his systematic reading of the playwright's works, which kept him occupied for precisely a year, formed only part of a larger plan to bring together, in the form of a book, striking references to music in the whole of world literature. Entitled *Dichtergarten* ("The Poet's Garden"), this collection would command Schumann's attention until just days before his suicide attempt in February 1854. The second project required less time for completion but was no less ambitious in scope. On 27 May 1852 Schumann began to assemble his writings on music (or "Davidsbündlerei," as he called them in the *Haushaltbücher*) with an eye toward publication of a collected edition. Finding a publisher, however, proved to be a difficult task. His proposal having been rejected by Breitkopf and Härtel, Schuberth, Brockhaus, and Hinze, Schumann finally negotiated a contract with Georg Wigand, whose firm issued an edition of his writings in late February 1854, just about a week before the composer was confined to the asylum where he would spend his last days.

By the late spring of 1852, Schumann was not a well man. In March, during his two-week stay in Leipzig, he had suffered a severe nervous attack. Exhausted by his conducting duties and out of sorts, he complained of "dreadful rheumatism" in early April. The celebration of his forty-second birthday on 8 June was marred by a fit of convulsive coughing, the first sign of a severe cold that prevented his attendance of the Weimar premiere of *Manfred* in the middle of the month.[21] Probably hoping to relive their pleasant idyll of the summer before, he and Clara planned another trip down the Rhine. Just before setting off, Schumann's compositional interests turned to narrative forms. On 13 June he composed *Die Flüchtlinge* (op. 122, no. 2), a setting of a ballad by Shelley for declamation (speaker) and piano. Between 18 and 22 June, he started sketching a far larger work, the third and greatest of his choral-orchestral ballades, *Vom Pagen und der Königstochter* (op. 140), on texts by Geibel. Work on the new ballade continued after he and Clara began their holiday on 26 June, but was impeded by a "bad attack" at Bad Godesberg on 2 July. According to entries in the *Haushalt-bücher*, Schumann was "still very ill" when he returned to Düsseldorf on 7 July; the next day he suffered from "nervous complaints" ("Nerven-leiden").[22] Thus, it would seem that the composer was in the throes of the same sort of depressive malady that had plagued him throughout much of the period between 1844 and 1846. Resorting to a remedy that had provided him with some relief in earlier years, he bathed almost daily in the Rhine. Now, however, the baths failed to have a palliative effect: he remained "in a bad state" throughout most of July, so bad that he had to leave off orchestrating *Vom Pagen und der Königstochter.*[23] His condition took a turn for the better by the very end of the month, but after conducting his overture to *Julius Caesar* at a male chorus festival held in Düsseldorf on 3 August, he experienced an "incredible weakening" of his powers.

Hence, on 12 August the Schumanns travelled to Scheveningen, a spa situated near The Hague on the Dutch coast, where Schumann again began a daily regimen of bathing, much as he had in Norderney during the summer of 1846. At first, the baths seemed to do him some good: before long he regained his appetite, slept more comfortably, took pleasure in the company of Jenny Lind and the conductor and composer Johann Verhulst, played dominos with family and friends in the evenings, and even returned to the scoring of *Vom Pagen und der Königstochter* (completed in early September). Still, the improvement in his condition turned out to be shortlived; on 29 August he complained of "continuous nervous agitation" and on 3 September of "a burning feeling in the back of the head."[24] Nor was Clara faring well. On 9 September she suffered a miscarriage, another remarkable parallel with the couple's experiences in Norderney. She felt better by her birthday on 13 September, when she was presented with a little song, *Gern macht' ich dir heute,* a joint effort by "Marie and Papa," but not so Schumann, who had an attack of "nervous dizziness" on the same day. His health was little improved when they departed for Düsseldorf on 17 September.

While the Schumanns were in Scheveningen, some of their friends had seen to their move into new lodgings; once again, the old neighborhood had proven too noisy for Schumann to concentrate on his work. Having settled into the roomy townhouse at Bilkerstrasse 1032 on 19 September, he was "feeling tolerably well,"[25] well enough to put the finishing touches on *Des Sängers Fluch* by early October. But since his health remained unstable through the middle of the month, he was compelled to ask his deputy, Julius Tausch, to assume the direction of the first two concerts (28 October and 18 November) of the Musikverein's 1852–53 season.[26] This was no doubt a wise move. On 21 November, Schumann experienced new and troubling symptoms that he described as "unusual aural disturbances."[27] Although he had complained of distorted hearing during the depressive phase of 1844 and 1845, the disturbances registered in the fall of 1852 were early signs of a fatal condition.

Only two days later, however, Schumann was well enough to resume rehearsals with the Gesangverein. (Clara, on the other hand, was now disturbed by fainting spells that persisted into mid-December). On 2 December he led his orchestra and chorus in the warmly applauded premiere of *Vom Pagen und der Königstochter.* (In preparing for this event, Schumann worked for the first time with the orchestra's new concertmaster, Rupert Becker, called in to replace Wasielewski, who had accepted a post as conductor of the Concordia Chorverein in Bonn.) Over the next days Schumann started on a new composition, his first in about three months, a cycle of five lieder on translations of texts attributed to Mary Queen of Scots. Brooding but eloquent, the *Gedichte der Königin Maria Stuart,* op. 135, were completed on 15 December. But although Schumann worked on this set, his last major contribution to the song literature, "with joy and trepidation," his joy would not last long. On 14 December he received an "impertinent" letter from Wortmann requesting that he consider limiting his conducting. The next day, however, he was given a vote of confidence by twenty-two members of the Allgemeiner Musikverein (including Tausch, the composer Albert

Dietrich, Joseph Euler, and his friend Dr. Richard Hasenclever), who voiced strong objections to the contents of Wortmann's letter. Nonetheless, Schumann could only claim a pyrrhic victory in his second skirmish with the administration of the Musikverein: he agreed to hand over the choral rehearsals to Tausch, thus leaving only the orchestra rehearsals and the direction of public concerts under his control.

By the end of the year, Schumann's life settled into a familiar (if hectic) routine. On 30 December he conducted his first complete concert with the Musikverein orchestra since the end of the previous season. His health apparently restored, he also regained his compositional stride, and would continue to produce steadily throughout most of 1853, though his focus shifted from vocal to instrumental music. In late December 1852 he started writing piano accompaniments for Bach's sonatas and partitas for solo violin, a task that occupied him until early February 1853. Between 28 February and 12 March he composed the last and most exuberant of the choral-orchestral ballades, *Das Glück von Edenhall*, op. 143, on a text by Uhland adapted for his purposes by Dr. Hasenclever. (As late as 7 February 1854 he corresponded with Hermann Rollett about the possibility of a fifth ballade text.) Then he returned to the harmonization project he had taken to calling "Bachiana," and by 10 April had provided Bach's suites for solo cello with keyboard accompaniments. On 23 March, during the second leg of the "Bachiana" phase, he added an evocative Offertorium to his Mass; the spiritual center of the work, it was perhaps intended for entry in a competition for "the best composition of two Masses and motets" sponsored by a British patron.[28] In mid-April his thoughts turned to the upcoming Lower Rhine Festival, slated to be held in Düsseldorf later in the spring. A festive event indeed, it would bring together noted conductors (Hiller and Schumann himself), soloists (including Joachim and Clara), an orchestra of 160, and a chorus of 490, for three days of music-making culminating in performances of Handel's *Messiah* and Beethoven's Violin Concerto and Ninth Symphony. Among Schumann's contributions was a work drafted between 15 and 19 April, the *Fest-Ouverture* on the *Rheinweinlied*, op. 123, for orchestra, solo tenor, and chorus (one of many compositions that should be required listening for those who still think that Schumann's late music is all gloom and doom).

Toward the end of the month the Schumanns discovered a new (and for us, unusual) pastime: table-turning or table-rapping—the act of moving a table or producing knocking sounds without apparent physical means, ascribed to a spiritual force with which the participants are thus able to communicate. Schumann voiced his astonishment over this mysterious practice in a letter to Hiller of 25 April 1853: "Yesterday we did some *table-turning* for the first time. What a remarkable power! Just think, I asked for the rhythm of the first two measures of [Beethoven's] C-minor Symphony! The table hesitated with the answer longer than usual, then finally it began . . . though at first quite slowly. When I said: 'but the tempo is quicker, dear table,' it rapped in the correct tempo. . . . We were all beside ourselves with amazement to be surrounded with such wonders."[29] While some biographers have interpreted Schumann's fascination with table-turning (unfortunately, an article he wrote on the subject does not survive) as a sign of impending madness, it should be noted that if the composer was mad for indulging in this party game, so too were his family and many of his friends: his personal physician and friend, Dr. Hasenclever, no less than Clara's friend, the pianist Rosalie Leser, joined in with an enthusiasm just as great as Schumann's. Even his seven-year-old daughter Julie had her own toy table ("Puppentisch").

With the start of rehearsals on 11 May for the Lower Rhine Festival, the Schumanns' table-turning sessions were temporarily suspended.[30] A co-director of the festival along with Tausch and Hiller, Schumann took an active role in the planning and execution of its activities: a series of four concerts held between 15 and 17 May. In addition to conducting a performance of Handel's *Messiah* on the opening concert, he was amply represented as a composer. By his own account, the performances of the Fourth Symphony, Piano Concerto (with Clara as soloist), and newly composed *Fest-Ouverture* generated incredible enthusiasm in the large and receptive audiences.

About a week after the festival, Schumann set to work again on one of his literary projects. Having completed his perusal of Shakespeare's plays on 6 April, he now turned to Jean Paul, still his favorite author, with an eye toward the references to music in his works. Although he had culled the pertinent excerpts by early July, he continued reading for pleasure well into the year; indeed, by October he had made his way through *Titan, Die unsichtbare Loge, Hesperus,* and *Siebenkäs.* Shortly after beginning the Jean Paul segment of *Dichtergarten* in late May, Schumann also resumed compositing with a set of contrapuntal pieces, *Sieben Clavierstücke in Fughettenform,* op. 126. If the pedagogical intent of this collection is implicit, it is explicit in the collection immediately following. Composed in mid- to late June, the *Drei Clavier-Sonaten für die Jugend,* op. 118, were dedicated to his daughters Julie, Elise, and Marie, each of whom received her own sonata.

During the same period Clara was also busily composing, though in her case for the first time in many years. Before the month of June was out, she had finished a set of Romanzen for piano (op. 21), a collection of lieder (op. 23), and a group of variations (op. 20) on the first of three *Albumblätter* from Schumann's *Bunte Blätter,* op. 99. (Another individual, soon to play a crucial role in the composer's life, also wrote a set of variations on the same theme). Clara's creative outburst came to an end in July with a set of *Romanzen* (op. 22) for violin and piano. Around this time there also came a brief hiatus in Schumann's compositional efforts. Channelling most of his energy into the study of Jean Paul's novels, he also experienced a "severe attack of rheumatism" late in July that may have blunted his will to produce. Early in the next month we find him occupied with a more purely secretarial task: the compilation of a catalogue listing the holdings of his music library; his preparation of an index of his own compositions on 18 August belongs in the same category.[31]

But the middle of August also marks the initiation of an amazing surge in Schumann's creativity—the last surge of its kind in the composer's life. By 17 August he had rounded out the *Faust* scenes with an overture, thereby bringing to an end a project dating back almost a decade. After "ordering" the *Albumblätter,* op. 124, a week later, he drafted the *Concert-Allegro mit Introduction,* op. 134, for piano and orchestra. A visit from Joachim, whose playing seemed to "cast a spell on everything," between 28 August and 1 September no doubt inspired him to compose a similar concert piece for violin and orchestra, the *Phantasie,* op. 131. (During Joachim's brief stay Schumann made note of "an unusual weakening" in his "power of speech"; quite unlike anything he had experienced before, this symptom was another early manifestation of the fatal condition mentioned earlier).[32] Then on 13 September, Clara's thirty-fourth birthday, Schumann presented his wife with the orchestral compositions he had been working on furtively for the last month, together with a little partsong for vocal quartet and piano, *Die Orange und Myrthe hier,* and a new piano he had purchased from the Klems firm at a reduced price of 204 thalers. His composing continued apace in the weeks after this "joyful day," first with the *Ballade vom Haideknaben* (op. 122, no. 1) for declamation and piano, and next with *Kinderball,* op. 130, a set of "six easy pieces" for piano four-hands. The composition to which Schumann at first referred casually as a "piece for violin" (Stück f. Violine) soon evolved into a full-blown concerto, sketched and scored between 21 September and 3 October.

While still at work on the Violin Concerto on 30 September, Schumann received a visit from a fair-haired young man from Hamburg who had been recommended to him by Joachim. A pianist and composer, his name was Johannes Brahms. Schumann at once recognized his twenty-year-old guest as a genius, hailing him in a letter to Joachim of

8 October 1853 as a "young eagle" and a "true apostle who will inscribe revelations that many Pharisees . . . will not unriddle for centuries to come."[33] During the course of the ensuing month, the young eagle and the established master met almost daily for sessions in which the former regaled Schumann, and Clara too, with his recently composed piano sonatas, or "veiled symphonies," as Schumann called them (including the F♯-minor Sonata, op. 2), smaller piano pieces such as the E♭-minor Scherzo (op. 4), songs, and other works now lost: a *Phantasie* for piano, sonatas for violin and piano, and string quartets.[34]

While Brahms has often been credited with inspiring the last up-surge in Schumann's creativity,[35] we can now recognize this conjecture as a distortion of the facts. As we have seen, Schumann had been pro-ducing steadily for two months before Brahms arrived. Of course, the first of Schumann's compositions begun after the younger man's arrival, *Märchenerzählungen,* op. 132, for clarinet (or violin ad libitum), viola, and piano, may owe something to his newly found soulmate, but it is just as firmly rooted in his plan to enrich the genres of *Hausmusik* through a series of pieces for melody instruments and piano, a project going back to the late 1840s. Still, there is no denying Brahms's role in rekindling Schumann's Davidsbündler spirit. The "Pharisees" to whom Schumann alluded in his letter to Joachim are no doubt offspring of the "Philistines" that he and his collaborators on the *Neue Zeitschrift* battled in the 1830s. Not surprisingly then, the day after singing Brahms's praises to Joachim, Schumann turned to the medium of music criticism for the first time in about a decade. If Schumann's writings of the 1830s are representative of criticism "in a new key," then his celebrated essay on Brahms, completed on 13 October and published in the 28 October 1853 issue of the *Neue Zeitschrift* as "Neue Bahnen" (New Paths), was conceived in a decidedly messianic key. Singled out as a kind of savior who would "give expression to the times in an ideal fashion," Brahms was also elected to preside over a new Davidsbund whose other mem-bers—like Christ's disciples, twelve in number—included Joachim, Die-trich, Gade, Woldemar Bargiel, Robert Franz, and Stephen Heller.[36]

On 14 October the most promising of these disciples, Joachim, paid a surprise visit to Düsseldorf, and the following day Schumann hatched the idea of composing, along with Brahms and Dietrich, a sonata based on the first letters of Joachim's personal motto: "Frei aber einsam" (Free but lonely). In about a week his contributions to the *F.A.E.* Sonata, an Intermezzo (second movement) and Finale, were complete; then be-tween 29 and 31 October he added two more movements of his own to these, the result being the Third Violin Sonata in A minor. On the same day that Schumann conceived the sonata on Joachim's motto, he made an unusual notation in the *Haushaltbücher:* "Diotima."[37] A reference to either the character of the same name in Plato's *Symposium* or the hero's beloved in Friedrich Hölderlin's *Hyperion,* both of them symbols of ideal beauty, Diotima figured in the original title of what Schumann would ultimately call *Gesänge der Frühe* (op. 133). A cycle of luminous, other-worldly piano pieces, the work was provisionally drafted by 18 October.[38] Three days later Schumann began on a project at once inspired by Joachim and redolent of the "Bachiana" of late 1852 and early 1853: a series of piano accompaniments to Paganini's Caprices for solo violin. Finally, on 2 November (the day of Brahms's departure, and two days after Joachim's), he started drafting a set of five *Romanzen* for cello and piano. Completed soon thereafter and subsequently tried out with Reimers, the pieces do not survive: finding them unworthy of her husband's genius, Clara destroyed them some forty years later.[39]

During the happy period of Brahms's and Joachim's visits, a major storm was brewing with the executive committee of the Musikverein. Its chairman, Julius Illing, and another member, J. E. Heister, had an unpleasant exchange with Schumann on 19 October, the subject of which was almost certainly the music director's increasingly problematic conducting. We know from eye-witness accounts that Schumann's unusual style could make a striking effect. Pohl, for instance, was deeply moved by the composer's rendition of his *Manfred* Overture at a performance in Leipzig in March 1852: "completely oblivious to the public, even paying little attention to the orchestral musicians, he lived only in his tones . . . he himself became Manfred."[40] But at times, it was difficult to say whether Schumann was merely self-absorbed or in fact incompetent. Already in October 1851 he had trouble negotiating the tempo and meter changes in Beethoven's Choral Fantasy. Early in the next year he and Wasielewski had serious disagreements over his strange fondness for exceedingly slow tempos. According to one observer, he was no longer able to "keep the masses together" during the rehearsals of Handel's *Messiah* for the Lower Rhine Festival in May 1853.[41] Then on 16 October 1853, three days before his conference with Illing and Heister, there was a genuine fiasco at a performance of Moritz Hauptmann's Mass at the Maximiliankirche: apparently unaware of what was going on around him, Schumann continued conducting after the music stopped. Understandably enough, the members of the Gesangverein refused to perform under his direction in the future. Nor did Schumann's behavior at the rehearsals for the upcoming subscription concert on 27 October, the last such event he would conduct in Düsseldorf, bode well. Joachim, whose *Hamlet* Overture was slated for performance, tells of Schumann's disappointment over the fact that the "magical horn solo" was inaudible during the first run-through of the work. After the younger composer tact-fully pointed out that the horn-player had not even come in, Schumann ran the overture again, but with no better results: either unwilling or unable to cue, he never did manage to elicit the magical solo from a player who was obviously averse to counting.[42]

The entry in the *Haushaltbücher* for 7 November reads: "Decisive day. Effronteries." Two members of the Musikverein's executive commit-tee, Illing and Joseph Herz, had paid a visit to Clara to suggest, as deli-cately as they could, that Schumann should limit his conducting to his own pieces and entrust Tausch with the direction of everything else, and also to request that she take up this suggestion with her husband. In-censed, Clara would have none of it. "What a shameful plot," she wrote in her diary, "and an affront to Robert, for it would force him, in es-sence, to resign his position; I told all this to the gentlemen without even consulting with Robert."[43] In Clara's view, Schumann's deputy was the villain in the affair: "Tausch behaves like a crude, uncultured indi-vidual . . . because under the prevailing circumstances, he shouldn't be conducting, but is nonetheless, even though Robert wrote him that if he did, he (Robert) could no longer consider him a well-intentioned human being."[44] On 9 November Schumann responded to the executive committee in writing, indicating that he viewed their plan as a violation of his contract and that he would give notice, if at all, by the prescribed time, October 1854.[45] (He informed Joachim on the same day that he and Clara were giving some thought to establishing themselves in Vi-enna.) A subscription concert was scheduled for the following evening, but as Clara noted laconically in her diary: "We stayed at home. Tausch conducted."[46] In failing to appear for the performance, Schumann of course left himself open to being charged with breach of contract, a fact of which he was gently reminded in a letter from Illing and Wortmann of 14 November: a "request," they wrote, is not a "demand," and a "de-mand" is not a "violation of contract," but the "Herr Doktor" should remember that "both sides have their responsibilities." And indeed, soon after dispatching this letter to Schumann, the executive committee in-formed the mayor, Ludwig Hammers, that Tausch would conduct the remainder of the 1853–1854 season and assume the directorship in the following year.[47] Convinced that the administrators of the Musikverein had broken their contractual agreement, Schumann replied bluntly in a letter of 19 November: "After such happenings, we can have nothing further to do with one another." With this last salvo, his tenure as Düs-seldorf's municipal music director came to an end.[48]

Probably to divert his mind from these unpleasantries, Schumann occupied himself in the next days with matters relating to the publication of his collected writings. Then on 24 November, he and Clara embarked on a month-long concert tour of the Netherlands that would prove to be a major triumph. Travelling through Utrecht, The Hague, Rotterdam, and Amsterdam, they were greeted with honor and Schumann's works (including the Second and Third Symphonies, the *Genoveva* Overture, the Piano Concerto and *Concert-Allegro,* the Piano Quintet, and *Der Rose Pilgerfahrt*), with enthusiasm.[49] Impressed by the generally "charming and cultured" audiences and also by the well-trained Dutch orchestras, Schumann was even more pleased with the handsome profits earned from the tour. But at the same time, his physical condition was becoming a cause for concern: at the beginning of the trip he suffered from "intolerable aural disturbances," and near the end, at an audience with the Queen, from "difficulty in hearing."[50] Back in Düsseldorf on 22 December, the Schumanns celebrated Christmas quietly with Joachim, Dietrich, and Reimers, and in the early part of the New Year, Schumann began excerpting passages from Schiller's poems and Hoffmann's *Kreisleriana* for *Dichtergarten*. On 19 January 1854 he and Clara journeyed to Hannover, where Joachim served as concertmaster of the court orchestra. The next twelve days were taken up with spirited conversation among friends—Schumann and Joachim were soon joined by Brahms and another young talent, Julius Otto Grimm—and a steady stream of music making: public performances of Schumann's Fourth Symphony and *Phantasie* for violin and orchestra; private readings of his three violin sonatas; and a rehearsal of his Violin Concerto with Joachim and the court orchestra. Schumann also found time to work on *Dichtergarten,* turning now to Goethe's correspondence and the poetry of *Des Knaben Wunderhorn.*

After returning to Düsseldorf on 30 January, Schumann drafted a brief introductory essay for the collected edition of his writings and culled quotations from the ancient Greeks and Romans for inclusion in *Dichtergarten*. But before long, his routine was brutally and irrevocably disrupted.[51] On the evening of 10 February, he was plagued by "very strong and painful aural disturbances" that took the form of a continually sounding pitch or pitches. This malady grew worse but also more "wondrous" in the next days, for by then he was hearing entire compositions (the chorale *Ein feste Burg ist unser Gott* among them) in "splendid harmonizations" and played by a "distant wind band."

Over the course of the following weeks, Schumann teetered on the brink between madness and lucidity. After Dr. Hasenclever was called in on 15 February, he took a turn for the better, but in the middle of the night on 17 February, he rose from bed to jot down a theme "dictated by the angels" (in conversation with Rupert Becker on 24 February, he ascribed the melody to the spirit of Schubert). By the next morning, however, the angelic voices had become the voices of demons, "tigers and hyenas" who sang "hideous music" and threatened to "hurl him into hell." Throughout the following week he was alternately hounded by good and evil spirits, but managed in his more rational moments to write a set of five variations on the "angelic" theme (commonly known as *Geistervariationen,* Schumann's last surviving keyboard work was actually entitled *Thema mit Variationen für das Pianoforte;* it bears a dedication to Clara).

By February 26, Schumann was well enough to play through a sonata by the young Martin Cohn for Dietrich, but afterward worked himself into such a state of "joyous exaltation" that he was bathed in sweat. Fearful he might harm Clara during the night, he demanded to be taken to an asylum. Although the physician called in to examine the overwrought composer, a Dr. Böger, was able to convince him to take to his bed, he awoke the next morning in a profoundly melancholy state, murmuring "Ah Clara, I am unworthy of your love." After working for a time on the fair copy of his variations, he slipped undetected from the house. Rupert Becker recorded the painful climax of the tale in his diary:

> Schumann snuck out of his bedroom at two in the afternoon (wearing felt slippers) and headed straight for the Rhine, jumping into the river from the middle of the bridge! Luckily he was noticed at the entrance to the bridge, and indeed because he offered his handkerchief as a pledge since he had no money for the toll! Fortunately several fishermen who had been observing this odd transaction came along with a little boat, immediately after he lept, and saved him. Once in the boat, he tried to jump into the water again, but the fishermen prevented him. The trip home must have been dreadful; he was transported by eight men and followed by a group of people (it was Carnival season) who amused themselves at his expense.[52]

Clara was kept from seeing her husband upon his return, his doctors (Hasenclever and Böger) surmising that the sight of her might increase his agitation; hence she passed the next days in nervous anticipation at the home of her friend Rosalie Leser. Nor was she informed of Schumann's attempted suicide, a desperate action motivated by numbing depression, pathological guilt (the probably cause of which we will take up later), and fears of harming his wife. In fact, she would not piece together the terrible truth until over two years later, when Schumann's wedding ring could not be located after his death. Then she remembered the contents of a note she had once found among his papers: "Dear Clara, I'm going to throw my wedding ring into the Rhine; do the same with yours, and then both rings will be united!"[53]

For his part, Schumann persisted in demanding to be institutionalized. In the first days of March, Dr. Hasenclever arranged for his removal to a private sanatarium run by Dr. Franz Richarz, a personal acquaintance, and located in Endenich, a suburb of Bonn. In the meantime, Brahms had arrived from Hannover and would remain in Düsseldorf at the side of Clara and her children for the better part of two years. His rapid assumption of some of the duties associated with the pater familias of the Schumann household—along with Clara, he maintained the *Haushaltbücher* until March 1856—and his growing passion for Clara long ago triggered speculation that theirs was more than a friendship. As of this writing, the possibility of a romance between Brahms and Clara remains speculation.[54]

Clara was prevented from bidding her husband farewell when he departed for Endenich on 4 March in the company of Hasenclever and two male attendants. Instead she "sat at Fräulein Leser's in a gloomy stupor," thinking to herself: "Now I'm done for."

The Late Styles

During the last four years of his career, Schumann produced no less than fifty compositions, many of them multi-movement cycles or collections. Among them we find representatives of practically all the major genres. These works are remarkably varied in style and content, and consistently high in quality. (For an overview of the works composed from 1850 to February 1854, see Table 12.1). Whoever hears signs of decay in the late music simply does not know it very well. Of course, not every one of the late works is an unqualified masterpiece. The overtures, for instance, are generally less successful than the "Rhenish" Symphony. But if a composition occasionally falls short, this is probably owing to Schumann's willingness to experiment, to take chances, to find new solutions to old problems, right up to the end of his career.

Schumann's creativity in the final phase of his career was guided by two principal impulses: the desire to build up a repertory commensurate with his position as municipal music director in an active (if provincial) center; and second, a level-headed concern to ensure commercial success. In addition, the trajectory of the late music was shaped by a re-enactment and completion of the march through the genres begun years before. From April through August 1850, a period when he anticipated moving to Düsseldorf, Schumann focused mainly on the composition of lieder. Installed in his new post by the fall of 1850, he concentrated on orchestral music through the early part of 1851, when his

Table 12.1. Compositions: 1850–1854

1850

January	*Neujahrslied,* op. 144 (sketch completed; see October)
March	*Drei Gesänge,* op. 83 (completed April)
April	*Der Handschuh,* op. 87 (?)
	Aufträge, from *Lieder und Gesänge,* op. 77, no. 5
	Drei Lieder für Drei Frauenstimmen, op. 114, no. 2
	Faust Scenes, Nos. 5 & 6 (completed May)
May	*Sechs Gesänge von Wilfried von der Neun,* op. 89
July	*Lieder und Gesänge,* op. 96
	Fünf heitre Gesänge, op. 125, nos. 2, 4, 5
	Lieder und Gesänge, op. 77, nos. 2 & 3
August	*Lieder und Gesänge,* op. 127, no. 4
	Sechs Gedichte von N. Lenau und Requiem, op. 90
October	*Neujahrslied,* op. 144 (orchestration completed)
	Cello Concerto, op. 129
November	Third Symphony, op. 97 (completed December)
December	*Spreu,* published as *Bunte Blätter,* op. 99 (1852) and *Albumblätter,* op. 124 (1854) (see also August 1853)
	Overture to Schiller's *Braut von Messina,* op. 100 (sketched)

1851

January	Overture to Schiller's *Braut von Messina,* op. 100 (orchestrated)
	Sechs Gesänge, op. 107, nos. 1–3, 6
	Fünf heitre Gesänge, op. 125, no. 3
	Overture to Shakespeare's *Julius Caesar,* op. 128
March	*Märchenbilder,* op. 113 (viola, ad libitum violin & piano)
	Vier Husarenlieder von Nikolaus Lenau, op. 117
April	*Der Rose Pilgerfahrt,* op. 112, version with piano (completed May; see also November)
	Der Königssohn, op. 116 (completed June)
May	*Romanzen und Balladen für Chorgesang,* op. 145, no. 3
	Mädchenlieder von Elisabeth Kulmann für zwei Frauenstimmen, op. 103 (completed June)
	Sieben Lieder von Elisabeth Kulmann, op. 104 (completed June)
June	*Ball-Scenen,* op. 109 (piano, four hands)
August	*Drei Fantasiestücke,* op. 111
September	*Drei Gedichte aus den Waldliedern von Pfarrius,* op. 119
	Sonata for Piano and Violin, op. 105
October	Piano Trio No. 3, op. 110
	Second Grand Sonata for violin and piano, op. 121 (completed November)
November	*Der Rose Pilgerfahrt,* op. 112, version with orchestra
December	Fourth Symphony, op. 120 (revision of 1841 D-minor Symphony)
	Overture to Goethe's *Hermann und Dorothea,* op. 136

1852

January	*Des Sängers Fluch,* op. 139 (polished October 1852)
February	*Messe [Missa sacra],* op. 147 (completed March; see also March 1853)
April	*Requiem,* op. 148 (completed May)
May	*Verzweifle nicht im Schmerzenstal,* op. 93, motet for double chorus & orchestra (scored)
June	*Die Flüchtlinge,* op. 122, no. 2 (declamation and piano)
	Vom Pagen und der Königstochter, op. 140 (completed September)
July	
September	*Gern macht' ich dir heute, Liedchen von Marie und Papa*
November	
December	[5] *Gedichte der Königin Maria Stuart,* op. 135
	Piano accompaniments to Bach, Sonatas and Partitas for unaccompanied violin (completed February 1853)

1853

January	
February	*Das Glück von Edenhall,* op. 143 (completed March)
March	Piano accompaniments to Bach, Suites for unaccompanied cello (completed April)
	Offertorium added to *Messe*
April	*Fest-Ouverture* on the *Rheinweinlied,* op. 123
May	*Sieben Clavierstücke in Fughettenform,* op. 126 (completed June)
June	*Drei Clavier-Sonaten für die Jugend,* op. 118
August	*Faust* Overture
	Die Orange und Myrthe hier (vocal quartet & piano)
	Albumblätter, op. 124 (put "in order")
	Concert-Allegro mit Introduction, op. 134 (piano & orchestra)
September	*Phantasie,* op. 131 (violin & orchestra)
	Ballade vom Haideknaben, op. 122, no. 1 (declamation & piano)
	Kinderball. Sechs leichte Tanzstücke, op. 130 (piano, four hands)
	Violin Concerto, WoO23 (completed October)
October	*Märchenerzählungen,* op. 132 (clarinet, ad libitum violin, viola, piano)
	Gesänge der Frühe, op. 133 (piano)
	Piano accompaniments to Paganini's 24 Caprices for violin solo (continued 1855, Endenich)
	Intermezzo and *Finale* of F. A. E. Sonata for Violin and Piano, WoO22 (movements 2 & 4; other movements by Albert Dietrich & Johannes Brahms)
	Third Sonata for Violin and Piano, WoO27 (two new movements added to *Intermezzo* & *Finale* of F. A. E. Sonata)
	Fünf Romanzen for cello and piano (lost)

1854

February	*Thema mit Variationen für das Pianoforte,* WoO 24

focus shifted to oratorical and balladic works. Up to this point, Schumann's creativity almost exactly replicates the motion from lied through
literary opera that informs the works of the 1840s. At the same time,
his cultivation of the larger forms during the early phase of his tenure
in Düsseldorf alternated with the production of various types of *Hausmusik,* including lieder, choral partsongs, and four-hand piano music, a
phenomenon we have already observed during the intensely productive
phase at the end of the 1840s. His turn in the fall of 1851 to instrumental chamber music, the genre in which public and private styles achieve
an ideal balance, represents a natural consequence of the alternation of
larger and smaller forms in the period just before. The year 1852 was
devoted mainly to vocal music, and here we note the convergence of
two patterns: a continuation of Schumann's review of the musical
genres, resulting in a revived interest in the choral-orchestral ballade
(and in operatic plans), and the culmination of this review in church
music. A new cycle of compositional activity began in 1853, this one
centered on instrumental music and comprising arrangements and collections, pedagogical works, orchestral and concertante compositions,
and finally, chamber music and piano works. Thus, the pattern of creativity that encompasses practically the whole of Schumann's career enfolds smaller patterns within it, while the course of the larger and the
smaller patterns was determined by a confluence of internal imperatives
and external needs.

Since Schumann's later music recapitulates, in microcosm, the
achievements of an entire creative life, it is not surprising to observe
that it embraces a broad diversity of styles. This music can be thought
of as the product of a varied array of personas, each dominant (by-
and-large) during progressively later phases of the last four years of the
composer's career, and each associated with a style and family of genres.
As a lyric poet, Schumann concentrated on lieder. As music director, he
cultivated a public style that is particularly prominent in his symphonic
works. Schumann the storyteller wrote oratorios, choral-orchestral ballades, and declamation ballads. Schumann the ecclesiastic produced not
only a Mass and Requiem, but also the final song of the Lenau cycle,
op. 90. His character as a collector shows through, naturally enough, in
his arrangements and collections. As a pedagogue, he wrote contrapuntal works and *Hausmusik* for children and adults. And finally, Schumann
the Davidsbündler displays an esoteric style that shows through most
obviously in the late chamber and piano music. Just as a single persona
may manifest itself in a variety of genres, so, conversely, may a single
genre be linked with a number of personae. Instrumental chamber music, for instance, proves to be a very mobile genre in this regard. The A-

minor Piano and Violin Sonata, with its alternation of Florestinian and Eusebian movements, nicely exemplifies the Davidsbündler persona. The D-minor Violin Sonata, on the other hand, is marked by the large dimensions, seriousness of tone, and thematic integration characteristic of the public style. As emphasized in their titles, the *Märchenbilder* and *Märchenerzählungen* reveal the narrative art of the musical storyteller. And last, Schumann's harmonizations of Bach's works for unaccompanied strings and Paganini's Caprices—chamber music of a sort—are indices of his passion for arranging and collecting.

Listing each of the personas in turn does not mean that they are absolutely fixed, impermeable characters. On the contrary, just as the younger Schumann brought together Florestan and Eusebius in the same composition, so do many of the later works conflate a variety of personas and styles. The outer movements of the Violin Concerto frame a central slow movement at once lyric and esoteric. The largely public, "secular" style of the Third Symphony gives way to an evocation of the sacred style in its fourth movement. The *Sieben Clavierstücke in Fughettenform* emanated from Schumann the pedagogue, collector, and Davidsbündler. In *Der Rose Pilgerfahrt*, the composer emerges as lyric poet, storyteller, and, given the focus on the theme of redemption, ecclesiastic as well. The Mass and Requiem display a similar mixture of lyric and sacred styles. Still, consideration of the personas in order has the advantage, first, of giving shape to an amazingly rich repertory, and second, of allowing the detection of relationships within this repertory that might otherwise go unnoticed.

Schumann shows himself best as lyric poet in his late lieder, a body of music just as compelling as the better-known works of the *Liederjahr*, 1840. Genuine lyricists focus on the inner lives of their subjects; this is precisely what Schumann does in the greatest of his late songs, the cycles on texts by Lenau and Elisabeth Kulmann, and the *Maria Stuart* lieder, each of which can be viewed as an analogue to one of the cycles of 1840. At the heart of the Lenau cycle (*Sechs Gedichte . . . und Requiem*, op. 90) are a series of lyrics on the theme of a lost love, over which the poet's grief steadily intensifies. As such, the poems unfold a kind of *Künstlerleben* or "Artist's Life" that makes the cycle into a pendant to *Dichterliebe*. The concluding Requiem, the "old Catholic poem" attributed to Heloïse, is at once a lament for the passing of the poet's life and a celebration of his transfiguration through death, his release from "feverish, burning love." The melancholy tone of Lenau's texts is a product of a sensuous palette of aural metaphors, many of them contrasting sound and silence, emblems for presence and absence respectively. Schumann's music mediates this contrast through an evocative array of echo and "tolling" effects (an echo, after all, synthesizes sound and silence), witness the resonant pedals in the first and fourth songs and the imitation of funeral chimes in the piano part of the sixth, the latter a somber conceit that ushers in the joyous strumming of angelic harps in the *Requiem*.

Schumann preceded each of the *Sieben Lieder*, op. 104, on Kulmann texts with comments that take us on a chronological tour of the poet's brief life, thus making explicit the cycle's conception as a sort of *Mädchenleben* ("Girl's Life") that finds its earlier equivalent in *Frauenliebe und Leben*. Given the prominence of syllabic settings, transparent accompaniments, and only slightly modified strophic forms, the style of Schumann's music is apparently simplicity itself. But this simplicity is often tinged with a musical response to the mystical overtones that attracted the composer to Kulmann's poems in the first place. The visionary quality of the sixth song, *Die letzten Blumen starben*, for instance, is a function of harmonic progressions attenuated by unusual voice-leading and bare textures in the accompaniment.

The *Gedichte der Königin Maria Stuart*, op. 135, count as another latter-day analogue to the *Frauenliebe und Leben*, only here the texts trace an eminently tragic course from the queen's departure from France to her plea for salvation in the moments before she was put to death. Schumann portrays this ill-fated life as a miniature drama through his recourse to a declamatory style and a flexible, prose-like syntax that seems to deny the regular rhymes of the poetry. Yet the drama of the cycle is an inner drama and therefore emerges as an utterance of the composer's lyric persona, who conflates these seemingly antithetical modes through the fusion of recitative and chorale in the second and fifth songs, and operatic melody and strophic form in the third and fourth.

The intimate style of the lieder gives way to a public style in the symphonic and concertante works of Schumann's final creative phase. Much of this music has earned an undeservedly bad reputation for grayness and gloom. But while it is possible to view the orchestral color of the later version of the Fourth Symphony, the *Faust* Overture, and the tutti passages in the first movement of the Violin Concerto as generally somber, it is equally important to observe that all of these works are in D minor, a key Schumann seems to have associated with solemn grandeur (the same holds for the opening of *Der Königssohn*, where the sonority of the trombone choir transports us into the distant realm of legend). In the overture to *Julius Caesar*, another arguably somber work, the uniformity of the orchestral color, which at times seems to prefigure Bruckner's massive sonic effects, is complemented by the extreme (perhaps too extreme) limitation of the thematic material. On the other hand, all of the concertante works are scored with the utmost discretion. Likewise, a delicate woodwind tone prevails in the overture to *Hermann und Dorothea,* no doubt a reflection of the content of Goethe's play, a pastoral set against the backdrop of the French Revolution. In each case, the quality of the orchestral sound—somber or airy—is intentionally calculated to create a specific effect.

The same desire to communicate a message clearly and directly (to make a public statement in tones) informs Schumann's choice of his musical materials, which in several cases strike a frankly popular tone. Consider, for example, the many allusions to the *Marseillaise* in the overture to *Hermann und Dorothea,* or the appearance of *Bekränzt mit Laub,* a well-known lied extolling the virtues of Rhine wine, in the *Fest-Ouverture,* op. 123. What is most striking, however, is the composer's artful handling of these materials. The *Fest-Ouverture,* to take one example, culminates in a jubilant presentation of the Rheinweinlied by tenor solo and chorus, but this climactic moment is prepared by a process of motivic evolution extending throughout the entire piece: fragments of the well-known tune insinuate themselves, at first obliquely, into the opening slow introduction, and then more obviously, into the ensuing *Lebhaft,* a sonata-allegro design. The boisterous statement of the Rhein-weinlied at the conclusion of the work is thus heard as the logical out-come of an on-going motivic argument.

Schumann once told Wasielewski that in the Third Symphony "popular elements should prevail, and the result, I think, has been a success."[55] More specifically, the undisputed success of the work lay in its nearly ideal fusion of these "popular elements" with the demands of high art. Once again, the technique of motivic evolution plays a crucial role in the process (Examples 12.1a–d). During the first episode of the Scherzo, a leisurely swinging waltz, or ländler, Schumann introduces a light-hearted, sequentially rising motive in sixteenth notes (a relative of the same idea takes on a considerably more demonic cast in the finale

Example 12.1a. Third Symphony: *Scherzo,* mm. 16–18 (cellos and bassoon).

Example 12.1b. Third Symphony: fourth movement, mm. 1–5 (horn and trombone).

Example 12.1c. Third Symphony: fifth movement, mm. 46–48 (horns).

Example 12.1d. Third Symphony: fifth movement, mm. 271–76 (winds and strings).

of the A-minor Piano and Violin Sonata). The motive, furthermore, provides the basis for the shape of the E♭-minor subject of the "solemn" *(feierlich)* fourth movement, Schumann's most compelling homage to the *stile antico*. During the last movement the motive reclaims its popular tone at the beginning of the transition to the second group and at the head of the development section, but, as a final gesture of synthesis in the coda, Schumann recalls the "solemn" form from the previous movement, now transformed into the parallel major and treated imitatively. Another idea figures in the thematic web. Appropriately enough, the final stretto is preceded by a call in the horns and trumpets based on the dancelike opening theme of the first movement. Through the recall and transformation of easily graspable ideas, the Third Symphony in effect becomes a popular epic.

If popular elements play a decisive part in establishing the public character of Schumann's late overtures and Third Symphony, then instrumental virtuosity takes on a corresponding role in ensuring the public dimension of his concertante works. Here too, the composer was faced with the challenge of speaking to his listeners (and interpreters) in a language they could understand, while at the same time not sacrificing the claims of art. Schumann addressed this concern both at the level of the detail and that of the larger design. Among the fingerprints of his virtuoso writing for violin is a predilection for rapid arpeggios connecting the extreme reaches of the instrument and often involving dramatic leaps. In the Violin Concerto (and also in the *Phantasie*, op. 131, and the finale of the Third Violin Sonata) passages such as these occur with some frequency: at the close of the exposition and recapitulation in the first movement, at the parallel spots in the dancelike finale, and last, at the very end of the finale[56] (Examples 12.2a and b). Schumann's violin writing is also characterized by highly ornamental figuration, by melodic lines peppered with short trills and other graces. Passages of this sort occur in the transitions from first to second group in

Example 12.2a. Violin Concerto: first movement, close of exposition, mm. 125–29. Violin and piano reduction by Georg Schunemann. © B. Schott's Soehne, Mainz, 1937. © renewed. All right reserved. Used by permission of European American Music Distributors Corporation, sole U.S. and Canadian agent for B. Schott's Soehne, Mainz.

Example 12.2b. Violin Concerto: third movement, coda, mm. 302–6. Violin and piano reduction by Georg Schunemann. © B. Schott's Soehne, Mainz, 1937. © renewed. All right reserved. Used by permission of European American Music Distributors Corporation, sole U.S. and Canadian agent for B. Schott's Soehne, Mainz.

the first and last movements of the Violin Concerto. Specific virtuoso styles, in other words, are not invoked for their own sake, but are rather put to the service of a specific musical function: extravagant arpeggiation aptly signals closure, while ornamental passage-work provides an effective means of moving from one idea to another.

Nowhere is Schumann's desire to fuse virtuosity and musical substance more obvious than in his written-out cadenzas for the Cello Concerto, the *Concert-Allegro* for piano, and the *Phantasie* for violin. In all of these pieces, the traditional site of soloistic display is neatly integrated with the thematic argument of the work, perhaps most skillfully in the *Concert-Allegro* and the *Phantasie*. Indeed, the cadenza of the former (much as in the far better-known Piano Concerto) amounts to no less than a secondary development section. (We find a similar approach in several of the concertos of the work's dedicatee, Johannes Brahms, though in the first movements of his Second Piano Concerto, op. 83, and Double Concerto, op. 102, the written-out cadenza is displaced from its usual spot to the opening of the piece.) In the cadenza of the *Phantasie* Schumann recalls a device already used to stunning effect in the first movement of Mendelssohn's E-minor Violin Concerto: the violin concludes with a series of *ricochet* figures over which the orchestra enters with the principal theme. The cadenza is thus seamlessly bound with the coda, while, at the same time, the traditional role of violin and orchestra are playfully reversed as the soloist assumes an accompanimental role.

The technique of thematic integration that we have observed in the Third Symphony is also much in evidence in the Cello Concerto and the Violin Concerto, both of which are unified by a web of motivic cross-references, some subtle and others more explicit. This is an essentially narrative, "epic" technique, a product of the storyteller persona. And to be sure, Schumann most clearly displays the storyteller's art—an art that reaffirms the importance of telling old tales and singing old songs—in the oratorical and balladic works of his last years. The fairy-tale oratorio *Der Rose Pilgerfahrt* resonates in many ways with *Das Paradies und die Peri*, composed nearly a decade before. Here too we encounter a series of flexibly designed scenes in which one number flows gracefully into the next, a broad range of vocal styles extending from folklike lyricism to the histrionic gestures of the *Rezitativischer Gesang*, a choral style notable for its elfin lightness, deftly wrought woodwind textures in the later orchestral version, and a focus on the poetic theme of redemption. In *Der Rose Pilgerfahrt*, however, the theme is further coupled with the notion of transfiguration: the central figure of the musical fairy tale begins as a rose, takes on human form through the agency of the Elf Princess, and ends her pilgrimage as an angel. Schumann beautifully portrays the main character's removal from the earthly to the spiritual realm in the final scene of the oratorio, "Rosa's Verklärung" (the title makes for an obvious parallel with the concluding installment in the *Faust* scenes), underscoring his heroine's transformation from human to divine status, her accession "to a higher light," through musical means at once simple but compelling: the poignant chromaticism of the

first part of the scene (in D♭ major) is replaced by the almost unadulter-
ated diatonicism of the second (in C major), where Rosa, like the Peri
before her, is greeted by the strains of an angelic choir.

Schumann's storytelling reached a highpoint in the four choral-
orchestral ballades composed between the spring of 1851 and the early
part of 1853. Based as they are on substantial texts of poetic quality,
these works may be viewed as pendants to the earlier literary operas,[57]
each of them representing a unique synthesis of the epic, lyric, and
dramatic modes. Not surprisingly, Schumann's approach to the first of
these modes is most apt to command our attention. In three of the
ballades (*Der Königssohn, Des Sängers Fluch*, and *Vom Pagen und der
Königstochter*), the narration of events is split among solo voices and
chorus, a strategy prompted by the overriding poetic theme of these
works. While the tale unfolded in *Der Rose Pilgerfahrt* centers on the
theme of redemption, the ballades take up an even more fundamental
aspect of the storyteller's art: the preservation of memory. Schumann's
dispersal of the narrative voice among soloists and chorus serves as a
powerful reminder that memory is at once an individual and a communal affair. The theme is underscored in other ways as well. In *Des Sängers Fluch*, a minstrel is put to death for seducing his queen with a sensual Minnelied; but the minstrel's companion, an old harper, avenges
his young friend's death by placing a curse on the king and his house.
At the end of the work the chorus tells us that what was once a splendid
palace is now a desolate wasteland and that the king and his name are
no longer remembered. The chorus's grim intonation of the final words,
"Versunken und vergessen, Das ist des Sängers Fluch," drives home the
essential point: to be forgotten, or to forget, is the worst fate of all. (The
theme possesses an unmistakably political dimension as well: without
the bard to preserve his memory in verse and song, even the mightiest
of rulers is doomed to oblivion.) Similarly, the phrase "Das Glück von
Edenhall" (the good fortune of Edenhall) is repeated again and again,
like a mantra, by the frenzied revellers in the ballade of the same name
in a desperate (and futile) attempt to imprint the phrase on their memories and thereby preserve the ephemeral good fortune that is the fortune of the house of Edenhall.

The poetic theme of memory goes hand in hand with the musical
devices of motivic recall and transformation, techniques employed masterfully in the greatest of the choral-orchestral ballades (actually a cycle
of four interrelated ballades on texts by Geibel, slightly reworked by
Schumann himself), *Vom Pagen und der Königstochter*. The young page
in Geibel's tale, much like the minstrel in *Des Sängers Fluch*, is put to
death after his tryst with the king's daughter is discovered. His body,

hurled into the sea by the king's henchmen, is claimed by a chorus of water nymphs who convince a "Meermann" (the male counterpart of a mermaid) to fashion the page's bones and golden hair into the frame and strings of a harp. After completing his task, the Meermann sings a beguiling melody to the accompaniment of the harp, a tune destined to have a disastrous effect on the royal household. During the wedding festivities for the king's daughter and the nobleman to whom she has been married against her will, the entire company is suddenly transfixed by the distant strains of the Meermann's lied; imagining that she hears the voice of her beloved page beckoning from afar, the king's daughter falls dead as her father and bridegroom flee from the hall. Schumann complements this allegory on the bewitching powers of memory with an equally bewitching web of motivic recurrences and transformations. The opening march tune of the first ballade, a fitting backdrop for the royal hunting expedition with which the tale opens, takes the form of a rollicking dance during the concluding wedding celebration (Example 12.3). The third ballade in turn opens with a lilting siciliano for the water nymphs, which will serve as the basis for the Meermann's melody (Example 12.4), the latter sumptuously scored for a mellow horn and trombone choir, and accompanied by rustling strings and punctuating harp chords. Naturally enough, the opening phrases of the melody recur in the moments before the final catastrophe, but by the end of the work only a fragment remains: the melody's head motif, a rising fourth, which is repeated by clarinet and horn as the chorus delivers its solemn but chilling account of the fate of the king's daughter.

If the storyteller endeavors to preserve memory, the ecclesiastic attempts to preserve souls. Schumann adopted some of the characteristics of this persona as well. Given to wearing almost exclusively black clothes during his Düsseldorf years, he was often mistaken by observers for a clergyman.[58] Yet Schumann's religiosity was devoid of dogmatism. In a self-characterization written in 1830, he described himself as "religious, but without religion"; according to Wasielewski, this description held into the 1850s.[59] The paradox of a religious person without religion found artistic expression in Schumann's composition of a Mass (and Requiem) intended for "the church service and concert use," and also provides a link between his sacred music and his oratorical works: the projected Luther oratorio, Schumann insisted in a letter to Pohl, "must be suitable for church and concert hall."[60]

Both the Mass and Requiem, Schumann's chief essays in the sacred style, are characterized by the "lofty simplicity and dignity" that E. T. A. Hoffmann singled out as the hallmarks of genuine church music.[61] The "simplicity" of the Mass manifests itself in a tonal orbit circumscribed

Example 12.3. Vom Pagen und der Königstochter: opening of Ballades I and IV

Example 12.4. *Vom Pagen und der Königstochter:* Ballade III: music for sea nymphs and "Meermann."

by only three keys (C, E♭, and A♭) and in the symmetrical framing of the whole (the Kyrie and Agnus Dei correspond in tone, if not in substance) and its parts (refrain and arch forms govern the Gloria, Credo, and Sanctus). In the opening movement of the Requiem, Schumann achieves a specifically "lofty" simplicity through a declamatory but understated setting of the text supported by gentle syncopations in the orchestra (Example 12.5). As the music is kept from submitting to the

Example 12.5. Requiem: first movement, mm. 1–6.

regular stresses of the C meter, the result is a notably speech-like quality, a chiselling of the words geared to present them as objects of pious devotion.

Composed within a short space of one another, the Mass and Requiem are related not only in style, but also in content. Both works make extensive use of a motive comprised of interlocking fourths, a relative of the "signature" motive we have identified in *Genoveva* and the *Faust* scenes, and presented in descending and ascending forms.[62] In addition, both share the same poetic theme: the notion of redemption that, as we have seen, also plays a crucial part in Schumann's oratorical works and literary operas. Hence the storyteller and the ecclesiastic are motivated by similar impulses. The poetic heartpiece of the Mass comes in the "added" movement, the Offertorium ("Tota pulchra es"), a prayer in which the Virgin is asked to intercede with God on behalf of the supplicant (much as Gretchen intercedes with the Mater Gloriosa on Faust's behalf). A reflective lied for soprano solo, obligato cello, strings, and organ, it is cast in a syllabic but syntactically flexible style whereby phrase elisions and hemiolas create the impression of one long-breathed melody. In the "Te decet," "Liber scriptus," and "Hostias" of the Requiem, the descending form of the signature motive becomes an emblem of the penitent sinner's longing for redemption. But when the redemptive moment arrives, it is articulated through the technique of motivic recall. The final words of the last movement, "Dona eis requiem" (Grant them rest), bring an allusion, first in the orchestra, then the chorus, to the very opening of the work.

Just as the ecclesiastic traffics in spiritual redemption, so is the collector concerned with material redemption, with the preservation of fragile objects that might otherwise perish, and the arrangement of these objects in a meaningful order. In a sense, Schumann was a passionate collector—of books, of musical fragments, of memories—throughout his life, though the tendency intensified during his later years. The literary manifestations of this persona include Schumann's selection, beginning in April 1852, of passages on music from the works of Shakespeare, Jean Paul, and other classics of world literature for his *Dichtergarten,* and also, beginning at about the same time, his assemblage of his own writings on music for publication in a collected edition. While living in Düsseldorf, he not only maintained his *Projektenbuch* and *Haushaltbücher,* but also a *Merkbuch* (notebook) in which he jotted down plans for future works (in one of its more surprising entries, we learn that Schumann was contemplating a *Deutsches Requiem* on texts by Rückert).[63] Finally, in August 1853 we find him preparing both a catalogue of his music library and an index to his compositions.

Schumann's passion for collecting had a musical side as well. Indeed, the figure of the collector serves as a powerful mediator between the composer's life and his art. Late in 1850 he began to bring together the nearly three dozen little piano pieces, most of them composed in the 1830s, that he would later publish as *Bunte Blätter,* op. 99, and *Albumblätter,* op. 124. There is no little irony in his original title for the collection: "Spreu." Literally, the word means "chaff," but chaff is also a metaphor for "worthless stuff," rags and tatters that one might just as well toss into the dustbin. In bringing together the rags and tatters of the earlier part of his career as a collection (or two collections), Schumann saved them from precisely that fate.

Once a group of objects has been assembled into a collection, it is imbued with an aura, an indefinable quality compounded of nearness and distance that inspires the beholder with awe. This too has a musical counterpart. In his "Bachiana" project, Schumann left the texts of Bach's sonatas and partitas for solo violin and suites for solo cello absolutely untouched: all he added were piano accompaniments. That is, he provided Bach's works for solo strings with an aura in the form of accompaniments that are generally discreet and often transparent, as transparent as the glass case through which we might view a collection of rare coins or stamps.

Like the collector, the pedagogue strives to impose order and to preserve, if not objects, then traditions. Schumann took on this persona when, in early February 1853, he supervised the fledgling attempts at composition of his daughters Elise and Marie. Not long afterward he returned to the pedagogical project begun in 1848 and 1849 with the *Album für die Jugend* and *Lieder-Album für die Jugend,* and continued in 1851 with the *Ball-Scenen,* rounding it off with *Sieben Clavierstücke in Fughettenform, Drei Clavier-Sonaten für die Jugend* (both composed in May and June of 1853), and *Kinderball* (composed in September 1853). All of these collections belong to the world of *Hausmusik* and disclose interesting relationships not only with one another but with other portions of Schumann's output as well. The *Ball-Scenen* and *Kinderball,* both for piano four-hands, obviously form a complementary pair, the earlier set intended for talented amateurs, the later one for aspiring children (more than a modicum of technical skill is necessary to negotiate *Ecossaise,* No. 7 of *Ball-Scenen,* or *Ringelreihe,* the sixth piece in *Kinderball*). Perhaps while working on the Violin Concerto in the fall of 1853 Schumann even thought back to the *Ball-Scenen,* whose second piece, like the finale of the later work, is a polonaise in D major.

While edification and conviviality intersect in the collections for piano four-hands, a poetic element is added to the mix in the *Sieben*

Clavierstücke and *Drei Clavier-Sonaten*. Many of the fugues in the former set are notable for their quiet lyricism and for a detached, almost abstract quality. In the last fugue, this quality arises from the syncopations and ties that take the edge from the rhythmic definition of the subject, thereby lending the piece a dreamy, Eusebian dimension. Each of the *Drei Clavier-Sonaten* is progressively more difficult—technically and musically—in accordance with the increasing capabilities of the set's dedicatees, Schumann's three eldest daughters: Julie (eight years old when the sonatas were written), Elise (ten), and Marie (twelve). The last movement of Marie's sonata bears the evocative title *Traum eines Kindes* (A Child's Dream). Dominated by a brisk but gently developed motive in $\frac{6}{8}$ meter, the amiable course of the movement is twice interrupted by the opening music of Julie's sonata, the first in the set. Ever a lover of allusion, Schumann here employs the device to a distinctly poetic end. The quotation of Julie's sonata in Marie's is an emblem for the elder daughter's recollection of the world of early childhood: a realm best accessible through dream.

To be sure, the poetic quality of Schumann's late music is largely a function of his Davidsbündler persona. As we have said before, this persona was no doubt stimulated by Schumann's contact with Brahms and Joachim—the key figures in the new Davidsbund proclaimed in "Neue Bahnen"—in the autumn of 1853, but it was already in evidence well before. Schumann's preparation, beginning in the spring of 1852, for a collected edition of his writings on music would have given him the opportunity to ponder anew the ideals of his younger days. Writing to Strackerjahn on 17 January 1854, soon before the collection appeared in print, he was pleased to observe that he had "hardly deviated at all from views expressed more than twenty years ago."[64] On 3 February he went on to offer the clearest exposition of the Davidsbund that we possess, describing it in the Introduction to his collected writings as "more than a secret society," its members including the "artist-characters" Florestan, Eusebius, and Raro, whose bond "runs like a red thread" through the pages of the *Neue Zeitschrift*.[65] Just three days later he reaffirmed a crucial element of the Davidsbündler philosophy in a letter to Richard Pohl, recently identified by Schumann as the apologist for the New German School who wrote under the pseudonym "Hoplit." Often interpreted as a reactionary jibe at the accomplishments of Wagner and Liszt, the letter is nothing of the kind. "Those whom [Hoplit and his party] take to be musicians of the future," Schumann maintained, "I consider musicians of the present, and those whom they take as musicians of the past (Bach, Handel, Beethoven) seem to me the best musicians of the future."[66] What we have, in other words, is a radical restatement of the philosophy of music history that informed Schumann's critical writings of the 1830s, according to which the ephemeral present is viewed as a site of imperfection and the past as the nurturing source for a "new poetic age" lying in the future.

Signs of the Davidsbündler persona emerge earlier still in the music of Schumann's final phase. Indeed, works redolent of the esoteric manner of his younger days are spread throughout the last years. The finale of the G-minor Piano Trio, composed during a spate of chamber music activity in the autumn of 1851, falls into a sonata-allegro form, but the design bears traces of the sectional, mosaic-like construction of many of the *Novelletten*. Written shortly before the G-minor Trio, the *Fantasiestücke*, op. 111, are shaped according to a principle familiar from the *Fantasiestücke*, op. 12: the central, Eusebian movement of the later cycle is flanked by a passionate Kreisler piece and a mock-pompous, Florestinian march. A similar alternation of characters unmasks the A-minor Sonata for Piano and Violin as a cycle of three character pieces, the second of which is the joint effort of Florestan and Eusebius. But the most compelling of the Wunderkinder's creations is without a doubt the third movement of the *Märchenerzählungen,* where Schumann's Eusebius persona removes us into a fairy-tale world by way of a deftly contrived musical texture, its elements consisting of a bass pedal, murmuring sixteenths supporting a descending arabesque in the right hand of the piano, and, hovering over it all, a gracefully shaped cantilena in the clarinet interwoven with the viola's counterline, the whole luxurious sound structure a subject for rhapsodic variations (Example 12.6).

To ensure the unity of the *Gesänge der Frühe,* composed, like the *Märchenerzählungen,* during the productive October of 1853, Schumann employs a network of subtle, "witty" connections much as he had in earlier cycles such as the *Davidsbündlertänze:* variants of the chorale-like melody of the first piece infiltrate the texture of the second, while the last two pieces dissolve into nothingness with the same plagal progression. In the Intermezzo and Finale of the *F.A.E.* Sonata, Schumann translates a verbal motto into a musical cipher, which then serves as the basis for a seemingly endless array of varied motivic shapes, a practice reminiscent of the generation of material in *Carnaval.* And finally, the treatment of the melody as a migrating cantus firmus in the *Thema mit Variationen,* Schumann's last surviving keyboard work, recalls a similar technique in the *Impromptus,* op. 5. Is it mere coincidence that both pieces are intimately connected with Clara?

In all of these instances, Schumann evokes the Davidsbündler style of the 1830s without simply repeating it. On the contrary, the earlier manner is refracted through the medium of an eminently "late" sensibil-

Example 12.6. Märchenerzählungen: third movement, mm. 1–9.

ity, perhaps nowhere more beautifully than in the first of the *Gesänge der Frühe*, where the bass and inner voices become curiously dislodged from the melody, as if to imitate the overlapping and clashing of sonorities in a great reverberatory space. The distance between the earlier and later manifestations of the Davidsbündler style is inscribed in the difference between the salon and the cathedral.

Our consideration of the Davidsbündler persona and its role in the music of Schumann's last years has brought us into contact with many motifs—the collected edition, the manifesto, the march, the fairy tale, the chorale, the cantus firmus, the cathedral—a motley throng, to be sure, but one whose members can be easily linked with his other personas. This may be significant. Perhaps it means that the Davidsbündler persona embodies all the rest and that it figures as an emblem for the musical novel we have subsumed under a rather colorless rubric: "The Late Styles." It would also mean that Schumann continued, up through the very end of his career, to carry on his musical pursuits as if they were a kind of literature.

"Do You Remember When . . . ?"

When Schumann first demanded to be taken to an asylum on 26 February 1854, the day before his suicide attempt, he is reported to have assured Clara: "It won't be for long, and I'll come back cured."[67] As it turned out, he was wrong on both counts. The composer would live out the last two-and-a-half years of his life in an asylum for the mentally disturbed in Endenich. For a man in Schumann's condition, it was not such a bad place to be. Located on a well-kept estate just outside of Bonn and with a view of the Rhine and the Siebengebirge (mountains), this private institution was originally designed to house only fourteen patients, though by the time Schumann was admitted, two more buildings had been opened to accommodate between forty and fifty more. The director of the operation, Dr. Franz Richarz, belonged to the more progressive group of thinkers among nineteenth-century psychiatrists. An adherent of the "no restraint" method championed by the English physician John Conolly, he neither force-fed his patients nor drugged them with strong medications. By the standards of his time, and even of our own, Schumann was quite well treated. What patient in a twentieth-century institution can claim, as Schumann did, a round-the-clock attendant? To be sure, one aspect in particular of Richarz's method will strike us an unusual: his conviction that in order to prevent untoward reversals in the state of his patients, their relatives should be kept away until all symptoms of illness had vanished. But this will at least account for the fact that Clara did not see Schumann until 27 July 1856, just two days before his death. She was strongly advised by her husband's doctors (Richarz and Peters, the latter officially in charge of Schumann's case) to stay away, and putting her faith in their ability to effect a cure, she did.[68]

Much light is shed on Schumann's final years in Endenich by the contents of the log-book or diary in which Dr. Richarz maintained a close record of his famous patient's condition.[69] Although the general trajectory of Schumann's illness has long been known, Richarz's diary affords us a sharper sense of its many ups and downs. While Schumann was severely psychotic when admitted to Endenich in March 1854, he took a turn for the better toward the end of April and improved steadily until late autumn (toward the end of this phase he even began corresponding with Clara and Brahms). Then, beginning in November 1854, his condition worsened dramatically up through October 1855. The period between November 1855 and January 1856 saw a slight improvement, but the final decline soon set in, leading inexorably to death in July 1856.

Not unexpectedly, the diary is rich in fascinating and often troubling details. Richarz made careful note of Schumann's temperature, pulse rate, pupillary condition, and other physical and psychological symptoms. In addition, he reported on his patient's food intake (and cigar-smoking), sleeping habits, and even the regularity and quality of his bowel movements. For the most part, Schumann was given only mild medications, including a harmless copper mixture commonly used as a sedative, and other benign treatments such as lukewarm baths. His doctors' fondness for administering enemas, however, was not met with equal enthusiasm on the part of his patient. Richarz's diary mentions the use of a straight jacket only once, in an entry of 20 April 1854, during a phase when Schumann was still manifesting symptoms of extreme psychosis.[70] Finally, the diary provides an account of Schumann's daily activities, which included walks to Bonn to visit the Beethoven monument, piano playing (Schumann had access to a Lipp piano in the room adjoining his own), composing, letter writing, and visits from friends such as Joachim, Brahms, Wasielewski, and the poetess Bettina von Arnim (often they were permitted to observe Schumann only from a distance, through a partially opened door, or through a little window in the wall of his room).

Many of the entries in Richarz's log make for painful reading. Consider, for instance, his report for 8 May 1855:

> Yesterday [Schumann was] continually agitated, talking drivel loudly and rapidly, also [while walking] in the garden he made fierce gesticulations; afterward [he] played the piano in a wild and crazy manner for almost two hours, hollering all the while; after dinner [he] was violent with the attendant, turned him out of his room while threatening him with a chair. At night, sleepless, uninterrupted ranting and raving, threatened the attendant again . . . Speech indistinct, like a drunkard . . .[71]

We can intuit from a reference (in an entry of 12 September 1855) to Schumann's "writing down all kinds of brief jottings and reflections" that the patient himself was keeping a diary.[72] On 11 January 1856, he made an urgent request for manuscript paper because "he wanted to compose something small." Perhaps this "something small" was the harmonization of the chorale *Wenn mein Stündlein vorhanden ist,* one of the few surviving bits of evidence relative to his compositional activity at Endenich. Be this as it may, we learn from Richarz that by 15 January he had composed a fugue and that in the next days he was "always busy composing."[73] Richarz's entries for mid-April 1856, however, give us a strong clue as to the probable fate of Schumann's late diary, his fugue, and perhaps his other compositions as well. On 16 April the doctor noted: "Last night and this morning [he] burned letters from his wife . . . but disputed the fact that he was actually burning letters," and on 17 April: "Burned papers again today."[74] Rational behavior and dementia often alternated at even closer intervals. On 11 March 1855, Schumann wrote perfectly lucid letters to Simrock, asking for a copy of the recently published piano-four-hand arrangement of his *Fest-Ouverture* on the Rheinweinlied, and to Brahms, requesting that he remind Clara to send a copy of Paganini's Caprices; but the next day, after suffering a convulsive attack, he claimed that he was being "pursued by Nemesis" and that "a demon had taken away his power of speech."[75]

Perhaps the most striking aspect of Richarz's diary is its contribution to our understanding of the nature and causes of Schumann's final illness and death. According to one recent theory, the composer in essence committed suicide through self-starvation.[76] The diary does not sustain this hypothesis. Although at various points throughout his stay at Endenich he refused food or drink under the delusional belief that they had been poisoned—on 10 October 1855, for instance, he "threw his wine in the chamber pot, saying it was urine"[77]—these phases alternated with others when he ate normally. On 13 July 1856 (just weeks before Schumann's death), Richarz reported: "ate quite well . . . willingly had wine"; but only two days later he "wouldn't eat breakfast, said it was poison"; and during the daily consultation with his doctors on 16 July, he maintained that "he was being fed the shit of other [patients]."[78] There is a terrible irony in all this: if Schumann sometimes refused nourishment, it was because he wanted to prolong his life, not end it.

Richarz's comments for 12 September 1855 bring us closer to the true cause of Schumann's demise. The full text of the entry, from which I have already quoted, runs as follows: "Recently [Schumann] has been writing down all kinds of brief jottings and reflections of melancholy content, e.g.: 'In 1831 I was syphilitic and treated with arsenic.'"[79] Although there has long been a strong suspicion that Schumann had earlier contracted syphilis, we can now be reasonably certain that this was indeed the case. Other pieces of the puzzle begin to fall into place. Most probably the source of Schumann's infection was the woman known to us only as "Christel" or "Charitas," who enters his diary in the spring of 1831.[80] In addition, Schumann alludes frequently during precisely this period to a "wound" that at first caused him "biting and gnawing pain," and that was in all probability a penile lesion, one of the most common manifestations of primary syphilis.[81] While there are no references in Schumann's diaries to symptoms of the secondary stage of the disease (which often sets in about two months after the appearance of the initial lesion and usually results in a rash), it is likely that many of the complaints Schumann registered during the latter half of 1852 and the autumn of 1853—rheumatoid pain, dizziness, aural disturbances, difficulty in speaking—represent the onset of tertiary syphilis after a long period of latency. The hallucinations and auditory delusions he experienced in February 1854 mark the full outbreak of the final stage of the disease: general paresis or progressive paralysis.[82]

While Schumann was at Endenich the symptoms of general paresis intensified drastically, their course complicated all the more by the fact that he continued to suffer from the depressive disorder that had plagued him for much of his adult life. The steady deterioration of his neurological system brought with it convulsive fits and, especially from March 1855, a gradual loss of the ability to speak understandably (in an entry of 6 September 1855, Richarz compared Schumann's speech to that of a person whose mouth is half full, adding that "only vowel sounds can be distinguished").[83] His dementia, likewise a consequence of general paresis, increased at an alarming rate, manifesting itself in delusional ideas (on 20 April 1854, he "saw his first [!] wife in heaven"; in early September of the same year, he insisted that Düsseldorf had been destroyed),[84] aggressive behavior, talking and sometimes singing to himself, and violent fits of cursing and screaming that left him hoarse.

Although we are able to detect signs during Schumann's final years in Endenich of several of the personas considered in the previous section of this chapter, we will be faced with the sad task of reporting on their disintegration. Indeed, the tragedy of Schumann's very last years exercises its fullest and most devastating impact if we recognize it for what it was: the story of a richly layered personality in decay.

After he began corresponding with Clara in September 1854, Schumann often asked to be sent copies of the recently published scores of his friends. The old Davidsbündler spirit shines through unmistakably in his letters to both Clara and Brahms, many of which include mini-critiques, in a stenographic but suggestive style, of the compositions he eagerly studied and played: Joachim's Variations for Viola and Piano, op. 20, Brahms's *Ballades*, op. 10, and the latter's Variations, op. 9 (dedicated to Clara, and based on the same theme from Schumann's *Bunte Blätter* on which Clara herself had written variations).[85] Indeed, his enthusiasm for Brahms's Variations no doubt inspired the "composition of new musical thoughts" that Richarz noted in a diary entry for 17 December 1854.[86] What these "new musical thoughts" might have been, we do not know: they probably perished when he consigned his papers to the flames in April 1856.

We catch glimpses of the storyteller persona as well in Schumann's

Endenich letters, especially those addressed to Clara. Repeatedly he calls up "blissful memories" of happier days gone by through allusions to the enthusiastic reception of his pieces at the 1853 Lower Rhine Festival and the subsequent concert tour of the Netherlands, and in references to the many trips the couple enjoyed together: to Switzerland, Heidelberg, The Hague, Belgium, and along the Rhine.[87] (This fixation on the past became a source of annoyance for Clara, who wondered why her husband did not think more toward the future). Again and again, he asks: "Do you remember . . . ?" He even closes his letter of 18 September 1854, the same letter in which he responded to news of the birth of his son Felix in June, with the words: "don't forget me." In his last letter to Clara, dated 5 May 1855, he encloses a portrait of Mendelssohn as an "Andenken," a "keepsake," but also a "remembrance."[88] To be sure, the "storytelling" in these letters to Clara goes beyond a mere rehearsal of past events: it represents a desperate attempt to preserve the past from oblivion, for by mid-1854 Schumann's memory was beginning to slip away from him. Early in June, Clara received an encouraging report from Schumann's doctors, who reported that "[Robert] is not talking in a confused way and has asked some questions indicating that he is beginning to recall the past." But by August, they noted that "after an hour or so [Schumann] has no idea of what he did the hour before." Writing in late December, Richarz found him "often absent-minded, digressive, and incoherent in conversation."[89] The storyteller, it would seem, was falling prey to the worst fate of all. Was he ever haunted by the final words of *Des Sängers Fluch*: "Versunken und vergessen . . ."—Lost and forgotten?

The related personas of the collector and arranger likewise figure prominently in Schumann's Endenich years. Sometime before August 1854 he began copying out poems from Scherer's *Liederwald*, perhaps for future use as song texts; between March and June 1855 he returned to the harmonization of Paganini's Caprices, a project begun in the fall of 1853, just months before his confinement; and at some point during his stay at Endenich he started to make a piano reduction of Joachim's *Heinrich* Overture. But by the spring of 1855, Schumann the collector had already begun to turn into a self-parody. In a letter to Brahms of March 1855, the same one in which he offered a mini-review in the Davidsbündler manner of Joachim's Variations, op. 20, he asked to be sent an atlas. Shortly after visiting him in May 1855, Joachim reported that he "showed me alphabetical lists of city names he had compiled," no doubt from the atlas. At his consultation with Richarz on 6 September of the same year, Schumann probably paid little attention to his doctor's questions, for he was "busily making geographical excerpts from a map." And finally, on 9 June 1856, less than two months before his death, Richarz again found him "busy with the atlas."[90]

Of course, by June 1856, Schumann was in a sorry state indeed. Often indignant and sullen, his expression vacant and squinting, his face and limbs twitching uncontrollably, frequently coughing up phlegm, unable to control his bladder, and eventually confined to bed due to the edema (swelling) in his feet, Dr. Richarz's illustrious patient was nearing the end. Clara, however, had little inkling of the dramatic decline in her husband's condition. The year before, she had received a report from Bettina von Arnim, who, after visiting with Schumann in May 1855, concluded that his recovery was actually being impeded by the "hypochondriacal" Dr. Richarz. Alarmed by this account, Clara dispatched Joachim to Endenich and soon thereafter was given the (overly) reassuring news that Schumann was cheerful, looked forward to future visits from Joachim and Brahms, and had finished accompaniments to all but four of the Paganini Caprices (the young violinist and composer tactfully omitted any reference to Schumann's recent interest in geography). Still concerned, Clara arranged to meet with Dr. Richarz in Brühl, a town about 20 kilometers from Endenich, during the early summer of 1855. At the time, Richarz gave her hope that Schumann might still recover, and there the matter stood for about a year (in the meantime, Brahms's attempts to find a more suitable institution for him proved fruitless).[91]

But in June 1856 Clara began to receive distressing reports once again. She finally learned from Brahms that for weeks Schumann had apparently done nothing but pick names out of an atlas. After discovering that his badly swollen feet kept him in bed, she resolved to investigate for herself. Arriving in Endenich for the first time on 14 July, she was informed by Richarz (who, as usual, advised against an encounter with his patient) that Schumann probably had less than a year to live. Having returned to Düsseldorf she received a telegram on 23 July urging her to depart at once for Endenich if she wanted to see her husband alive. Both she and Brahms rushed to the asylum the same day, but were told upon arrival that the immediate danger had passed. And once again, Clara was discouraged from seeing Schumann, this time by both Richarz and Brahms, who claimed that the experience might be too much of a shock for her.[92]

Although Clara went home to Düsseldorf, she did not remain there for long. Unable to bear the separation any longer, she set off for Endenich for the third and last time on 27 July, determined to see her husband. When she finally did, between 6 and 7 P.M. on the same day, he was barely strong enough to embrace her, though he did appear to recognize her as his beloved wife. Clara provides a moving account of these moments of reunion and recognition in her diary: "Once I could make out 'my,' and certainly he wanted to say 'Clara,' because he gazed at me in such a friendly manner, and then 'I know'—'you'. . . ."[93] During the next forty-eight hours, neither she nor Brahms strayed far from the dying man's side. On 28 July Clara fed him a couple of spoonfuls of tea and a bit of jelly and wine as well: "he slurped up the wine from my fingers—ah, he knew it was I. . . ."[94] Richarz reports that by evening he was expectorating great quantities of phlegm, a consequence of the pneumonia that claimed his life, and that by the afternoon of 29 July his breathing was labored, his pulse just barely detectable. Schumann died that day at 4 P.M. quietly and alone, Clara having gone to the train station to meet Joachim, who had been summoned from Heidelberg to join her and Brahms. She arrived at her husband's bedside just a half hour after his death: "Today I saw him for the last time; I lay a few flowers on his brow so that he might take my love with him."[95]

The burial service, a simple affair in accordance with Clara's wishes, took place two days later. Wasielewski's Concordia Chorverein provided a chorale, and Ferdinand Hiller came from Cologne to pay his final respects, but otherwise the only notable mourners included Otto Jahn, Julius Grimm, and of course the major lights of the new Davidsbund: Dietrich, Joachim, and Brahms. According to the poet Klaus Groth, a friend of Brahms who was also in attendance, as the small cortège wound its way through the streets of Bonn the townspeople came "flooding from every street and alleyway as if to see a prince pass by . . . it was as if the people of Bonn, quite suddenly and involuntarily, had felt the message run through their minds that one of the noblest of Germans was on his last journey." Schumann was interred at 7 P.M. in the cemetery near the Sternentor in Bonn. Then, as Clara put it in her diary: "A new life began for me."[96]

Epilogue: A Place to Recall Schumann and His Music

Although Schumann's memory was all but effaced during his years in Endenich, the memory of the composer's achievements remained very much alive. No one remembered them better than Brahms. While he once quipped, with characteristic irony, that the only art he ever learned from Schumann was the art of playing chess, his comments in a letter of January 1873 are probably closer to the mark: "The remembrance ["Andenken"] of Schumann is sacred to me. I will always take this noble, pure artist as my model."[1] Indeed, Schumann's musical language exerted a decisive impact on Brahms's approach to melody, tonal planning, counterpoint, and form. His fondness for melodies constructed largely from chains of thirds—especially in late works such as *O Tod, wie bitter bist du* from the *Vier ernste Gesänge* (op. 121), or the outer movements of the Fourth Symphony (op. 98)—resonates with a similar feature in Schumann's *Mein Wagen rollet langsam* (op. 142, no. 4) and in the coda of the finale of his D-minor Piano Trio. Though Brahms's disposition of thematic groups in tonalities a third apart certainly owes much to Schubert, it owes just as much to Schumann's *Fantasie* (op. 17) and the opening movement of his First Symphony. One of the key aspects of Schumann's New Way, the configuration of a thematic idea as a contrapuntal duo, is echoed frequently in Brahms's work: in the opening movements of the First Symphony (op. 68) and the C-minor Piano Trio (op. 101), to cite only the most obvious examples. Schumann's "fantasy variations," as Brahms himself called them, not only served as models during the younger composer's early years (in the Variations, op. 9, for instance), but in his maturity as well (consider the slow movement of the Second String Quintet, op. 111). And last, the blurring of the border between development and recapitulation, one of Brahms's favorite means of imparting further continuity to the sonata form, was a favorite trick of Schumann's too, witness the outer movements of his F-major Piano Trio (op. 80), and the opening movements of the Cello Concerto, A-minor Sonata for Piano and Violin, and G-minor Piano Trio.

Brahms's contemporary Anton Bruckner likewise owes a debt to Schumann. His conception of the symphony as a quasi-religious genre is unthinkable without the example provided by Schumann's Second Symphony. Similarly, the apotheotic moments of "breakthrough" (*Durchbruch*) in Mahler's symphonies find striking parallels in Schumann's First and Third Symphonies. And we can be certain that Mahler closely studied Schumann's setting of the concluding scene of *Faust*, Part Two, before fashioning his own musical counterpart to the same text as the gargantuan second movement of the Eighth Symphony. As a composer of lieder, Hugo Wolf drew liberally on Schumann's legacy, while as a critic he paid tribute to the older composer's piano music, chamber music, and choral works.

Nor was Schumann's impact confined to the German sphere. Though critical of his orchestration, Tchaikovsky was an ardent devotee of Schumann's symphonic works, chamber music, and piano pieces, all of which seemed to him to reveal "a whole world of new musical forms" and to touch "heart-cords which have never yet vibrated at the bidding of his predecessors."[2] From this "world of new musical forms," two elements in particular seem to have fascinated the Russian composer: Schumann's sharply chiselled musical mottos (such as we hear at the opening of his First Symphony and Tchaikovsky's Fourth) and the irresistible surge of his codas (in, for instance, the finale of the Fourth Symphony and the finale of Tchaikovsky's First).

Schumann's effect was felt in France as well. Debussy thought highly enough of the canonic *Studien* for *Pedal-Flügel*, op. 56, to arrange them for two pianos and paid the older composer an even more telling tribute in confiding to the publisher André Durand that it was his highest wish for his piano music to assume a place "to the left of Schumann or the right of Chopin."[3] A lover of literature like no other composer of the nineteenth century, Schumann in turn played a part in stimulating a literary movement inextricably linked with the French: Symbolism. For

Camille Mauclair, a poet and friend of Stephan Mallarmé, Schumann had already "realized everything the Symbolists only dreamed of." Mauclair's first attempts at *vers libre* were even conceived as verbal analogues to the composer's keyboard miniatures.[4]

Thus, while Nietzsche came close to writing off Schumann's music as a "merely German phenomenon,"[5] history has proven the philosopher overly hasty in his assessment. Still, there is no denying that our composer exerted his greatest influence on future generations of German artists. Some of the most significant manifestations of this influence are also the least obvious. We might not at first think of pairing Schumann and Alban Berg, for example, but on reflection it appears that they had much in common: born song-writers, they also shared a predilection for quotations from their own works and those of others, encoded messages, and musical ciphers. Theodor Adorno put his finger on another aspect of the affinity between these cabalistic lyricists: "Among the great composers Schumann was the one who . . . discovered the musical *gestus* of remembering, looking and listening back. That, along with Schumann's impassioned exuberance, echoes throughout Berg's oeuvre. . . ."[6] In a polemical exchange with Hans Pfitzner on the relationship between analysis and value judgment, Berg argued that the "beauty" of *Träumerei* was a direct consequence of its motivic structure, implying that the motivicism of his own music (and of Schoenberg's as well) was not so far removed from that of Schumann.[7]

Before closing, I would like to indulge in a brief digression—a rhetorical strategy that would have appealed to the subject of this biography. Writing in 1836, and reflecting on his youthful enthusiasm for Uhland's chivalric ballads, Heinrich Heine exclaimed: "But since then so much has happened!" Now the poet is sitting in a house on the Boulevard Montmartre in Paris, and "here the wildest waves of the times break; here screech the loudest voices of the modern age; there is laughing, roaring, and beating of drums; the National Guard marches past in quick double time; and everyone is speaking French." Then he asks: "Is this the place to read Uhland's poems?"[8]

I am sitting in a café on Commonwealth Avenue in Boston; outside, noisy streetcars lumber along; inside, university students on their way to or from summer-term classes are sipping lattés and munching on scones; rock music pours (fortunately, not too loudly) from speakers overhead; and (nearly) everyone is speaking English. So I feel compelled to ask: Is this the place to recall Schumann's life? to ponder his writings? and above all, to think about his music? Since I cannot presume to answer for everyone, I will respond for myself: yes to the first question, because the tragic end of Schumann's life calls to mind the devastation wrought by the plagues of the past and quickens my desire that cures will be found for the plagues of the present; yes to the second, because Schumann's writings remind me that the present is fraught with imperfections, but that precisely these imperfections may hold out the greatest promise for the future; and yes to the third, because Schumann's music may just yet inspire a sense for poetry in a largely unpoetic age.

Appendix: *from* Flegeljahre
by Jean Paul

Chapter 63: "Titanium—Black Tourmaline—Masked Ball"

"We'll see one another tonight," said Vult to Walt on the morning of the fancy-dress ball, and with this valediction departed as if unveiling a veil. In his loneliness, Walt the notary found that the day burned too brightly for the beautiful night, out of which and for which this day had come into being. At dinner he longed for his brother, whose empty casing seemed even emptier, since he was supposed to meet Vult that evening, though without knowing in what form.

Walt went to a costume-shop and searched long for an Apollo- or Jupiter-mask; he couldn't understand, he said, why people almost always picked ugly masks. Since Vult had enjoined him to appear in the packed ballroom no earlier than 11 o'clock, he leisurely prepared his finery, getting out of his old clothes like dream-honey pours slowly from a calyx.

The thought of future events—especially the idea that he would play a role in this great Shrove Tuesday celebration—colored, as if in a romantic glow, his undressing and practically simultaneous dressing-up again as well as the late-night hustle and bustle of the city and in the house. How differently the rumbling of the carriages sounds if one knows that he will follow along after, as if hearing them while standing before the bedboard with a nightcap on!

As he left his little room, he prayed to God that he might find it again happily; he felt like a hero who, thirsty for fame, sets out for his first battle. [1] With warm, domestic feelings, and in the double-costume of a miner and a wagoner (as if he were at home peering out of two attic windows), he carried himself like a sedan chair across the street, and could hardly believe that he was strolling along everywhere, with all his spirit-wheels, so splendidly unnoticed and encased twice over, as if he were a pocketwatch. *By making a wrong turn, as he was often wont to do, he first entered the punch room, which he mistook for the ballroom, and into which beautifully muted music was wafting from a considerable distance.* [2] But he was not sufficiently astonished to forget to take off his miner's cap, which broke into the shimmering Baumannshöhle[2] of figures. As he boldly looked out of his mask at the window, he was amazed, in glancing around him, to notice the several uncovered faces of people with worn-out masks in one hand and punch glasses in the other. He attributed the general dipping into the mineral spring or goblet of distinction to the laws of the ball, and forthwith asked for one glass and then—taking his cue from a gentleman in an admiral's costume at the head of the line—yet another. *He couldn't spot Wina, nor was there any trace of Vult.* [2] A lady knight from the Order of the Slavegirls of Virtue made her way nimbly through the crowd, and gazed deeply into his eyes. Finally she grasped his hand, opened it, and traced an H on his palm; but since he knew nothing of this long- or short-range telegraphic code, he pressed her hand gently instead of writing on it.

Finally, since he wanted to investigate the bustle in the adjoining hall, he made his way into the resonant and brightly lit ballroom, full of fluttering figures and fancy hats, all of them in an enchanted frenzy. What a fertile zodiac-heaven of criss-crossing, zigzagging shapes! [2] He felt poetically elevated, when, like an ascending terrestrial globe on the First Day, he caught sight of this crazy mix of wild animals, old knights, ecclesiastics, goddesses, Moors, Jews, nuns, Tyrolians, and soldiers. For a long time he followed a Jew, who was bedecked with payment claims snipped out of the official gazette, and read him over, much like he did another fellow who was done up with the danger notices, attached to the appropriate limbs, from the princely gardens. From a huge wig full of curling-papers, which the bearer unravelled and distributed, he took one for himself, but found nothing inside except a common encomium to his charming eyes.

He and his imagination were most drawn to a giant boot that was gliding along, wearing and carrying itself, [3] until an old-fashioned schoolmaster with a walking stick stared at him severely, shaking his head in a gesture of reprimand, so that he became quite confused, and sought the offending source in himself and his wagoner's costume. When the pedagogue noticed this, his nodding and his motions of disapproval became all the more vehement, until our notary—who, terrified, looked into his threatening eyes—dove into the crowd. He found it frightful to gaze into dark, unknown eyesockets (as if into the open mouth of a projectile) and to receive, in return, the vivid stare of a stranger.

He had not yet seen Vult or Wina, and in the end he wondered anxiously whether he would find them in this ocean as pearls or islands.

All at once a maiden with a wreath of flowers on her head appeared before him; from the mouth of her mask hung a slip of paper, on which was written: "I am Spes, the personification of Hope, who is represented with a wreath of flowers on her head and a lily in her right hand; with her left arm she supports herself on an anchor or a mighty pillar (S. Damm's *Mythologie*, newly edited by Levezow, section 454)." Walt, who was plagued by the silliest thoughts when first confronted with anything, inwardly wanted to take counsel with Wina, if only the figure had been more elegant and a bit larger. *But Hope quickly turned around; first a masked shepherdess appeared, and then a simply clad nun with a half-mask and a fragrant bouquet of auriculas.* [4] The shepherdess took Walt's hand and traced an H on it; he pressed hers, as was his habit, and shook his head, because he believed that she wanted to sign her name with the H. Suddenly he looked hard at the half-mask, that is, the half-face of the nun, and in the fine but pert line of the rosey lips and the chin full of determination, he at once recognized Wina, who merely looked out of the darkness with gentle, starry eyes. His hand was already on its way to his cap, which he then—in accord with the freedom from strict manners allowable at a masked ball—put back close to its former place. "O how blissful," he said quietly. "And you are Mademoiselle Raphaela?" Both nodded. "O what more could one desire in such an intoxicating time, when two people, disguised as spirits without bodies, recognize one another in the Elysian Fields?"

A footman came along and swept Raphaela onto the dance-floor: "Best wishes, Herr Miner!" he said in departing, so that Walt recognized him as the Alsatian. *For a second he stood alone next to the quiet maiden—the crowd momentarily served as a mask—with freshness and charm the half-rose and lily of her face emerged from the half-mask as if from the blossom of a drooping bud.—From behind their dark masks they gazed at one another like foreign spirits from two distant planets, as if they were two stars in a solar eclipse, and each soul observed the other from a great distance, wanting thereby to appear all the more distinct.*[5]

But since Walt, finding himself in this situation, made a face as if he wanted to celebrate a jubilee, Wina asked him, as Spes passed by searching for the Slave-girl of Virtue, whether he wouldn't dance. Immediately he was whirled into the billowing crowd, and helped to whirl it along, since he danced like the Romans, for whom, according to Böttiger, mimetic dancing consisted in nothing other than the movement of the hands and arms. His feet danced passionately to the waltzes until

a sign was given to halt, whereupon the dashing masses arranged themselves, one after the other, into a stationary throng. He however believed
himself to be flying after a summer aflutter with butterflies. *Just as a
youth touches the hand of a great and famous writer for the first time, so
he gently touched—like butterfly wings, like auricula powder—Wina's
back, and put himself in a position whereby he could best look into her
life-breathing face. If there's a harvest dance that is itself a harvest, if there's
a Catherine-wheel of loving enchantment, then Walt the wagoner had
both.* [8] But since he couldn't move his feet without also moving his
tongue, the dance hall became his grand pulpit; and he described it to
her as they danced: how even the body became music—how humanity
rushes past while life stands still—how two souls lose consciousness of
the crowd around them and solitary, like celestial bodies in ethereal
space, circle about themselves according to their own law—how only
those souls who love each other should dance in order to reflect the
spiritual side of this artful illusion in harmonic motion. As they stood
and he surveyed the fancy-dress ball with its dancing battalions, he said:
"How sublime the coats and the great hats of the men look, like cliffs
overlooking a women's garden party! A masked ball is perhaps the highest means through which life is able to make a postlude to poetry's
prelude. Just as all social stations and historical epochs are equal before
the poet, and all external trappings a mere camouflage, but everything
within is joy and resonance, so here people poeticize themselves and
their lives,—the most ancient fashions and customs are revived and take
their place next to the most recent—the remotest savage, the finest and
the coarsest classes alike, the mocking caricature, even different seasons
and religions, the fiendish and the friendly—all these are rounded into
one light and happy circle, and the circle is splendidly set into motion,
as if through a metrical power, namely through music, that land of
spirits, just like fancy-dress outfits are the land of bodies.—And there
only *one* being remains serious, unhidden, and unmasked, and governs
the cheerful play."—He thought of the jacketed Master of the Ball, with
his small unmasked face and head, whom he looked at attentively and
with some irritation.

Wina answered quietly and quickly: "Your visage is itself the art of
poetry. So the history of the human race might appear, to such a higher
being, as but a grander masked ball."—"We are a fireworks display,"
Walt countered quickly, "that a mighty spirit burns off in different
shapes", and continued with his awkward waltzing. The longer he flailed
before stopping, the more intensely he praised the springtime that
greeted him, aromatically, in the soaring dance. "O, if only today I might
sacrifice myself to the most beautiful spirit of them all, then I'd be the

happiest of men," he said. Hope (Spes) always stood at his side as he spoke. Wina the nun, like a gentle dove with an olive branch in its mouth, failed to notice how impetuously he spoke, and seemed, out of boldness, not to trouble over misinterpreting him, just as he, out of ignorance, didn't misinterpret himself.

Today she appeared completely perfect to him, although up to now he believed that he had already taken the full measure of her worth, just as the moon, before it hangs over us full and radiant, appears to rise as a perfectly formed disk.

After the end of the German dance he asked her—since her forbearance gradually grew into a triumphal arch of his art—for an English dance, merely so that he could often grasp her hand, and face her charming lips and eyes without having to leap up and down. Quietly she said: "Yes!"

Even more quietly he heard his name; Spes stood behind him and said: "Go at once through the great hall portal, and look around toward the left." It was Vult. Thus to his joy he found amidst all these strangers a dear friend whom he might lead onto his own Elysian island. He went out; Spes was in the fifth little dressing-room; she signalled for him to enter through a door. Walt wanted to embrace his brother, but Vult retreated to the door-jambs: "Consider the nature of our costumes!" and closed the door behind him. *He tore off his mask, and a peculiarly hot desert-drought (or dry fever-heat) broke through his facial expressions and words. "If you've ever harbored any love for your brother," he began with a parched voice, taking off his garland and untying his woman's garb, "if the fulfillment of one of your brother's most sincere wishes, the importance of which you'll learn in twenty-four hours, means something to you; and if you're not indifferent to his experience of the smallest or greatest joys, in short, if you want to grant one of his most fervent entreaties [7]:* then get out of your clothes (that's half the request); dress up as Hope, and I'll take the wagoner's costume (that's the whole of it)."

"Dear brother," Walt answered fearfully, and at the same time let out the breath he'd been holding in expectantly, "to your request, it goes without saying, I can only give one reply: with joy."

"Then hurry up," retorted Vult, without thanking him.[9] Walt added that his brother's solemn tone had nearly frightened him, and also that he little understood the purpose of their costume exchange. Vult said that by tomorrow all would turn out well, and that he himself was not at all irritated but rather full of high spirits. During their alternate pupation and de-pupation, Walt suddenly wondered whether he, costumed as a woman, would be able to dance the English dance he had promised to Wina: "Oh, I so much look forward to it," he said to his brother;

"just between us, it will be the very first *angloise* I've danced in my life, so I'll have to rely somewhat on my costume and my present happiness." A vivid expression then took hold of Vult's lean face. "Heaven, Hell," he said, "Rather than mimic (as you might think), I'll sneeze ever so lightly after the beat, or put my flute behind me and stretch out my arms. *For up to now—don't be offended—you've glided through the hall, horizontally as the wagoner and vertically as the miner, with good imitation-waltzes* [6], but my friend, an English dance! and which one? It was devilish, not even Irish. And do you consider your dancing partner—who indeed follows along, blushing and pale as a knight's melancholy lady—to be your mourning crossbearer as soon as you falter, bump, and dash like a comet?—But I can put this right splendidly. The crowd will soon see that the wagoner can unmask himself and make this dance into something serious, because I'll dance the *angloise* in your costume. Even in Poland I passed for a dancer, not to mention here, where the only pole-dance is Ursa Major's."

Walt remained quiet for a few minutes, then he said: "The lady I'm thinking of, and whom I've just now detained, is Wina Zablocki. But since she's promised me and my costume a dance, how will you excuse our exchange?"—"But this will be precisely our triumph," said Vult, "and you won't divine how I've brought it off any sooner than to-morrow."

Then he disclosed to his brother that today he had won so much at faro that he would have to consider a gold coin from him as thoroughly imperfect matter for chopping up into bits, even if it were only so that he might have something to do among the onlookers in the buffet room; thereupon he recommended that Walt, as Spes, should have nothing to do with any of the female maskers, because Hope's goodness easily turns into its opposite.

Walt's evening star gradually assumed its full brightness, and as he fitted the half-bust onto Vult, and looked into his very serious face and eyes, he said passionately: "May you be ever more happy! Joys are man's wings, his pinions. I'm too intoxicated by all that's happened today to express finely enough my wish that you should love even better than I."

"But to speak in your flute language," Vult retorted, "love is an eternal torment, either a sweet or a bitter one; it is an endless night in which no star rises without another disappearing behind my back— friendship is a day in which nothing sets except the sun; and then the devil appears out of the darkness.—

"But seriously, love is a bird of paradise and a joker—a phoenix of delicate ashes but without sunshine—to be sure, it belongs to the female race, yet like a goat it has horns and a beard, just as a husband can actually give milk.[3] It's practically immaterial what one says or plans about love, for everything is true in its own time.—Herewith I invest you with the floral wreath and the costume you'll wear as a disguise, that of Spes. Go into the ballroom through my door (as I'll go in through yours)—take care, be quiet, and drink up!"

Upon entering the hall, it seemed to Walt as if everyone was aware of the costume-exchange and espied his innermost being more easily through this, his second casing, than through his first. A few women observed that behind her flowers Hope now had blonde instead of black hair as before, but they attributed this difference to the wig. Also Walt's step, as befits Hope, was smaller and more feminine than Vult's.

But soon he forgot himself and the hall and everything else, for without ado Vult the wagoner set Wina, whom everyone knew, at the very head of the English dance, and now, to the astonishment of his partner, artfully traced out a dance-sketch with her, and like some artists, painted as it were with his feet, only with larger decorative strokes. Wina was amazed, since she thought she was dancing with Walt the wagoner, whose voice and inflection Vult (contrary to Walt's presupposition) convincingly mimicked from behind his mask, so that he wouldn't be deemed an impostor who was only trying to pass himself off as the notary.

Late in the dance, amidst hasty hand gestures, criss-crossings, and dashing turns to and fro, Vult let slip more and more Polish expressions— mere whiffs of the language: half-mad, sea-blown butterflies from a distant isle. His speech wafted down to Wina like that rare lark-song in late summer.[10] A bonfire blazed from behind her half-mask. How she yearned beyond the single-syllable English dance and toward the linguistically richer waltz, since she wanted to tell Vult of her astonishment and delight with more than just happy glances—all this his own glances took in, but not happily.

It happened. But the praise blowing toward him regarding his long-concealed talents turned over the leaves in the book of his life onto yet another talent: his modesty. Drawing on his best Polishisms, he said of himself that he had so little worldliness, but so much simplicity (an uncommon trait for a notary), and that he was rightly called Gottwalt, namely "may God prevail"! Yet his heart was warm, his soul pure, his life quietly poetic; and, as he had mentioned during the first waltz, he attended the masked ball in the Erdensaal with pleasure and happiness, from the country dances and the shepherds' ballet to the war-dance and the *danse macabre.*

Since the music for the second part of the dance sank into an ardent superabundance that, like deep waves, passionately elevates the innermost foundations of longing from out the sea more powerfully than any Adagio—and since the people and the candles darted about and whirled—and since the distant ringing and rushing masked the maskers another time over—so Vult said hastily, but in Polish: "Pleasure rushes around us with luxuriantly foliated garlands. Why, Sister, am I the only person here who dies unceasingly because he has neither heaven nor earth—for you are both to me? I want to tell you everything, I am animated by pain and pleasure—do you want to make a god-forsaken man out of a god-governed one, out of a Gottwalt? Oh, give me a sign, a word! I entrust the executioner's job to my tongue alone; may it be my sword, if only Sister, it moves you thereby!"

"Gottwalt," said Wina (dancing all the while) more affectedly and seriously than he, "how could you think of a human tongue in this way?—How can you so torture yourself and me?"—"Sister," he continued, "the sound of your voice is my sword"—"But it's even stronger still," she answered softly. "You torment me more severely with silence than others do with speech."

Now he had everything, namely her avowal of love for his pseudo-self or his sham-Walt, and he laughed at the real Walt, who was little more than Hope, both as player's-part and as reality; only his anxious spirit refused to submit to shadowy thoughts; resolute and silent he danced away, suddenly disappearing from the circle of merry-making guests.

For a long time Spes had remained nearby with the noisy blessings of a double joy, and had congratulated himself and Wina as the best dancers, and (since he was of the opinion that Wina had been told what he was representing) he referred her celestial glances completely to himself. Unfortunately he found himself right in the punch room, just as the boring English dance wound down, and after the end of which he planned to make his speech—Vult was poised for his dancing avowal of love, and Spes, waiting in vain, stood with the wreath on "her" head and with the inscribed slip fluttering from "her" chin, all the while observing the long drawn-out waltz. Shortly before the dance abruptly broke off, the Slave-girl of Virtue pulled Spes into an adjoining room. Spes hoped for a hundred of the most unusual incidents to come to pass. "So, don't you recognize me any more," asked the masker. "Then you know me?" asked Spes.

"If you would just please close your eyes for a moment, I'll untie your mask and mine as well," she said. He did as he was told. She kissed him quickly on the mouth and said: "I've seen you somewhere." It was Jakobine. Just then General Zablocki entered through a second door: "Ah Jakobine, so you're with Hope again?" he said and then withdrew. "What did he mean by that?" she asked. But Walt ran terrified and half undressed into the ballroom, and with some difficulty fastened the displaced mask onto his garlanded head.

Wina and Vult were nowhere to be seen; after searching and hoping for some time he had to return home as Hope without exchanging his costume. Hence the masked ball, so full of intentional disguises, drew to a close with unintentional ones of a graver sort.

[Schumann originally placed the following sentence, the last in Chapter 64 and in the novel, at the head of the manuscript for the *Papillons:* "Walt, enraptured, listened to the fleeing tones [of Vult's flute] as they resounded upward from the street, for he didn't notice that with them his brother too was fleeing."]

Notes

Introduction

1. Benjamin, "Goethes Wahlverwandtschaften," p. 157.
2. Barthes, "The Death of the Author," p. 142.
3. These issues are rehearsed in greater detail in Dahlhaus, "Wozu noch Biographien," p. 82 and *Idem, Ludwig van Beethoven: Approaches to his Music*, pp. 1–18.
4. See Dahlhaus, *Ludwig van Beethoven*, pp. 4–5, 12–15, 31–42.
5. Laux, *Robert Schumann*, p. 5.
6. Ostwald, *Schumann: The Inner Voices of a Musical Genius*, pp. 53–54.
7. Schumann, *Tagebücher* (hereafter cited as *TB*) 1, pp. 252 ("Voluptuous scandal"), 257 ("The inaccessible barmaid"), 261 ("The homosexual" and "Coffeehouse"), and 262 ("Real fear").
8. A Pavian professor.
9. Schumann writes in Italian: "si Signore!!—questo [sic] Signora è certamente dalla Campagna."
10. With the phrase "ruhig Sitzenbleiben" Schumann depicts himself as one who is left at a ball without a partner.
11. *TB* 1, p. 261. All translations are mine unless noted otherwise.
12. Cf. Ostwald, *Schumann*, p. 42, and *TB* 1, p. 177.
13. Cf. Ostwald, *Schumann*, p. 42, and *TB* 1, p. 178.
14. *TB* 1, p. 85.
15. *TB* 1, p. 344.
16. *TB* 1, p. 177.
17. Ostwald, *Schumann*, pp. 102–104.
18. *Jean Paul Werke*, 2, p. 48.
19. Hans Lenneberg makes a similar point in his review of Ostwald's book (p. 82), but he too suggests that Schumann had at least one homosexual encounter (with the Leipzig publisher Heinrich Probst) on the basis of selective quoting. Lenneberg takes as evidence the phrase "Probst von hinten u. von vorne," which, when placed within its original context (a description of convivial music-making at Friedrich Wieck's in late November 1828), probably means no more than that Probst gave Schumann a congratulatory embrace after a successful performance: "coffee at Wieck's—*Trio by Hünten*—Probst['s embrace] from the front and behind—*Trio by Schubert* and the critics—Wieck's delight and rapture—*G. W. Fink*—his wife, a pupil of Field—*Müller* the violinist and Grabau [the 'cellist] enraptured over the *Trio*" *TB* 1, p. 150–51. Cf. Lenneberg, Review, p. 82.
20. See *TB* 1, pp. 419–23.
21. Ostwald, *Schumann*, pp. 54, 102.
22. Letter of 31 May 1936 to Arnold Zweig; quoted in Ellman, "Freud and Literary Biography," p. 260.

23. See, among several other studies, Boetticher, "Weitere Forschungen an Dokumenten zum Leben und Schaffen Robert Schumanns," pp. 43–52.

24. See Rosener, "Studies in Schumann Manuscripts," pp. 326–27, 341–43, 365–74, 401–403; and Rosener, "Schumann's revisions in the First Movement of the Piano Sonata in G minor, Op. 22," pp. 102–9.

25. Finson, *Robert Schumann and the Study of Orchestral Composition*, p. 63.

26. Finson, "The Sketches for Robert Schumann's C Minor Symphony."

27. See Claudia Macdonald's (1992) review of Draheim's reconstruction, pp. 144–51.

28. Waldura, *Monomotivik, Sequenz und Sonatenform im Werk Robert Schumanns.*

29. See Kapp, *Studien zum Spätwerk Robert Schumanns;* and Struck, *Die umstrittenen späten Instrumentalwerke Schumanns.*

30. On the troublesome gaps in Schumann's correspondence, see Boetticher, "Über die Unbekannte 'Familienkassette' Robert und Clara Schumanns," pp. 47–48; "Das Erbe Robert Schumanns in jüngeren Schriften," p. 248; and "Weitere Forschungen an Dokumenten zum Leben und Schaffen Robert Schumanns" (according to which the author is in the process of preparing a *Gesamtausgabe* of the letters for Schott), p. 53. The materials of the *Familienkassette* have been published as *Briefe und Gedichte aus dem Album Robert und Clara Schumanns.*

31. See Boetticher, *Einführung*, pp. 668ff.; and "Das Erbe Robert Schumanns," pp. 248–49.

32. To date, only three volumes of choral music (including the *Romanzen* for women's chorus, opp. 69 and 91, the *Missa sacra*, op. 147, and the Requiem, op. 148), and the Third Symphony, op. 97 have appeared. Editions of the *Konzertstück* for four horns and orchestra, op. 86, and the Cello Concerto, op. 129, were slated for publication as early as 1992. Unless otherwise noted, the examples in this book are based on the collected edition of Schumann's works published by Breitkopf & Härtel (1881–93), and edited by Clara Schumann, Johannes Brahms, and others.

33. See Boetticher, "Zum Problem eines 'Urtextes' bei Robert Schumann und Anton Bruckner," pp. 405–6.

34. See Wendt, "Zu Robert Schumanns Skizzenbüchern," pp. 109–11, 114.

35. Boetticher, in "Weitere Forschungen," pp. 44–45, calls attention to Schumann's use of varying dynamics in each hand and his frequent limitation of accent marks to one note in a chord.

36. Danuser, "Kann Poetik die Biographik retten?" p. 287.

37. Eggebrecht and Holland, "Eine Schumann-Diskographie und ihre Kriterien," p. 366.

38. Benjamin, "Goethes Wahlverwandtschaften," p. 156.

39. Letter of 21 March 1855 to Clara Schumann, from Litzmann, ed., *Clara Schumann—Johannes Brahms: Briefe*, 1, p. 100.

40. See the minutes of Schumann's literary club (12 December 1825–16 February 1826) as reproduced in Schoppe, "Schumanns *Literarischer Verein*," pp. 23–31.

41. See *TB* 3, pp. 626–638, *passim.*

42. See Nauhaus, "Schumanns *Lektürebüchlein* [1845–1852]," pp. 78–79; and Appel, "Katalog," p. 160.

43. Rumenhöller, "Botschaft von Meister Raro," p. 227.

44. *The New York Review of Books* 40, nos. 1 & 2 (January 14, 1993), p. 3.

45. Diary entry of late 1827, *TB* 1, p. 82.

46. "Etuden für das Pianoforte," *Neue Zeitschrift für Musik* (hereafter cited as *NZfM*) 11 (1839), p. 121. Quoted in Gurlitt, "Robert Schumann und die Romantik in der Musik," p. 13.

47. Quoted in Gurlitt, "Robert Schumann und die Romantik in der Musik," p. 13.

48. Entry of 4 June 1832, *TB* 1, p. 404.

49. See the letter to Clara of 7 April 1839 in Clara Schumann, ed., *Jugendbriefe von Robert Schumann,* p. 301.

50. *TB* 2, p. 143.

51. Quoted from Boetticher, *Robert Schumann: Einführung,* p. 330.

52. From a letter to Ferdinand Hiller, in *Briefe, Neue Folge,* p. 326.

53. See, e.g., Ostwald, "Leiden und Trauern," p. 127.

54. Dahlhaus, *Ludwig van Beethoven,* p. 10.

55. Brendel, "Robert Schumann mit Rücksicht auf Mendelssohn-Bartholdy," p. 91.

56. Boetticher, *Einführung in die musikalische Romantik,* p. 106.

57. Richard Ellman, "Freud and Literary Biography," p. 263.

58. Rauchfleisch, *Robert Schumann: Leben und Werk—Eine Psychobiographie.*

59. Ostwald, *Schumann,* pp. 1–9 ("Crisis, 1854"). Similarly, Charles Rosen begins the Schumann chapter of his *The Romantic Generation* (pp. 646ff.) with a section entitled "The Irrational."

60. Heuberger, *Erinnerungen,* p. 94.

61. See Brendel, "Robert Schumann," p. 114; and his review of Schumann's second symphony in *NZfM* 25 (1846), p. 181.

62. See, for instance, Knepler, "Robert Schumann," pp. 779–94; Lippman, "Robert Schumann," cols. 313–19; Chissell, *Schumann,* pp. 95–97; Abraham, "Robert Schumann," pp. 850–54; Edler, *Robert Schumann und seine Zeit,* pp. 104–5, 305; and Boetticher, *Einführung in die musikalische Romantik,* pp. 107, 111–12, 140–41.

63. Entry of 1 June 1846; *TB* 2, 402.

64. Karl Laux, for instance, dispenses altogether with period divisions in his study of Schumann's life and works, opting instead for a focus on four "creative complexes"—piano music, songs, large instrumental and vocal forms, and instrumental and vocal chamber music—that occupied Schumann throughout his career, but with varying degrees of emphasis. See Laux's *Robert Schumann,* p. 261.

65. See Kapp, *Studien zum Spätwerk Robert Schumanns,* pp. 3–75, *passim.*

66. In her review of the De Beenhouwer-Draheim reconstruction of the D-minor *Konzertsatz* for piano and orchestra (1839), Claudia Macdonald emphasizes the similarity between the principal theme of the movement's second group and *Der Dichter spricht* from *Kinderscenen* (p. 146). Another of Schumann's unfinished works, the C-minor Symphony drafted in September 1841, discloses an even more tangible link with the keyboard works. The *Scherzo* of the symphony, with only slight alterations, reappears as no. 13 of *Bunte Blätter,* op. 99. See Finson, "The Sketches for Robert Schumann's C Minor Symphony," p. 405.

67. Matthias Wendt notes that many of the dated entries from the first of the so-called "Wiede" Sketchbooks (1831–32) are devoted to difficult passages copied from various keyboard works, thus making for a kind of *Übungtagebuch;* see "Zu Robert Schumanns Skizzenbüchern," p. 102.

68. *TB* 2, pp. 448–49.

69. Schoenberg, "New Music, Outmoded Music, Style and Idea" (1946), in *Style and Idea,* p. 113.

70. See the review of *Genoveva,* probably by Eduard Krüger, in *NZfM* 34 (1851), p. 129.

71. See his review in *NZfM* 37 (1852), pp. 117–20. Uhlig's negative judgment extended even to one of the best-received of the late works, the Third ("Rhenish") Symphony (see pp. 117–18).

72. Brendel, "Die Schumannfeier in Zwickau," *NZfM* 52 (1860), p. 223.

73. For a complete account of the curious reception history of the Violin Concerto, see Struck, *Robert Schumann: Violinkonzert D-moll,* pp. 15–23.

74. For a discussion of the suppression of Schumann's late works by his intimates, see Melkus, "Zur Revision unseres Schumann-Bild," pp. 186–88; and the dissenting voice raised by Eismann in "Zu Robert Schumanns letzten Kompositionen," pp. 151–57.

75. On this point, see especially Struck, "*Die umstrittenen späten Instrumentalwerke Schumanns*, pp. 711–12.

76. See Truscott's comments on the *Faust* Overture, the *Konzert-Allegro* for Piano and Orchestra (op. 134), and the violin concerto, in "The Evolution of Schumann's Last Period," pp. 105–111.

77. See Nagler's analysis of the *Faust* Overture in, "Gedanken zur Rehabilitierung," pp. 336–43; Kapp's analysis of the orchestral exposition of the violin concerto in *Studien zum Spätwerk*, pp. 79–101; and Struck, *Die umstrittenen späten Instrumentalwerke Schumanns*, p. 710.

78. Melkus, "Zur Revision," pp. 189–90; Hopf, "Fehlinterpretation eines Spätstils am Beispiel Robert Schumanns," pp. 245–47; and Nagler, "Gedanken zur Rehabilitierung," p. 337.

79. See Nietzsche, *Beyond Good and Evil*, p. 181; and Liszt, "Robert Schumann," pp. 156–57, 178–82.

80. Rumenhöller, "Botschaft von Meister Raro," pp. 228–29.

81. Wolff, "Robert Schumann: Der Klassizist," pp. 47–51.

82. Dahlhaus, *Nineteenth-Century Music*, p. 145.

83. Kapp, *Studien zum Spätwerk*, pp. 3–75, *passim*.

Chapter 1

1. From August Schumann's *Staats-, Post- und Zeitungslexikon von Sachsen* (1814–), quoted in Eismann, *Quellenwerk* 1, p. 9.

2. See Schumann's *Lebensskizze* of 1840, drafted in connection with his application for a doctorate from the University of Jena, and quoted in Eismann, *Quellenwerk* 1, p. 15. Schumann's school friend Emil Flechsig presented a similar account of the elder Schumann in his *Lebenserinnerungen*, also quoted in Eismann, *Quellenwerk* 1, p. 15.

3. Quoted from one of four autobiographical sketches of similar content, all drafted ca. 1840, in Eismann, *Quellenwerk* 1, p. 18.

4. Quoted from his *Erinnerungsblätter für gebildete Leser aus allen Ständen* (1813), in Eismann, *Quellenwerk* 1, p. 23.

5. Appel, "Katalog," in *Robert Schumann und die Dichter*, ed. Appel and Hermstrüwer, p. 164. "Skülander" may have been read by some biographers as a fanciful form of "Alexander," which is sometimes given as Schumann's middle name (see, e.g., Gerald Abraham's article in *The New Grove*, 16, p. 831). In none of the pertinent documents (baptismal, marriage, and death certificates or letters), however, does Schumann appear as "Robert Alexander."

6. Quoted from an autobiographical account of 1825 or 1826 in Eismann, *Quellenwerk* 1, p. 10.

7. See Ostwald, "Leiden und Trauern," p. 122.

8. Eismann, *Quellenwerk* 1, p. 11.

9. *Ibid.*

10. Schumann, *Selbstbiographische Notizen*, ed. Schoppe; see also Eismann, *Quellenwerk* 1, p. 12. Kuntsch was the dedicatee of Schumann's canonic *Studien für den Pedal-Flügel*, op. 56 (1845).

11. Schumann, *Selbstbiographische Notizen*, ed. Schoppe; and Eismann, *Quellenwerk* 1,

p. 17. These dances, now lost, are the first works listed in Schumann's *Projektenbuch,* begun in 1840 and maintained until the end of his career, a record of completed and planned creative works.

12. Eismann, *Quellenwerk* 1, p. 13.

13. *Ibid.,* p. 14.

14. *Ibid.*

15. Eismann, *Quellenwerk* 1, p. 20–21, note 1.

16. *Ibid.,* pp. 31–32.

17. *Ibid.,* p. 18.

18. *TB* 2, p. 402. See also Schumann, *Selbstbiographische Notizen,* ed. Schoppe; and the entry in the *Projektenbuch* for 1822 or 1823, in Eismann, *Quellenwerk* 1, p. 17.

19. Entry of ca. 1847, *TB* 2, p. 402.

20. See Eismann, *Quellenwerk* 1, p. 17; and Pelker, *Konzertouvertüre,* vol. 2, p. 715. The manuscript, consisting of a full score with underlaid piano reduction (perhaps for rehearsal purposes), still survives and is currently in private hands.

21. Eismann, *Quellenwerk* 1, p. 17.

22. *TB* 2, p. 402.

23. Schoppe, "Schumanns Litterarischer Verein," p. 21.

24. *Ibid.,* pp. 23–31.

25. The other Schiller plays studied by the members of the *Verein* were *Fiesko, Die Jungfrau von Orleans, Maria Stuart, Wilhelm Tell, Die Räuber, Kabale und Liebe,* and *Don Carlos.* See Schoppe, "Schumanns Litterarischer Verein," pp. 24–30.

26. The relevant passage begins "Theaterpassion (1823–27)." See Eismann, *Quellenwerk* 1, p. 18.

27. Schoppe, "Schumanns Litterarischer Verein," p. 31.

28. See Boetticher, ed., *Briefe und Gedichte,* p. 198. The essay appears in Appel and Hermstrüwer, eds., *Robert Schumann und die Dichter,* pp. 33–39.

29. Schoppe, "Schumanns Litterarischer Verein," p. 22.

30. Schumann, *Selbstbiographische Notizen,* ed. Schoppe.

31. See Schoppe, "Schumanns frühe Texte," p. 13; and *TB* 1, p. 22.

32. See Eismann, *Quellenwerk* 1, p. 18; Appel, "Katalog," in Appel and Hermstrüwer, eds., *Robert Schumann und die Dichter,* p. 165; and Schoppe, "Schumanns frühe Texte," p. 10.

33. For a more detailed discussion of the contents of the manuscript, preserved in the Robert-Schumann-Haus in Zwickau as A RSH Z I 4, see Schoppe, "Schumanns frühe Texte," p. 10.

34. *Ibid.,* p. 11.

35. The essay appears in Boetticher, *Robert Schumann in seinen Schriften,* pp. 4–6.

36. See Schumann, "Warum erbittert uns," in Appel and Hermstrüwer, eds., *Robert Schumann und die Dichter,* pp. 35–36.

37. *TB* 1, p. 30. Schumann renders "Know thyself," the inscription over the portal of Apollo's Temple at Delphi, in Greek.

38. *TB* 1, pp. 22, 24, 25, 30.

39. Schumann may have touched on these subjects—lovesickness for Liddy and grief over his sister's demise—in a conversation of late January 1827 with his friend Otto Walther. His response to Walther's soothing words strikes a grim chord in the light of Schumann's own end: "An inability to compose myself—no, that I couldn't overcome; a suicide!!—ugh, how I shudder when these two thoughts come to mind." *TB* 1, p. 25.

40. *TB* 1, p. 22.

41. *Ibid.*

42. *TB* 1, p. 21.

43. *Ibid.*, pp. 26–27.

44. The fancy-dress ball not only serves as the poetic starting point for such works from the 1830s as *Papillons* and *Carnaval;* in 1849 Schumann would set a lyric by Rückert, very similar in spirit to his own early attempt at a *Tanzlied,* as the first of the *Vier Duette,* op. 78.

45. *TB* 1, p. 21.

46. *Ibid.*, p. 30.

47. Eismann, *Quellenwerk* 1, p. 20.

48. Schumann, *Selbstbiographische Notizen,* ed. Schoppe.

49. Eismann, *Quellenwerk* 1, p. 17.

50. See Schumann, *Selbstbiographische Notizen,* ed. Schoppe; and Flechsig's *Lebenserinnerungen,* in Eismann, *Quellenwerk* 1, p. 16.

51. Schumann, *Selbstbiographische Notizen,* ed. Schoppe.

52. Eismann, *Quellenwerk* 1, p. 17.

53. See Eismann, *Quellenwerk* 1, p. 18; and *TB* 1, p. 105.

54. On this point, see Schoppe, "Schumanns frühe Texte," p. 11.

55. *TB* 1, p. 112. By 20 August, Agnes Carus had "learned to understand the songs better"; see *TB* 1, p. 119.

56. *Klage,* mentioned along with *Hirtenknabe* and *Erinnerung* in a diary entry of 16 August 1828 (*TB* 1, p. 114), has been lost; the same may also be true of one to three of the "10–12 lieder" mentioned in the *Projektenbuch* for 1828; see Eismann, *Quellenwerk* 1, p. 81. Most of the extant songs have been published: *Sehnsucht, Die Weinende, Erinnerung, Kurzes Erwachen, Gesanges Erwachen,* and *An Anna* in Robert Schumann, *Sechs frühe Lieder,* ed. Karl Geiringer (Vienna: Universal, 1933), and *An Anna II, Im Herbste,* and *Hirtenknabe* in Series 14 of the Breitkopf Collected Edition.

57. *Briefe, Neue Folge,* pp. 6–7. Since Schumann's letter is dated 15 July 1828, he almost certainly enclosed the following lieder for Wiedebein's inspection: *Kurzes Erwachen* (completed 29 June 1828), *An Anna I* (2 July 1828), *Gesanges Erwachen* (10 July 1828). *Im Herbste,* another Kerner setting, though undated, was probably included as well. Likewise, he may have sent along *An Anna II* (dated 31 July 1828) in an earlier draft. According to Flechsig, Wiedebein received six lieder from Schumann; see Eismann, *Quellenwerk* 1, p. 44.

58. Eismann, *Quellenwerk* 1, pp. 39–40.

59. *Ibid.*, p. 28.

60. See Flechsig's *Lebenserinnerungen,* in Eismann, *Quellenwerk* 1, p. 16.

61. Schumann, *Selbstbiographische Notizen,* ed. Schoppe.

62. *Jugendbriefe,* pp. 22–23.

63. Letter of 13 June 1828; *Jugendbriefe,* p. 24.

64. Eismann, *Quellenwerk* 1, p. 44. Perhaps Flechsig stretched the truth as well. A certificate dated 17 January 1831, intended for inclusion with Schumann's application materials for a doctorate from the University of Jena, speaks to his attendance of a Professor Krug's lectures on basic philosophy, logic, and metaphysics during the summer semester of 1828; Eismann, *Quellenwerk* 1, p. 46. Still, Schumann's approach to his legal studies was probably comparable to that of Eugène Rastignac, the impoverished law student and aspiring socialite from Balzac's *Père Goriot:* "The student studied no longer. He went to his lectures to answer to his name and, having attested to his presence, made off. He had persuaded himself, as most students do, that he should postpone his studies until it was time to sit for his examinations; he would let his second and third years' work pile up, and then apply himself to learning law seriously in one last spurt at the last moment." Quoted from Marion Ayton Crawford's translation (Penguin: London and New York, 1951), p. 110.

65. See Flechsig's *Lebenserinnerungen,* in Eismann, *Quellenwerk* 1, p. 44; and Schumann's letter of 22 August 1828 to his mother, in *Jugendbriefe,* pp. 32–33.

66. Eismann, *Quellenwerk* 1, p. 44.

67. *Ibid.*

68. Eismann, *Quellenwerk,* p. 45.

69. See Schumann, *Selbstbiographische Notizen,* ed. Schoppe; and Boetticher, *Robert Schumann: Einführung,* p. 245.

70. Between May and October of that year, he read *Hesperus, Titan* (twice!), *Flegeljahre, Siebenkäs,* and *Der Komet* in this fashion. See *TB* 3, pp. 626–38.

71. *TB* 1, p. 76.

72. *Ibid.,* pp. 82, 170.

73. *Jugendbriefe,* p. 17.

74. *TB* 1, pp. 40, 55; see also Schumann's letter of 25 April 1828 to his brother, in *Jugendbriefe,* p. 19.

75. *Briefe, Neue Folge,* p. 5.

76. Quoted in Jacobs, "Schumann and Jean Paul," p. 252.

77. Casey, ed., *Jean Paul: A Reader,* p. 169.

78. See the commentary on this passage in Berger, *Jean Paul,* pp. 90–91.

79. See *Athenäum* Fragment 421, in Schlegel, *Kritische Ausgabe,* vol. 2, pp. 246–47.

80. *TB* 1, p. 168.

81. Casey, ed., *Jean Paul: A Reader,* p. 230.

82. *TB* 1, p. 82.

83. *Ibid.*

84. Entry for 29 May 1828, in *TB* 1, p. 83.

85. *TB* 1, p. 82. See also the entry for 16 November 1828, in *TB* 1, p. 142: "No life is purely poetic, just as none is purely tragic: all too often prose and humor peer through; Jean Paul understood this very well, and therefore after every poetic passage he douses [the reader] with a bucketful of ice-cold wit."

86. Entry for 4 August 1828, in *TB* 1, pp. 103–4.

87. Entry for 13 August 1828, in *TB* 1, p. 105. Comments such as this indicate that, contrary to the opinion of some biographers, Schumann maintained just as healthy an interest in Jean Paul's aesthetic writings as in his imaginative prose. See also his reference to Jean Paul's theory of comic drama in *TB* 1, p. 124 (entry of 5 September 1828).

88. Entry for 29 July 1828 in *TB* 1, p. 98.

89. See *TB* 1, pp. 99–100, 105, and 115. For a transcription of the six extant chapters of the work, see, Otto, *Robert Schumann als Jean Paul-Leser,* pp. 25–43.

90. For examples, see Chapter 9, "Schwefelblumen" ("Sulphur-flowers") of *Flegeljahre.* Some of Jean Paul's *Streckverse* are no longer than a few phrases, e.g., "The Children," which reads: "Stay close to God, ye little ones, for the smallest bit of earth is indeed nearest the sun." See also Schumann's diary entry for 25 April 1828 (*TB* 1, p. 55): "Jean Paul's grave— deep pain . . . his room and chair . . . pleasant memories . . . Polymeter."

91. Schumann designated the work as an *Erzählung* or "tale," but to judge from the surviving drafts, its intended scope was more along the lines of a novella.

92. See *TB* 1, p. 140. Drafts for the following chapters of the novel made their way into *Hottentottiana: Mitternachtsstück* (9 November 1828), *Harmonika-Altarblatt* (9 November 1828), *Vorabende* (14 November 1828), *Nachtpläne* (19 November 1828), and *Vorfrühling* (20 November 1828); see *TB* 1, pp. 134–40, 145–46. By 29 November, Schumann had decided on a plan for the entire work, though it was never completed; see *TB* 1, p. 150.

93. Jean Paul himself appears frequently in his own novels; according to the original

plan for *Selene,* Schumann likewise intended to introduce Jean Paul as a character; see *TB* 1, p. 150.

94. *TB* 1, pp. 146, 150.

95. *Ibid.,* p. 139.

96. *Ibid.,* p. 135. It should be recalled in this context that "Selene" was the moon-goddess of Greek mythology and an emblem of enchantment.

97. The passage appears in translation in Casey, ed., *Jean Paul: A Reader,* pp. 179–83. Like Schumann's scene, Jean Paul's plays in a nocturnal realm dominated by the image of a dark and desolate church, its tall stained-glass windows illuminated by moonlight.

98. *TB* 1, p. 137.

99. *Ibid.,* p. 138.

100. *Ibid.,* p. 96.

101. *Ibid.,* p. 96.

102. Entry of 4 July 1832, in *TB* 1, p. 411.

103. *TB* 1, pp. 96, 111.

104. Entry of 4 August 1828, in *TB* 1, p. 104.

105. Entry of 13 August 1828, in *TB* 1, p. 113.

106. In response to a request for a definition of "tone," Lühe wrote back to Schumann on 27 July 1828. The essay in its entirety, "with improvements and comparisons by Willibald v. d. Lühe," is reproduced in Otto, *Schumann als Jean Paul-Leser,* pp. 66–75.

107. Otto, *Schumann als Jean Paul-Leser,* p. 72.

108. *Ibid.,* pp. 74–75. Schumann describes just the kind of Biedermeier scene with which some of his later keyboard music, notably the *Album für die Jugend,* would be associated.

109. *Ibid.,* p. 74.

110. Cf. *TB* 1, p. 99; and Otto, *Schumann als Jean Paul-Leser,* p. 67.

111. Otto, *Schumann als Jean Paul-Leser,* p. 68.

112. In Section 13 of the *Clavis Fichtiana* from the "Comic Appendix" to *Titan,* Jean Paul refers similarly to "Reali- und Aseitäten oder Gottheiten" ("reali- and aseities or deities").

113. Otto, *Schumann als Jean Paul-Leser,* p. 110.

114. *Ibid.,* p. 111. The references in Schumann's diary to champagne consumption, inebriation, and hangovers might too easily contribute to an image of a dissipated youth. The exhortation "à la Jean Paul" at the head of the essay on geniality—"Youths! Drink as much champagne as you like; but above all, be ingenious and *remain so!*"—feeds into the same myth. We might temper this view, however, with Flechsig's assertion that Schumann, during his first stint in Leipzig, "was not only the most ambitious, but also the most industrious, tireless man that I knew. Apart from the little time he spent in the evening at a tavern, he sat for the whole day, from morning on, engrossed in whatever project was at hand . . ." Eismann, *Quellenwerk* 1, p. 16.

115. Otto, *Schumann als Jean Paul-Leser,* pp. 112–13.

116. *Ibid.,* p. 111. Here too, Schumann was coming to grips with his own aspirations to genius, a quality for which he would *have to work.* His student friend Eduard Röller put it a little uncharitably in a letter of 11 October 1856 to Flechsig: "Just between us, I always thought his ambition exceeded his innate genius." Eismann, *Quellenwerk* 1, p. 69.

117. See Schoppe, "Schumanns frühe Texte," p. 14. The title of the collection recalls a Jean-Paulian designation such as *Blumen-, Frucht-, und Dornenstücke (Flower-, Fruit-, and Thornpieces),* from the full title of *Siebenkäs.*

118. Eismann, *Quellenwerk* 1, p. 44.

119. *Jugendbriefe,* pp. 32–33.

120. *TB* 1, pp. 177–178, 181–83, 185, 192.

121. Eismann, *Quellenwerk* 1, p. 44.

122. *TB* 1, p. 119.

123. See the diary entries for 17 and 19 August 1828 (*TB* 1, p. 116), 3 January 1829 (*TB* 1, p. 165), 9 January 1829 (*TB* 1, p. 166), and 11 January 1829 (*TB* 1, p. 166).

124. *TB* 1, p. 111.

125. Letter of 6 November 1829, in *Jugendbriefe*, p. 83.

126. *Jugendbriefe*, p. 83.

127. *TB* 1, pp. 82, 119.

128. Entry of 24 September 1828, in *TB* 1, p. 124.

129. See Draheim, "Schumanns Jugendwerk," p. 186.

130. Entry of 5 September 1828, in *TB* 1, p. 124.

131. Entry for 9 October 1828, in *TB* 1, p. 125. Nonetheless, Schumann would later turn to his "dull and tedious" Polonaises as a source of material for *Papillons*: portions of the A section of Polonaise IV resurface in *Papillons*, No. 11; the Trio theme of Polonaise VII in turn serves as the main theme of *Papillons*, No. 5.

132. *TB* 1, p. 180.

133. *Ibid.*, p. 151. Cf. also Flechsig's comment on Schumann's reaction to Schubert's death, quoted above, in Eismann, *Quellenwerk* 1, p. 44. Whether or not the quartet represented a sublimation of Schumann's grief over Schubert's death however, as Peter Ostwald has suggested ("Leiden und Trauer," pp. 124–25), is difficult to say.

134. *TB* 1, p. 172.

135. *Ibid.*, p. 174.

136. Entry for 21 March 1829, in *TB* 1, p. 182.

137. *TB* 1, pp. 183–84.

138. Entry for 7 January 1830, in *TB* 1, p. 214.

139. *TB* 1, p. 152. The trio was rendered by Adolph Wendler (piano), Christian Müller (violin), and Johann Grabau ('cello; the dedicatee of Schumann's *Fünf Stücke im Volkston*, op. 102).

140. Entry for 21 March 1829, in *TB* 1, p. 182.

141. *TB* 2, p. 402.

Chapter 2

1. *Jugendbriefe*, pp. 30–31.

2. Letter of 25 May 1829, in *Jugendbriefe*, p. 49.

3. *Jugendbriefe*, pp. 62–63.

4. See Eismann, *Quellenwerk* 1, pp. 69–71.

5. See his letters of 3 August 1829 to his mother (*Jugendbriefe*, pp. 67–68); 3 June 1830 to his brother (*Jugendbriefe*, p. 112); 1 July 1830 to his mother (*Jugendbriefe*, pp. 114–15); and Röller's letter of 11 October 1856 to Flechsig; in Eismann, *Quellenwerk* 1, p. 69.

6. Letter of 3 June 1830, in *Jugendbriefe*, p. 112.

7. *Jugendbriefe*, pp. 67–68.

8. Schumann, *Selbstbiographische Notizen*, ed. Schoppe.

9. Letter of 6 November 1829, in *Jugendbriefe*, p. 81.

10. Schumann abandoned his *Jünglingswallfahrten* after drafting an account of the hero's first journey. See Schoppe, "Schumanns frühe Texte," p. 13.

11. See Töpken's letter to Wasielewski, in Eismann, *Quellenwerk* 1, pp. 54–55.

12. Eismann, *Quellenwerk* 1, p. 55.

13. See the diary entry for 26 January, in *TB* 1, p. 222.

14. *TB* 1, pp. 211–12.

15. See *Jugendbriefe*, p. 104; and Töpken's comments on Schumann's performance, in Eismann, *Quellenwerk* 1, p. 55. For a discussion of Schumann's preparation for the 24 January concert, see Macdonald, "Schumann's earliest compositions," pp. 264–65.

16. *Jugendbriefe*, p. 105.

17. *TB* 1, p. 230.

18. Entry for 18 January, in *TB* 1, p. 218.

19. *TB* 1, p. 304.

20. Thibaut, *Ueber Reinheit der Tonkunst*, p. 1.

21. Entry for 11 April 1830, in *TB* 1, pp. 282–83.

22. Eismann, *Quellenwerk* 1, p. 69.

23. Letter of 20 August 1831, in *Briefe, Neue Folge*, p. 32.

24. *TB* 1, p. 242.

25. *Jugendbriefe*, pp. 114–15.

26. *Ibid.*, pp. 116–119.

27. Eismann, *Quellenwerk* 1, p. 62.

28. *Ibid.*, pp. 64–65.

29. *Ibid.*, p. 65. Writing to his guardian, Rudel, on 21 August, Schumann promised to resume his legal studies if, after six months' time, Wieck was dissatisfied with his progress; see *Briefe, Neue Folge*, pp. 26–27.

30. Eismann, *Quellenwerk* 1, pp. 67–68. Schumann returned the favor in 1832 by dedicating a now lost *Exercise fantastique* for piano to Kuntsch.

31. Letter of 21 August, in *Briefe, Neue Folge*, p. 25.

32. Eismann, *Quellenwerk* 1, p. 81.

33. Nos. 1, 6, and 7 of *Papillons* draw on *Walzer* 6, 4, and 5, respectively.

34. *Jugendbriefe*, pp. 84–85. In a note, Schumann further claims to have initiated something of a rage for Schubert, whose "name is hardly known here," among the musical elite of Heidelberg.

35. Schumann, *Selbstbiographische Notizen*, ed. Schoppe.

36. See Boetticher, *Schumanns Klavierwerke* 1, pp. 103, 124–25; and *Schumanns Klavierwerke* 2, p. 56.

37. *TB* 1, p. 362. As Claudia Macdonald has convincingly argued, Schumann finished a first draft of the solo exposition (modelled to a large extent on the Hummel A-minor Concerto, op. 85, that he had studied and performed in 1828–29) by the time he left Heidelberg for Leipzig in the early fall of 1830. Then in the winter, spring, and summer of 1830–31 in Leipzig, he added a solo development and recapitulation (the "second" and "last" solos from the diary quotation) that betray the influence of Henri Herz's A-major Concerto, op. 34. The tuttis never proceeded past the sketch stage. See Macdonald, "Models," pp. 159–89.

Over the course of the decade, Schumann began to look askance at the then typical practice of writing solos and tuttis separately. Reviewing Kalkbrenner's Fourth Piano Concerto in 1836, he took the composer and many of his contemporaries to task for completing the solos before the tuttis, and only then "inserting" the latter into the musical fabric. See Schumann, *Gesammelte Schriften* (hereafter cited as *GS*) 1, p. 155.

38. *TB* 1, p. 330.

39. *Ibid.*, pp. 376, 413. For a summary account of Schumann's work on the F-major concerto, see Macdonald, "Schumann's earliest compositions," pp. 267–71.

40. Cf. note 37. At one point, Schumann even contemplated dedicating the concerto to Hummel. See Macdonald, "Models," p. 189.

41. *TB* 1, p. 361. Cf. his comments, in the *Kurztagebuch*, on the "romantic" spirit in the Trio theme of his C-minor Piano Quartet (1828–29); *TB* 2, p. 402.

42. Letter of 20 August 1831, in *Briefe, Neue Folge*, p. 32.

43. Schumann's *Kompositions-Verzeichnis* gives May 1830 and July 1832 as the dates for the first version and its elaboration, respectively; see *Briefe, Neue Folge*, p. 536. In the *Projektenbuch*, the second version is dated 1833/Leipzig; see Eismann, *Quellenwerk* 1, pp. 81–82.

44. For a more detailed comparison of the first version, now in the Pierpont Morgan Library, and the second, see Boetticher, "Weitere Forschungen," pp. 46–47.

45. See Eismann, *Quellenwerk* 1, p. 83.

46. According to the *Projektenbuch*, only half of the originally drafted variations were published; see Eismann, *Quellenwerk* 1, p. 81.

47. *TB* 1, pp. 373, 376.

48. *Ibid.*, pp. 377–78.

49. *Ibid.*, pp. 424–25.

50. For a transcription of the forty-measure sketch for an orchestral introduction, see Boetticher, *Schumanns Klavierwerke* 1, pp. 37–39. Scholars disagree on the dating of the sketch: while Boetticher places it in the fall of 1829, Macdonald ("Schumann's earliest compositions," p. 282, note 101) argues for a summer 1831 dating on the basis of its proximity to the final revisions for the exposition of the F-major Piano Concerto. Macdonald may indeed be correct, for by the later date Schumann had already become familiar with a similarly conceived work that soon became a favorite: Chopin's Variations on *Là ci darem la mano*, op. 2, for piano and orchestra.

51. Schumann employs a similar effect to create a sense of suspended time in the closing moments of *Papillons*, No. 12.

52. See Töpken's letter to Wasielewski of 30 September 1856, in Eismann, *Quellenwerk* 1, p. 70. The name might also have been suggested by the Abegg brothers, August and Otto, who like Schumann, were students in Heidelberg. See *TB* 1, pp. 225, 227, 233, and 295 for references to either or both of the brothers; perhaps not coincidentally, the first three of these entries date from February and March 1830, the period when Schumann had begun to draft the *"Abegg"* Variations.

53. *TB* 1, pp. 424–25.

54. Letter from Schumann to his mother, 15 December 1830, in *Jugendbriefe*, pp. 136ff.

55. Schumann, *Selbstbiographische Notizen*, ed. Schoppe.

56. See the entries for 11, 12, and 25 May 1831, in *TB* 1, pp. 329–30, 333.

57. Schumann's five early sketchbooks (Universitätsbibliothek Bonn, Schumann 13–17), of which only the first was maintained as a continuously paginated, self-contained volume by the composer himself, passed first into the hands of Dr. Alfred Wiede, superintendent of mines in Zwickau-Weissenborn. For a discussion of the relationship between the *Übungtagebuch* and the other contents of Schumann 13, see Wendt, "Zu Robert Schumanns Skizzenbüchern," p. 102.

58. See Wendt, "Zu Robert Schumanns Skizzenbüchern," p. 102.

59. *Jugendbriefe*, p. 134.

60. Letter to his mother of 15 May 1831, in *Jugendbriefe*, p. 144.

61. Letter of 15 December 1830, in *Jugendbriefe*, p. 138.

62. Letter to Hummel of 20 August 1831, in *Briefe, Neue Folge*, p. 32.

63. Entry of 23 August 1832, in *TB* 1, p. 413.

64. Entry of 13 July 1831, in *TB* 1, p. 349.

65. See Schumann, *Selbstbiographische Notizen,* ed. Schoppe; and the entries for 30 July and 13 October 1831, in *TB* 1, pp. 358, 371.

66. *TB* 1, p. 371.

67. Cf. Chapter 1, pp. 31–33.

68. Letter to Wasielewski of 7 September 1856, in Eismann, *Quellenwerk* 1, p. 74.

69. See Schumann's letters to Dorn of 25 April 1832 (*Briefe, Neue Folge,* p. 35) and Kuntsch of 27 July 1832 (*Jugendbriefe,* p. 187); and the entry of 15 May 1832, in *TB* 1, p. 390.

70. *TB* 1, p. 405.

71. *Jugendbriefe,* p. 187.

72. *TB* 1, pp. 336–37.

73. *Ibid.*

74. *TB* 1, pp. 334, 336.

75. Christel, whom Schumann continued to see for five or six years, first enters his diary on 12 May 1831 (*TB* 1, p. 330), but since he had only then resumed regular entries after a more than year-long hiatus, it is possible that their relationship extended back to his relocation in Leipzig during the fall of 1830. The fact that Schumann never mentions her surname, but only refers to her by the diminutive "Christel," lends credence to Ostwald's conjecture that she was perhaps a servant in Wieck's household (see *Schumann: Inner Voices,* p. 75). The "consequences in January 1837" attributed to his having "sought her out" the year before were almost certainly a sexually transmitted disease (see *TB* 1, p. 422).

76. *TB* 1, p. 339.

77. Entry of 15 June 1831, in *TB* 1, pp. 342–43.

78. *TB* 1, pp. 379, 382.

79. See Schoppe, "Schumanns frühe Texte," p. 13.

80. *TB* 1, p. 344.

81. See Ostwald, *Schumann: Inner Voices,* pp. 78–79; and *TB* 1, p. 339. Schumann drafted only the first scene of his planned Abelard drama (see *TB* 1, pp. 463–64, note 329).

82. *GS* 1, pp. 119. In the years to come, Schumann often marked off the three adjacent name-days in the *Haushaltbücher.* See the entries for 12–14 August 1838, 1839, and 1846 in *TB* 3, pp. 46, 73, and 287–88. In 1853, only Clara's and Aurora's days were so indicated (*TB* 3, pp. 632–33). Did Schumann thereby disavow the youngest of the child prodigies?

83. Diary entry of 27 May 1831, in *TB* 1, p. 334.

84. For a record of Schumann's attempt to master Chopin's Opus 2, see *TB* 1, pp. 344, 346, 348–50, 354, and 358.

85. *TB* 1, pp. 354, 358.

86. *Ibid.,* p. 351.

87. "Von K. [*sic*] Schumann. Ein Opus II," in *Allgemeiner musikalischer Zeitung* (hereafter cited as *AmZ*) 33, cols. 805–8. As Leon Plantinga has pointed out (*Schumann as Critic,* p. 35), Schumann's letter of 28 April 1832 to Ignaz Castelli, editor of the *Allgemeiner musikalischer Anzeiger,* indicates that Fink, editor of the *AmZ,* had only published half of the original review. The other half has never surfaced. See *Briefe, Neue Folge,* p. 36.

88. *AmZ* 33 (1831), cols. 808–11.

89. See the diary entry of 30 July 1831, in *TB* 1, p. 358.

90. *TB* 1, p. 222. According to a report of Schumann's physical condition written by Dr. Moritz Emil Reuter early in 1841, the composer had already noticed as a youth that the index *and* middle fingers of his right hand lacked "strength and flexibility." See Rothe, "Neue Dokumente," p. 319.

91. See Schumann, *Selbstbiographische Notizen*, ed. Schoppe; and Eismann, *Quellenwerk* 1, p. 78.

92. While some writers (see, e.g., Sams, "Schumann's Hand Injury," p. 1156) have viewed the diary references from the early 1830s to a "wound" and to "biting, gnawing pain" (see, e.g., the entry for 12 May 1831, in *TB* 1, p. 330) as evidence that Schumann may have contracted syphilis, Ostwald points out that even if the composer did acquire the disease at this time, the symptoms of tertiary syphilis would not have manifested themselves so early (see Ostwald, "Florestan," pp. 18–19). Ostwald's masturbation hypothesis, however, probably reads too much into Schumann's plea for the forgiveness of unnamed sins in a diary entry of 21–30 June 1831: "Evil days. May God and my conscience grant me pardon!" (see "Florestan," p. 21; and *TB* 1, p. 344).

93. Ostwald, "Florestan," p. 22.

94. See the diary entries for 7 May and 12/13 June 1832, in *TB* 1, pp. 386 and 409.

95. Entry in the *Projektenbuch* for October 1831, in Eismann, *Quellenwerk* 1, p. 78.

96. See *TB* 1, pp. 386 (entries of 7 and 9 May 1832), 394, and 410.

97. See *Jugendbriefe*, p. 188. Although Ostwald argues that the treatment forced the young man "to participate in a ritualized public act of necrophilia," and therefore may have had devastating psychological consequences (see "Florestan," p. 23), the report in the letter to his mother seems to indicate that Schumann took it all in stride.

98. *Jugendbriefe*, p. 194.

99. *Ibid.*, p. 234.

100. Letter to his mother of 28 June 1833, in *Jugendbriefe*, p. 210.

101. *Jugendbriefe*, p. 295.

102. Lippman, "Theory and Practice," p. 320.

103. According to the *Projektenbuch*, the work was completed in 1831 in Leipzig, but included several "shorter pieces" dating from 1829 in Heidelberg (see Eismann, *Quellenwerk* 1, pp. 81–82). Schumann's *Kompositions-Verzeichnis* places Nos. 1, 5, 6, and 7 (of the finished set) in April 1830 (Heidelberg), and the others in January 1832, though the year should certainly read 1831 (see Boetticher, *Schumanns Klavierwerke* 1, p. 49). Boetticher offers an account of the relationship between the *6 Walzer* and *Papillons*, noting that the sketch for what became Opus 2, no. 9 was originally designated "Valse" as well (*Schumanns Klavierwerke* 1, pp. 62–68). In his letter of 30 September 1856 to Wasielewski, Töpken ascribes Nos. 1, 3, 4, 6, and 8 to Schumann's Heidelberg period (see Eismann, *Quellenwerk* 1, p. 70). Töpken's recollection of having heard No. 8 in D minor (as opposed to its ultimate C♯ minor/D♭ major) is confirmed by an overview of a movement-sequence for *Papillons* preserved in Wiede Sketchbook III (see Boetticher, *Schumanns Klavierwerke* 1, pp. 75–76).

104. The persistent grace-note figures in Opus 2, no. 11 likewise recall similar gestures in No. 6 of the *VIII Polonaises*.

105. See Boetticher, *Schumanns Klavierwerke* 1, pp. 75–76.

106. Like several of the pieces in the final version (Nos. 4, 11, 12), this diminutive movement makes prominent use of horn fifths. See Boetticher, *Schumanns Klavierwerke* 1, p. 76.

107. Although Daniel Steibelt published a *Papillons* as his Opus 69 (1819), there is no evidence that Schumann was familiar with this collection.

108. For a discussion of the importance of butterfly imagery in Schumann's youthful poems (1825), see Schoppe, "Schumanns frühe Texte," p. 10. A poem entitled *Raupe und Schmetterling* (Caterpillar and Butterfly), possibly dating from 1830, was included in *Allerley aus der Feder Roberts an der Mulde* (see *TB* 1, p. 323).

109. *TB* 1, p. 332.

110. *Ibid.*, p. 340.

111. Letter of 19 March 1838, in Schumann, Clara and Robert, *Briefwechsel: Kritische Gesamtausgabe* (hereafter cited as *BrKG*) 1, p. 125.

112. The entire chapter appears in translation as Appendix 1.

113. *Jugendbriefe*, pp. 166–67.

114. *Ibid.*, pp. 167–68.

115. Letter of 22 August 1834, in *Briefe, Neue Folge*, p. 54. The reference to a "giant boot in F♯ minor" links the third of the *Papillons* with the passage from the masked ball scene beginning: "He [Walt] and his imagination were most drawn to a giant boot that was gliding along, wearing and carrying itself. . . ." Cf. the more qualified statement in a letter from Schumann to Gottfried Weber (editor of *Cäcilia*) of 11 January 1834: "*[Papillons]* arose in part from the last chapter of Jean Paul's *Flegeljahre* . . . I assembled [the movements] in such a way that one might detect in them something of the masked ball and also perhaps something of Wina's eyes peering from behind her mask." See *Briefe, Neue Folge*, p. 46.

116. *TB* 1, p. 359. In calling 2 June 1831 a "Hundetag" (dog-day), Schumann makes an oblique allusion to Jean Paul's *Hesperus*, whose chapters are delivered to the author by way of a "dog-post." See *TB* 1, 336.

117. *TB* 1, p. 401. Schumann copied Rellstab's review of 25 May 1832 into his diary (see *TB* 1, pp. 426).

118. *Briefe, Neue Folge*, p. 54.

119. For a concise account of Schumann's notations, see Lippman, "Theory and Practice," pp. 314–16. The marked spots are numbered as follows: (1)—"As he left his little room . . . for his first battle." (2)—"By making a wrong turn . . . considerable distance." "He couldn't spot Wina, nor was there any trace of Vult." "Finally, since he wanted to investigate . . . zigzagging shapes!" (3)—"He and his imagination . . . wearing and carrying itself." (4)—"But Hope quickly turned around . . . bouquet of auriculas." (5)—"For a second he stood alone . . . observed the other from a great distance." (8)—"Just as a youth touches . . . Walt the wagoner had both." (7)—"He tore off his mask. . . one of his most fervent entreaties" (9)—" 'Dear brother . . . with joy'." (6)—"For up to now . . . imitation-waltzes" (10)—"Upon entering the hall . . . lark song in late summer." The complete text for these passages is given in Appendix 1.

120. Cf. also the passages linked with Nos. 1, 3, and 5 in note 119.

121. Cf. also the passages linked with Nos. 2, 8, and 10 in note 119.

122. The attempts of various writers to pinpoint specific connections between the two may therefore amount to a futile exercise. See Chailley, "Zum Symbolismus," pp. 60–64; and especially Mayeda, *Schumanns Weg zur Symphonie*, pp. 111, 114–16.

123. *Briefe, Neue Folge*, p. 148.

124. See Lippman, "Theory and Practice," p. 322; and Struck, "Literarischer Eindruck," p. 112.

125. See Chapter 1, pp. 28–29.

126. This addition first appears in the engraver's copy, or *Stichvorlage*, over an erasure in the original; see Boetticher, "Weitere Forschungen," p. 46. According to Julius Knorr's program for *Papillons*, published in 1861 in his *Führer auf dem Felde der Klavierunterrichtsliteratur*, the closing passage of the *Finale* represents the subsiding of the hubbub on carnival night as the tower clock strikes 6; see *GS* 2, p. 456. (Moreover the fourth edition of *Papillons*, issued in 1860, includes the following notation toward the end of the *Finale*: "The carnival-night bustle is silenced. The tower clock strikes 6.") While the entire program of Schumann's fellow Davidsbündler may not, as he claimed, transmit the composer's own thoughts on the content of *Papillons*, Knorr's description of the last piece probably does reflect Schumann's

intent. Brendel published a similar interpretation in his 1845 essay "Robert Schumann mit Rücksicht auf Mendelssohn-Bartholdy" (*NZfM* 22, p. 83); hence even if the program did not originate with Schumann, it was at least a product of his immediate circle.

127. Letter of 5 April 1833, in *Briefe, Neue Folge*, p. 43.

128. See *GS* 2, p. 207. Consider also the following from the *Denk- und Dichtbüchlein* (1833) of Meister Raro, Florestan, and Eusebius: "[Music] would be a paltry artform if it consisted only of tones, possessing neither a language of nor signs for the states of the soul.— Florestan" (*GS* 1, p. 22); in a subsequent aphorism, Eusebius similarly insists that music should have both "script and signs" for all the various soul-states (*GS* 1, p. 22).

129. *AmZ* 35 (1833), col. 616. Schumann's own view on the restrictiveness of a fixed program is implicit in his account of the "spirit of individuality" *(Particulargeist)* and its manifestation in music: "The more a piece of music is individualized and suggestive to the listener of a variety of images, the more all-inclusive, eternal, and new for all times it will be." (Diary entry for June 1832, in *TB* 1, p. 410).

130. Even Schumann's compositional method at this stage of his career reveals a fragmentary, cut-and-paste approach to musical construction: a piece designated "Intermezzo" in Wiede Sketchbook III begins with the first sixteen measures of what became *Papillons*, no. 10 (but in D$\flat$) and proceeds with music that subsequently made its way into *Papillons*, no. 8. See Dietel, *'Eine neue poetische Zeit'*, p. 56. For an intriguing account of the relationship between fragmentation in *Papillons* and the concept of romantic irony, see Bracht, "Schumann's 'Papillons,'" pp. 73–84. More comprehensive discussions of Schumann's engagement with the fragment include my *Nineteenth-Century Music*, pp. 49–88; and Rosen, *Romantic Generation*, pp. 41–115, *passim*.

131. Entry of 28 May 1832, in *TB* 1, p. 399.

132. Quoted from a letter from Sörgel to Schumann, in *TB* 1, p. 399 (entry of 26 May 1832).

133. Letter of 24 May 1832, in Boetticher, ed., *Briefe und Gedichte*, p. 91.

134. Review of Schumann's Opp. 1–5 in *Caecilia* (1834); see Eismann, *Quellenwerk* 1, p. 82.

135. See *TB* 1, p. 426.

136. See also Weber's 1834 review, quoted in Eismann, *Quellenwerk* 1, p. 82; and Kossmaly, "Über Schumann's Clavier-Compositionen," col. 17.

137. *TB* 1, p. 427.

138. *TB* 1, p. 407, entry of 9 June 1832.

139. For a discussion of tonal and motivic cross-reference in *Papillons*, see Kaminsky, "Aspects of harmony," pp. 140–45, and "Principles of Formal Structure," pp. 209–10.

140. See Lacoue-Labarthe and Nancy, *The Literary Absolute*, pp. 11–12, 30–35, 82.

141. Letters of 22 August 1834 to Henriette Voigt, in *Briefe, Neue Folge*, p. 54; and 8 May 1832 to his mother, in *Jugendbriefe*, p. 174.

142. *TB* 1, pp. 401, 413. According to the diary, the idea for "a second volume of *Papillons*, whose first piece will have the character of a monastic hymn," was not broached until 6 May 1832, even though the designation on the Kistner print suggests an earlier origin; see *TB* 1, p. 385. This is supported by a list of "plans for the future" in a diary entry of 13 October 1831. Included with projected variation sets on J. P. Pixis's *Glöckchenthema* (probably his "Les trois clochettes," op. 120) and the *Zigeunermarsch* from Weber's *Preciosa* is a reference to "fluttering *Papillons*." See *TB* 1, p. 372.

143. *Briefe, Neue Folge*, p. 414.

144. A comparison of the *Albumblätter*, a collection of brief keyboard works composed between 1832 and 1845, with an overview of the projected contents of the 12 *Burle* (tran-

scribed in Boetticher, *Schumanns Klavierwerke,* 1, p. 101) suggests the following correspondences: *Scherzino* (op. 124, no. 3) = *Burla* 6; *Larghetto* (op. 124, no. 13) = *Burla* 8; *Burla* (op. 124, no. 12) = *Burla* 5.

145. See Boetticher, *Schumanns Klavierwerke* 1, p. 59.

146. See Boetticher, *Schumanns Klavierwerke* 1, pp. 59, 146; and Boetticher, *Schumanns Klavierwerke* 2, pp. 96, 260, 261.

147. See Boetticher, *Schumanns Klavierwerke* 1, p. 54; and Schumann's letter to Töpken of 5 April 1833, in *Briefe, Neue Folge,* p. 43.

148. Among the earliest references to the new cycle is a diary entry of 29 April 1832: "The image of the *Intermezzi* is alive within me; only some small details are lacking." (*TB* 1, p. 381). The completion of the work in mid-July coincides with the drafting of a now lost *Exercise fantastique* dedicated to Kuntsch (see the diary entry of 22 July 1832, in *TB* 1, p. 412).

149. See Rellstab's review of 10 January 1834 in *Iris,* quoted in Boetticher, *Schumanns Klavierwerke* 1, p. 113.

150. Consider the diary entry of 22 May 1832: "The *Intermezzi* should really be something—I plan to weigh every note in the balance. This morning I began with Marpurg [*Abhandlung von der Fuge*] and understand him more quickly and easily than I did several months ago." (*TB* 1, p. 394).

151. *TB* 1, p. 379; see also Eismann, *Quellenwerk* 1, p. 82.

152. Entry of 30 May 1832, in *TB* 1, p. 401.

153. Entry of 20 April 1832, in *TB* 1, p. 379.

154. Entry of 4 June 1832, in *TB* 1, p. 404. The picture to which Schumann refers was probably Johann Peter Lyser's widely circulated "Karrikatur auf die Wiener Konzerte 1828."

155. See *TB* 1, p. 389; and the letter of 27 July 1832, in *Jugendbriefe,* p. 187.

156. Eismann, *Quellenwerk* 1, p. 82.

157. The overview is reproduced in Boetticher, *Schumanns Klavierwerke* 1, p. 101. The works-in-progress listed in the diary include *2 Burle* and *Papillons, Livr.* 2 as well (see *TB* 1, p. 413).

158. *TB* 1, p. 388.

159. *Ibid.,* p. 403.

160. See Münster, "Beethoven-Etuden," p. 53.

161. *TB* 1, p. 381.

162. On 1 May 1832, Schumann's thoughts turned to the plot of the *Wuderkinder* novel, newly christened as *Florestan* (*TB* 1, p. 382). The *Acht Bilder . . . Florestaniana* may therefore refer to a projected set of prose poems after the manner of the last section of the "Tonwelt" essay.

163. For a summary of the contents of the three versions (the third titled simply *Exercises*), see Münster, "Beethoven-Etuden," pp. 53–56. The dating of the latter two is open to conjecture; while Clara placed them both in 1833, Schumann's overview of his activities for 1835 alludes to the "drafting of a fair copy of the *Etuden über eine Beethoven'sches Thema*;" see *TB* 1, p. 421. Robert Münster's edition of all the completed variations from the three versions was published by Henle Verlag in 1976. As Münster points out ("Beethoven-Etuden," pp. 53–54), the seventh variation from the first version alludes to the *Scene am Bach* from Beethoven's Sixth Symphony as well.

164. *TB* 1, p. 421.

165. The latter is mentioned in the *Projektenbuch;* see Eismann, *Quellenwerk* 1, p. 82.

166. The reference in the *Projektenbuch* to "symphonic beginnings" (1829/Heidelberg) may allude to no longer extant sketches for yet another symphony. See Eismann, *Quellenwerk* 1, p. 81.

167. See the entry of 25 October 1828, in *TB* 1, p. 128: "Theatre—Shakespeare's Hamlet."

168. *Jugendbriefe,* p. 133.

169. For a more detailed discussion of these symphonic sketches and their relationship to the *Hamlet* project, see Draheim, "Schumann und Shakespeare," pp. 241–42; Dusella, "Symphonisches," pp. 217–23; and Finson, "Schumann and Shakespeare," pp. 129–32.

170. Schumann, *Selbstbiographische Notizen,* ed. Schoppe.

171. See the entry for the Symphony (designated *Oeuv. 7*) in Schumann's *Kompositions-Verzeichnis,* in *Briefe, Neue Folge,* p. 537.

172. *TB* 1, p. 472, note 436. A reviewer for a local newspaper offered a warmer appraisal, criticizing not the orchestration but the orchestra, which was not "strongly constituted" enough for a work that was obviously intended, in his view, for a large, professional ensemble such as the Leipzig Gewandhaus Orchestra. (See *TB* 1, p. 429). That venerable institution did perform the movement on 29 April 1833, but again without much effect. The first modern-day performance of the completed portions of the work, edited by Marc Andreae, took place at the Swiss-Italian Broadcasting Studios in Lugano on 8 April 1971.

173. See the entry of 8 March 1833, in *TB* 1, p. 416.

174. Schumann includes "the last movement of my symphony" under "Plans" and "Works-in-Progress" in a diary entry of 8 March 1833; interestingly enough, "English grammar" appears in the same list. See *TB* 1, p. 417. May 1833 is given as the terminal date of work on the symphony in Schumann's *Kompositions-Verzeichnis;* see *Briefe, Neue Folge,* p. 537.

175. See the entry of 29 May 1832, in *TB* 1, p. 400.

176. For more detailed accounts of the genesis of the work, see Abraham, "Schumann's Jugendsinfonie"; Mayeda, *Schumanns Weg,* pp. 172–84, 202–9; and Dusella, "Symphonisches," p. 213.

177. For further discussion on this point, see Mayeda, *Schumanns Weg,* pp. 190–91.

Chapter 3

1. *TB* 1, pp. 417, 419.

2. Entries in what Schumann called a "kleines Tagebuch" cover the period 28 July 1836 to 28 October 1837; see *TB* 2, pp. 22–42.

3. *TB* 1, pp. 419–23.

4. See *Briefe, Neue Folge,* p. 537.

5. The case for a period of heated compositional activity in the first half of 1833 is further strengthened by the Vienna précis, where Schumann notes that immediately after drafting the *Impromptus* [26–30 May], he set to work on the F♯-minor Sonata, and "more or less finished [it] up to the last part." See *TB* 1, p. 419.

6. This is one of the central arguments of Kapp's *Studien zum Spätwerk;* see, e.g., pp. 9, 32–34, 41, 57–58, 61–62.

7. *GS* 1, p. 63.

8. For a discussion of the Berlin sketch and transcriptions of the *Intermezzo* and several of the *Ritornelli,* see Boetticher, *Schumanns Klavierwerke* 1, pp. 87–90. A presumably later sketch, once part of a private collection in Munich, but now lost, also bears the title *Scenes musicales;* see Boetticher, *Schumanns Klavierwerke* 1, pp. 85–86.

9. Schumann, *Selbstbiographische Notizen,* ed. Schoppe.

10. For an excellent summary of the genesis of Schumann's themes, see Becker, "New

Look," pp. 570–77. As Becker points out, the opening of Clara's theme bears an uncanny resemblance to a four-measure sketch drafted by Schumann on 30 September 1830 while en route from Paderborn to Detmold (see *TB* 1, p. 321). Since Clara's composition probably dates from 1831 (and since even if it dates from 1830, Schumann, who was in Heidelberg at the time, would not have seen it), Becker convincingly argues that after resettling in Leipzig in October 1830 Schumann may have shared his sketch with Clara, who then elaborated it as the theme of her *Romance*. As Becker also notes, "Clara's" theme was destined for a long history. When Clara and Brahms wrote variations on the fourth piece in Schumann's *Bunte Blätter*, op. 99—Clara's Variations, op. 20 (1853) were dedicated "to HIM," that is, Robert, while the manuscript of Brahms's Opus 9 (1854) refers to Variations on a "theme by HIM" and "dedicated to HER"—they both alluded to the theme of Clara's youthful *Romance* (see mm. 201–6 of Clara's Variations, and Variation 10, mm. 30–31, of Brahms's). Clara's theme, in other words, had evolved into an emblem for shared artistic ideals among the members of Schumann's circle.

11. The resemblance between Schumann's and Beethoven's variations was not lost on Liszt. See the comments on the *Impromptus* in his 1837 review of Schumann's Opp. 5, 11, and 14 for the *Gazette musicale*, reproduced in Wasielewski, *Schumann*, p. 521.

12. See *Selbstbiographische Notizen*, ed. Schoppe; and *TB* 1, p. 400. On Schumann's debt to Bach in the *Impromptus*, see also Rosen, *Romantic Generation*, pp. 664–668. As Rosen points out, Schumann draws upon (but transforms) the tradition of the fugal gigue in the finale of the work.

13. To be sure, Schumann's revision of the *Impromptus*, published in 1850, in which he excised the rhapsodic No. 11 altogether and made the concluding references to Clara's theme more explicit, undercuts this interpretation. For a thorough account of the differences, great and small, between the two versions of the work, see Becker, "A Study of Robert Schumann's *Impromptus*," and "A New Look," pp. 583–85. Becker makes a good case for the affective "imbalance" of the revision. In my view as well, the later version lacks the poetry of the original.

14. *TB* 1, p. 419.

15. *Ibid.*

16. *Jugendbriefe*, pp. 227–28. The last quotation, omitted from the *Jugendbriefe*, is cited from Ostwald, *Schumann: Inner Voices*, p. 103.

17. Litzmann, *Clara Schumann* 1, pp. 84–85. This letter, when considered along with Schumann's reference to his move from a fifth-floor to a ground-floor apartment, strengthens the conjecture that he may have contemplated suicide by flinging himself out of his apartment window on the "most frightful evening" of 17 October 1833; see *TB* 1, p. 419. Wasielewski notes, however, that while some individuals supported the claim, others denied it. See Wasielewski, *Schumann*, p. 11.

As we have already seen (Introduction, pp. 5–7), there is little evidence to support Ostwald's claim that "homosexual panic" hastened the onset of Schumann's illness. True, a group of "attractive young men," many of them eventual collaborators on his journal, had begun to gather around him, and to be sure, "revelry as well as rivalry" prevailed in that circle, but the composer's supposed "desire for intimacy with men" was probably more of a cultural than a sexual phenomenon. Cf. Ostwald, *Schumann: Inner Voices*, pp. 102–4.

18. These together with related symptoms (depression, anxiety, fear of death, physical weakness, trembling in the limbs, insomnia) would recur with greater intensity about a decade later. But the effects of the breakdown that Schumann suffered following his return from a Russian tour with Clara in 1844 would persist for almost three years. See *TB* 2, p. 396; Litzmann, *Clara Schumann* 2, p. 76; and Wasielewski, *Schumann*, p. 352.

19. *Jugendbriefe,* p. 227.

20. *TB* 1, p. 417.

21. See Schumann's letter to his mother of 28 June 1833, in *Jugendbriefe,* p. 209; and *TB* 1, p. 419.

22. Jansen, *Davidsbündler,* p. 53. See also *TB* 1, p. 420; and Schumann's Introduction to the collected editions of his writings (1854), in *GS* 1, p. 1.

23. *Jugendbriefe,* pp. 209ff. Likewise, Schumann was not indifferent to the possible material benefits of the enterprise. See the letter of 19 March 1834 to his mother (*Jugendbriefe,* p. 233): "Apart from honor and fame, I can also expect some profit [from the journal], so that you can really rest easier about my getting along in the future."

24. See Marc Andreae's Preface to Schumann, *Sinfonie G-moll für Orchester* (Frankfurt, London, New York: Litolff's Verlag/Peters, 1972).

25. *TB* 1, p. 419.

26. *Ibid.*

27. *Jugendbriefe,* p. 232.

28. *TB* 1, p. 420.

29. See Schumann's letter of 25 August 1834 to Henriette Voigt, in *Briefe, Neue Folge,* p. 55; and *TB* 1, p. 420.

30. *NZfM* 2 (1835), p. 146.

31. A somewhat abridged version of the article appears in *GS* 2, pp. 260–72.

32. See *TB* 1, pp. 339, 342–44, 379, 382; and Schoppe, "Schumanns frühe Texte," p. 13.

33. Schlegel, *Kritische Friedrich Schlegel Ausgabe* (cited hereafter as *KFSA*) 2, p. 271.

34. See the entry for 6 June 1831, in *TB* 1, p. 337.

35. Warrack, *Weber,* p. 104.

36. The leading lights of Leipzig's cultural elite belonged to the Tunnel über der Pleisse; other members whom Schumann knew well included the music dealer and publisher Friedrich Hofmeister, Karl Herlosssohn, and Heinrich Dorn. Although Schumann never joined the group, he did attend some of the functions it sponsored. A diary entry for January 1837, for example, reads: "Masked ball at the Tunnel" (*TB* 2, p. 31). For an excellent summary of the activities of the Ludlamshöhle, the Tunnel über der Spree, and the Tunnel über der Pleisse, along with an account of their relationship to Schumann's Davidsbund, see, Appel, "Schumanns Davidsbund," pp. 1–15.

37. *GS* 1, p. 2.

38. Letter of 14 September 1836 to Dorn, in *Briefe, Neue Folge,* p. 77.

39. There are some differences of opinion over the identities of the individuals masked by these Davidsbündler names. "Knif," for instance, may refer to Gottfried Fink, the editor of the rival *Allgemeine musikalische Zeitung* ("Knif" = "Fink" in reverse); or to Julius Knorr, who also appears in the *Neue Zeitschrift* simply as "Julius." Jansen (*Davidsbündler,* p. 31) held to the first view, Kreisig (*GS* 2, p. 460, note 520) to the second.

40. Entry for 8 June 1831, in *TB* 1, p. 339.

41. As Appel points out, Leipzig enjoyed a relatively loose enforcement of the censorship laws in the period after the enactment of the Carlsbad Decrees (1819); see "Schumanns Davidsbund," pp. 17–18.

42. In the months leading up to the founding of the journal, the makeup of the editorial committee underwent several changes. Schumann included Ortlepp, Wieck, and two unnamed music teachers among the journal's "directors" in a letter to his mother of 28 June 1833 (*Jugendbriefe,* p. 210); a week before the March 1834 contract was drawn up, he listed Ferdinand Stegmeyer (who, according to the final arrangements, was retained as a tie-breaker should the four editors fail to reach a concensus), Knorr, Schunke, Wieck, and himself as

editors; see *Jugendbriefe*, p. 233, and Kross, "Aus der Frühgeschichte," p. 432.

43. The contract is reproduced in Kross, "Aus der Frühgeschichte," pp. 429–32.

44. *GS* 2, p. 273.

45. *Jugendbriefe*, p. 242.

46. *TB* 1, p. 420.

47. For a detailed account of the entire affair and a transcription of the 24 December 1834 contract, see Kross, "Aus der Frühgeschichte," pp. 426–29, 433–38.

48. *GS* 1, p. 1.

49. Kross, "Aus der Frühgeschichte," p. 445.

50. *TB* 1, pp. 420, 473 (notes 447, 448).

51. See Boetticher, *Schumanns Klavierwerke* 2, p. 47.

52. See Boetticher, *Schumanns Klavierwerke* 2, p. 47.

52. See Eismann, *Quellenwerk* 1, p. 124; and *TB* 1, pp. 420–21.

53. *TB* 1, p. 419.

54. See Plantinga, *Schumann as Critic,* pp. 82–85. Before the founding of the *Neue Zeitschrift* in 1834, Schumann is known to have studied two books dealing with music history: C. F. D. Schubart's *Ideen zu einer Aesthetik der Tonkunst* (1806), and Thibaut's *Über Reinheit der Tonkunst* (1825/26), both of them highly unreliable on matters of historical fact. Only around 1840, and perhaps under the influence of C. F. Becker, who reviewed publications on historical themes for the *Neue Zeitschrift,* did Schumann make a serious effort to improve his knowledge in this area. After selling the journal in 1844, he continued along the same course; among the entries in the *Lektürebüchlein* for 1847 are Forkel's biography of Bach, Mattheson's biography of Handel, and Kiesewetter's *Geschichte der Europaeisch-Abenalaendischen oder unsrer heutigen Musik* (1834/1846); see Nauhaus, "Schumanns *Lektüre-büchlein,*" pp. 71, 83. As Boetticher has pointed out, Schumann also read Baini's biography of Palestrina during this period; see *Schumann: Einführung,* pp. 291–292.

55. *NZfM* 2 (1835), p. 3.

56. *GS* 1, p. 60.

57. As early as May 1828 Schumann expressed the same conceit in even more starkly existential terms: "The past is the angel of destruction of the present, and every moment a victim of suicide, for a single beautiful moment kills not only itself but also millions of its future sisters." See *TB* 1, p. 89; and Mayeda, "Schumanns Gegenwart," p. 18.

58. *TB* 1, p. 110; and *GS* 1, p. 23.

59. See Szondi, "Friedrich Schlegel and Romantic Irony," pp. 57–59. For discussions of the points of contact between Schumann's thinking and Schlegel's, see Botstein, "History, Rhetoric," pp. 23–29; Dahlhaus, *Analysis,* p. 16; Dahlhaus, *Klassische und Romantische,* p. 260; and my *Nineteenth Century Music,* p. 12. Other precedents for Schumann's philosophy of history include Heine's faith in a future informed by the spirit of progress (as articulated in *Zur Geschichte der Neueren Schönen Literatur in Deutschland* [1833]) and Jean Paul's conviction that the past and future can only be experienced poetically, as "memory" and "hope" (see "Über die Realität des Ideals" from *Titan,* in *Jean Paul Werke* 3, p. 221). For further commentary on the relationships among Schumann, Heine, and Jean Paul, see Knepler, *Musikgeschichte,* p. 774; and Mayeda, "Schumann's Gegenwart," p. 13.

60. *Briefe, Neue Folge,* p. 52.

61. For excerpts from Schumann's *Chronologische Geschichte,* see Boetticher, *Schumann: Einführung,* pp. 291–92.

62. *Briefe, Neue Folge,* pp. 177–78. Schumann's reference to the "profound combinatorial power" of Bach's music resonates with the critical categories of Jena Romanticism. For

Friedrich Schlegel, the combinatorial power *par excellence* is *Witz* (wit), the faculty that allows us to discern similarities between apparently dissimilar entities. See, e.g., *Athenäum* Fragment 220 (*KFSA* 2, p. 200), *Ideen* Fragment 123 (*KFSA* 2, p. 268), *Philosophische Fragmente, Zweite Epoche II*, no. 729 (*KFSA* 18, p. 381), and especially the commentary on the literary fragment in *Lessings Gedanken und Meinungen* (*KFSA* 3, p. 83).

63. 1838 review of Czerny's edition of the *WTC*, in *GS* 1, p. 354.

64. *GS* 1, p. 9.

65. *TB* 1, p. 348.

66. *Leipziger Musikleben 1837/38*, in *GS* 1, p. 380.

67. *GS* 2, p. 74.

68. 1839 review in *GS* 1, p. 401.

69. 1841 review of the 13th through 16th subscription concerts of the Leipzig Gewandhaus Orchestra, in *GS* 2, p. 54. By the following year, Schumann had somewhat tempered this position. In a review of recently composed string quartets, he noted that while Hirschbach took Beethoven as his model, "many fruit-laden trees still stand in the gardens of Mozart and Haydn." *GS* 2, p. 75.

70. *NZfM* 1 (1834), p. 78.

71. *NZfM* 1 (1834), p. 62.

72. *NZfM* 1 (1834), p. 38. For further discussion of Schumann's politicization of the current musical scene, see Dahlhaus, *Nineteenth-Century Music*, 247–48; Dahlhaus, *Klassische und Romantische*, p. 261; and Knepler, *Musikgeschichte*, p. 773.

73. Boetticher, *Schumann: Einführung*, p. 292.

74. See Plantinga, *Schumann as Critic*, pp. 102–3.

75. Review of Heller's *Drei Impromptus*, op. 7, in *NZfM* 7 (1837), p. 70. Cf. also Schumann's 1839 New Year's editorial, *NZfM* 10 (1839), p. 1; and his letter to Keferstein of 31 January 1840, in *Briefe, Neue Folge*, pp. 177–78. As Plantinga further points out, Schumann and his confrères were often dubbed "*neoromantics*," a term emphasizing their position as restorers of tradition, by contemporary writers; see *Schumann as Critic*, p. 107.

76. *NZfM* 2 (1835), p. 3.

77. *Fastnachtsrede von Florestan*, in *NZfM* 2 (1835), p. 116.

78. *NZfM* 1 (1834), p. 63.

79. *Ibid.*, p. 4.

80. Schlegel, *KFSA* 1, p. 35.

81. *GS* 1, p. 252. See also "Etüden für das Pianoforte" (1839), *GS* 1, p. 76.

82. See *NZfM* 1 (1834), p. 151; *NZfM* 1 (1834), pp. 113–14; *NZfM* 10 (1839), p. 74; and *NZfM* 16 (1842), p. 174.

83. *NZfM* 5 (1836), p. 63; *NZfM* 10 (1839), p. 134; *NZfM* 10 (1839), p. 6; *NZfM* 11 (1839), p. 1.

84. *NZfM* 5 (1836), p. 63; *NZfM* 15 (1841), p. 141; *NZfM* 4 (1836); p. 163; *NZfM* 3 (1835), p. 33.

85. "Sonaten für Clavier," *NZfM* 10 (1839), p. 134.

86. *GS* 1, p. 30.

87. *Athenäum* Fragment 80, *KFSA* 2, p. 176.

88. *Philosophische Fragmente, Erste Epoche, II*, no. 927, *KFSA* 18, p. 106.

89. See *Kritische Fragmente* 117, *KFSA* 2, p. 183; and "Vom Wesen der Kritik" (1804), in *KFSA* 3, p. 55.

90. See Benjamin, *Begriff der Kunstkritik*, pp. 60–63.

91. *GS* 1, p. 44.

92. Otto, *Schumann als Jean-Paul Leser,* p. 75.

93. "Der Davidsbündler," *GS* 2, p. 263.

94. "An Chiara" (1835), *GS* 1, pp. 121–22.

95. *GS* 1, p. 2.

96. *Ibid.,* p. 13.

97. *Ibid.,* p. 14.

98. *Ibid.,* pp. 52–53.

99. For a discussion of the points of contact between hermeneutics and Schumann's critical strategies, see Bent, *Music Analysis* 2, pp. 122–23.

100. See the entry for 31 May 1831, in *TB* 1, p. 335.

101. *GS* 2, pp. 210–11.

102. Dahlhaus, *Nineteenth-Century Music,* p. 54.

103. The "first kiss," which Florestan locates in Variation 5, occurs in G♭ major, not B♭ major as he says. See *GS* 1, pp. 6–7.

104. *NZfM* 3 (1835), pp. 1–2, 33–35, 37–38, 41–51. For translations, see Cone, *Berlioz,* pp. 220–248; and Bent, *Music Analysis* 2, pp. 166–94.

105. Hoffmann's review, first published in 1810 in the *AmZ,* begins with a florid account of Beethoven's ability to awaken "just that infinite longing which is the essence of romanticism" and proceeds with a demonstration of the thematic unity of the Fifth Symphony, supported by numerous musical examples. See Hoffmann, *Schriften* 5, pp. 34–51. Three years later, Hoffmann combined material from this review with another on Beethoven's piano trios, op. 70; the newly titled essay, "Beethovens Instrumentalmusik," was published in the *Zeitung für die elegante Welt.* The essay also appeared in the *Kreisleriana* section of the *Fantasiestücke in Callot's Manier* (1814–1815).

106. Cf. *NZfM* 3 (1835), p. 37; and the gloss on Schumann's analysis in Cone, *Berlioz,* pp. 250–261.

107. Though Fétis is not mentioned by name, Schumann published his 1 February 1835 review *(Revue musicale)* in the 19 and 23 June 1835 issues of the *Neue Zeitschrift* and thus knew it well. See Bent, *Music Analysis,* vol. 2, pp. 162–63.

108. As Bent also points out, it is remarkable that Schumann should have come to such insightful conclusions working from Liszt's piano transcription of the score alone. See Bent, *Music Analysis,* vol. 2, p. 161.

109. *NZfM* 3 (1835), pp. 50–51.

110. Berlioz was much heartened by Schumann's review. In a letter of 28 December 1836, he expressed his wish for a meeting with Schumann; this, however, did not take place until February 1843 (Boetticher, ed., *Briefe und Gedichte,* pp. 35ff. and 232ff.) As time went on, Schumann grew more uncertain of Berlioz's ability to make good on this promise. In an 1839 review of the *Waverley* Overture, he wrote: "If one traces the derivation of isolated thematic ideas, they often seem conventional, even trivial in themselves. But the whole exerts an irresistible charm on me, in spite of its assault on a German ear unused to such things. Berlioz reveals himself differently in all of his works and charts out new territory in each: it's difficult to know whether he should be called a genius or a musical adventurer." (*NZfM* 10 [1839], p. 187). Four years later, Schumann's reaction to Berlioz's music had cooled further: "At present, I confess, I would certainly be harsher with much of his work. The years make one more severe, and the unlovely things I found in Berlioz's earlier music . . . have not become more beautiful in the interim. But I also maintain that a divine spark resides in this musician." (*NZfM* 19 [1843], pp. 177–78).

Chapter 4

1. *Briefe, Neue Folge,* p. 170.

2. Letter of 22 September 1837, in *Briefe, Neue Folge,* pp. 101–2. See also the similar comments in the letters to Moscheles of 23 August 1837 (again on *Carnaval*), to Simonin de Sire of 15 March 1839, and to Dorn of 5 September 1839 (on *Kinderscenen*); *Briefe, Neue Folge,* pp. 92, 148, 170.

3. *TB* 2, p. 55.

4. For a summary of Schumann's experiments with order in *Carnaval*, the *Etudes Symphoniques,* the *Fantasiestücke, Davidsbündlertänze,* and *Kinderscenen* (as well as the earlier *Papillons* and Paganini *Etudes,* op. 3), see Boetticher, "Weitere Forschungen." Newcomb ("Schumann and the Marketplace," pp. 280–82, 311) considers two further instances of the same phenomenon: the *Quasi Variazioni* movement of the *Concert sans Orchestre,* and the *Novelletten.* Similarly, the *Nachtstücke* were rapidly conceived in late March and early April of 1839, but only put "completely in order" by January of the following year; see Schumann's letter to Clara of 17 January 1840, in Robert and Clara Schumann, *Briefe einer Liebe,* p. 247.

5. See *GS* 1, p. 389; and *GS* 2, p. 348.

6. *Briefe, Neue Folge,* p. 110.

7. *Ibid.,* pp. 148–49.

8. *Ibid.,* p. 227.

9. *Ibid.*

10. Consider also Schumann's remarks to Hermann Hirschbach in a letter of 28 May 1839: "My *Fantasie* in C major (Opus 17, I believe) was recently published by Breitkopf und Härtel; have a look at the *first* movement, with which, when I wrote it three years ago, I thought to have achieved the highest—now I obviously view matters differently." *Briefe, Neue Folge,* p. 156.

11. *BrKG* 1, p. 146. Cf. his remarks to de Sire (letter of 8 February 1838): "I'm understood only by a very few"; *Briefe, Neue Folge,* p. 110.

12. *Briefe, Neue Folge,* p. 227.

13. Letter to Schumann of 5 June 1839; in *Liszt's Briefe,* vol. 1, p. 27. When Liszt performed *Carnaval* at a benefit concert in Leipzig on 30 March 1840, he programmed only about half of the cycle's movements. See *TB* 2, p. 500, note 378.

14. See *NZfM* 5 (1836), pp. 135–37; and Wasielewski, *Schumann,* p. 157. For other references to the "confused" quality of Schumann's earlier keyboard music by generally supportive critics, see Brendel, "Robert Schumann," p. 92; and Kossmaly's essay in *AmZ* 46 (1844), cols. 17, 19–20.

15. Quoted in Newcomb, "Schumann and the Marketplace," p. 307, note 38.

16. Litzmann, *Clara Schumann* 1, p. 311.

17. *Briefe, Neue Folge,* p. 434.

18. See his letter to Kossmaly of 5 May 1843, in *Briefe, Neue Folge,* p. 227.

19. See Newcomb, "Schumann and the Marketplace," pp. 274–77.

20. *GS* 1, p. 28.

21. *Jugendbriefe,* p. 243.

22. Litzmann, *Clara Schumann* 1, p. 85. See also *TB* 1, p. 421.

23. *Briefe, Neue Folge,* pp. 101–2.

24. Quoted in *TB* 2, p. 467, note 112.

25. *GS* 1, p. 484.

26. *Ibid.* Cf. Schumann's similar comments on *Papillons* in *TB* 1, p. 399.

27. For a detailed discussion of unifying strategies in *Carnaval*, see Kaminsky, "Principles," pp. 211–216.

28. Letter of 1 December 1839; in *BrKG* 2, p. 809. Brendel also called attention to the "witty" side of Schumann's music in general and of *Carnaval* in particular. See "Robert Schumann," p. 91.

29. See Jean Paul, *School for Aesthetics*, pp. 121–46; and my *Nineteenth-Century Music*, pp. 71–73.

30. Schumann's reference to the work in his *Projektenbuch* includes the amplifying phrase "actually variations on a theme of Herr von Fricken"; Eismann, *Quellenwerk* 1, p. 124.

31. "Etüden für Pianoforte," in *NZfM* 4 (1836), p. 16.

32. "Variationen für Pianoforte," in *NZfM* 5 (1836), p. 67.

33. These five variations were first published as late as 1873, in the version of the *Etudes* edited by Brahms. They appear in the Supplement volume of Schumann's *Werke*, Series 14, pp. 40–47.

34. See his letter of 16 February 1869 to Adolf Schubring; in *Briefwechsel* 8, p. 218.

35. *TB* 1, p. 421.

36. See Schumann, "Aufzeichnungen," pp. 107, 110–12.

37. *TB* 1, p. 421.

38. Schumann's fragmentary draft and sketches for the Fandango are preserved in the Gesellschaft der Musikfreunde in Vienna. A facsimile appears in Harold Bauer's edition of Opus 11 (New York: Schirmer, 1945). The later sonata movement deviates from the Fandango in a number of respects, including the addition of a lengthy introduction and the recomposition of the exposition's original transition to allow for an excursion to E♭ minor. The sketches for the Fandango's development section unfold the dotted motive that, in varied form, heads off the sonata movement's introduction. For discussions of the ramifications of some of these differences, see Harwood, "Robert Schumann's Sonata," pp. 17–18; and Lester, "Robert Schumann," p. 201.

39. Litzmann, *Clara Schumann* 1, p. 238. Interestingly enough, the motive does not appear in the Fandango.

40. The original finale first appeared in print in 1866. For an account of the genesis of the G-minor Sonata with emphasis on its first movement, see Roesner, "Schumann's Revisions."

41. For a more detailed discussion of these features and their possible debt to Beethoven, see Barry, "Image and Imagination."

42. Litzmann, *Clara Schumann* 1, p. 186.

43. Hans-Christian Schmidt, Liner Notes to *Robert Schumann: Piano Sonatas 1–3*, Volker Banfield (CPO Digital 999 217-2, Berlin, 1993), p. 11.

44. *TB* 1, p. 422.

45. *Jugendbriefe*, p. 268.

46. *Briefe, Neue Folge*, p. 68.

47. *TB* 2, pp. 29–30.

48. *BrKG* 1, pp. 67–68.

49. See *TB* 1, p. 422; and *TB* 2, p. 28.

50. *TB* 2, p. 29.

51. *Ibid.*, pp. 23, 25, 28.

52. *Ibid.*, p. 25.

53. Letter of 14 September 1836, in *Briefe, Neue Folge*, pp. 78–79.

54. *NZfM* 15 (1841), pp. 141–42.

55. *TB* 2, p. 26.

56. Schumann, "Aufzeichnungen," p. 111.

57. Selections from Henriette Voigt's diary appear in Boetticher, "Weitere Forschungen," pp. 53–55. It is interesting to compare Voigt's and Schumann's accounts of the same events. Voigt noted in her diary on 1 October 1836, for instance, that she and the Polish violin virtuoso Karol Lipinski read through Beethoven's "Kreutzer" Sonata and several of Bach's sonatas for violin and keyboard (Boetticher, p. 55). Little did she suspect, however, that Schumann was less than impressed with her Bach interpretation, which he found "dry and lacking in understanding" (*TB* 2, p. 27).

58. Jansen, *Davidsbündler*, p. 74. Jansen later realized that Schumann's improvisation was incorporated into one of the *Nachtstücke*, op. 23. According to another contemporary listener, Hieronymus Truhn, Schumann's interpretation of his own works (*Kinderscenen, Kreisleriana, Novelletten*) was "indescribable." He moved his fingers "with almost anxious speed, as if ants were crawling on the keyboard; [he played] with little accentuation, but with generous use of the pedals" (Jansen, p. 75).

59. Boetticher, "Weitere Forschungen," p. 55.

60. For a more detailed account, see Roesner, "Autograph of Schumann's Piano Sonata in F minor."

61. As Newcomb has shown, even these variations underwent significant revisions in order and number before the final form was achieved. See "Schumann and the Marketplace," pp. 280–282.

62. *BrKG* 2, p. 495.

63. *BrKG* 2, p. 126.

64. *Ibid.*

65. See Marston, *Schumann: Fantasie*, pp. 7–8; and " 'Im Legendenton'," p. 230. The autograph of the *Fantasie* is currently in private hands and unavailable for examination. The title page is transcribed in Erler, *Robert Schumann's Leben*, vol. 1, p. 101. Marston reproduces two pages from the autograph that were used to illustrate Sotheby's auction catalogues of November 1977 and November 1984; see *Schumann: Fantasie*, Plates 1 and 2, between pp. 32 and 33.

66. Entry of 9 September 1836, in *TB* 2, p. 25.

67. *Briefe, Neue Folge*, p. 421. See also the diary entry for December 1836: "Work on a sonata for Beethoven. Finished, except for details, by the beginning of the month" (*TB* 2, p. 30).

68. As indicated in Schumann's diary, the new sonata occupied him from December 1836 to February 1837 (*TB* 2, pp. 30–31). He may have even completed a draft of the entire work: a "Sonate in Fm" appears as Opus 16 in a list of works copied into the diary in the autumn of 1837. The *Fantasie* is designated in the same list as "[Opus] 15. Sonate f. Beethoven" (*TB* 2, p. 42).

69. See *TB* 2, pp. 52–53. On the implications of "Fata Morgana," see Marston, *Schumann: Fantasie*, pp. 32–33. This title obviously intrigued Schumann. A diary entry for 13 November 1838 reads: "Thoughts of a *Fata Morgana* for Clara" (*TB* 2, p. 82). The composition was published as the fourteenth piece, *Vision*, in the *Alblumblätter*, op. 124. For a summary of the various titles linked with the *Fantasie*, see my *Nineteenth-Century Music*, pp. 46–47; and Marston, *Schumann: Fantasie*, p. 23.

70. *NZfM* 3 (1835), p. 33. In his often quoted review of Chopin's Piano Sonata in B♭ Minor, op. 35, Schumann observed: "That [Chopin] called it a sonata is certainly a caprice, if not a downright presumption, for he has simply harnessed together four of his maddest children, hoping, with this name, to smuggle them into a place where they wouldn't otherwise be admitted." (*NZfM* 14 [1841], p. 39). Schumann's children, while not as mad as

Chopin's, are an unruly lot nonetheless; perhaps for this reason he finally decided to bring them together as a *Fantasie*.

71. "Monument für Beethoven: Vier Stimmen darüber," *NZfM* 4 (1836), p. 212. The article appeared on 24 June, precisely when Schumann was drafting the first movement of what became the *Fantasie*.

72. *BrKG* 2, p. 562.

73. An examination of the engraver's copy of the *Fantasie* reveals the surprising fact that the last movement was to have ended with an almost exact recall of this music. In the long run, Schumann decided against this strategy, perhaps because it struck him as an overly obvious means of binding the work into a unity. See Marston, *Schumann: Fantasie*, pp. 18–20, 74.

74. See Roesner, "Schumann's 'Parallel' Forms."

75. See my *Nineteenth-Century Music*, pp. 24, 46; and "Schumann's 'Im Legendenton.'"

76. Schumann likewise attributes these features to Chopin's B♭-minor Sonata, a work no less rich in "new forms" than his own *Fantasie*. See *NZfM* 14 (1841), p. 39.

77. This interpretation is supported by the manuscript sources for the *Fantasie*. The sketches for the *Im Legendenton* (transcribed in Marston, *Schumann: Fantasie*, p. 11) suggest that it may have been originally conceived as a character piece independent of the work in which it was ultimately embedded. Just as the *Fantasie* as a whole was renamed again and again, so too was the *Im Legendenton*. Many of these titles are rich in implications for a view of this section as an embedded narrative: "Romanza" (a song telling of a tragic or amorous incident), "Legende" (a tale from religious history), and most suggestive of all, "Erzählend im Legendenton" ("narrated in the tone of a legend"). See Marston, *Schumann: Fantasie*, pp. 17, 20–21; Marston, " 'Im Legendenton,' " pp. 230, 234–38; and Schneider, " 'Im Legendenton,' " pp. 556–57.

78. *TB* 2, p. 30.

79. *Ibid.*, pp. 31–34.

80. *TB* 1, p. 422.

81. *TB* 2, p. 33.

82. *Jugendbriefe*, p. 298.

83. *TB* 2, p. 33.

84. *TB* 1, p. 422; and *TB* 2, p. 32.

85. Litzmann, *Clara Schumann* 1, pp. 118–119; and *Briefe, Neue Folge*, pp. 97–98.

86. Litzmann, *Clara Schumann* 1, pp. 119–120. Consider also Clara's words in a letter from the beginning of October 1837: "I'm prepared for everything, even the worst. . . . Through you, I've grown strong—your heart and your noble pride have given me self-esteem as well." See Litzmann, *Clara Schumann* 1, p. 131.

87. See *BrKG* 1, pp. 133–56.

88. *TB* 2, p. 34.

89. *Ibid.*

90. *BrKG* 1, p. 75. In a letter to Clara of 6 February 1838, Schumann similarly referred to the *Davidsbündlertänze* as a "Polterabend," an evening festivity before a wedding, featuring games and all-round good cheer; see *BrKG* 1, p. 93.

91. Schumann held Clara's cycle in high regard. In a review of 12 September 1837, he wrote that the pieces of her *Soirées musicales* were "like the buds before the wings of color are exploded into open splendor, captivating and significant to view, like all things that contain the future within themselves." Translation quoted from Reich, *Clara Schumann*, p. 238. To cite just one detail from Clara's Mazurka that probably caught his attention, the metric

displacement of the motto in the coda is just the sort of witty gesture that Schumann often employed in his own music.

92. See Roesner, "Sources," p. 58.

93. See Fiske, "Schumann Mystery"; and Sams, "Tonal Analogue," pp. 113–14.

94. See his description of the genesis of *Carnaval* in *GS* 1, p. 484.

95. According to Charles Rosen's suggestive analysis of this gesture of recall, "Schumann does everything possible to make the return of the *Ländler* [No. 2] sound like the involuntary resurfacing of a buried memory, the rediscovered existence of the past within the present." (*Romantic Generation*, p. 235.)

96. Litzmann, *Clara Schumann* 1, pp. 126–27.

97. *TB* 2, p. 35.

98. *TB* 3, p. 47.

99. *TB* 2, p. 33.

100. *TB* 2, pp. 36, 38.

101. *Ibid.,* p. 38.

102. *Ibid.,* p. 39.

103. *Ibid.,* pp. 40–41.

104. *Ibid.,* p. 40. A diary entry for 8 November 1837 also alludes to "thoughts about a polonaise." (*TB* 2, p. 45). Sketches and drafts for these compositions do not survive; perhaps they should be counted among the "small things" to which Schumann referred in the *Projektenbuch* for 1837; see Eismann, *Quellenwerk* 1, p. 125.

105. *TB* 2, p. 44.

106. For a description of the contents of the *Fugengeschichte* and a thematic catalogue of the fugue subjects contained therein, see Boetticher, *Robert Schumann: Einführung,* pp. 604–7, 639. As Boetticher has noted on several occasions, Schumann may have treated this material as a repository for thematic ideas in his later works.

107. *TB* 2, p. 45.

108. An entry in the *Haushaltbücher* for 18 November 1837 refers to "a gift for C[haritas]." *TB* 3, p. 32.

109. *TB* 2, p. 47.

110. *Ibid.,* pp. 47–49.

111. *Ibid.,* p. 50.

112. During the "ordering" process, one of the pieces, a B-minor Scherzo, was eliminated. It later appeared as the ninth item in *Bunte Blätter,* op. 99.

113. Letter of 3 April 1838 to Joseph Fischhof, in *Briefe, Neue Folge,* p. 118. Cf. also his letter of 30 June 1839 to Hermann Hirschbach, where he describes the *Novelletten* as "intimately connected and composed with great joy." *Briefe, Neue Folge,* p. 158.

114. *BrKG* 1, pp. 98, 100.

115. Letter of 6 February 1838, in *BrKG* 1, p. 90.

116. Letter of 30 June 1839, in *BrKG* 2, p. 608.

117. According to Schumann's letter to Clara of 19 March 1838, he had originally composed "thirty cute little things" from which he selected "twelve" (ultimately, thirteen) for his cycle. Robert Polansky claims to have located the sketches for the "rejected" *Kinderscenen* in a manuscript now located in the Library of Congress (Washington, DC), which also contains fair copies for a number of the *Albumblätter,* op. 124. See Polansky, "Rejected *Kinderscenen.*"

118. *Briefe, Neue Folge,* p. 423.

119. *Jugendbriefe,* p. 280.

120. *Briefe, Neue Folge,* p. 290.

121. *Jugendbriefe,* p. 276.

122. *TB* 2, p. 57.

123. The first reference to plans for a quartet, actually three quartets, comes in Schumann's letter to Clara of 11 February 1838 quoted above (*BrKG* 1, p. 100). Clara responded enthusiastically on 3 March, but begged her fiancé, for neither the first nor the last time, to *"be really clear."* (*BrKG* 1, p. 108; for Schumann's response, see his letter of 19 March in *BrKG* 1, p. 121.) On Beethoven's Opus 131 as a possible source of inspiration for Schumann's quartet plans in February and March, see *TB* 2, p. 51. The April 1838 letter to Fischhoff appears in *Briefe, Neue Folge,* p. 118. On Schumann's abortive attempt at quartet writing in the summer of 1838, see his letter to Clara of 13 April (*BrKG* 1, p. 140), and his diary entries for 15–24 June (*TB* 2, p. 58).

124. *TB* 2, p. 52.

125. Entry of 3 May 1838, in *TB* 2, p. 55.

126. Eismann, *Quellenwerk* 1, p. 125.

127. See his letter of 15 March 1839 to Simonin de Sire, in *Briefe, Neue Folge,* pp. 148–49.

128. For a provocative discussion of Schumann's possible attempt to realize Kreisler's compositional style as described by Hoffmann, see Münch, "Fantasiestücke in Kreislers Manier," pp. 256–269.

129. *TB* 2, p. 63.

130. Litzmann, *Clara Schumann* 1, p. 222.

131. Barthes, "Rasch," in *The Responsibility of Forms,* p. 302.

132. For more detailed discussions of the peculiarly Hoffmannesque narrative elements in *Kreisleriana,* see Crisp, *Kreisleriana,* pp. 14–17; and my *Nineteenth-Century Music,* pp. 61–62.

133. *TB* 2, p. 56.

134. *Ibid.*

135. *TB* 2, p. 57. Wieck divorced Clara's mother, *née* Marianne Tromlitz, in 1825 and three years later married Clementine Fechner. Clara's mother, herself a musician, married Adolf Bargiel, a piano teacher and colleague of Wieck's, just months after the finalization of her divorce.

136. *TB* 2, p. 59.

137. *Ibid.,* p. 61.

138. *Ibid.,* p. 62.

139. *Ibid.,* pp. 61–63.

140. *Ibid.,* p. 65.

141. *GS* 1, p. 327.

142. *TB* 2, pp. 64–66.

143. *Ibid.,* p. 70.

144. See his letter to his brothers of 19 March 1838, in *Briefe, Neue Folge,* pp. 113–15; and the diary entry of 24 March 1838: "It's been decided about Vienna, if heaven wants to ensure our happiness" (*TB* 2, p. 53).

145. *TB* 2, pp. 71–75.

146. *Ibid.,* p. 80.

147. *BrKG* 1, p. 291.

148. *TB* 2, p. 81.

149. See the entry for 24 November 1838, in *TB* 2, p. 82; and the letter to Zuccalmaglio of 10 March 1839, in *Briefe, Neue Folge,* p. 147. In the letter, Schumann attributes the failure of his scheme to the censor's intransigence.

150. *TB* 2, pp. 72, 75, 77.

151. See the entry for 9 November 1838 in *TB* 2, p. 81: "Might I perhaps work up [Johann Günzburg's novella] *Astorga* as an opera?"

152. Entry of 28 October 1838, in *TB* 2, p. 78.

153. *TB* 2, p. 73.

154. *Briefe, Neue Folge,* pp. 424–25.

155. *NZfM* 12 (1840), p. 82.

156. See Eismann, *Quellenwerk* 1, pp. 109–10.

157. *TB* 2, p. 89.

158. *TB* 3, pp. 30, 35, 41, 45, 49.

159. On this point, see Newcomb, "Schumann and the Marketplace," pp. 267–68.

160. The *Fughette* was probably composed in early September 1839, well after Schumann's return to Leipzig. See his letter of 5 September 1839 to Fischhof, in *Briefe, Neue Folge,* p. 172; and *TB* 2, p. 95.

161. See *TB* 2, pp. 84–85; and Eismann, *Quellenwerk* 1, p. 125.

162. "Das Clavier-Concert," *NZfM* 10 (1839), pp. 5–7.

163. Letter of 24 January 1839, *BrKG* 2, p. 367.

164. According to Schumann's diary, some of the material employed in the *Arabeske* predates the trip to Vienna; *TB* 2, p. 87.

165. *Briefe, Neue Folge,* p. 169.

166. *Ibid.,* p. 167.

167. *BrKG* 2, p. 435.

168. Jean Paul, *School for Aesthetics,* pp. 88–92.

169. Letter of 7 August 1839 to Ernst Becker, in *Briefe, Neue Folge,* p. 166.

170. Cf. Schumann's remark on the composition of the *Humoreske* in his letter of 11 March 1839 to Clara: "The whole week I sat at the piano . . . laughing and crying at the same time." *BrKG* 2, p. 435.

171. Jean Paul, *School for Aesthetics,* p. 92.

172. *TB* 2, p. 88. In the *Projektenbuch,* Schumann lists only the first movement as having been completed in Vienna; see Eismann, *Quellenwerk* 1, p. 125.

173. See Eismann, *Quellenwerk* 1, p. 125; Schumann's letter to Clara of 24 January 1840, in Robert and Clara Schumann, *Briefe einer Liebe,* p. 247.

174. Several writers have even speculated that Schumann had the *Faschingsschwank* in mind when he included a "grossen *romantischen Sonate*" in a list of works for 1839. See Erler, *Schumann's Leben* 1, pp. 193–94. Although Newcomb takes this to be a reference to a never completed Sonata in F Minor (the preliminary materials for which do not survive), his case does not strike me as convincing; see "Schumann and the Marketplace," pp. 304–5. The F-minor sonata was sketched in 1836 and appears in an October 1837 list of works as Opus 16 (*TB* 2, p. 42). The complete entry from the 1839 list, however, indicates that work on the "romantic Sonata" was still in progress at that time: "Anfang eines Concertes [D minor], und einer grossen *romantischen Sonate*." This concords well with the unfinished state of the *Faschingsschwank* in 1839.

175. *TB* 2, p. 87.

176. *Ibid.,* p. 89.

177. See *TB* 2, p. 89; and Schumann's letter to Clara of 17 January 1840, in Robert and Clara Schumann, *Briefe einer Liebe,* p. 247.

178. *TB* 2, p. 90.

Chapter 5

1. See *TB* 2, pp. 90, 114; and Schumann's letter to Clara of 19 April 1839, in Boetticher, *Robert Schumann in seinen Schriften*, p. 247.

2. Litzmann, *Clara Schumann* 1, p. 312.

3. For Clara's letters of 1 and 2 May 1839 to her father and Schumann, respectively, see Litzmann, *Clara Schumann* 1, pp. 316–22. Schumann's written response to Clara's letter does not survive, though his less than enthusiastic reaction can be inferred from later comments. As chance would have it, a letter from Schumann of 4 May 1839 crossed with Clara's letter of 2 May. In it he estimated his capital at 10,040 thalers: 1,000 in government bonds, 7,540 held jointly with his brothers, and another 1,500 from Eduard's estate; see *BrKG* 2, p. 515. For Schumann's reply to Clara's assurance of 13 May, see *TB* 2, p. 90.

4. See *Briefe, Neue Folge*, pp. 159–60; and *TB* 2, p. 90.

5. Schumann's petition to the Leipzig court (written with the help of his friend Friedrich Hermann, an assessor) and his letter to Clara appear in Eismann, *Quellenwerk* 1, pp. 108–109, 117–18.

6. See *TB* 2, p. 91; Boetticher, *Robert Schumann in seinen Schriften*, p. 250; *BrKG*, pp. 127, 569–71; and *Briefe, Neue Folge*, p. 158. Schumann's enthusiasm for quartet composition was no doubt stimulated by his contact with Hermann Hirschbach, whose reviews of Beethoven's late quartets, for which Schumann also had a passion, would appear in several of the summer 1839 issues of the *Neue Zeitschrift* (see Marston, "Schumann's Monument," p. 249). All that we have of Schumann's pair of quartets are drafts for the openings of movements in D and E♭. These sketches, now in the Deutsche Staatsbibliothek, are transcribed in Marston, "Schumann's Monument," pp. 250–51.

7. See *TB* 2, p. 97; *TB* 3, p. 69; and *Briefe, Neue Folge*, p. 160.

8. *TB* 2, p. 91.

9. *Ibid.*, p. 92; *TB* 3, p. 71; and Litzmann, *Clara Schumann* 1, pp. 360ff.

10. *TB* 2, p. 93.

11. *Ibid.*, p. 93.

12. *Ibid.*, pp. 93 and 497 (note 358).

13. *Ibid.*, p. 94.

14. Eismann, *Quellenwerk* 1, p. 110; Clara later added: "From my portfolio. How often I've read these lines!"

15. *TB* 2, p. 96.

16. *Ibid.*, p. 95.

17. *Ibid. BrKG* 2, p. 734.

18. *Briefe, Neue Folge*, pp. 227, 234. Schumann noted his completion of a fair copy of the cycle in a letter of 11 December 1839 to Carl Becker (*Briefe, Neue Folge*, p. 175). The "two little *Blumenstücke*" mentioned in the same letter cannot refer to the *Blumenstück*, op. 19 (which was published in August 1839) and must therefore have been lost.

19. Litzmann, *Clara Schumann* 1, p. 355.

20. See Reich, *Clara Schumann*, p. 97.

21. Eismann, *Quellenwerk* 1, p. 121.

22. *Ibid.*

23. *Briefe, Neue Folge*, p. 178; see also Schumann's letter to Clara of 20 February 1839, in Boetticher, *Robert Schumann in seinen Schriften*, p. 231.

24. Letter to Keferstein of 8 February 1840, in *Briefe, Neue Folge*, p. 180.

25. Letter to Reinhold of 17 February 1840, in *Briefe, Neue Folge*, pp. 182–183.

26. *Briefe, Neue Folge,* p. 187. Schumann's diploma, in the original Latin and in German translation, is reproduced in Eismann, *Quellenwerk* 1, pp. 116–117.

27. *TB* 2, p. 96; and Eismann, *Quellenwerk* 1, p. 147.

28. Although it has been suggested that some of the fifty pieces Schumann claimed to have begun in his 10 October 1839 letter to Clara may have been songs, this seems to me unlikely. At the time, his creative thinking was still very much centered on piano music. The works he either completed (the G-minor *Fughette,* the *Drei Romanzen*) or projected (Preludes) in the fall and early winter of 1839 were all conceived for the keyboard.

29. See *Jugendbriefe,* p. 309; *Briefe, Neue Folge,* p. 428; and Robert and Clara Schumann, *Briefe einer Liebe,* pp. 262–263. Writing away from the piano will also figure in "the completely new manner" of composition that Schumann adopted in 1845. See Chapter 9, pp. 305–306.

30. See his letter to Kistner of 7 March 1840, in *Briefe, Neue Folge,* pp. 128ff.; and Turchin, "Robert Schumann's Song Cycles," p. 411.

31. Boetticher, *Robert Schumann in seinen Schriften,* pp. 327, 340; Litzmann, *Clara Schumann* 1, p. 411; and *Jugendbriefe,* p. 314.

32. *TB* 3, pp. 95, 114, 155, 158.

33. *Jugendbriefe,* p. 314; and Boetticher, *Robert Schumann in seinen Schriften,* p. 340. On 22 June, Schumann replaced the opening song of the cycle, *Der Frohe Wandersmann* with *In der Fremde.* The former was published over a decade later as the first song in the *Lieder und Gesänge,* op. 77. See also Turchin, "Robert Schumann's Song Cycles," p. 412.

34. *Dein Angesicht* (op. 127, no. 2), *Es leuchtet meine Liebe* (op. 127, no. 3), *Lehn' deine Wang* (op. 142, no. 2), and *Mein Wagen rollet langsam* (op. 142, no. 4). The collections in which these songs first appeared were issued in 1854 and 1858.

35. See *TB* 3, pp. 116 and 700, note 129.

36. See *TB* 2, pp. 97 and 500, note 382.

37. *TB* 3, p. 158.

38. *TB* 3, p. 155.

39. Sams, *Songs of Robert Schumann,* p. 51.

40. Eismann, *Quellenwerk* 1, pp. 124–25.

41. *TB* 2, p. 99.

42. Entry for 21 September, in *TB* 2, pp. 103–4.

43. Entries for mid-November, in *TB* 2, pp. 122–23.

44. Entry for 12 October, in *TB* 2, pp. 112–13. The "nice book" formed the basis for Schumann's *Dichtergarten,* a volume assembled in his last years, and comprised of selected quotations on music from world literature.

45. Entry for 21 September, in *TB* 2, p. 103.

46. Entry for 9 October, in *TB* 2, p. 111.

47. Entry for late September, in *TB* 2, p. 107.

48. Entry for 27 September–4 October, in *TB* 2, p. 107.

49. *Ibid.*

50. Entry for early October, in *TB* 2, p. 110.

51. Entry for early November, in *TB* 2, p. 121. Clara would concertize in Denmark in the early spring of 1842, but without Schumann. See Chapter 7, p. 243.

52. *TB* 2, p. 124.

53. See *TB* 2, pp. 114, 116, 130, 138.

54. *TB* 2, p. 105.

55. *Ibid.,* pp. 122, 129.

56. *Ibid.*, p. 108.

57. See *TB* 2, p. 112; and *TB* 3, p. 164. On the controversial dating of these sketches, which might also be linked to entries in the *Haushaltbücher* of 21–22 January 1841 (*TB* 3, p. 172), see Chapter 6, note 24.

58. His setting of a lied from August Schmidt's musical journal *Orpheus* does not survive. See *TB* 3, p. 164.

59. *TB* 2, p. 127.

60. According to entries in the *Haushaltbücher,* Schumann "composed" and "orchestrated" Heine's *Tragödie* between 27 October and 7 November 1841 (*TB* 3, p. 198). This orchestral version, now lost, probably served as the basis for the version with piano published in 1847 as part of the *Romanzen und Balladen,* op. 64. "Es fiel ein Reif" remains the only text known to have been set by both Robert and Clara, another sign, perhaps, that the latter did not want to engage in open competition with her husband.

61. *TB* 2, p. 134. Cf. his comments in a letter of 13 June 1839: when he and Clara are finally wed, they will publish jointly "so that posterity will regard us as one heart and soul, and be unable to tell what is by you and what is by me." *BrKG* 2, p. 571.

62. Edvard Grieg, "Robert Schumann," *The Century Magazine* 47 (1894), pp. 447–48; quoted in Komar, *Schumann: Dichterliebe,* p. 119.

63. See Turchin, "Schumann's Conversion."

64. Robert and Clara Schumann, *Briefe einer Liebe,* p. 278.

65. *Jugendbriefe,* pp. 309, 314; and *TB* 2, p. 122.

66. *Briefe, Neue Folge,* p. 164.

67. See Eismann, *Quellenwerk* 1, p. 18; and *TB* 1, pp. 105, 146, 155.

68. See *TB* 1, p. 417; and Edler, *Robert Schumann,* p. 213.

69. *Briefe, Neue Folge,* p. 158.

70. "Drei gute Liederhefte," *NZfM* 13 (1840), p. 118.

71. According to Nicholas Marston ("Schumann's Monument," pp. 252–64), Schumann's cultivation of the lied in 1840 should not be viewed as an abandonment of instrumental genres. Specifically, Marston provocatively suggests that *Dichterliebe* was modelled on Beethoven's C♯-minor Quartet, op. 131, and thus represents a sublimation of Schumann's attempt at quartet composition in 1839 (and in 1838 as well).

72. *NZfM* 5 (1836), p. 175.

73. *NZfM* 19 (1843), p. 35.

74. *NZfM* 18 (1843), p. 120.

75. "Drei gute Liederhefte," *NZfM* 13 (1840), p. 119.

76. One gets the impression, from reading Schumann's historical sketch of the lied in an 1843 review of collections by Kossmaly, Helsted, and Franz, that Bach and Beethoven were of greater significance in furthering the aesthetic aims of the genre than Schubert. See *NZfM* 19 (1843), p. 35.

77. "Aus Franz Schubert's Nachlass," *NZfM* 8 (1838), p. 177.

78. *NZfM* 11 (1839), p. 71.

79. *NZfM* 19 (1843), p. 35.

80. "Drei gute Liederhefte," *NZfM* 13 (1840), p. 118.

81. Rufus Hallmark has dealt with the ticklish issue of Schumann's occasional alterations of individual words in his poetic texts, arguing that some of these may have been slips of the pen on Schumann's part (in his setting of Heine's "Du bist wie eine Blume" [*Myrthen,* op. 25, no. 24], for instance, he renders "so hold, und schön, und rein" as "so schön, so rein, und hold") or on the part of an inattentive copyist (Hallmark cites examples from *Dichter-*

liebe and *Frauenliebe und Leben*). See Hallmark, "The Poet Sings," p. 17; "Schumanns Behandlung"; and "Textkritische," pp. 110–12. Although Hallmark has drawn fire for his suggestion that the original text should be restored in these cases (especially when Schumann's autographs transmit it unaltered), this seems to me a perfectly viable editorial practice.

82. Clara's setting of Geibel's "Die stille Lotosblume" (composed in July 1843 and published in her *Sechs Lieder,* op. 13, of 1844) may have been conceived in response to these favorites among the songs that Schumann presented to her as a wedding gift in September 1840. The texts of all three play at the delicate border between purity and sensuousness, and Clara projects this play much as her husband had done: the A♭ tonality of *Die stille Lotosblume* echoes the tonic of *Du bist wie eine Blume* and the key associated with the magical moment in *Die Lotosblume* where the lotus blossom turns her face to her "paramour," the moon; likewise, the pulsing chords and lush chromatic part-writing in Clara's song recall similar features in Schumann's settings.

83. Debussy, "What should one set to music: Good Poetry or Bad Poetry, Free Verse or Prose?" (1911), in *Debussy on Music,* p. 250.

84. Cf., for instance, Eric Sams's comments on the Heine *Liederkreis:* "Schumann is always aware of the pretty colours of a Heine lyric rather than of the sting in the tail." (*Songs of Robert Schumann,* p. 45). More recent writers have begun to recognize that Schumann did have an eye, and an ear, for the sting in Heine's verses. See Dill, "Romantic Irony," p. 184; Geck, *Von Beethoven bis Mahler,* pp. 188–189; Killmayer, "Schumann und seine Dichter," pp. 232–233; and Rosenberg, "Paradox," pp. 10–11.

85. Quoted in Dill, "Romantic Irony," pp. 181–82.

86. Letter of 9 June 1828 to a Dr. Kurrer in Augsburg, in Eismann, *Quellenwerk* 1, p. 35.

87. It is interesting to observe that Clara also took the edge from Heine's irony in the revised version of her setting of "Ihr Bildnis," one of the three songs she presented to Schumann for Christmas 1840. Lost in dreams, the speaker in the poem gazes at his (or her) beloved's portrait, which miraculously begins to take on a life of its own. But the poem ends on a discordant note as the speaker bursts into tears at the realization "that I have lost you!" ("dass ich dich verloren hab'!"). In her first setting, Clara highlighted this bitter twist with a startling deception: the vocal line does not close on the expected tonic, E♭, but rather on E, supported by a biting diminished seventh chord in the piano. When she revised the song for publication in 1843, Clara eliminated the deceptive cadence, thus allowing voice and piano to come together, as expected, on the E♭-major tonic.

88. Robert and Clara Schumann, *Briefe einer Liebe,* p. 262. Cf. also his comments in a letter of 23 February 1840 to Breitkopf and Härtel on the publication of the Heine *Liederkreis:* "You will no doubt agree to a division [of the *Liederkreis*] into two volumes ['Hefte'], though actually I would prefer the collection ['Sammlung'], which forms a whole, to appear in one volume." *Briefe, Neue Folge,* p. 428.

89. See Robert and Clara Schumann, *Briefe einer Liebe,* p. 262; *Briefe, Neue Folge,* p. 428; *TB* 2, p. 132; and Ozawa, *Quellenstudien,* p. 27.

90. *TB* 2, p. 550, note 727. The first documented public performance of Schubert's *Schöne Müllerin* as a cycle came as late as 1856, in a Viennese *Liederabend* organized by the baritone Julius Stockhausen. See Dürr, *Das deutsche Sololied,* pp. 245–246.

91. The term "Liederkreis," though usually translated as "song cycle," would have had additional implications for nineteenth-century devotees of song literature. As Luise Eitel Peake notes, a *Liederkreis* was also a "song club," a group of individuals dedicated to the

cultivation of the art of song. The appearance of the term in the title of a publication would therefore signal, to the potential buyer, the convivial nature of the lieder contained therein. See Peake, "Liederkreis," in *The New Grove,* vol. 10, p. 847.

92. *NZfM* 19 (1843), p. 34.

93. *NZfM* 5 (1836), p. 143.

94. Letter of 31 May 1840, in Robert and Clara Schumann, *Briefe einer Liebe,* p. 279.

95. Carl Loewe's *Frauenliebe* closes with the last poem of Chamisso's lyric cycle, "Traum der eignen Tage," in which the woman finds consolation for her loss in the lives of her children and grandchildren. Composed in 1836 and published the following year, Loewe's song cycle was probably not unknown to Schumann, given the melodic and formal similarities between their respective settings of the first, second, and fourth songs.

96. See Fischer-Dieskau, *Robert Schumann: Words and Music,* p. 89. For a provocative interpretation of Chamisso's poems and Schumann's songs as "*impersonations* of a woman by the voices of a male culture," see Solie, "Whose life?" It may be worth noting that the rhetoric of some of Clara's entries in the marriage diary sometimes approaches that of the female speaker in *Frauenliebe.* Consider the following, written shortly after her wedding in September 1840: "For me, it is as if I loved you more every minute, and I can truly say that I live *only* in you. It is my highest wish that you should be satisfied with me, and if you find that something is amiss, please tell me immediately; won't you do that, my dear husband?" *TB* 2, p. 102. As we have seen, subsequent entries show a considerably less docile side of Clara's personality.

97. Hallmark, *Genesis,* p. 115.

98. For a detailed account of the compositional and publication history of the cycle, see Hallmark, *Genesis;* and "Sketches for *Dichterliebe.*"

99. See Finson, "Intentional Tourist." For a discussion of two further dispositions connected with the genesis of the cycle, the order in which Clara copied out the poems for her future husband's use and the order in which the poems were set to music, see McCreless, "Song Order," pp. 18–19.

100. According to his letter of 7 March 1840 to Kistner, the first volume of *Myrthen* was to include: *Widmung, Die Lotosblume, Jemand, Mutter, Mutter! Lass mich ihm am Busen hangen,* and *Mein Herz ist im Hochland.* When the cycle was published in September of that year, these songs appeared as Nos. 1, 7, 4, 11, 12, and 13, respectively. (See *Briefe, Neue Folge,* p. 429). For an account of the preliminary orderings of the Rückert cycle, see Hallmark, "Rückert Lieder," pp. 8–11.

101. On this point, see Rosen, *Romantic Generation,* pp. 210–12.

102. Eismann, *Quellenwerk* 1, pp. 126–27.

103. Brendel, "Robert Schumann," p. 121.

104. Cf. "Robert Schumanns Gesangkompositionen," *AmZ* 44 (1842), cols. 31–32; and *NZfM* 23 (1845), p. 14.

105. Cf. "Ludwig Berger's gesammelte Werke," *NZfM* 16 (1842), p. 174; and *NZfM* 19 (1843), p. 35.

106. *TB* 2, p. 122.

Chapter 6

1. *BrKG* 2, p. 826.

2. Czerny, *School of Practical Composition* 2, p. 34.

3. *BrKG* 2, p. 345. Cf. also Clara's letter of six days later: "So, my dear, will you come

around to writing for orchestra? Do you find my wish improper? Certainly not. The piano is not sufficient for you; the whole world says so; and in this case the world is certainly correct." *BrKG* 2, p. 351.

4. *TB* 2, p. 155.

5. *Ibid.*, p. 154.

6. See *TB* 2, p. 159, entry of 11–25 April 1841; and *TB* 3, p. 198, entries of 28 October and 4 November 1841.

7. See *TB* 3, pp. 175, 183, 186–88.

8. *Ibid.*, 160.

9. *Ibid.*, pp. 160, 164.

10. *TB* 3, p. 175, entry of 21 February 1841.

11. *TB* 2, p. 151. Cf. also the entries in the *Haushaltbücher* for 22 February ("Feeling unwell. In general, I suffer from an ever sickly strain."), 24 February ("Always melancholy."), and 25 February ("Melancholy. Longing for debauchery."); *TB* 2, p. 175.

12. *TB* 2, p. 167.

13. *Ibid.*, p. 188.

14. *Ibid.*, p. 189.

15. *Ibid.*, p. 156; entry of 22–29 March 1841.

16. *Ibid.*, pp. 155, 191.

17. *Ibid.*, pp. 195–97.

18. *TB* 3, pp. 176, 197.

19. *TB* 2, p. 187, entry of 27 September–24 October 1841.

20. *Ibid.*, p. 167.

21. See *TB* 2, pp. 164, 177.

22. *TB* 2, p. 177, entry of 9–10 July 1841.

23. *Ibid.*, p. 177.

24. There has been some controversy over the dating of these sketches. Both Edler ("Ton und Zyklus," p. 195) and Nauhaus ("Final-Lösungen," pp. 309–10) align them with the references to symphonic "attempts" and "beginnings" in the *Haushaltbücher* for October 1840 (*TB* 3, p. 164). Finson (*Robert Schumann and the Study of Orchestral Composition*, pp. 29–32), however, makes a good case for linking the sketches with entries of 21–22 January 1841 ("Beginning of a symphony in C minor," *TB* 3, p. 172); in an earlier study ("Sketches for Schumann's C minor Symphony," p. 395), Finson opts for the 1840 dating.

25. *TB* 3, p. 195.

26. Indeed, the connections between this movement and Schumann's piano music of the 1830s are set in relief by the similarities between a prominent gesture in the Trio of the Scherzo and a comparable figure in the *Préambule* and *March des Davidsbündler* from *Carnaval*.

27. While the orchestral version is lost, a version for soprano, tenor, and piano was published as the third of the *Romanzen und Balladen,* op. 64 (1847).

28. *TB* 2, p. 177.

29. For references to Schumann's engagement with the *Peri* text, see the diary entry for 18 July–8 August 1841 (*TB* 2, p. 179); and the entries in the *Haushaltbücher* for 4–5 August, 8 August, 22 August, 30 August, 21 December, and 26 December (*TB* 3, pp. 189–92, 202–3).

30. For an overview of this material, see Dusella, "Symphonisches in den Skizzenbüchern."

31. Dahlhaus, *Nineteenth-Century Music,* p. 152.

32. See in particular *Neue Sinfonien für Orchester* (1839), *GS* 1, p. 424. For a thorough analysis of this problem in the light of Schumann's own D-minor symphony, see Mark Evan

Bonds, *After Beethoven: Imperatives of Originality in the Symphony* (forthcoming), Chapter 4.

33. "Die C-dur-Sinfonie von Franz Schubert," *GS* 1, p. 463.

34. See the frequent references to these works in the diaries from 1828 to 1830: *TB* 1, pp. 108, 113, 150–52, 156, 161, 168, 171, 180, 208, and 223.

35. Tovey, *Essays in Musical Analysis* 2, p. 48.

36. Letter to Schumann of 20 January 1843, quoted in Schneider, *Schumann: I. Symphonie*, p. 56.

37. *AmZ* 43 (1841), col. 330.

38. *TB* 3, pp. 172–73.

39. See Rothe, "Neue Documente," pp. 318–20.

40. For a detailed discussion of these revisions, see Finson, *Schumann and the Study of Orchestral Composition*, pp. 69–75, 103.

41. *TB* 2, p. 157.

42. See Fink's review in *AmZ* 43 (1841), col. 330; and August Kahlert's somewhat longer essay in *AmZ* 44 (1842), cols. 265–266.

43. Finscher, " 'Zwischen absoluter und Programmusik," pp. 104–11. See also Mayeda, *Schumanns Weg*, pp. 307–48, *passim*.

44. *GS* 1, p. 84.

45. *GS* 1, p. 65. Schumann made the same point in an 1843 review of Spohr's symphonies 6 and 7 (*GS* 2, p. 129).

46. Review of 1836, *GS* 1, p. 143.

47. *Briefe Neue Folge*, p. 223.

48. *TB* 2, pp. 143, p. 510.

49. The original poem is reproduced in Jansen, *Davidsbündler*, p. 294.

50. See his letter to Wilhelm Taubert of 10 January 1843; *Briefe Neue Folge*, p. 224.

51. Kapp, "Tempo und Charakter," p. 206.

52. See, for instance: Tovey, *Essays in Musical Analysis* 2, p. 46; Chissell, *Schumann*, pp. 95–96; Abraham, "Robert Schumann," p. 852; Finson, *Schumann and the Study of Orchestral Composition*, pp. 63–64; and Schneider, *Schumann: I. Symphonie*, p. 15.

53. See Tovey, *Essays in Musical Analysis* 2, pp. 49–50; Schneider, *Schumann: I. Symphonie*, p. 29; and Dahlhaus, *Nineteenth-Century Music*, p. 159.

54. See Tobel, *Die Formenwelt der klassischen Instrumentalmusik*, p. 78; Edler, *Robert Schumann und seine Zeit*, p. 152; and Roesner, "Studies in Schumann Manuscripts," p. 368. Other possibilities have been raised as well. Finson (*Schumann and the Study of Orchestral Composition*, pp. 42–44) hears the reprise displaced to the middle of the development section, where the winds state the first *Allegro* theme in D major. For Mayeda ("Skizzen Robert Schumanns," pp. 134–35; and *Schumanns Weg*, pp. 369, 375–77), the *tutti* statement of the motto marks an ambivalent point between development and recapitulation.

55. In the autograph full score, only the third phrase (which descends from A to D) is presented as a $\frac{4}{4}$ *Maestoso*.

56. *GS* 1, pp. 59, 67–68.

57. Dörffel, *Geschichte*, p. 96.

58. *AmZ* 50 (1848), col. 129.

59. Dörffel, *Geschichte*, pp. 5–6, 65–66.

60. *TB* 3, pp. 179–81. For a complete account of the work's genesis and Schumann's revisions to the *Finale* in October 1845, see Finson, "Schumann, Popularity," pp. 4–10.

61. See *TB* 3, p. 183 (entry of 8 May: "finished with the '*Suite*' "); and *TB* 2, p. 164 (entry of 10–22 May: "the *Symphonette* is completely orchestrated").

62. *Briefe, Neue Folge*, pp. 434, 539. The reviewer for the *Leipziger Allgemeine Zeitung* (9 December 1841) referred to the work as "Dr. Schumann's Third [!] Symphony"; the review is quoted in Just, *Schumann: Symphonie Nr. 4*, p. 58.

63. *AmZ* 43 (1841), col. 1100.

64. See his letter of 8 January 1842 to Carl Kossmaly in *Briefe Neue Folge*, p. 212.

65. Finson, "Schumann, Popularity," pp. 25–26.

66. *TB* 2, p. 159.

67. *Ibid.*

68. *AmZ* 43 (1841), col. 332. Spohr's letter to Schumann of 20 January 1843 is quoted in Schneider, *Schumann: I. Symphonie*, pp. 55–56.

69. See the entries in the *Haushaltbücher* for 4 May ("A Fantasy—with orchestra—begun"), 6–7 May ("[Work] on scoring of the last movement [of op. 52]"), 8 May ("Finished with the 'Suite' [= op. 52]"), and 13 May ("Worked on the Fantasy); *TB* 3, pp. 181–82.

70. Apparently the 13 August trial run supplied the impetus for minor revisions (see the entry in the *Haushaltbücher* for 20 August; *TB* 3, p. 191). For discussions of the rather complicated genesis of the *Phantasie* and the transformations it underwent when, in June and July 1845, Schumann rounded out his original conception with a slow movement and Rondo (the result being the A-minor Piano Concerto, op. 54), see Frager, "The Manuscript of the Schumann Piano Concerto," p. 83; Boetticher, "Das Entstehen," pp. 45–52; and Boetticher, "Die Frühfassung."

71. *TB* 2, p. 180.

72. Letter to Clara of 26 January 1839; *BrKG* 2, p. 367.

73. Specifically: Weber's F-minor *Konzertstück* for piano and orchestra, op. 79; and Spohr's Violin Concerto No. 8, *in modo di scena cantante*. For a discussion of the form of the *Phantasie* in light of Schumann's critical prescriptions for a concerted work that would conflate sonata-form and multi-movement designs (*NZfM* 4 [1836], p. 123), see Macdonald, "Mit eine eignen," pp. 242, 252–57.

74. Schumann, however, may have influenced the choice of key in the first place. See his letter of 10 January 1833 to Friedrich Wieck; *Jugendbriefe*, p. 201.

75. For a penetrating analysis of the "avant-garde" qualities of Clara's sadly underrated concerto, see Macdonald, "Critical Perception," pp. 24–37.

76. See Janina Klassen's prefatory remarks to her edition of Clara Schumann, *Konzert*, p. vii.

77. See, however, Schumann's poetic account of Clara's A-minor Concerto in *NZfM* 3 (1835), p. 182. As Macdonald points out ("Critical Perception," pp. 27–28), he praised the work's imaginative ideas, but found its overall form wanting in direction and coherence. Perhaps by 1841 his outlook had changed.

78. *TB* 2, p. 141.

79. *Ibid.*, p. 157.

80. *Ibid.*, p. 166.

81. *Ibid.*, pp. 169, 179; *TB* 3, pp. 184, 189, 192–93, 196.

82. *TB* 3, p. 200.

83. *Ibid.*, pp. 579–80.

84. Czerny, *School of Practical Composition* 1, pp. 83–86.

85. See *TB* 3, pp. 579–580, entries of 12, 17, and 19 December 1851. The first page of the autograph full score (1851) originally carried the title: "Phantasie für Orchester." "Phantasie" was subsequently crossed out and replaced with "Symphonie." (See the facsimile in Zlotnik, "Orchestration Revisions," p. 592).

86. Entry of 31 May 1841; *TB* 2, p. 166. Cf. her similar remark of several weeks later:

"Robert is finished with the new symphony in one movement, that is, with the sketches" (*TB* 2, p. 169). The Breitkopf and Härtel edition of 1853 retains the same notion (of a "symphony in one movement") in the somewhat unwieldy title: "Symphonie / No. IV. D moll / Introduction, Allegro, Romanze, Scherzo und Finale / in einem Satz . . . op. 120." See Hofmann, *Erstdrucke,* pp. 260–261.

87. Review quoted in Just, *Schumann: Symphonie Nr. 4,* pp. 58–59. The reviewer arrives at "five parts" by reckoning the slow introduction in his count. On the slight but telling differences between the 1841 version and the Wüllner/Brahms *Bearbeitung* of 1891, see Andreae, "Die vierte Symphonie," pp. 38–39.

88. *AmZ* 43 (1841), cols. 1100–1101.

89. *Ibid.,* col. 1101.

90. *TB* 2, p. 154.

91. *Ibid.,* p. 185, entry of 17 September 1841.

Chapter 7

1. See the entries for 30 January, 6–8, 10–12, and 14 February in *TB* 3, pp. 206–7.

2. *TB* 2, p. 211.

3. *Ibid.,* p. 226.

4. See Litzmann, *Clara Schumann* 2, p. 41; and *TB* 2, p. 203.

5. *TB* 2, p. 206.

6. *Ibid.,* pp. 202–3, 206–7.

7. Entry for 28 February, *TB* 2, p. 209.

8. *TB* 2, p. 209.

9. Entry for early October 1842, *TB* 2, pp. 249–50.

10. Entry of 17 February 1843, *TB* 2, p. 255.

11. *TB* 2, p. 525, note 536.

12. Entry for 16 August 1842, *TB* 2, p. 240. Clara did oblige the guests at the Majorin Serre's the next evening with a rendition of one of the *Novelletten* (*TB* 2, p. 243).

13. Entry for 12 August, *TB* 2, p. 238.

14. *TB* 2, 250.

15. *Ibid.,* p. 255.

16. *Major Writings of Germaine de Staël,* p. 318.

17. *TB* 2, p. 206.

18. *Ibid.,* p. 212.

19. *TB* 3, p. 210.

20. See the entries for 20 March, 5 April, 25 May, and 16 June in *TB* 3, pp. 209–10, 215, 217.

21. *TB* 2, p. 250; *TB* 3, p. 226.

22. *Ibid.,* p. 255.

23. *TB* 3, p. 232.

24. *TB* 2, p. 217.

25. *Ibid.,* p. 216.

26. *Ibid.,* p. 232.

27. *Ibid.,* p. 218.

28. *Ibid.,* pp. 240–242.

29. Entry for late July, *TB* 2, p. 233.

30. *TB* 2, p. 251.

31. *Ibid.*

32. See Kohlhase, *Kammermusik Robert Schumanns* 1, p. 7.

33. *Jugendbriefe,* p. 280.

34. *Briefe, Neue Folge,* p. 118.

35. *GS* 1, pp. 333–47.

36. See his letter to Clara of 13 June 1839, in *BrKG* 2, pp. 570–71. Schumann's sketches, limited to the openings of the two works, are transcribed in Marston, "Schumann's Monument," pp. 250–51.

37. *TB* 3, pp. 216–20.

38. *Ibid.,* pp. 225–33.

39. Dickinson, "The Chamber Music," in Abraham, *Schumann: A Symposium,* p. 140.

40. *Briefe, Neue Folge,* p. 450.

41. "Streichquartette" (1842), *GS* 2, p. 75.

42. "Zweite Quartettmorgen" (1838), *GS* 1, p. 338–39.

43. "Erster Quartettmorgen" (1838), *GS* 1, p. 335; see also "Streichquartette," *GS* 2, p. 75.

44. "Dritter Quartettmorgen" (1838), *GS* 1, pp. 341–42.

45. "Preisquartett von Julius Schapler" (1842), *GS* 2, p. 380.

46. "Streichquartette," *GS* 2, pp. 75–76.

47. See the entry in the *Haushaltbücher* for 29 May: "Began fugues with Clara." (*TB* 3, p. 215). According to Boetticher (*Robert Schumann: Einführung,* p. 639), the volume of fugal sketches ("Fugengeschichten") that dates from about this time may have been intended as a *Lehrbuch* for Clara.

48. "Streichquartette," *GS* 2, p. 75.

49. *TB* 2, pp. 200, 220, 229; *TB* 3, pp. 210, 213.

50. See Sisman, *Haydn and the Classical Variation,* pp. 150–63; and "Haydn's Hybrid Variations," pp. 509–515.

51. A more complete account of the rationale for the form is provided in my "From 'Concertante Rondo' to 'Lyric Sonata': A Commentary on Brahms's Reception of Mozart," in *Brahms Studies,* ed. David Brodbeck (Lincoln & London: University of Nebraska Press, 1994), pp. 115–19.

52. See, e.g., Schnebel's discussion of the first movement of Opus 41, no. 3, in "Rück-ungen—Ver-rückungen," pp. 70–71.

53. *TB* 2, p. 253.

54. *TB* 3, p. 212.

55. "Leipziger Musikleben 1837/38," in *GS* 1, p. 380.

56. See "Preisquartett von Julius Schapler" (1842), *GS* 2, p. 72; and "Streichquartette" (1842), *GS* 2, p. 74.

57. "Preisquartett von Julius Schapler," *GS* 2, p. 71.

58. *TB* 2, p. 249.

59. Roesner, "Schumann's 'Parallel' Forms," pp. 265–278. For an alternate account of the finale of Opus 41, no. 3, see Newcomb, "Schumann and Late Eighteenth-Century Narrative Strategies," pp. 170–74; and Kohlhase, *Kammermusik* 1, pp. 158–61, and 2, pp. 69–74. Both writers view the movement as a kind of rondo form; while the finale does feature a recurrent, though altered refrain, the rondo interpretation does not address the larger symmetries of the "parallel" form.

60. See Schumann's brief description of the event in *TB* 2, p. 255.

61. *AmZ* 49 (1847), col. 230.

62. As Schumann put it ("Zweite Quartettmorgen" [1838], *GS* 1, p. 336), the four mem-

bers of a string quartet, unlike the members of a symphony orchestra, "constitute their own public." The same idea serves as the foundation for Adorno's analysis of the changing social function of chamber music in the nineteenth and twentieth centuries; see his *Introduction to the Sociology of Music,* pp. 85–86.

63. *TB* 2, p. 297.

64. Schumann's piano quintet figured on one of Vieuxtemps's matinées in St. Petersburg; see the brief notice in *AmZ* 50 (1848), col. 23.

65. See his letter of 14 December 1847 to Raimund Härtel: "The published parts of such works [Opus 41, nos. 1–3] seem to me like a man split into four segments: one can't know how to grasp or seize hold of him. . . . There are seldom four musicians who, without a score, would know how to understand the difficult [motivic/contrapuntal] combinations of musical works like these even after several play-throughs. What is the result? The players set the pieces aside after a cursory reading. With a score in hand they could more easily do justice to the composer. Therefore, I'm certain that a published score would help the sale of the parts." Schumann had his way. On 9 October of the following year he wrote to Härtel, thanking him for publication of the scores for the Opus 41 quartets. See *Briefe Neue Folge,* pp. 452, 456.

66. "Trios für Pianoforte mit Begleitung" (1840), *GS* 1, p. 497.

67. *GS* 1, p. 501.

68. See the review of a 12 April 1844 performance in St. Petersburg, in *AmZ* 46 (1844), cols. 332–333. For a succinct account of the Quintet's warm reception at both private soirées and public concerts during the late winter and early spring of 1844, see also *TB* 2, pp. 288–89, 297, 337.

69. *AmZ* 49 (1847), col. 553.

70. See Wagner's letter to Schumann of 25 February 1843; quoted in Edler, *Robert Schumann,* p. 170.

71. As Kohlhase points out, the revisions were probably motivated by suggestions from the members of Ferdinand David's quartet, the first interpreters of Schumann's chamber music for strings. See "Die klanglichen und strukturellen Revisionen," pp. 53–77.

72. See Westrup, "The Sketch for Schumann's Piano Quintet," pp. 369–370. The sketches for the discarded *Scena* are transcribed in Kohlhase, *Kammermusik* 3, p. 29.

73. See Kohlhase, *Kammermusik* 1, p. 227, and 2, p. 79. A transcription of the projected *Trio* appears in 3, pp. 24–26.

74. *AmZ* 46 (1844), cols. 148–49.

75. Tovey, *Essays in Musical Analysis: Chamber Music,* p. 151.

76. Other examples include the recurrence of the slow, descending scalar segment from the beginning of the first movement's development section as a transition into the second movement's central *Agitato.* For more complete accounts of the inter-movement thematic relationships in the Piano Quintet, see Conrad, "Zu Schumanns Klavierquintett," pp. 343–56; and Kohlhase, "Robert Schumanns Klavierquintett," pp. 164–68.

77. Kohlhase's (*Kammermusik* 1, pp. 162–66) and Edler's (*Robert Schumann,* p. 171) classification of the movement as an unusual sonata-rondo form ignores the larger parallelisms that make for a more tightly integrated structure. Schumann's sketches for the movement (which correspond closely to the final version up to m. 137, but then present a series of empty bars with only occasional motivic entries until the equivalent of m. 212 in the final version) likewise support the notion of a "parallel" form. See Westrup, "Sketch for Schumann's Piano Quintet," p. 371.

78. The effect of this gesture of return precisely reverses the course of Schumann's com-

positional process; as Kohlhase points out (*Kammermusik* 1, p. 51), the first movement of the quintet was probably sketched after the other movements of the work. For a discussion of the Bachian quality of the reprise (and of the Quintet as a whole), see Wollenberg, "Schumann's Piano Quintet."

79. "Trios für Pianoforte mit Begleitung," *GS* 1, p. 498.

80. Dahlhaus, *Ludwig van Beethoven*, p. 203.

81. As Dadelsen has pointed out ("Schumann und die Musik Bachs," p. 54), Schumann's incorporation of fugal textures into the works of his Chamber Music Year generally owes more to Classical than to Baroque, Bachian models.

82. "Brief über den Roman," from *Gespräch über die Poesie* (1800), *KFSA* 2, p. 333.

83. *TB* 3, p. 231.

84. *Briefe, Neue Folge*, p. 229.

85. "Trios für Pianoforte mit Begleitung," *GS* 1, p. 498.

86. See Brendel's "Robert Schumann," p. 121; and his review of Schumann's Second Symphony in *NZfM* 25 (1846), p. 181.

87. Entries of 7 April and 27 June 1842, in *TB* 3, pp. 211 and p. 218.

88. Mayeda, *Robert Schumanns Weg*, pp. 518–21.

89. See Kohlhase, *Kammermusik* 1, p. 51; and "Robert Schumanns Klavierquintett," pp. 151–152. The tragedy is foreshadowed at the beginning of the first movement's development section, where the idea first occurs. For a comparison of the opening idea of the Piano Quintet with material from Prelude 7 of the First Book of Bach's *WTC*, see Wollenberg, "Schumann's Piano Quintet," pp. 300–302.

90. Kohlhase, "Robert Schumanns Klavierquintett," pp. 157–163.

91. "Streichquartette" (1842), *GS* 2, p. 76.

92. "Trios für Pianoforte mit Begleitung," *GS* 1, pp. 498–99. See also Schumann's comparable remarks on Léon de St. Lubin's allusions to Mozart's Symphony 40 and Rossini's *Guillaume Tell* Overture in his E♭-major string quintet, op. 88 ("Sechster Quartettmorgen" [1838], *GS* 1, p. 346).

93. "Streichquartette," *GS* 2, p. 74.

Chapter 8

1. *TB* 2, p. 267.

2. "Neue Oratorien," *GS* 2, p. 3.

3. *TB* 3, pp. 236–37; and *TB* 2, p. 255.

4. *Briefe, Neue Folge*, pp. 435–36, 539 (note 530). Apart from the obvious scoring differences, the two versions diverge on a number of points. The two-piano setting, for instance, lacks the transition between Variations 5 and 6. Likewise, the second version features a much more compact coda than its earlier counterpart. These changes were probably motivated by the new scoring medium: the transitional passage and the original coda represent two of the relatively few spots where the 'celli and horn come into their own.

5. *Briefe, Neue Folge*, p. 436.

6. From his *Davidsbündlerbrief*; quoted in Nauhaus, "Schumanns Peri," p. 145.

7. *TB* 2, p. 269.

8. *AmZ* 46 (1844), cols. 303–4.

9. Wieck's first visit ran from 17 to 22 March. He returned to Leipzig on 19 May (with his whole family) and remained for over a week, devoting most of his energies to Clara's

half-sister Marie, who like Clara before her was being primed for a career as concert pianist. According to an entry in the marriage diary, the Schumanns had scarcely any contact with Wieck, though he was still the source of some annoyance; as Clara put it: "His frightful agitation, [not to mention] the restlessness of his body and spirit alike, won't allow him—or those around him—to enjoy life peacefully." At the beginning of August, Wieck and Marie visited with Robert and Clara for a day. See *TB* 2, pp. 260, 264, 268. Wieck's letter to Schumann of 16 December is quoted in Eismann, *Quellenwerk* 1, p. 136.

   10. *TB* 2, p. 258.
   11. See *TB* 2, p. 254. The *Lektionsplan* for the conservatory appeared in *NZfM* 18 (17 April 1843), p. 126; other instructors listed here include: Henriette Bünau-Grabau (voice), Moritz Klengel (violin), F. Böhme (voice and choral music), Ernst Wenzel (piano), and Louis Plaidy (piano).
   12. Entry for 5 April 1843, in *TB* 2, p. 261.
   13. *TB* 2, p. 271.
   14. See Meissner, *Geschichtsrezeption*, p. 100.
   15. *TB* 2, p. 259.
   16. *Ibid.*, p. 257.
   17. See *TB* 2, p. 256; and *TB* 3, pp. 236–38.
   18. Berlioz, *Memoirs*, p. 285.
   19. *TB* 2, p. 256. Clara did not share her husband's generally positive feelings about Berlioz as man or artist: "He is cold, aloof, sullen—a musician like myself can't warm to him. Robert is of another opinion and has become very fond of him. As for his music, I agree with Robert; it is full of interesting and ingenious things, but I can't keep from saying that it doesn't give me much pleasure, and I have no desire to hear any more of it. Pardon me, my dear Robert, but why shouldn't I express my true feelings [?]" *TB* 2, pp. 258–59.
   20. See Nauhaus, "Schumanns *Peri*," pp. 134–35; and Edler, *Schumann*, pp. 232.
   21. See *TB* 3, p. 223, 282 (according to an entry in the *Haushaltbücher*, Schumann returned to Immermann's text on 15 June 1846); and Schumann's letter of 1 September 1842 to Kossmaly, *Briefe, Neue Folge*, p. 220.
   22. *TB* 2, p. 270. In the same entry Schumann listed two possibilities for opera texts: "Der verschleierte Prophet v. Khorassan" (The Veiled Prophet of Khorassan), the first of the verse tales from Moore's *Lalla Rookh* and "Till Eulenspiegel." Anton von Zuccalmaglio was Schumann's librettist of choice for both projects, neither of which materialized.
   23. Letter of 5 May 1843; *Briefe, Neue Folge*, pp. 226–227.
   24. See *TB* 3, pp. 189–92, 202–4; and Wasielewski, *Robert Schumann*, p. 327. For an excellent discussion of these and other issues pertinent to the text, see Nauhaus, "Schumanns *Peri*," pp. 134–39.
   25. See, however, the brief reference for 21 September 1842 in the *Haushaltbücher.* "Dr. [Friedrich Wilhelm] Lindner [professor of philosophy at Leipzig University] mit Peri" (*TB* 3, p. 225). Nauhaus reports that Schumann's copy of the *Peri* text (now in the Heinrich-Heine-Institut, Düsseldorf) contains two important musical notations: a nine-bar melody sketch for the orchestral introduction to No. 1, and the opening of the ensuing alto solo, *Vor Eden's Thor.* Unfortunately, neither of these can be dated with any certainty. See Nauhaus, "Schumanns *Peri*," p. 139.
   26. *TB* 3, p. 238.
   27. *TB* 2, p. 260.
   28. *TB* 3, p. 248; *TB* 2, pp. 261, 263.
   29. *TB* 2, p. 263. See also *TB* 2, p. 265; and *TB* 3, pp. 251–52.
   30. While 16 June is given as the date of completion in both the marriage diary (*TB* 2,

p. 265) and the *Haushaltbücher* (*TB* 3, p. 254) the last page of the autograph score includes the following inscription: "Completed, with thanks, on 17 June 1843 in Leipzig/Dedicated to my dear Clara/Rob. Schumann" (*TB* 3, p. 729, note 375). Between 18 and 22 July, and again on 1 September, Schumann subjected the score to an overall check ("Durchsicht") (*TB* 3, pp. 256, 351). And finally, on 20 September he reworked and expanded the last half of the closing chorus (No. 9) of Part I (*TB* 3, p. 353, and p. 741, note 475). The piano-vocal score (largely prepared by Clara during the summer and fall of 1843), together with the solo and choral parts, was issued by September 1844; the full score appeared in January 1845 under the imprint of Breitkopf and Härtel.

31. See the entries for 8 and 9 March, 12 May, 26 June, and 7 July in *TB* 3, pp. 239, 251, 254, 255.

32. *TB* 2, pp. 265–66.

33. See the unsigned reviews of the December 1843 Leipzig performances in: *AmZ* 45 (1843), col. 953; and *Leipziger Zeitung* (7 December 1843), quoted in Nauhaus, "Schumanns Peri," p. 144. Cf. also Dörffel, *Gewandhausconcerte*, pp. 107–8 (quotations from positive accounts by Moritz Hauptmann and Julius Becker); *AmZ* 46 (1844), col. 28 (unsigned review of the 23 December 1843 Dresden performance); Brendel, "Robert Schumann," p. 121; [J. C. Lobe], review in *AmZ* 49 (1847), col. 144. The most extensive review of the *Peri* to appear during Schumann's lifetime was written by Eduard Krüger, a frequent contributor to the *Neue Zeitschrift* who visited with the composer and his wife in July 1843, just after the oratorio was completed, and appeared in four installments (20 and 27 August, 3 and 10 September 1845) in the *Allgemeine musikalische Zeitung*. (See *AmZ* 47 [1845], cols. 561–70, 585–89, 606–11, 617–622). For an analysis of Krüger's review, which touches on matters of genre, textual content, melodic style, and form, see my "Schumann's 'New Genre for the Concert Hall'."

34. *TB* 2, p. 275.

35. Wasielewski, *Robert Schumann*, p. 340.

36. For an account of the 4 and 11 December performances of *Peri*, see Dörffel, *Gewandhausconcerte*, pp. 107–108. On the episode with the troublesome tenor soloist, see the review by O[swald] L[orenz] in *AmZ* 45 (1843), col. 955; Dörffel, *Gewandhausconcerte*, p. 216; and *Briefe, Neue Folge*, p. 515, note 293.

37. The poem, entitled "Die Perle," and dated 4 December 1843, is reproduced in Boetticher, ed., *Briefe und Gedichte*, pp. 183–84.

38. Nauhaus, "Schumanns Peri," p. 133, note 1.

39. See the entry for 30 December 1847 in *TB* 3, p. 449; and Schumann's letter of 1 January 1848 to Ferdinand Hiller, in *Briefe, Neue Folge*, p. 280.

40. With fifty-three documented performances (compared to the *Peri*'s fifty), only the First Symphony, op. 38, was given more frequently during the composer's lifetime. See Nauhaus, "Schumanns Peri," p. 133.

41. Dahlhaus, "Zur Problematik der musikalischen Gattungen," p. 857.

42. Letter of 20 February 1847, in *Briefe, Neue Folge*, p. 267.

43. Liszt, "Robert Schumann," pp. 169–70.

44. Quoted in Nauhaus, "Schumanns Peri," p. 136. See also the framing narrative to "Paradise and the Peri," in Moore, *Poetical Works*, p. 406.

45. de Ford, *Thomas Moore*, p. 42. The poet himself cast the Peri tale in an ironic light through the caustic remarks of the Great Chamberlain Fadladeen, who says in the prose narrative following the poem: "it is a waste of time and patience to dwell longer upon a thing so incurably frivolous." See Moore, *Poetical Works*, p. 413.

46. Letter of 19 June 1843 to Johannes Verhulst, in *Briefe, Neue Folge*, p. 230. Cf. Flech-

sig's letter to Schumann of 8 August 1841, in Boetticher, ed., *Briefe und Gedichte*, p. 57.

47. *NZfM* 19 (1843), p. 192; and *AmZ* 46 (1844), col. 28.

48. *Briefe, Neue Folge*, p. 228. The reference to "heitre Menschen" is to be understood in relation to a passage from Goethe's *Maximen und Reflexionen* that Schumann had copied into his *Mottosammlung;* Goethe differentiates between "heilig" (sacred) and "profan" (secular) music, the defining characteristic of the latter being "Heiterkeit" (cheerfulness). On this point, see Probst, *Robert Schumanns Oratorien*, pp. 15–16.

49. The projected oratorio *Luther*, which occupied Schumann in the early 1850s, was to be "suitable for both the church and the concert hall"; see his letter to Richard Pohl of 14 February 1851; *Briefe, Neue Folge*, p. 336.

50. Peter Ostwald sees in the "ambisexual Peri" a "lovely symbol of Schumann's guilty innocence." (*Schumann*, p. 182). As provocative as this hypothesis may be, it does not square well with the facts. As shown in the Introduction, the argument for Schumann's sexual ambivalence rests on very flimsy evidence indeed. As for the Peri, "she/he" answers to the feminine pronoun *sie* throughout Schumann's text.

51. See Schumann's reviews of Marschner's *Klänge aus Osten* (1840; *GS* 2, pp. 41–42); Hiller's *Die Zerstörung Jerusalems* and Sobolewski's *Der Erlöser* (1841, *GS* 2, pp. 3–10); and Loewe's *Johann Huss* (1842; *GS* 2, pp. 99–105).

52. See the entries for 1–2 February 1843 in *TB* 3, p. 236.

53. Cf. Kapp, *Studien zum Spätwerk*, p. 264, note 1512.

54. *GS* 2, p. 42.

55. Cf. *GS* 2, pp. 41–42, and Schumann's letter of 20 February 1847, in *Briefe, Neue Folge*, p. 267. Brendel did not fail to recognize the innovative structure of the *Peri*; in a review of Schumann's *Genoveva*, he called attention to the oratorio as a milestone on the way toward an ideal dramatic form in which "each act [of an opera] *proceeds with the uninterrupted flow of a Finale*"; see *NZfM* 33 (1850), p. 3.

56. It is interesting to note that Wagner also toyed with the idea of setting Moore's poem to music. He abandoned the project because, as he wrote to Schumann in a letter of 21 September 1843: "I couldn't find the proper form in which to render it [Moore's *Peri*] and congratulate you on having succeeded in doing so." Quoted from Wagner, *Sämtliche Briefe* 2, p. 326.

57. For a discussion and transcription of Schumann's structural plan, see Nauhaus, "Schumanns *Peri*," pp. 135–37, 146–48.

58. "Erster Quartettmorgen," *GS* 1, pp. 335.

59. Brendel, "Robert Schumann," p. 115.

60. See Introduction, pp. 15–16.

61. I use the term, after the German *Literaturoper*, to mean a musico-dramatic work based on a practically unaltered poetic text not originally intended for musical setting. Debussy's *Pélleas et Mélisande* (on Maeterlinck's play) and Berg's *Wozzeck* (on Büchner's fragmentary drama) are prime examples.

62. In a letter of June 1848 to Friedrich Whistling, Schumann himself noted that both the musical and poetic content of the *Schlussszene* of *Faust* were prefigured in the corresponding scene from the *Peri; Briefe, Neue Folge*, p. 454. Liszt was among the first writers to point out the relationships between the *Peri* and Schumann's later works involving chorus and orchestra (the *Faust* music; the *Manfred* music, op. 115; the *Requiem für Mignon*, op. 98b; and *Der Rose Pilgerfahrt*, op. 112); see Liszt, "Robert Schumann," pp. 169–70. Cf. also Edler, *Schumann*, p. 235; and Probst, *Schumanns Oratorien*, pp. 33–34, 130.

Chapter 9

1. *TB* 2, p. 269.

2. Apparently Clara had enlisted Mendelssohn's aid; in a letter of 9 December 1843 she thanked him for bringing her husband round to an agreement on the tour. See Litzmann, *Clara Schumann* 2, pp. 84–85.

3. *TB* 3, p. 360.

4. *TB* 2, p. 269.

5. Clara's programs mixed the usual virtuosic fare (Weber's F-minor *Konzertstück;* Thalberg's Fantasies on themes from Rossini's *Mosé in Egitto, La Donna del Lago,* and *Semiramide;* Henselt's Variations on themes from Donizetti's *L'elisir d'amore;* and Liszt's paraphrase of Donizetti's *Lucia* and his transcription of Schubert's *Erlkönig*) with more serious works, including sonatas (or sonata movements) by Scarlatti and Beethoven (Opus 27, no. 2; Opus 31, no. 2; Opus 57), Mendelssohn's G-minor Piano Concerto, op. 25, and selections from her husband's *Fhantasiestücke,* op. 12, and *Romanzen,* op. 28.

6. Entry of 8 February 1844, in *TB* 2, p. 323.

7. See the description of Riga's Hotel Stadt London in *TB* 2, p. 321.

8. *TB* 2, p. 322. The journeymen's society of Riga (the "Schwarzhäupter") had reserved the hall in which Clara was scheduled to play for cleaning on the day of her concert.

9. See the entry for 16 March 1844, in *TB* 2, p. 337.

10. See *TB* 2, pp. 311–12; and *TB* 3, p. 268. The bulk of this sum derived from four concerts in St. Petersburg (the last of which brought in over a thousand thalers) and three in Moscow. We can get a sense for the buying power of the total intake from the Russian tour by keeping in mind that a year's rent in Dresden would cost the Schumanns 200 thalers; see the quarterly entries from 1845 in *TB* 3, pp. 384, 392, 401, and 410.

11. Entries for 4 March, 5 March, and 26 March 1844, in *TB* 2, pp. 330–31, 344.

12. Entry for [10] April 1844, in *TB* 2, p. 351.

13. *TB* 2, p. 352.

14. Entry for 18 April 1844, in *TB* 2, p. 356.

15. *TB* 2, p. 352.

16. Entry for 7 February 1844, in *TB* 2, p. 323.

17. *TB* 2, p. 309.

18. *Ibid.,* p. 324.

19. *Ibid.,* p. 327.

20. *Ibid.,* pp. 332, 353.

21. Entry for 8 March 1844, in *TB* 2, p. 333.

22. Entry of 4 May 1844, in *TB* 2, p. 366. See also the description of the "abominable liturgical singing" that Schumann heard at the Kremlin, in *TB* 2, p. 359.

23. *TB* 2, pp. 341, 365–66.

24. *Ibid.,* p. 341.

25. Entry for 18 March 1844, in *TB* 2, p. 338.

26. Entry for 7 March 1844, in *TB* 2, p. 333.

27. *TB* 2, pp. 309, 290.

28. *Ibid.,* pp. 297, 365.

29. Entry for 7 February 1844, in *TB* 2, p. 322.

30. Entry for 8 March 1844, in *TB* 2, p. 333.

31. Entry for 20 March 1844, in *TB* 2, p. 339.

32. Entries of 23 and 24 March 1844, in *TB* 2, pp. 342–43.

33. Entries of 17 and 24 March 1844, in *TB* 2, pp. 337, 342–43.

34. Entries of 28 April and 1 May 1844, in *TB* 2, pp. 360, 363.

35. Entries of 27 and 28 April 1844, in *TB* 2, p. 360.

36. Entries of 21–29 February 1844, in *TB* 2, pp. 283–84, 328–29.

37. See *TB* 2, pp. 335, 337.

38. *TB* 2, pp. 293, 354.

39. *Ibid.,* pp. 300, 357.

40. Litzmann, *Clara Schumann* 2, pp. 74–75.

41. Eismann, *Quellenwerk* 1, p. 144.

42. *TB* 2, p. 339.

43. Entry of February 1843, *TB* 2, p. 255.

44. From *On Literature* (1800), in *Major Writings of Germaine de Staël,* p. 201.

45. *TB* 2, p. 294.

46. *Ibid.,* p. 356.

47. Entries of 25 and 27 February 1844, in *TB* 2, pp. 284, 329.

48. Entry of 13 March 1844, in *TB* 2, p. 287.

49. The poems date from late April 1844; see *TB* 2, pp. 355–56, 359. The two poems to Napoleon mentioned in Clara's diary entry of 16 April (*TB* 2, p. 355) comprise sections III and IV of the four-part *Die Glocke von Iwan Welikii;* a fifth poem on the French retreat from Moscow *(Die Franzosen vor Moskau)* is thematically related to the Napoleon poems, but eschews references to the imposing bell tower at the Kremlin. All are reproduced in *TB* 2, pp. 375–86. For translations, see Nauhaus, *Marriage Diaries,* trans. Ostwald, pp. 312–27.

50. Ostwald, *Schumann,* p. 188.

51. *TB* 2, p. 375.

52. *Ibid.,* p. 376.

53. *Ibid.*

54. *TB* 2, p. 377.

55. *Ibid.,* p. 379.

56. *Ibid.*

57. *TB* 2, pp. 380–83.

58. See the entry for 16 March 1846, in *TB* 3, p. 416. At about this time Schumann also began to keep a record of his intimate life with Clara, designating each sexual encounter with a diagonally drawn "F" in the *Haushaltbücher* and his travel diaries. The first of these indications appears on 13 April 1846, the last on 14 February 1854. The Schumanns' sex life fell into a remarkably consistent rhythm. Apart from periods of abstinence just before and after Clara gave birth, they generally had intercourse twice a week.

59. *TB* 2, pp. 397–402, 411, 421.

60. *TB* 3, p. 366.

61. *Ibid.,* p. 245.

62. Ostwald, *Schumann,* p. 196.

63. For a facsimile and diplomatic transcription (by Gerd Nauhaus) of the *Lektürebüchlein,* see Appel and Hermstrüwer, eds., *Robert Schumann und die Dichter,* pp. 52–85. The "Zeitungmaterial für spätere Zeit" appears on pp. 54–57.

64. See the entries for 1–3 September 1846, in *TB* 2, p. 290.

65. See *TB* 3, pp. 347, 348, 426. Collected as a *Theaterbüchlein* for the years 1847–1850, the essays appear in *GS* 2, pp. 160–63.

66. *Briefe, Neue Folge,* p. 244.

67. See Litzmann, *Clara Schumann* 2, p. 76.

68. See the entries for 19 October, and 22–24 November 1845, in *TB* 3, pp. 406–7.

69. Entry for 17 March 1846, in *TB* 2, p. 398.

70. *TB* 2, p. 244.

71. Litzmann, *Clara Schumann* 2, p. 104.

72. *TB* 3, p. 384.

73. *Ibid.*, p. 244.

74. See Litzmann, *Clara Schumann* 1, p. 85; Wasielewski, *Robert Schumann*, p. 110; and my commentary in Chapter 3, pp. 110.

75. *TB* 3, pp. 364, 369–71.

76. Litzmann, *Clara Schumann* 2, p. 76.

77. *Briefe, Neue Folge*, p. 244. See also the letter of 25 November 1844 to Ferdinand David (quoted on p. 517, note 312), where Schumann complains that there is "so little music to hear" in Dresden; "but this suits by situation, since I'm still suffering from nerves, and everything exhausts me."

78. *TB* 3, pp. 376–78.

79. *Ibid.*, p. 379.

80. Entry for 6 March 1844, in *TB* 3, p. 382.

81. *TB* 3, p. 393.

82. See *TB* 2, pp. 393–94.

83. Entry for 6 March 1846, in *TB* 3, p. 415.

84. See the entries for 27–28 March 1845, in *TB* 3, pp. 383–84.

85. Entry of 12 August 1846, in *TB* 3, p. 287.

86. Helbig's account is quoted in Wasielewski, *Schumann*, pp. 351–353. Schumann's anxiety as regards heights mixed fear with awe. While on holiday with Clara in the Harz region (10–18 September 1844), he made his way up the Ramberg and to the tower at its summit "with apprehension." At the same time he was deeply moved by the breathtaking view from the mountain-situated Schloss Falkenstein. He and Clara were so taken with the whole area that they contemplated a return trip for the following year. See *TB* 2, p. 387–88.

87. *TB* 2, p. 396.

88. See *TB* 2, p. 401. The examination took place on 1 June 1846 in Maxen.

89. Entry for 11 September 1844, in *TB* 2, p. 387.

90. Entry for 13 September 1844 (Clara's birthday), in *TB* 2, p. 388.

91. "Wie sie schnarchen, wie sie blasen!" See *TB* 2, p. 389. The scene from Goethe's play is set in the Harz mountains.

92. *TB* 2, pp. 389 and 547 (note 695).

93. See Foucault, *Madness and Civilization*, pp. 166–72.

94. *TB* 3, p. 371.

95. *Ibid.*, pp. 377–78.

96. Wasielewski, *Schumann*, p. 352.

97. See *TB* 3, pp. 391–98.

98. Entry for 15 July 1846, in *TB* 3, p. 405.

99. *TB* 3, pp. 285–86.

100. *Ibid.*, pp. 285–86, 288.

101. Cf. Wasielewski, *Schumann*, p. 351; and *Briefe, Neue Folge*, p. 244.

102. See Wasielewski, *Schumann*, p. 353; and *TB* 3, p. 416.

103. Entry for 12 June 1845, in *TB* 2, p. 391.

104. Schnebel, "Rückungen—Ver-rückungen," pp. 71–72.

105. Dadelsen, "Schumann und Bach," p. 56.

106. Walsh, "Schumann and the Organ," p. 743.

107. According to the *Haushaltbücher*, Schumann's work on *Corsar* extended from 28 June to mid-July; see *TB* 3, pp. 366–67. The surviving fragments, edited by Joachim Draheim

(Wiesbaden: Breitkopf and Härtel, 1983), include a Chorus of Corsairs, an orchestral interlude (featuring Schumann's first experiment with melodrama), and the beginnings of an aria for Conrad, the opera's hero.

108. *TB* 3, p. 364.

109. *Ibid.*, pp. 378, 408; see also Schumann's letter to Mendelssohn of 18 November, in *Briefe, Neue Folge*, p. 255.

110. See *TB* 2, p. 404; and Appel and Hermsträuwer, eds., *Robert Schumann und die Dichter*, p. 63.

111. The librettist for the project was to have been Julius Hammer, who may also have been tapped for the King Arthur opera. See *TB* 3, pp. 382 and 749 (note 528); and *TB* 2, p. 399.

112. *TB* 3, p. 384. Schumann noted the idea again in an entry in the *Kurztagebuch* for 1 April 1846; see *TB* 2, p. 400.

113. *Ibid.*, pp. 364–65.

114. *Ibid.*, pp. 368, 376.

115. In a list compiled during the summer of 1845, Schumann did, however, number the setting of the closing scene from *Faust* among his recently completed works; *TB* 2, p. 395.

116. *Briefe, Neue Folge*, pp. 517 (note 313) and 244.

117. *Ibid.*, p. 454.

118. *TB* 2, p. 402. Cf. Schumann's advice to Carl van Bruyck in a letter of 10 May 1852: "Accustom yourself . . . to conceiving music freely from your imagination, without the aid of the piano; only in this way are its inner wellsprings revealed, thus appearing in ever greater clarity and purity." *Briefe, Neue Folge*, p. 356.

119. Unfortunately, Schumann never wrote the article "On Composing away from and at the Piano," one of a number of titles listed under "Journal material for a later time" in the *Lektürebüchlein*. See Appel and Hermsträuwer, eds., *Schumann und die Dichter*, p. 57.

120. *TB* 3, pp. 381, 382.

121. Published by Boetticher as *Briefe und Gedichte*.

122. *TB* 3, p. 387.

123. *Ibid.* Charles Rosen suggests that the invention of this instrument was stimulated by nineteenth-century musicians' practice of trying out Bach's organ works at the piano. (See Rosen, *Romantic Generation*, p. 668.)

124. Clara was to have been the featured performer at the inaugural concert of the Dresden series, but was precluded from appearing due to poor health. On Schumann's behalf, Wieck travelled to Leipzig to retain Joachim as substitute soloist. See *TB* 3, pp. 405 and 745 (note 561).

125. Schumann in fact continued to polish the B-A-C-H fugues sporadically until 31 March of the next year. See *TB* 3, p. 273.

126. See, e.g., Dadelsen, "Schumann und Bach," pp. 58–59; Dahlhaus, "Bach," p. 16; Walsh, "Schumann and the Organ," pp. 742–43; and Schnebel, "Rückungen—Ver-rückungen," pp. 71–72. Klaus-Jürgen Sachs ("Robert Schumanns Fugen") is practically alone in providing a sympathetic account of Schumann's B-A-C-H fugues.

127. *Briefe, Neue Folge*, p. 446.

128. *GS* 1, p. 354.

129. *GS* 1, pp. 253–54.

130. See, e.g., "Bach," in Schoenberg, *Style and Idea*, pp. 396–97.

131. For an account of Schumann's Opus 60 fugues stressing their distance from Bach

in matters of development, voicing, syntax, and form, see Sachs, "Robert Schumanns Fugen," pp. 151, 159–68.

132. Schumann's own comments on countersubjects in his *Lehrbuch der Fugenkomposition* (1848), prepared in part for the instruction of his pupil Alexander Ritter, are highly revealing: "The countersubject of a fugue can be presented simultaneously with the principal subject. But an even greater effect can be achieved if the countersubject is introduced a little at a time, because the perception of two themes and their elaboration requires a highly developed power of aural comprehension." (See Boetticher, *Robert Schumann: Einführung*, p. 615).

133. *Briefe, Neue Folge*, p. 438.

134. See Schumann's letters to Kistner (31 December 1845) and Härtel (21 January 1846), in *Briefe, Neue Folge*, pp. 444–45. Apparently Schumann negotiated with both firms over the publication of the Piano Concerto and the *Ouverture, Scherzo und Finale*, op. 52. The latter eventually appeared under Kistner's imprint.

135. *TB* 3, pp. 391–94. The autograph title page of the Concerto retains the designation *Allegro quasi Fantasia, Intermezz* [sic] *und Rondo*, though it was deleted as a heading for the movement itself. See Roe, "Schumann's Piano Concerto," pp. 77–79.

136. *TB* 3, p. 394. After the private première of the *Phantasie* in the summer of 1841, Schumann probably returned to the opening movement several times for revision. See Roe, "Schumann's Piano Concerto," p. 77.

137. Tovey, *Essays* 3, p. 182.

138. *NZfM* 26 (1847), p. 18.

139. Litzmann, *Clara Schumann* 2, p. 138.

140. Letter of 18 November 1845, in *Briefe, Neue Folge*, p. 255.

141. Appel, "Überleitung," pp. 255–61.

142. For a more detailed account of Hölderlin's theory, see my "The *Wechsel der Töne* in Brahms's *Schicksalslied*," *JAMS* 46 (1993), pp. 97–104.

143. *Briefe, Neue Folge*, p. 249.

144. *TB* 3, p. 408.

145. *Ibid.*, p. 410.

146. *Ibid.*, p. 414.

147. *Ibid.*, pp. 328–329.

148. See Dörffel, *Geschichte*, p. 114.

149. *NZfM* 28 (1848), pp. 97, 100.

150. *NZfM* 32 (1850), p. 159.

151. *NZfM* 25 (1846), p. 181.

152. See Chapter 6, note 24.

153. See, e.g., Edler, "Ton und Zyklus," p. 201.

154. On this point, see Newcomb, "Once More," p. 247. The motive is likewise embedded in the chorale melody itself (mm. 230–32).

155. Gerd Nauhaus also points out that the buildup to the Finale's coda (mm. 344–51) makes reference to the peroration (mm. 131–35) of Schumann's sixth B-A-C-H fugue. See "Final-Lösungen," pp. 317–18.

156. *AmZ* 50 (1848), cols. 369–70.

157. The principal discussions include: Edler, "Ton und Zyklus," p. 201; Idem, *Schumann und seine Zeit*, pp. 177–78; Eichhorn, "Melancholie," p. 11; Nauhaus, "Final-Lösungen," pp. 316–18; Newcomb, "Once More," pp. 233–47; and Roesner, "Tonal Strategy," pp. 302–5.

158. As Jon Finson has shown, the special demands of the Finale motivated a shift in

Schumann's sketching technique. While the customary continuity drafts are preserved for some portions of the movement, Schumann made and retained multiple drafts for especially troublesome spots: the opening group, the ensuing transition, and the coda. The drafts for the latter are of particular interest, for they document Schumann's efforts to increase the cross-referential density of the closing pages of his symphony and hence to ensure greater coherence for the work in its entirety. See Finson, "Sketches for Fourth Movement," pp. 152–67.

159. For excellent comments on this point, see Newcomb, "Once More," pp. 240–47; and Roesner, "Tonal Strategy," p. 302.

160. *Briefe, Neue Folge,* p. 262.

161. *Briefe, Neue Folge,* p. 300.

162. *TB* 3, p. 328.

163. See, e.g., Edler, *Schumann und seine Zeit,* pp. 177–78; Mayeda, *Schumanns Weg,* pp. 523–28; Newcomb, "Once More," pp. 234, 237; and Roesner, "Tonal Strategy," p. 296.

164. Review in *NZfM* 29 (1848), p. 113.

165. Letter to Whistling of 15 March 1846, in *Briefe, Neue Folge,* p. 446.

166. See Reich, *Clara Schumann,* p. 244; and *TB* 3, pp. 292, 428–29.

167. The story is somewhat complicated by the fact that two months before rounding off the draft of the F-major Trio in late October, Schumann returned to elaborate the sketches for the D-minor Trio. (See *TB* 3, p. 438; Kohlhase, *Kammermusik* 2, p. 111; and Litzmann, *Clara Schumann* 2, p. 173). In the later trio, Schumann departed from his usual compositional practice in another way as well: the elaboration of the first and second movements (7–16 October) predates the completion of the continuity draft for the work as a whole. See Kohlhase, *Kammermusik* 2, p. 133.

168. Reich, *Clara Schumann,* p. 245.

169. See the entries for 2–3 October in *TB* 3.

170. *NZfM* 29 (1848), p. 115.

171. Kohlhase's study of the preliminary material for the D-minor Trio has brought to light sketches and an almost complete draft of a second episode that, if retained, would have imparted an overall ABACA shape to the movement. The ultimately rejected C section, like its earlier counterpart (B), features a contrapuntally dense texture with violin, cello, and piano in close imitation practically throughout. See Kohlhase, *Kammermusik* 3, pp. 43–47, for transcriptions of Schumann's sketch and draft.

172. Letter to Louis Ehlert of 26 November 1849, in *Briefe, Neue Folge,* p. 319.

173. Letter to C. Reinecke of 1 May 1849, in *Briefe, Neue Folge,* p. 303.

174. Alluding to a famous verse from the closing scene of Goethe's *Faust,* Part II, Dörffel heard this passage as an emanation "from higher spheres." See *NZfM* 29 (1848), p. 114.

175. Kohlhase notes that the slow movement of the F-major trio was originally to have included a passage based on the song *Dein Bildnis wunderselig,* which, as we have seen, figures in the development (and in the coda) of the first movement as well. All that remains, in mm. 14–17 of the final version, is an attenuated reference to the song's head motif. See Kohlhase, *Kammermusik* 1, p. 53, and 2, p. 59.

176. Schumann, "Aufzeichnungen," pp. 99–104, 111–13.

177. *Ibid.,* p. 103.

Chapter 10

1. A CD of the performance, conducted by Kurt Masur and featuring Edda Moser in the title role, Dietrich Fischer-Dieskau (Siegfried), Peter Schreier (Golo), Gisela Schröter

(Margaretha), the Gewandhausorchester Leipzig, and the Rundfunkchor Berlin, was issued in 1992 (Berlin Classics BC 2056-2). A live performance (with numerous cuts) under Gerd Albrecht (Philharmonisches Staatsorchester Hamburg) appeared on the Orfeo label (C 289 932 H) in 1993. The first of these two recordings is by far the better, musically and sonically. Although *Genoveva* was not totally forgotten after its Leipzig premiere on 26 June 1850, the 150 or so performances it received between then and the early 1970s do not represent an impressive number; see Oliver, "Robert Schumanns vergessene Oper," pp. 162–64; and Siegel, "A Second Look," pp. 17, 32, for accounts of the opera's performance history.

2. See, e.g., Abraham, "Robert Schumann," pp. 853–54. This view is deeply rooted in nineteenth-century thought; Johann Christian Lobe's comments (reproduced in Eismann, *Quellenwerk* 1, p. 166) on *Genoveva*, which he described in 1869 as "a great through-composed lied," are typical.

3. *Briefe, Neue Folge*, p. 330.

4. Liszt, "Robert Schumann," p. 170.

5. Letter of 12 December 1830 to his mother; *Jugendbriefe*, p. 133.

6. Entry for 21 November 1843 in *TB* 2, p. 270.

7. Review of Karl Reissiger's *Adele de Foix*, in *GS* 2, p. 94.

8. See the entries for 5 September 1842 and 15 June 1846 in *TB* 3, pp. 223 and 282.

9. See Hoy-Draheim, "Robert Schumanns Opernpläne," p. 101.

10. Reproduced in Schumann, *Korsar*, ed. Draheim, pp. xvi–xvii.

11. See the letters of 8 October 1848 to Carl Wettig, and 6 December 1851 to Liszt, in *Briefe, Neue Folge*, pp. 291–92, 352.

12. See also the summary in Oliver, "Schumanns vergessene Oper," pp. 10–21.

13. *GS* 2, p. 95.

14. *Ibid.*, p. 94.

15. *GS* 1, pp. 319–20.

16. See his letters of 25 December 1848 to Schindelmeisser, and 27 August 1850 to Spohr, in *Briefe, Neue Folge*, pp. 297 and 331.

17. Review of *Lieder* by J. P. E. Hartmann and Karl Banck (1842), in *GS* 2, p. 250. In his review of W. Reuling, Piano Trio, op. 75 (1842), Schumann goes on to say: "the highest peaks of Italian art don't extend to the first beginnings of the truly German; one cannot stand with one foot on an Alp and the other on a comfortable meadow." See *GS* 2, p. 89.

18. Review of Reuling's Piano Trio, in *GS* 2, pp. 88–89.

19. Review of *Lieder* by Hartmann and Banck, in *GS* 2, p. 250. Cf. the similar remarks in the *Musikalische Haus- und Lebensregeln* (1848): "But there are melodies of a different sort [from those praised by dilettantes], and if you turn to Bach, Mozart, and Beethoven, you will see them in a thousand different guises; hopefully you will soon tire of the impoverished monotony of the latest Italian opera melodies." See *GS* 2, p. 169.

20. Wagner, *Zukunftsmusik* (1860), in *Gesammelte Schriften* 7, p. 127.

21. Letter of 22 October 1845, in *Briefe, Neue Folge*, p. 252.

22. The *Haushaltbücher* make reference to an evening conversation with Wagner devoted to *Tannhäuser* (entry for 24 November 1845, in *TB* 3, p. 407). It is tantalizing to speculate on the nature of the composers' exchanges (of which there were several during Schumann's Dresden years). According to an entry in the *Kurztagebuch* for 17 March 1846, "Wagner possesses an enormous gift of gab . . . one can't listen to him for long" (*TB* 2, p. 398). In contrast, Wagner found Schumann to be "a highly gifted musician, but an impossible human being. When I came to Dresden from Paris, I visited Schumann, told him of my Parisian experiences, spoke of the musical situation in France and Germany, and spoke of literature and politics—but he remained as good as silent for almost an hour. Certainly one can't

conduct a conversation *alone!* An impossible human being!" (Quoted in Eismann, *Quellenwerk* 1, pp. 133–34).

23. Letter of late November 1845, in *Briefe, Neue Folge*, p. 254. Clara, however, remained decidedly skeptical toward Wagner and his works: "I can't agree with Robert [on the merits of *Tannhäuser*]; for me, this music isn't music at all, though I won't deny that Wagner will enjoy a successful career in the theatre. But I would rather be silent altogether about Wagner, for I can't deny my convictions, and I feel for this composer not the tiniest spark of sympathy." Litzmann, *Clara Schumann* 2, p. 109.

24. See the commentary in Meissner, *Geschichtsrezeption*, pp. 102–3.

25. *Briefe, Neue Folge*, p. 256.

26. *Briefe, Neue Folge*, p. 373.

27. *Briefe, Neue Folge*, pp. 291–92.

28. For a detailed discussion of Schumann's scenario, see Hoy-Draheim, "Robert Schumanns Opernpläne," pp. 101–4.

29. The essay appears in translation as "Berlioz and his Harold Symphony" in Strunk, *Source Readings in Music History: The Romantic Era*, pp. 107–33.

30. Liszt, "Berlioz," pp. 123–26.

31. Liszt, "Berlioz," p. 128.

32. Dahlhaus, "Zur Dramaturgie der Literaturoper," pp. 295–303.

33. *TB* 2, pp. 413 and 551 (note 729).

34. Litzmann, *Clara Schumann* 2, pp. 145–46.

35. The Schumanns just about broke even in Vienna only because of Jenny Lind's collaboration in Clara's 10 January concert; they netted a mere 96 thalers in Berlin. See the entries for 22 January 1847 in *TB* 3, p. 342; and 25 March 1847 in *TB* 2, p. 420.

36. Litzmann, *Clara Schumann* 2, p. 155.

37. See *TB* 2, p. 415; and Litzmann, *Clara Schumann* 2, pp. 154–58.

38. See the entries for 5 January, 26–27 January, 17–19 March, and 21–22 March 1847, in *TB* 2, pp. 412–13, 419, and *TB* 3, p. 340. Clara's diary makes reference to the debilitating effect that preparations for the Singakademie concert had on Schumann's nerves; see Litzmann, *Clara Schumann* 2, p. 157.

39. *TB* 2, p. 411.

40. See *TB* 2, pp. 413, 415, 417, 418, and 420.

41. Litzmann, *Clara Schumann* 2, p. 149.

42. *TB* 2, p. 420.

43. *TB* 2, p. 419.

44. Wasielewski, *Schumann*, pp. 382–83. In a letter to Hiller written during the summer of 1847, Schumann portrayed Reinick as "a good, friendly fellow, but dreadfully sentimental"; see *Briefe, Neue Folge*, p. 273.

45. See his letter of July 1847 to Hiller, in *Briefe, Neue Folge*, p. 273.

46. *Briefe, Neue Folge*, p. 268.

47. *Ibid.* On Hebbel's own account, his meeting with Schumann on 27 July 1847 during a visit to Dresden was an utter failure. Schumann, the poet wrote in his diary, was "not merely stubborn, but downright unpleasant in his taciturnity." Completely "imprisoned in his talent," he appeared "to listen just as little as he spoke." In a letter to a friend, Hebbel claimed that Schumann "gaped" at him in silence for the duration of their meeting, then remained just as incommunicative on the half-hour walk back to his hotel. When Hebbel heard his "child . . . clad in music" a decade later, he expressed nothing but displeasure. See Edler, *Schumann*, pp. 244, 266 (note 45); and Sietz, "Zur Textgestaltung," p. 400.

48. Quoted in Sietz, "Zur Textgestaltung," p. 401. Unfortunately, Reinick's version of the text (two acts of which Schumann mentioned in his letter to Hebbel) is no longer extant. In a letter written shortly before the June 1850 premiere of the opera, Schumann claimed to have retained only about 200 of Reinick's lines; see Sietz, p. 402. He was, however, intent on expressing his appreciation for the poet's labors: in a letter to C. F. Peters (27 February 1850) concerning the publication of his score, he asked for 160 louis d'or, of which 20 were to go to the "partial author" of the text; see *Briefe, Neue Folge*, p. 466. In the end, Schumann only received 100 louis, 15 of which he offered to Reinick; see Sietz, p. 402.

49. *Briefe, Neue Folge*, p. 268.

50. Schumann's dogged labor on the opera and little else must have taken a financial toll. Unable to come up with the 36 thalers due in rent, he wrote to his brother Carl on 19 June 1848 for a loan. See *Briefe, Neue Folge*, p. 283.

51. *TB* 3, p. 466.

52. *Briefe, Neue Folge*, p. 296. See also the entry for 15 November 1848, in *TB* 3, p. 475.

53. *Ibid.*, p. 289.

54. Letter to Rietz of 3 February 1849, in *Briefe, Neue Folge*, p. 299.

55. *Briefe, Neue Folge*, p. 327.

56. See the entries for 22 May, 20 and 22 June 1850, in *TB* 3, pp. 527, 530.

57. *TB* 3, p. 530.

58. See Schumann's letters to Spohr of 27 August 1850 and 13 December 1852, in *Briefe, Neue Folge*, pp. 331, 363. Spohr was taken by Schumann's elimination of "the unnatural interruption of the action by a wearisome and constant repetition of words," a technique the older composer traced to his own *Die Kreuzfahrer* (1843–44); see *Louis Spohr's Autobiography* 2, p. 297.

59. For an account of the slightly revived interest in *Genoveva* since the centenary of its premiere, see Oliver, "Robert Schumanns vergessene Oper," pp. 162–64; Siegel, "A Second Look," p. 17; and Note 1 above.

60. Brendel, "Schumann's Oper," p. 18.

61. *Ibid.*, p. 3.

62. Cf. Brendel, "Schumann's Oper," p. 18; and Brendel, "Einige Worte," p. 265.

63. Hanslick, "Robert Schumann als Opernkomponist," p. 262.

64. *Ibid.*, p. 258.

65. *NZfM* 34 (1851), p. 130.

66. Eismann, *Quellenwerk* 1, p. 166.

67. Brendel, "Schumann's Oper," p. 3.

68. Shaw, Review of *Genoveva* (13 December 1898), in *Great Composers*, p. 199. Wagner likewise had reservations about the effectiveness of the text. In his autobiography, he registered his frustration over Schumann's reactions to his suggestions: "[Schumann] invited me to hear him read his libretto, which was a combination of the styles of Hebbel and Tieck. When, however, out of a genuine desire for the success of his work, about which I had serious misgivings, I called his attention to some grave defects in it, and suggested the necessary alterations, I realized how matters stood with this extraordinary person: he simply wanted me to be swayed by himself, but deeply resented any interference with the product of his own ideals, so that thenceforward I let matters alone." *My Life* 1, p. 386.

69. Quoted in Sietz, "Zur Textgestaltung," pp. 398–99.

70. Opitz, *Prosodia Germanica* (ca. 1650), quoted from Benjamin, *Origin*, p. 62.

71. For preliminary observations on the links between Schumann's text and the "mannerism" of baroque theatre, see Wolff, "Schumanns 'Genoveva'," pp. 89–92.

72. Benjamin, *Origin*, pp. 65, 69.

73. In the spring of 1829, Schumann read *La Vida es Sueño* (*Life is a Dream*), one of the Spanish dramatist's most famous plays (*TB* 1, p. 183). Calderón's *La Puente de Mantible* (*The Bridge of Mantible*) and *El Magico Prodigioso* (*The Marvelous Magician*) were considered for operatic treatment in 1841 (Schumann's scenario for a text based on the former is preserved in the Robert-Schumann-Haus; see *TB* 2, pp. 177, 179, 515 [note 476]). In his letter of October 1848 to Carl Wettig, Schumann included Calderón among the masters of world drama to whom an aspiring opera composer might turn for a subject (*Briefe, Neue Folge*, p. 291).

74. Benjamin, *Origin*, p. 81.

75. *Ibid.*

76. As Hoy-Draheim points out ("Robert Schumanns Opernpläne," p. 103–4), Schumann deviated from Hoffmann in likewise planning a happy ending for the projected opera on *Doge und Dogaressa*.

77. Ostwald (*Schumann*, p. 214) views the opera as an embodiment of Schumann's ambivalent feelings toward Clara, since on the one hand it is obviously a paean to womanly virtue, while on the other, Siegfried's condemnation of Genoveva may represent the composer's subconscious desire to punish his wife for her professional successes. Stephen Meyer's argument ("Trope of the Double") for Schumann's identification with the dualistic personality of Golo is less far-fetched, but still beside the point.

78. *Briefe, Neue Folge*, p. 314.

79. As pointed out in Siegel, "Second Look," p. 18, the chorale is based on the tune *Ermuntre dich mein schwacher Geist.*

80. Quoted from Benjamin, *Origin*, p. 72.

81. *Ibid.*, p. 74.

82. This scenario is well exemplified by Rosauro's attempts to reclaim her tarnished honor in Calderón's *Life is a Dream*.

83. The bipartition recalls the large-scale structure of the *Peri* and likewise looks forward to the disposition of the projected *Romeo and Juliet* opera of 1850; see Hoy-Draheim, "Schumanns Opernpläne," pp. 102–3.

84. Brendel, "Schumann's Oper," p. 3.

85. Benjamin, *Origin*, p. 71.

86. *Ibid.*, pp. 159–235.

87. On the dialectical nature of the courtier in the *Trauerspiel*, see Benjamin, *Origin*, p. 98.

88. Schumann described Marschner's *Templer* in an entry in the *Theaterbüchlein* for 8 May 1847 as "the most important German opera of recent times after Weber"; *GS* 2, p. 160.

89. Weber's *Euryanthe* (like *Genoveva*, an underrated masterpiece) was one of Schumann's favorite operas. Shortly after attending a performance of the work on 23 September 1847, he described Weber's opera as "a chain of sparkling jewels from beginning to end—highly ingenious throughout." *GS* 2, p. 161.

90. It is probably not a coincidence that the motive articulating Golo's arrival and his subsequent presentation of Siegfried's sword and ring (a derivative of the idea given as Example 10.3) bears a marked similarity to the motive from Weber's scene representing Adolar's resolve to punish his former beloved.

91. Benjamin, *Origin*, p. 66.

92. *Ibid.*, p. 81; emphasis in quotation mine.

93. *Ibid.*, p. 76.

94. *Ibid.*, pp. 215–20.

95. *TB* 3, p. 466. Schumann read Byron's drama in the 1839 translation of "Posgaru," pseudonym for Karl Adolf Suckow.

96. *Works of Byron* 4, p. 80.

97. See the entry for 26 March 1829 in *TB* 1, p. 183: "Bedtime reading: Byron's *Manfred*—dreadful night." Byron's *Childe Harold* produced a similar effect three days later.

98. Wasielewski, *Schumann*, p. 398.

99. A letter of 31 May 1849 to Liszt indicates that Schumann had made some revisions in the score by that time. See *Briefe, Neue Folge*, p. 306.

100. *Briefe, Neue Folge*, p. 527. Schumann was unable to attend the performance due to an attack of "Rheuma."

101. Letter to Liszt of 25 December 1851, in *Briefe, Neue Folge*, p. 353.

102. Review of 30 March 1884, quoted in Zanoncelli, "Von Byron zu Schumann," p. 131.

103. The music for this scene made a deep and lasting impression on the young Brahms, who wrote to Clara in a letter of 21 March 1855: "I often find the melodramas [in *Manfred*] incredible, for instance, Astarte's appearance and utterances [in No. 11]. Here is musical speech ["Musiksprache"] of the highest order; it penetrates to the depths of the heart." Litzmann, ed. *Clara Schumann—Johannes Brahms: Briefe* 1, p. 100.

104. See, e.g., Abraham, "Dramatic Music," in Abraham, ed., *Schumann: A Symposium*, p. 263; and Zanoncelli, "Von Byron zu Schumann," p. 134.

105. Letter of 5 November 1851, in *Briefe, Neue Folge*, p. 350.

106. Letter of 25 December 1851, in *Briefe, Neue Folge*, p. 353. Cf. also the similar remark in his letter to Liszt of 5 November 1851, in *Briefe, Neue Folge*, p. 350.

107. Letter of 15 February 1817, in *Works of Lord Byron* 4, pp. 54–55. Cf. his similar description of *Manfred* in a letter of 17 June 1817: "it is not a drama properly—but a dialogue, still it contains poetry and passion" (*Works of Lord Byron* 4, p. 138).

108. The inclusion of incest in Byron's drama obviously reflects the poet's own affair with his half-sister, Augusta Leigh.

109. Szondi, *Theory of the Modern Drama*, pp. 7–41.

110. Nietzsche, *Beyond Good and Evil*, p. 181. Tovey, practically alone among critics, saw "no substantial contradiction to Byron in [Schumann's] thus heightening the effect of the close." (*Essays* 4, p. 113). More recently, Zanoncelli has justified the composer's ending by viewing it as a projection of "that real, unresolved family tragedy, whose principal characters were Robert and Clara Schumann" ("Von Byron zu Schumann," p. 134).

111. See Chapter 9, pp. 303–304.

112. *Briefe, Neue Folge*, p. 250.

113. *Ibid.*, p. 244.

114. On 21 March 1847, Schumann attended a soirée for the Grand Duchess of Mecklenburg at which several selections from Radziwill's *Faust* (1835), including the ballad *Der König von Thule*, Gretchen's *Mein Ruh' ist hin*, and *Neige, neige, Du Ohnegleiche* (from the *Schlussszene*), were performed; see *TB* 2, p. 419. Schumann had first become acquainted with Radziwill's settings, which he found full of inadequacies but "interesting," in 1837; see *GS* 1, pp. 313–14.

115. Letter of 26 June 1848, in *Briefe, Neue Folge*, p. 454.

116. The first version of the Chorus mysticus as it now stands was probably completed in essence during 1844. In his *Projektenbuch* for 1847, Schumann alludes only to a "second *Schlusschor* for the Faust scene;" see Eismann, *Quellenwerk* 1, p. 169.

117. Schumann had conceived the idea of a "Chorverein" or "Caecilienverein" (ulti-

mately called a Verein für Chorgesang) on 29 November 1847 (*TB* 3, p. 445) and continued to direct the group, which first met on 5 January 1848, until his departure for Düsseldorf in September 1850. In 1898, the organization celebrated its fiftieth anniversary as the Robert Schumann'sche Singakademie.

118. Although Schumann had hoped that his music for the *Schlussszene* would form part of the official celebration, he was passed over in favor of the Hofkapellmeister, Karl Reissiger. Obviously unwilling to suffer another insult at the hands of the individual who had intrigued against his *Genoveva*, Schumann organized and directed a performance at the Palais des Grossen Gartens that, in addition to his *Faust* setting, also included Mendelssohn's *Erste Walpurgisnacht*. At precisely the same time, Schumann's setting was performed for Goethe festivals in Weimar (under Liszt's direction) and Leipzig.

119. According to entries in the *Haushaltbücher*, he first sketched No. 3 and then turned to Nos. 1 and 2; see *TB* 3, p. 498.

120. *TB* 3, p. 526.

121. Quoted in Mintz, "Schumann as Interpreter," p. 236. Given his outlook on the melodic style in the *Peri* and *Genoveva*, it is hardly surprising that Krüger took exception to the supposed Wagnerisms in the *Faust* scenes: "In writing *hardly memorable melodies . . .* Schumann takes the same path as Wagner; the predominantly psychological recitation, tone-painting, and orchestral texture all impede melodic memorability" (quoted in Probst, *Schumanns Oratorien*, p. 118). Writing in 1874, Alfred Ehrlich viewed a portion of Faust's monologue from No. 4 ("So ist es also") as a "perfect example of endless melody according to Wagnerian principles," nor did he intend this observation as a compliment; see Probst, *Schumanns Oratorien*, p. 118.

122. Liszt, "Robert Schumann," p. 170.

123. For an excellent summary of Schumann's alterations, see Mintz, "Schumann as Interpreter," pp. 254–56.

124. "Farbigen" in the original.

125. As early as 1882, Philipp Spitta argued that the *Faust* scenes did not constitute a "self-contained artwork;" see his "Lebensbild," p. 92. For more recent expressions of essentially the same opinion, see Abraham, "The Dramatic Music," in Abraham, ed., *Schumann: A Symposium*, p. 266; Sams, "Schumann and Faust," p. 546; and Edler, *Schumann*, p. 257, who views the fragmentary nature of Schumann's scenes as a sign of "resignation" in the face of the unattainability of the unity associated with "the integrated classical work."

126. Wasielewski, *Schumann*, p. 434.

127. *Ibid.*

128. Wasielewski, *Schumann*, p. 440.

129. Adorno, "On the Final Scene of *Faust*," from *Notes to Literature* 1, p. 119; Goethe, *Conversations*, p. 307, entry for 13 February 1829.

130. Lukács, *Theory of the Novel*, p. 76.

131. The tripartition of *Abtheilung* III is supported by both internal and external evidence. On one hand, No. 7/iii is set off from 7/iv by the tonal cleft between them: Bb-Ab; on the other, Schumann allowed that a brief pause should be made between No. 7/iv and 7/v. See his letter of 21 August 1849 to Montag, in *Briefe, Neue Folge*, p. 523 (note 384).

132. See Dällenbach, *Mirror in the Text*, pp. 36–38, 67–70; and my *Nineteenth-Century Music*, p. 36.

133. For a fascinating discussion of the relationship between D minor and "Hallen" (an architectural conceit specific to German Romanticism that attempts to conflate the open halls of Greek antiquity with the closed Gothic halls of the Middle Ages) in late Schumann, see Kapp, *Studien zum Spätwerk*, pp. 134–44. In Kapp's view, D minor represents Schumann's

ideal tonal analogue for the dialectic between free and enclosed space implicit in the nineteenth-century "Halle."

134. Mintz's argument for a network of what he calls "symbolic" or "interpretive" cells is unconvincing largely because the neutral character of the cells mitigates against their assumption of a referential role; see Mintz, "Schumann as Interpreter," pp. 239–53.

135. Schumann's motive is possibly traceable to Bach. At the conclusion of the second movement of his Cantata 161, *Komm, du süsse Todesstunde*, a very similar figure is employed as a musical cipher for the soul's longing for death. In any case, the Faustian signature motive obviously had an abiding personal significance for Schumann: it appears, among other instances, in the Mass (op. 147) and Requiem (op. 148).

136. If anything, Schumann heightens the contrast by revising the ending of Goethe's scene much as he had the ending of Byron's *Manfred*. While Goethe closes with Mephistopheles's speech in praise of negation and "the Eternally-empty" ("das Ewig-Leere"), Schumann deleted these lines, closing instead with the chorus's repetition of Mephistopheles' "Es ist vollbracht" (It is fulfilled) and a reflective orchestral chorale.

137. Letter of 10 August 1849 to Liszt, in *Briefe, Neue Folge*, p. 310.

138. Letter of 1 September 1849 to Brendel, in *Briefe, Neue Folge*, p. 311.

139. A closely related figure serves as fugue subject in *And with his stripes* from Handel's *Israel in Egypt*, the Kyrie from Mozart's Requiem, and the Finale of Haydn's F-minor String Quartet, op. 20, no. 5.

140. In his *Lektürebüchlein* for 1847, Schumann listed, under "Musical Studies," all of Handel's major English oratorios with the exception of *The Triumph of Time and Truth*. Some of these works obviously impressed him less than others; *L'Allegro, il Penseroso ed il Moderato*, for instance, was written off as "A frightfully outdated thing, hardly worthy of mention among [Handel's] oratorios. Bach could never imagine, let alone compose, something so superficial and insignificant." Schumann's readings for the same year included the Handel biographies of Burney and Mainwaring (in Mattheson's translation). See Appel and Hermstrüwer, eds., *Schumann und die Dichter*, pp. 71, 83, 85.

141. The tone, timbre, and melodic-gestural content of this section hearken unmistakably to the Peri's *Sei dies, mein Geschenk*.

142. *NZfM* 31 (1849), p. 115.

143. Letter of 26 June 1848 to Whistling, in *Briefe, Neue Folge*, p. 454.

144. See his letter to Brendel of 18 September 1849; in *Briefe, Neue Folge*, p. 312.

145. The second version of the *Schlusschor* offers compelling evidence of the inherent unity in Schumann's literary operas of 1847–1850. The fugue subject of its central section prefigures the motive associated with Margaretha from the Act I Finale of *Genoveva* (Example 10.2). Its opening melody looks forward to the lyric orchestral motive that supports much of the heroine's prayer in *Genoveva*, Act IV, No. 16. Schumann's first, like his last completed literary opera, effects a synthesis of the mundane and the divine.

146. Kaufmann, "Goethe's Faith and Faust's Redemption," in *From Shakespeare to Existentialism*, pp. 73–76.

147. Eichner, "The Eternal Feminine: An Aspect of Goethe's Ethics," in Goethe, *Faust*, Norton Critical Edition, pp. 617–24.

Chapter 11

1. *Briefe, Neue Folge*, p. 302.

2. Letter of 31 May 1849, in *Briefe, Neue Folge*, p. 306.

3. Letter of 26 November 1849, in *Briefe, Neue Folge*, p. 319.

4. *TB* 3, pp. 452, 511.

5. See the letters of 27 February 1849 (to Härtel), 1 May 1849 (to Reinecke), and 8 May 1853 (to C. van Bruyck), in *Briefe, Neue Folge*, pp. 458, 303–4, and 372.

6. See Litzmann, *Clara Schumann* 2, p. 121; and *Briefe, Neue Folge*, pp. 522–23 (note 379).

7. Nietzsche, *Beyond Good and Evil*, p. 182.

8. *Briefe, Neue Folge*, p. 305.

9. Boetticher, *Einführung*, pp. 111, 140. Cf. also Gurlitt, "Robert Schumann," pp. 20–21, and Edler, *Robert Schumann*, p. 190, for discussions of the Biedermeier quality in much of Schumann's later keyboard music. Dahlhaus notes a similar tone in the oratorio *Der Rose Pilgerfahrt;* see his *Nineteenth-Century Music*, p. 169.

10. Newcomb, "Schumann and the Marketplace," pp. 267–268.

11. Edler, *Schumann*, p. 103.

12. *Ibid.*, p. 107. See also Knepler, "Robert Schumann," p. 794.

13. Boetticher puts it in no uncertain terms; for him, the later *Hausmusik* involving piano represents "a frightful descent into [the composition of] homely commodities." See *Einführung*, p. 140.

14. See, e.g., Newcomb, "Schumann and the Marketplace," pp. 301–302.

15. *Briefe, Neue Folge*, p. 470. The work he had in mind, the *Fantasiestücke* for piano, op. 111, would prove to be as little a favorite with the public as *Genoveva*.

16. Quoted from J. P. Stern, *Idylls and Realities: Studies in Nineteenth-Century German Literature* (London, 1971), in Sheehan, *German History*, p. 538.

17. Sheehan, *German History*, p. 541.

18. Dahlhaus, *Nineteenth-Century Music*, pp. 174–78.

19. Letter of 10 April 1849 to Hiller, in *Briefe, Neue Folge*, p. 302.

20. One of these had already been composed on 11 January 1841; see *TB* 3, p. 171.

21. The first strophe of the last song in the set, *Deutscher Freiheitsgesang*, was first published by Julien Tiersot as late as 1913 in an arrangement for voices and piano as a supplement to the April issue of the *Revue Musicale*. The first two songs, *Schwarz-Rot-Gold*, and *Zu den Waffen*, were published in 1913 and 1914 respectively.

22. *Briefe, Neue Folge*, p. 294.

23. *TB* 3, p. 445.

24. *Briefe, Neue Folge*, p. 302.

25. See Meissner, *Geschichtsrezeption*, p. 100.

26. Only three pieces from the third volume *(Romanze von Gänsebuben, John Anderson*, and *Der Schmidt)* date from 1849 (March/August); the other two (*Die Nonne* and *Die Sänger*) were added by 1851.

27. Review of Schumann's *Romanzen und Balladen*, Heft I, op. 67, in *NZfM* 31 (1849), pp. 189–90. In a fragment probably dating from the late 1840s, Schumann presented his own views on the textual requirements of the choral lied: "Sharp individualization of characters even in word-expression. Avoidance of too many trochaic meters, also of feminine endings. . . . Avoidance of the overused rhyme: 'Herz-Schmerz.' In lyric poems it is very good if the first four or eight lines can be repeated at the end if necessary. Energy and brevity throughout. As many rhymes as possible. Care in the choice of epithets. In general, not too much epithesis." See Boetticher, *Schumann in seinen Schriften und Briefen*, p. 433.

28. For a discussion specifically addressing Schumann's enrichment of the *Romanze*, a genre known to most mid-nineteenth-century Germans through its popular but aesthetically trivial French counterpart, the *romance*, see Best, *Romanzen*, p. 189.

29. *TB* 3, p. 459. Schumann's *Zigeunerleben*, Opus 29, no. 3, for solo quartet (and ad libitum triangle and tambourine) was performed as well.

30. Letter of 30 April 1849 to Friedrich Kistner, in *Briefe, Neue Folge*, pp. 459–60. In a note appended to the *Stichvorlage*, Schumann further indicated that when the work was given in "sociable circles," the fourth and sixth lieder in the final version of the *Liederspiel* could be cut in the interest of greater concision; see Mahlert, *Fortschritt und Kunstlied*, p. 96.

31. Letter of 1 May 1849 to C. Reinecke, in *Briefe, Neue Folge*, pp. 303–4.

32. See, for instance, Edler, *Robert Schumann*, p. 225.

33. *TB* 3, pp. 490 and 776 (note 702).

34. See Mahlert, *Fortschritt und Kunstlied*, p. 97.

35. Schumann also recognized the usefulness of such distinctions. As he put it in the *Musikalische Haus- und Lebensregeln:* "In judging compositions you must distinguish between those belonging to the realm of art *[Kunstfach]* and those intended merely for dilettantish entertainment *[Unterhaltung]*. Stand up for the former and don't be annoyed by the latter." *GS* 2, p. 169.

36. From the *Vorwort* to Riehl's collection; quoted in Petrat, " 'Hausmusik' um 1840," p. 259.

37. Quoted in Newcomb, "Schumann and the Marketplace," p. 273.

38. *Briefe, Neue Folge*, p. 290. On 31 August 1848, Schumann presented his daughter Marie, on the occasion of her seventh birthday, with an album of little piano pieces ("Kindermelodieen") including eight of his own and several others by Bach, Handel, Mozart, Beethoven, and Schubert. Six of Schumann's eight appeared later in the *Album für die Jugend*. See *TB* 2, p. 399; and *TB* 3, pp. 469 and 769 (note 660).

39. *Briefe, Neue Folge*, p. 312; cf. also Schumann's letter of 10 April 1849 to Hiller (p. 303).

40. *TB* 3, p. 669.

41. Excerpts from the *Lehrbuch* appear in Boetticher, *Robert Schumann: Einführung*, pp. 614–15, 627. Among the most intriguing ideas articulated in the *Lehrbuch* is Schumann's conviction that "almost all masterworks, even those in freer compositional styles, can be related to fugal form."

42. For a discussion of the negligible quality of much of the *Hausmusik* that flooded the German market in the mid-1840s, see Petrat, " 'Hausmusik' um 1840," pp. 256–57.

43. For a comprehensive account of the genesis of the *Album für die Jugend*, see Appel, " 'Actually, Taken Directly from Family Life'. "

44. *GS* 2, p. 179.

45. Similarly, the *Lieder-Album für die Jugend* proceeds from simple settings to the musically (and psychologically) challenging Mignon lied, *Kennst du das Land*.

46. Cf. the entry of 13 April in the *Kurztagebuch* occasioned by a walk in the woods with Marie: "The happy days of childhood—one relives them through children." *TB* 2, p. 400.

47. *Briefe, Neue Folge*, p. 290. Alfred Dörffel, in a review of 1849, differentiated the sets in remarkably similar terms. In the *Kinderscenen*, he maintained, Schumann appears as "an artistic personality, thinking back on the long-gone period of his youth and losing himself in dreamy recollections . . . [in] musical poems ["Dichtungen"] alien to a child's understanding." In contrast, "that which in the *Kinderscenen* was a removal into the far distant past approaches, in the *Album für die Jugend*, ever closer to present-day life: recollections are transformed into lived experiences." See *NZfM* 30 (1849), pp. 89–90.

48. As Bernhard Appel points out (" 'Actually, Taken Directly from Family Life', " p. 188), Schumann quotes the two principal phrases of the *Grossvatertanz* in reverse order, his

standing the tune on its head thus making for a gentle touch of irony.

49. Quoted in Casey, ed., *Jean Paul: A Reader*, p. 69.

50. *Ibid.*, p. 74.

51. *NZfM* 30 (1849), p. 90.

52. Cf. also the entry for 25 November 1848 in *TB* 3, p. 476.

53. See Knechtges, *Schumann im Spiegel*, p. 115.

54. See *TB* 3, pp. 479–81; and Eismann, *Quellenwerk* 1, p. 169. For an account of Schumann's revisions, see Jensen, "A New Manuscript," pp. 75–80.

55. For a discussion and transcription of these mottos, see Jensen, "A New Manuscript," pp. 81–84. The verses earmarked for *Vogel als Prophet* come from Eichendorff's *Zwielicht*, which Schumann had set as the tenth song in his Opus 39 *Liederkreis*. His male chorus settings of the verses intended for *Jäger auf der Lauer* and *Jagdlied* appeared in the *Fünf Gesänge aus H. Laubes Jagdbrevier*, op. 137 (composed May 1849).

56. Pfarrius's *Waldlieder*, the source for the mottos for *Eintritt* (No. 1) and *Abschied* (No. 9), was first published in 1850. See Struck, "Literarischer Eindruck," p. 114. Schumann set three of the lyrics from Pfarrius's *Waldlieder* for voice and piano in September 1851 (*Drei Gedichte*, op. 119).

57. According to the *Haushaltbücher*, *Abschied*, probably intended as the final piece from the start, was completed on 1 January 1849, with *Vogel als Prophet* following on 6 January (see *TB* 3, pp. 480–81). The title page of the manuscript (now in the Bibliothèque Nationale in Paris) used as engraver's copy for the publication of the *Waldscenen* indicates that the cycle, as originally drafted, was to include only eight pieces. See Jensen, "A New Manuscript," p. 73.

58. One recollective moment even extends beyond the frame of the cycle: the allusion, at the final cadence of *Abschied*, to the closing gesture that Schumann appended to the *An die ferne Geliebte* reference in the first movement of the *Fantasie*, op. 17.

59. See E. Bernsdorf's brief review of the *Fantasiestücke* in *NZfM* 32 (1850), p. 59.

60. Quoted in Edler, *Robert Schumann*, p. 104.

61. The sketch was complete by 20 February 1849, less than a week after the drafting of the *Adagio und Romanze*, while the orchestration occupied Schumann until March 11. See *TB* 3, pp. 484–86. The first private reading of the work took place at the home of the Dresden court chamber musician Joseph Levy on 15 October, with Levy and three other horn players from the Dresden court orchestra taking the solo parts. The piece was premiered on 25 February 1850 at the Leipzig Gewandhaus with Rietz conducting. Probably at the suggestion of his publisher Schuberth, Schumann arranged the *Concertstück* for piano and orchestra (and perhaps also for two pianos). See the Preface to Robert Schumann, *Konzertstück nach Opus 86 für Klavier und Orchestra*, ed. Marc Andreae, ed. for 2 pianos (Frankfurt & New York: Litolff's Verlag/Peters, 1986), p. 4.

62. See the entry for 15 October 1849, in *TB* 3, p. 506.

63. See Meissner, *Geschichtsrezeption*, p. 106.

64. See *TB* 3, pp. 503–4; and Gebhardt, *Robert Schumann als Symphoniker*, p. 173. Tovey, one of the work's few apologists, was unable to account for the neglect of a piece that seemed to him "one of Schumann's happiest and most inventive" creations. See *Essays in Musical Analysis* 3, *Concertos*, p. 189.

65. See the 1836 and 1839 reviews of concerti by Moscheles and Mendelssohn in *GS* 1, pp. 163 and 386.

66. See the entry for 6 March 1844, in *TB* 2, p. 332. In this he might have turned to Weber's F-minor *Konzertstück* for piano and orchestra, op. 79, as a model.

67. There are echoes of the Piano Concerto as well. The sequential phrases soon after

the soloist's first entry in the *Allegro* clearly hearken to a passage from the second group of the concerto's first movement (see mm. 77ff. and 330ff.).

68. Sheehan, *German History*, p. 657.

69. For Krüger, writing in 1852, the serious artist had no other choice: the "outer tumult" demanded a retreat into an "inner realm." See *NZfM* 36 (1852), p. 41.

70. *Briefe, Neue Folge*, p. 306. Contemporary critics heard something of this quality in Schumann's music as well, though it sometimes failed to elicit their approbation. Krüger, for instance, viewed the "coarse naturalism" in *Genoveva* as sign of "a time that cannot sing joyfully, because it has other tasks." See *NZfM* 34 (1851), p. 144.

71. *TB* 1, p. 77.

72. Eismann, *Quellenwerk* 1, p. 158.

73. On 13 April 1848, for instance, Schumann and his friend Bendemann took opposite sides in a discussion of the Prussian advance into Schleswig-Holstein. See *TB* 3, p. 458; and Litzmann, *Clara Schumann* 2, p. 178.

74. See the entries for 28 February, 5 March, 16 March, 19 March, and 27 March 1848, in *TB* 3, pp. 454–56.

75. *Lektürebüchlein*, in Appel and Hermstrüwer, eds., *Robert Schumann und die Dichter*, pp. 73, 77.

76. Entry for 2 March 1848, in *TB* 3, p. 454.

77. *TB* 3, p. 490; see also Litzmann, *Clara Schumann* 2, p. 185.

78. Litzmann, *Clara Schumann* 2, p. 186.

79. *Ibid.*, pp. 186–87.

80. *TB* 3, pp. 490–91.

81. Litzmann, *Clara Schumann* 2, pp. 187–88.

82. *TB* 3, p. 491.

83. Litzmann, *Clara Schumann* 2, p. 189.

84. *TB* 3, p. 491.

85. Letter of 31 May 1849; in *Briefe, Neue Folge*, p. 306.

86. Litzmann, *Clara Schumann* 2, p. 191.

87. Ostwald, *Schumann*, p. 220. Not all writers subscribe to this point of view. According to Ulrich Mahlert, the "social and artistic will to progress of the revolutionary years" left an indelible stamp on Schumann's production (*Fortschritt und Kunstlied*, p. 183). For a comprehensive (and at times provocative) account of Schumann's engagement with revolutionary themes, see Kapp, "Schumann nach der Revolution."

88. *Briefe, Neue Folge*, p. 463.

89. Entry for 23 May 1849, in *TB* 3, p. 492.

90. See Litzmann, *Clara Schumann* 2, p. 192. The text for the motet was drawn from the *Makamen des Hariri*, the poetic source for the *Bilder aus Osten*.

91. See Eismann, *Quellenwerk* 1, 170.

92. Entry for 8 January 1848, in *TB* 3, p. 450.

93. Jon Finson has noted political overtones even in the unassuming songs of the *Lieder-Album für die Jugend*, which, he argues, neither "constitute a flight from political reality" nor "mark the beginning of an artistic regression." Among the best-represented poets in the collection is the "uncompromising republican" August Heinrich Hoffmann von Fallersleben, author of *Deutschland, Deutschland, über alles* ("Schumann's Mature Style," pp. 228–29). See also Kapp, "Schumann nach der Revolution," pp. 359, 387.

94. See the entries for 12–15 June 1849, in *TB* 3, p. 494.

95. *Briefe, Neue Folge*, p. 461.

96. Wagner, "Beethoven," in *Prose Works* 5, p. 124. Schumann had perhaps been con-

templating a Meister-related project for some time. In early March 1847, while in Berlin for a performance of the *Peri,* he read Goethe's novel for the third time. See *TB* 2, pp. 417–18; and *Lektürebüchlein,* in Appel and Hermstrüwer, eds., *Robert Schumann und die Dichter,* p. 67.

97. *Athenäum* Fragment no. 216, in *KFSA* 2, p. 198.

98. Novalis, *Fragmente und Studien,* no. 536, in *Schriften* 3, p. 646.

99. Goethe, *Wilhelm Meister's Apprenticeship,* p. 320.

100. Schumann's cycle omits only the *Spottlied, Ich armer Teufel, Herr Baron* from Book III of the novel. Wolf surely studied Schumann's settings very carefully. Both composers shaped the Harper's *Wer nie sein Brot* as a *crescendo* to a mighty climax followed by a dissolution into immobility. Likewise, Wolf's setting of *An die Thüren* shares its key (C minor) and languid chromatic voice-leading with Schumann's. Wolf's Mignon, also like Schumann's, is at once disarmingly naïve and wracked by emotional turmoil.

101. See, for instance, Theodor Uhlig's review in *NZfM* 35 (1851), pp. 219–21. For more recent, but equally unflattering appraisals, see Sams, *Songs of Robert Schumann,* pp. 220–27; and Stein, "Musical Settings," pp. 139–40, 142.

102. See *TB* 3, pp. 491, 495–97. Schumann composed Philine's lied, *Singet nicht in Trauertönen,* on 1 July. Placed just after *Wer sich der Einsamkeit ergiebt,* Philine's light-hearted encomium to nocturnal bliss is an ironic rejoinder to the Harper's nightly encounters with pain, grief, and torment.

103. *Briefe, Neue Folge,* p. 232.

104. Goethe, *Wilhelm Meister's Apprenticeship,* p. 72.

105. See Sams, *Songs of Robert Schumann,* p. 216; Edler, *Robert Schumann,* p. 223; Ostwald, *Schumann,* p. 221; and Mahlert, *Fortschritt und Kunstlied,* p. 149. For Finson ("Schumann's Mature Style," p. 249), who perhaps presses the point too far, the political connotations of the cycle emerge in Schumann's liberation of the vocal line from the "tyranny of cantabile melody."

106. Quoted in Casey, ed., *Jean Paul: A Reader,* p. 61.

107. *GS* 2, p. 166.

108. See the entries for 26 November, 30 November, and 3 December 1848, in *TB* 3, pp. 476–77.

109. *Briefe, Neue Folge,* p. 460.

110. See the letter of 17 January 1854 to Strackerjahn, in *Briefe, Neue Folge,* p. 391; and Wasielewski, *Robert Schumann,* p. 406.

111. *Briefe, Neue Folge,* p. 460.

112. *Ibid.* Similarly, Schumann referred to *Verzweifle nicht im Schmerzenstal* as a "religiöser Gesang." See Wasielewski, *Robert Schumann,* p. 403.

113. *Ideen,* no. 13, in *KFSA* 2, p. 257.

114. The celebrated theme that grows out of the opening F-A♭-F motto of Brahms's Third Symphony, op. 90, has often been traced to an idea in the first movement of Schumann's "Rhenish" Symphony. At the same time, the shape of Brahms's theme is suspiciously close to that of the concluding "sleep" motive from the *Nachtlied.* Given the younger composer's high regard for Schumann's choral music, it may not be too far-fetched to assume that he also drew on the *Nachtlied* as a source for his symphonic theme. This hypothesis furthermore imparts a "poetic" dimension to the quiet close of Brahms's finale: the motive becomes a cipher for the "sleep" into which the symphony's "hero" drifts after weathering many a turbulent storm.

115. Adapted from Goethe, *Wilhelm Meister's Apprenticeship,* p. 352.

116. See *TB* 3, pp. 496–97, 503.

117. For a detailed discussion of the thematic and motivic connections between the

Meister lieder and the *Requiem für Mignon,* see Mahlert, *Fortschritt und Kunstlied,* pp. 152–56.

118. "Goethe's Career as a Man of Letters" (1932), in Mann, *Essays of Three Decades,* p. 49.

Chapter 12

1. Mendelssohn, who served in Düsseldorf from 1833 to 1835, was less than enthusiastic about the city's orchestra: "At the beat, they all come in separately . . . , and in the *pianos* the flute is always too high, and not a single Düsseldorfer can play a triplet clearly, . . . and every *Allegro* leaves off twice as fast as it began, and the oboe plays E-natural in C minor." Quoted in Porter, "Schumann Legacy," p. 58.

2. *Briefe, Neue Folge,* p. 318.

3. *Ibid.,* p. 323.

4. Letter of 26 August 1850, in *Briefe, Neue Folge,* p. 467.

5. *TB* 3, p. 786, note 770.

6. See Bischoff, *Monument für Beethoven,* pp. 352–57. As Bischoff notes, apart from the occasional addition of a *decrescendo,* Schumann hardly altered the text; his concern was with as "authentic" a performance as possible.

7. Kapp, "Das Orchester Schumanns," p. 198.

8. The reviewer who covered the premiere of the work on 6 February 1851 for the *Rheinische Musikzeitung* already noted that the symphony as a whole presented "a piece of Rhenish life." See Lichtenhahn, "Sinfonie als Dichtung," p. 18.

9. Wasielewski, *Robert Schumann,* p. 455.

10. Kapp, "Das Orchester Schumanns," p. 198. As regards the image of Schumann "with his head buried in the score," we should keep in mind that he was severely nearsighted and, refusing to wear glasses, made do clumsily with a lorgnette.

11. See Pohl, "Reminiscences of Robert Schumann," pp. 237–41, 248, 255.

12. According to Edler, the only known example of the genre before Schumann is C. A. Schumacher's (rather undistinguished) *Erlkönig* of 1838. See *Robert Schumann und seine Zeit,* p. 261. Mendelssohn's *Die erste Walpurgisnacht,* op. 60 (1841), a setting of a balladic text by Goethe, should certainly be added to the list of precedents for Schumann's ballades.

13. There is evidence that some of the works attributed to the young poet were written, either in whole or in part, by her mentor and biographer Karl Friedrich von Grossheinrich. See Lossewa, "Neues über Elisabeth Kulmann."

14. See Litzmann, *Clara Schumann* 2, p. 240; and *TB* 3, p. 571.

15. For a summary of the orchestrational and structural differences between the 1841 and 1851 versions of the D-minor symphony, see Zlotnik, "Orchestration Revisions," pp. 225–32; and Andreae, "Die vierte Symphonie," pp. 35–41. As Andreae notes, Breitkopf and Härtel published what amounts to a third version in 1891. The product of an editorial collaboration between Brahms and the conductor Franz Wüllner, it retains most of the features of the 1841 version while incorporating some aspects of the later reorchestration. The title page of the 1851 revision reads: "Symphonistische Phantasie für grosses Orchester"; similarly, the first page of the score bears the designation "Phantasie für Orchester." Schumann later crossed out the word "Phantasie," replacing it with the more neutral "Symphonie."

16. On Schumann's consideration of *Hermann und Dorothea* as an operatic subject, see Pohl, "Reminiscences of Robert Schumann," p. 253. On his reactions to Wagner's seminal tract, see *Briefe, Neue Folge,* p. 352.

17. Pohl, "Reminiscences of Robert Schumann," pp. 242–43, 249.

18. Letter of 13 January 1851, in *Briefe, Neue Folge,* p. 335. Strackerjahn was an amateur singer and member of a Berlin club whose members were all great fans of Schumann's music. The group called itself "Die Bande Bob."

19. Quoted in *Robert Schumann Neue Ausgabe* IV/3/2, p. xi.

20. *TB* 3, p. 669.

21. See *TB* 2, p. 432; and *TB* 3, pp. 590, 595.

22. *TB* 2, p. 434; and *TB* 3, p. 597.

23. *TB* 3, pp. 597–599.

24. *TB* 2, pp. 436–37.

25. *TB* 3, p. 602.

26. The leave of absence brought with it a reduction in Schumann's quarterly salary from 162 thalers to 137 thalers. Tausch normally received only 25 thalers per quarter for his services. See *TB* 3, pp. 668–69.

27. *TB* 3, p. 608.

28. See Appel, Critical Notes to *Robert Schumann Neue Ausgabe* IV/3/2, pp. xxv–xxvii.

29. *Briefe, Neue Folge,* pp. 370–71.

30. See, however, the entries in the *Haushaltbücher* for 1 August 1853 ("Toward evening, table-turning with the dinner guests") and 17 October 1853 ("Unsuccessful attempt at table-rapping"); *TB* 3, pp. 631, 639.

31. In 1925 Martin Kreisig made a copy of the former list that is now housed in the Robert-Schumann-Haus in Zwickau. From it we learn that Schumann's music library contained about 500 titles, most of them scores, among which are represented all the major categories of composition: church music, operas, orchestral music, instrumental chamber music, and *Hausmusik* (choral partsongs, lieder, and piano music). See Bischoff, *Monument für Beethoven,* pp. 364–65.

32. *TB* 3, p. 634.

33. *Briefe, Neue Folge,* p. 379.

34. See *TB* 3, pp. 637–38.

35. See, e.g., Schoppe, "Schumann und Brahms," pp. 86–88.

36. *NZfM* 39 (1853), pp. 185–86.

37. *TB* 3, p. 639.

38. For a detailed discussion of the cycle's rather complicated genesis and also of the connotations of its original title *(An Diotima),* see Struck, *Die umstrittenen späten Instrumentalwerke Schumanns,* pp. 465–77.

39. See Heuberger, *Erinnerungen,* p. 60.

40. Kapp, "Das Orchester Schumanns," pp. 198–99. As Kapp notes in "Schumann nach der Revolution" (pp. 348, 352), Schumann was also convinced that a conductor should not rule over his orchestra like a dictator; under ideal circumstances, the orchestra would operate "like a republic."

41. *Ibid.,* p. 200.

42. See Moser, *Joseph Joachim* 1, pp. 382–83.

43. Eismann, *Quellenwerk* 1, p. 181.

44. *Ibid.,* p. 182.

45. Litzmann, *Clara Schumann* 2, pp. 248–49. Schumann's contracts were negotiated yearly in October and went into effect in April of the following year.

46. Eismann, *Quellenwerk* 1, p. 182.

47. Litzmann, *Clara Schumann* 2, p. 252.

48. See *TB* 3, p. 810, note 924a. Clara sent a copy of Schumann's letter to Hammers,

who wrote back on 6 December suggesting that the matter be arbitrated by a subcommittee of the town council, but Schumann never responded. (At the time he considered taking over the direction of Julius Stern's Gesangverein in Berlin.) The city continued to pay his salary until March 1855; as implied in his letter of 9 November 1853, he had probably settled his contract for the 1854–55 season in October 1853.

49. Writing to Strackerjahn on 17 January 1854, Schumann noted with amazement that his music was "more intimately known in Holland than in Germany." *Briefe, Neue Folge*, p. 390.

50. *TB* 2, pp. 441, 446.

51. My account of Schumann's last weeks in Düsseldorf is based on *TB* 3, pp. 648–49; Litzmann, *Clara Schumann* 2, pp. 295–302; and Eismann, *Quellenwerk* 1, pp. 190–91.

52. Eismann, *Quellenwerk* 1, p. 191.

53. Litzmann, *Clara Schumann* 2, p. 301.

54. For a fair-minded analysis of this ticklish subject, see Reich, "Clara Schumann and Johannes Brahms," pp. 41–44.

55. Wasielewski, *Robert Schumann*, p. 456.

56. Deemed unplayable by many performers, the rapid passage-work in the finale of the Violin Concerto is perfectly manageable if Schumann's metronome marking ($\bullet$ = 63) is observed. Among modern virtuosi, only Gidon Kremer has had the courage to take Schumann at his word, with stunning results. For a convincing refutation of the old hypothesis that Schumann's metronome was defective, see Dietrich Kämper, "Zur Frage der Metronombezeichnungen Robert Schumanns."

57. For a discussion of Schumann's (and his collaborators') alterations made to the original texts, see Jarczyk, *Die Chorballade*, pp. 38–59, 86–91.

58. See Edler, *Robert Schumann*, p. 262.

59. See *TB* 1, p. 243; and Wasielewski, *Robert Schumann*, pp. 233–34, 404.

60. Letter of 14 February 1851, in *Briefe, Neue Folge*, p. 336.

61. "Old and New Church Music," in Charlton, ed., *E. T. A. Hoffmann's Musical Writings*, p. 358.

62. The ascending form of the motive, which figures in the Credo of the Mass and the "Te decet" of the Requiem, approximates the shape of the principal idea of the fourth movement of the Third Symphony and thus provides a bridge from the sacred to the public style.

63. See Appel, Critical Notes to *Robert Schumann Neue Ausgabe* IV/3/2, pp. xv–xvi.

64. *Briefe, Neue Folge*, pp. 390ff.

65. *GS* 1, p. 2.

66. Pohl, "Reminiscences of Robert Schumann," p. 259.

67. Litzmann, *Clara Schumann* 2, p. 299.

68. For a thorough and thoughtful account of this issue, see Reich, *Clara Schumann*, pp. 145–47.

69. Portions of this document have only recently been made available for study. Placed in the archive of the Akademie der Künste, Berlin, by Aribert Reimann (Richarz's great grand-nephew), in 1991, the diary was withheld from public examination for ethical reasons. Excerpts appear in Franken, "Robert Schumann," pp. 17–24. The parts of the diary covering the periods from 4 March 1854 (when Schumann was admitted) to 6 April 1854, and 28 April to 6 September 1854, were destroyed at the end of the Second World War.

70. Franken, "Robert Schumann," p. 17.

71. *Ibid.*, p. 20.

72. *Ibid.*, p. 21.

73. *Ibid.*, p. 22.

74. *Ibid.*, pp. 22–23.

75. Cf. *Briefe, Neue Folge*, p. 408; Hanslick, "Robert Schumann in Endenich," p. 282; and Franken, "Robert Schumann," pp. 19–20.

76. See Ostwald, *Schumann*, pp. 278, 292, 307.

77. Franken, "Robert Schumann," p. 21. See also the entries for 22 January and 25 July 1855 (pp. 18, 21).

78. *Ibid.*, p. 23.

79. *Ibid.*, p. 21.

80. Christel figures regularly in Schumann's diary between 12 May 1831 (though it is clear from the tenor of this and subsequent entries that he had regular sexual contact with her before) and 13 July 1832. (See *TB* 1, pp. 330, 332, 339, 342–44, 350, 355, 372, 374, 386–87, 390, 394). The first reference to her is also the most intriguing: "In the afternoon Christel [was] pale—disclosures—only guilt gives birth to Nemesis." Did the "disclosures" involve a recently contracted venereal disease? Was Schumann visited by Nemesis, the goddess of retribution (whom we encounter on 12 March 1855 in Endenich) on the morning of the day he lept into the Rhine? I am tempted to answer both questions in the affirmative.

81. Although the ulcerations that may appear during the primary stage of the disease are generally painless, I am informed by Dr. Reed Drews (Professor of Medicine, Beth Israel Hospital, Brookline, Massachusetts) that a lesion accompanied by painful sensations is not out of the question. I would like to thank Dr. Drews for his advice on this and other questions regarding Schumann's illness.

82. In his autopsy report on Schumann, discovered in 1973 by Gerd Nauhaus, the director of the Robert-Schumann-Haus in Zwickau, Richarz described a process of organic decay or atrophy of the brain and ascribed Schumann's death to a "progressive paralysis" whose final manifestation was pneumonia. Though it did not draw the connection with syphilis, Richarz's diagnosis should be taken seriously. See Franken, "Robert Schumann," pp. 9, 14, 15. It should also be mentioned that Schumann apparently did not transmit the disease to Clara, who died of a stroke at the age of seventy-six. Obviously, he was not in sexual contact with her during the initial outbreak of infection, when the disease is highly contagious. (According to the *Haushaltbücher*, he and Clara had intercourse for the last time on 14 February 1854, just as general paresis began to set in; see *TB* 3, p. 648.) Thus, the mental illness of his son Ludwig (1848–1899), who like Schumann died in an asylum, cannot be ascribed to the transmission of syphilitic infection through Clara.

83. Franken, "Robert Schumann," p. 21.

84. *Ibid.*

85. See his letters of 27 November 1854, 6 January 1855, and mid-March 1855, in Hanslick, "Robert Schumann in Endenich," pp. 277, 281, 283.

86. Franken, "Robert Schumann," p. 18.

87. See his letters to Clara of 14 September 1854, 18 September 1854, 10 October 1854, and 12 October 1854, in Hanslick, "Robert Schumann in Endenich," pp. 273, 274, 276.

88. Litzmann, *Clara Schumann* 2, p. 374.

89. See Litzmann, *Clara Schumann* 2, pp. 319–29; and Franken, "Robert Schumann," p. 18. For Dagmar Hoffmann-Axthelm, the most tragic aspect of Schumann's final years was his loss of the ability to communicate with others. See his *Robert Schumann*, pp. 10–11.

90. See Hanslick, "Robert Schumann in Endenich," pp. 278, 283; and Franken, "Robert Schumann," pp. 21 and 23.

91. See Litzmann, *Clara Schumann* 2, pp. 375–76; Joachim and Moser, *Briefe* 1, pp. 287, 290; and Kalbeck, *Johannes Brahms* 1, pp. 271–72.

92. Litzmann, *Clara Schumann*, 2, pp. 413–14.

93. Eismann, *Quellenwerk* 1, p. 197. Richarz confirmed this account, but added that Schumann became violent soon after Clara left for the evening and would not allow his attendant to spend the night in his room; Franken, "Robert Schumann," p. 24.

94. See Eismann, *Quellenwerk* 1, p. 197; and Franken, "Robert Schumann," p. 24.

95. Franken, "Robert Schumann," p. 24; and Eismann, *Quellenwerk* 1, pp. 197–98.

96. See Porter, "The Schumann Legacy," p. 198; and Eismann, *Quellenwerk* 1, p. 198.

Epilogue

1. See Floros, *Brahms und Bruckner,* p. 115; and Brahms, *Briefwechsel* 3, p. 121.

2. See Newmarch, *Tchaikovsky,* pp. 132–33.

3. Letter of January 1907; quoted in Edler, *Robert Schumann,* p. 309.

4. See Edler, *Robert Schumann,* pp. 309–10.

5. Nietzsche, *Beyond Good and Evil,* p. 182.

6. Adorno, *Alban Berg,* p. 21.

7. See Berg, "The Musical Impotence."

8. Heine, *The Romantic School,* pp. 114, 116.

Appendix

1. In his copy of *Flegeljahre,* Schumann underlined several passages from this chapter and noted, in the margin, the number of the piece from *Papillons* (perhaps in one of its earlier manifestations) to which they corresponded. The underlined passages are indicated here in italics; Schumann's numbers appear in square brackets.

2. The Baumannshöhle was a stalactite cave on the left bank of the river Bode in the Harz mountains, and had been something of a tourist attraction since the late seventeenth century. The Schumanns visited it on 13 September 1844. See *TB* 2, pp. 388 and 728.

3. According to Bechstein and other natural scientists goats (as well as Americans) have milk; the old proverb is correct. [Jean Paul's footnote]

Bibliography

Abert, Hermann. "Robert Schumann's 'Genoveva'" (1910). In *Musik-Konzepte Sonderband: Robert Schumann II*, ed. Heinz-Klaus Metzger and Rainer Riehn. Munich, 1982.

Abraham, Gerald. *A Hundred Years of Music*, 3d ed. Chicago: Aldine, 1964.

―――. "Robert Schumann." In *The New Grove*, ed. by Stanley Sadie, vol. 16. London: Macmillan, 1980.

―――. "Schumann's *Jugendsinfonie* in G minor." *Musical Quarterly* 37 (1951): 45–60.

―――, ed. *Schumann: A Symposium*. London: Oxford University Press, 1952.

Adorno, Theodor W. *Alban Berg: Master of the Smallest Link*, trans. Juliane Brand and Christopher Hailey. Cambridge: Cambridge University Press, 1991.

―――. "Coda: Schumanns Lieder." In *Noten zur Literatur I*. Berlin and Frankfurt, 1958.

―――. *Introduction to the Sociology of Music*, trans. E. B. Ashton. New York: Continuum, 1976.

―――. *Notes to Literature*, vol. 1, trans. Shierry Weber Nicholsen. New York: Columbia University Press, 1991.

Alain, Olivier. "Schumann und die französische Musik." In *Sammelbände der Robert-Schumann Gesellschaft* I/1961. Leipzig: VEB Deutscher Verlag für Musik, 1961.

Alf, Julius, and Joseph A. Kruse, eds. *Robert Schumann: Universalgeist der Romantik. Beiträge zu seiner Persönlichkeit und seinem Werk*. Düsseldorf: Droste Verlag, 1981.

Andreae, Marc. "Die vierte Symphonie Robert Schumanns, ihre Fassungen, ihre Interpretationsprobleme." In *Robert Schumann: Ein romantisches Erbe in neuer Forschung. Acht Studien*, ed. Robert-Schumann-Gesellschaft Düsseldorf. Mainz: Schott, 1984.

Appel, Bernhard R. "'Actually, Taken Directly from Family Life': Robert Schumann's *Album für die Jugend*," trans. John Michael Cooper. In *Schumann and His World*, ed. R. Larry Todd. Princeton, Princeton University Press, 1994.

―――. "Katalog." In *Robert Schumann und die Dichter*, ed. Appel and Hermsträuwer. Düsseldorf: Droste Verlag, 1991.

―――. "Ein produktives Missverständnis: Robert Schumanns 'Kinderszenen' Op. 15 in der Kritik Ludwig Rellstabs." *Musikforschung* 40 (1987): 109–15.

―――. "Robert Schumann als Leser." In *Robert Schumann und die Dichter*, ed. Appel and Hermsträuwer. Düsseldorf: Droste Verlag, 1991.

————. "Schumanns Davidsbund: Geistes- und sozialgeschichtliche Voraussetzungen einer romantischer Idee." *Archiv für Musikwissenschaft* 38 (1981): 1–23.

————. "Die Überleitung vom 2. zum 3. Satz in Robert Schumanns Klavierkonzert Opus 54." *Musikforschung* 44 (1991): 255–61.

————, ed. *Schumann Forschungen.* Vol. 3, *Schumann in Düsseldorf.* Mainz and London: Schott, 1993.

Appel, Bernhard R., and Inge Hermstrüwer, eds. *Robert Schumann und die Dichter: Ein Musiker als Leser.* Düsseldorf: Droste Verlag, 1991.

Barry, Barbara. "Image and Imagination in Schumann's G-minor Sonata." *Journal of the Science and Practice of Music* (The Music Research Center, Hanyang University, Seoul, Korea) 4 (1987–88): 57–73.

Barthes, Roland. "The Death of the Author." In *Image Music Text,* trans. Stephen Heath. New York: Hill and Wang, 1977.

————. *The Responsibility of Forms,* trans. Richard Howard. New York: Hill and Wang, 1985.

Beaufils, Marcel. "Mythos und Maske bei Robert Schumann." In *Sammelbände der Robert-Schumann Gesellschaft* II/1966. Leipzig: VEB Deutscher Verlag für Musik, 1967: 66–76.

Becker, C. F. "Zur Geschichte der Hausmusik in früheren Jahrhunderten." *NZfM* 7 (1837): 25ff., 177ff.; 8 (1838): 45ff.; 9 (1838): 115ff., 195ff.; 10 (1839): 105ff., 121ff.

Becker, Claudia Stevens. "A New Look at Schumann's Impromptus." *Musical Quarterly* 67 (1981): 568–86.

————. "A Study of Robert Schumann's *Impromptus,* Op. 5: Its Sources and a Critical Analysis of its Revisions." D.M.A. diss., Boston University, 1977.

Bellman, Jonathan. *"Aus alten Märchen:* The Chivalric Style of Schumann and Brahms." *Journal of Musicology* 13/1 (1995): 117–35.

Benjamin, Walter. *Der Begriff der Kunstkritik in der deutschen Romantik.* 1919–20. Frankfurt: Suhrkamp, 1973.

————. "Goethes Wahlverwandschaften" [1921/22]. In *Gesammelte Schriften,* I/1, ed. Rolf Tiedemann and Hermann Schweppenhäuser. Frankfurt: Suhrkamp, 1980.

————. *The Origin of German Tragic Drama* [1925], trans. John Osborne, intro. by George Steiner. London: Verso, 1985.

Bent, Ian, ed. *Music Analysis in the Nineteenth Century.* Vol. 1, *Fugue, Form, and Style.* Cambridge: Cambridge University Press, 1994.

————. *Music Analysis in the Nineteenth Century.* Vol. 2, *Hermeneutic Approaches.* Cambridge: Cambridge University Press, 1994.

Berg, Alban. "The Musical Impotence of Hans Pfitzner's 'New Aesthetic.'" In Willi Reich, *The Life and Works of Alban Berg,* trans. Cornelius Cardew. New York: Da Capo, 1982.

Berger, Dorothea. *Jean Paul Friedrich Richter.* New York: Twayne, 1972.

Berger, Karol. *"Diegesis* and *Mimesis:* The Poetic Modes and the Matter of Artistic Presentation." *Journal of Musicology* 12 (1994): 407–33.

Berlioz, Hector. *Memoirs*, trans. Rachel and Eleanor Holmes; annotated, and the translations revised by Ernest Newman. New York: Dover, 1966.

Best, Walther. *Die Romanzen Robert Schumanns*. Frankfurt: Lang, 1988.

Bischoff, Bodo. *Monument für Beethoven: Die Entwicklung der Beethoven-Rezeption Robert Schumanns*. Cologne-Rheinkassel: Verlag Dohr, 1994.

Blackall, Eric A. *Goethe and the Novel*. Ithaca and London: Cornell University Press, 1976.

———. *The Novels of the German Romantics*. Ithaca and London: Cornell University Press, 1983.

Boetticher, Wolfgang. *Einführung in die musikalische Romantik*. Wilhelmshaven: Heinrichshofen's Verlag, 1983.

———. "Das Enstehen von R. Schumanns Klavierkonzert: Textkritische Studien." In *Festschrift Martin Ruhnke zum 65. Geburtstage*. Stuttgart: Hänssler-Verlag, 1986.

———. "Das Erbe Robert Schumanns im jüngeren Schrifttum." *Neue Zeitschrift für Musik* 1981: 248–51.

———. "Die Frühfassung des ersten Satzes von Robert Schumanns Klavierkonzert op. 54 und das Problem seiner Durchführung." In *Festschrift Arno Forchert zum 60. Geburtstag*. Kassel: Bärenreiter, 1986.

———. "Neue textkritische Forschungen an R. Schumanns Klavierwerk." *Archiv für Musikwissenschaft* 25 (1968): 46–76.

———. *Robert Schumann: Einführung in Persönlichkeit und Werk*. Berlin: Hahnefeld, 1941.

———. *Robert Schumann in seinen Schriften und Briefen*. Berlin: Hahnefeld, 1942.

———. *Robert Schumanns Klavierwerke—Neue biographische und textkritische Untersuchungen, Teil I, Opus 1–6*. Wilhelmshaven: Heinrichshofen's Verlag, 1976.

———. "Schumanns frühe Klavierquartett c-Moll (1828/29)." *Musikforschung*, 31 (1978): 465–67.

———. "Über die unbekannte 'Familienkassette' Robert und Clara Schumanns." In *Scritti in Onore di Luigi Ronga*. Milan: Ricciardi, 1973.

———. "Weitere Forschungen an Dokumenten zum Leben und Schaffen Robert Schumanns." In *Robert Schumann: Ein romantisches Erbe in neuer Forschung*. Mainz: Schott, 1984.

———. "Zum Problem eines 'Urtextes' bei Robert Schumann und Anton Bruckner." In *Bericht über den Internationalen Musikwissenschaftlichen Kongress Bayreuth 1981*. Kassel: Bärenreiter, 1984.

———, ed. *Briefe und Gedichte aus dem Album Robert und Clara Schumanns*. Leipzig: VEB Deutscher Verlag für Musik, 1979.

Bonds, Mark Evan. *After Beethoven: Imperatives of Originality* in the Symphony (forthcoming).

Borris, Siegfried. "Kontroverse Aspekte zur Hausmusik." *Musica* 40 (1986): 413–15.

Botstein, Leon. "History, Rhetoric, and the Self: Robert Schumann and Music Making in German-Speaking Europe, 1800–1860." In *Schumann and His World*, ed. R. Larry Todd. Princeton: Princeton University Press, 1994.

Bracht, Hans-Joachim. "Schumanns 'Papillons' und die Ästhetik der Frühromantik." *Archiv für Musikwissenschaft* 50 (1993): 71–84.

Brahms, Johannes. *Briefwechsel,* 16 vols. Berlin: Deutsche Brahms Gesellschaft, 1907–1922.

Brendel, Franz. "Einige Worte über Richard Wagner." *Neue Zeitschrift für Musik* 34 (1851): 264–66.

———. "R. Schumann's Oper: Genoveva." *Neue Zeitschrift für Musik* 33 (1850): 1–4, 17–18.

———. "Robert Schumann mit Rücksicht auf Mendelssohn-Bartholdy, und die Entwicklung der modernen Tonkunst überhaupt." *Neue Zeitschrift für Musik* 22 (1845): 63–67, 81–83, 98–92, 113–15, 121–23, 145–47, 149–50.

———. "Vergangenheit, Gegenwart und Zukunft der Oper." *Neue Zeitschrift für Musik* 23 (1845): 33–35, 37–39, 41–43, 105–8, 109–12, 121–24, 149–152; and 24 (1846): 57–60, 61–64.

Brion, Marcel. *Schumann and the Romantic Age,* trans. Geoffrey Sainsbury. New York: Macmillan, 1956.

———. "Schumann et l'âme du romantisme allemand." In Marcel Brion, *Schumann.* [Paris]: Hachette, [1970].

Brodbeck, David. "The Joachim-Brahms Counterpoint Exchange; or Robert, Clara, and 'The Best Harmony Between Jos. and Joh.'" In *Brahms Studies,* vol. 1, ed. D. Brodbeck. Lincoln and London: University of Nebraska Press, 1994.

Brown, Thomas Alan. *The Aesthetics of Robert Schumann.* New York: Philosophical Library, 1968.

———. "Schumann's Baroque Organ Compositions." *The Diapason,* 68/5 (April 1977): 4–5, 20.

Bula, Karol. "Zu den Beziehungen Chopins zu Schumann." In *Robert-Schumann-Tage 1985,* ed. Günther Müller. Wissenschafliche Arbeitstagung zu Fragen der Schumann-Forschung in Zwickau, 1985.

Burde, Wolfgang. "Robert Schumann—ein moderner Komponist." *Neue Zeitschrift für Musik* 3 (1981): 221.

Byron, George Gordon, Baron. *The Complete Poetical Works,* ed. Jerome J. McGann, vol. 4. Oxford: Clarendon Press, 1986.

———. *Lord Byron's Correspondence,* ed. John Murray, vol. 2. London: Murray, 1922.

———. *The Works of Lord Byron: Letters and Journals,* vol. 4. London: Murray, 1904.

Cacciopo, Curt. "Poem to Music: Schumann's 'Mondnacht' Setting." *College Music Symposium* 30/2 (1990): 46–56.

Casey, Timothy J., ed., and Erika Casey, trans. *Jean Paul: A Reader.* Baltimore and London: The Johns Hopkins University Press, 1992.

Cerny, Miroslav K. "Schumann und die tschechischen Komponisten um die Mitte des 19. Jahrhunderts." In *Robert-Schumann-Tage 1985,* ed. Günther Muller. Wissenschaftliche Arbeitstagung zu Fragen der Schumann-Forschung in Zwickau, 1985.

Chailley, Jacques. "Zum Symbolismus bei Robert Schumann mit besonderer Berücksichtigung der *Papillons* op. 2," in *Robert Schumann: Ein romantisches Erbe in neuer Forschung*. Mainz: Schott, 1984.

Charlton, David, ed. *E. T. A. Hoffmann's Musical Writings: Kreisleriana, The Poet and the Composer, Music Criticism*. Cambridge: Cambridge University Press, 1989.

Chisell, Joan. *Schumann*. Rev. ed. London: Dent, 1967.

Cone, Edward T. *Berlioz: Fantastic Symphony* (Norton Critical Score). New York: Norton, 1971.

Conrad, Dieter. "Zu Schumanns Klavierquintett." In *Musik-Konzepte Sonderband: Robert Schumann II*, ed. Heinz-Klaus Metzger and Rainer Riehn. Munich, 1982.

Correll, Linda E. [see also Roesner, Linda]. "Structural Revisions in the String Quartets Opus 41 of Robert Schumann." *Current Musicology* 7 (1968): 87–95.

Crisp, Deborah. "The *Kreisleriana* of Robert Schumann and E. T. A. Hoffmann: Some Musical and Literary Parallels." *Musicology Australia* 16 (1993): 3–18.

Czerny, Carl. *School of Practical Composition*, trans. John Bishop, 3 vols. London: R. Cocks, [1848].

Dadelsen, Georg. "Schumann und die Musik Bachs." *Archiv für Musikwissenschaft* 14 (1957): 46–59.

Dahlhaus, Carl. *Analysis and Value Judgment*, trans. Siegmund Levarie. New York: Pendragon, 1983.

————. "Bach und der romantische Kontrapunkt." *Musica* 43 (1989): 10–22.

————. *Between Romanticism and Modernism: Four Studies in the Music of the Later Nineteenth Century*, trans. Mary Whittall. Berkeley and Los Angeles: University of California Press, 1980.

————. *Klassische und Romantische Musikästhetik*. Laaber: Laaber Verlag, 1988.

————. *Ludwig van Beethoven: Approaches to his Music*, trans. Mary Whittall. Oxford: Clarendon Press, 1991.

————. *Die Musiktheorie im 18. und 19. Jahrhundert*, 2 vols.; *Geschichte der Musiktheorie*, vols. 10 & 11. Darmstadt: Wissenschaftliche Buchgesellschaft, 1984.

————. *Nineteenth-Century Music*, trans. J. Bradford Robinson. Berkeley: University of California Press, 1979.

————. "Romantik und Biedermeier: Zur musikgeschichtlichen Charakteristik der Restaurationszeit." *Archiv für Musikwissenschaft* 31 (1974): 22–41.

————. "Wozu noch Biographien?" *Melos/Neue Zeitschrift für Musik* 1 (1975): p. 82.

————. "Zur Dramaturgie der Literaturoper." In *Vom Musikdrama zur Literaturoper: Aufsätze zur neueren Operngeschichte*. Munich: Piper, 1989.

————. "Zur Problematik der musikalischen Gattungen im 19. Jahrhundert." In *Gattungen der Musik in Einzeldarstellungen: Gedenkschrift Leo Schrade*. Bern and Munich: Francke Verlag, 1973.

Dällenbach, Lucien. *The Mirror in the Text*, trans. Jeremy Whiteley with Emma Hughes. Chicago: University of Chicago Press, 1989.

Danuser, Hermann. "Kann Poetik die Biographik retten?" *Melos/Neue Zeitschrift für Musik* 1 (1975): 286–87.

Daverio, John. "From 'Concertante Rondo' to 'Lyric Sonata': A Commentary on Brahms's Reception of Mozart." In *Brahms Studies,* vol. 1, ed. David Brodbeck. Lincoln and London: University of Nebraska Press, 1994.

———. *Nineteenth-Century Music and the German Romantic Ideology.* New York: Schirmer Books, 1993.

———. "Reading Schumann by Way of Jean Paul and his Contemporaries." *College Music Symposium* 30/2 (1990): 28–45.

———. "Schumann's 'Im Legendenton' and Friedrich Schlegel's *Arabeske.*" *19th Century Music* 11/2 (1987): 150–63.

———. "Schumann's 'New Genre for the Concert Hall': *Das Paradies und die Peri* in the Eyes of a Contemporary." In R. Larry Todd, ed., *Schumann and His World.* Princeton: Princeton University Press, 1994.

Debussy, Claude. *Debussy on Music,* trans. and ed. Richard Langham Smith. New York: Knopf, 1977.

de Ford, Miriam Allen. *Thomas Moore.* New York: Twayne, 1967.

Degen, Johannes D. "Schumanns Einfluss auf die skandinavischen Schüler und Schülernachfolger." In *Robert-Schumann-Tage 1985,* ed. Günther Müller. Wissenschaftliche Arbeitstagung zu Fragen der Schumann-Forschung in Zwickau, 1985.

Demmler, Martin. " 'Nicht zuviel Kreuze und Bee': Die Tendenz zum Populären in Schumanns späten Vokalwerk." *Musica* 43 (1989): 483–86.

Dietel, Gerhard. *'Eine neue poetische Zeit': Musikanschauung und stilistische Tendenzen im Klavierwerk Robert Schumanns.* Kassel: Bärenreiter, 1989.

Dill, Heinz J. "Romantic Irony in the Works of Robert Schumann." *Musical Quarterly* 73 (1989): 172–95.

Dörffel, Alfred. "Für Pianoforte: Robert Schumann, op. 68, Album für die Jugend." *Neue Zeitschrift für Musik* 30 (1849): 89–91.

———. *Geschichte der Gewandhausconcerte zu Leipzig vom 25. November 1781 bis 25. November 1881.* Leipzig, 1884. (Reprint ed., Leipzig: VEB Deutscher Verlag für Musik, 1980).

Draheim, Joachim. "Robert Schumann als Übersetzer." In *Robert Schumann und die Dichter,* ed. Appel and Hermstrüwer. Düsseldorf: Droste Verlag, 1991.

———. "Schumann Erstdrucke: Versuch einer bibliographischen Ergänzung." *Musikforschung* 46 (1993): 53–60.

———. "Schumann und Shakespeare." *Neue Zeitschrift für Musik* (1981): 237–47.

———. "Schumanns Jugendwerk: Acht Polonaisen op. III für Klavier zu 4 Händen." In *Schumanns Werke,* ed. Mayeda and Niemöller. Mainz: Schott, 1987.

Dürr, Walther. *Das deutsche Sololied im 19. Jahrhundert: Untersuchungen zu Sprache und Musik.* Wilhelmshaven: Heinrichshofen's Verlag, 1984.

Dusella, Reinhold. "Symphonisches in den Skizzenbüchern Schumanns." In *Probleme der Symphonischen Tradition,* ed. Kross. Tutzing: Schneider, 1990.

Edler, Arnfried. "Aphoristik und Novellistik: Versuch über das Private in Schumanns Klaviermusik." In *Musica Privata—Die Rolle der Musik im privaten Leben—*

Festschrift zum 65. Geburtstag von Walter Salmen, ed. Monika Fink, Rainer Gastrein, Günter Mössmer. Innsbruck: Helbling, 1991.

———. *Robert Schumann und seine Zeit.* Laaber: Laaber Verlag, 1982.

———. "Ton und Zyklus in der Symphonik Schumanns." In *Probleme der Symphonischen Tradition im 19. Jahrhundert,* ed. Kross. Tutzing: Schneider, 1990.

Eggebrecht, Harald. "Töne sind höhere Worte." In *Musik-Konzepte, Sonderband, Robert Schumann I,* ed. Heinz-Klaus Metzger and Rainer Riehn. Munich, 1981.

Eggebrecht, Harald, and Dieter Holland. "Eine Schumann-Diskographie und ihre Kriterien." In *Musik-Konzepte Sonderband: Robert Schumann II,* ed. Heinz-Klaus Metzger and Rainer Riehn. Munich, 1982.

Eichner, Hans. "Germany/Romantisch-Romantik-Romantiker." In *'Romantic' and Its Cognates—The European History of a Word,* ed. H. Eichner. Toronto: University of Toronto Press, 1972.

Einstein, Alfred. *Music in the Romantic Era.* New York: Norton, 1947.

Eismann, Georg. "Nachweis der internationalen Standorte von Notenautographen Robert Schumanns." In *Sammelbände der Robert-Schumann Gesellschaft* II/1966. Leipzig: VEB Deutscher Verlag für Musik, 1967.

———. *Robert Schumann: Eine Biographie in Wort und Bild.* Leipzig: VEB Verlag, 1956.

———. *Robert Schumann: Ein Quellenwerk über sein Leben und Schaffen,* 2 vols. Leipzig: Breitkopf & Härtel, 1956.

———. "Zu Robert Schumanns letzten Kompositionen." *Beiträge zur Musikwissenschaft* 10 (1968): 151–57.

Ellman, Richard. "Freud and Literary Biography." In Richard Ellman, *a long the river run: Selected Essays.* New York: Knopf, 1989.

Emans, Reinmar, and Matthias Wendt, eds. *Beiträge zur Geschichte des Konzerts: Festschrift Siegfried Kross zum 60. Geburtstag.* Bonn: Gudrun Schröder Verlag, 1990.

Epstein, David. *Beyond Orpheus: Studies in Musical Structure.* Oxford and New York: Oxford University Press, 1987.

Erler, Hermann. *Robert Schumann's Leben aus seinen Briefen geschildert,* 2 vols. Berlin: Ries and Erler, 1887.

Fellerer, Karl Gustav. *Studien zur Musik des 19. Jahrhunderts. Band 1: Musik und Musikleben im 19. Jahrhundert.* Regensburg: Bosse, 1984.

Fellinger, Imogen. "Brahms's 'Way': A Composer's Self-view." In *Brahms 2: biographical, documentary and analytical studies,* ed. Michael Musgrave. Cambridge and London: Cambridge University Press.

Ferris, David. "From Fragment to Cycle: Formal Organization in Schumann's Eichendorff *Liederkreis.*" Ph.D. diss., Brandeis University, 1993.

Finscher, Ludwig. " 'Zwischen absoluter und Programmusik': Zur Interpretation der deutschen romantischen Symphonie." In *Festschrift Walter Wiora zum 70. Geburtstag: Über Symphonien,* ed. Christoph-Hellmut Mahling. Tutzing: Schneider, 1979.

Finson, Jon W. "The Intentional Tourist: Romantic Irony in the Eichendorff *Lie-*

derkreis of Robert Schumann." In R. Larry Todd, ed., *Schumann and His World*. Princeton: Princeton University Press, 1994.

———. *Robert Schumann and the Study of Orchestral Composition: The Genesis of the First Symphony, Op. 38.* Oxford: Clarendon Press, 1989.

———. "Schumann and Shakespeare." In *Mendelssohn and Schumann*, ed. Finson and Todd. Durham: Duke University Press, 1984.

———. "Schumann, Popularity, and the *Ouverture, Scherzo, und Finale,* Opus 52." *Musical Quarterly* 69 (1983): 1–26.

———. "Schumann's Mature Style and the 'Album of Songs for the Young'." *Journal of Musicology* 8 (1990): 227–50.

———. "The Sketches for Robert Schumann's C Minor Symphony." *Journal of Musicology* 1 (1982): 395–418.

———. "The Sketches for the Fourth Movement of Schumann's Second Symphony, Op. 61." *Journal of the American Musicological Society* 39 (1986): 143–68.

Finson, Jon W., and R. Larry Todd, eds. *Mendelssohn and Schumann: Essays on Their Work and its Context.* Durham: Duke University Press, 1984.

Fischer-Dieskau, Dietrich. *Robert Schumann—Words and Music: The Vocal Compositions,* trans. Reinhard G. Pauly. Portland, Oregon: Amadeus Press, 1988.

Fiske, Roger. "A Schumann Mystery." *Musical Times* 105 (1964): 574–78.

Floros, Constantin. "Brahms der 'Messias' und 'Apostel': Zur Rezeptionsgeschichte des Artikels 'Neue Bahnen'." *Musikforschung* 36 (1983): 24–29.

———. *Brahms und Bruckner—Studien zur musikalischen Exegetik.* Wiesbaden: Breitkopf & Härtel, 1980.

———. "Schumanns musikalische Poetik." In *Musik-Konzepte, Sonderband, Robert Schumann I,* ed. Heinz-Klaus Metzger and Rainer Riehn. Munich, 1981.

Foucault, Michel. *Madness and Civilization: A History of Insanity in the Age of Reason,* trans. Richard Howard. New York: Vintage, 1965.

———. "What is Enlightenment?" trans. Catherine Porter. In *The Foucault Reader,* ed. Paul Rabinow. New York: Pantheon, 1984.

Forchert, Arno. "Mahler und Schumann." In *Mahler-Interpretation: Aspekte zum Werk und Wirken von Gustav Mahler,* ed. Rudolf Stephan. Mainz: Schott, 1985.

Fowler, Andrew. "Robert Schumann and the 'Real' Davidsbündler." *College Music Symposium* 30/2 (1990): 19–27.

Frager, Malcolm. "The Manuscript of the Schumann Piano Concerto." *Current Musicology* 15 (1973): 83–87.

Francke, Kuno, and W. G. Howard, eds. *The German Classics of the Nineteenth and Twentieth Centuries.* New York: AMS Press, 1969.

Franken, Franz Hermann. "Robert Schumann in der Irrenanstalt Endenich." In *Robert Schumanns letzte Lebensjahre: Protokoll einer Krankheit. Archiv Blätter 1* of the Stiftung Archiv der Akademie der Künste, Berlin. Berlin, March 1994.

Gal, Hans. *Schumann Orchestral Music.* BBC Music Guides. Seattle: University of Washington Press, 1979.

Gebhardt, Arnim. *Robert Schumann als Symphoniker.* Vol. 20 of *Forschungsbeiträge zur Musikwissenschaft.* Regensburg: Bosse, 1968.

Geck, Martin. *Von Beethoven bis Mahler: Die Musik des deutschen Idealismus.* Stuttgart and Weimar: Metzler, 1993.

Gerstmeier, August. *Robert Schumann: Klavierkonzert A-moll, op. 54.* Munich: Wilhelm Fink Verlag, 1986.

Gieseler, Walter. "Schumanns frühe Klavierwerke im Spiegel der literarischen Romantik." In *Robert Schumann: Universalgeist der Romantik,* ed. Alf and Kruse. Düsseldorf: Droste Verlag, 1991.

Godwin, Robert Chandler. "Schumann's Choral Works and the Romantic Movement." D.M.A. diss., University of Illinois, 1967.

Goethe, Johann Wolfgang von. *Conversations with Eckermann (1823–1832),* trans. John Oxenford. San Francisco: North Point Press, 1984.

———. *Faust,* trans. Walter Arndt, ed. Cyrus Hamlin. Norton Critical Edition. New York: Norton, 1976.

———. *Wilhelm Meister's Apprenticeship,* ed. and trans. Eric A. Blackall. Vol. 9 of *Goethe's Collected Works.* New York: Suhrkamp, 1989.

Gregor-Dellin, Martin. *Richard Wagner: His Life, His Work, His Century,* trans. J. Maxwell Brownjohn. San Diego and New York: Harcourt Brace Jovanovich, 1983.

Gülke, Peter. "Zur 'Rheinischen Sinfonie'." In *Musik-Konzepte Sonderband: Robert Schumann II,* ed. Heinz-Klaus Metzger and Rainer Riehn. Munich, 1982.

Gurlitt, Wilibald. "Robert Schumann und die Romantik in der Musik." In *Robert Schumann: Universalgeist der Romantik,* ed. Alf and Kruse. Düsseldorf: Droste Verlag, 1981.

Hallmark, Rufus. *The Genesis of Schumann's Dichterliebe: A Source Study.* Ann Arbor: University of Michigan Press, 1979.

———. "Die handschriftlichen Quellen der Lieder Robert Schumanns." In *Robert Schumann: Ein romantische Erbe in neuer Forschung.* Mainz: Schott, 1984.

———. "The Poet Sings." In German Lieder in the Nineteenth Century, ed. R. Hallmark New York: Schirmer Books, 1996.

———. "The Rückert Lieder of Robert and Clara Schumann." *19th Century Music* 14/1 (1990): 3–30.

———. "Schumanns Behandlung seiner Liedtexte: Vorläufige Bericht zu einer neuen Ausgabe und zu einer Neubewertung von Schumanns Liedern." In *Schumanns Werke,* ed. Mayeda and Niemöller. Mainz: Schott, 1987.

———. "A Sketch Leaf for Schumann's D-minor Symphony." In *Mendelssohn and Schumann,* ed. Finson and Todd. Durham: Duke University Press.

———. "The Sketches for *Dichterliebe*." *19th Century Music* 1/2 (1977): 110–36.

———. "Textkritische und aufführungspraktische Probleme in Schumanns Liedern." In *Schumann Forschungen,* vol. 4, ed. Wendt. Mainz and London: Schott, 1993.

Hanslick, Eduard. "Robert Schumann als Opernkomponist." In *Die Moderne Oper.* Berlin: Hofmann, 1875.

————. "Robert Schumann in Endenich." In *Am Ende des Jahrhunderts* [1895–1899]. Berlin: Allgemeiner Verein für Deutsche Litteratur, 1899. (Translation by Susan Gillespie in R. Larry Todd, ed., *Schumann and His World.* Princeton: Princeton University Press, 1994.)

Harwood, Gregory. "Robert Schumann's Sonata in F♯ minor: A Study of Creative Process and Romantic Inspiration." *Current Musicology* 29 (1980): 17–30.

Hebbel, Friedrich. *Werke in Zwei Bänden,* vol. 1. Munich: Hanser, 1978.

Heine, Heinrich. *The Romantic School,* trans. Helen Mustard. In *The Romantic School and Other Essays,* ed. Jost Hermand and Robert C. Holub. New York: Continuum, 1985.

Henius, Carla. "Erfahrungen mit Schumanns *Liederkreis*—und mit Adorno." In *Musik-Konzepte Sonderband: Robert Schumann II,* ed. Heinz-Klaus Metzger and Rainer Riehn. Munich, 1982.

Heuberger, Richard. *Erinnerungen an Johannes Brahms: Tagebuchnotizen aus den Jahren 1875 bis 1897,* ed. Kurt Hofmann. Tutzing: Schneider, 1971.

Höckner, Berthold. "The 'Multiple Persona' and Robert Schumann's *Heine-Liederkreis* op. 24." Paper delivered at the 59th Annual Meeting of the American Musicological Society, Montreal, November 1993.

————. "Spricht der Dichter oder der Tondichter? Die multiple *persona* und Robert Schumanns *Liederkreis* op. 24" in *Schumann Forschungen,* vol. 4, *Schumann und Seine Dichter,* ed. Matthias Wendt. Mainz and London: Schott, 1993; pp. 18–32.

Hoffmann, E. T. A. *Fantasie- und Nachtstücke.* Munich: Winkler, 1976.

————. *Schriften zur Musik.* Munich: Winkler, 1977.

Hofmann, Kurt. *Die Erstdrucke der Werke von Robert Schumann.* Tutzing: Hans Schneider, 1979.

Hoffmann-Axthelm, Dagmar. *Robert Schumann: "Glücklichsein und tiefe Einsamkeit."* Stuttgart: Reclam, 1994.

Hopf, Helmuth. "Fehlinterpretation eines Spätstils am Beispiel Robert Schumann." In *Robert Schumann: Universalgeist der Romantik,* ed. Alf and Kruse. Düsseldorf: Droste Verlag, 1981.

Hoy-Draheim, Susanne. "Robert Schumanns Opernpläne nach Dramen von William Shakespeare." In *Robert Schumann und die Dichter,* ed. Appel and Hermstrüwer. Düsseldorf: Droste Verlag, 1991.

Husmann, Heinrich. "Schumann als Gestalter: Die Einheit und Form in seinen Symphonien." *Musica* 10 (1956): 456–60.

Jacobs, Robert L. "Schumann and Jean Paul." *Music and Letters,* 30 (1949): 250–58.

Jamison, Kay Redfield. *Touched with Fire: Manic-Depressive Illness and the Artistic Temperament.* New York: The Free Press, 1993.

Jansen, Gustav. *Die Davidsbündler: Aus Robert Schumanns Sturm- und Drangperiode.* Leipzig: Breitkopf & Härtel, 1883.

Jarczyk, Michael. *Die Chorballade im 19. Jahrhundert.* Munich and Salzburg: Musikverlag Emil Katzbichler, 1978.

Jensen, Eric Frederick. "A New Manuscript of Robert Schumann's *Waldszenen* Op. 82." *Journal of Musicology* 3 (1984): 69–89.

Joachim, Joseph. *Letters from and to Joseph Joachim,* selected and trans. Nora Bickley. London: Macmillan, 1914.

Joachim, Joseph, and Andreas Moser. *Briefe von und an Joseph Joachim,* 2 vols. Berlin: Bard, 1911.

Just, Martin. *Robert Schumann: Symphonie Nr. 4 D-moll.* Munich: Wilhelm Fink Verlag, 1982.

Kaden, Werner. "Zum Verhältnis von Musikästhetik und Musikkritik bei Robert Schumann." In *Robert-Schumann-Tage 1985,* ed. Günther Müller. Wissenschaftliche Arbeitstagung zu Fragen der Schumann-Forschung in Zwickau, 1985.

Kalbeck, Max. *Johannes Brahms,* 4 vols. Berlin: Deutsche Brahms-Gesellschaft, 1912–1921.

Kallberg, Jeffrey. "The Harmony of the Tea Table: Gender and Ideology in the Piano Nocturne." *Representations* 39 (1992): 102–33.

Kaminsky, Peter M. "Aspects of Harmony, Rhythm and Form in Schumann's 'Papillons,' 'Carnaval' and 'Davidsbündlertänze'," 2 vols. Ph.D. diss., University of Rochester, 1990.

———. "Principles of Formal Structure in Schumann's Early Piano Cycles." *Music Theory Spectrum* 11/2 (1989): 207–25.

Kämper, Dietrich. "Zur Frage der Metronombezeichnungen Robert Schumanns." *Archiv für Musikwissenschaft* 21 (1964): 141–55.

Kang, Mahn-Hee. "Robert Schumann's Piano Concerto in A minor: A Stemmatic Analysis of the Sources." Ph.D. diss., Ohio State University, 1992.

Kapp, Reinhard. "Das Orchester Schumanns." In *Musik-Konzepte Sonderband: Robert Schumann II,* ed. Heinz-Klaus Metzger and Rainer Riehn. Munich, 1982.

———. "Robert Schumann: Sinfonie Nr. 4 d-moll op. 120." *Neue Zeitschrift für Musik* 143 (June/July 1982): 54–56.

———. "Schumann nach der Revolution: Vorüberlegungen, Statements, Hinweise, Materialien, Fragen." In *Schumann Forschungen,* vol. 3, ed. Appel. Mainz and London: Schott, 1993.

———. *Studien zum Spätwerk Robert Schumanns.* Tutzing: Schneider, 1984.

———. "Tempo und Charakter in der Musik Schumanns." In *Schumanns Werke,* ed. Mayeda and Niemöller. Mainz: Schott, 1987.

Kast, Paul, ed. *Schumanns rheinische Jahre.* Düsseldorf: Droste Verlag, 1981.

Kaufman, Walter. *From Shakespeare to Existentialism.* Princeton: Princeton University Press, 1980.

Keil, Sigmar. *Untersuchungen zur Fugentechnik in Robert Schumanns Instrumentalschaffen.* Hamburger Beiträge zur Musikwissenschaft 11. Hamburg: Wagner, 1973.

Kerman, Joseph and Alan Tyson. "Ludwig van Beethoven." In *The New Grove,* ed. Stanley Sadie, vol. 2. London: Macmillan, 1980.

Killmayer, Wilhelm. "Schumann und seine Dichter." *Neue Zeitschrift für Musik* 1981: 231–36.

Kirchmeyer, Helmut. *Robert Schumanns Düsseldorfer Brahms-Aufsatz Neue Bahnen und die Ausbreitung der Wagnerschen Opern bis 1856.* Berlin: Akademie Verlag, 1993.

Knaus, Herwig. *Musiksprache und Werkstruktur in Robert Schumanns "Liederkreis."* Munich: Katzbichler, 1974.

Knechtges, Irmgard. *Robert Schumann im Spiegel seiner späten Klavierwerken.* Regensburg: Bosse, 1985.

Knepler, Georg. "Robert Schumann." In *Musikgeschichte des 19. Jahrhunderts,* vol. 2. Berlin: Henschel Verlag, 1961.

Koch, Heinrich Christoph. *Musikalisches Lexikon.* Frankfurt, 1802.

Kohlhase, Hans. *Die Kammermusik R. Schumanns, stilistische Untersuchungen. Hamburger Beiträge zur Musikwissenschaft,* vol 19. Hamburg: Wagner, 1979.

————. "Die klangliche und strukturellen Revisionen im Autograph der Streichquartette op. 41." In *Schumanns Werke,* ed. Mayeda and Niemöller. Mainz: Schott, 1987.

————. "Robert Schumanns Klavierquintett op. 44." *Musik-Konzepte Sonderband: Robert Schumann I:* 148–73.

Komar, Arthur, ed. *Schumann: Dichterliebe* (Norton Critical Score). New York: Norton, 1971.

Kossmaly, Carl. "Über Robert Schumann's Claviercompositionen." *Allgemeine musikalische Zeitung* 46 (1844) cols. 17–21, 33–37. (Translation by Susan Gillespie. In *Schumann and His World,* ed. R. Larry Todd. Princeton: Princeton University Press, 1994.)

Kramer, Lawrence. "*Carnaval,* Cross-Dressing, and the Woman in the Mirror." In *Musicology and Difference,* ed. Ruth Solie. Berkeley and Los Angeles: University of California Press, 1993.

————. *Music and Poetry: The Nineteenth Century and After.* Berkeley and Los Angeles: University of California Press, 1984.

————. *Music as Cultural Practice 1800–1900.* Berkeley and Los Angeles: University of California Press, 1990.

Kristeva, Julia. *Black Sun: Depression and Melancholia,* trans. Leon S. Roudiez. New York: Columbia University Press, 1989.

Kross, Siegfried. "Aus der Frühgeschichte von Robert Schumanns Neuer Zeitschrift für Musik." *Musikforschung* 34 (1981): 423–45.

————. "Brahms und Schumann." In *Brahms-Studien,* vol. 4. Hamburg: Wagner, 1981.

————, ed. *Probleme der Symphonischen Tradition im 19. Jahrhundert.* Tutzing: Schneider, 1990.

Krüger, Eduard. Review of Schumann, *Das Paradies und die Peri,* Op. 50. In *Allgemeine musikalische Zeitung* 47 (1845); cols. 561–70, 585–89, 606–11, and 617–22.

————. Review of Schumann, *Genoveva,* Op. 81. In *Neue Zeitschrift für Musik* 34 (1851): 129–31, 141–44.

Krummacher, Friedhelm. "Synthesis des Disparaten. Zu Beethovens späten Quartetten und ihrer frühen Rezeption." *Archiv für Musikwissenschaft* 37 (1980): 99–134.

Kruse, Joseph A. "Robert Schumanns Lektüre: Zeitgenössischer Kanon, individuelle Schwerpunkte, kompositionsspezifische Auswahl und seine Urteile als Leser." In *Robert Schumann und die Dichter*, ed. Appel and Hermstrüwer. Düsseldorf: Droste Verlag, 1991.

Lacoue-Labarthe, Philippe, and Jean-Luc Nancy. *The Literary Absolute*, trans. Philip Barnard and Cheryl Lester. Albany: State University of New York Press, 1988.

Laux, Karl. *Robert Schumann*. Leipzig: Reclam 1972.

———. "Was ist ein Musikschriftsteller? Carl Maria von Weber und Robert Schumann als Vorbild." In *Sammelbände der Robert-Schumann Gesellschaft* II/ 1966. Leipzig: VEB Deutscher Verlag für Musik, 1967.

Lenneberg, Hans. Review of Peter Ostwald, *Schumann: The Inner Voices of a Musical Genius*. In *19th-Century Music* 10/1 (1986): 80–83.

Lester, Joel. "Reading and Misreading: Schumann's Accompaniments to Bach's Sonatas and Partitas for Solo Violin." *Current Musicology* 56 (1994): 24–53.

———. "Robert Schumann and Sonata Forms." *19th Century Music* 18/3 (1995): 189–210.

Lichtenhahn, Ernst. "Sinfonie als Dichtung: Zum geschichtlichen Ort von Schumanns 'Rheinischer.'" In *Schumanns Werke*, ed. Mayeda and Niemöller. Mainz: Schott, 1987.

Lippman, Edward A. *A History of Western Musical Aesthetics*. Lincoln and London: University of Nebraska Press, 1992.

———. "Robert Schumann." In *MGG*, ed. Friedrich Blume, vol. 12. Kassel: Bärenreiter, 1965.

———. "Theory and Practice in Schumann's Aesthetics." *JAMS* 17 (1964): 310–45.

Liszt, Franz. "Berlioz and his Harold Symphony" (1855). In *Source Readings in Music History: The Romantic Era*, Oliver Strunk. New York: Norton, 1965.

———. *Briefe*, ed. La Mara. Leipzig: Breitkopf & Härtel, 1893–1905.

———. "Robert Schumann" (1856). In *Gesammelte Schriften*, vol. 4. Leipzig: Breitkopf & Härtel, 1882.

Litzmann, Berthold. *Clara Schumann: Ein Künstlerleben*, 2 vols. Leipzig: Breitkopf & Härtel, 1902 and 1905.

———, ed. *Clara Schumann—Johannes Brahms: Briefe aus den Jahren 1853–1896*. Leipzig: Breitkopf & Härtel, 1927.

Locke, Ralph, and Jurgen Thym. "New Schumann Materials in Upstate New York: A First Report on the Dickinson Collection, with Catalogue of its Manuscript Holdings." *Fontes Artis Musicae* 27 (1980): 137–61.

Lossewa, Olga. "Neues über Elisabeth Kulmann." In *Schumann Forschungen*, vol. 4, ed. Wendt. Mainz and London: Schott, 1993.

Lukács, Georg. *The Theory of the Novel*, trans. Anna Bostock. Cambridge: MIT Press, 1971.

Macdonald, Claudia. "Critical Perception and the Woman Composer: The Early Reception of Piano Concertos by Clara Wieck Schumann and Amy Beach." *Current Musicology* 55 (1993): 24–55.

———. " 'Mit eine eignen ausserordentlichen Composition' ": The Genesis of Schumann's Phantasie in A Minor." *Journal of Musicology* 13/2 (1995): 240–59.

————. "The Models for Schumann's F-major Piano Concerto of 1831." *Studi Musicali* 21 (1992): 159–89.

————. Review of Robert Schumann, *Konzertsatz für Klavier und Orchester d-moll,* reconstructed and completed by Jozef De Beenhouwer, ed. by Joachim Draheim (Wiesbaden: Breitkopf & Härtel, 1988). In *JAMS* 45 (1992): 143–53.

————. "Robert Schumann's F-major Piano Concerto of 1831 as Reconstructed from his First Sketchbook: A History of its Composition and Study of its Musical Background." Ph.D. diss., University of Chicago, 1986.

————. "Schumann's Earliest Compositions and Performances." *Journal of Musicological Research* 7 (1987): 259–83.

Mahlert, Ulrich. *Fortschritt und Kunstlied: Späte Lieder Robert Schumanns in Licht der liedästhetischen Diskussion ab 1848.* Munich und Salzburg, 1983.

Mahling, Christoph-Hellmut. "Nähe und Distanz: Bemerkungen zum Verhältnis von Robert Schumann zu Frédéric Chopin und Franz Liszt." In *Gattungen der Musik und ihre Klassiker,* ed. Hermann Danuser. Laaber: Laaber Verlag, 1988.

Mainka, Jürgen. "Schumann und der Realismus." In *Wegzeichen: Studien zur Musikwissenschaft,* ed. Jürgen Mainka and Peter Wicke. Berlin: Verlag Neue Musik, 1985.

Maintz, Marie Luise. " '. . . in neuverschlungener Weise'—Schuberts Einfluss auf die Symphonien Schumanns." In *Probleme der Symphonischen Tradition,* ed. Kross. Tutzing: Schneider, 1990.

————. "Konzept statt Konzert: Schumanns 'Concertsatz' in d-moll." In *Beiträge zur Geschichte des Konzerts,* eds. Emans and Wendt. Bonn: Gudrun Schröder Verlag, 1990.

Maniates, Maria Rika. "The D minor Symphony of Robert Schumann." In *Festschrift für Walter Wiora zum 30. Dezember 1966.* Kassel: Bärenreiter, 1967.

Mann, Thomas. *Essays of Three Decades,* trans. H. T. Lowe-Porter. New York: Knopf, 1976.

Marsoner, Karin. "Das Sonatenkonzept Robert Schumanns in Theorie und Praxis." In *Gustav Mahler: Sinfonie und Wirklichkeit.* Graz: Edition für Institut für Wertungsforschung, 1977.

Marston, Nicholas. " 'Im Legendenton': Schumann's 'Unsung Voice.'" *19th Century Music* 16/3 (1993): 227–41.

————. *Schumann: Fantasie, Op. 17.* Cambridge: Cambridge University Press, 1992.

————. "Schumann's Monument to Beethoven." *19th Century Music* 14/3 (1991): 247–64.

Martin, Uwe. "Ein unbekannte Schumann-Autograph aus dem Nachlass Eduard Krügers." *Musikforschung* 12 (1959): 405–15.

Mayeda, Akio. *Robert Schumanns Weg zur Symphonie.* Zurich: Atlantis Verlag, 1992.

————. "Schumanns Gegenwart." In *Robert Schumann: Ein romantisches Erbe.* Mainz: Schott, 1984.

————. "Die Skizzen Robert Schumanns als stilkritische Erkenntnisquelle." In *Robert Schumann: Ein romantisches Erbe.* Mainz: Schott, 1984.

Mayeda, Akio and Klaus Wolfgang Niemöller, eds. *Schumanns Werke: Text und Interpretation—16 Studien*. Mainz: Schott, 1987.

McCreless, Patrick. "Song Order in the Song Cycle: Schumann's *Liederkreis*, Op. 39." *Music Analysis* 5 (1986): 5–28.

McFarland, Thomas. *Romanticism and the Forms of Ruin: Wordsworth, Coleridge, and Modalities of Fragmentation*. Princeton: Princeton University Press, 1981.

McGann, Jerome J. *The Romantic Ideology: A Critical Investigation*. Chicago and London: University of Chicago Press, 1983.

Meissner, Bernhard. *Geschichtsrezeption als Schaffenskorrelat: Studien zum Musikgeschichtsbild Robert Schumanns*. Bern: Francke, 1985.

Melkus, E. "Zur Revision unseres Schumann-Bildes." *Österreichische Musikzeitschrift* 15 (1960): 182–90.

Mendelssohn, Felix. *Letters*, ed. G. Selden-Goth. New York: Pantheon, 1945.

Mennemeier, Franz Norbert. "Fragment und Ironie beim jungen Friedrich Schlegel: Versuch der Konstruktion einer nicht geschriebenen Theorie" [1968]. In *Romantikforschung seit 1945*, ed. Klaus Peter. Königstein: Verlagsgruppe Athenäum-Hain-Scripter-Hanstein, 1980.

Meyer, Stephen. "The Trope of the Double in Schumann's *Genoveva*." *The Opera Journal* 27 (1994): 4–26.

Michaelis, C. F. "Ueber das Humoristische oder Launige in der musikalischen Komposition." *Allgemeine musikalische Zeitung* 9 (1807): cols. 725–729.

Mintz, Donald. "Schumann as an Interpreter of Goethe's *Faust*." *JAMS* 14 (1961): 235–56.

Molnár, Antal. "Die beiden Klavier-Trios in d-Moll von Schumann (op. 63) und Mendelssohn (op. 49)." In *Sammelbände der Robert-Schumann Gesellschaft* I/1961. Leipzig: VEB Deutscher Verlag für Musik, 1961.

Moore, Thomas. *Poetical Works*. New York: Appleton, 1846.

Moser, Andreas. *Joseph Joachim: Ein Lebensbild*, 2 vols. Berlin: Deutsche Brahms-Gesellschaft, 1908.

Müller, Günther, ed. *Robert-Schumann-Tage 1985: 10. Wissenschaftliche Arbeitstagung zu Fragen der Schumann-Forschung in Zwickau*. [Zwickau], 1985.

Münch, Stephan. " 'Fantasiestücke in Kreislers Manier': Robert Schumanns 'Kreisleriana' op. 16 und die Musikanschauung E. T. A. Hoffmanns." *Musikforschung* 45/3 (1992): pp. 255–74.

Münster, Robert. "Die Beethoven-Etuden von Robert Schumann aus Anlass ihrer Erstausgabe." *Die Musikforschung* 31 (1978): 53–56.

Musgrave, Michael. *The Music of Brahms*. London: Routledge and Kegan Paul, 1985.

Musik-Konzepte Sonderband: Robert Schumann I, ed. Heinz-Klaus Metzger and Rainer Riehn. Munich: Edition Text & Kritik, 1981.

Musik-Konzepte Sonderband: Robert Schumann II, ed. Heinz-Klaus Metzger and Rainer Riehn. Munich: Edition Text & Kritik, 1982.

Mustard, Helen Meredith. *The Lyric Cycle in German Literature*. New York: Columbia University, 1946.

Nagler, Norbert. "Gedanken zur Rehabilitierung des späten Werks," *Musik-Konzepte*

Sonderband: Robert Schumann I, ed. Heinz-Klaus Metzger and Rainer Riehn. Munich, 1981.

———. "Das konfliktuöse Kompromiss zwischen Gefühl und Vernunft im Frühwerk Schumanns." In *Musik-Konzepte Sonderband: Robert Schumann I,* ed. Heinz-Klaus Metzger and Rainer Riehn. Munich, 1981.

Nauhaus, Gerd. "Final-Lösungen in der Symphonik Schumanns." In *Probleme der Symphonischen Tradition,* ed. Kross. Tutzing, Schneider, 1990.

———. *The Marriage Diaries of Robert and Clara Schumann: From their Wedding Day through the Russia Trip,* trans. Peter Ostwald. Boston: Northeastern University Press, 1993.

———. "Quellenuntersuchungen zu Schumanns 'Das Paradies und die Peri'. " In *Robert-Schumann-Tage 1985,* ed. Günther Müller. Wissenschaftliche Arbeitstagung zu Fragen der Schumann-Forschung in Zwickau, 1985.

———. *Robert Schumann: Scenen aus Goethes 'Faust.'* Zwickau: Kulturhaus, 1981.

———. "*Der Rose Pilgerfahrt,* op. 112: Schumanns Abschied vom Oratorium." In *Schumann Forschungen,* vol. 3, ed. Appel. Mainz and London: Schott, 1993.

———. "Schumanns *Das Paradies und die Peri:* Quellen zur Entstehungs-, Aufführungs- und Rezeptionsgeschichte." In *Schumanns Werke,* ed. Mayeda and Niemöller. Mainz: Schott, 1987.

———. "Schumanns *Lektürebüchlein.*" In *Robert Schumann und die Dichter,* ed. Appel and Hermstrüwer. Düsseldorf: Droste Verlag, 1991.

———. "Zur Edition der Haushaltbücher Robert Schumanns." In *1. Schumann-Tage des Bezirkes Karl-Marx-Stadt 1976.*

Neighbour, Oliver. "Brahms and Schumann: Two Opus Nines and Beyond." *19th Century Music* 7/3 (1984): 266–70.

Nelson, John D. "Progressive Tonality in the Finale of the Piano Quintet, Op. 44 of Robert Schumann." *Indiana Theory Review* 13 (1992): 41–52.

Neumeyer, David. "Organic Structure and the Song Cycle: Another Look at Schumann's *Dichterliebe.*" *Music Theory Spectrum* 4 (1982), pp. 92–105.

Newcomb, Anthony. "Once More Between Absolute and Program Music: Schumann's Second Symphony." *19th Century Music* 7/3 (1984): 233–50.

———. "Schumann and Late Eighteenth-Century Narrative Strategies." *19th Century Music* 11/2 (1987): 164–74.

———. "Schumann and the Marketplace: From Butterflies to *Hausmusik.*" In *Nineteenth-Century Piano Music,* ed. R. Larry Todd. New York: Schirmer, 1990.

Newmarch, Rosa. *Tchaikovsky: His Life and Works, with Extracts from his Writings, and the Diary of his Tour Abroad in 1888,* ed. Edwin Evans. London: G. Richards, 1900.

Niemöller, Klaus Wolfgang. "Robert Schumanns Cellokonzert in der Instrumentation von Dmitri Schostakowitsch: Ein Beitrag zur Schumann-Rezeption in der Sowjetunion." In Emans and Wendt, eds., *Beiträge zur Geschichte des Konzerts.* Bonn: Gudoun Schröder Verlag, 1990.

———. "Zur analytischen Interpretation der Musik Robert Schumanns." In *Schumanns Werke,* ed. Mayeda and Niemöller. Mainz: Schott, 1987.

Nietzsche, Friedrich. *Beyond Good and Evil*, trans. Walter Kaufman. New York: Vintage, 1966.

Novalis. *Schriften*. Vol. 3, *Das philosophische Werk II*, ed. Richard Samuel. Stuttgart: Kohlhammer, 1960.

Oechsle, Siegfried. "Schubert, Schumann und die Symphonie nach Beethoven." In *Probleme der Symphonischen Tradition*, ed. Kross. Tutzing: Schneider, 1990.

Oliver Jr., Willie-Earl. "Robert Schumanns vergessene Oper 'Genoveva'," Ph.D. diss., Freiburg im Breisgau, 1976.

Orlova, Alexandra. *Tchaikovsky: A Self-Portrait*, trans. R. M. Davison. Oxford and New York: Oxford University Press, 1990.

Ostwald, Peter. "Florestan, Eusebius, Clara, and Schumann's Right Hand." *19th Century Music* 4 (1980/81): 17–31.

———. "Leiden und Trauern im Leben und Werk Robert Schumanns." In *Schumanns Werke*, ed. Mayeda and Niemöller. Mainz: Schott, 1987.

———. *Schumann: The Inner Voices of a Musical Genius*. Boston: Northeastern University Press, 1985.

Otto, Frauke. *Robert Schumann als Jean Paul-Leser*. Frankfurt am Main: Herchen Verlag, 1984.

Ozawa, Kazuko. *Quellenstudien zu Robert Schumanns Liedern nach Adelbert von Chamisso*. Frankfurt: Peter Lang, 1989.

Paul, Jean. *Jean Paul Werke*, ed. Norbert Miller, 6 vols. Munich: Carl Hanser Verlag, 1960–63.

Peake, Luise Eitel. "The Antecedents of Beethoven's Liederkreis." *Music and Letters* 63 (1982): 242–60.

———. "Song Cycle." In *The New Grove*, vol. 17. London: Macmillan, 1980.

———. "The Song Cycle: A Preliminary Inquiry into the Beginnings of the Romantic Song Cycle and the Nature of an Art Form," Ph.D. diss., Columbia University, 1968.

Petman, Rudolf. "Schumanns Schaffensästhetik im Lichte seiner Zeit." In *Robert-Schumann-Tage 1985*, ed. Günther Müller. Wissenschaftliche Arbeitstagung zu Fragen der Schumann-Forschung in Zwickau, 1985.

Pelker, Bärbel. *Die deutsche Konzertouvertüre (1825–1865): Werkkatalog und Rezeptionsdokumente*, 2 parts. Frankfurt: Lang, 1993.

Peterson, John David. "Schumann's Fugues on B-A-C-H: A Secret Tribute." *The Diapason*, 73/5 (1982): 12–13.

Petrat, Nicolai. *Hausmusik des Biedermeier im Blickpunkt der zeitgenössischen musikalischen Fachpresse (1815–1848)*. Hamburg: Karl Dieter Wagner, 1986.

———. " 'Hausmusik' um 1840." *Musica* 42 (1988): 255–60.

Plantinga, Leon. *Romantic Music: A History of Musical Style in Nineteenth-Century Europe*. New York: Norton, 1984.

———. *Schumann as Critic*. New Haven: Yale University Press, 1967.

———. "Schumann's Critical Reaction to Mendelssohn." In *Mendelssohn and Schumann*, ed. Finson and Todd. Durham: Duke University Press, 1984.

Pleasants, Henry, trans. and ed. *The Music Criticism of Hugo Wolf*. New York and London: Holmes and Heier, 1979.

Pohl, Richard. "Reminiscences of Robert Schumann" (1878), trans. John Michael Cooper. In *Schumann and His World,* ed. R. Larry Todd. Princeton: Princeton University Press, 1994.

Polansky, Robert. "The Rejected *Kinderscenen* of Robert Schumann's Opus 15." *Journal of the American Musicological Society* 31 (1978): 126–31.

Porter, Cecelia Hopkins. "The Schumann Legacy in Germany's Heartland." *The American Organist* 29/2 (February 1995): 56–62.

Pousseur, Henri. "Schumann ist der Dichter: Fünfundzwanzig Momente einer Lektüre der *Dichterliebe.*" In *Musik-Konzepte Sonderband: Robert Schumann II,* ed. Heinz-Klaus Metzger and Rainer Riehn. Munich, 1982.

Probst, Gisela. *Robert Schumanns Oratorien.* Wiesbaden: Breitkopf & Härtel, 1975.

Ramroth, Peter. *Robert Schumann und Richard Wagner im geschichtsphilosophischen Urteil von Franz Brendel.* Frankfurt: Lang, 1991.

Rauchfleisch, Udo. *Robert Schumann: Leben und Werk. Eine Psychobiographie.* Stuttgart: Kohlhammer, 1990.

Reber, Arthur S. *The Penguin Dictionary of Psychology.* New York: Viking, 1985.

Reich, Nancy B. "Clara Schumann and Johannes Brahms." In *Brahms and His World,* ed. Walter Frisch. Princeton: Princeton University Press, 1990.

———. *Clara Schumann: The Artist and the Woman.* Ithaca: Cornell University Press, 1985.

———. "The Lieder of Clara Schumann." *American Brahms Society Newsletter* 12 (Autumn 1994): 1–4.

———. "Women as Musicians: A Question of Class." In *Musicology and Difference,* ed. Ruth A. Solie. Berkeley and Los Angeles: University of California Press, 1993.

Riasanovsky, Nicholas V. *The Emergence of Romanticism.* New York and Oxford: Oxford University Press, 1992.

Richter, Jean Paul. *School for Aesthetics,* trans. Margaret Hale, as *The Horn of Oberon.* Detroit: Wayne State University Press, 1973.

Rienäcker, Gerd. "Romantisches in Robert Schumanns 'Genoveva'. " In *Robert-Schumann-Tage 1985,* ed. Günther Müller. Wissenschaftliche Arbeitstagung zu Fragen der Schumann-Forschung in Zwickau, 1985.

Robert-Schumann-Gesellschaft Düsseldorf, ed. *Robert Schumann: Ein romantisches Erbe in neuer Forschung. Acht Studien.* Mainz: Schott, 1984.

Roe, Stephen. "The autograph manuscript of Schumann's Piano Concerto." *Musical Times* 131/2 (1990): 77–79.

Roesner, Linda Correll. "The Autograph of Schumann's Piano Sonata in F minor." *Musical Quarterly* 61 (1975): 98–130.

———. "Brahms's Editions of Schumann." In *Brahms Studies: Analytical and Historical Perspectives,* ed. George Bozarth. Oxford: Clarendon Press, 1990.

———. "The Sources for Schumann's *Davidsbündlertänze,* Op. 6: Composition, Textual Problems, and the Role of the Composer as Editor." In *Mendelssohn and Schumann: Essays on Their Work and Its Context,* ed. Finson and Todd. Durham, N.C.: Duke University Press, 1984.

———. "Schumann's 'Parallel' Forms." *19th Century Music* 14/3 (1991): 265–78.

————. "Schumann's Revisions in the First Movement of the Piano Sonata in G minor, Op. 22." *19th Century Music* 1/2 (1977): 97–109.

————. "Studies in Schumann Manuscripts," Ph.D. diss., New York University, 1973.

————. "Tonal Strategy and Poetic Content in Schumann's C-major Symphony, Op. 61." In *Probleme der Symphonischen Tradition,* ed. Kross. Tutzing: Schneider, 1990.

Rosen, Charles. *The Romantic Generation.* Cambridge: Harvard University Press, 1995.

————. *Sonata Forms.* New York: Norton, 1980.

Rosenberg, Wolf. "Paradox, Doppelbödigkeit und Ironie in der *Dichterliebe.*" *Dissonanz/Dissonance* 15 (1988): 8–12.

Rothe, Hans-Joachim. "Neue Dokumente zur Schumann-Forschung aus dem Leipziger Stadt-Archiv." In *Bericht über den Internationalen Musikwissenschaftlichen Kongress Leipzig 1966.* Kassel: Bärenreiter, 1970.

Rothenberg, Albert. *Creativity and Madness: New Findings and Old Stereotypes.* Baltimore and London: Johns Hopkins University Press, 1990.

Rumenhöller, Peter. "Botschaft von Meister Raro: Zum Verständnis von Robert Schumann heute." *Neue Zeitschrift für Musik* 1981: 226–30.

Sachs, Klaus-Jürgen. "Robert Schumanns Fugen über den Namen BACH (op. 60)." In *Johann Sebastian Bach und seine Ausstrahlung auf die nachfolgenden Jahrhunderte.* Mainz, 1980.

Sammons, Jeffrey L. *Heinrich Heine: The Elusive Poet.* New Haven and London: Yale University Press, 1969.

Sams, Eric. "Brahms and his Clara Themes." *Musical Times* 112 (1971): 432–34.

————. "Did Schumann Use Ciphers?" *Musical Times* 106 (1965): 584–91.

————. "Schumann and Faust." *Musical Times* 113 (1972): 543–46.

————. "Schumann and the Tonal Analogue." In *Robert Schumann: The Man and His Music,* ed. Alan Walker. London: Barrie and Jenkins, 1972.

————. "Schumann's Hand Injury." *Musical Times* 112 (1971): 1156–1159.

————. *The Songs of Robert Schumann,* 3d ed. Bloomington and Indianapolis: Indiana University Press, 1993.

————. "The Tonal Analogue in Schumann's Music." *Proceedings of the Royal Musical Association* 96 (1969/70): 103–19.

Schauffler, Robert Haven. *Florestan: The Life and Works of Robert Schumann.* New York: Holt, 1945.

Schelling, Friedrich Wilhelm Joseph. *The Philosophy of Art,* ed. and trans. Douglas W. Stott. Minneapolis: University of Minnesota Press, 1989.

Schilling, Gustav, ed. *Encyclopädie der gesammten musikalischen Wissenschaften oder Universal-Lexikon der Tonkunst.* 7 vols. Stuttgart: Köhler, 1835–1842.

Schlegel, Friedrich. *Kritische Friedrich Schlegel Ausgabe,* ed. Ernst Behler, Jean-Jacques Anstett, and Hans Eichner, 35 vols. Munich, Paderborn, Vienna: Schöningh, 1958–.

Schmid, Manfred Hermann. *Musik als Abbild: Studien zum Werk von Weber, Schumann und Wagner.* Tutzing: Schneider, 1981.

Schmitz, Arnold. "Die ästhetischen Anschauungen Robert Schumanns in ihren Beziehungen zur romantischen Literatur." *Zeitschrift für Musikwissenschaft,* 3 (1920–21): 111–18.

Schnebel, Dieter. "Postscriptum zu Schumanns Spätwerken." In *Musik-Konzepte Sonderband: Robert Schumann II,* ed. Heinz-Klaus Metzger and Rainer Riehn. Munich, 1981.

———. "Rückungen—Ver-rückungen: Psychoanalytische Betrachtungen zu Schumanns Leben und Werk." In *Musik-Konzepte Sonderband: Robert Schumann I,* ed. Heinz-Klaus Metzger and Rainer Riehn. Munich, 1981.

Schneider, Frank. " 'Im Legendenton': Fragwürdiges zu einem musikalischen Topos." In *Gattungen der Musik und ihre Klassiker,* ed. Hermann Danuser. Laaber: Laaber Verlag, 1988.

Schneider, Norbert J. *Robert Schumann: I. Symphonie B-dur Op. 38.* Munich: Wilhelm Fink Verlag, 1982.

Schoenberg, Arnold. *Fundamentals of Musical Composition,* ed. Gerald Strang and Leonard Stein. London: Faber and Faber, 1967.

———. *Style and Idea,* ed. Leonard Stein, trans. Leo Black. Berkeley and Los Angeles: University of California Press, 1984.

Schoppe, Martin. "Die Anfänge der Schumann-Rezeption." In *1. Schumann-Tage des Bezirkes Karl-Marx-Stadt 1976.*

———. "Robert Schumanns frühe Texte und Schriften." *Robert-Schumann-Tage 1985,* ed. Günther Müller. Wissenschaftliche Arbeitstagung zu Fragen der Schumann-Forschung in Zwickau, 1985.

Schoppe, Martin. "Schumann und Brahms—Begegnung in Düsseldorf." In *Brahms-Studien,* vol. 7. Hamburg: Johannes Brahms-Gesellschaft, 1987.

———. "Schumanns Litterarischer Verein." In *Robert Schumann und die Dichter,* ed. Appel and Hermstrüwer. Düsseldorf: Droste Verlag, 1991.

Schubring, Adolf. "Schumanniana No. 4: The Present Musical Epoch and Robert Schumann's Position in Musical History" (1861), trans. John Michael Cooper. In *Schumann and His World,* ed. R. Larry Todd. Princeton: Princeton University Press, 1994.

Schumann, Clara. *Konzert für Klavier und Orchester a-moll, op. 7,* ed. Janina Klassen. Wiesbaden: Breitkopf & Härtel, 1990.

Schumann, Clara, ed. *Jugendbriefe von Robert Schumann,* 2d ed. Leipzig: Breitkopf & Härtel, 1886.

Schumann, Clara, and Johannes Brahms. *Briefe aus den Jahren 1853–1896,* ed. Berthold Litzmann. Vol. 1 (1853–1871). Leipzig: Breitkopf & Härtel, 1927.

———. *Letters . . . 1853–1896,* 2 vols., ed. Berthold Litzmann. New York: Longmans, Green, 1927.

Schumann, Clara, and Robert. *Briefwechsel: Kritische Gesamtausgabe,* 2 vols., ed. Eva Weissweiler. Frankfurt: Stroemfeld/Roter Stern, 1984.

Schumann, Eugenie. *Ein Lebensbild meines Vaters.* Leipzig, 1931.

———. *Memoirs,* trans. Marie Busch. London: Eulenberg, 1985.

Schumann, Robert. "Aufzeichnungen über Mendelssohn," annotated by Heinz-Klaus

Metzger and Rainer Riehn. In *Musik-Konzepte 14/15: Felix Mendelssohn Bartholdy* (1980): 97–122.

———. *Briefe, Neue Folge*, 2d ed., ed. Gustav Jansen. Leipzig: Breitkopf & Härtel, 1904.

———. *Gesammelte Schriften über Musik und Musiker*, 5th ed., 2 vols., ed. Martin Kreisig. Leipzig: Breitkopf & Härtel, 1914.

———. *Jugendbriefe*, 2nd ed., ed. Clara Schumann. Leipzig: Breitkopf & Härtel, 1886.

———. *Konzertsatz für Klavier und Orchester d-moll*, reconstructed by Jozef de Beenhouwer, ed. Joachim Draheim. Wiesbaden: Breitkopf & Härtel, 1988.

———. *Der Korsar: Opernfragment* [1844], ed. Joachim Draheim. Wiesbaden: Breitkopf & Härtel, 1983.

———. *Robert Schumann: Neue Ausgabe sämtlicher Werke*, ed. Robert-Schumann-Gesellschaft, by Akio Mayeda and Klaus Wolfgang Niemöller, in collaboration with the Robert-Schumann-Haus Zwickau. Mainz: Schott, 1991–.

———. *Selbstbiographische Notizen—Faksimile*, ed. Martin Schoppe. Robert-Schumann-Gesellschaft [n.d.].

———. *Symphony Opus 38*. New York: Robert Owen Lehman Foundation, 1967. [Facsimile ed. of manuscript sketches and full score of 1841 version]

———. *Tagebücher, Band I: 1827–1838*, ed. Georg Eisman. Leipzig: VEB Deutscher Verlag für Musik, 1971.

———. *Tagebücher, Band II: 1836–1854*, ed. Gerd Nauhaus. Leipzig: VEB Deutscher Verlag für Musik, 1987.

———. *Tagebücher, Band III; Haushaltbücher*, Pts. 1 (1837–47) and 2 (1847–1856), ed. Gerd Nauhaus. Leipzig: VEB Deutscher Verlag für Musik, 1982.

Schumann, Robert, and Clara. *Briefe einer Liebe*, ed. Hanns-Josef Ortheil. Königstein: Athenäum, 1982.

Seyfarth, Winfried. "Die unvollendeten 'Faust-Szenen': ein bedeutender Beitrag Robert Schumanns zu den Goethe-Gedächtnisfeiern im Jahre 1849." In *1. Schumann-Tage des Bezirkes Karl-Marx-Stadt 1976*.

Shaw, George Bernard. *The Great Composers: Reviews and Bombardments*, ed. Louis Crompton. Berkeley: University of California Press, 1978.

Sheehan, James J. *German History 1770–1866*. Oxford: Clarendon Press, 1989.

Siegel, Linda. *Music in German Romantic Literature—A Collection of Essays, Reviews, and Stories*. Novato, California: Elra Publications, 1983.

———. "A Second Look at Schumann's *Genoveva*." *Music Review*, 36/1 (1975): 17–41.

Siegmund-Schultze, Walter. "Zu den Beziehungen Robert Schumanns und Johannes Brahms." *Robert-Schumann-Tage 1985*, ed. Günther Müller. Wissenschaftliche Arbeitstagung zu Fragen der Schumann-Forschung in Zwickau, 1985.

Sietz, Reinhold. "Zur Textgestaltung von Robert Schumanns 'Genovefa." *Musikforschung*, 23 (1970): 395–410.

Sisman, Elaine R. *Haydn and the Classical Variation*. Cambridge and London: Harvard University Press, 1993.

————. "Haydn's Hybrid Variations." In *Haydn Studies,* ed. Jens Peter Larsen, Howard Serwer, and James Webster. New York: Norton, 1981.

Smallman, Basil. *The Piano Trio: Its History, Technique, and Repertoire.* Oxford: Clarendon Press, 1990.

Solie, Ruth A., ed. *Musicology and Difference: Gender and Sexuality in Music Scholarship.* Berkeley and Los Angeles: University of California Press, 1993.

————. "Whose Life? The Gendered Self in Schumann's *Frauenliebe* Songs." In *Musik and Text: Critical Inquiries,* ed. Steven Scher. Cambridge: Cambridge University Press, 1992.

Spitta, Phillipp. "Ein Lebensbild Robert Schumanns." In *Sammlung musikalischer Vorträge,* Reihe 4, ed. Paul Graf Waldersee. Leipzig: Breitkopf & Härtel, 1882.

Spohr, Louis. *Louis Spohr's Autobiography.* London: Longman, 1865. (Da Capo Press reprint, 1969).

Staël, Germaine de. *Major Writings of Germaine de Staël,* trans. and with an Introduction by Vivian Falkenflik. New York: Columbia University Press, 1987.

Stearns, Peter N. *1848: The Revolutionary Tide in Europe.* New York: Norton, 1974.

Sterk, Valerie Stegink. "Robert Schumann as Sonata Critic and Composer: The Sonata from Beethoven to 1844, as reviewed by Schumann in the *Neue Zeitschrift für Musik,*" 2 vols., Ph.D. diss., Stanford University, 1992.

Stein, Jack M. "Musical Settings of the Songs from *Wilhelm Meister.*" *Comparative Literature* 22 (1970): 125–46.

Steinbeck, Susanne. *Die Ouvertüre in der Zeit von Beethoven bis Wagner: Probleme und Lösungen.* Munich: Katzbichler, 1973.

Struck, Michael. "Am Rande der 'grossen Form'—Schumanns Overtüren und ihr Verhältnis zur Symphonie." In *Probleme der Symphonischen Tradition,* ed. Kross. Tutzing: Schneider, 1990.

————. "Gerüchte um den 'späten' Schumann." *Neue Zeitschrift für Musik* 143 (May 1982): 52–56.

————. " 'Gewichtsverlagerungen': Robert Schumanns letzte Konzertcompositionen." In *Schumanns Werke,* ed. Mayeda and Niemöller. Mainz: Schott, 1987.

————. "Literarischer Eindruck, poetischer Ausdruck und Struktur in Robert Schumanns Instrumentalmusik" in *Robert Schumann und die Dichter,* ed. Appel and Hermstrüwer. Düsseldorf: Droste Verlag, 1991.

————. *Robert Schumann: Violinkonzert D-moll (WoO 23).* Munich: Wilhelm Fink, 1988.

————. *Die umstrittenen späten Instrumentalwerke Schumanns. Hamburger Beiträge zur Musikwissenschaft 29.* Hamburg: Wagner, 1984.

————. "Zur Relation von Quellenbefunden und analytischen Erkenntnisgewinn im Spätwerk Robert Schumanns." *Musikforschung* 44 (1991): 236–54.

Strunk, Oliver. *Source Readings in Music History: The Romantic Era.* New York: Norton, 1965.

Sutherland, Stuart. *The International Dictionary of Psychology.* New York: Continuum, 1989.

Szondi, Peter. "Friedrich Schlegel and Romantic Irony, with Some Remarks on

Tieck's Comedies." In *On Textual Understanding and Other Essays,* tr. Harvey Mendelssohn. Minneapolis: University of Minnesota Press, 1986.

———. *Theory of the Modern Drama,* ed. and trans. Michael Hays. Cambridge: Polity Press, 1987.

Taylor, Ronald. *Robert Schumann: His Life and Work.* New York: Universe, 1982.

Temperley, Nicholas. "Schumann and Sterndale Bennett." *19th Century Music* 12/3 (1989): 207–20.

Thibaut, Anton Friedrich. *Ueber Reinheit der Tonkunst,* 7th ed. Freiburg and Leipzig: Mohr, 1893.

Thym, Jurgen. "Schumann in Brendel's *Neue Zeitschrift für Musik* from 1845 to 1856." In *Mendelssohn and Schumann,* ed. Finson and Todd. Durham: Duke University Press, 1984.

———. "The Solo Song Settings of Eichendorff's Poems by Schumann and Wolf," Ph.D. diss., Case Western Reserve University, 1974.

Tobel, Rudolf von. "Die Formenwelt der klassischen Instrumentalmusik." Diss., University of Bern, 1931.

Todd, R. Larry, ed. *Mendelssohn and His World.* Princeton: Princeton University Press, 1991.

———. "On Quotation in Schumann's Music." In *Schumann and His World,* ed. R. Larry Todd. Princeton: Princeton University Press, 1994.

———, ed. *Schumann and His World.* Princeton: Princeton University Press, 1994.

Tovey, Donald Francis. *Essays in Musical Analysis: Chamber Music.* London: Oxford University Press, 1944.

———. *Essays in Musical Analysis. Vol. 2: Symphonies.* London, Oxford University Press, 1935.

———. *Essays in Musical Analysis. Vol. 3: Concertos.* London: Oxford University Press, 1936.

———. *Essays in Musical Analysis. Vol. 4: Illustrative Music.* London: Oxford University Press, 1937.

———. *Essays in Musical Analysis. Vol. 6: Supplementary Essays, Glossary and Index.* London: Oxford University Press, 1939.

Truscott, Harold. "The Evolution of Schumann's Last Period." *The Chesterian* 21/ no. 190 (London, 1957): 76–84; 103–11.

Turchin, Barbara. "Robert Schumann's Song Cycles in the Context of the Early Nineteenth-century Liederkreis," Ph.D. diss., Columbia University, 1981.

———. "Robert Schumann's Song Cycles: The Cycle within the Song." *19th Century Music* 8/3 (1985): 231–44.

———. "Schumann's Conversion to Vocal Music: A Reconsideration." *Musical Quarterly* 67 (1981): 392–404.

Vitercik, Greg. "Mendelssohn the Progressive." *Journal of Musicological Research,* 8 (1989): 333–74.

Wagner, Richard. *Gesammelte Schriften,* 4th ed., 10 vols., Leipzig: Siegel, 1907.

———. *My Life,* 2 vols., authorized translation from the German. New York: Dodd and Mead, 1911.

———. *Prose Works*, 8 vols., trans. and ed. William Ashton Ellis. London: Routledge and Kegan Paul, 1892–1899.

———. *Sämtliche Briefe*, ed. Gertrud Strobel and Werner Wolf. Leipzig: VEB Verlag für Musik, 1967–.

Waldersee, Paul Graf. "Robert Schumann's Manfred." In *Sammlung musikalischer Vorträge*, Reihe 2, ed. Paul Graf Waldersee. Leipzig: Breitkopf & Härtel, 1880.

Waldura, Markus. *Monomotivik, Sequenz und Sonatenform im Werk Robert Schumanns*. Saarbrücken: Saarbrücker Druckerei und Verlag, 1990.

———. "Zitate vokaler Frühgesänge in Schumanns 'Gesänge der Frühe': Überlegungen zur Deutung eines irritierenden Titels." In *Schumann in Düsseldorf: Werke—Texte—Interpretationen. Bericht über das 3. Internationalen Schumann-Symposium am 15. und 16. Juni 1988*. Mainz: Schott, 1993.

Walker, Alan. *Schumann*. London: Faber and Faber, 1976.

Walsh, Stephen. "Schumann and the Organ." *Musical Times* 111 (1970): 741–43.

Warrack, John. *Carl Maria von Weber*, 2d ed. Cambridge: Cambridge University Press, 1976.

Wasielewski, Wilhelm Joseph von. *Robert Schumann: Eine Biographie*, enlarged ed. Leipzig: Breitkopf & Härtel, 1906.

Weber, Gottfried. *Versuch einer geordneten Theorie der Tonkunst*. Mainz, 1817–21.

Wehnert, Martin. "Zu Robert Schumanns kunsttheoretischer Position: 'Gefühlsästhetik'?" *Robert-Schumann-Tage 1985*, ed. Günther Müller. Wissenschaftliche Arbeitstagung zu Fragen der Schumann-Forschung in Zwickau, 1985.

Weingartner, Felix. "On Schumann as Symphonist" (1904–1906). In R. Larry Todd, ed., *Schumann and His World*. Princeton: Princeton University Press, 1994.

Wendt, Matthias. "Zu Robert Schumanns Skizzenbüchern." In *Schumanns Werke*, ed. Mayeda and Niemöller. Mainz: Schott, 1987.

———, ed. *Schumann Forschungen*. Vol. 4, *Schumann und seine Dichter*. Mainz and London: Schott, 1993.

Westrup, Jack. "The Sketch for Schumann's Piano Quintet op. 44." In *Convivium musicorum: Festschrift Wolfgang Boetticher*. Berlin: Merseburger, 1974.

Wolff, Helmuth Christian. "Robert Schumann: Der Klassizist." *Musica* 2 (1948): 47–54.

———. "Schumanns 'Genoveva' und der Manierismus des 19. Jahrhunderts." In H. Becker, ed., *Beiträge zur Geschichte der Oper*. Regensburg: Bosse, 1969.

Wollenberg, Susan. "Schumann's Piano Quintet in E flat: The Bach Legacy." *Music Review* 52 (1991): 299–305.

Wörner, Karl H. *Robert Schumann*. Zurich, 1949.

Young, Percy M. *Tragic muse: the life and works of Robert Schumann*. London: Dobson, 1961.

Zanoncelli, Luisa. "Von Byron zu Schumann oder Die Metamorphose des 'Manfred.'" *Musik-Konzepte Sonderband: Robert Schumann I*, ed. Heinz-Klaus Metzger and Rainer Riehn. Munich, 1981.

Zlotnik, George Asher. "Orchestration Revisions in the Symphonies of Robert Schumann," Ph.D. diss., Indiana University, 1972.

General Index

Strackerjahn, August, 447, 566n18
Strauss, Richard, 335
Strauss Sr., Johann, 124, 309
Struck, Michael, 8
Suckow, Karl Adolf, 341, 361
Szondi, Peter, 361–62

Täglichsbeck, Johann Friedrich, 49
Tausch, Julius, 446, 450–52, 456
Tchaikovsky, Peter I., 490
Telemann, Georg Philipp, 205
Thalberg, Sigismund, 173
Thibaut, Anton Friedrich, 55, 56, 59–61
Tieck, Ludwig, 42, 43, 330, 338–39, 344–45, 348–49, 361
Töpken, Anton, 57–58, 66, 80, 85
Tovey, Donald Francis, 228, 256, 313

Uhland, Ludwig, 447, 491
Uhlig, Theodor, 16
Uhlmann, Johann, 185

Verdi, Giuseppe, 334
Verhulst, Johann, 248, 265, 449
Viardot-Garcia, Pauline, 269, 288
Vieuxtemps, Henri, 162, 255
Voigt, Henriette, 82–85, 90, 112, 143, 149–50, 163, 186, 527n57

Wackenroder, Heinrich, 42, 43
Wagner, Richard, 12, 256, 270, 276, 278, 282, 296, 303, 329, 331, 336–37, 343, 351, 381. *See also* Schumann, Robert, on Wagner
and Dresden revolution, 423
on RS, 553n22, 555n68

Waldura, Markus, 8
Wasielewski, William Joseph von, 338, 356, 369, 372, 442, 446, 450, 483, 488
Weber, Carl Maria von, 22, 24, 30, 50, 277–78, 343
Harmonische Verein, 114
RS's reception of, 354–55, 556n89
Weber, Gottfried, 87, 128
Widemann, Carl, 342
Wieck, Clara. *See* Schumann, Clara
Wieck, Clementine, 169, 184
Wieck, Friedrich, 34, 46–47, 49–51, 62, 66, 68, 99, 117, 144, 147–48, 155, 160–61, 168–70, 172, 199, 207, 223–24, 269, 296, 336, 543n9
complexity of relationship with RS, 169
and Dresden orchestral concerts, 307
legal battle with RS and Clara, 182–89, 193–96
as "Meister Raro," 72
and *Neue Zeitschrift für Musik*, 114, 115, 116
as pedagogue, 68–69
on RS's use of chiroplast, 77
Wiedebein, Gottlob, 31–32
Wielhorski, Count Matvei, 288
Wielhorski, Michail, 288–90
Wigand, Georg, 448
Wildenhahn, Carl August, 195–96
Wolf, Hugo, 357–58, 428, 490
Wolff, Helmuth Christian, 19
Wortmann, Wilhelm, 445–46, 450–51, 456
Wüllner, Franz, 239

Zachariä, Karl, 56, 58

Index of Schumann's Works
discussed in this book

A note on the orthography of the titles of Schumann's published works: Here and throughout the text, spellings are generally given as they appear in the first edition of the composition.

Dramatic Music

Der Korsar (chorus, melodrama, and aria fragment), 302, 304, 331, 334
Hamlet (projected), 99, 330
Scenen aus Göthe's Faust (WoO 3), 14–15, 19, 284, 292, 294, 297, 301–05, 322–23, 329–330, 334–36, 340, 342, 353, 364–87, 392, 398, 434, 437, 440, 453, 464, 469, 476, 490
op. 81, *Genoveva*, 16, 284, 303, 322, 329–32, 334–36, 338–56, 361, 367, 370–71, 373, 394, 428, 440–41, 476
op. 115, *Manfred*, 15, 284, 329–31, 334–36, 341, 356–65, 371, 389, 435, 449, 455

Works for Voices and Orchestra

Deutsches Requiem (projected), 476
Luther (oratorio; projected), 443–44, 471
Overture & Chor von Landleuten, 23
Psalm 150 (lost), 23
Tragödie (lost), 534n60. *See also* **Lieder,** op. 64
op. 50, *Das Paradies und die Peri,* 15–16, 136, 220, 227, 267–69, 271–85, 304–337, 345, 359, 362–63, 386, 434–35, 440–41, 469
op. 71, *Adventlied,* 389, 434–36
op. 84, *Beim Abschied zu singen* (with winds or piano), 339–434
op. 93, *Verzweifle nicht im Schmerzenstal* (men's chorus and organ or orchestra). *See* **Choral partsongs and motets,** op. 93
op. 98b, *Requiem für Mignon,* 391, 395, 399, 434, 436–38, 442
op. 108, *Nachtlied,* 391, 434–35
op. 112, *Der Rose Pilgerfahrt* (originally with piano), 434, 444, 446–47, 463, 469–70
op. 116, *Der Königssohn,* 433, 444, 464, 470
op. 139, *Des Sängers Fluch,* 426, 433, 447, 450, 470, 486
op. 140, *Vom Pagen und der Königstochter,* 12–13, 433, 449–50, 470–74
op. 143, *Das Glück von Edenhall,* 433, 451, 470
op. 144, *Neujahrslied,* 391, 393, 434–36, 440, 442
op. 147, Mass, 284, 434, 447, 451, 463, 471, 474, 476
op. 148, Requiem, 284, 434, 448, 463, 474–76

Choral Partsongs and Motets

Drei Freiheitsgesänge (WoO13–15; men's chorus), 397, 426, 560n21
op. 33, *Sechs Lieder* (men's chorus), 191, 397
op. 55, *Fünf Lieder* (mixed chorus), 315, 399
op. 59, *Vier Gesänge* (mixed chorus), 315, 399
op. 62, *Drei Gesänge* (mixed chorus and *ad libitum* winds), 397, 426

Arrangements